The Intellectual and Cultural World of the Early Modern Inns of Court

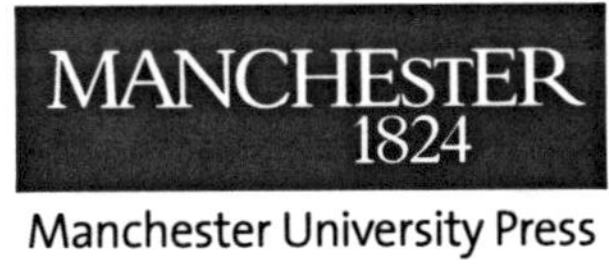

Manchester University Press

The Intellectual and Cultural World of the Early Modern Inns of Court

edited by
JAYNE ELISABETH ARCHER,
ELIZABETH GOLDRING,
and SARAH KNIGHT

Manchester University Press
Manchester and New York

distributed exclusively in the USA by Palgrave Macmillan

Published by Manchester University Press
Oxford Road, Manchester M13 9NR, UK
and Room 400, 175 Fifth Avenue, New York, NY 10010, USA
www.manchesteruniversitypress.co.uk

Distributed in the United States exclusively by
Palgrave Macmillan, 175 Fifth Avenue,
New York, NY 10010, USA

Distributed in Canada exclusively by
UBC Press, University of British Columbia, 2029 West Mall,
Vancouver, BC, Canada V6T 1Z2

British Library Cataloguing-in-Publication Data is available

Library of Congress Cataloging-in-Publication Data is available

ISBN 978 0 7190 9009 7 paperback

First published by Manchester University Press in hardback 2011

This paperback edition first published 2013

The publisher has no responsibility for the persistence or accuracy of URLs for any external or third-party internet websites referred to in this book, and does not guarantee that any content on such websites is, or will remain, accurate or appropriate.

Printed by Lightning Source

Contents

Contents

List of illustrations

Map

Plates

Plates appear between pages 142 and 143

Figures

Every effort has been made to obtain copyright for the images included in this book.

Notes on contributors

Hugh Adlington

Dr Hugh Adlington is Lecturer in English at the University of Birmingham. He has published numerous journal articles and book chapters on early modern literature, religion, law, and politics. He is a volume editor of the *Oxford Edition of the Sermons of John Donne* (forthcoming), and co-editor of the *Oxford Handbook of the Early Modern Sermon* (forthcoming).

Jayne Elisabeth Archer

Dr Jayne Elisabeth Archer is Lecturer in Medieval and Renaissance Literature in the Department of English and Creative Writing at Aberystwyth University. She is an Associate Fellow of the Centre for the Study of the Renaissance, University of Warwick. She is General Editor of *John Nichols's The Progresses and Public Processions of Queen Elizabeth I: A New Edition of the Early Modern Sources* (Oxford University Press, forthcoming) and co-editor of an essay collection: *The Progresses, Pageants, and Entertainments of Queen Elizabeth I* (Oxford University Press, 2007). She has published articles on Elizabethan and Jacobean masques, early modern women's receipt books, and alchemy in early modern literature, and is currently working on a book-length study of the relationship between housewifery and natural philosophy in early modern England.

J. H. Baker

Sir John Baker, QC, is Downing Professor of the Laws of England at the University of Cambridge and Professorial Fellow of St Catharine's College. A member of both the Inner Temple and Gray's Inn, he is an Honorary Bencher of the Inner Temple and Literary Director of the Selden Society. Sir John is the leading expert on early modern English legal history, with a particular interest in the history of the legal profession and of the Inns of Court in this period. His many publications include *An Introduction to English Legal History* (Butterworths, 1971; 4th edn 2002), *The Legal Profession and the Common Law* (Hambledon Press, 1986), *Readings and Moots at the Inns of Court in the Fifteenth Century* (with Samuel E. Thorne; Selden Society, 1990), and *The Law's Two Bodies: Some Evidential Problems in English Legal History* (Oxford University Press, 2001). He is also General Editor of the multi-volume

Oxford History of the Laws of England (Oxford University Press, 2003–), as well as the author of volume six of that series, which covers the period 1483–1558.

Tarnya Cooper
Dr Tarnya Cooper, Sixteenth-Century curator at the National Portrait Gallery, was sole curator for the 2006 exhibition *Searching for Shakespeare* and edited the exhibition catalogue of the same name. In 2003, she was co-curator of the National Maritime Museum's *Elizabeth* exhibition and contributed to the accompanying exhibition catalogue. An expert on Tudor portraiture and specifically portraits of the professional classes in early modern England, Dr Cooper is currently completing a book entitled *Citizen Portraiture: Portrait Painting and the Urban Elite in Tudor and Jacobean England and Wales*.

Bradin Cormack
Bradin Cormack is Associate Professor in the English Department at the University of Chicago and Director of the Nicholson Center for British Studies there. His publications include *A Power to do Justice: Jurisdiction, English Literature, and the Rise of Common Law, 1509–1625* (University of Chicago Press, 2007) and *The Forms of Renaissance Thought: New Essays on Literature and Culture*, co-edited with Leonard Barkan and Sean Keilen (Palgrave Macmillan, 2008). He is currently at work on two books, a study of Shakespeare's sonnets and a monograph on *Shakespeare and Law*.

Mark Girouard
Dr Mark Girouard, formerly Slade Professor of Fine Art at Oxford University (1975–76) and George Lurcy Visiting Professor at Columbia University (1987), is the leading historian of English architecture of his generation. A member of the Royal Fine Art Commission (1972–96) and the Royal Commission on Historical Monuments (1976–81), he is the author of numerous books, including *Robert Smythson and the Architecture of the Elizabethan Era* (Country Life, 1963; published in a revised form as *Robert Smythson and the Elizabethan Country House* by Yale University Press, 1983) and *Life in the English Country House* (Yale University Press, 1978), the latter of which won the Duff Cooper Memorial Prize as well as the W. H. Smith Award for 1979. His *Elizabethan Architecture: Its Rise and Fall, 1540–1640* was published by Yale University Press/The Paul Mellon Centre for Studies in British Art in 2009.

Elizabeth Goldring
Dr Elizabeth Goldring is an Associate Fellow of the University of Warwick's Centre for the Study of the Renaissance and a Consultant to English Heritage. Her research interests encompass sixteenth- and seventeenth-century court culture, England and the Continental Renaissance, and relations between literature and the visual arts. Publications include: (General Editor) *John Nichols's The Progresses and Public Processions of Queen Elizabeth I: A New Edition of the Early Modern Sources* (Oxford University Press, forthcoming); (co-editor) *The Progresses, Pageants, and*

Entertainments of Queen Elizabeth I (Oxford University Press, 2007); (Associate General Editor) *Europa Triumphans: Court and Civic Festivals in Early Modern Europe* (Ashgate, 2004); and (co-editor) *Court Festivals of the European Renaissance: Art, Politics and Performance* (Ashgate, 2002). She has also published articles in journals such as *ELR: English Literary Renaissance*, *The Burlington Magazine*, [*The*] *British Art Journal*, and *English Heritage Historical Review*. Current projects include a book on painting and patronage at the Elizabethan court.

Paula Henderson

Dr Paula Henderson is an independent scholar who specialises in early modern architectural and garden history. Her many publications include articles in *Garden History*, *Architectural History*, and *Country Life*, as well as essays in Lucy Gent (ed.), *Albion's Classicism: The Visual Arts in Britain, 1550–1660* (Yale University Press, 1995) and in Pauline Croft (ed.), *Patronage, Culture and Power: The Early Cecils, 1558–1612* (Yale University Press, 2002). Her first book, *The Tudor House and Garden: Architecture and Landscape in the Sixteenth and Early Seventeenth Centuries* (Yale University Press, 2005), won the Berger Prize for British Art History.

Lorna Hutson

Lorna Hutson is Berry Professor of English Literature and Head of the School of English at the University of St Andrews. She is co-editor (with Victoria Kahn) of *Rhetoric and Law in Early Modern Europe* (Yale University Press, 2001) and has recently edited a special forum of *Representations* on Ernst Kantorowicz entitled 'Fifty Years of *The King's Two Bodies*' (vol. 106, Spring 2009). Her most recent book, *The Invention of Suspicion: Law and Mimesis in Shakespeare and Renaissance Drama* (Oxford University Press, 2007) won the Roland H. Bainton Prize for Literature in 2008.

Sarah Knight

Dr Sarah Knight is Senior Lecturer in Shakespeare and Renaissance Literature, School of English, University of Leicester. Her main research and teaching interests are in early modern English and Latin literature, and in the intellectual and literary culture of the English universities during the sixteenth and early seventeenth centuries; she is particularly interested in academic drama, representations of adolescence, and the relationship between satire and education. She has edited and translated Leon Battista Alberti's *Momus* and the accounts of Elizabeth I's visits to Oxford in 1566 and 1592 for the new edition of John Nichols's *Progresses*, and is preparing an edition and translation of John Milton's *Prolusions*, and new editions of the plays of Fulke Greville and the college play *The New Moone*.

Richard McCoy

Richard McCoy is Professor of English, Queens College and Graduate Center, CUNY. His publications include *Alterations of State: Sacred Kingship in the English Reformation* (Columbia University Press, 2002), *The Rites of Knighthood: The Literature and Politics of Elizabethan Chivalry* (University of California Press, 1989), and *Sir Philip Sidney: Rebellion in Arcadia* (Rutgers University Press, 1979). He is currently working on *Faith in Shakespeare: Theology and Performance*, a study of links between Reformation liturgical theology and contemporary performance theory in early modern drama. He has published many articles in journals such as *Shakespeare Survey*, *Criticism*, the *Historical Journal*, and the *Journal of Medieval and Renaissance Studies*.

Alan H. Nelson

Alan H. Nelson is Professor Emeritus in the Department of English at the University of California, Berkeley. His specialisations are palaeography, bibliography, and the reconstruction of the literary life and times of medieval and Renaissance England from documentary sources. His most recent publication is *Monstrous Adversary: The Life of Edward de Vere, Seventeenth Earl of Oxford* (Liverpool University Press, 2003). He is one of the four editors of *Records of Early English Drama: Oxford*, 2 vols (University of Toronto Press, 2004). Professor Nelson is currently working on *London: Inns of Court*, also for *REED*. His monograph, *The Library of Humphrey Dyson*, is forthcoming from the Oxford Bibliographical Society.

Damian X. Powell

Dr Damian X. Powell is Principal of Janet Clarke Hall and a Senior Fellow in the School of Historical Studies within The University of Melbourne. He writes on aspects of British and Australian legal and military history. Previous publications include 'Remembrance Day: Memories and Values in Australia since 1918', *Victorian Historical Journal* (2004), 'Coke in Context: Personal and Professional Observation in Sir Edward Coke's *Reports*', *Journal of Legal History* (2000), and *James White-locke's Liber Famelicus, 1570–1632: Law and Politics in Early Stuart England* (P. Lang, 2000).

Wilfrid R. Prest

Professor Emeritus in History and Law at the University of Adelaide, Wilfrid Prest is the author of *The Inns of Court under Elizabeth I and the Earl Stuarts, 1590–1640* (Longman, 1972), *The Rise of the Barristers: A Social History of the English Bar, 1590–1640* (Clarendon Press, 1986), *Albion Ascendant: English History, 1660–1815* (Oxford University Press, 1998), and most recently *William Blackstone: Law and Letters in the Eighteenth Century* (Oxford University Press, 2008), together with articles and chapters on law, the legal profession, the Inns of Court, and aspects of religious, social, and political history in early modern Britain, *circa* 1550–1800.

Paul Raffield

Dr Paul Raffield is Associate Professor in the School of Law, University of Warwick, and a member of Gray's Inn. He is the author of a monograph, *Images and Cultures of Law in Early Modern England: Justice and Political Power, 1558–1660* (Cambridge University Press, 2004) and has published articles on various aspects of the relationship between law and literature in early modern England, in *Law and Literature*

(2009, 2005), *Law and Critique* (2002, 1997), *International Journal for the Semiotics of Law* (2000), and *Journal of Legal History* (1999). In 2007, he co-organised a conference on 'Shakespeare and the Law', hosted by The University of Warwick, papers from which were published in an edited collection: Paul Raffield and Gary Watt (eds), *Shakespeare and the Law* (Hart Publishing, 2008). He is currently writing a monograph, *Shakespeare's Imaginary Constitution: Late-Elizabethan Politics and the Law*, to be published by Hart in 2010.

Emma Rhatigan

Dr Emma Rhatigan is currently a lecturer at Sheffield University. Her 2006 DPhil dissertation explored John Donne's Lincoln's Inn sermons, tracing the history of preaching at Lincoln's Inn, and examining how the sermons Donne preached in the pulpit can be interpreted in terms of his intimate relationship with the Society. She is currently adapting her thesis into a book-length study of preaching at Lincoln's Inn between 1580 and 1642 and in conjunction with this work is editing a volume of Donne's Inns of Court sermons for the recently commissioned *Oxford Edition of the Sermons of John Donne*. She is also editing, with Hugh Adlington and Peter McCullough, *The Oxford Handbook to the Early Modern Sermon*. Her publications include essays in *John Donne Journal* (2004), *Journal of Ecclesiastical Studies* (forthcoming), and *The Oxford Handbook of John Donne Studies* (forthcoming).

Geoffrey Tyack

Dr Geoffrey Tyack is a Fellow of Kellogg College, Oxford, Director of the Stanford University Centre in Oxford, editor of the *Georgian Group Journal*, and a Fellow of the Society of Antiquaries. He has published widely on English architectural history and is an expert on the collegiate architecture of Oxford and Cambridge. His many publications include *Sir James Pennethorne and the Making of Victorian London* (Cambridge University Press, 1992), *Oxford: An Architectural Guide* (Oxford University Press, 1998), and *Modern Architecture in an Oxford College: St John's College, 1945–2005* (Oxford University Press, 2005). He has recently contributed a chapter on William Dugdale and the Warwickshire country house to C. Dyer and C. Richardson (eds), *William Dugdale, Historian, 1605–1686* (Boydell Press, 2009), and his revision of the Berkshire volume in the Pevsner *Buildings of England* series was published by Yale University Press in 2010.

Jessica Winston

Jessica Winston is Assistant Professor of English at Idaho State University. She has published several articles on early Elizabethan poetry and drama, including 'Seneca in early Elizabethan England' (*Renaissance Quarterly*, 2006), 'National history to foreign calamity: *A Mirror for Magistrates* and early English tragedy', in Dermot Cavanagh, Stuart Hampton-Reeves, and Steve Longstaffe *(eds)*, *Shakespeare's Histories and Counter-Histories* (Manchester University Press, 2006), 'Expanding the political nation: *Gorboduc* at the Inns of Court and succession revisited' (*Early Theatre*, 2005), and 'A Mirror for Magistrates and public political discourse in Elizabethan England' (*Studies in Philology*, 2004).

Acknowledgements

This volume of essays developed from the research interests of the editors during their employment as postdoctoral research fellows at the AHRC Centre for the Study of Renaissance Elites and Court Cultures at the University of Warwick's Centre for the Study of the Renaissance. All fifteen of the essays in this collection were first presented as papers at a conference, 'The Intellectual and Cultural World of the Early Modern Inns of Court', which was held in London at the Courtauld Institute and selected venues within the Inns of Court in September 2006. The conference was organised under the auspices of Warwick's Centre for the Study of the Renaissance, and with the generous support of the British Academy, the Modern Humanities Research Association, the Paul Mellon Centre for Studies in British Art, the Society for Renaissance Studies, the Humanities Research Centre (Warwick), the Registrar (Warwick), the History of Art Department (Warwick), and the School of English (Leicester). The editors are grateful to Nicholas Orchard, Jackie Sullivan, and the personnel at the Courtauld Institute, and to the Honourable Society of Lincoln's Inn and the Honourable Society of the Middle Temple for providing congenial settings for the formal and informal proceedings of the conference. Special thanks are due to Anthony Arlidge, QC, who helped the organisers liaise with the Middle Temple. We are also grateful to all those who attended the conference, whether as chairs, delegates, or presenters; their questions, comments, and observations provided the editors and contributors with invaluable feedback that helped shape and refine the structure and contents of the collection. This essay collection has in turn received grants from the Paul Mellon Centre for Studies in British Art, the Society for Renaissance Studies, and the Society for Theatre Research to meet the costs associated with illustrating the volume.

Our thanks are due to Professor Julian Gardner, Professor Steve Hindle, and Dr Ingrid De Smet, successive directors of the Centre for the Study of the Renaissance, each of whom has shown unflagging enthusiasm and support for the conference and essay collection. We are grateful to staff at Warwick who advised on and contributed to these projects at their inception and throughout: Linda Bromley; Jayne Brown; Lisa Cook; Dr Elizabeth Clarke; Dr Lawrence Green; Dr Liese Perrin; and Dr Andrew Roadnight. Professor Wilfrid R. Prest and Professor John Morrill gave helpful feedback on the publishing prospectus for this essay collection. We would also like to express our gratitude to Professor Malcolm Airs, Professor Gordon Campbell, Dr Susan Foister, and Professor Peter Mack. In preparing this volume, the editors have received invaluable advice and assistance from Matthew Bailey, Assistant Collections Manager at the National Portrait Gallery; Colin Davidson at the Middle Temple; John Fisher, Prints and Maps Section, the Guildhall Library, London; Kate Harris, Archivist, Longleat House, Wiltshire; Guy Holborn of Lincoln's Inn Library; Andrew Mussell, Archivist of Gray's Inn; Sandra Powlette, Permissions Manager at the British Library, London; David Raymont, Librarian, The Actuarial Profession/Staple Inn Hall; Julia Steele, Collections Manager at the Society of Antiquaries of London; Lesley Whitelaw, Archivist at the Middle Temple Library; Clare Rider and Celia Pilkington, successive Archivists of the Inner Temple Library; and Robert Yorke, Archivist at the College of Arms. Finally, we are indebted to the staff at Manchester University Press for their support in bringing this volume to completion.

Jayne Elisabeth Archer, Elizabeth Goldring, and Sarah Knight

Abbreviations

BL   British Library, Department of Manuscripts, St Pancras, London

Black Books   *The Records of the Honourable Society of Lincoln's Inn: The Black Books*, ed. W. P. Baildon, R. Roxburgh, and P. V. Baker, 6 vols (London: Lincoln's Inn, 1897–2001)

Bodleian   Bodleian Library, Oxford

Calendar of the Middle Temple   *A Calendar of the Middle Temple Records*, ed. C. H. Hopwood (London: Printed by the Masters of the Bench and sold by Butterworth & Co., 1903)

CUL   Cambridge University Library, Cambridge

Inner Temple Records   *A Calendar of the Inner Temple Records*, ed. F. A. Inderwick and R. A. Roberts, 5 vols (London: Published by Order of the Masters of the Bench, 1896–1919)

ITL   Inner Temple Library, London

LI   Lincoln's Inn Library, London

Middle Temple Records   *Middle Temple Records*, ed. C. H. Hopwood, 4 vols (London: Printed by the Masters of the Bench and sold by Butterworth & Co., 1904–5)

Minutes of the Middle Temple   *Minutes of the Parliament of the Middle Temple*, trans. and ed. Charles Trice Martin, 4 vols (London: Middle Temple/Butterworth & Co., 1904–1905)

MTL   Middle Temple Library, London

NA   The National Archives, Kew, London

ODNB   Oxford Dictionary of National Biography, online edn www.oxforddnb.com

OED   Oxford English Dictionary, online edn, www.oed.com

Pension Book of Gray's Inn   *The Pension Book of Gray's Inn: Records of the Honourable Society, 1569–1800*, ed. Reginald J. Fletcher, 2 vols (London: Chiswick Press for the Masters of the Bench, 1901–10)

Records of Lincoln's Inn   *The Records of the Honourable Society of Lincoln's Inn. Admissions (and Chapel Registers)*, 2 vols (London: Lincoln's Inn, 1896)

TCD   Trinity College Library, Dublin

Unless otherwise indicated, all references to Shakespeare are taken from *Arden Shakespeare Complete Works*, ed. Ann Thompson, Richard Proudfoot, and David Scott Kastan (London: Thomson Learning, 2007).

Introduction

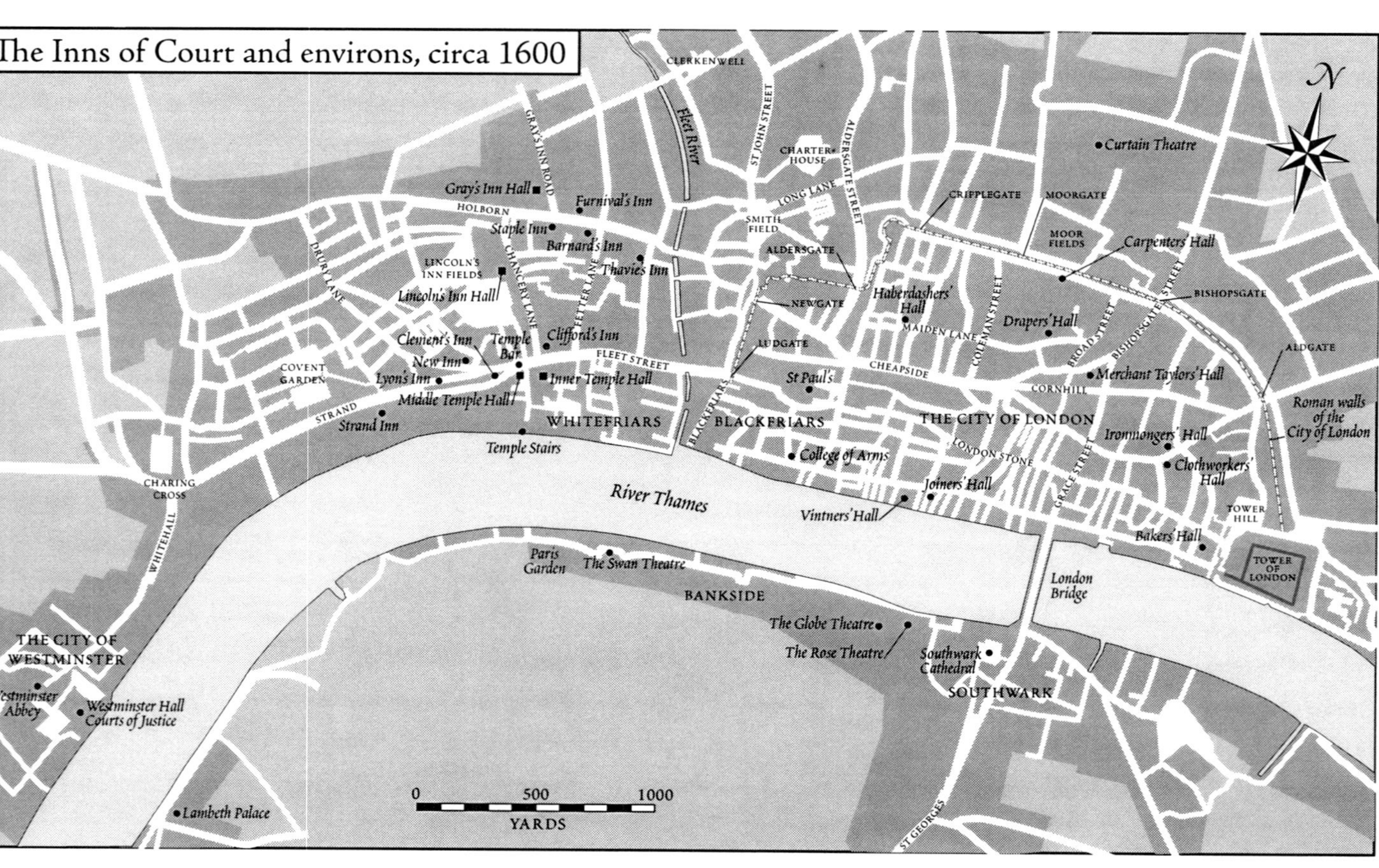

The Inns of Court and environs, circa 1600
N
CLERKENWELL
Fleet River
ST JOHN STREET
CHARTER HOUSE
ALDERSGATE STREET
LONG LANE
Curtain Theatre
GRAY'S INN ROAD
Gray's Inn Hall
Furnival's Inn
HOLBORN
CRIPPLEGATE
MOORGATE
Staple Inn
SMITH FIELD
MOOR FIELDS
Barnard's Inn
ALDERSGATE
Carpenters' Hall
LINCOLN'S INN FIELDS
Thavies Inn
DRURY LANE
CHANCERY LANE
NEWGATE
Haberdashers' Hall
BISHOPSGATE
Lincoln's Inn Hall
FETTER LANE
COLEMAN STREET
Drapers' Hall
BISHOPSGATE STREET
MAIDEN LANE
Clement's Inn
Temple Bar
Clifford's Inn
LUDGATE
CHEAPSIDE
ALDGATE
COVENT GARDEN
New Inn
FLEET STREET
St Paul's
CORNHILL
Merchant Taylors' Hall
Lyons Inn
Inner Temple Hall
Roman walls of the City of London
STRAND
Middle Temple Hall
BLACKFRIARS
BLACKFRIARS
THE CITY OF LONDON
Ironmongers' Hall
CHARING CROSS
Strand Inn
WHITEFRIARS
College of Arms
LONDON STONE
GRACE STREET
Clothworkers' Hall
Temple Stairs
Joiners' Hall
WHITEHALL
River Thames
Vintners' Hall
TOWER HILL
Bakers' Hall
Paris Garden
The Swan Theatre
BANKSIDE
London Bridge
TOWER OF LONDON
THE CITY OF WESTMINSTER
The Globe Theatre
The Rose Theatre
Southwark Cathedral
Westminster Abbey
Westminster Hall
Courts of Justice
SOUTHWARK
Lambeth Palace
0   500   1000
YARDS
ST GEORGES

Preface

Jayne Elisabeth Archer, Elizabeth Goldring, and Sarah Knight

The Intellectual and Cultural World of the Early Modern Inns of Court examines an important but hitherto neglected aspect of early modern English life: the artistic and intellectual patronage of the Inns of Court and their influence on religion, politics, education, rhetoric, and culture from the late fifteenth through the early eighteenth centuries. This period witnessed the height of the Inns' status as educational institutions: emerging from an earlier incarnation as fairly informal associations in the fourteenth century, the Inns of Court in the fifteenth and sixteenth centuries had developed sophisticated curricula for their students, leading to their description in the early seventeenth century as an integral part of England's 'third university'.[1] Some of the most influential politicians, writers, intellectuals, and divines – as well as lawyers – of Tudor and Stuart England passed through the Inns: men such as Edward Hall (1497–1547; entered Gray's Inn by 1521), William Lambarde (1536–1601; Lincoln's Inn, 1556), Sir Edward Coke (1552–1634; Inner Temple, 1572), Francis Bacon (1561–1626; Gray's Inn, 1576), John Donne (1572–1631; Lincoln's Inn, 1592), John Webster (1578x80–1638?; Middle Temple, 1598), and John Selden (1584–1654; Inner Temple, 1603). Time spent at the Inns of Court was highly influential and personally formative for all of these individuals, and each would go on to reflect in print on his time at the Inns, through the various authorial processes of improving and codifying laws, generating new legislative and educational theories, and crystallising social and institutional observations in literary form.

Recent work in early modern literary, cultural, and historical studies has shown a marked interest in the law and legal institutions.[2] Such scholarship is indebted to the pioneering historical studies on the Inns of Court and Chancery by Sir John H. Baker, Eric Ives, and Wilfrid R. Prest.[3] This historical work on the organisation, curricula, and development of the early modern Inns has been complemented by literary research on the extra-curricular dramatic performances that were a regular part of life at the Inns, most notably in Marie Axton's analyses of the revels at the Inner Temple and Gray's Inn (1970; 1977); D. S. Bland's edition *Three Revels from the Inns of Court* (1984); Philip J. Finkelpearl's examination of John Marston's time at the Middle Temple (1969); and, more recently, in essays on plays performed by and/or at the Inns, such as Shakespeare's *The Comedy of Errors* (1594–95) and

Norton and Sackville's *Gorboduc* (1561–62), which has been the topic of essays by Henry James and Greg Walker, and Jessica Winston among several others.[4] Over the past few years, four book-length studies of literary representations of law and legal culture, focused at least in part on the Inns, have propelled our understanding of the early modern Inns still further forward: Subha Mukherji's *Law and Representation in Early Modern Drama* (2006), Kieran Dolin's *A Critical Introduction to Law and Literature* (2007), Lorna Hutson's *The Invention of Suspicion* (2007), and Bradin Cormack's *A Power to Do Justice* (2007) have deepened our understanding of how English law functioned during this period, and how authors responded to and represented its status and influence.[5]

This literary and historical scholarship has highlighted the need for interdisciplinary approaches to the Inns of Court and to the law in early modern England. Paul Raffield's *Images and Cultures of Law in Early Modern England: Justice and Political Power, 1558–1660* (2004), following the work of Peter Goodrich, argues for the importance of ritual, symbolism, and the material culture of the Inns in helping shape and reinforce a sense of communal identity and political authority.[6] Such work suggests that the Inns can be usefully regarded as societies, and this term, with its implications of both exclusiveness and communality, seems particularly appropriate for a consideration of the early modern Inns' unusual function as privileged, expensive institutions of learning, with their own idiosyncratic and venerable rituals, as well as urban clusters of young men living geographically near to some of London's most demotic, colourful areas.

Three recent interdisciplinary essay collections have also drawn attention to the interconnectedness of law, politics, and culture in the early modern period. *Rhetoric and Law in Early Modern Europe*, edited by Victoria Kahn and Lorna Hutson (2001), has brought together studies from a range of disciplines, which discuss several different legal systems, in order to examine the role of rhetoric and law in the formation of concepts of authorship and subjectivity.[7] *Literature, Politics and Law in Renaissance England*, edited by Erica Sheen and Lorna Hutson (2005), includes essays on legal discourse, its structures of meaning and language, and their representation in early modern culture – popular as well as elite.[8] Finally, *Women, Property and the Letters of the Law in Early Modern England*, edited by Nancy E. Wright, Margaret W. Ferguson, and A. R. Buck (2004), has explored women's relationship with property and law in literary and non-literary texts of the period.[9]

In the wake of these studies which have expanded our understanding of the impact of law and legal culture on all levels of early modern society, the present collection also considers the diversity of people who contributed to life at the Inns: the builders, gardeners (female and male), architects, professional actors, craftspeople, cooks, and municipal functionaries, among others, who worked at the Inns alongside the lawyers, students, and visiting court dignitaries we might more typically expect to find there. The chapters in *The Intellectual and Cultural World of the Early Modern Inns of Court* apply a variety of interdisciplinary approaches –

extending its methodological scope to give new emphasis to material and visual culture – to the Inns, both as self-governing institutions, and in terms of their wider influence on Elizabethan and Stuart society. In devising the content and structure of this volume, we have been guided by four main objectives: firstly, to encourage and showcase cutting-edge work on the early modern Inns, with particular attention to new archival findings and to innovative analyses of the culture and organisation of the Inns; secondly, to foster interdisciplinary work on the Inns by providing a forum for the cross-fertilisation of ideas and discoveries between scholars working in different fields; thirdly, to commission and foreground new research into hitherto neglected aspects of the Inns, in particular their (and their members') patronage of architecture, gardens, and the visual arts more generally; and finally, to define and provide foundations for areas of future research on the early modern Inns of Court.

The collection begins with an essay by Professor Sir John H. Baker, QC, Downing Professor of the Laws of England at the University of Cambridge, and Literary Director of the Selden Society. Setting the scene for the following chapters, his introductory chapter provides an account of the composition and role of the medieval and early Tudor Inns of Court and Chancery, and describes their gradual transformation into their early modern incarnations as important centres of learning. The fourteen remaining chapters are grouped in three overlapping sections, corresponding broadly to different disciplinary approaches and areas of focus. Across these three sections, the Inns are understood as unique, distinctive institutions in their own right, but also as places embedded within larger cultural, political, and artistic contexts and networks.

Part I, 'History: education, religion, politics, and the law', foregrounds historical scholarship, and encompasses education, religion, politics, legal practice, and the administration and governance of the early modern Inns. Part II, 'Art, architecture, and gardens', brings together new and innovative work by leading historians of art, architecture, and gardens, whose findings collectively open up the visual and material culture of the early modern Inns and their members. Part III, 'Literature and drama', contains essays on poetic and dramatic texts written and/or performed by members of the Inns, often with a wider audience in mind. This final section builds on the former two sections, by outlining the ways in which literary and dramatic works reflect on and intervene in contemporary political, social, and religious issues, and by attending to the physical settings of the Inns and their function as performance spaces. Critical attention is also given here to new formal and generic developments in the literary and performance culture of the Inns, which attracted many innovative, bold authors during this period. As befits the interdisciplinary nature of this collection, many individuals make multiple appearances, albeit in different guises, across the volume. The judge and Lincoln's Inn bencher Sir Randolph Crewe, for example, is discussed in Part I as the dedicatee of various sermons preached at Lincoln's Inn, and in Part II as the builder of Crewe Hall, Cheshire, the screen for which may have been modelled on that in Lincoln's 'Old Hall'[10] (See Figure 11).

Each of the three sections is prefaced by a short introduction which reflects on recent research on the Inns and associated theoretical and methodological developments in the relevant disciplines. In these section introductions, the chapters – both within and across disciplines – are set in conversation with one another, and areas of comparison and potential dissonance are highlighted. Finally, directions for, and areas of, future research on the early modern Inns are identified.

Much new work remains to be done within this burgeoning field. While this collection offers varied, innovative approaches to the study of the early modern Inns across numerous academic disciplines, it is also clear that the Inns would reward still more scholarly attention in the future. It is hoped that the chapters that follow will provide – both individually and collectively – a baseline from which such research might proceed and that the work of the scholars in this volume will soon be complemented by new work on these singular sites of early modern cultural activity.

Notes

1 George Buc[k], *The third universitie of England. Or A treatise of the foundations of all the colledges, auncient schooles of priviledge, and of houses of learning, and liberall arts, within and above the most famous cittie of London* (London: Thomas Dawson, 1615), pp. 968–78. See also John H. Baker, *The Third University of England: The Inns of Court and the Common-Law Tradition* (London: Selden Society, 1990).

2 See, for example, the multi-volume *Oxford History of the Laws of England* (gen. ed.) John H. Baker, 6 vols (Oxford: Oxford University Press, 2003–); Christopher W. Brooks, *Law, Politics and Society in Early Modern England* (Cambridge: Cambridge University Press, 2008); Bradin Cormack, *A Power to Do Justice: Jurisdiction, English Literature, and the Rise of Common Law, 1509–1625* (Chicago, IL: University of Chicago Press, 2008); Lorna Hutson, *The Invention of Suspicion: Law and Mimesis in Shakespeare and Renaissance Drama* (Oxford: Oxford University Press, 2007); and Alan H. Nelson's edition of dramatic texts and documents relating to the early modern Inns of Court (forthcoming with University of Toronto Press, in association with Records of Early English Drama).

3 See, for example, John H. Baker, *An Inner Temple Miscellany: Papers Reprinted from the Inner Temple Yearbook* (London: The Honourable Society of the Inner Temple, 2004), *Readers and Readings in the Inns of Court and Chancery* (London: Selden Society, 2000), and *The Third University of England*; Eric W. Ives, *The Common Lawyers of Pre-Reformation England. Thomas Kebell: A Case Study* (Cambridge: Cambridge University Press, 1983), and 'Some aspects of the legal profession in the late fifteenth and early sixteenth centuries' (PhD dissertation, University of London, 1955); Wilfrid R. Prest, *The Inns of Court under Elizabeth I and the Early Stuarts, 1590–1640* (London: Longman, 1972).

4 Marie Axton, 'Robert Dudley and the Inner Temple revels', *Historical Journal*, 13:3 (1970), 365–78, and *The Queen's Two Bodies: Drama and the Elizabethan Succession* (London: Royal Historical Society, 1977); Desmond S. Bland (ed.), *Three Revels from the Inns of Court* (Amersham: Avebury, 1984); Philip J. Finkelpearl, *John Marston of the Middle Temple: An Elizabethan Dramatist in his Social Setting* (Cambridge, MA: Harvard University Press, 1969); Robert S. Miola (ed.), *The Comedy of Errors: Critical Essays* (New York, NY: Garland; Routledge, 1997); Henry James and Greg Walker, 'The politics of

Gorboduc', *English Historical Review*, 110 (1995), 109–21; Jessica Winston, 'Expanding the political nation: *Gorboduc* at the Inns of Court and succession revisited', *Early Theatre*, 8:1 (2005), 11–34.

5 Subha Mukherji, *Law and Representation in Early Modern Drama* (Cambridge: Cambridge University Press, 2006); Kieran Dolin, *A Critical Introduction to Law and Literature* (Cambridge: Cambridge University Press, 2007); Hutson, *The Invention of Suspicion*; Cormack, *A Power to Do Justice*.

6 Paul Raffield, *Images and Cultures of Law in Early Modern England: Justice and Political Power, 1558–1660* (Cambridge: Cambridge University Press, 2004); Peter Goodrich, 'Eating law: commons, common land, common law', *Journal of Legal History*, 12 (1991), 246–67, and *Languages of Law: From Logics of Memory to Nomadic Masks* (London: Weidenfeld & Nicolson, 1990).

7 Victoria Kahn and Lorna Hutson (eds), *Rhetoric and Law in Early Modern Europe* (New Haven, CT: Yale University Press, 2001).

8 Erica Sheen and Lorna Hutson (eds), *Literature, Politics and Law in Renaissance England* (Basingstoke: Palgrave Macmillan, 2005).

9 Nancy E. Wright, Margaret W. Ferguson, and A. R. Buck (eds), *Women, Property and the Letters of the Law in Early Modern England* (Toronto; London: University of Toronto Press, 2004).

10 See Chapters 3 (pp. 53, 62, below) and 7 (p. 153, below).

1

The third university 1450–1550:
law school or finishing school?

J. H. Baker

I have been asked to introduce this collection with a general account of life in the Inns of Court and Chancery in the period 1450–1550. Perhaps I may be allowed to begin that task in the first person. I am currently engaged in two projects relating to 'the third university'. One is an edition of the statutes of the Inns of Chancery. When I first undertook this editorial project, only two sets of statutes out of the nine were known; now we have four, which is almost half, and they contain many mutual similarities. They offer our best hope of finding out how the lesser Inns worked, though I fear we shall never know as much about them as we do about the Inns of Court. But this is a subject I will pass over in this chapter.[1] The other project, on which I have been engaged for a very long time, is a biographical dictionary of the Inns of Court and Chancery, and of what I loosely call 'men of court', for the period 1440 to 1550. It will include all relevant people mentioned in that period – which means that some of the biographical material runs back to 1400 and some runs forward to 1600. There are about ten thousand names, and inevitably many of the entries are obscure or ambiguous. It is, nevertheless, a substantial sample from which some general conclusions may be drawn. It is probable that most 'men of court' – that is, men who practised law as counsel, attorneys, or office-holders in the central courts – were members of the Inns, except perhaps for the lowliest of under-clerks.

On the other hand, it is evident that only a small proportion of the members of the Inns were men of court in the professional sense in which I have defined them. That seems to have been as true in 1450 as in 1550. It may be asked how it is possible to know this, since the official membership records are very defective until the 1550s. Fortunately, a great deal of information about the membership of all the Inns can be recovered from the plea rolls of the Common Pleas, which for almost every term from the mid-1440s onwards record actions of debt against groups of members for dues owed to the societies. Comparison of the Lincoln's Inn actions for dues with the *Black Books* of that Inn, which record most of the admissions during the relevant period, shows that the proportion of members put in suit was quite high. The plea-roll lists therefore give us a very good cross-section, especially of the non-legal members – who were more likely to go out of residence with debts unpaid.

Early membership

Let us take as an example the Middle Temple. The first Common Pleas suit was brought in 1479 by William Poulet, as '*thesaurarius Medii Templi*', against forty-five men, claiming £10 from each of them. Poulet (or Paulet) is probably the Somerset justice of that name, later knighted, who was seated at Hinton St George and died in 1488. A similar action was brought in 1486 by William Copley as treasurer against one knight, two esquires, two clerks, and sixty-two gentlemen, mostly of London, also for £10 each. A third action, in 1498, was brought by Andrew Dymmok, second baron of the Exchequer, Richard Empson, and Thomas Englefield, the three governors of the Inn, and Henry Harman as treasurer, against five knights, four esquires, and eleven gentlemen, of various places, again for £10 each.[2] Empson was perhaps the most famous Middle Templar of Henry VII's reign. Englefield (later Sir Thomas Englefield) was also a leading figure in public affairs, since he was speaker of the House of Commons and would become, with Empson, one of the King's executors. Harman was clerk of the Crown in the King's Bench.

The defendants are of a rather different character, mostly west-country gentlemen. The 1498 action is particularly interesting in that connection. The benchers who brought the action were not themselves from the west country: Empson was from Northamptonshire, Englefield from Berkshire, Dymmok from Lincolnshire, and Harman from Kent. On the other hand, four of the five knights and one of the esquires were from Somerset: Sir John Byconell (of North Perrott), Sir Hugh Luttrell (of Dunster), Sir John Speke (of White Lackington), Sir John Wadham (of Merrifield), and Thomas Malet (of Currypool). Other Somerset names in the list include John Wyndham of Orchard, who was to be knighted in 1487 after the Battle of Stoke and executed for treason in 1502. In the 1486 suit we also find Sir John Paulet, Robert Hill, esquire, and Amyas Paulet, esquire – who was knighted with Wyndham in 1487, and as Sir Amyas was still being pursued by the Inn for his debts in 1504 and 1516. This Sir Amyas Paulet (1457–1538) was a son of the Sir William mentioned above as treasurer, and became an important figure in the history of the Inn, for in 1520 he served as treasurer and at his own costs rebuilt the gate-house in Fleet Street.

Not all the Somerset members of the Middle Temple were laymen. They included a fair share of eminent lawyers, including four chiefs: Sir William Hody (Chief Baron of the Exchequer), Sir John Fitzjames and Sir William Portman (Chief Justices of the King's Bench), and Sir James Dyer (Chief Justice of the Common Pleas). But the knights and esquires in these fifteenth-century actions were not lawyers. The evidence suggests that fewer than ten per cent of Inns of Court men in the fifteenth and sixteenth centuries took to the legal profession as a career. The laymen were a distinct group within the Inn, and we can imagine what they were like. Indeed, we do not have to indulge our imagination too far because we may read a complaint of around 1539 that the 'learners' in the Middle Temple were much troubled by the noise made by 'them that be no learners'.[3]

This was a university in the modern sense, a place to grow up, to learn about life, to make useful contacts, even to misbehave a bit; and a considerable part of the gentry of England went through the system, if only for a brief spell of residence. It seems from these actions for dues that the Middle Temple was, apart from everything else, a club for the landed families of Somerset. Even a century later, as Wilfrid Prest has shown for the period 1590–1639, one third of entrants to the Inn came from the six western counties of Cornwall, Devon, Dorset, Gloucestershire, Somerset, and Wiltshire.[4] By then, the Inn also admitted more members from Northamptonshire and Warwickshire than any of the others. These local connections no doubt began through personal contacts; the Warwickshire link with the Middle Temple went back at least to the early 1500s, with John Rastell and Christopher St German. The other Inns had similar links, though none of them quite as durable. Gray's Inn, for instance, recruited heavily from Sussex and Yorkshire, Lyon's Inn from Devon. An action for dues brought on behalf of Gray's Inn in 1486 mentions no fewer than four knights from prominent Yorkshire families (Sir William Gascoigne of Gawthorpe, Sir Robert Constable and Sir Ralph Bygot of Flamborough, and Sir John Savile of Thornhill),[5] while an Inner Temple suit in the same term is distinctly concentrated upon the Home region: there are only five defendants, Sir William Say (of Broxbourne, Hertfordshire), William Paston (of Paston, Norfolk), John Clopton (of Long Melford, Suffolk), John Bame (of Gillingham, Kent), and John Faunt (of Wistow, Huntingdonshire).[6] But these were not exclusive catchment areas. Gray's Inn also had strong Sussex connections, while the Inner Temple recruited numerous members from the middle and north-western parts of England, from Northamptonshire through the Midlands to Shropshire and Cheshire. Nor were families rigidly linked with particular Inns: William Paston's brother John was a fellow Inner Templar, but John's son William went to Lincoln's Inn, as did John Clopton's son William. As with the Middle Temple suits, the defendants in these actions, whether knights, esquires, or gentlemen, were generally not professional lawyers.

It is difficult to say whether the 'non-learners' would have read much law during their spell of residence. It would certainly have made sense for all of them at least to buy a *Littleton*, a statute-book, and a book on justices, to acquaint them with the minimal knowledge necessary to run their estates and their counties. Elementary law books are sometimes found inscribed with the names of men who are not known to have become lawyers. The non-learners may even have been expected to attend and watch the public manifestations of learning, unless they bought exemption with a 'special admission'. The evidence for their presence is sketchy. The plea-roll entries mentioned above do not particularise the bills on which members were sued; and although most of the debts were probably for pensions, or room-rents, the dates of residence are not given. The only continuous records of residence are those in the *Black Books* of Lincoln's Inn, which – from the 1420s until the reign of Elizabeth I (at least) – list those due to attend the Lent, Autumn, and Christmas vacations, marking those who were absent. These lists were omitted from the printed *Black*

Books, but are of some importance. They show that most of the members attended at least a few learning vacations, and so they would presumably have been exposed to the readings and moots. Perhaps that was enough to put most of them off, though some went on to be called to the bar without, to our knowledge, becoming practitioners. The reports of moots in this period do not give enough names for any generalisations to be made; but some of the Elizabethan and Jacobean moots are packed with names, and it would be an interesting study to find out what proportion of an Inn's members took part in them.

Non-legal activity

If they did not read law, what did the non-learners do? Wilfrid Prest and other contributors to this volume have provided us with much detail about the non-legal activities in which members of the Inns were involved in the second half of the sixteenth and early seventeenth centuries, especially drama and literature.[7] We must be cautious about extrapolating these details backwards, since the evidence is more scanty, but it seems likely that similar diversions were available in the fifteenth and early sixteenth centuries. Sir John Fortescue, who had been a member of Lincoln's Inn in the 1420s, wrote fifty years later that: 'In these inns … there is, besides the law school, a kind of academy of all the manners which inform *nobiles*. They learn to sing and practise all kinds of music; they also engage in dancing, and sports suitable for gentlemen, just like those brought up in the king's household.'[8] *Nobiles* has generally been translated by editors as noblemen. Fortescue said that all the members of the Inns were the sons of *nobiles*; but the Inns received very few sons of the nobility, as later understood, and Fortescue clearly meant gentlemen. Nobility and gentry were equivalent concepts in medieval times.[9] Most of the entrants probably were indeed sons of the gentry, very often eldest sons; but the list of defaulters derived from the plea rolls includes a few Pickbones and Squeles, for whom admission to an Inn of Chancery was probably seen as a kind of transition from yeoman status to that of gentleman.

Fortescue should not be taken to mean that the Inns provided instruction in singing and dancing. They simply kept alive the traditional songs and measures, to which new members were doubtless introduced by their seniors. Like everything else in the law, entertainment was governed to some extent by custom and precedent. And most of it was limited to the Christmas vacation, attendance at which was compulsory for new members. The carol, or ring-dance, was central to the festivities. The Lincoln's Inn ring-dance, or 'howe', had set steps, recorded in a fifteenth-century moot book now at Cambridge; and on the last leaf is the carol 'Nowel, out of your slepe', which is still not wholly forgotten.[10] So inveterate were these customs that the Inner Temple kept up its stately ring-dance, performed at walking pace, until the last solemn revels in 1734. The principal carol sung on these occasions, known as the 'old song of mirth and solace', may have been of medieval origin: 'Some mirth and solace now let's make / To cheer our hearts, and sorrows slake'.[11]

The earliest evidence of the way Christmas was kept in the Inns comes from some extracts made in the seventeenth century from the lost records of Furnival's Inn for 1407.[12] There were twenty-six members of the Inn keeping commons over Christmas that year, and their kitchen bills reveal that on Christmas Day they were treated with meat pies, mortreux of pork (stew), baked chickens and rabbits, with apples and raisins for dessert. This was washed down with five gallons of red wine and two of sweet wine – a very generous ration, it would seem, though it perhaps refers to the whole twelve days. There is mention of a minstrel (*citherator*) – who played a stringed instrument, probably a harp or lute – and of an allowance of bread for the *revellours*. A few years later there is expenditure on 'players' (*lusores, ludenses*), who are probably identical in kind with the revellers of 1407. Such players no doubt performed the 'interlude', which is mentioned on Christmas Day 1412. They seem to have come from without the society – perhaps from the parish of St Andrew's, perhaps from the City. They may be identifiable in turn with the waits mentioned in 1481 and 1485, and again in 1500, when the waits of London came to the Candlemas revels together with a harpist. In 1502 and 1503, the guests at the banquet included members of Thavie's Inn and other Inns of Court and Chancery; the occasion was one 'whereat was much dancing and revelling, and for that purpose the minstrelsy of the lady princess and her servants were here, with the waits of London, the harper, and other musical instruments'. Besides venison and other meats, the delicacies included jellies, candied fruit, sweets, comfits, cream, almonds, blanch-powder, fritters ('*panpuffes*'), and something called '*tardburgoine*' – presumably some kind of French tart. Besides the musical and alimentary entertainments were zoological displays: in 1473, 1494, and 1496 a lion, and in 1485 a baboon. There is also an item in the 1407 accounts, which recurs in 1491, of payments for 'harness' from an armourer, suggesting that there may have been some kind of tournament or military show. A mock royal court, with a student king, is mentioned in 1450. And in 1505 there was a boar, with holly to deck the hall. This was truly the old English Christmas tradition.

The other Inns of Chancery celebrated the season in much the same way. The lost records of Clifford's Inn apparently contained even fuller information than those of Furnival's Inn about Christmas entertainments. The following note was made by someone who saw them in the seventeenth century:

> By the pension rolls of this house, and stewards' books there, it appeareth divers grand Christmas times have been in this house solemnly held and right commendably and sumptuously performed by the gentlemen of this Society, namely one in the 22nd year of King Edward the fourth [1482], which was with great reputation, much cost and diligence magnificently managed and performed, the same continuing from the Vigil of the Feast day of Saint Thomas the Apostle until the twentieth day of Christmas following. In which time every day, daily, the company exceeded in largess of diet, their tables being replenished with store of venison, and costly viands, change of 12 wines, selected songs, choice music, majestical masques, stately stage-plays, bountiful

banquetings, dicing, dancing, and many other rare invented courtly pastimes, with like rarity of oratory speeches, whereby was unfolded the brave wits and ingenious capacity of sundry persons resorting thither, to enrich with their personal presence the honour of this house as best beseemed the same.[13]

The larger societies keeping term in the Inns of Court observed Christmas with at least equal splendour. Three members of each society were elected as steward, marshal, and master of the revels, to oversee the festivities and keep the accounts. There are scattered references to Christmas throughout the *Black Books* of Lincoln's Inn in the fifteenth century, chiefly concerned with the duties of attendance and service. At Christmas 1498, the society was entertained by the waits, by the king's players (*lusores*), and by minstrels, showing that at that date these were different entities, and the Inn also paid 3*s*. 4*d*. to a singer for 'the carol' at Christmas. Boars and spiced delicacies were the traditional fare here also. An 'interlude' is mentioned in a note of 1489 on the flyleaf of a book in the Inn's library,[14] and there are several references to 'disguisings'.[15]

Something of the atmosphere on these occasions was preserved for us by John Spelman (*c.*1480–1546), the future judge, who set down an eye-witness account of a Gray's Inn Christmas soon after he joined that society around 1500.[16] Here too, there was a student 'king', elected by the youngest students – the 'clerks of the third table'. This king dined in state with his court, including 'lords', a chancellor, constable, and other officers, and whenever he rose from table the company shouted '*Vive le roy*'. Grace at the end of the meal was preceded by the anthem *Nesciens mater*. When the members went to church – presumably St Andrew's, Holborn – the marshal gave each of them a silver badge, and they went in procession, the most junior in front, singing 'What shall we sing in worship of this day?'[17] At church, the marshal paid for a carol. The returning procession sang 'There shall none rain down rain', followed by 'Round about the fire', which was performed *accelerando* with a shout at the end. Each day in the evening supper was followed by revels, a 'constable's court', and then a late snack (the 'rere-supper'). On Twelfth Night, the marshal and steward came by torchlight to the fire in hall, singing 'Farewell and have good day', after which they broke their staves of office and cast them into the fire. The student constable then sat to hold his court, but as soon as the 'Oyez' was proclaimed the other students set upon him and the treasurer – no doubt the mock lord treasurer rather than the Master Treasurer – and gave them 'many friendly blows'.

Spelman also indicates that cards and dice were allowed over the holiday period. He does not mention the interludes or disguisings, but in 1526 there was a notable scandal in Gray's Inn when a play performed by the students there was deemed – doubtless correctly – to represent a satire on Cardinal Wolsey, the King's chief minister. The principal author, John Roo, an alumnus of Gray's Inn who had become a serjeant at law, was sent to prison for contempt.[18] But the dramatic spirit could not be extinguished. In a report made on the state of the Inns of Court in 1539, it was stated that 'ordinarily they have some interlude or tragedy played by the gentlemen of the same house, the ground and matter whereof is devised by some of the gentlemen of the house'.[19] The members of the Inns were thus beginning to take over the Christmas entertainments from the medieval waits and to perform plays of their own making, a tradition which would flower in the Elizabethan period. The last notorious Christmas entertainment in the medieval manner, with a mock court and grand officers, was that attended by King Charles II in Lincoln's Inn in 1662.[20]

The music, the 'disguising and pastimes', and the courtly ceremony associated with the Christmas vacation – and also with All Saints and Candlemas[21] – could be said to have provided the Renaissance gentleman with polite accomplishments and to have laid the foundations of an English musical and dramatic tradition. But it is anachronistic to suppose that the play-writing and performing occupied the high ground on which it has been placed by modern academia. They began as diversions and casual entertainments, and it has to be admitted that they had a rougher side. The atmosphere of the Christmas festivities, as we can see from Spelman, was at times like that of a rumbustious children's party, although it also managed to recall the social ritual of an age long gone by: a curious mixture of officially tolerated horse-play and carefully preserved medieval tradition. The young man elected as lord of misrule sometimes over-indulged his dramatic licence, and in 1518, Lincoln's Inn felt obliged to abolish the custom of electing a mock traitor (Jack Straw); five years later, a lord of misrule elsewhere actually killed someone.[22] Quite apart from Christmas, student behaviour was often rude and sometimes violent. On several occasions in Henry VII's reign, the Inns were in trouble before the Privy Council for rioting, sometimes resulting in death; gaming and loose living were rife; and in 1506, a future chief justice was fined for frequenting a brothel.[23] The misbehaviour may have been worse than that of the students in the contemporary universities, who were younger and *in statu pupillari*. There were no tutors in the Inns of Court, where most entrants were around twenty-one years of age, and perhaps the traditional scholarly virtues were less valued by men of the world. Yet the frequency of disorderly incidents over the period as a whole compares favourably with modern universities, and for the realities of serious student life we should look rather at the students' notebooks than at the disciplinary records which fate has so unkindly preserved.

Legal education

The main function of the Inns was legal education. Fortescue, quoted earlier, had begun his account of the Inns of Court and Chancery by explaining that they were a large law school or *studium* unique to England. In his student days, they were perhaps less than a century old, representing a collegiate development within an older law school which had arisen to train the apprentices of the bench in the reign of Henry III (r.1216–72). We know nothing about the original educational arrangements – not even where the law school was situated – though the most likely location was the Common Bench itself. By the time of Edward II (r.1307–27), perhaps from 1293, the apprentices had their enclosed area in the court, called the 'crib', where they were herded to watch and learn, and might occasionally be treated to a helpful word of explanation from the chief justice. Perhaps they stayed on in court after it had risen (in the middle of the day) for their academical instruction, which consisted of lectures and disputations. That at least would explain the lack of any known premises for the school. The formal association of the apprentices with the Bench was doubtless lost in the fourteenth century with the rise of the Inns.

The conclusion that the collegiate system came into being around 1340 and immediately took over the more advanced teaching – a contention first put forward in 1990[24] – was a daring departure from the tale as told by Samuel E. Thorne in 1959, which had been treated as gospel for the previous thirty years.[25] Thorne had supposed that the bare provision of lodgings came first, and that education was added much later – probably in the early fifteenth century – as a means of generating income. It was not a firm conclusion, but a tentative thesis put forward for testing. The immediate source for this hypothesis appears to have been the historical appendix to C. P. Snow's widely acclaimed novel, *The Masters*, which was first published in 1951. Snow claimed of the early Cambridge students:

> The university offered them nothing but lectures, to which they went if they pleased. They found their own lodging, often in the garrets of the little town. Their time was their own, to talk, gamble, drink, fornicate. They seem to have been unusually active with their knives … The students liked their life, but no one else did … So, almost from the origin of the university, there were attempts to get them out of their lonely lodgings into boarding-houses … These boarding-houses had nothing to do with teaching; the students just lodged there, and went off in the morning to the schools. They were simply a sensible means of keeping these youths from the wilder excesses. Some of them were given money, rules, and became known as colleges, but their purpose remained the same.[26]

Much of this passage occurs, verbatim, in Thorne's lecture.[27] It is a neat, colourful, and plausible hypothesis, but – at any rate for the Inns of Court – wrong. It is probably wrong in respect of the universities as well. The earlier period in which we have ventured to place the origins of our legal colleges was, as it happens, the most active period of college-founding at Paris, Oxford, and Cambridge. That wave of new foundations can hardly have gained its momentum from bare coincidence; and in all three places it seems that colleges were intended from the outset to provide students with a stricter academical as well as social discipline.

Unlike the universities and their colleges, the Inns of Court were unincorporated, and this enabled their constitutions to evolve over time. As far as we can tell, their original constitutions were independent of the degree system which grew up during the fifteenth century. All the members – including the youngest students – were regarded as members of the *societas* or fellowship, and were described in the sixteenth century as fellows (or *socii*). Even on a formal monumental inscription, it was appropriate to describe a bencher as 'one of the fellowship of the Middle Temple',[28] while as late as 1660, a mere student could be described likewise as a 'fellow of the Middle Temple'.[29] The fellowship was divided into two 'companies', known as clerks' commons and masters' commons, alluding to their separate tables in hall. Clerks were newly admitted students, who paid lower dues and had cheaper commons (or food rations) in return for waiting on the masters in hall, like sizars at Cambridge. They remained in this station for about two years, until they were themselves 'called' to masters' commons by the benchers. The masters were divided into benchers (or masters of the bench), utter barristers (or masters of the utter bar), and 'no utter barristers' (or masters of the inner bar).

Each Inn was self-governing, in the sense that the whole society of masters made orders for its regulation, and once a year elected three or four governors to act as an executive governing body for the next twelve months. The full assembly of the society was known in each of the Temple societies as a 'Parliament'; in Lincoln's Inn it was the 'Council', and in Gray's Inn a 'Pension'. Decisions of the Middle Temple parliaments in Henry VIII's reign were recorded as having been made by the 'company' (*comitiva*) or 'fellowship' (*societas*) rather than by the bench. In the course of the early Tudor period, the government of the inns gradually passed from the fellowship at large, and their elected governors, to the masters of the bench (or benchers): that is, those masters who had graduated from the utter bar to the bench of their societies. The Temple Parliaments, the Lincoln's Inn Council, and the Gray's Inn Pension still act as the governing bodies of the Inns today, but they are composed exclusively of benchers.

The 'learners', as noted above, were but a minority of the younger members, and it follows that the educational system – though sophisticated and demanding – was not compulsory, any more than it was (for example) in early Victorian Cambridge. The principal sanction was self-qualification. No one was obliged to attend an Inn of Chancery, though he might find it more difficult or expensive to join an Inn of Court if he did not, and he might be daunted by the lack of elementary preparation if he intended to pursue the law. No one was obliged to join an Inn of Court, but he could not advance in the law beyond the status of an attorney unless he did so; and if he meddled in litigation without being a member of an Inn he was probably guilty of the offence of maintenance.[30] No one who joined an Inn was obliged to attend its learning exercises, provided he was prepared to pay a fine or find a substitute; but he could not become a barrister or a bencher without performing at least some of them to a suitable standard, and indeed in 1568, the Middle Temple went so far as to decree that benchers who were elected without having read were to have no voice or place in parliaments.[31] These unwritten incentives were enough of a sanction for those intending to live from the law, and the new serjeants called from the Middle Temple in 1503 were doubtless sincere in praising the Inn for 'binding them to study by the good rules ordained by the company, which restrained them in their youth from their disinclination to study'.[32]

Exercises of learning

Reading facilities were minimal: libraries were small and insecure, and members of the Inns had to rely on small private libraries, containing manuscript as well as printed books, and to make good the deficiencies by loan or exchange. The only communal meeting place, apart from the Round of Temple Church (or the chapels of Gray's and Lincoln's Inns), was the hall. That was used not only for dinner (served at around mid-day), but also for the learning exercises. The learning exercises which developed in the medieval Inns were taken over from the system which had been developing for at least eighty years before they came into existence, and consisted of lectures (or 'readings') and disputations (the readers' cases and the moots).[33] At their best, these provided students with a rigorous introduction both to legal practice and to legal method. The readings became more and more sophisticated as propositions were challenged and polished over the generations; the lecturers were not expected to work up lectures from scratch, but passed on a refined body of 'inherited learning'; most of the fourteenth- and fifteenth-century readings are anonymous, because they were not perceived as individual performances.

The readings of the fifteenth and sixteenth centuries exposed the audience to close textual analysis, to historical and purposive interpretation, and to some pretty intricate law, while the debates upon the readers' cases initiated them in the techniques of legal argument and enabled them to see leading members of the profession – including judges and serjeants – exercising their wits on pure questions of law. The moots, on the other hand, were vocational exercises in the recondite art of pleading.[34] In that respect they differed materially from moots as we understand them today. There was no final judgment in a moot, because there was no trial and therefore no established facts; the exercise was predicated on the first stage of legal proceedings, when the issue – the question to be tried later – was thrashed out in open court by skilled pleaders, and the only decisions commonly required from the bench were interlocutory rulings on points of form. Oral pleading was still the core of a lawyer's art in the reign of Edward III (r.1327–77), when the first moot-cases were compiled, and it is not surprising that it was given prominence in the educational system of that period.

It is true that the records of the Inns do not place as much emphasis on these exercises as on living arrangements and social discipline; but that should not mislead us as to the primacy of legal education. The system was governed largely by unwritten custom, and therefore only the occasional tinkering needed to be put in writing. The division of exercises into lectures and disputed cases reflected the educational system in the universities, and it resulted in a parallel graduation system. Utter barristers, corresponding with bachelors, were those who took part in disputations by arguing cases in hall as if at the bar of a court – that is, outside the bar; and for centuries, a barrister could only take that degree at a moot. In the universities, likewise, bachelors graduated by arguing a *quaestio* in the schools. The process of self-graduation, by performing an exercise, was more significant than the 'call' which authorised it: so much may be deduced from the absence of any formal record of the making of utter barristers until the sixteenth century. Benchers, corresponding to masters or doctors, were those who had delivered a course of lectures and thereafter sat on the bench at moots. Masters likewise graduated by giving lectures and then presided over disputations. We might note also that if a bencher went on to become a serjeant at law, the central point of the graduation was a pleading exercise, by reciting a 'count' in law-French at the bar of the Common Pleas: even at that level, although a call from the monarch was a prerequisite, it was still for the serjeant to make himself a graduate by performing the act.

The readings were not given in term time, but in the two 'grand' vacations, during Lent and the early autumn (August).[35] This seemingly odd arrangement had the perfectly simple explanation that term-time was dedicated to Westminster Hall, where the students flocked to watch the proceedings and perhaps to discuss them afterwards. These grand vacations were the chief events in the educational cycle, and were regularly attended by those judges and serjeants who were former benchers of the Inn. Each lecture course originally lasted about four weeks, though they became shorter in later centuries. They were always given on statutory texts, not because statutes were superior to the common law, but because (as in the universities) readings had to be on texts, and the common law was *lex non scripta*. In the fourteenth and early fifteenth centuries, it seems to have been the custom to proceed through the *statuta vetera* from Magna Carta (1215) until the reign of Edward I (r.1272–1307), each reader beginning where his predecessor left off. From early Tudor times, however, we find some readers breaking from the old cycle, doubtless in order to make a mark and impress the Crown with their usefulness: the earliest known example is Edmund Dudley's reading in Gray's Inn on *Quo Warranto*, around 1485, and ten years later, at least two of the new serjeants read on *Prerogativa Regis*.[36] Once readers had acquired a free choice, there was the possibility of introducing an element of practical usefulness into a course which was still necessarily random in its coverage. After 1530, it was not at all unusual to expound the statutes of Henry VIII, including those concerned with technical matters. On the other hand, the result was to turn the readings into unique performances, of variable quality, in place of the 'core of inherited learning' which the old system had passed on.

The readings, like *lecturae ordinariae* in the universities, consisted of exposition followed by disputation. The reader read a clause of his statute each day, commented upon it, and then explained its operation with the aid of a spectrum of illustrative cases. The fifteenth-century tradition was to gloss each phrase in the statute *seriatim*, and this method was still followed by some readers in the earlier Tudor period. But the new form of reading introduced by Dudley and his contemporaries laid more emphasis on the analytical treatment of a topic, ranging if need be far away from the wording of the set text. Both the old and the new traditions recognised the importance of interactive exercises, and the most intellectually testing part of the reading was the disputation of the readers' 'cases'. Each day a few of the put-cases were challenged for argument by the barristers, benchers, serjeants, and judges who were present. The process is described in a report on the Inns of Court written by Thomas Denton, Nicholas Bacon, and Robert Cary in 1540:

> [The reader], openly in the hall before all the company, shall read from one such act or statute as shall please him to ground his whole reading on for all that vacation; and that done doth declare such inconveniences and mischiefs as were unprovided for, and now by the same statute be [remedied], and then reciteth certain doubts and questions which he hath devised that may grow upon the said statute, and declareth his judgment therein; that done, one of the younger utter barristers rehearseth one question propounded by the reader, and doth by way of argument labour to prove the reader's opinion to be against the law; and after him the rest of the utter barristers and readers one after another in their ancienties do declare their opinions and judgments in the same; and then the reader who did put the case endeavoureth himself to confute objections laid against him, and to confirm his own opinion; after whom the judges and serjeants, if any be present, declare their opinions; and after they have done the youngest utter barrister again rehearseth another case, which is ordered as the other was. Thus the reading ends for that day: and this manner of reading and disputations continues daily two hours, or thereabouts … And besides this daily, in some houses, after dinner, one at the reader's board before they rise propoundeth another of his cases to him, put the same day at his reading, which case is debated by them in like form as the cases are used to be argued at his reading; and like order is observed at every mess at the other tables; and the same manner always observed at supper, when they have no moots.[37]

These disputations in the course of readings have sometimes been confused with moots, but they were an entirely different exercise.[38] Moots were primarily vocational pleading exercises, founded upon sets of facts provided to the students for the purpose, like examination questions. The problems were mostly taken from moot-books of some antiquity, in which some of them are given mnemonic names such as Jacob and Esau, The Rod (*Le virge*), The Rose between Thorns (*Rosa inter spinas*), The Sparrowhawk (*Lesperver*), and The Little Rose (*Parva rosa*). The cases were extremely complex. The object was not to thrash out a contested point of law in a single sitting, but to practise the art of pleading, and incidentally of oral argument, in an exercise divided up into manageable instalments. The first task would be to draw a writ in Latin, and then suitably elaborate pleadings in law-French bringing out all the questions in the case, recited orally and with argued exceptions at each stage. A prolonged '*casus notabilis*' in the Inner Temple in the 1490s proceeded as far as a demurrer to a surrebutter.[39] The exercise could occupy many days, or even a whole vacation. Law school was no soft option.

The daily commitment to learning was not supposed to end with call to the bar or bench. The utter barrister was expected to participate in some of the exercises, and after about five years to read in one of the Inns of Chancery. By the sixteenth century, each Inn of Chancery was attached to a parent Inn of Court, though it is not known how this arrangement came about. Readings 'in Chancery' were also on statutes, with disputations; but they were given in term time as well as the grand vacations, were less demanding, and were attended by students from all the Inns. Barristers of still greater seniority were appointed to 'read in court', that is, in an Inn of Court. After reading they became benchers, but they were in a way still learning, since lawyers never stop doing so; they had their own continuing educational routine, besides the readings at which they assisted, since cases could be moved at 'the board' or 'the board's end' (the high table in hall).

The readings underwent something of a decline in the sixteenth century.[40] There is telling evidence of this in the notebook of a Middle Temple student, now in the British Library.[41] After attending Henry Archer's reading in 1580, the student noted that everyone rejoiced when the reader had finished, because he was the worst reader that ever was or ever would be, both for learning and good cheer, and was derided by everyone. This implies, of course, that the standard was usually markedly better. And the student may have been unduly influenced by the lack of 'good cheer', because later in the same year he praised John Boys as a reader in that every day he had provided such liberal and exceeding good cheer as had never been seen before in the memory of any of the utter barristers. A more authoritative critic, no doubt, was Sir Edward Coke (1552–1634), who complained that:

> the cases are long, obscure, and intricate, full of new conceits, liker rather to riddles than lectures, which when they are opened they vanish away like smoke, and the readers are like to lapwings, who seem to be nearest their nests when they are furthest from them, and all their study is to find nice evasions out of the statute.[42]

Coke was in a good position to know, because his own reading in the Inner Temple (1592) amply illustrates these defects. The greatest days of the Inns as an academical institution were already over. The educational system was stuck in the fourteenth century, and in any case the common law was increasingly coming to be associated with judicial pronouncements rather than with the 'old common learning' of the Inns of Court. Readings were becoming isolated events, associated with food and drink, rather than an educational routine; and the moots were becoming a graduation ceremony rather than an introduction to practice.

Importance of the law school

In 1642, the system collapsed completely and was not effectively replaced until modern times. But legal historians have been too slow to look back beyond this educational collapse and to appreciate the true significance of 'the third university' in its vital period between 1340 and 1640. It may no longer be obvious to the common-law mind why law schools should influence legal development at all. The common law accords little or no weight to doctrinal writing as a source of law; the law is what the courts say and do, not what professors say and write. That is a proposition which has certainly influenced legal historians, in that the history of the common law has been for many of our precursors a history of what courts said and did, to the exclusion of all else. But the fact that the bulk of manuscript readings and moots for the fifteenth century may exceed that of the law reports is enough to alert us to an important additional dimension. So also is the fact that early Tudor lawyers in their study-notebooks mixed material from Gray's Inn or the Inner Temple with cases from Westminster Hall, as if the source made little or no difference.

The common law was the common learning of the men of law belonging to the Inns of Court.[43] What passed as law in the readings and moots was just as much 'law' as what passed as law in the courts; it guided lawyers in their practice, affected their advice, and of course controlled the intellectual horizons of judges and counsel arguing cases in court. It would not be inherently surprising to find that the law of the Inns of Court was sometimes ahead of the law of Westminster Hall; new learning is more readily tested and assimilated in the classroom before dangerous experiments are made in real cases. Nevertheless, it is not appropriate in relation to this law school to distinguish too sharply between *doctrine* and *jurisprudence*; there was no separate profession of Doctor of English Law, because mooting and lecturing were an essential preliminary to becoming an advocate and a judge. There were no royal judges who had not been law professors; and the link between legal education and practice has never been so close in any common-law country since. For all the extra-curricular achievements of its large and wide-ranging membership, this was first and foremost one of the most influential law schools the world has known. And perhaps that influence, in a cultural as well as a technical sense, even extended to the ninety per cent of members who were not lawyers, the knights of the shire and the Justice Shallows of Clement's Inn, whose everyday lives would inevitably be governed by parchment and wax and legal terminology.

Notes

1 See John H. Baker, *Learning in the Early Inns of Chancery* (London: Selden Society, 1990), pp. xxx–xxxiii, and 'The Inns of Chancery', in John H. Baker (ed.), *The Oxford History of the Laws of England*, 6 vols (Oxford: Oxford University Press, 2003–), VI, 453–9.

2 NA, CP 40/870, m. 440, continued at m. 530 (1479); CP 40/871, m. 477 (exigent, 1480); CP 40/896, m. 181[d] (1486); CP 40/947, m. 201[d] (exigent, 1498). A summary of these actions will be provided in *The Men of Court 1440–1550: A Prosopographical Survey of the Inns of Court and Chancery, and the English Legal Profession* (forthcoming in the Selden Society Supplementary Series).

3 'State of the Fellowship of the Middle Temple' (*c.*1539), BL, Cotton MS Vitellius C. 9, fols 319–23[v], printed in William Dugdale, *Origines Juridiciales or, historical memorials of the English laws*, 3rd edn (London: Printed for Christopher Wilkinson, Thomas Dring, and Charles Harper, 1680), pp. 193–7 (p. 195). There is a modern edition by R. M. Fisher in *Journal of the Society of Public Teachers of Law*, 14 (1977), 111–17.

4 Wilfrid R. Prest, *The Inns of Court under Elizabeth I and the Early Stuarts, 1590–1640* (London: Longman, 1972)

5 There is also one Cornish knight (Sir John Trefry of Fowey), though most Cornishmen went to Lincoln's Inn.

6 NA, CP 40/896, m. 97^{d} (suit by the treasurer and governors of the Inner Temple) and m. 501^{d} (suit by John Strete, who acted on behalf of Gray's Inn). The local additions are not given in the roll, but are from the author's unpublished biographical dictionary.

7 Prest, *The Inns of Court under Elizabeth I and the Early Stuarts, 1590–1640*, and *The Rise of the Barristers: A Social History of the English Bar, 1590–1640* (Oxford: Clarendon Press, 1986). See also Walter Cecil Richardson, *A History of the Inns of Court: With Special Reference to the Period of the Renaissance* (Baton Rouge, LA: Claitor's Publishing Division, 1978).

8 John Fortescue, *De Laudibus Legum Angliae*, ed. and trans. Stanley B. Chrimes (Cambridge: Cambridge University Press, 1942), p. 118.

9 See G. R. Sitwell, 'The English gentleman', *The Ancestor*, 1 (1902), 58–103 (esp. 69–71).

10 For example, there is a recording by *Pro Cantione Antiqua* and Medieval Wind Ensemble, published by Innovative Music Productions Ltd in 1986 (PCD 844), track no. 25. The publishers were, of course, unaware of the Lincoln's Inn connection.

11 For further details of Christmas in the Inns, and references, see John H. Baker, *An Inner Temple Miscellany: Papers Reprinted from the Inner Temple Yearbook* (London: The Honourable Society of the Inner Temple, 2004), ch. 4.

12 All these references to Furnival's Inn are from the 'Brerewood manuscript' in MTL, partly edited by Desmond S. Bland in *Early Records of Furnival's Inn* (Newcastle upon Tyne: Department of Extra Mural Studies, King's College, 1957).

13 Unpublished part of the MTL 'Brerewood Manuscript', fol. 57. There are notes of some further Christmas records there, written with the same annoyingly vague verbosity.

14 See John Spelman, *The Reports of Sir John Spelman*, ed. John H. Baker, 2 vols (London: Selden Society, 1977–78), II, 130, n. 9. There is another interlude mentioned in 1500 (*Black Books*, I, 121).

15 *Black Books*, I, 132; and see *Lisle Letters*, ed. Muriel St Clare Byrne, 6 vols (Chicago, IL: Chicago University Press, 1981), II, 20 ('The inns of court hath kept revel this Christmas [1533] with such disguisings and pastimes as hath not been seen.')

16 Spelman, *The Reports of Sir John Spelman*, ed. Baker, I, 233–4.

17 There is a reference to these badges in the Middle Temple records for 1510, though the mystified editor rendered *signorum* as swans (*Middle Temple Records*, I, 30); their significance remains unclear.

18 Edward Hall, *Hall's Chronicle: Containing the history of England during the reign of Henry the Fourth, and the succeeding monarchs, to the end of the reign of Henry the Eighth*, ed. Henry Ellis (London: Printed for J. Johnson; F. C. and J. Rivington; T. Payne; Wilkie and Robinson; Longman, Hurst, Rees and Orme; Cadell and Davies; and J. Mawman, 1809), p. 719; John Foxe, *Actes and Monuments* (London: John Day, 1563), p. 448. Also implicated were Thomas Moyle, an ancient (later a bencher), and the more revolutionary Simon Fish.

19 Spelman, *The Reports of Sir John Spelman*, ed. Baker, II, 130, n. 9.

20 *The Diary of John Evelyn*, ed. E. S. de Beer, 5 vols (Oxford: Clarendon Press, 1955), III, 307–8.

21 The feast of the Purification of the Blessed Mary (2 February). Lincoln's Inn paid for minstrels at Candlemas in 1503 (*Black Books*, I, 132).

22 *Black Books*, I, 189–90; *Letters and Papers, Foreign and Domestic of the Reign of Henry VIII*, ed. J. S. Brewer, 37 vols (London: Longman, Green, Longman, & Roberts, 1862–1932), IV, 390. One of the Inns of Chancery even saw fit to legislate on the matter: 'If any gentle-

man of this house shall take upon him to be Christmas Lord or any such like, without the consent of the principall and sage company then remaining in the same house, he and all such as shall assist and take part with him therein shall be expulsed the house, any use to the contrary notwithstanding' (manuscript statutes of Staple Inn (1624, but incorporating earlier texts) in the writer's possession, fol. 17ᵛ, no. 46).

23 See Spelman, *The Reports of Sir John Spelman*, ed. Baker, II, 131.

24 John H. Baker, 'The third university of England: the Inns of Court and the common-law tradition' (Selden Society lecture, 1990); repr. in Baker, *The Common Law Tradition: Lawyers, Books, and the Law* (London: Hambledon Press, 2000), ch. 1; and in *The Selden Society Lectures 1952–2001* (Buffalo, NY: W. S. Hein, 2003), pp. 565–614.

25 Samuel E. Thorne, 'Early history of the Inns of Court', *Graya*, 50 (1959), 79–96, reprinted in Samuel E. Thorne, *Essays in English Legal History* (London: Hambledon Press, 1985), pp. 137–54.

26 Charles P. Snow, 'Reflections on the college past', in *The Masters* (Harmondsworth: Penguin, 1956), pp. 300–12.

27 Thorne, *Essays in English Legal History*, pp. 140–2.

28 Inscription formerly in Temple Church for '*Johannes Portman quondam unus societatis Medii Templi*' (1521) (Dugdale, *Origines Juridiciales*, p. 173). Portman was reader of the Inn in 1509 and 1515.

29 Monument formerly in Temple Church for Edward Barnard, who died aged twenty-two in 1660 (Dugdale, *Origines Juridiciales*, p. 174 ('*socius*')). There is an example of 1655 on the same page in Dugdale.

30 John H. Baker, *The Legal Profession and the Common Law: Historical Essays* (London: Hambledon Press, 1986), pp. 109–11, 135–49.

31 *Middle Temple Records*, I, 166.

32 John H. Baker, *The Order of Serjeants at Law: A Chronicle of Creations with Related Texts* (London: Selden Society, 1984), p. 267; *Middle Temple Records*, I, 8.

33 For what follows, see John H. Baker, Introduction, in Samuel E. Thorne and John H. Baker (eds), *Readings and Moots at the Inns of Court in the Fifteenth Century. Vol. 2: Moots and Readers' Cases* (London: Selden Society, 1990), pp. xv–lxxvi, and John H. Baker, *Readers and Readings in the Inns of Court and Chancery* (London: Selden Society, 2000).

34 Not in the sense of advocacy, but the technical process of defining an issue for trial.

35 On the use of the readings, see Chapters 4 and 6, pp. 79–83 and pp. 110–20, below.

36 Serjeants at law had to leave their Inns of Court, and it was the custom for the junior serjeant-elect in each Inn to deliver a reading (displacing the ordinary reading) before doing so.

37 The report was first printed in Edward Waterhous, *Fortescutus Illustratus* (London: Printed by Thomas Roycroft for Thomas Dicas, 1663), pp. 544–5.

38 For what follows, see Baker, 'Learning exercises in the Inns of Court', in Baker (ed.), *The Oxford History of the Laws of England*, VI, 463–7.

39 Thorne and Baker (eds), *Readings and Moots at the Inns of Court in the Fifteenth Century*, pp. 179–92. The order of pleadings was: count (plaintiff), plea (defendant), replication (plaintiff), rejoinder (defendant), surrejoinder (plaintiff), rebutter (defendant), surrebutter (plaintiff). A demurrer took exception to the legal effect of the pleading which immediately preceded it.

40 On the 'decline' in the readings, see Chapter 6, p. 20, below.

41 BL, Additional MS 16169, fols 198^{v}, 237; printed in Baker, *Readers and Readings in the Inns of Court and Chancery*, pp. 353, 354.

42 Edward Coke, *Commentary on Littleton* (London: Printed [by Adam Islip] for the Societie of Stationers, 1628), fol. 280.

43 For this theme, see John H. Baker, 'Common erudition', in Baker, *The Law's Two Bodies: Some Evidential Problems in English Legal History* (Oxford; New York, NY: Oxford University Press, 2001), pp. 67–70.

Part I

History: education, religion, politics, and the law

Introduction

Education, religion, politics, and the law at the early modern Inns of Court

Jayne Elisabeth Archer

As the full title of this section implies, 'historical' scholarship on the early modern Inns of Court brings together diverse methodologies and encompasses matters including the role and nature of education at the Inns; religious allegiances within and between the Inns; the contribution of Innsmen to political debates in the febrile period leading up to the civil wars; and, of course, the purpose and practice of the law itself. Many more topics could be added to this list, but it is these four central and overlapping concerns – education, religion, politics, and the law – which the chapters in this section scrutinise. Sir John H. Baker's chapter on the origins, composition, and function of the early modern Inns has already introduced these topics, and it is Baker's scholarship over the last three decades, along with that of Eric Ives and Wilfred R. Prest, which provides much of the foundation for the historical research presented here.[1] Prest himself contributes the final chapter in this section, and his essay opens with some reflections on recent work on the historiography of the early modern Inns.[2] In this Introduction, I won't repeat what Prest provides so eloquently elsewhere. Instead, I want to use this short Introduction to do three things: firstly, to foreground common areas of interest and practice shared by the contributors to this section; secondly, to draw attention to areas of relevance to and shared concern with the chapters in Parts II and III; and finally, to identify topics for future research into the history of the early modern Inns.

The profiles of the authors of chapters in this section demonstrate the fact – indeed, the necessity – that research on the early modern Inns is interdisciplinary: the contributors are currently based in Schools of English Literature, Law, Politics, and History. This interdisciplinarity is the first aspect of the work in this section – and, indeed, the essay collection as a whole – to which I wish to draw attention. Interdisciplinarity is, of course, a fundamental characteristic of work on the early modern period more generally. As Erica Sheen and Lorna Hutson remark in the Introduction to their edited collection *Literature, Politics and Law in Renaissance England* (2005): 'the sixteenth and seventeenth centuries in England constitute a period anterior to the full emergence of distinctions between legal, literary and political discourses'.[3] But the Inns, which inhabited a physical and conceptual space that was simultaneously central and marginal in early modern London and the nation more generally, seem to demand an especially rigorous redefinition of traditional disciplinary boundaries and methodologies. Consequently, the chapters in this section draw upon a wide range of sources in order to illuminate not simply the life and administration of the Inns, but the mental worlds of the Innsmen themselves. Thus, over the following pages, the history of the early modern Inns is reconstructed and scrutinised using personal letters; accounts and receipts; menu plans; diaries and commonplace books; memoirs and life-writing; entertainment texts; books of heraldry; poems; sermons; and the early printed histories written by Innsmen such as George Buc[k] and William Dugdale.[4]

Buc,[5] in a famous quotation that is often taken out of context, saw the Inns of Court and Chancery as members of the collection of colleges and centres of learning which together comprised 'the third Vniuersitie of England'.[6] Thus the Inns were perceived as part of a complex of institutions, all situated within the 'cittie of London', that included 'the Colledge of Herauldes', the 'colledge of Physitians', 'Gresham Colledge', 'Saint Peters of Cornehill' (one of the three 'Schoole-churches' mentioned by Buc), and 'S. Anthonies Colledge' and 'the Monastery of Gray-fryers or Christes church' (both schools for children of the poor), to name but a few.[7] Together, Buc explains, these institutions encompass an eclectic range of disciplines, including:

> the Arts of Grammar, of Rhetorike, of Arithmetike, of Musicke, of Geometry, of Astronomy, of Geographie, of Historiographie: Likewise the other Mathematicall learnings, and Philosophie, Phisicke, and Metaphisicke, the lawes Ecclesiasticall, Municipall, and Ciuill. As also the Artes of Riding, Gladiatorie, Alchimy, Optics, Memoratiue, Geodesie [land surveying], Poetrie, Haraldrie [sic], Graphice, Charactery, Brachigraphie [shorthand], and diuers Languages, holy, learned, and strange.[8]

As Baker argues elsewhere in this volume, although the Inns' main purpose was legal education, they also provided the sons of the gentry with an opportunity to acquire learning in a more general sense.[9] Buc's inclusion of such diverse and sometimes heady topics should alert us not simply to the need for interdisciplinarity in our approaches to the Inns, but also to the possibility of future research both into the Inns' relations with other London-based centres of learning – such as Gresham College and the College of Arms – and into the influence of other intellectual traditions on Innsmen's conception and practice of the law.

The reciprocal influences of the discourses of law and natural philosophy – to identify just one potential link for future research – should come as no surprise when we consider that the Inns helped produce men such as Francis Bacon (1561–1626),[10] John Preston (1587–1628) – who, as Hugh Adlington notes in his chapter in this section, combined his role as preacher to the Honourable Society of Lincoln's Inn (1622–28) with a lifelong interest in natural philosophy[11] – and John Selden (1584–1654).[12] Further work on Innsmen's knowledge and patronage of natural philosophy might help give us a better sense of the interpenetration of this evolving discourse with that of the law. It might also explain the presence of natural philosophy in a number of entertainments performed as part of Inns' revels. For example, the Gray's Inn revels of 1594–95, which are discussed in several of the chapters in Part III,[13] included the Second Counsellor's speech 'advising the Study of Philosophy', which advocates *the Conquest of the Works of Nature*. 'The Masque of Proteus', also featured, is structured around the central conceit of the power of the loadstone (or magnet) to attract and repel.[14] Similarly, the 'Masque of Mountebanks', performed at Gray's Inn in 1618, satirises the purveyors of quack remedies and elixirs of youth with a confidence and degree of detail that testifies to the members' familiarity with medical and, specifically, Paracelsian discourse.[15]

If Buc, in *The third universitie of England* (1615), reminds us of the interdisciplinary nature of knowledge and learning in early modern England, he also alerts us to the importance of their physical location. For Buc, the Inns, being situated in close proximity to Westminster and the law courts, are able to produce men who 'attayne to great places and dignities and offices in the law and in the common-wealth', including 'famous lawyers, Worthy members of the common-wealth, and great and much-honoured magistrates'.[16] But he also draws attention to the Inns as physical spaces, whether as emblems of civic pride, or as sites that helped fashion communities – social, cultural, and intellectual – of like-minded men. In this respect, the Inns can be usefully compared to the guilds and livery companies. As with the guilds, the physical and textual spaces of the Inns are concerned with what Ian W. Archer has called 'the importance of continuity and longevity in providing legitimation'.[17]

The chapters in this section all give emphasis to the importance of spaces – physical, textual, and mental – in the historiography of the early modern Inns. This point is made powerfully by Damian X. Powell in his examination of the Middle Templar James Whitelocke (1570–1632):

> the early Stuart Inns of Court were physical spaces as much as intellectual ones. For Whitelocke and for the other lawyers, at any stage in their association with their societies, the architectural setting defined and reinforced the social and intellectual hierarchies of the Inns as they gathered for Michaelmas, Hilary, Easter, and Trinity term. As always, the politics of space spoke to the politics of identity.[18]

Research on the 'architectural setting' of the Inns, such as that presented in Part II of the present collection,[19] can thus help shed light on the ways in which 'social and intellectual hierarchies' and also ideas of 'continuity and longevity' assumed physical form. So also, historiographical analysis can help reconstruct the function and meaning of those spaces and the mental worlds of those who inhabited them. The chapters in this and the following two sections take us through just some examples of these physical and imaginative spaces: there is, of course the architecture of the Inns themselves, including the halls, members' rooms, and gardens, but there are also libraries (personal and institutional); muniments rooms and archives; seating arrangements; heraldic and emblematic devices; costumes; dance; and the gestures assumed in performances such as readings, moots, revels, and sermons.

These 'social and intellectual hierarchies' also existed to be challenged and refined, and the Christmas and New Year revels, involving as they did the brief reign of the 'Lord of Misrule', showcase the myriad physical forms in and through which the Inns presented and contested 'ideas' of themselves. Thus, as Paul Raffield demonstrates in his discussion of the influence of Neoplatonism and Aristotelianism on the rituals enacted in Hall, entertainment texts – textual spaces – such as the Inner Temple revels of 1561–62, can be used to help recreate physical, social, and conceptual spaces.[20] For Raffield, the seemingly secular revels helped encode 'prevailing doctrinal orthodoxy, concerning the semiotic status of sacrament and ceremony'.[21] Hugh Adlington's and Emma Rhatigan's contributions to this section also make use of the proximity of textual and physical spaces in order to bridge both the secular and the spiritual and the literary and the legal.[22] Whilst Adlington examines the sermon styles and confessional allegiances of the preachers who served at each of the four Inns, Rhatigan focuses on the most famous of these preachers: John Donne. Both chapters remind us that the services held in the Inns chapels provided important occasions in which – like the readings, moots, and revels – the various members of the honourable societies could be brought together in a shared, communal experience.

Notes

1 For examples of work by Baker, Ives, and Prest, see the Preface, p. 6, n. 3, above.

2 See Chapter 6, esp. 'Recent work on the early modern Inns of Court', pp. 107–10, below.

3 Erica Sheen and Lorna Hutson, 'Introduction: Renaissance, law and literature', in Sheen and Hutson (eds), *Literature, Politics and Law in Renaissance England* (Basingstoke: Palgrave Macmillan, 2005), pp. 1–22 (p. 18). On the issue of interdisciplinarity with regard to the 'Law and Literature' movement, see Subha Mukherji, '"Understood relations": law and literature in early modern studies', *Literature Compass*, 6:3 (2009), 706–25.

4 George Buc[k], *The third universitie of England. Or A treatise of the foundations of all the colledges, auncient schooles of priviledge, and of houses of learning, and liberall arts, within and above the most famous cittie of London* (London: Thomas Dawson, 1615); William Dugdale, *Origines Juridiciales. Or historical memorials of the English laws* (London: F. & T. Warren, 1666).

5 Buc[k] (*bap.*1560, *d.*1622) was a probationer at Thavie's Inn before becoming a member of New Inn and, in 1585, the Middle Temple.

6 Buc, *The third universitie of England*, p. 905.

7 *Ibid.*, pp. 979, 980, 982, 983, 987.

8 *Ibid.*, p. 905.

9 See Chapter 1, esp. p. 10, above.

10 Bacon entered Gray's Inn on 27 June 1576 and was admitted in November of the same year. On the relationship between law and natural philosophy in Bacon's thinking, see Stephen Gaukroger, *Francis Bacon and the Transformation of Early-Modern Philosophy* (Cambridge: Cambridge University Press, 2001), pp. 57–67.

11 See Chapter 3, p. 64, below.

12 Selden was admitted to Clifford's Inn in 1602 and to the Inner Temple in November 1603. There is no comprehensive account of Selden's interest in natural philosophy and its possible relationship to his legal writings and career. Yet he was, for example, a friend of the physician and occultist Robert Fludd (*bap.*1574, *d* 1637), whom he acknowledges in the prefatory material to his *Titles of Honor* (London: Printed by William Stansby for John Helme, 1614), sig. A3ʳ. According to John Beale (Sheffield University Library, Hartlib Papers, 62/25/2ʳ–3ᵛ), writing in 1659, Selden co-authored *A Choice Manuall. Or, Rare and Select Secrets in Phisick and Chyrurgery: Collected, and Practiced by the Right Honourable, the Countesse of Kent* (19 editions, 1653–87), which includes formulae for Paracelsian and chymical medicines. Selden demonstrated a thorough knowledge of alchemical and Hermetic traditions in his learned 'illustrations' to Michael Drayton's *Poly-Olbion* (1612 and 1622): see Anne Lake Prescott, 'Marginal discourse: Drayton's muse and Selden's "story"', *Studies in Philology*, 88 (1991), 307–28, and Douglas Brooks-Davies, *The Mercurian Monarch: Magical Politics from Spenser to Pope* (Manchester: Manchester University Press, 1983), pp. 154–60. And in his most famous work, *Table Talk* (London: Printed for E. Smith, 1689), Selden quotes George Ripley ('*Riply* the Alchymist') in his notes on 'Gold' (p. 22). On Selden's relations with Fludd and his knowledge of natural philosophy, see Christopher Hill, *Intellectual Origins of the English Revolution Revisited*, rev. edn (Oxford: Clarendon Press, 1997), p. 134, and David Sandler Berkowitz, *John Selden's Formative Years* (London: Associated University Presses), pp. 29–30.

13 See Chapters 12 (pp. 258–9), 13 (pp. 264–85), and 14 (pp. 286–301), below.

14 The text of the *Gesta Grayorum* survives in a publication dating from 1688: *Gesta Grayorum, or, The history of the high and mighty prince, Henry Prince of Purpoole ... who reigned and died, A.D. 1594: together with a masque, as it was presented (by His Highness's command) for the entertainment of Q. Elizabeth, who, with the nobels of both courts, was present thereat* (London: Printed for W. Canning, 1688), pp. 34, 58–68. The speech is usually attributed to Francis Bacon, and the 'Masque of Proteus' to Francis Davison (1573/4–1613x19), who was admitted to Gray's Inn in 1593.

15 The 'Masque of Mountebanks', which was performed by and for members of Gray's Inn and the Middle Temple, has been attributed to John Marston, who entered the Middle Temple before 1592. The 'Masque' has been edited by Desmond S. Bland in *Three Revels from the Inns of Court* (Amersham: Avebury, 1984).

16 *Ibid.*, p. 969.

17 Ian W. Archer, 'Discourses of history in Elizabethan and early Stuart London', *Huntington Library Quarterly*, 68:1/2 (2005), 205–26 (205).

18 See Chapter 4, esp. 'Finding a place at the Inns', pp. 77–8, below.

19 See Chapters 7 (pp. 138–56, below) and 10 (pp. 199–213, below).

20 See Chapter 2, pp. 32–50, below.

21 See Chapter 2, p. 32, below.

22 See Chapters 3 (pp. 51-74, below) and 5 (pp. 90–106, below).

2

The Inner Temple revels (1561–62) and the Elizabethan rhetoric of signs: legal iconography at the early modern Inns of Court

Paul Raffield

In 1532, the bar attained statutory recognition as an independent body of practitioners, enabling the institutional expansion of a secularised legal profession. The standardisation of legal practice was reflected in the acquisition of systematised rhetorical skills by professional advocates. Advances in printing technology facilitated the mass-publication of rhetorical training manuals, the techniques of which replicated those of the ancient world. An increased level of professionalism inevitably diminished the relevance of the sacerdotal role that the political theorist Sir John Fortescue (*c*.1397–1479), a member of Lincoln's Inn, had attributed to the prototypical lawyer.[1] As Abraham Fraunce observed in *The Lawiers Logike* (pub.1588), lawyers of the late Elizabethan period were operating in an ethical vacuum, beholden not to God but to a set of saleable rhetorical skills, which were acquired at the Inns of Court. For Fraunce (member of Gray's Inn and practising barrister), the study of common law lacked method and reason, and was consequently 'hard, harsh, unpleasant, unsavoury, rude and barbarous'.[2]

In this chapter, I argue that the Inns attempted to redress the perceived ethical deficit by inventing an order of signs that was purposely invested with a persuasive humanist content, reflecting the efforts of the legal community to assert its symbolic, self-appointed status as the embodiment of justice and the font of divine wisdom. My analysis of the institutional iconography at the Inner Temple precedes a consideration of the influence of the European Renaissance over institutional existence at the Elizabethan Inns of Court. In particular, I consider the effects of Neoplatonic humanism on the rituals enacted in Hall, of which the religious act of dining and the concomitant educational exercises were pre-eminent. These phenomena are examined in the context of prevailing doctrinal orthodoxy, concerning the semiotic status of sacrament and ceremony. Finally, I address the unique contribution of Richard Hooker (1554–1600) to the synthesis of classical philosophy and Christian theology and to their representation in the iconography of the legal community at the Inns of Court.

Reformation of the image

With due deference, both to the oral tradition of English law and the ordered conviviality that characterised formal relationships between the gentlemen of the Inns of Court, I begin with an anecdote. It was related for the first time in 1612 by Sir George Buc, member of the Middle Temple, Gentleman of the King's Privy Chamber, Master of His Majesty's Office of the Revels, and author of *The Third Universitie of England*, from which the anecdote is taken. In a passage explaining the provenance of the emblems of the four Inns of Court, Buc states that the original device of the medieval Knights Templar was 'a horse (as Mathew Paris writeth) with two menne ryding upon him: and this (as hee sayeth) was engraven in their common Seale'.[3] This device can be witnessed in monumental form outside the Temple Church, where two bronze knights sit astride a bronze horse, atop a stone plinth.[4] As Buc explains, the chosen emblem 'had a very honourable beginning and was a symbole of piety'. He goes on to say that the emblem signified 'Love, and Charitie' and was 'a true Herogliffe of ingenious kindenesse, and Noble courtesies of Souldiers'.[5] The intention of the Order was to depict in graphic form the charitable and honourable ethos of the Knights Templar: a gallant knight rescues a comrade, whose horse has presumably been killed or fled the battlefield, and bears him to safety on his own horse. But as the Reformation was conclusively to demonstrate, the meaning of signs was ambiguous and invariably contentious. In the case of the original emblem of the Templars, Buc expresses indignation that 'they which loved to deprave, and make scandalous, and ridiculous, interpretations ... would have it supposed that it was taken, and devised to shew and express the poore, and needy beginnings ... of this order, as being driven for lacke of horses to ride two upon one Horse'.[6] Buc is referring presumably to the claim of the antiquarian and Inner Templar Joseph Holland (d.1605) that 'These Templers were at the first so poor as they had but one house [*sic*] to serve two of them, in token whereof they gave in their seal two men riding on one horse'.[7]

Public ridicule and the implication of impoverishment provided a suitable incentive for the Order of Knights Templar to change its heraldic device, and the emblem of the two knights sitting astride one horse was replaced by one that depicted the paschal lamb and flag of England. After the eviction of the Knights Templar, at the instigation of Pope Clement I,[8] their land was conferred upon the Knights of the Order of Saint John of Jerusalem. Eventually, in the reign of Edward III, it was leased in perpetuity to 'the reverend, auncient professors of the Lawes'.[9] It is a reasonable observation of Buc's that the two ancient devices of the Templars would have made suitable emblems for the Inner Temple and the Middle Temple, instead of which the former chose the figure of Pegasus, while at the time Buc was writing *The Third Universitie*, the Middle Temple had not 'as yet to my knowledge chosen, or appropriated any ensigne'.[10] Robert A. Pearce argues that the device of the paschal lamb and flag was a victim of the Henrician destruction of religious images and that the sixteenth-century Inner and Middle Temples dissociated themselves from the emblem in order to dispel suspicions, concerning their true allegiance to the reformed Church of England.[11] But it should be remembered also that the paschal lamb and flag was strongly associated with Richard II (notably in the Wilton Diptych).[12] It is equally probable that the decision not to adopt this emblem reflected a collegiate desire of the two Inns not to be linked by association with the absolute rule of a deposed and heirless King, least of all during the reign of Elizabeth I. This might explain why the emblem of the lamb and flag was not chosen by the Middle Temple until some years after the death of Elizabeth I, who in conversation with William Lambarde was supposed to have commented: 'I am Richard II know ye not that?'[13]

Pegasus and the mythical iconography of common law

In *A Guide to the Inns of Court and Chancery*, Robert A. Pearce asserts that Gerard Legh is usually credited with the suggestion that the Inner Temple adopt Pegasus as its heraldic device.[14] Legh's *The Accedens of Armory* (pub.1562) includes an account of the author's visit to the Inner Temple during the Christmas revels of 1561. These were the extravagant revels described with some degree of licence by the antiquary William Dugdale in *Origines Juridiciales* (1666), at which Lord Robert Dudley (later Earl of Leicester) enacted the role of Palaphilos, the High-Constable of the goddess of war, Pallas Athena.[15] Legh's curious book, for the most part, provides a graphically illustrated exposition of heraldic devices. But when he describes the heraldic significance of Pegasus, Legh's imaginative powers are given full rein. Following his description of the arms as 'Azure, a Pegasus Argent, called the horse of honour' and 'a shielde of antiquitie worthelye borne of olde, for honours sake', he invents a dialogue between two fictionalised versions of himself: 'Legh', whom he describes as a 'Calighate knight'; and 'Gerard', who (like his creator) is 'an Herehaught', i.e. herald.[16] Having established the ancient, honourable credentials of the Inner Temple, thereby legitimising the claim of the common law to embody the supreme authority of the Ancient Constitution,[17] Legh weaves a narrative that entwines the indigenous customs of the Inner Temple (of which Legh was a member) with classical precepts of natural law – represented in the narrative by archetypes such as Palaphilos, Pegasus, and Pallas Athena.

Legh's is a literary evocation of the juristic framework that the legal writer and Middle Templar Christopher St German (*c*.1460–1540/41) provided in his *Two Dialogues in English, Between a Doctor of Divinity and a Student in the Laws of England* (1528). In this seminal work, divine law, natural law, and common law are represented as co-existent and indivisible; while equity is presented as a guiding principle of English law.[18] It is important to note, in the context of the Inns of Court and their influence over the development of common-law principles and doctrines, that St German's *Doctor and Student* was a set text there.[19] Notwithstanding the justifiable claim of Wilfrid R. Prest that education at the Elizabethan and Jacobean Inns was more concerned with technical aspects of property law than with constitutional jurisprudence,[20] it is undeniable that the just governance of society is an underlying theme of St German's work.[21]

Legh portrays the Inner Temple as a sovereign city-state, embodying both the classical model of the state provided in Plato's *Republic* and the Christian model of Saint Augustine's *City of God*.[22] Of course, the Temple was (and remains) a self-governing municipal authority. Its independent status facilitated Legh's portrait of its environs as an 'Iland, wherein are the store of Gentilmen of the whole Realme, that repaire thither to learne to rule, and obey by lawe'.[23] Legh is not alone among early modern commentators in identifying right relations between men, and between man and God, as definitive features of the Inns of Court. In *De Laudibus Legum Angliæ*(*c.*1470), Sir John Fortescue's eulogy to English law and its institutions, the Lord Chancellor informs the Prince that 'there is a constant Harmony amongst them [members of the Inns], the greatest Friendship and a general Freedom of Conversation'.[24] The philosophical precept that links Plato, Saint Augustine, and Christopher St German to Legh's imaginative description of the Inner Temple is *Justitia*, or righteousness: an ethical, rather than a legal, principle that refers to the ideal goodness of society.

The influence of the classical world over the development of the Elizabethan and Jacobean Inns cannot be overestimated. It appears that this was partly due to their architectural development as miniature city-states or *poleis*, enabling their governance as Aristotelian communities; or, conversely, that their physical development in this form reflected the influence of classicism over prevailing, insular norms. If, as Aristotle asserts, 'justice is the bond of men in states',[25] then the Inns provided a template for the creation of the ideal constitution. Legh's description of the Inner Temple is dependent on allusions and tropes of a distinctive literary and classical type, and can reasonably be described as Aristotelian: it depicts the state of the Inner Temple as a creation of nature, whose ultimate purpose (*telos*) is the enablement of a good life.[26]

Legh relates the ancient myth of Pegasus, striking with his hooves 'the highest toppe of Mount Helicon, from whence immediatelye, rose the fountaine (Hypocrene)'.[27] The waters of the Hippocrene were supposed to impart poetic inspiration and the Inns of Court were perhaps best known during the early modern period for presenting a poetics (or aesthetics) of law through their arcane rites – of which the Inner Temple revels of Christmas 1561 are exemplary. The extent to which learning in general had been affected by the influx of humanism, facilitated by advances in the printing process,[28] can be partly gauged from Legh's extended use of the 'Hippocrene' metaphor. The waters of the inspirational stream have, according to Legh, 'watered the growinge plantes of the pleasaunt countries adjoining. And latelye, so wythe cleare streames hath abounded, as exceeding tholde lymittes, burste foorthe the bankes, reaching themselfe, to countries, farther distant, sweetlye moystinge the soiles thereof. And emongst other, pleasauntlye washte over tholde forworen Temples'.[29]

There is no evidence to suggest that educational exercises in the Elizabethan Inns of Court were influenced by external factors such as the flood of books, which as Maitland remarked (unintentionally adopting Legh's aquatic metaphor), 'poured from the press' during the sixteenth century.[30] Formal legal education still took the form of moots and readings.[31] As J. H. Baker has noted, the readings themselves contributed to the corpus of English law, particularly in relation to criminal jurisdiction.[32] But in addition to their obvious importance as the principal means through which knowledge of common law was attained, the form of the moots and readings of the Elizabethan period demonstrate that the Inns had assimilated the ideals of an Aristotelian commonwealth, in which the bonds of friendship formed the basis of the *polis*. The communal ethos of the Inns extended to the educational exercises, which were inextricably linked to the rites of dining in Hall. Dugdale describes a typical vacation exercise at the Inner Temple, in which a moot was staged in the library, involving three members of the Inn. The most junior, 'after the Case brought in, repeats the pleading Verbatim, and takes as many exceptions to the insufficiency of the pleading, as he can; and all this Ex tempore'. The second barrister 'answers those exceptions ... then argues the points in Law, contrary to the first Barristers Argument'. The third (and most senior) barrister considers 'all the Exceptions taken by both the puisne [more junior] Barristers', and states (in his opinion) the law relating to the case in question. Crucial to the notion of law as an expression of communality and sociality, when all three arguments have been made in the library, 'the *Barristers* repair to their Table in the Hall, and sit there according to their Antiquity'. Once seated, the 'Exceptions spoken of in the Library, are again toucht'.[33] At a symbolic level, the above exercise represents the Platonic idea of order as a sign of perfection – the achievement of which is only possible through the performance by each individual of his allotted role.[34]

Forensic rhetoric and the absence of ethics

Whilst the records of moots and readings instance the immutability and insularity of formal education at the early modern Inns of Court, the aesthetic rites of the legal community reveal the visible influence of classicism over the nationalistic predilections of common law. Attendance at the seasonal revels was compulsory for members, which suggests that the relevance of these to collegiate life at the Inns was more than incidental. As festive diversions from the austere regimen of Clerks Commons exercises, the revels provided seasonal respite from the study of law, which Abraham Fraunce described in *The Lawiers Logike* as 'confusedly scattered and utterly undigested'.[35] Fraunce's primary contribution to the criticism of Elizabethan legal education was to identify the absence of an intellectual and ethical context in which the common law was learnt. In a typical, flamboyant diatribe, Fraunce describes common lawyers thus:

so many upstart Rabulae Forenses, which under a pretence of Lawe, become altoge-ather lawlesse, to the continuall molestation of ignorant men, and general overcharging of the countrey, with an overflowing multitude of seditious cavillers: who, when their fathers have made some lewde bargayne in the countrey, run immediately to the Innes of Court, and having in seaven yeares space met with six French woordes, home they ryde lyke brave Magnificoes, and dashe their poore neighboures children quyte out of countenance, with Vilen in gros, Villen regardant, and Tenant per le curtesie.[36]

The target of Fraunce's spectacular polemic is the forensic rhetoric that was learnt at the Inns of Court and practised in the courts of justice. It is ironic, given his theme, that Fraunce should employ a highly rhetorical style in order to condemn the particular use to which rhetoric was put at the Inns (although, as Aristotle observed, exaggeration is a stylistic device that is often associated with epideictic rhetoric – the ends of which are honour or disgrace). But as Peter Goodrich has noted, it was not rhetoric itself to which Fraunce objected; rather, he abhorred the unscholarly and unethical employment of rhetoric by forensic orators.[37]

If the innovative printing processes of the sixteenth century had facilitated the dissemination of ideas from the ancient world, they had also enabled the publica-tion of an unprecedented number of rhetorical manuals. Works such as *The Arte or Crafte of Rhetoryke* (1529) by Leonard Cox; *The Art of Rhetorique* (1553) by Thomas Wilson; *The Arte of English Poesie* (1589) by George Puttenham; and *The Garden of Eloquence* (1593) by Henry Peacham sought to standardise the teaching of rhetorical skills. Whilst making grandiose claims for the persuasive power of rhetoric, such as Wilson's assertion that 'if the worthinesse of Eloquence maie move us, what worthier thing can there bee, then with a word to winne Cities and whole Countries',[38] it is notable that none of these writers refers to the Aristotelian corre-lation between rhetoric and justice. Given that Aristotle describes one of the four uses of rhetoric as 'the means by which truth and justice maintain and assert their natural superiority to falsehood and injustice',[39] this oversight might seem perverse were it not for the fact that these works were regarded by their authors and readers as handbooks, intended purely for the acquisition of skills in forensic oratory.

The growth throughout the sixteenth century of what might be described as the rhetoric industry created a potential crisis in the professional identity of the legal community at the Inns of Court. On the one hand, the establishment of an independent, secular legal profession required that its members be uniformly skilled in the practice of advocacy. Hence, the judge and Middle Templar Sir John Dodde-ridge (1555–1628) delineated the essential qualities of a common lawyer as: 'Sharp-ness of wit & judgment, Memory, Ready speech, Liberal Arts, Skill in Latin, Logic'.[40] On the other hand, if the legal profession was to retain its self-proclaimed status as the receptacle and mouthpiece of God's law, and was to be publicly perceived as such, then education at the Inns of Court had to be seen to be more than the ability to engage in mooting exercises or to argue readers' cases. Dodderidge had shown himself to be in favour of a broad legal education, in which the professors of law were 'furnished with the knowledge of all good literature of most of the Sciences liberall … And if the knowledge of the Law, doe receive ornament by those eruditions (and I think no man can denie) it shall be very expedient and well befitting to the student of the Lawes.'[41] But the reality of formal education at the Inns was that the training was intended to produce rhetoricians and legal technocrats, rather than humanists and philosophers.

Along with the vacation moot, an important educational exercise was the reading: a biannual event, taking place during Lent and early autumn. According to Dugdale, at 'about 8. or 9. of the Clock', the 'Mornings Reading' takes place. The reader 'utters some divisions and expositions of the Statute, whereon he is to read'. His case is taken up and argued by 'the antientest Utter Barrister in Commons', after which 'the Judges and Benchers argue according to their antiquity'. During the evening, immediately after dinner, 'the *puisne Vacationer Utter-Barrister* … argues the Case at the *Bench Table*, after Dinner'. Then, every bencher present argues the case before the reader gives his opinion on the law. Finally, he thanks those present for 'their company, pains, and attendance, costs, and chardges'.[42] Dugdale's description of a reading at the Inner Temple demonstrates the unexpected congruity of hierarchy and fraternity that characterised formal relationships between members of the Inns. The readings (like the vacation moots) were sophisticated rhetorical exercises, designed to instil in the participants not only the skills of forensic oratory, but also unquestioning respect for the immutable certainties of English law. The learning exercises reinforced the idea of law as tradition or ancient custom, passed down from generation to generation. Hence, the emphasis on the 'antiquity' of the judges and benchers, and the implied legitimacy that such seniority attaches to their pronouncements on any aspect of the law.

Visual rhetoric and the representation of *Res Publica*

Some educational exercises were still conducted in law-French, but despite the obvious association of this hybridised language with France and the 'Norman yoke', its continued use had the paradoxical effect of uniquely distinguishing common law from canon and civil law.[43] Rather, it is the symbolic representations of law, presented during the revels, which provide evidence of external influence over the ancient customs of English law. The Inner Temple revels that Gerard Legh attended in 1561 were indicative of the pervasive effects of the European Renaissance on the English legal institution. Legh writes approvingly of the Hippocrene bursting its banks, watering the soil of distant countries and washing over old, foreign temples. He likens the Inner Temple to a Platonic academy, in which the members not only learn to govern and to serve their 'prince and common weale', but also 'to use all other exercises of bodye and minde whereunto nature most aptly serveth, to adorn by speaking, countenance, gesture, & use of apparel, the person of a gentleman, wherby amitie is obtained & continued'.[44]

On his arrival at the Inn, Legh is welcomed by Palaphilos, 'a king of arms, who courteouslie saluted me saying, for that I was a straunger, and seeming by my demeanour a lover of honour I was his geste of right'.[45] It is, of course, an idealised portrait that Legh paints. The truth was that strangers were not welcomed by the Inns, whether or not they were lovers of honour. Indeed, at the Inner Temple, legislation existed to the effect that 'no Stranger … should be admitted to take any Repast, or to be in Commons in the time of Christmass'; while, at Middle Temple, legislation was passed, 'forbidding any Gentleman to lodg any Stranger in his Chamber'.[46] The sharing of its *arcana* with strangers was not a quality for which the sixteenth-century English legal institution is best remembered, although of course members of the Inns during this period often performed their entertainments before the exclusive audience of the royal court.[47]

Insularity extended to the dissemination of legal knowledge as much as it did to the exclusive practices of the legal community within the Inns of Court. Discourse on the subject of law was best left to lawyers – an opinion shared by generations of eminent common lawyers, from Sir Thomas More (1478–1535) to Sir Edward Coke (1552–1634).[48] Nor was it necessarily considered useful for common lawyers to have bathed in the waters of the Hippocrene. Not all lawyers shared Dodde-ridge's preference for a broad legal education: in an undated letter to Sir Edward Coke, Sir Francis Bacon criticised his great rival on the grounds that 'while you speake in yor own Element, the Law, no man ordinarily equalls you, but when you wander indeed … you converse with bookes not men, and bookes especially humane'.[49] This might be thought an odd accusation, of a lawyer whom J. G. A. Pocock suggested was notable for the peculiar insularity of his mind,[50] but it is indicative of a particular narrowness of vision on the part of the letter's author and is symptomatic of a restrictive interpretation of the law in its cultural, social, and political context.

Legal education at the Inns of Court was concerned exclusively with the applica-tion of rhetorical skills to particular cases and statutes. Despite this, Legh insists that the inclusive scholasticism of the Inner Temple was conducive to the creation of a body of lawyers whose public function beyond the confines of the Inn is to serve the commonwealth, applying the equitable principles of the *polis* to the administra-tion of justice in the state. Legh's narrative is notable for its representation of the Inner Temple as the embodiment of *justitia* (in the Platonic sense of right relations between men), rather than of formal law. The bonds of friendship, engendered by the collegiate ethos of the Inn, are responsible (according to Legh) for forming 'such unitie of minds and manners, as lightly never after is severed, then which is nothinge more profitable to the common-weale'.[51] The identical sentiment is repeated on the next page where, once again, Legh asserts the ethical principle of justice, rather than the legalistic notion of formal law, as the foundation of the ideal state: 'For that the best of their people from tender yeres trained up in precepts of Justice, it could not chose, but yelde forth a profitable people to a wise common weale.'[52]

The 'common-weale' to which Legh refers was a familiar, early modern translation of the Latin *Res Publica*, in which political arrangements were directed to promote the maximum good of the citizen body. *Res Publica* did not imply opposition to the notion of kingship, *per se*; rather, under such a polity (as Alan Cromartie has noted), the power of the monarch was limited by law, and was anyway simply a means to an end: that of promoting the public good in the best interests of the subjects of law.[53] Cromartie makes the accurate observation that generations of common lawyers, from Fortescue to Coke, regarded the common law as natural law in an English context. He further notes that such theories tended to emerge when common lawyers considered their authority to be threatened by rival jurisdictions.[54] The most insidious threat to the constitutional supremacy of common law was the *imperium* of the monarch, which effectively rendered the king under God but not law, because the king *was* the law. The imperial theory of kingship was, as John Guy has noted, incompatible not only with humanist theories of republicanism, but also with the common law itself.[55]

It is not my intention to speculate over the political connotations of the Inner Temple revels of 1561–62.[56] But it is possible to infer from their content that the lawyers who devised and performed the entertainment were presenting, in symbolic form, a vision of community in which ancient English custom fused with humanist-classical political theory to create a unique template for the ideal governance of the common-weal.[57] Whilst the masque that was presented on St Stephen's Day 1561 cannot be categorised as a learning exercise of equivalence to the moots and readings, it demonstrates at least an interest in examining alternative forms of governance and their applicability to the English constitution. Consequently, it can be seen that an awareness of constitutional jurisprudence was a peripheral aspect of the broad, humanist education to which Legh alludes.

The first scene of the masque, performed after the first course at dinner (described by Legh as 'served with tender meates, sweete fruites & dainty delicates'),[58] is distinctive for its depiction of an idyllic, pastoral scene. Characters include a Master of the Game (played by the future Lord Chancellor, Christopher Hatton, who had been admitted to the Inner Temple in 1560), dressed in green velvet; and a forest ranger, dressed in green satin. In his idiosyncratic style, Dugdale provides a generic description of the scene, thus:

> bearing in his hand a green Bow, and divers Arrows, with either of them a Hunting Horn about their necks; blowing together three blasts of Venery, they pace round about the fire three times ... This Ceremony also performed, a Huntsman cometh into the Hall, with a Fox and a Purse-net; with a Cat, both bound at the end of a staff; and with them nine or ten Couple of Hounds, with the blowing of Hunting-Hornes.[59]

The fox and the cat are set upon by the hounds and 'killed beneath the fire', whereupon the Constable-Marshal (played by Lord Robert Dudley, admitted to the Inner Temple in 1561) directs the participants to their 'several appointed places'.[60]

At one level, the above scene can be interpreted as a pantomimic expression of 'Merrie England', in which the participants are prototypes of the English subjects of law, who, according to Fortescue, 'are Rich in Gold, Silver, and in all the Necessaries and Conveniencies of Life'.[61] Both Fortescue's vision of England and the hunting scene described above are utopian depictions of a self-sufficient and exclusive realm.[62] But it is impossible to ignore the congruency of indigenous custom (here expressed by the antique rituals of hunting), natural law (represented by the order and reason of the sylvan community),[63] and divine law, which the hunting scene implies: the deity being honoured in the ceremonial slaughter of the fox and cat, and by the sacrificial burning of these animals under the direction of Palaphilos, High Constable of Pallas Athena and Marshal of the Inner Temple.[64] The scene represents the triangular relationship between distinct, but related, jurisdictions.

That English law was the distillation of immemorial custom was an axiom of common-law ideology. In the words of St German, 'the Law of England standeth upon divers general Customs of old time used through all the Realm, which have been accepted and approved by our Sovereign'.[65] In *circa* 1470, approximately fifty years before the publication of *Doctor and Student*, Fortescue insisted that England has 'been constantly governed by the same Customs, as it is at present'.[66] Of course, an axiom of equal importance to jurists was that common law was 'the absolute perfection of reason'.[67] So, if the custom upon which law was based did not conform to the imperative of reason, what then? For Fortescue, this apparent paradox was simply resolved: 'if they [customs] were not above all Exception Good, no Doubt but some or other of these Kings from a Principle of Justice, in Point of Reason, or mov'd by Inclination, would have made some Alteration or quite abolished them'.[68] As J. G. A. Pocock observes, logic such as this can hardly be described as rational, based as it is on a 'technical and traditional' interpretation of customary law.[69]

The legal fiction that the common law derived from ancient, English custom eventually and inevitably confronts the fact of the Norman Conquest. Dugdale concedes that William I introduced Norman customs into English law, such as 'that Pleadings should thenceforth be in French, and that Language taught in Schools'.[70] But common lawyers and commentators (notably Sir Edward Coke) remained adamant that subsequent monarchs were sympathetic to the indigenous customs of the ancient English nation. For example, Dugdale cites Coke's approval of the actions of Henry I: 'Because he abolished such Customes of Normandy, as his Father had added to our Common Laws he is said to have restored the antient Laws of England.'[71]

The rhetorical triangle and the communication of ideas

Returning to the congruency of divine law, English law, and natural law: the image of the triangular relationship between God, human society, and the natural order was one with which early modern jurists were to become increasingly familiar.

Fortescue had stated authoritatively that human laws derive from three possible sources: nature, customs, or statutes.[72] Subsequently, St German asserted that the mysteries of eternal law were revealed by 'the light of Natural Reason; Secondly, by Heavenly Revelation; Thirdly, by the order of a Prince or any other secondary Governor that hath power to bind his Subjects to a Law'.[73] In the seventeenth century, Dugdale begins his history of English law with the statement of the Jacobean Lord Chancellor, Thomas Egerton, Baron Ellesmere, that 'the Common Laws of England are grounded upon the Law of God, and extend themselves to the original Law of Nature, and the universal Law of Nations; and that they are not originally *Leges scriptae*'.[74] Ellesmere describes an equilateral triangle, albeit with God at its apex, in which natural law, common law, and the law of nations are co-extensive and indivisible. His deliberate emphasis on the predominantly unwritten character of English law is relevant to the thesis that law can be understood or represented only in images.[75]

The triangular congruency of divine law, natural law, and human law can be viewed as a communicative device, which was intended to convey the basis of an ethical relationship between lawmaker, law, and subject of law. The rhetorical triangle is instanced in the second scene of the St Stephen's Day masque at the Inner Temple, which took place after supper. During this spectacular event, the Queen's representative at the revels, Robert Dudley, played the role of Palaphilos. Dugdale provides the following description of the performance:

> [Palaphilos] presenteth himself with Drums afore him, mounted upon a Scaffold, born by four men; and goeth three times round about the Harthe, crying out aloud, *A Lord, A Lord,* &c. Then he descendeth & goeth to dance &c. and after he calleth his Court, every one by name, one by one, in this manner.
>
> Sir *Francis Flatterer* of *Fowleshurst*, in the County of *Buckingham.*
> Sir *Randle Rackabite,* of *Rascall Hall,* in the County of *Rake Hell.*
> Sir *Morgan Mumchance,* of *Much Monkery* in the County of *Mad Mopery.*
> Sir *Bartholomew Baldbreech,* of *Buttocks-bury,* in the County of *Brekeneck.*
>
> This done, the Lord of Misrule addresseth himself to the Banquet: which ended with some Minstralsye, mirth, and dancing.[76]

The alliterative titles of the members of the fictional court simultaneously exaggerate and exemplify the exalted status of the 'courtiers', while implying their emblematic status as 'Gentlemen of bloud, possessing virtue',[77] and hence as worthy advisers to the sovereign. They suggest well-defined and circumscribed symbolic positions, notably the Aristotelian role of friends, counsellors or *amici principis*. These friends of the prince are (as Guy has noted in connection with Sir Thomas Elyot's *The boke named the Gouernour*) drawn from the English nobility and gentry, and limit the power of the monarch by advising the king and guiding his actions; thus, the citizen or *politikon zoon* is redefined as a counsellor to the magistrate.[78] In figurative terms, one side of the equilateral triangle is provided by the ruler (Palaphilos); a second by his counsellors (Sir Francis Flatterer *et al.*); and a third by the commonwealth (represented by the membership of the Inner Temple, which celebrates and reflects the amity and harmony between ruler and counsellors, with 'Minstralsye, mirth, and dancing'). The rhetorical function of the exercise is to depict the harmonious relations that exist between ruler and subject of law, engendered by the co-existence of complementary organs in the body politic.

Of course, the most potent communicative device available to the English legal institution was the common lawyer himself. Fortescue succinctly defended the role of the judge as a minister (or messenger) of God, by asserting that 'we, who are the Ministerial Officers, who sit and preside in the Courts of Justice, are therefore not improperly called, *Sacerdotes* (Priests). The import of the Latin Word (*Sacerdos*) being one who gives or teaches Holy Things'. Fortescue attributes to the judiciary a rabbinical function: the laws of men, if they are good laws, are synonymous with the laws of God, and are to be expounded only by his ministers. In Fortescue's words, 'to study the Laws, tho' of Human Institution, is in effect to study the Laws of God'.[79]

The role of the common lawyer as divine agent, whose primary purpose was to impart the word of God, can be traced to the clerical foundations of the English legal profession;[80] and belief in the spiritual role of the common lawyer did not expire with the secularisation of the legal profession. If anything, the need to assert the superiority of common law to rival jurisdictions encouraged jurists to claim that the common law and its practitioners were the sanctified embodiment of a unique, divinely appointed jurisprudence. Hence, in 1599, in a chapter entitled 'Of the good qualities wherewith the Student of the lawe ought to be furnished', the lawyer and historian William Fulbecke (*b.*1559/60, *d.* in or after 1602), a member of Gray's Inn, insisted that 'The first and chiefe thing that I doe require in him, is, to have the true knowledge, and feare of God, without which his other knowledge is but as a sword in the hand of a frantike person.' Allied to the pre-eminence of knowledge and the fear of God is an injunction against pride. Fulbecke advises the prospective student of common law that 'the way to the hight of knowledge is by humilities gate. Let not the increase of his skil make his mind to increase, and swell.'[81]

It appears certain that one effect of the educational exercises of the Inns, in which hierarchy was enforced and rank delineated according to experience and antiquity, was to engender humility in the presence of God's law. The dramatic rites enacted during the revels depict in symbolic form not only the humility of common lawyers, but also their sacerdotal status as messengers of God. At the end of the Inner Temple revels of St Stephen's Day 1561, Palaphilos conducts a ceremony in which the particupants are created knights of Pallas Athena. They are enjoined to: 'Advance your honours by your dedes, / to lyve for evermore, / As Pallas knightes, by Pallas helpe, / Pallas serve ye therefore.'[82]

In his concluding eulogy to the members of the Inner Temple, Legh places the classical imagery in a specific Judaeo-Christian context, observing that the Knights of Pallas Athena are angelic servants of God: 'Herein I might compare your state (but that you are men) unto the heavenly Ierarches [Hierarchs], for that you have the three thinges that Ierarches have, that is, Order, cunning, and working. In your order is office, in your cunning, readiness, and in your working is service.'[83] The Knights of Pallas represent the idea that the existence of a harmonious political community is contingent upon the presence and maintenance of justice. Legh's interpretation of the scene unites the precepts of classical, political philosophy and the teachings of Judaeo-Christian theology. The fusion of these distinct philosophical strands was a notable feature of juristic thought during the Elizabethan period. Coke, for example, claims that natural law (the codification of which he attributes to Aristotle, 'nature's secretary') 'is that which God at the time of creation of the nature of man infused into his heart.'[84]

Common law and the mixed polity

By the end of the sixteenth century, the sacerdotal role of the lawyer had been subjugated to the imperatives of a standardised legal profession. In *The Lawiers Logike*, Abraham Fraunce suggested that rhetoric had supplanted ethics as the cornerstone of English legal education. The vocabulary of signs had been degraded and Fraunce prescribed the reformation of the legal profession through its rediscovery of an ethical purpose, predicated upon reason and method. In a parallel development, marked by the publication of *Of the Laws of Ecclesiastical Polity* (the first five books of which were published between 1593 and 1597), Richard Hooker attempted to restore to visual rhetoric its moral purpose of maintaining the natural superiority of truth and justice over falsehood and injustice. As Patrick Collinson has argued, for Hooker the Sacraments were not mere signs, but rather the means which facilitate assimilation into the body of Christ.[85] Hooker wrote (concerning the Sacraments) that 'These sensible things which Religion hath allowed, are resemblances framed according to things spirituall understood, whereunto they serve as a hand to leade, and a way to direct.'[86] He reaffirmed St Augustine's description of the Sacraments as visible signs of invisible grace (the description was employed in the 1604 *Book of Common Prayer*). In other words, he was aware that the Sacraments and ceremonies of the Anglican Church acted upon the human faculties in an iconic manner, directing the subject to an understanding and revelation of the infinite and the invisible. Leaving aside the substantive, metaphysical aspect of the Sacraments (in which Hooker clearly believed), it is evident from the above statement that Hooker was profoundly conscious of the persuasive power of the image and of its utility in expressing the intangible concepts of unwritten law. He understood and respected the persuasive power of rhetoric and its utility in asserting the superiority of truth to falsehood.[87] As Master of the Temple, between 1585 and 1591, Hooker had been uniquely placed to observe and comment upon developments in the Church and the English legal community. His vision of a triangular constitution, in which the imperatives of crown, church, and commonwealth were co-extensive and indivisible, provided the template for the modern English state.

The acceptance by Elizabeth I of Hooker's ceremony-based version of Anglicanism facilitated the emergence in the Jacobean period of more complex institutional iconography.[88] For example, echoing Hooker's authorial preoccupation with angels,[89] the Jacobean Inns of Court employed the extravagant ceremony of the masque with which to depict their members as angelic messengers of God. In *The Masque of the Inner Temple and Grays Inn*, written by Francis Beaumont – who had been admitted to the Inner Temple in 1600 – and performed in February 1612 at the Banqueting House in the presence of James I, the lawyer-masquers played the roles of 'Olympian Knights', appearing 'as consecrated persons all in vailes, like to Coapes, of silver Tiffinie.'[90] In *The Inner Temple Masque or Masque of Heroes*, written by Thomas Middleton and performed by members of the Inner Temple in 1619, the masquers are 'themselves discovered, sitting in Arches of Clouds, being nine in Number, Heroes Deified for their Vertues'. The function of these seraphic figures is anything but ornamental: 'Yet in their love to humane good, / In which estate themselves once stood, / They all descend to have their worth / Shine, to Imitation, forth.'[91] The angelic spirits, in human form, descend to earth from their celestial home in order to impart the divine message of the law.

The educational function of the Inns of Court was, of course, to equip its members with the requisite knowledge and skills for successful careers at the bar. In order to fulfil this purpose, the acquisition of forensic, rhetorical techniques was necessary. A secondary function was, as Fortescue suggested, 'not so much to make the Laws their Study, much less to live by the Profession (having large Patrimonies of their own) but to form their Manners.'[92] But there was another, more abstruse, function, not unconnected with the threat posed to the constitutional supremacy of common law by the burgeoning power of the Executive and the rival jurisdictions of civil and canon law.[93] The legal community at the Inns of Court sought to represent itself as the defender of a mixed polity, in which the triangular relationship between crown, church, and commonwealth was regulated by the supreme authority of common law, as interpreted and administered by its professors – the common lawyers. The dramatic medium of the masques and revels was employed to depict, in emblematic terms, an ideal constitution, which combined the classical, civic virtues of the ancient *polis* with Christian principles of fairness and equity. These devices complemented the more mundane educational exercises of the moots and readings. They placed rhetoric in an ethical framework – a development that, in Aristotelian terms, was crucial if rhetoric was to be effective in supplanting falsehood with truth, and inequity with justice.

Notes

1 Sir John Fortescue, *De Laudibus Legum Angliæ*, ed. John Selden (London: R. Gosling, 1737), pp. 4–5. On Fortescue, his 'philosophy' and *De Laudibus*, see John G. A. Pocock, *The Machiavellian Moment: Florentine Political Thought and the Atlantic Republican Tradition* (Princeton, NJ: Princeton University Press, 2003), pp. 9–30.

2 Abraham Fraunce, *The Lawiers Logike, exemplifying the precepts of logike by the practise of the common lawe* (London: T. Gubbin & T. Newman, 1588), fol. q2ᵛ. For a discussion of Fraunce, see Peter Goodrich, *Languages of Law: From Logics of Memory to Nomadic Masks* (London: Weidenfeld & Nicolson, 1990), pp. 18–52.

3 George Buc, *The Third Universitie of England* (London, 1615), in John Stow and Edmund Howes, *The Annales or a Generall Chronicle of England* (London: Thomas Dawson for Thomas Adams, 1615), p. 972.

4 The monument was erected and dedicated in 2000, to commemorate the start of the third millennium. It is situated on the site of the former cloister courtyard of the Knights Templar.

5 Buc, *The Third Universitie*, p. 972.

6 *Ibid.*, p. 972.

7 Joseph Holland, *The Question is, of the Antiquity use and privilege of places for Students and Professors of the common law* (1601), in Thomas Hearne (ed.), *A Collection of Curious Discourses, written by eminent Antiquaries upon several heads in our English antiquities* (Oxford: Thomas Hearne, 1720), p. 128.

8 The Order was arraigned on charges 'of Heresie, of Idolatrie, of Sodomie, and of other horrible crimes' (Buc, *The Third Universitie*, p. 971).

9 *Ibid.*, p. 971.

10 *Ibid.*, p. 973.

11 The depiction of *Agnus Dei*, the Lamb of God, was prohibited by statute in 1570. 13 Eliz. I C. 2 describes such emblems as 'vain and superstitious things'.

12 See J. H. Harvey, 'The Wilton Diptych: a re-examination', *Archaeologia*, 98 (1961), 1–28; also, D. Crouch, *The Image of Aristocracy in Politics, 1000–1300* (London: Routledge, 1992); J. Alexander and P. Binski (eds), *Age of Chivalry: Art in Plantagenet England, 1200–1400* (London: Royal Academy of Arts, in association with Weidenfeld & Nicolson, 1987).

13 Quoted in E. K. Chambers, *William Shakespeare: A Study of Facts and Problems*, 2 vols (Oxford: Clarendon Press, 1930), II, 237. On the use of imagery by Richard II to imply imperial majesty and absolute power, see Nigel Saul, 'Richard II and the vocabulary of kingship', *English Historical Review*, 110 (1995), 854–77.

14 Robert A. Pearce, *A Guide to the Inns of Court and Chancery* (London: Butterworths, 1855), pp. 219–20.

15 William Dugdale, *Origines Juridiciales or, historical memorials of the English laws* (London: F. & T. Warren, 1666), pp. 150–3. On the Inner Temple revels of 1561–62, see Paul Raffield, *Images and Cultures of Law in Early Modern England: Justice and Political Power, 1558–1660* (Cambridge: Cambridge University Press, 2004), pp. 90–105. On *The Accedens of Armory* and the semiotics of law, see Peter Goodrich, 'Eating law: commons, common land, common law', *Journal of Legal History*, 12 (1991), 246–67.

16 Gerard Legh, *The Accedens of Armory* (London: R. Tottel, 1576), fol. 118ʳ.

17 On belief among common lawyers in the existence of an ancient constitution of immemorial origin, see John G. A. Pocock, *The Ancient Constitution and the Feudal Law: A Study of English Historical Thought in the Seventeenth Century – A Reissue with a Retrospect* (Cambridge: Cambridge University Press, 1987).

18 See John Guy, 'Thomas More and Christopher St German: the battle of the books', in Alistair Fox and John Guy (eds), *Reassessing the Henrician Age: Humanism, Politics and Reform, 1500–1550* (Oxford: Blackwell, 1986), pp. 95–120 (p. 102); also, John Guy, *Christopher St. German on Chancery and Statute* (London: Selden Society, 1985), p. 19.

19 John Guy, 'Tudor monarchy and its critiques', in John Guy (ed.), *The Tudor Monarchy* (London: Arnold, 1997), pp. 78–104 (p. 88).

20 Wilfrid R. Prest, *The Inns of Court under Elizabeth I and the Early Stuarts, 1590–1640* (London: Longman, 1972), p. 221.

21 See, for example, the assertion that 'if any general Custom were directly against the Law of God, or if any Statute were made directly against it … the Custom and Statute were void' (Christopher St German, *Two Dialogues in English, between a doctor of divinity and a student in the laws of England, of the grounds of the said laws, and of conscience* (London: the Assigns of R. & E. Atkins, 1709), p. 18). On St German and constitutionalism, see Mark D. Walters, 'St German on reason and parliamentary sovereignty', *Cambridge Law Journal*, 62 (2003), 335–70.

22 On the architecture of the early modern Inns as the representational synthesis of Augustinian and Platonic ideals, see Paul Raffield, 'Bodies of law: the divine architect, common law and the ancient constitution', *International Journal for the Semiotics of Law*, 13 (2000), 333–56.

23 Legh, *The Accedens of Armory*, fol. 119^v.

24 Fortescue, *De Laudibus Legum Angliæ*, ed. Selden, p. 112.

25 Aristotle, *The Politics*, in *The Politics and The Constitution of Athens*, ed. S. Everson (Cambridge: Cambridge University Press, 1996), bk. 1, 1253a, p. 14.

26 *Ibid.*, bk. 1, 1252b, p. 13.

27 Legh, *The Accedens of Armory*, fol. 118^v.

28 On the printing revolution in early modern Europe, see Elizabeth L. Eisenstein, *The Printing Press as an Agent of Change* (Cambridge: Cambridge University Press, 1980).

29 Legh, *The Accedens of Armory*, fol. 118^v.

30 Frederick W. Maitland, *English Law and the Renaissance* (Cambridge: Cambridge University Press, 1901), p. 29.

31 On the readings, see Chapter 1, pp. 17–20, above, and Chapter 6, pp. 110–20, below.

32 See John H. Baker, *The Third University of England: The Inns of Court and the Common-Law Tradition* (London: Selden Society, 1990), p. 20, and Baker's 'Why the history of English law has not been finished', *Cambridge Law Journal*, 59 (2000), 2–84 (82).

33 Dugdale, *Origines Juridiciales*, p. 159.

34 See bk. 4 of Plato, *The Republic*, trans. Desmond Lee (London: Penguin, 1987), 427D–434C, 441C–445B. On the cosmos, temperance, and justice, see Plato, *Gorgias*, in *Lysis, Symposium, Gorgias*, trans. W. R. M. Lamb (London: W. Heinemann, 1946), 507E–508A.

35 Fraunce, *The Lawiers Logike*, fol. q3^v.

36 *Ibid.*, fols q4^r–q4^v. On the public perception of attorneys-at-law in early modern England, see Christopher W. Brooks, *Pettyfoggers and Vipers of the Commonwealth: The 'Lower*

Branch' of the Legal Profession in Early Modern England (Cambridge: Cambridge University Press, 1986).

37 Goodrich, *Languages of Law*, p. 30.

38 Thomas Wilson, *The Art of Rhetorique* (London: G. Robinson, 1585), p. 2.

39 Aristotle, *The Rhetoric*, trans. J. E. C. Welldon (London: Macmillan, 1886), preface, p. x.

40 John Dodderidge, *The English Lawyer: Describing a method for the managing of the lawes of the land* (London: I. More, 1631), p. 17.

41 *Ibid.*, p. 35.

42 Dugdale, *Origines Juridiciales*, pp. 159–60.

43 John H. Baker, 'The three languages of the common law', *McGill Law Journal*, 43 (1998), 5–24. See also J. H. Baker, *Manual of Law French* (Amersham: Avebury, 1979).

44 Legh, *The Accedens of Armory*, fols 118ᵛ, 119ᵛ.

45 *Ibid.*, fol. 120ʳ.

46 Dugdale, *Origines Juridiciales*, pp. 149, 192.

47 See for example, the performance in January 1562 by members of the Inner Temple, of *The Tragedy of Gorboduc*, in the presence of Elizabeth I. The play was written by two common lawyers, Thomas Norton and Thomas Sackville; it was published as *The tragedie of Ferrex and Porrex* (London: J. Daye, 1570).

48 'Be they of the church or the realm … to put out books in writing abroad among the people against them, that I would neither do myself, nor in the doing commend any man that does' (Thomas More, *The Debellacyon of Salem and Bizance* (London: W. Rastall, 1533), fols qviiiʳ–qixʳ). According to Coke, it was 'a desperate and dangerous matter for civilians and canonists (I speak of what I know, and not without just cause) to write either of the Common Laws of England which they profess not, or against them which they know not' (Edward Coke, *The Reports of Sir Edward Coke, Knt. in English*, ed. George Wilson, 7 vols (London: Rivington, 1777), V, xvii).

49 Letter to Edward Coke from Sir Francis Bacon: BL, Sloane MS 1775, fol. 79ᵛ. Although undated, Bacon refers to Coke's conduct of the prosecution in the trial of the alleged conspirators, following the Gunpowder Plot of 1605.

50 Pocock, *The Ancient Constitution*, p. 56.

51 Legh, *The Accedens of Armory*, fol. 119ᵛ.

52 *Ibid.*, fol. 120ʳ.

53 Alan Cromartie, 'The constitutionalist revolution: the transformation of political culture in early Stuart England', *Past and Present*, 163 (1999), 76–120 (100).

54 *Ibid.*, 82.

55 Guy, 'Tudor monarchy and its critiques', p. 89.

56 On the political symbolism of *Gorboduc* and other dramatic entertainments at the Elizabethan Inns of Court, see Raffield, *Images and Cultures of Law*, pp. 127–31. On drama as a stylistic expression of art, government, and the visibility of power, see Ian Ward, 'A kingdom for a stage, princes to act: Shakespeare and the art of government', *Law and Critique*, 8 (1997), 189–213. For the argument that the political symbolism in *Gorboduc* 'was probably a source for Shakespeare's *Titus Andronicus*', see Dympna Callaghan and Chris R. Kyle, 'The wilde side of justice in early modern England and *Titus Andronicus*', in Constance Jordan and Karen Cunningham (eds), *The Law in Shakespeare* (Basingstoke: Palgrave Macmillan, 2007), pp. 38–57 (p. 41).

57 Guy argues that the political culture of the Tudor period can be fully understood only if

it is interpreted in the context of a 'humanist-classical culture' ('Tudor monarchy and its critiques', p. 104).

58 Legh, *The Accedens of Armory*, fol. 123ᵛ.

59 Dugdale, *Origines Juridiciales*, pp. 155–6.

60 *Ibid.*, p. 156.

61 Fortescue, *De Laudibus Legum Angliæ*, ed. Selden, p. 83.

62 On medieval utopias, see Herman Pleij, *Dreaming of Cockaigne: Medieval Fantasies of the Perfect Life*, trans. Diane Webb (New York, NY: Columbia University Press, 2001).

63 St German defined natural law in terms of laws of reason and reasonable creatures (*Two Dialogues in English*, p. 2). On the influence of Thomist theories of natural law over positive law, see R. H. Tawney, *Religion and the Rise of Capitalism* (Harmondsworth: Penguin, 1984), pp. 51–2.

64 On the rituals of ancient Greek sacrifice, see George Hersey, *The Lost Meaning of Classical Architecture* (Cambridge, MA: MIT Press, 1988), pp. 15–16.

65 St German, *Two Dialogues in English*, p. 21.

66 Fortescue, *De Laudibus Legum Angliæ*, ed. Selden, p. 30.

67 Edward Coke, *The Second Part of the Institutes of the Lawes of England* (London: M. Flesher & R. Young, 1642), p. 179.

68 Fortescue, *De Laudibus Legum Angliæ*, ed. Selden, pp. 30–1.

69 Pocock, *The Machiavellian Moment*, p. 16.

70 Dugdale, *Origines Juridiciales*, p. 7.

71 *Ibid.*, p. 7.

72 Fortescue, *De Laudibus Legum Angliæ*, ed. Selden, p. 28. For a discussion of Fortescue and natural law, see E. F. Jacob, *Sir John Fortescue and the Law of Nature* (Manchester: Manchester University Press, 1934); Jacob emphasises that natural law was not of purely academic interest during the fifteenth century, but 'might be appealed to in the courts' (p. 19).

73 St German, *Two Dialogues in English*, p. 3.

74 Dugdale, *Origines Juridiciales*, p. 3.

75 On law as an iconic order, and the central role of the image in 'capturing' the soul of the subject of law, see Pierre Legendre, *Law and the Unconscious: A Legendre Reader*, ed. Peter Goodrich, trans. Alain Pottage and Anton Schütz (Basingstoke: Macmillan, 1997), pp. 211–54.

76 Dugdale, *Origines Juridiciales*, p. 156. On the St Stephen's Day masque of 1561 at the Inner Temple, see Raffield, *Images and Cultures of Law*, pp. 90–4.

77 John Ferne, *The Blazon of Gentrie* (London: J. Windet for T. Cooke, 1586), p. 86.

78 Guy, 'Tudor monarchy and its critiques', pp. 81, 82, 85.

79 Fortescue, *De Laudibus Legum Angliæ*, ed. Selden, pp. 4–5.

80 On the monastic origins of the English bar, see John H. Baker, *The Order of Serjeants at Law: A Chronicle of Creations with Related Texts* (London: Selden Society, 1984); also, Paul Brand, *The Origins of the English Legal Profession* (Oxford: Blackwell, 1992).

81 William Fulbecke, *A Direction or Preparative to the study of the Lawe* (London: T. Wight, 1600), fols 10ʳ, 11ᵛ.

82 Legh, *The Accedens of Armory*, fol. 130ᵛ.

83 *Ibid.*, fol. 135ᵛ.

84 Coke, 'Postnati. Calvin's case', in *The Reports of Sir Edward Coke*, ed. Wilson, IV, fol. 12ᵛ.

85 Patrick Collinson, 'Hooker and the Elizabethan Establishment', in Arthur S. McGrade (ed.), *Richard Hooker and the Construction of Christian Community* (Binghamton, NY: Medieval and Renaissance Texts and Studies, 1997), pp. 141–81 (p. 175). Hooker defined sacraments as 'those which are signes and tokens of some generall promised grace, which always really descendenth from God unto the soule that duly receiveth them' (Richard Hooker, *Of the Lawes of Ecclesiasticall Politie* (London: William Stansbye, 1622), bk. 4.1, p. 130).

86 Hooker, *Of the Lawes of Ecclesiasticall Politie*, bk. 4.1, p. 130.

87 On the importance of rhetoric in Hooker's work, and the influence of the Erasmian, humanist education he received at Corpus Christi College, Oxford, see R. J. Schoeck, 'From Erasmus to Hooker: an overview', in McGrade (ed.), *Richard Hooker and the Construction of Christian Community*, pp. 59–74.

88 Hooker died in 1600, three years before the accession to the English throne of James VI of Scotland. A. S. McGrade observes that, in doctrinal terms, Hooker represented the established church of his day, and that his version of Anglicanism probably came closest to that favoured by Queen Elizabeth (*Of the Laws of Ecclesiastical Polity*, ed. A. S. McGrade (Cambridge: Cambridge University Press, 1989), pp. xv–xvi).

89 McGrade suggests that bk. 1 of the *Laws*, especially, encourages the reader to interpret Hooker 'as an Anglican angelic doctor, serenely above the controversies of his day' (*ibid.*, p. xx).

90 Francis Beaumont, *The Masque of the Inner Temple and Grayes Inn. Presented before his Maiestie in the Banquetting House at White-hall on Saturday the twentieth day of Februarie, 1612* (London: G. Norton, 1612), fol. C3.

91 Thomas Middleton, *The Inner-Temple Masque or Masque of Heroes. Presented (as an entertainment for many worthy Ladies) by Gentlemen of the same Ancient and Noble House* (London: J. Browne, 1619), fol. C2. On designs for the masques, see John Peacock, 'Inigo Jones's stage architecture and its sources', *Art Bulletin*, 64 (1982), 195–216.

92 Fortescue, *De Laudibus Legum Angliæ*, ed. Selden, p. 112.

93 See, for example, *Cawdrey's Case* (1591), concerning the imperial prerogative of the Queen (Coke, 'Caudrey's Case. Of the King's ecclesiastical law', in *The Reports of Sir Edward Coke*, ed. Wilson, III, fols i[r]–xli[r]). This case is discussed in John Guy, 'The Elizabethan Establishment and the ecclesiastical polity', in John Guy (ed.), *The Reign of Elizabeth I: Court and Culture in the Last Decade* (Cambridge: Cambridge University Press, 1995), pp. 126–49 (pp. 131–2).

3

Gospel, law, and *ars praedicandi* at the Inns of Court, *c*.1570–*c*.1640

Hugh Adlington

In October 1602 the law student John Manningham (*c*.1575–1622) attended a sermon preached by Francis Marbury at the Temple Church. The experience was not a happy one. Manningham confided to his diary that 'I may not write what he [Marbury] said, for I could not hear him; he pronunces [*sic*] in manner of a common discourse.' Unable even to note the main heads of the sermon, let alone paraphrase or quote flights of eloquence, Manningham concluded with understandable frustration: 'I love not the sound of the sermon, except the preacher will tell me what he says.'[1] Manningham's tetchy declaration touches on many of the most pressing questions related to preaching at the early modern Inns of Court. Who preached what, in which ways, and to whom? And how did the preaching of religion reflect or shape the doctrinal, ecclesiastical, and moral character of the Inns? This chapter's enquiry into the nature of preaching at the Inns may thus serve as a lens by which to examine the role played by religion in the broader cultural life of the Inns of Court, and how that role may have changed between *c*.1570 (when preachers were first installed on a permanent basis) and *c*.1640 (when the political situation had begun to depress attendance at the Inns).[2]

The nature of religious life at the Inns of Court has been addressed to some extent by historians of early modern law and religion. Wilfrid Prest's remains the foundational work in this area. Prest shows how permanent preachers were formally appointed for the first time at the Inns in the mid-1570s in what seems to have been an effort to extirpate popery from their precincts.[3] Changes in the religious climate in the 1580s and 1590s brought about changes in preaching personnel. Increasing concern over non-conformity and separatism meant that godly ministers such as William Charke (d.1617; Gray's Inn preacher, *c*.1575–*c*.1580), Richard Alvey (d.1584; Master of the Temple, 1560–84), and Walter Travers (1548?–1635; Temple preacher, 1580–86) gave way to more conformable churchmen such as Richard Field (1561–1616; Lincoln's Inn preacher, 1594–96), Roger Fenton (1565–1616; Gray's Inn preacher, 1598–1616), and Richard Hooker (1554–1600; Master of the Temple, 1585–91).

Despite this shift towards the ecclesiastical centre, the Inns retained throughout the Jacobean period a discernible tendency, with some exceptions, towards appointing what Prest calls 'evangelical' preachers.[4] Why should this be so? 'Puritanism', or the various degrees of Calvinist conformity in matters of doctrine and ecclesiology which this term loosely connotes, held a number of attractions for common lawyers.[5] These included anticlericalism, the equation of worldly success with spiritual election, and an emphasis on preaching as the prime means to lead men to God. As Prest comments: 'A lawyer could appreciate and criticise sermons on his own terms, for logic, rhetoric and argument from authority were also his basic stock in trade.'[6] In many ways, the relationship between preaching and the practice of common law was reciprocal. Inns of Court sermons often employed courtroom terms concerning witness, testimony, and judgment for exegetical ends; scriptural exposition proceeded via legal techniques of case-putting and argument; and, at a higher level of abstraction, theological concepts themselves bore a distinctly juridical stamp: the Covenant theology of preachers such as John Preston (1587–1628), for example, might well be construed in terms of Tudor-Stuart laws of contract.[7]

The closeness of this association between common lawyers and Reformed doctrine and churchmanship can be overstated. Not only did the balance of what Prest calls 'this temporary and incomplete alliance between clergy and judiciary' differ between the Inns, it also changed over time.[8] Prest, Paul Seaver, and R. M. Fisher have all shown how throughout this period external political pressure was brought to bear on the appointments of preachers according to the demands of current events. Well-documented examples of outside interference in the nominally autonomous, extra-parochial jurisdiction of the Inns include the notorious quarrel over the appointment of Richard Hooker to the Temple in 1584; the Middle and Inner Temples' rebuff of a royally sponsored candidate, Alexander Simpson, to succeed William Crashawe in 1613; and William Laud's intervention in the religious affairs of the Inns in the 1630s.[9] Evidently, the association between the religious and legal cultures of the Inns is not straightforwardly, or *a priori*, ideological; by undertaking a study of preaching at the Inns (considering the rhetorical style and doctrinal and ecclesiological content of sermons), this chapter aims to contribute to a fuller, more complex picture of the flexible, shifting relationships between religion, politics, and law in the period.

Sources and methodology

Existing research in this area, chiefly undertaken by literary scholars, tends to focus on single preachers, such as John Donne (1572–1631) or Richard Sibbes (1577?–1635). Such studies often regard their subjects' appointments as Inns of Court preachers as phases in larger careers.[10] Other accounts tend to concentrate on single institutions, such as recent valuable research on the preaching context at Lincoln's Inn by Jeffrey Johnson, Emma Rhatigan, and Katrin Ettenhuber;[11] or on sermons preached by Inns of Court divines at other venues, such as Andrew

Fitzmaurice's study of Richard Crakanthorpe's sermon to the Virginia Company;[12] or on the religious and political significance of sermons in print (such as those of John Preston), yet with little or no attention paid to preaching venue or occasion.[13]

One obvious reason for the lack of concentrated study in this area is bibliographical: very few sermons preached at the Inns survive, either in manuscript or print. A number of printed sermon treatises by celebrated preachers such as Sibbes and Preston announce themselves as 'the substance' of 'divers' or 'sundry' sermons preached at Gray's Inn or Lincoln's Inn,[14] but only thirty-eight printed texts of single-sermon length, preached at the Inns of Court and Chancery and published between 1570 and 1640, are now extant.[15] Such a number appears paltry when compared to the thousands of sermons preached at the Inns in this period, and the broad corpus of surviving printed sermons preached at Paul's Cross, Whitehall, the Spital, and the universities. It looks even more trifling when John Donne's twenty-two sermons preached at Lincoln's Inn (1616–22), and his single sermon preached at the Temple, are removed from the total.[16] For publishers and booksellers, perhaps, Inns of Court sermons were simply not commercially viable, holding only limited public appeal. Of the few Inns of Court sermons printed and sold as stand-alone items, the majority were delivered by celebrated visiting preachers, such as Joseph Hall (1574–1656), or were dedicated to powerful legal grandees such as Sir John Dodderidge (1555–1628), Sir Henry Hobart (c.1554–1625), or Sir Randolph Crewe (1559–1646).[17] Moreover, a good proportion of these extant texts were sold through booksellers located in the heart of London's legal district – at St Dunstan's, Chancery Lane, and near the Temple – suggesting that lawyers themselves made up the majority of their readership.

What, then, can be learned from the relatively few printed early modern Inns of Court sermons that do survive? 'Sermon style', Perry Miller has argued, 'was not a matter of taste and preference, it was a party badge.'[18] Analysis of sermons' rhetorical structures and exegetical styles, then, may reveal something of the types of theology and ecclesiology listened to and sponsored by the gentlemen students and lawyers of the Inns. Yet care needs to be taken in correlating manner so closely with matter in the printed prose of this period. As Neil Rhodes puts it, 'Hooker's Ciceronianism may have helped to legitimise the Anglican Church, but Milton's Ciceronianism was put to the service of a revolutionary Puritan government.'[19] *Pace* Miller, then, sermon style may not be indexed quite so simply to political or religious positions. The reductive categorisations of 'Puritan plain style' and the 'metaphysical' or 'witty' style of Laudian or *avant-garde* conformity, endorsed by Miller and W. Fraser Mitchell, and later by Horton Davies, hardly do justice to the protean nature of religious belief and expression in the period.[20] In reality, the diverse temperaments, educational attainments, and oratorical abilities of individual preachers attuned to exigencies of occasion, auditory, and venue, resulted in the deployment of an array of rhetorical means to achieve doctrinal, political, and edifying ends in English sermons of the sixteenth and seventeenth centuries.

Contemporary theories of preaching, *artes praedicandi*, must also be taken into account. Failure to understand the role of such theories in sermon composition means that 'we are not well-placed to determine what their [the sermons'] characteristics imply for the politics, ideologies or theologies of the writers'.[21] Bearing such methodological and theoretical considerations in mind, the following analyses of sermons preached at the Inns of Court between 1570 and 1640 seek to gauge not only the nature and extent of the correlation between rhetorical style and religious, legal, and political alignment, but also how far such an evaluation is possible.

Gray's Inn: continuity in conformity?

Of the four houses, Gray's Inn appears at first sight to have enjoyed the most consistency in religious politics between 1570 and 1640. Gray's Inn boasts the smallest turnover of preachers (five) in this period, with the Presbyterian anti-Catholicism of William Charke and Thomas Crooke (*c*.1545–98) in the 1580s and 1590s succeeded by the Anglican conformity of Roger Fenton, the moderate Reform of Richard Sibbes, and, after 1635, the peaceable religious diplomacy of Hannibal Potter (1592–1664).[22] The earliest surviving Gray's Inn printed sermons were delivered not by permanent appointees, however, but by occasional preachers: John Barlow's vigorous defence of the godly in *The Joy of the Upright Man* (1619), and Joseph Hall's urbane yet impassioned call for personal moral reform in *The Great Impostor* (1623). Little is known of Barlow, though church records suggest that he served as rector of Chiddingfield, Surrey (1616–40).[23] Since Chiddingfield fell under the jurisdiction of the Canterbury Province, Barlow may have benefited from the patronage of the godly Archbishop of Canterbury, George Abbot. Certainly, the uncompromisingly Calvinist tenor of the sermon is consistent with Abbot's own doctrinal orientation. Barlow's aim, stated clearly in his letter of dedication, is to confute 'the opinion of those, that hold there is no mirth or comfort in a Christian course; who cry out, what? turne Puritane? become a Precisian? then farewell all ioy, and welcome melancholy'.[24]

To achieve that end, Barlow's sermon follows the tripartite method of doctrine, reason, and use, advocated by William Perkins (1558–1602) in *The Arte of Prophesying* (1592; trans. 1607). Each word of the sermon's scriptural text (Psalm 97: 11) is subjected to literal and tropological (moral) analysis.[25] Proof texts are drawn from the Geneva Bible (1587), with not a single reference to patristic, scholastic, or Reformed commentary; nor is there any use of ancient languages. Local analogies illustrate spiritual truths: 'Yong Conuerts (to speake with reuerence) are not vnlike some of your London Cockneyes; tell them when they come into the Countrye, that wheate is wheate … they will not credit you, for they haue no experience in matters of that nature' (p. 16). The theological emphasis throughout is Christological, and firmly Calvinist on the doctrine of justification (good works are useless; Christ alone is the source of subsequent grace), although Barlow acknowledges that such a doctrine may appear severe: 'I know that this is a hard position to settle in [your] minds' (p. 23). The uncompromising manner is maintained to the end: 'if thou finde not the doctrine true, cast off righteousnes, goe to thy old course, count me a false prophet, and curse me when thou diest' (p. 36).

Whether the Gray's Inn congregation held Barlow to his word is not known. Even if it were, however, it would be unwise to draw conclusions about the religious culture of Gray's Inn on the evidence of occasional sermons delivered by visiting preachers. It is certainly the case that Barlow's deliberate use of everyday analogies, his recourse to the Geneva Bible, and his avoidance of classical, patristic, and scholastic authorities reflect a firmly Reformist sensibility that has substantially different intellectual priorities to the overt erudition of contemporary university sermons. Yet quite opposite inferences about the religious orientation of Gray's Inn could be drawn from Joseph Hall's 1623 Candlemas sermon, *The Great Impostor*. Later to become Bishop of Exeter, and then of Norwich, Hall in 1623 held the post of Dean of Worcester. Like Barlow, Hall too was a beneficiary of George Abbot's patronage.[26] In place of Barlow's doctrinal logic, intense Biblicism, and fervent admonition, however, Hall offers suavity, wit, and a rich array of learned reference. Hall's punning dedication to the Society of Gray's Inn – 'At Whose Barre This Impostor was openly arraigned' – establishes the playful manner to follow. The studiedly hyperbolic exordium to Hall's sermon, preached on Jeremiah 17: 9 ('The heart is deceitfull above all things'), exemplifies the gently ironical tone of a man at ease in his surroundings:

> I know where I am; in one of the famous Phrontiseries of Law and Iustice: wherfore serues Law and Iustice, but for the preuention or punishment of fraud and wickednesse? Giue me leaue therefore to bring before you, Students, Masters, Fathers, Oracles of Law and Iustice, the greatest Cheator and Malefactor in the world, our owne Heart.[27]

Greek and Latin *sententiae* and Hebrew quotations stud Hall's address; these combine with a vigorous call-and-response prose rhythm that compels engagement:

> Would the Israelites be deuout? they are idle; Doth *Dauid* daunce for ioy before the Arke? he is a foole in a Morris: Doth Saint *Paul* discourse of his heauenly Vision? too much learning hath made him mad. Doe the Disciples miraculously speake all the tongues of Babel? They are full of new wine: Doe they preach Christs Kingdome? they are seditious; The resurrection? they are bablers. Is a man conscionable? he is an Hypocrite: Is he conformable? he is vnconscionable: Is he plaine dealing? he is rudely vnciuill: Is he wisely insinuatiue? he is a flatterer. (pp. 33–5)

Unlike Barlow's sermon, however, Hall's vivid eloquence is not put to controversial doctrinal or ecclesiological ends. Hall focuses instead on individual examination of conscience and the need for conformity. All groups which fall outside the English Church – 'blind-folded Papists' and 'Squint-eied Schistmaticks' alike – are equally pitied for their spiritual blindness, for their 'mesprison, superstition, [and] conceitednesse' (p. 12).

Perhaps it is no surprise that Hall, preaching on one of the Church's four 'Grand Days' to an audience of eminent judges as well as barristers and law students, and speaking just months after the issue of *Directions to Preachers* (August 1622), chooses to steer clear of sensitive matters of state (such as James VI & I's unpopular pacific diplomacy) or of religion (such as controversial doctrines of predestination and salvation).[28] Yet Hall's tact, compared to Barlow's more forthright statement of belief, cannot simply be attributed to immediate political pressures. Royal attempts to muzzle the pulpits had been made before (including proclamations in 1620 and 1621 'against excess of lavish speech'), and in this, Barlow's 1619 Gray's Inn sermon was just as much subject to official scrutiny as Hall's. Inherent differences in sensibility, rather than a willingness to serve the times, lie at the root of the stylistic divergence between the two sermons. *Stilus virum arguit*; the style betrays the man. In playing host to sermons of such distinctly dissimilar character, though, Gray's Inn chapel should not be seen as unusual. Within the Jacobean Church, diverse sermon styles might be tolerated in even the most politically charged pulpits, such as the chapels royal of James VI & I.[29] Nevertheless, while James was willing to listen to a moderately broad range of preaching styles and viewpoints, those with which he associated himself in print tended to support his political objectives.[30] It seems unlikely that the Inns had any such aim: both Barlow's and Hall's Gray's Inn sermons were published under the auspices of their authors, not of the Society of Gray's Inn itself.

Preaching style, as I have been using it so far, is a compound term. Relevant subdivisions of style derive from the canons of classical rhetoric (*inventio, divisio, dispositio, elocutio, memoria,* and *actio*), all of which are addressed by early modern sermon manuals, or *artes praedicandi*. The most influential of these manuals for English preachers in the early seventeenth century included Desiderius Erasmus's *Ecclesiastes* (1535), Philipp Melanchthon's (1497–1560) four tracts on preaching, Nils Hemmingsen's *The Preacher, or Methode of Preachinge* (trans. I. H.) (1574), Andreas Hyperius's *The Practise of Preaching* (trans. John Ludham) (1577), Batholomaeus Keckermann's *Rhetoricæ Ecclesiasticæ* (1606), William Perkins's *The Arte of Prophesying* (1592; trans. 1607), and Richard Bernard's *The Faithfull Shepheard* (1607). Four basic sermon structures (*dispositio*) were available to early modern preachers: homilies, thematic, classical oration, doctrine-reason-use. Preaching manuals also bore upon the sermon's *amplificatio*: the kinds of non-scriptural texts cited (patristic, scholastic, classical, humanist). As well as structure, and citations, a vital element of style was *elocutio*, a term which comprised considerations of syntax, diction, and rhetorical devices. *Pronuntiatio* and *actio* were also crucial aspects of preaching style.[31] The rules, methods, and aims of *ars praedicandi*, as understood by English preachers in this period, thus provide the theoretical and practical framework for analysing sermon style.

What can be said of the *ars praedicandi* of Richard Sibbes, the only permanent Gray's Inn preacher for whom we have extant printed sermons? Out of the thirty volumes of Sibbes's sermons that appeared in his lifetime, and the many more that were collected and published after his death, just four sermons, close to the form in which he is likely to have preached them at Gray's Inn, survive in print.[32] Educated at St John's College, Cambridge, Sibbes had been public lecturer at Holy Trinity Church, Cambridge before being chosen, by the influence of Sir Henry Yelverton (1566–1630), as Reader of Divinity at Gray's Inn in 1617.[33] The Presbyterian minister Thomas Manton (1620–77) observed of Sibbes's preaching style that his listeners termed him: '*The sweet dropper*; sweet and heavenly distillations … *dropping* from him with such a *native elegancie* as is not easily to be imitated'.[34]

The impression given, of a mild and holy eloquence, is borne out by the evidence of Sibbes's surviving Gray's Inn sermons. In a sermon preached on Isaiah 7: 14 ('The Lord himselfe shall give a signe, Behold a virgin shall conceive and bare a Sonne, and shall call his name Imanuell'), Sibbes begins with a pithy assertion of the error to be rectified: 'Man unsubdued by the spirit of God, admires the devices of men, and the fabricke of his owne braine.'[35] The sermon proceeds by a *per verbum* explication of its scriptural text, in a style that advances through a combination of logic, biblical paraphrase, and conversational narrative:

> We had need of strong grace to apprehend these strange things. And therefore God hath provided a grace suitable, above reason, and above nature, and that is faith. Reason mocketh at this. The devil knoweth it and envyeth it. The Angels know, and wonder at it. The soule it selfe without grace sutable to the admirablenesse of the thing, can never apprehend it. And therefore well may it be said, Behold, a virgin shall conceive and beare a sonne. (p. 8)

Sibbes's oratorical style strives for clarity, eschews ornamentation or displays of scholarship, deploys an unfussy vernacular diction, rarely uses Latin, and in its *amplificatio* sticks largely to the scriptures with little expositional reference to patristic, scholastic or even Reformation authorities. His prose is paratactic and Senecan in manner, with little use of legal terms beyond the most common: evidence, witness, testimony. His doctrinal stance is firmly conformist Calvinist, as witnessed by his emphasis in the passage quoted on 'sutable' grace, yet the equipoise of Sibbes's style dampens rather than enflames potential controversy. The well-attested success of Sibbes's Gray's Inn ministry suggests that such a rhetorical approach, and the kind of moderate conformism which it connotes, were broadly in tune with the religious sensibilities of his auditory.

Just how Sibbes stood with Archbishop William Laud (1573–1645) in the 1630s is a matter of debate. In 1627 Sibbes, along with William Gouge (1575–1653), Thomas Taylor (1576–1632), and John Davenport (*bap.*1597, *d.*1670), had been reprimanded by Laud for raising aid for destitute ministers in the Upper Palatinate. Yet evidence from Sibbes's last two sermons preached at Gray's Inn in 1635, just days before his own death, suggests he remained uncowed. In the second of the sermons, Sibbes alludes overtly to the importance of maintaining faith, 'When there comes ill tidings of the Church abroad, and at home'.[36] Preaching on John 14: 1 ('Let not your hearts be troubled, ye beleeve in God, beleeve also in me'), Sibbes calls for spiritual steadfastness in times of affliction. He warns against giving in to despair, illustrating his admonition with the biblical example of Achan, who brought disaster upon the Judahites by his covetousness (Joshua 7: 19–26):

> *Iosuah* was much cast downe when he saw it went not well with *Israel*: but get thee up *Iosuah*, saith God, what doest thou lying here? up and do thy duty; consider what is amisse: There is an *Achan* in the Campe: and so when things go not well, let not your thoughts be conversant about the matters of trouble, so much as about your duty.[37]

The Achan reference, while certainly referring in the spiritual realm to man's own traitorous impulse against confidence in God, may also signify something more topical and controversial. At first glance, Sibbes appears to be mollifying both the spiritual and political fears of his auditory ('let not your thoughts be conversant about the matters of trouble'); in other words, to be quiescent, to avoid controversy. But this is only the first part of Sibbes's exhortation. The second part is a call to follow the example of Joshua and 'do thy duty'. In Joshua 7, 'doing thy duty' means rooting out the pariah in the Judahites's midst, Achan, and stoning him to death. When this typology is applied topically, in the context of Laudian ceremonial and liturgical innovations and the dangers facing the Gray's Inn congregation in the increasingly embittered religious atmosphere of Charles I's personal rule, 'duty' acquires a sharper edge.

Sibbes also makes oblique allusion to contemporary political and religious affairs on several occasions via reference to the curse of Meroz (Judges 5: 23), a city and people cursed by the angel of God because its inhabitants failed to come to the aid of the Israelites in battle.[38] In the 1620s and 1630s, this verse was frequently used by preachers, such as Edward Gee in *The Curse and Crime of Meroz* (1620) preached at the Exeter assizes, as a thinly veiled attack on royal inaction in the face of persecution of Protestant clergy and lay persons abroad. Sibbes's careful use of typology in his Gray's Inn sermons does not contradict Mark Dever's recent recasting of Sibbes as a cautious rather than radical Reformer; yet it does suggest that at least a faint accent of dissent may still be heard beneath the sermons' conciliatory and moderate rhetorical surface.

Notable features of Sibbes's manner of delivery, his sermons' *elocutio*, which bear comparison with Hall (though not in doctrine), are his conversational register and autobiographical references. Nowhere is this more apparent than in Sibbes's final two sermons of 1635. The scriptural text taken by Sibbes, John 14: 1, contains the departing words of Christ to his disciples at the Last Supper; Sibbes's two sermons on this text would be his own valedictory words to his Gray's Inn auditory. A careful reading of Sibbes's sermons also uncovers his recurring use of mechanical imagery for the dysfunctional workings of the soul and commonwealth: 'like an Instrument out of tune, made fit for nothing, or like a limbe out of joynt'; 'The soule is as it were put out of joynt by it; we make actions difficult unto us, the wheeles of the soule are thereby taken off; joy and comfort are as it were oyle to the soule'.[39] And again: 'A limbe out of ioynt can doe nothing without deformity and paine; deiection takes off the wheeles of the soule'.[40] For those gathered at Gray's Inn chapel who knew him well, and there must have been many after his eighteen years as their preacher, these metaphors of spiritual break-down must have gained additional resonance from the knowledge of Sibbes's origins in Suffolk: he had been born and raised the son of a wheelwright, and put to apprenticeship in a wheelwright's shop before being diverted into a career in the ministry.[41]

Sibbes's Gray's Inn sermons certainly contain more autobiographical references than do his sermons preached elsewhere. For comparison, a Sibbes sermon of 1634 preached at St Mary's in Cambridge avoids all personal references. This is in spite of the fact that Sibbes might have been expected to know many of his congregation due to his long association with Cambridge, culminating in his appointment in 1626 as Master of St Catharine's College, and his presentation in 1633 to the perpetual curacy of Holy Trinity, Cambridge. Nevertheless, the public nature of the St Mary's pulpit and the ritual nature of the occasion (a Gunpowder Plot sermon) meant that Sibbes adopted a broader register, quite different in tone from the implied intimacy of his sermons preached at Gray's Inn. Indeed, the strong spirit of fellowship that existed at Gray's Inn is referred to frequently by Sibbes in his sermons: 'and so [we] may be as friends, enjoying acquaintance and communion together'.[42]

One thing immediately strikes the reader of the extant sermons preached *in situ* at Gray's Inn (by Barlow, Hall, and Sibbes): stylistic difference (in *dispositio*, *amplificatio*, and *elocutio*), rather than similarity, is their defining characteristic. Yet for seventeenth-century hearers and readers the sermons of both Hall and Sibbes were regarded as 'witty' or 'elaborate' (where the latter term, in seventeenth-century usage, conveys the sense of: 'subjected to processes of art' (*OED*, B1)). William Chappell's *Art and Method of Preaching* (1656) contains an index listing 'elaborate' preachers, among whom are Hall and Sibbes, and other Inns of Court ministers such as Joseph Caryl (1602–73), John Preston, and John Donne.[43] While it is no surprise to find these names accompanied in the lists of the 'elaborate' by star turns such as Lancelot Andrewes, Robert Sanderson, and Jeremy Taylor, it comes as a shock to discover that the same category also contains such godly luminaries as William Perkins and Richard Greenham (p. 29). And yet Thomas Fuller's remarks on the sermons of Perkins might equally be applied to those of Sibbes: 'his sermons were not so plain but that the piously learned did admire them, nor so learned but that the plain did understand them'.[44] Audience expectations are vital. Both Hall and Sibbes accommodate those expectations in their Gray's Inn sermons, establishing a personal rapport, handling controversial points with tact, and stimulating the senses with flashes of learning and oratory. Barlow does none of these things. It would be fascinating to know how his sermon was received.

Lincoln's Inn: stronghold of Puritanism?

Lincoln's Inn employed at least eleven permanent preachers between 1581 and 1647, and it is generally regarded as 'the real stronghold of Puritanism among the four inns'.[45] That Lincoln's Inn counted such a zealous anti-Laudian pamphleteer as William Prynne (1600–99) among its number is certainly no disqualification from this title. Among its preachers, the most obviously Reformist in sensibility were Richard Crakenthorpe (1568–1624), Thomas Gataker (1574–1654), John Preston, and Joseph Caryl. Edward Reynolds (1599–1676), Richard Field (1561–1616), and John Aglionby (1566/67–1610) might be placed approximately in the Anglican doctrinal and ecclesiological middle, while the chaplain and vacation preacher Edward May stands out as the lone admirer of 'the beauty of holiness'; May was dismissed from his post in 1621 for his sermon attack on the anti-sacral piety of the benchers.[46] John Donne is notoriously difficult to place on a religio-political spectrum, although Peter McCullough's tripartite formula offers a useful guide: zealous in preaching, liberal in theology, and willing to conform in ceremonial matters.[47] The four preachers for whom we have sermons preached at Lincoln's Inn are Thomas Gataker, John Donne, Edward May, and John Preston.

Thomas Gataker, educated at St John's College, Cambridge, took up his post as Divinity Reader at Lincoln's Inn in 1601. He remained there for ten years, continuing as a guest preacher at both Lincoln's Inn and Serjeants' Inn thereafter. In his lifetime he published over fifty tracts and sermons, in which he evolved moderate positions on controversial questions, including a flexible definition of justification and a delicate balance of episcopacy and Presbyterianism in matters of church governance. A prodigious scholar, Gataker was 'addicted to sprinkling his texts with classical references';[48] his pulpit oratory consequently steers more towards the unabashedly learned style of court preachers such as Joseph Hall and Lancelot Andrewes (1555–1626) than the unadorned prose of Richard Sibbes or Roger Fenton. In the Westminster Assembly of 1644, Gataker went so far as to defend his preaching style, protesting that the Perkinsian pattern of doctrine, reason, use was 'too strait for the variety of gifts, and occasion doth claim liberty'.[49]

Gataker's only surviving Lincoln's Inn sermon, delivered in the first decade of the seventeenth century but not published until 1623, provides a representative sample of his pulpit oratory. Gataker's text is Hebrews 11: 7, on God's warning to Noah of the Flood, and the sermon integrates both scholastic and humanist methods of sermon construction in its *inventio, divisio,* and *amplificatio.* Gataker exhorts his auditory to follow Noah's example by responding faithfully to divine warnings of impending danger. The publication of such an exhortation in 1623 was hardly coincidental. In that year domestic controversy over the Spanish Match reached a pitch with the futile journey of Prince Charles and the Duke of Buckingham to Madrid. Gataker's sermon joins his voice in apocalyptic terms to those urging military support for the *causa communis* of international Protestantism:

> Cast we our eyes abroad into foraine parts almost on euery side of vs, and see if the fire
> of Gods wrath be not gone out alreadie, and hath taken hold of our neighbours houses,
> yea and burnt diuers, and not a few of them, downe to the ground: And it concerneth
> vs, as wee say, not them alone, to looke to it, when our neighbours houses are on fire.[50]

Gataker's learned apparatus is evident from the dense citational thickets of tiny print in the sermon's margins. He quotes church fathers Augustine, Basil, and Ambrose, and classical rhetors Ovid, Seneca, and Virgil; he launches into biblical history and frequently inserts parenthetical qualifications and digressions. His periods, though multi-clausal, are forcefully propositional, yoking what M. W. Croll and George Williamson saw as the Ciceronian strain in early modern English prose with what Janel Mueller has called 'Scripturalism', a syntax and rhythm modelled on the cadences, alliteration, and phrasal parallelism (antithetical and correlative) of both Old and New Testaments.[51] Gataker's sermons thus constitute a resounding challenge to the facile equation of elaborate style with Laudianism, and plain style with Puritanism.

In all of his sermons, not least those preached at Lincoln's Inn and Serjeants' Inn, Gataker's enthralling fusion of scriptural and classical sources and prose styles is put in the service of a resolute defence of the godly:

> If he be conuersant in Gods word, and diligent in frequenting the ministery of it;
> he is a *Bible-bearer*, and *a gadder* vp and downe *after Sermons*. If he *make conscience
> of an oath*, and will reproue others when they sweare; he is *a superstitious fellow*, too
> straitlaced, more nice than wise. If hee will not swill and swagger, drinke healths
> and play the goodfellow, goe for company to *a Brothel-house*, or to *a Play-house*, little
> better, *the very seminaries and nurseries of all filthinesse and prophanenesse*; he is a man
> altogether vnsociable, of *a melancholy disposition*, little better than *a lunaticke*, as they
> said sometime of *Iohn the Baptist*.[52]

Nor is Gataker shy of pin-pointing the specific spiritual weaknesses of his Lincoln's Inn congregation. Sparing in his use of legal terminology, Gataker warns that a mere intellectual assent to faith in God, the kind of conceptual game-playing or speculation familiar to lawyers trained in mooting and bolting hypothetical cases, is insufficient to attain salvation: 'For that *faith* or *knowledge* that swimmeth only in the braine, but sinketh not downe into the heart, that consisteth only in speculation, and proceedeth no further, doth not at all pierce into, or worke vpon the affections, it is *no sound knowledge, no true faith*; it is but as the glittring of *a glow-worme, a light without heat*.'[53]

In his Serjeants' Inn sermons too, a principled constancy characterises Gataker's willingness to hold his legal auditory to moral account: 'If others then shall see you riding in your circuits on the Sabbath, will not they thinke within themselues? And why may not I as well ride on the Sabbath to a Faire, as the Iudge may to the place of Assise?'[54] No doubt Gataker's reputation for personal probity (including frequent refusals of lucrative preferment) and his closeness and loyalty to senior lawyers combined to sugar the pill.

All four dedicatees of his Inns of Court sermons were eminent figures in legal London: Sir Henry Hobart, Chief Justice of the Common Pleas; his son and heir, Sir John Hobart; Sir Randolph Crewe (sergeant at law and Lincoln's Inn bencher); and Sir James Ley (Chief Justice of the King's Bench). Each of Gataker's dedicatory epistles adopts the modesty topos in claiming plainness of speech ('I was neuer furnished with any store of *Rhetoricall lights*'),[55] yet each vigorously defends his use of pagan writers, which 'purged of their *Heathenish drosse* ... may well and warrantably ... be ... applied also to *the vse of the Sanctuarie and of Gods seruice therein*.'[56] Such topoi recur throughout Gataker's corpus of sermons. Indeed, Gataker's preaching style and doctrinal and ecclesiological stance remain remarkably consistent whatever the occasion (marriages, funerals, church visitations) and wherever the venue (Lincoln's Inn, Serjeants' Inn, Rotherhithe, Black Friars, and the Free School of Tunbridge, Kent). Gataker, clearly, was a known quantity when appointed by Lincoln's Inn in 1601; his staunch godliness, profound scholarship, and impressive network of legal connections must have recommended him highly. And the evidence of his printed sermons suggests that he did not disappoint; only John Donne among his successors at Lincoln's Inn can rival Gataker for the sustained verbal brilliance, learnedness, and moral imagination of his preaching ministry.

Given Emma Rhatigan's chapter in the present volume, little needs to be said here about Donne's stint as Divinity Reader at Lincoln's Inn (1616–22).[57] For the present purposes, just three aspects of Donne's preaching style warrant brief attention. The first is the significant part played by philology in his biblical exegesis, something that distinguishes him from other permanent Inns of Court preachers, and that links him with the so-called metaphysical preaching style of court divines such as Lancelot Andrewes and Joseph Hall. Time and again, comparative textual analysis, etymology, and grammar are the humanist instruments by which Donne purges his scriptural text of the accretion of errors in commentary. In a Lincoln's Inn Trinity Sunday sermon on 2 Corinthians 1: 3, that begins 'Blessed be God', Donne's thought turns immediately to parts of speech: 'There is not a better Grammar to learne, then to learne how to blesse God, and therefore it may be no levity, to use some Grammar termes herein. God blesses man *Dativè*, He gives good to him; man blesses God *Optativè*, He wishes well to him; and he blesses him *Vocativè*, He speaks well of him.'[58]

Legal terms and allusions too, can be found in far greater profusion than in the sermons of Sibbes or Gataker: 'the importunate sutor, the widow, is not blamed in the Gospel for her importunity to the Judge'; 'yet *Moses* puts a case'; and papists, 'when they will pray the Virgin *Mary* to assist her Son', then they will 'make her a Chancellor to mitigate his common Law'.[59] The third aspect of Donne's preaching style at Lincoln's Inn is his shrewd appreciation of the common lawyer's professional mental dexterity, juggling hypotheses, putting cases, batting suits back and forth between *proponens* and *respondens*, able to remain in dialectical suspension until the verdict is reached. Like Gataker, Donne sees the spiritual redundancy in such a purely speculative engagement with religion. He exhorts his auditory to climb higher, firing their affections as well as their intellects, urging them to 'proceed a step farther, to feele this fire burning out, thy faith declared in works, thy justification growne into sanctification, And then thou wilt be upon the last staire of all, That great day of thy glorification will breake out even in this life.'[60]

To judge from the evidence of the *Black Books* of Lincoln's Inn, students and benchers cherished the scintillating pulpit oratory of Gataker and Donne even where they might demur on points of doctrine or church politics. The same cannot be said for the house's attitude to Edward May, chaplain and vacation preacher (1616–22). In October 1621, the Council of the Honourable Society of Lincoln's Inn remarked on 'the scandalles and indiscreet passages' contained in May's *A Sermon of the Communion of Saints*, preached in the Hilary term of that year, finding them to be 'taxacious and imputacious to some of this House.'[61] May's mock dedication to an unnamed bishop mounts a withering attack on the Reformist sensibilities of some of his auditory, censuring those who:

> grow old in affected-Ignorance, learned mis-interpretation, zealous malice, and in an holy contempt of all Sacred and spirituall things, as sacred *deriuation of the holy Ghost*; sacred *imposition of hands*, sacred *succession of Bishops and Presbyters*; sacred *orders*; sacred *offices*; sacred *ceremonies*; the sacred *patrimony of the Crucified*; the *necessitie of* sacred *repentance*; th'*Authoritie of* the sacred *Church*.[62]

The sermon itself flirts with danger by its ecumenism ('And here we shall see how farre we may, and must communicate with the vniuersall Church? How farre with the Church of *Rome*?' (p. 12)), but the real damage may well have been inflicted by May's *ad hominem* protest against the maltreatment of the clergy: 'I am sensible of contempt and persecution, and Greatnes complaines shee is disgraced, if perchance once a yeare she bee seene in companie of a poore Priest, when as their Greatnesse hath made vs poore' (p. 8). Whether these remarks were aimed at particular benchers, or at the 'Great' in general, is not known for certain; the resolution of the Lincoln's Inn Council, however, was clarity itself: Edward May was to be 'amoved and absolutelie discharged of and from his said place.'[63]

The last word in the affair goes to May himself. In a prefatory letter to the second impression of the sermon, printed shortly after his dismissal, he promises 'charitable reuenge' for the suppression of the sermon and for his own committal 'vnto darknesse.'[64] To that end, May proposed a larger work that would consider how far the doctrines of the Council of Trent will admit reunion between the Churches of Rome and England.[65] Despite May's attempt to present his dismissal in terms of competing visions of the Church, no record of the proposed work survives. The reference in the *Black Books* to May's 'taxacious and imputacious' passages against members of Lincoln's Inn seems therefore to suggest that May's downfall was as attributable to his want of tact as to sharp differences in doctrine or churchmanship.

The final preacher for whom we have a sermon preached at Lincoln's Inn, John Preston, possessed tact in abundance. A student of natural philosophy and medicine at King's and Queens' Colleges, Cambridge, Preston had been converted by an evangelical university sermon in Great St Mary's in 1611 or 1612, and elected to succeed John Donne as preacher at Lincoln's Inn in 1622. Once in post, and capitalising on the prestige of his mastership of Emmanuel College, Cambridge, and his royal chaplaincy to Prince Charles, Preston built a formidable godly network that reached across court, commons, and university circles. Notable Lincoln's Inn allies included William Noy, Henry Sherfield, and William Hakewill, and intimate friends included, among others, the Earls of Warwick, Lincoln, Pembroke, and Bedford. Christopher Hill places Preston at the centre of this powerful social web, calling it 'a nominal roll of the Puritan opposition'.[66] Contrary to hostile caricatures of Preston as a 'nasal-whining Puritan',[67] Hill portrays him as a socially and politically successful scholar and courtier, a view endorsed by more recent biographical accounts. Jonathan Moore, for example, offers a picture of Preston as a type of ecclesiastical push-me-pull-you, the 'conforming reformer': an advocate of English hypothetical universalism in matters of grace, anti-papal and anti-Arminian in matters of sacrament, and moderate in regard of outward conformity yet nonetheless critical of the increasing formalism he saw in the state church.[68]

Preston's *A Profitable Sermon Preached at Lincolnes Inne*, based on Genesis 22: 14 and published posthumously in 1633, contains some typical aspects of his sermon style. Like Donne, Preston makes frequent use of legal jargon: 'Therefore the Lord suffers us, as it were, to forfeit our Leases, that he may renew them; otherwise we should thinke our selves to bee Free-holders'; 'The Lord doth it for proofe and tryall'; 'And put the case thy name and credit bee lost'.[69] Like Gataker, Preston also makes overt reference to the fortunes of beleaguered co-religionists on the Continent: 'Now the scope of this place is, to helpe us against discouragements, when wee see it goe hard with the Church that there is no hope for them' (sig. P2[r]). Yet Preston's unadorned preaching style differs appreciably from that of either Gataker or Donne, or for that matter from that of Sibbes, Barlow, or Hall. The following passage is representative of Preston's unforced, colloquial fluency, here alluding to the dire state of the Reformed Churches in Germany, and exhorting his auditory to take spiritual solace in affliction:

> let us not thinke of our afflictions as of things that will undoe us, but as tryals that will bring us profit ... so it is with many amongst us, when they see afflictions befall the Church and people of God, O they presently are afraid, and therefore they say, Who would be as these men? ... And therefore let this be our practice concerning the estate and condition of the Church at this time, and needfull it is wee should so doe; for doe you not see the dangers that they and we are in, and the confusion that is almost throughout all *Europe*? (sig. R4[v])

Preston's exposition flows like a well-channelled water course, page after page, relentless and hypnotic, powering the mills of religious persuasion. Long conjunctive periods combine to form massive, imperturbable blocks of text. Frequently punctuated with rhetorical questions, Preston's periods suggest rapid, concentrated composition, with virtually no marginal notation, qualification, or correction. The pattern of doctrine, reason, and use found in a large number of Preston's published sermons, preached in Cambridge, London, and elsewhere, also reflects a consistently strong emphasis on practical piety. Personal touches are rare in Preston's Lincoln's Inn sermons – whether such touches were excised by his editors (Richard Sibbes, John Davenport, and Thomas Godwin and Thomas Ball) is not known – yet contemporary records of responses to Preston's preaching, and multiple editions of his works, stand testament to the success of his ministry at Lincoln's Inn.

In the late 1620s, Preston's influence in court and church circles began to wane; the 1626 York House conference signalled a new anti-Calvinist direction in church politics. There is no evidence, however, that Preston's social and professional ties with Lincoln's Inn suffered as a consequence. Perhaps Preston's enduring popularity at Lincoln's Inn can be explained by an element of self-recognition on the part of the benchers. For the sheer unstoppable tide of his eloquence Preston would have been the match of any utter barrister in his auditory.

The Temple Church: religious weathervane?

Of the three Inns of Court pulpits, the Temple Church shows perhaps the greatest flexibility in its religious politics in response to current affairs. The situation at the Temple is complicated, however, by the fact that preaching duties were shared between the Master of the Temple and the preacher or lecturer. The mastership was the only post at the Inns held within the gift of the Crown; the Temple preacher, by contrast, was appointed by joint decision of the Middle and Inner Temple benchers alone. Seven such permanent preachers were appointed between 1571 and 1630, with occasional preachers filling in as required. The Temple's willingness to adapt to suit the times is most evident in the appointment of the orthodox Richard Hooker in 1584, as a counterweight to the avowed Presbyterian Walter Travers; but also in 1627, in the installation of the moderate Laudian Paul Micklethwaite (1588/89–1639) in response to the ascendancy of the Durham House group in ecclesiastical affairs. Scarcity of evidence, though, makes it difficult to correlate religious politics and preaching styles at the Temple with any degree of confidence. Only three printed sermons preached at the Temple in this period survive, and all three were delivered by occasional preachers: one undated sermon by John Donne, and two by Thomas Aylesbury, both published in 1624.

Donne's sermon, preached on Esther 4: 16, deals chiefly with a biblical case of conscience – Esther's refusal to obey the king, that no man or woman should, on pain of death, approach him without royal summons. One possible date for the sermon is 21 June 1615, derived from a contemporary reference to Donne preaching at the Temple in a letter dated 'Midsom^r day 1615', written to 'Sr Edw Herbert att Paris' by 'Richard Prythergh'. The letter reads: 'this day Mr Donn preached att our Temple / he had to much learninge in his sermon for ignoramus'.[70] As Potter and Simpson point out, this is a topical allusion to George Ruggles's Latin comedy *Ignoramus*, first staged at Cambridge University before James VI & I in 1615, in which Ignoramus is a common lawyer.[71] Donne's sermon on Esther 4: 16 may not, of course, have been the one attended by Richard Prythergh (Donne may have preached other sermons at the Temple). Nevertheless, this particular sermon would certainly have held much of interest for an audience of lawyers. Donne states the nub of the issue at the outset: 'How far Humane Laws do bind the conscience ... hath been a perplexed question in all times, and in all places'.[72] In addressing this question, Donne alludes to the moral reasoning of both Protestant and Catholic casuists, makes learned references to an array of patristic sources, reviews Jewish history, discusses points of common and civil law, and compares Latin and Hebrew versions of scripture. Though impossible to tell whether or not this sermon was the one referred to by Prythergh, what is certain is that if Donne was aiming to impress his Temple Church auditory with his erudition and eloquence, he certainly would not have been the first nor the last visiting preacher to make the attempt.

Thomas Aylesbury (*bap.*1597, *d.*1660/61) is another prime example. A graduate of Christ's College, Cambridge, and client of both John Williams, Bishop of Lincoln, and Henry Wriothesley, 3rd Earl of Southampton (who was admitted to Gray's Inn in 1589), Aylesbury delivered two sermons at the Temple in 1623. His near-Arminian hypothetical universalism – that 'God tenders grace to al, if men ioyne but to make it efficacious' – is demonstrated in the first, *Christus Redivivus*;[73] and his criticism of both Roman Catholic eucharistic theology and of Brownist separatism is evident in the second, *Paganisme and Papisme Parallel'd*.[74] Yet, unlike the renowned lucidity of the legal arguments of John Dodderidge, to whom the first sermon was dedicated, Aylesbury's oratory tends towards the long-winded. His is a mannered, over-curious style, lending his words an affected, sententious air rather than the courtly sophistication at which he is aiming:

> We neuer read that Christ rode but once, and that vpon an Asse, when the people spred the way with branches, and the children welcomed him with *Hosannah & benedictus* in their mouths; if silence had beene imposed to those little ones, *etiam saxa* [even stones], stones would not haue wanted tongues to haue expressed the Creators worth: and though the earth, & men vpon the earth lay their hands vpon their mouths, when they should display a *Sauiours* goodnesse, yet *Cœli enarrant* [the Heavens tell us]: a *Metaphysicall* Starre shall be a *Cynosura* to conduce the *Sages* to *Christ*, folded in the armes of his mother the blessed *Virgin*: and a celestiall Angell shall wait vpon the same Sauiour, wrapped in the bowels of the earth, our common mother.[75]

Some account must be taken of Aylesbury's youth. In 1623 he was just twenty-five years old, and no doubt determined to impress in the prestigious pulpit of the Temple. His desire to ingratiate himself with his auditory may be seen in his assiduous incorporation of legalese into his exposition: 'the Lord entailes his special blessings vpon his children' (p. 10); and 'thus you see Reason stands in competition with Religion, and boasts to haue the more clients' (p. 42). Both of his sermons draw repeatedly on patristic sources: Latin, Greek, and Hebrew tags pepper each text. Conventionally anti-Catholic in sacramental matters, Aylesbury encourages the dedicatee of his second sermon, Henry Wriothesley, to 'encrease dayly your Zeale to his true worship'.[76] Such apparent markers of Calvinist conformity, however, are balanced by Aylesbury's liberality on the doctrine of grace, and the painful erudition of his style. Given Aylesbury's evident ambition, his ostentatious imitation of the courtly style may perhaps say more about Aylesbury than about the religio-political preferences of the benchers of the Inner and Middle Temples themselves.

Further clues as to the styles of churchmanship and oratory preferred at the Temple may be inferred more generally. The first permanent Temple preacher for whom printed material survives is William Crashawe (1572–1626), father of the poet and Catholic convert Richard Crashawe (1612–49). Another alumnus of St John's College, Cambridge, Crashawe held the post of preacher to the Inner and Middle Temples between 1605 and 1613, the last five years of which saw Crashawe struggle to retain his position amid constant petitions and negotiations over the payment of his stipend. Although none of Crashawe's sermons preached at the Temple Church were printed, his anti-Roman Catholic treatise on sin, *Parable of Poyson* (1618), 'Begun before the Prince his Highnesse, proceeded in at Greyes Inne, and the Temple, and finished at St. Martins in the fields', offers at least a snapshot of Crashawe's vigorous, controversialist style.[77] Dedicated to Attorney-General Sir Henry Yelverton, staunch supporter of godly clergy, the treatise adheres firmly to the *sola scriptura* precept of Reform exegesis in that nearly all of its proof texts are citations from the Old and New Testaments.

As a godly preacher, Crashawe also performs his public duty by warning his auditory to 'take heede of the Theater, where (if the olde Fathers may be trusted) a man can hardly escape acquaintance with the Diuell, and our daily and dreadfull experience tels vs, that not one of a thousand get any good there' (p. 9). And in this controversial mode, Crashawe's heavy irony seems calculated to appeal to his auditory's lawyerly sensibilities. He cleverly deploys the argument made by Bishop John Jewel in *Apologia pro Ecclesia Anglicana* (1562) that in fact the primitive British Church preceded that of Rome, thus standing the Roman Catholic argument against the novelty of the Reformation on its head:

> as you forsooke vs and the ancient religion, which we will keepe and maintaine; so he hath now giuen vs power ouer you, to conquer your kingdome and deface your religion, as it hath deserued: therefore neuer labour to bring vs to your noueltie and new fangled religion; but rather come home to vs and to the auntient religion of our forefathers: neuer endeuour to seduce vs into your secret and schismaticall, and inuisible Church; but rather come you into the light and sun-shine of our glorious, vniuersall, and catholike Church.[78]

After Crashawe, Abraham Gibson (1587–1629), chaplain in ordinary to James VI & I, preached at the Temple between 1614 and 1618. Gibson makes explicit his allegiance to undecorated preaching in the epistle dedicatory to a sermon he delivered at Paul's Cross in 1613: '*Plaine it was in the* Preaching, *more plaine it is in the* Printing: *Some* Quotations *I have omitted, and interposed in the* Margent, *to the end it may no way be obscure, but plaine to the plainest.*'[79] Like Crashawe, Gibson is fiercely anti-Catholic and strongly supportive of sermon-centred piety. Like Crashawe, too, he is at his most eloquent in passages of indignant denunciation, making effective use of alliteration and aphorism to roundly reject royal attempts to muzzle the pulpits: 'must wee, with the false prophets, speake pleasing things, sowing Pillowes vnder mens arme-holes, and flattering them in their sinnes? ... The calmest Sunne-shine doth lesse purifie the aire than the terriblest thunder and lightning. The pleas-antest Potion doth seldom purge so kindly as the bitterest Pill' (p. 5).

Both Crashawe and Gibson appear to be more determinedly Calvinist than the visiting preachers Donne and Aylesbury in matters of doctrine and ritual, and on questions of church governance. A conclusion might be drawn, therefore, about the kind of churchmanship preferred at the Temple in this period. Yet the documentary evidence is sparse, and records of disputes over religious principle or politics are more than outweighed by surviving evidence of squabbles over benefices and prece-dence, and clashes in personality (not only between preachers and benchers, but also between the governing bodies of the Middle and Inner Temples themselves).

Such tensions are present in even the most apparently unremarkable of places. Edward Dalton, for example, in his 1624 sermon, *Doubtings dounfall*, dedicated to 'To the Gentlemen of the Inns of Court, especially of the Temples', paints an ideal picture of the reciprocity of the legal and clerical professions:

> Without you [the lawyers], we must confesse, not any in our Gouernment ... contin-ueth or recouereth a certainty in his Estate Temporall, as you doe and will, I hope acknowledge, that you your selues attaine to, and find comfort in, that certainty of your future well-fare by the Ministery, which as a Conduit pipe conuaies it to you from the Sacred Word, that *Will of Saluation.*[80]

Dalton's portrayal, however, reads more like a grudging apology than a celebration of a functioning partnership. Heavily loaded qualifiers such as, 'we must confesse', and, 'as you doe and will, I hope acknowledge', are terms indicative rather of arbitration and reconciliation than of blissful union. Always sensitive, and sometimes fractious, the uneasy jurisdictional and professional relationship between law and clergy in the early seventeenth century is thus an essential context for understanding issues of religious politics, and even of prose style, in the period.

Conclusion

This survey of preaching has attempted to gauge the nature of the relationship between the literary style of sermons preached at the Inns and the religio-political inclinations of their authors and auditors. In passing, this enquiry has touched upon a number of related questions: how far can the kinds of religion preached at the Inns be distinguished from those preached at other educational, social, and vocational centres, such as the universities? What differences existed in preaching culture between the four houses? And to what extent did sermons intersect or engage with legal readings and law exercises, and with other branches of arts and learning, to constitute the Inns' institutional culture and identity? At least two salient features of the religious culture of the early modern Inns of Court emerge from the survey. The first is the tendency at the Inns towards the appointment of the more godly sort of churchman: fiercely anti-Catholic, actively sympathetic to the plight of the continental European Reformed Churches, and advocating a staunch belief in the primacy of the preaching ministry. Indeed, the pronounced orientation of the Inns towards godliness by the second decade of James's rule is suggested by a 1612 pamphlet attack on William Crashawe, written by Jesuit and religious controversialist John Floyd (1572–1649). Floyd addresses his prefatory epistle to 'The Students of the Common Law in his Maiesties Innes of Court', and offers: 'this fan of truth to cleanse your Temples, which more then any other place haue been filled with these cobwebs, where the deceyuer hath hid himselfe these many yeares in a fayre shew of feygned Godlynesse, to intangle his credulous Auditours, in wicked & damnable hatred of that faith, which our Forefathers did most gloriously professe'.[81]

The second feature that becomes apparent is the rich array of preaching styles that co-existed within this evangelically inflected religious culture. As Thomas Manton puts it: 'There is a diversity of gifts as there is of tempers, and of tempers as there is of faces.'[82] F. P. Wilson, fifty years ago, drew from this a pessimistic conclusion about the chances of successfully connecting a preacher's style with his beliefs: 'There are sermons plain and colored, Attic and Asiatic, simple and learned, dry and watery, dialectical and rhetorical. Is it possible to prophesy from a man's creed what style of sermon he would preach? Not very surely.'[83] Unlike early modern drama, poetry, and the prose of canonical figures such as Milton, the language of pulpit literature still awaits the attentions of computational stylistics. In the absence of such analysis, studies such as the present chapter can only speculate on the nature and causes of such stylistic diversity evident in printed Inns of Court sermons. Two brief points here must suffice. In the first instance, it can be argued that such diversity has a wider significance for understanding the literary culture of the Inns in this period. As W. Fraser Mitchell puts it, 'The sermon, therefore, may be regarded not only as itself providing a species of prose, but as a kind of index of what men were likely to attempt or applaud in contemporary literature.'[84] Furthermore, and most importantly, the stylistic variety on show in the pulpits of the Inns of Court suggests that political, theological, and ecclesiastical affiliations are only parts of the historical account of early modern religious culture, and the most classifiable, abstract parts at that. The less tangible aspects of historical enquiry, the force of individual personality, speech, and expression, and the sometimes unexpected social frictions or alliances that can result, are far harder to recover and to name. All that essays such as this one can hope to achieve, therefore, is to bring us just a little closer to the experience, as well as to the idea, of the intellectual and religious culture of the Inns of Court.

Notes

I am grateful to Katrin Ettenhuber for her valuable comments on an early draft of this chapter.

1 *The Diary of John Manningham of the Middle Temple 1602–1603*, ed. Robert Parker Sorlien (Hanover, NH: The University Press of New England, 1976), p. 115.

2 Wilfrid R. Prest, *The Inns of Court under Elizabeth I and the Early Stuarts, 1590–1640* (London: Longman, 1972), pp. 8–9.

3 *Ibid.*, pp. 192–3; R. M. Fisher, 'The origins of Divinity Lectureships at the Inns of Court, 1569–1585', *Journal of Ecclesiastical History*, 29 (1978), 145–62; R. M. Fisher, 'Privy Council coercion and religious conformity at the Inns of Court, 1569–1584', *Recusant History*, 15 (1981), 305–24; R. M. Fisher, 'The reformation of the clergy at the Inns of Court, 1530–1580', *Sixteenth Century Journal*, 12:1 (1981), 69–91.

4 Prest, *The Inns of Court under Elizabeth I and the Early Stuarts, 1590–1640*, p. 189. For sixteenth-century use of the term 'evangelical' applied to English Protestants, see Ashley Null, 'Thomas Cranmer and Tudor evangelicalism', in Kenneth J. Stewart and Michael A. G. Haykin (eds), *The Emergence of Evangelicalism: Exploring Historical Continuities* (Nottingham: Apollos, 2008), pp. 221–51.

5 For recent influential re-evaluations of 'puritanism', as a term designating an identifiable set of beliefs and behaviour, see Patrick Collinson, *Godly People: Essays on English Protestantism and Puritanism* (London: Hambledon Press, 1983); Peter Lake, 'Calvinism and the English Church, 1570–1635', *Past and Present*, 114 (1987), 32–76; Peter Lake, *Anglicans and Puritans? Presbyterianism and English Conformist Thought from Whitgift to Hooker* (London: Allen and Unwin, 1988); Anthony Milton, *Catholic and Reformed: The Roman and Protestant Churches in English Protestant Thought, 1600–1640* (Cambridge: Cambridge University Press, 1995); Peter Lake and Michael Questier, *Conformity and Orthodoxy in the English Church, c.1560 to 1660* (Woodbridge: Boydell, 2000).

6 Prest, *The Inns of Court under Elizabeth I and the Early Stuarts, 1590–1640*, p. 210.

7 John H. Baker, *An Introduction to English Legal History*, 4th edn (London: Butterworths, 2002), pp. 317–21. Preston succeeded Donne as preacher to Lincoln's Inn in 1622.

8 Prest, *The Inns of Court under Elizabeth I and the Early Stuarts, 1590–1640*, p. 211.

9 Fisher, 'Privy Council coercion and religious conformity at the Inns of Court, 1569–1584'; Prest, *The Inns of Court under Elizabeth I and the Early Stuarts, 1590–1640*, pp. 193–4, 206, 211; Paul S. Seaver, *The Puritan Lectureships: The Politics of Religious Dissent, 1560–1662* (Stanford, CA: Stanford University Press, 1970), p. 216; ITL, 1/1/1, 1/1/2; P. J. Wallis, *William Crashawe, The Sheffield Puritan* (London: Transactions of the Hunter Archaeological Society, 1963), p. 27.

10 Jeanne Shami, *John Donne and Conformity in Crisis in the late Jacobean Pulpit* (Cambridge: D. S. Brewer, 2003); Mark E. Dever, *Richard Sibbes: Puritanism and Calvinism in Late*

Elizabethan and Early Stuart England (Macon, GA: Mercer University Press, 2000).

11 Jeffrey Johnson, 'Consecrating Lincoln's Inn Chapel', *John Donne Journal*, 23 (2004), 139–60; Emma Rhatigan, 'Knees and elephants: John Donne preaches on ceremonial conformity at Lincoln's Inn', *John Donne Journal*, 23 (2004), 185–213; Katrin Ettenhuber, '"Take heed what you hear": re-reading Donne's Lincoln's Inn sermons', *John Donne Journal*, 26 (2007), 127–57.

12 Andrew Fitzmaurice, '"Every man, that prints, adventures": the rhetoric of the Virginia Company sermons', in Lori Anne Ferrell and Peter McCullough (eds), *The English Sermon Revised: Religion, Literature and History, 1600–1750* (Manchester: Manchester University Press, 2000), pp. 24–42.

13 Christopher Hill, 'The political sermons of John Preston', in Hill, *Puritanism and Revolution: Studies in the Interpretation of the English Revolution of the 17th Century*, rev. edn (New York, NY: St Martin's Press, 1997), pp. 216–47.

14 Richard Sibbes, *A Fountain Sealed: or, The duty of the sealed to the Spirit, and the worke of the Spirit in sealing ... Being the substance of divers sermons preached at Grayes Inne* (London: Printed by Thomas Harper for Lawrence Chapman, 1637); Richard Sibbes, *The Saints Cordialls delivered in sundry sermons at Graies-Inne, and in the citie of London* (London: Printed by M[iles] F[lesher] for Henry Overton [and R. Dawlman], 1637); John Preston, *An Elegant and Lively Description of Spirituall Life and Death delivered in divers sermons in Lincolnes-Inne, November the 9.th, M.DCXXIII. upon Iohn, 5.25* (London: Printed by Thomas Cotes, for Michaell Sparke, 1632).

15 To my knowledge there are no extant manuscript or printed texts of sermons preached between *circa* 1570 and *circa* 1640 at any of the following Inns of Chancery: Clement's Inn, Thavie's Inn, Clifford's Inn, Barnard's Inn, Staple Inn, Lyon's Inn, New Inn, and Furnival's Inn.

16 This is the number of Donne's sermons that state Lincoln's Inn or Serjeants' Inn as place of preaching in their early printed titles.

17 Thomas Aylesbury, *Christus Redivivus: Or the first fruits of them that sleepe. Deliuered in a sermon at the Temple Church, in Easter Tearme last, 1623* (London: G. E. for Leonard Becket, 1624); Thomas Gataker, *Gods Parley with Princes with an appeale from them to him* (London: Printed by Edw: Griffin, 1620); Thomas Gataker, *A Sparke Toward the Kindling of Sorrow for Sion, A Meditation on Amos 6. 6* (London: Printed by J[ohn] H[aviland] for William Sheffard, 1621).

18 Perry Miller, *The New England Mind: The Seventeenth Century* (New York, NY: Macmillan, 1939), p. 333.

19 Neil Rhodes (ed.), *English Renaissance Prose: History, Language, and Politics* (Tempe, AZ: Medieval and Renaissance Texts and Studies, 1997), p. 16.

20 Miller, *The New England Mind*; W. Fraser Mitchell, *English Pulpit Oratory from Andrewes to Tillotson: A Study of its Literary Aspects* (London: SPCK, 1932); Horton Davies, *Worship and Theology in England: From Andrewes to Baxter and Fox, 1603–1690* (Princeton, NJ: Princeton University Press, 1975).

21 Mary Morrissey, 'Scripture, style and persuasion in seventeenth-century English theories of preaching', *Journal of Ecclesiastical History*, 53 (2002), 686–706 (706).

22 Although Potter's Arminianism eventually proved too much for Gray's Inn; he was dismissed in 1641 for his indiscreet criticism of Marian protestant matyrs (Prest, *The Inns of Court under Elizabeth I and the Early Stuarts, 1590–1640*, p. 202).

23 Clergy of the Church of England Database (CCED), www.theclergydatabase.org.uk/jsp/

DisplayAppointment.jsp?CDBAppRedID=205788.

24 John Barlow, *The Joy of the Upright Man in a sermon preached at Grayes Inne* (London: Imprinted by Felix Kyngston for Nathaniel Newbery, 1619), sig. A2ᵛ.

25 On the use of the Psalms in Donne's sermons, see Chapter 5, pp. 90–106, below.

26 Richard A. McCabe, 'Hall, Joseph (1574–1656)', *Oxford Dictionary of National Biography*, Oxford University Press, Sept. 2004; online edn, Jan. 2008 www.oxforddnb.com/view/article/11976 (accessed 25 April 2009); CCED.

27 Joseph Hall, *The Great Impostor Laid Open in a Sermon at Grayes Inne, Febr. 2. 1623* (London: Printed by J. Haviland for Nathaniel Butter, 1623), pp. 1–2. The bantering tone is captured in Hall's use here of the word 'Phrontiseries', meaning a 'thinking shop' (*OED*); a term applied by Aristophanes in *The Clouds* to ridicule the school of Socrates.

28 Some of the topics proscribed by the *Directions* include anti-papist invective, predestination, matters of state, and personal slanders (*Visitation Articles and Injunctions of the Early Stuart Church*, Church of England Record Society, vol. 1, ed. Kenneth Fincham (Woodbridge: The Boydell Press, 1994), pp. 211–14).

29 Peter McCullough, *Sermons at Court: Preaching, Religion and Politics in Elizabethan and Jacobean England* (Cambridge: Cambridge University Press, 1998), pp. 101–68.

30 *Ibid.*, pp. 138–9.

31 Catherine J. Armstrong, '"Error vanquished by delivery": elite sermon performance in Jacobean England' (DPhil dissertation, University of Oxford, 2008).

32 Richard Sibbes, *Two Sermons Upon the First Words of Christs Last Sermon John XIIII. I* (London: Printed by Thomas Harper, for Lawrence Chapman, 1636); *A Miracle of Miracles or Christ in our Nature wherein is contained the wonderfull conception, birth, and life of Christ* (London: Printed by E[dward] G[riffin, and John Norton?], 1638); *A Learned Commentary or Exposition: upon the first chapter of the second Epistle of S. Paul to the Corinthians Being the substance of many sermons formerly preached at Grayes-Inne, London* (London: Printed by J. L. for N. B., 1655).

33 Mark E. Dever, 'Sibbes, Richard (1577?–1635)', *Oxford Dictionary of National Biography*, Oxford University Press, Sept. 2004; online edn, May 2007 www.oxforddnb.com/view/article/25498 (accessed 25 April 2009).

34 Sibbes, *A Learned Commentary or Exposition*, sig. Aᵛ.

35 Sibbes, *A Miracle of Miracles*, p. 2.

36 Richard Sibbes, *The Soules Conflict with it Selfe, and victory over it self by faith a treatise of the inward disquietments of distressed spirits, with comfortable remedies to establish them* (London: Printed by Miles Flesher for Robert Dawlman, 1635), p. 67.

37 Sibbes, *Two Sermons*, pp. 18–19.

38 Sibbes, *A Miracle of Miracles*, p. 24; *The Saints Safetie in Evill Times delivered at St Maries in Cambridge the fift of November, upon occasion of the Powder-Plot* (London: Printed by Miles Flesher for Robert Dawlman, 1634), p. 23.

39 Sibbes, *Two Sermons*, pp. 11, 13.

40 Sibbes, *The Soules Conflict with it Selfe*, sig. A4ᵛ.

41 Dever, 'Richard Sibbes'. See n. 33, above.

42 Sibbes, *Two Sermons*, p. 51.

43 William Chappell, *The Preacher, or the Art and Method of Preaching* (London: Printed for Edward Farnham, 1656), sig. L2ʳ.

44 Thomas Fuller, *The Holy State and the Profane State* (Cambridge: Printed by Roger Daniel

for John Williams, 1648), p. 81.

45 Prest, *The Inns of Court under Elizabeth I and the Early Stuarts, 1590–1640*, p. 204.

46 *Black Books*, II, 224–5.

47 Peter McCullough, 'Donne as preacher at court: precarious "Inthronization"', in David Colclough (ed.), *John Donne's Professional Lives* (Cambridge: D. S. Brewer, 2003), pp. 179–204 (pp. 192–3).

48 Brett Usher, 'Gataker, Thomas (1574–1654)', *Oxford Dictionary of National Biography*, Oxford University Press, Sept. 2004; online edn, Jan. 2008 www.oxforddnb.com/view/article/10445 (accessed 25 April 2009).

49 John Lightfoot, 'The journal of the proceedings of the assembly of divines: from January 1, 1643, to December 31, 1644', in *The Whole Works of the Rev. John Lightfoot, D.D.* ed. J. R. Pitman, 13 vols (London: J. F. Dove, 1824), XIII, 278.

50 Thomas Gataker, *Noah his Obedience: A Meditation on Hebrews 11.7* (London: Printed by John Haviland, 1623), in *Two Sermons tending to direction for Christian cariage* [sic] *both in afflictions incumbent, and in judgements imminent: the former on Psalm 13.1, the latter on Hebr. 11.7* (London: Printed by John Haviland, 1623), p. 89.

51 Morris W. Croll, *'Attic' and Baroque Prose Style: The Anti-Ciceronian Movement*, ed. J. Max Patrick, Robert O. Evans, and John M. Wallace (Princeton, NJ: Princeton University Press, 1969); George Williamson, *The Senecan Amble: A Study in Prose Form from Bacon to Collier* (London: Faber & Faber, 1951); Janel M. Mueller, *The Native Tongue and the Word: Developments in English Prose Style 1380–1580* (Chicago, IL; London: University of Chicago Press, 1984).

52 Gataker, *Noah his Obedience*, pp. 118–19.

53 *Ibid.*, p. 105.

54 Gataker, *Gods Parley with Princes*, pp. 12–13.

55 Gataker, *Noah his Obedience*, sig. M1^v.

56 *Ibid.*, sig. M2^r.

57 On Donne's sermons at Lincoln's Inn, see Chapter 5, pp. 90–106, below. On a portrait of Donne that was 'almost certainly on display in a private chamber of a member of Lincoln's Inn', see Chapter 8, pp. 172–4, below, and Plate 3.

58 *The Sermons of John Donne*, ed. George R. Potter and Evelyn M. Simpson, 10 vols (Berkeley; Los Angeles, CA: University of California Press, 1953–62), III, 238–9.

59 *Ibid.*, III, 261, 263.

60 *Ibid.*, III, 273.

61 *Black Books*, II, 224–5.

62 Edward May, *A Sermon of the Communion of Saints* (London: Printed by John Dawson for George Lathum, 1621), sigs A2^v–A3^r.

63 *Black Books*, II, 224–5.

64 Edward May, *A Sermon of the Communion of Saints* (London: Printed by John Leggat for George Lathum, 1621), sigs B1^r–B1^v.

65 *Ibid.*, sig. B1^v.

66 Hill, 'The political sermons of John Preston', p. 217.

67 *Ibid.*, p. 245.

68 Jonathan D. Moore, 'Preston, John (1587–1628)', *Oxford Dictionary of National Biography*, Oxford University Press, Sept. 2004; online edn, Jan. 2008 www.oxforddnb.com/view/article/22727 (accessed 25 April 2009).

69 John Preston, *A Profitable Sermon Preached at Lincolnes Inne*, in *A liveles life: Or, Mans spirituall death in sinne. Being the substance of severall sermons upon Ephes. 2. 1, 2, 3* (London: Printed by J. Beale for Andrew Crooke, 1633), sigs P3^v, P4^v, Q1^v.

70 NA, Powis MS 30/53/7/11.

71 *The Sermons of John Donne*, ed. Potter and Simpson, V, 15.

72 *Ibid.*, V, 224–5.

73 Aylesbury, *Christus Redivivus*, p. 17.

74 Thomas Aylesbury, *Paganisme and Papisme: Parallel'd and set forth in a sermon at the Temple-Church, upon the feast day of All-Saints 1623* (London: George Eld for Leonard Becket, 1624), pp. 9–10, 19.

75 Aylesbury, *Christus Redivivus*, pp. 2–3.

76 Aylesbury, *Paganisme and Papisme*, sig. A2^v.

77 William Crashawe, *The Parable of Poyson. In fiue sermons of spirituall poyson* (London: T[homas] S[nodham] for Richard Moore, 1618).

78 William Crashawe, *The Sermon preached at the Crosse, Feb. xiiij. 1607*, 2nd impression (London: H. L[ownes]. for Mathew Lownes, 1609), p. 20.

79 Abraham Gibson, *The Lands Mourning For Vaine Swearing: Or the downe-fall of Oaths* (London: T. S. for Ralph Mab, 1613), sig. A4^r.

80 Edward Dalton, *Doubtings dounfall first, prouing the communitie of the Saints assurance. Secondly, disprouing Bellarmines and his fellowes false allegations and friuolous exceptions against that truth* (London: Printed by B. A[lsop]., 1624), sig. A3^r.

81 John Floyd, *The Overthrow of the Protestants pulpit-Babels, convincing their preachers of lying & rayling, to make the Church of Rome seeme mysticall Babell* ([Saint-Omer]: [English College Press], 1612), p. 22.

82 Sibbes, *A Learned Commentary or Exposition*, sigs A1^r–A1^v.

83 F. P. Wilson, *Seventeenth-Century Prose* (Cambridge: Cambridge University Press, 1960), p. 92.

84 Mitchell, *English Pulpit Oratory from Andrewes to Tillotson*, p. 382.

4

The Inns of Court and the common law mind: the case of James Whitelocke

Damian X. Powell

In 1619 James Whitelocke (1570–1632) copied notes from a speech he gave, upon leaving the Middle Temple for Serjeant's Inn, into his *Liber Famelicus* or 'family book'. 'I hold it verye unpleasing to a sociable disposition to be deprived of the dayly conversation of ancient frends', he reflected after twenty-six years as a Middle Templar. 'I am likely to be sensible of this, for, thoughe I have found yow all my worthye frends, and assure myself of the continuance of your loves, yet I fear that by my remove I shall misse sum of the effects of it.'[1] Whitelocke paid tribute to a professional cohort he called 'my *coœtanei*, for we began togeather in the universitye, came hether togeather, and have lived togeather ever sithence, and our loves and affections have grown up togeather'. Theirs was a bond, Whitelocke noted, which had deepened as 'collegues, for we have lived together ever sithence in the participation of studyes, in doing of exercises, in taking our degrees, and for 28 years, almost compleat, have been *collaterales*, and sat on by the others side'. It would be 'verye uncouthe to me to be cut of[f] from these contentments, and to lighte upon new men and new manners', he concluded. 'It is not my meaning so to do. I shall *solum mutare non animum*, and my remove shall cawse only separation of our bodyes, not a divorce of our mindes.'[2]

Were these just words, a trope among the myriad public rituals of the Inns, a public courtesy? Or is it still possible to speak purposefully, as John Pocock once did, of the 'common law mind'?[3] Lawyers and historians from Sir John Fortescue to J. H. Baker have remarked upon the role of the 'third university of England' as the vehicle for the construction of a distinctive professional and constitutional voice.[4] This chapter questions 'sum of the effects' of the Middle Temple upon Whitelocke, in light of the varied claims made for a distinctive professional outlook formed at the early modern Inns of Court.

Historiography, sources, approaches

Arguing that the Western legal tradition is one 'of inescapable institutions and institutional life', Peter Goodrich and Paul Raffield have placed the Inns of Court at the centre of early Stuart constitutionalism in their recent studies of the Inns.[5] Drawing from radically different inspirations and ideas than the defining work of J. H. Baker and Wilfrid Prest, theirs is a new style of 'counter revisionism'.[6] As Raffield and Goodrich have engaged with the cultural repertoire of the Inns from dress and dinner codes to plays and revels in search of the 'aesthetics of law', they have argued that the distinctive professional outlook, fostered at the Inns in the reigns of Elizabeth and James I, nurtured and reinforced confidence in English law as a check on royal absolutism.[7] Raffield sums up thus: 'The Inns of Court, which developed on an unprecedented scale throughout this period, were symbols and embodiments not only of the self-proclaimed status of the legal profession as legitimate guardians of the constitution, but also of the values inherent in the constitution itself.'[8] Once a champion in the Whig tradition of English history, James Whitelocke presents a test case for this assertion.[9] His *Liber Famelicus* offers as many insights into the mind of a common lawyer as anything else that survives from the reign of the early Stuarts. It complements – at times intriguingly – the public records of the day. A rare source of colour and candour, it begs its readers to consider the currency of Whitelocke's views in his professional and social milieu. One might further ask to what extent Whitelocke's constitutional perspective – famously distilled in a 1610 parliamentary speech which suggested that 'the power of the king in parliament is greater than his power out of parliament, and doth rule and control it' – was influenced by his formation within the Middle Temple.[10]

The records which attest to James Whitelocke's own engagement with the Inns of Court shed light upon what Goodrich calls the 'practical and material forms' of the common-law tradition: its 'rituals, its repetitions, its texts, its symbols, its icons, its other media of circulation and inscription'.[11] Whitelocke wrote as much in them as anyone did in this period on the ritual, the intellectual, the social, and the ceremonial elements which flowed through the fabric of the Inns of Court in early Stuart times. Most survive in his own hand. They range from his much-copied 1619 reading on benefices to his law commonplace books, notes he made on the rituals of the Inns, and asides he salted throughout the *Liber Famelicus* on the professional solidarity and political concerns of his brother lawyers. Taken together, they reflect back upon a written and intellectual engagement which occurred over a twenty-year span. Beyond his own hand, his son Bulstrode Whitelocke's *Annals of his own life Dedicated to his Children* offers reflections upon James Whitelocke's outlook.[12] And the *Minutes of the Parliament of the Honourable Society of the Middle Temple* help to delineate the pragmatic and domestic realities which surrounded his progression.

Finally, this chapter reflects upon Whitelocke's constitutional pronouncements during his time at the Inns of Court, and their professional milieu.[13] In his 1610 parliamentary speech on Impositions, Whitelocke marked out strong ground for parliament by seating sovereign power 'in the king: but in the king is a two-fold power; the one in parliament, as he is assisted with the consent of the whole state; the other out of parliament, as he is sole, and singular, and guided merely by his own will', arguing that the personal prerogative was always responsive to a '*suprema potestas'* achieved with parliamentary sanction.[14] Twenty years later in Whitelocke's 1630 ruling in John Eliot's case, this Coke-like view had vanished in his advocacy for 'one super-eminent power, which is not subject to be questioned by any other, and that is the king in this commonwealth'.[15]

The first view was expressed in the middle of Whitelocke's long engagement with the Middle Temple, ten years after his call to the bar and nine years before his election as bencher and autumn reader. The second was given eleven years after he had left his Inn to preside over the royal courts of justice. Had an unwanted divorce of minds been forced upon Whitelocke during these years, under the pressure of royal demands, from the formational influences of the Inns? Or is it just too much, or just too hard, to speak of a coherent intellectual and professional formation at the Inns of Court in the decades before the civil wars? Navigating Whitelocke's path through the Inns opens to investigation the formative influences of the Inns of Court in the decades before political trust broke down and war broke out.

Finding a place at the Inns

Beyond the written record, the early Stuart Inns of Court were physical spaces as much as intellectual ones. For Whitelocke and for the other lawyers, at any stage in their association with their societies, the architectural setting defined and reinforced the social and intellectual hierarchies of the Inns as they gathered for Michaelmas, Hilary, Easter, and Trinity term. As always, the politics of space spoke to the politics of identity. Whitelocke's engagement with the spaces within and beyond the Middle Temple suggests an ambition to rise, as it were, with the barristers, drawing upon the social and professional cachet of his Inn to push forward in society. Plotting his movements within and beyond the Inns sheds interesting light upon his ambitions, but equally shows up the constraints upon his resources.

James Whitelocke was one of only eight scholars who proceeded to the Inns of Court from the Oxford BCL between 1571 and 1603, and the sole BCL to progress to the bench of the Middle Temple in the early modern period.[16] The fourth, twin son of a merchant and a classic 'middling sort' who saw his chance for Oxford at the Merchant Taylors' School, Whitelocke confessed in the *Liber Famelicus* that while accepting scholarship to study for the degree of Bachelor of Civil Law, his ambition 'had a farther reatche, for I ever had a purpose to ayme at the study of the common law'.[17] His movements from Oxford to London underline the strains placed upon his reserves of time and energy in meeting the dual responsibilities of his Inns and his university college. For if Whitelocke's joint ambition in common and civil law training was unusual, his method was audacious.

From 1590, James Whitelocke journeyed between London and St John's College, Oxford, keeping up the separate appearances and requirements of two law codes side by side. He was obviously proud enough of this dual pursuit of legal qualifications to make mention of it in the *Liber Famelicus* – but the somewhat cursory nature of his comments may betray the basic insecurity, behind the audacity, in this course of action. Indeed Whitelocke's peregrinations between Oxford and the Inns of Court and Chancery suggest a man stretching his financial and social resources to their limits in terms of time, money, and communal obligation. For eight years, Whitelocke 'kept in commons' in London, in his words, 'at all sutche times as I coulde have dayes, by ordinarye licence, by grace, or for furthering of the colledge businesse, to be absent from thence', before he was finally asked to vacate his St John's scholarship in 1598.[18]

As he pushed the spirit and the letter of the College statues to the limits, he faced the prospect of finding at least £30 a year to maintain residence at the Middle Temple.[19] Admission in 1590 into New Inn, the Middle Temple's nursery Inn of Chancery, allowed Whitelocke to pay a reduced admission fee to enter the Middle Temple three years later.[20] More fundamentally, it equipped him for low-level legal work as a 'common solicitor of causes' through which to subsidise his income; Whitelocke is listed as legal attorney in a 1597 case in the Exchequer Appearance Books three years before his call to the bar.[21] From 1594, Whitelocke lived with his Oxford friend Humphrey May 'in the middle chamber of the house late belonging to Thomas Dashe, gardner of the Middle Temple', also receiving May's brother Thomas into these surely unassuming digs in 1600.[22] His eventual status in his Inn was nowhere guaranteed in these earlier years, and it must have seemed hard going.

Legal education at the Inns

Historians are ambivalent about the practical utility or efficacy of the education provided by the learning exercises of the Inns of Court, the exact nature and calibre of which are difficult to assess.[23] Whitelocke's legal notes, which survive in the characteristic professional pastiche of English, Latin, and law-French of his day, suggest that the arcana of legal 'reason' was explored, for a serious junior lawyer such as himself, as much in watching and listening to his seniors as in drawing from the written wisdom of the yearbooks, digests, manuals, and reports.[24]

Participation in the life of the Middle Temple, including as a spectator, provided one way to discern patterns of juridical interpretation and Whitelocke's own notes, taken during and after dinnertime discussion, moots, and law readings, helped him to clarify what counted for good law and what did not.[25] While these learning exercises might throw up theoretical conundrums more worthy of academic consideration than practical value, they helped to shape the techniques and habits of a successful lawyer.[26]

Just beyond their physical realm but equally within the educational life of the Inns, Westminster encouraged regular rounds of court-watching during Whitelocke's time in London. By sitting in court, students were able to observe at first hand the public engagement in which the labours of opposing lawyers would wither or bear fruit. As well as giving students a feel for the business of the bar, court-watching thus had a serious educational function: by note-taking, students could begin to work out for themselves what counted for good legal argument and what did not. The importance of court-watching, an exercise as old as legal education itself, is amply demonstrated in notes Whitelocke compiled from cases he heard from 1597 to 1599 during his last two years as a student at the Middle Temple.[27] Exploring the relationship between the professional memory and written authority of early modern common law, Adam Fox has rightly noted 'a preference for the immediacy and the personal contact implied by vocal delivery'.[28] Whitelocke's surviving commonplace books distil the role of personal observation in the professional memory of the Inns of Court. They emphasise the immediacy of an education sharpened in first-hand observation of lawyers plying their trade and expounding upon their statutes.

Whatever their educational benefits or limitations, engagement with the learning exercises underlined the reputation and authority of the most senior members of the Middle Temple. From his admission in 1593 until his departure in 1619, James Whitelocke had to climb a carefully articulated ladder of competencies and exercises as he progressed through the ranks of his Inn. His surviving records reflect every level of his progression. Whitelocke was required to assist, by way of preparation for his call to the bar of the Middle Temple, in learning exercises conducted during the 'grand' vacations at the Inns of Chancery in 1599.[29] In his role as moot-sitter, he served as a *de facto* judge in moots held under the supervision of Nicholas Overbury, a senior barrister who served for this purpose as Chancery reader.[30] In the year before his call to the bar, Whitelocke twice assisted in the moots conducted at Furnival's Inn, New Inn, and Clifford's Inn, and once at Lyon's Inn; it seems likely that his Chancery role presaged his call to the bar by Overbury in August 1600.[31] Thereafter, Whitelocke acquired a more active role in the educational life of the Middle Temple during the grand vacations which formed the academic highlight of the year. In 1611, he was one of those appointed to provide a reader's feast, and in 1617, he was ordered to 'stand at the cupboard' (today a table at which the newly called barristers stand to enter their names in the books of the Inn), and thus to lead the debate for Walter Pye, Lent reader for that year.[32] In August 1618, Whitelocke noted in the *Liber Famelicus*, 'being on[e] of the cubberdmen of the Middle Temple, I went up to argue at the reading, the reader being Mr. Ford of Devonshire, to whome I gave a buck at 14s.'[33] Further ordered to the cupboard for William Rives in Lent 1619, Whitelocke's assistance at these readings was preparatory to his own election as autumn reader for 1619.[34] As the Middle Temple held only two readings a year, and restricted full membership of its bench to readers, election to read represented the culmination of the social and intellectual hierarchy. Whitelocke may thus have been secretly gratified as he wrote in his *Liber Famelicus* that 'the untimely deathe of Mr Stirrell' prompted the benchers to nominate him as autumn reader for 1619.[35]

James Whitelocke's 1619 reading on Benefices, hailed by historians as a 'classic' and 'notable' example, elucidates the form of this learning exercise peculiar to the Inns, its application to practice and learning of common law, and its socio-cultural significance within and beyond the Inns of Court.[36] A close analysis of the reading is beyond the scope of this chapter, but a few observations are possible.[37] It survives in large numbers of manuscript copies, suggesting its currency in scribal circles for those who sought to defend, or to curtail, church ambitions for clergy in increasingly controversial circumstances.[38] For his reading, Whitelocke drew upon a considerable knowledge of benefices, gained partly in his dual training in civil *and* common law, but also in his work as steward of St John's College and private legal work for a range of bishops. Whitelocke's experience added immediacy and authority to his analysis of benefices, plurality, and non-residence. Its topical and practical utility swam against a broader current, in the 'dogmatic and disputatious' exercises of the Inns, in which the readings were losing relevance in the development of the law.[39]

Ritual and culture of the Inns

Bulstrode Whitelocke remembered his father as a 'most laborious student all his dayes' of 'industry indefatigable', and one has no reason to doubt his assessment.[40] Of course, many others at the Inns showed lesser dedication to their studies; for the benchers who had to govern both the inspired and the unruly, the social rituals of the Inns offered one way to impress their own authority as much as the authority of the law. The success or failure of such cultural enterprise is open to question. In the most comprehensive modern study of the Inns, Wilfrid Prest identifies a challenge to the authority of the benchers from their students less enamoured of the traditional forms and rituals of their ancient societies.[41] Paul Raffield's *Images and Cultures of Law* places emphasis upon the 'invisible curriculum' of the Inns – from poetry and plays to masques and dining rituals – in the reinforcement of a coherent, and carefully cultivated identity. The Middle Temple Hall, he writes, 'was the setting for the continuous and undeviating repetition of legal ritual. Participation in these ceremonial rites affirmed the faith of students and practitioners in the legitimacy of the common law. Such rites were exclusive: only members of the Inn could practise them on a regular basis.'[42] The cumulative force of the symbols and dramaturgical actions of the Inns, he argues, represented a real challenge, as a nursery school for articulate opposition, to claims of royal absolutism. What, then, does Whitelocke's experience suggest of the strengths and limitations of the ritual and cultural production of the early modern Inns of Court?

In the close, closed community of less than two hundred barristers and benchers which made up the Middle Temple in James Whitelocke's day, social acts of conformity or non-conformity sent powerful political signals to those who presided, sometimes nervously, over large numbers of young men. As Paul Raffield expounds upon the cultural production of the Inns, he draws emphasis to the social-sacramental and ritualistic nuances of the Inns in such acts as the regulation of costume, beards, and diet. Whitelocke's example hints at the gap which existed between the imagined ideals of the Inns and the day-to-day realities of domestic life within them. Indeed, beyond professed communal beliefs, his example draws attention to the never-ending 'housekeeping' issues which confronted institutions such as the Middle Temple. For example, while Raffield stresses the religious imperatives at work in the daily rituals of the Inns (the forms of which, it should be noted, are still observed today in many collegial institutions founded – as all such places were – on the Benedictine model), regulations such as those governing sumptuary etiquette and attendance were probably framed as much by financial pressures and the need to exclude free-loading guests as by 'the bonds of apostolic fraternity'.[43] The regulation of dress within the Inns may well have been, as Raffield puts it, 'an important means of expressing the propriety, authority and indivisibility of divine and common law' – but may just as well have expressed the propriety, authority, and indivisibility of the benchers themselves.[44] Their frowning upon excessive flourishes in clothing may hint as much at the fragile power relations at work between those lawyers who had risen from middling sorts to great influence in their Inns, and those young grandees who had come to the Inns armed with wealth and influence.

In such a tight balancing act over the central issues of stated and real power, the revels presided over at the Middle Temple – a Rabelasian inversion of the normal order by a 'Lord of Misrule' called, by the Middle Templars, the 'Prince of Love' – offered a kind of pressure release valve out of term time as 'processions, feasts, music, masques and plays predominated'.[45] The *Liber Famelicus* offers little comment on these important rituals. While some of Whitelocke's 'middling' contemporaries at the Middle Temple (for example John Davies and John Ford) made a name of sorts for themselves through their sometimes boisterous engagement with prose and pun, Whitelocke sought recognition beyond the cultural and literary pursuits which tied the Inns, through their masques and revels, to the artistic orbit of the royal court. His approach may have been shaped by the sobering examples of his twin brother William – who abandoned his school studies and died at sea with Drake aged twenty-seven, or his eldest brother Edmund – who abandoned his legal studies at Lincoln's Inn for a life of courtly patronage, leading to his incarceration on suspicion of treason before his early death 'in the mirthe and good company of the earl of Northumberland'.[46] Whitelocke himself lacked the resources and probably the temperament to gain the most from the 'invisible curriculum' of the Inns or the grand vacations which balanced the formational role of the learning exercises – but he noted the symmetry at work in the life of his room-mate and lifelong friend Humphrey May, considering himself fortunate to associate with this 'towardly student and principal reveller' as he undertook (again in his own words) 'a long and tedious course of study' to ensure his own progress.[47]

Whitelocke's fullest observations on the social rituals of his Inn come in his account of his 1619 reading, the most complete account of any reading to survive from this period. In light of Prest's observations about an 'era of collective disobedience' which began at the Middle Temple in 1617 and continued 'until the end of the seventeenth century', Whitelocke's account suggests his own strong concerns.[48]

Referring to the masques and Christmas revels in the opening remarks of his reading, Whitelocke noted that the Middle Temple's reputation 'of late hath been impayred in the excercises of young gentlemen which touch gentry and honour, and would soon be so in the exercises of the Ancients which touch learning and proficiency if good affection to the publick did not prevent it'.[49] In his mind, cultural disorder threatened educational standards – and given that groups of Middle Temple barristers were protesting against the compulsory observance of fast days at this time, there is a hint of desperation in his reflection that, over the course of his reading, he 'went to churche ... accompanied with sutche benchers, cubberdmen, and senior barristers as wolde goe with me'.[50] There are other hints in his account that lack of interest in, and engagement with, the ceremonial aspects of his reading reflected a general apathy towards the whole exercise. It must have been a disappointment to Whitelocke that John Ford and William Rives both failed to oblige the benchers when asked to assist at his reading, forcing him to invite George Shurley and Richard Hadsor to help John Tynte and Thomas Tryst take up and elaborate upon his central arguments.[51] If not for the work of Hadsor and Shurley, and the vigorous participation of John Hoskins (whom Whitelocke would go on to support at his reading in Lent 1620), the reading might have descended into a professional embarrassment before the 'galaxy of grandees' who assembled at the Middle Temple for the occasion.[52]

Whitelocke provides 'the most complete surviving guest list for any reader's feast before the Civil War'.[53] His guests ranged from the archbishops of Canterbury (George Abbot) and Spalata (Marc Antonio de Dominis) to the bishops of London (John King) and Rochester (John Buckeridge), to the ambassador of the Low Countries (Sir Albertus Joachimi), old friends such as Sir Thomas Coventry, who now served as Solicitor-General, influential courtiers, legal luminaries, and patrons such as Sir Julius Caesar and Sir Lionel Cranfield (and potential patrons such as Sir John Davies and Sir Robert Heath – both poorly regarded by Whitelocke in private), among 'divers knightes and men of good qualitye'.[54] This assembly of the great and the good within the overlapping circles of legal, religious, and political power of the day underlines the wider importance of the reading and its associated ceremony, which put the Inns for this moment at the heart of London's cultural polity. On the other hand, Whitelocke's comments speak also to the fragility of arrangements within the Inns, threatening an imagined order celebrated in the ritual endeavours of the Inns of Court.

There was 'nothing more needfull to the upholding of civill society (as this wherein we live)', Whitelocke noted in his opening remarks to those assembled for his reading, 'then that every particular member thereof doe undergoe such burden as custome or order doe impose'.[55] Commitment to its educational life and continuance of 'the ancient formes of exercises in our profession' were, he remarked, necessary 'to preserve order' and 'maintaine the glory of our Societies'.[56] If the professed ideals of the common law elaborated in the rituals of the Inns were open to subversion and inversion, then the actions of even a dedicated lawyer such as Whitelocke show the pragmatic realities at work in the communal life of the Inns. While Whitelocke lamented decay in the forms and rituals of the Middle Temple, his own quest for status and power offer one example of the never-ending threat of corruption for those who regulated the Inns' affairs. In 1604, Whitelocke was fined 20s. for 'absence and being out of commons' during the August reading.[57] He might be forgiven for this lapse – but his exploitation of the statutes of admission, upon becoming a bencher, was insidious. Manipulating the vague requirement that a student have eight years of 'learning and continuance' before his call to the bar at a time when 'continuance was coming to be interpreted in the sense of membership of the society, rather than residence in commons', he gained admission for his fourteen-year-old son three years before Bulstrode Whitelocke first made appearance at the Inn.[58] By this time, the politics of space which reflected the politics of power had changed a great deal for James Whitelocke. Along with his son, he was able to lodge his servant Richard Oakely (and thus to qualify him also for the call to the bar) in what were now significant chambers with a large study, a bedchamber, and two separate smaller studies. Indeed, his son was granted residence without fine because, the benchers noted, his father had 'spent money in building and enlarging the chamber and studies'.[59] Whitelocke draws us away from Paul Raffield's imagined world of 'Eating, learning and revering the law' and back to the inconsistencies and tensions of everyday life.[60] Such tensions were at work around and within those who drew from the status and ritual of the early modern Inns of Court.

Conclusion

At the end of James Whitelocke's life, his son eulogised that his father's:

> reason was clear and strong, and his learning deep and general … exactly knowing in the history of his own country … most conversant in the studies of antiquity and heraldry; he was not excelled in the knowledge of his profession of the common law of England, wherein his knowledge of the civil law (whereof he was a graduate in Oxford) was a help to him: his learned arguments both at the bar and the bench will confirm this truth.[61]

James Whitelocke was no more typical than anyone within the Inns of Court – but he was, I think, an exemplar of the professional identity which came to the most serious practitioners of its educational life. The social confidences and insecurities which he felt as a result of his professional formation flowed largely from his appropriation of a legal language with inherent assumptions and methods of argumentation.

And what, then, of the once famous 'common law mind'? In summing up the influence of the Inns of Court on Whitelocke's formation, it is important to see that his outlook was not determined by the physical boundaries and rituals of the Middle Temple. Nor was it determined by the boundaries of his knowledge, which encompassed classical and theological understanding, a grounding in continental law, and a lifetime's engagement with English law and custom. His outlook was determined, rather, by the psychological assurances which held his world together. As Whitelocke's contemporary John Selden remarked, 'When men comfort themselves with philosophy, 'tis not because they have gott two or three sentences, but because they have digested these sentences, and made them their own.'[62]

Alongside many lawyers of his generation, Whitelocke had a clear but abstract appreciation of continental jurisprudence. He was able to see the polemical promise of a wider perspective, recounting in his *Liber Famelicus* that in the noted sixteenth-century civil lawyer Richard Cosin's *An apologie of, and for sundrie proceedings by jurisdiction ecclesiasticall* (1591), 'I saw how great use he made of his knowledge of the common law to upholde the authority of his owne profession.'[63] Yet it is not enough, as Brookes and Sharpe once did, to cite Whitelocke's civil law training as evidence of the receptivity of English common lawyers to continental legal and historical traditions.[64] Such knowledge was always held in tension with a fundamental ambiguity about 'foreign' laws as a symbol of national, political, and religious difference. Trained in mental genuflexion towards what Sir Edward Coke called 'immemorial custom', Whitelocke's understanding of the common law and its sources was (as Baker has suggested in the case of Coke himself) 'a guide not to the past but to the present', while the sense of continuity which they conveyed to him was often 'of rhetorical and emotional and political, rather than historical value'.[65] As Whitelocke demonstrated in an account he prepared for the Society of Antiquaries 'Of the Antiquity, Use, and Privilege of Places for Students and Professors of the Common Laws', such a reading of the past could be highly selective in its critical capacity when it came to the Inns of Court.[66] A basic sensitivity about the status and prestige of his own profession formed one aspect of a somewhat bipolar oscillation between confidence in, and anxiety about, the destiny and relative strength of English law when weighed against the inheritance of the Catholic, European states which practiced civil law. Thus, although Whitelocke demonstrated his intellectual confidence through an assize charge he delivered in Latin before some 'foreigners ... of quality', he was at pains to inform 'these strangers and scholars of the ability of our judges, and the cause of our proceedings in matters of law and justice'.[67] His was an anxiety that the legal education of the Inns sought to obviate, perhaps as much in the social ritual of the learning exercises as in their intellectual content itself.

Raffield concludes that: 'In the English legal system, paternal power did not vest in the king. Rather it existed in the artificial bonds of kinship that the institutional structures of common law sought to represent.'[68] A revealing passage in the *Liber Famelicus* distils, for its readers, Whitelocke's awareness of the kinship and identity formed in those brought up in the rituals of the Inns of Court. He noted that after a 1615 sermon at Windsor, Sir Edward Coke sought him out as one 'of his own coate'. When Whitelocke questioned him on his reluctance to dine at the royal court, Coke replied 'that whilest he stood by the king at dynner, he wolde be ever asking of him questions of that nature as he had as life to be out of the roome'. 'I guesse', Whitelocke reflected, 'it was concerning matters of the prerogative, which the king wolde take ill if he wear not answered in them as he wolde have it'.[69] At this time, Whitelocke assumed that these disagreements were personal, and could be resolved. Yet James I's arguments with Sir Edward Coke have played out in history because they were, in fact, insoluble.

As Whitelocke left the Middle Temple for Serjeant's Inn in 1619, he left one world for another. I believe that thereafter the unwanted divorce of minds he had feared was indeed forced upon him – not through absence alone, but by the policies of King Charles I.[70] From the 1620s, the 'vivid account' provided by the *Liber Famelicus* became 'quite cryptic'.[71] What we know of Whitelocke's time at the bench suggests that during these years crown policy stretched political consensus towards breaking point.[72] Like many historians today, Whitelocke understood the changes around him primarily within frameworks of personal and factional interest, falling privately into silence as he reached an intellectual impasse between the rights of the subject and the King's prerogative power.

Alan Cromartie has rightly concluded that in 1642, parliamentarians asserted the 'unapologetically provincial common law' to make the case for opposition to perceived royal excesses.[73] 'It was the availability of this legitimating theory [of English law]', he argues, 'that gave opponents of the crown their opportunity'.[74] James Whitelocke was dead by the time his 1610 speech on Impositions, which asserted that 'the power of the king in parliament is greater than his power out of parliament, and doth rule and control it', was published as *A Learned and Necessary Argument to Prove that Each Subject hath a Propriety in his Goods*.[75] This was in 1641, as part of the propaganda war which was shortly to culminate in open warfare between King and parliament. There can be little doubt that this confident language, formed in some large measure in the rituals of the Inns of Court, helped to define both the language and the character of resistance as England stumbled from political opposition to civil war.

Notes

1 *Liber Famelicus of Sir James Whitelocke, a Judge of the Court of King's Bench in the Reigns of James I and Charles I*, ed. John Bruce (London: Camden Society, 1858), p. 82. Bruce transcribed the original manuscript (BL, Additional MS 53725).

2 *Liber Famelicus*, ed. Bruce, p. 82.

3 John G. A. Pocock, *The Ancient Constitution and the Feudal Law: A Study of English Historical Thought in the Seventeenth Century* (London: Cambridge University Press, 1957), updated in Pocock's *The Ancient Constitution and the Feudal Law: A Study of English Historical Thought in the Seventeenth Century – A Reissue with a Retrospect* (Cambridge: Cambridge University Press, 1987).

4 Whitelocke quoted Fortescue from *A Learned Commendation of the Politique Lawes of Englande … And newly translated into Englishe by Robert Mulcaster* (London: Rychard

Tottill, 1567). John H. Baker, *The Third University of England: The Inns of Court and the Common-Law Tradition* (London: Selden Society, 1990). Sir Edward Coke declared the Inns 'the most famous university for profession of laws only, or of any human science, that is in the world' (Coke, *Third Report* (London, 1602), 'Preface').

5 Peter Goodrich, *Languages of Law: From Logics of Memory to Nomadic Masks* (London: Weidenfeld & Nicolson, 1990), p. 2.

6 cf. John H. Baker, *The Legal Profession and the Common Law: Historical Essays* (London: Hambledon Press, 1986), and *An Introduction to Legal History*, 4th edn (London: Butterworths, 2002), Wilfrid R. Prest, *The Inns of Court under Elizabeth I and the Early Stuarts, 1590–1640* (London: Longman, 1972), and *The Rise of the Barristers: A Social History of the English Bar, 1590–1640* (Oxford: Clarendon Press, 1986), with Paul Raffield, *Images and Cultures of Law in Early Modern England: Justice and Political Power, 1558–1660* (Cambridge: Cambridge University Press, 2004), and Peter Goodrich, *Languages of Law*, and 'Signs taken for wonders: community, identity, and *A History of Sumptuary Law*', *Law and Social Inquiry*, 23 (1998), 707–28.

7 Raffield, *Images and Cultures of Law*, p. 2.

8 *Ibid.*, p. 2.

9 J. R. Tanner, *Constitutional Documents of the Reign of James I, A.D. 1603–1625: With an Historical Commentary*, 2nd edn (Cambridge: Cambridge University Press, 1962), pp. 245–6; J. P. Kenyon, *The Stuart Constitution, 1603–1688: Documents and Commentary* (Cambridge: Cambridge University Press, 1966), p. 56.

10 *Complete Collection of State Trials and Proceedings for High Treason and other Crimes and Misdemeanors from the Earliest Period to the … Present Time*, ed. William Cobbett, Thomas Bayly Howell, and Thomas Jones Howell, 34 vols (London: Longman, 1809–28), II, col. 482.

11 Goodrich, *Languages of Law*, pp. 2–3.

12 While not a diary, it has been edited by Ruth Spalding as *The Diary of Bulstrode Whitelocke, 1605–1675*, Records of Social and Economic History, New Series XIII (Oxford: Published for The British Academy by Oxford University Press, 1990).

13 For the significance of Whitelocke's consititutional pronouncements, see, for example, Conrad Russell, *Parliaments and English Politics 1621–1629* (Oxford: Clarendon Press, 1979), p. 364; Theodore K. Rabb and Derek Hirst, 'Revisionism revised: two perspectives on early Stuart parliamentary history', *Past and Present*, 92 (Aug. 1981), 55–78, 79–99 (88); J. P. Sommerville, *Politics and Ideology in England, 1603–1640* (London: Longman, 1986), p. 179; Richard Cust, *The Forced Loan and English Politics 1626–1628* (Oxford: Clarendon Press, 1987), p. 152; Robert Ashton, *The English Civil War: Conservatism and Revolution, 1603–1649*, 2nd edn (London: Weidenfeld & Nicolson, 1989), p. 12; Glenn Burgess, *The Politics of the Ancient Constitution: An Introduction to English Political Thought, 1603–1642* (Basingstoke: Macmillan, 1992), pp. 143–4; Alan Cromartie, 'The constitutionalist revolution: the transformation of political culture in early Stuart England', *Past and Present*, 163 (May 1999), 76–120 (96–7); and James S. Hart, *The Rule of Law, 1603–1660: Crowns, Courts and Judges* (Harlow: Pearson Longman, 2003), pp. 97–8.

14 *Complete Collection of State Trials and Proceedings for High Treason and Other Crimes and Misdemeanors*, ed. Cobbett *et al.*, II, col. 482.

15 *Ibid.*, III, col. 308.

16 Prest, *The Rise of the Barristers*, pp. 111–12; John Barton, 'The Faculty of Law', in James McConica (ed.), *The History of the University of Oxford, Vol. 3: The Collegiate University* (Oxford: Clarendon Press, 1986), pp. 257–83 (p. 282).

17 *Liber Famelicus*, ed. Bruce, pp. 13–14.

18 *Ibid.*, pp. 14, 15; Damian X. Powell, *Sir James Whitelocke's Liber Famelicus, 1570–1632: Law and Politics in Early Stuart England* (Bern; New York, NY: Peter Lang, 2000), p. 30.

19 Prest, *The Inns of Court under Elizabeth I and the Early Stuarts, 1590–1640*, pp. 27–9.

20 *Middle Temple Records*, II, 164, 171. The fee varied from 20s. upon entry from a nursery Inn of Chancery to £5 for someone who could show no association with the Middle Temple.

21 Thomas G. Barnes, 'Star Chamber litigants and their counsel, 1596–1641', in J. H. Baker (ed.), *Legal Records and the Historian: Papers Presented to the Cambridge Legal History Conference, 7–10 July 1975, and in Lincoln's Inn Old Hall on 3 July 1974* (London: Royal Historical Society, 1978), pp. 7–28 (p. 24); NA, E2/2 (unfoliated) E. 39.

22 *Middle Temple Records*, I, 345, 401.

23 cf., for example, John H. Baker, 'Learning exercises in the medieval Inns of Court and Chancery', in Baker, *The Legal Profession and the Common Law*, pp. 7–23; Wilfrid R. Prest, 'The learning exercises at the Inns of Court', *Journal of the Society of Public Teachers of Law*, n. ser., 9 (June 1967), 301–13.

24 For a different view on the importance of book learning against that of the learning exercises see Prest, *The Inns of Court under Elizabeth I and the Early Stuarts, 1590–1640*, p. 134. On the languages of the law, see John H. Baker, *The Common Law Tradition: Lawyers, Books and the Law* (London: Hambledon Press, 2000), pp. 225–46.

25 Whitelocke's notes of exercises at the Inns of Court and Chancery survive in his hand in a commonplace book (CUL, MS Dd. 5. 7), organised under heads and titles.

26 cf. J. H. Baker, 'The Inns of Court and legal doctrine', in Thomas M. Charles-Edwards, Morfydd E. Owen, and D. B. Walters (eds), *Lawyers and Laymen: Studies in the History of Law* (Cardiff: University of Wales Press, 1986). pp. 274–86 (p. 276); Baker, 'Learning exercises', pp. 22–3; Gareth H. Jones, *The History of the Law of Charity, 1532–1827* (Cambridge: Cambridge University Press, 1969), p. 238.

27 CUL, MS Dd. 8. 48, fols 1–137.

28 Adam Fox, 'Custom, memory and authority of writing', in Paul Griffiths, Adam Fox, and Steve Hindle (eds), *The Experience of Authority in Early Modern England* (Basingstoke: Macmillan, 1996), pp. 89–116 (p. 94).

29 *Pension Book of Clement's Inn*, ed. Cecil T. Carr (London: Selden Society, 1960), pp. xxiii, xxx; *Middle Temple Records*, II, 536.

30 Samuel E. Thorne and John H. Baker (eds), *Readings and Moots at the Inns of Court in the Fifteenth Century. Vol. 2: Moots and Readers' Cases* (London: Selden Society, 1990), p. lxxi.

31 CUL, MS Dd. 5. 7, fol. 218ᵛ.

32 *Middle Temple Records*, II, 407, 546, 624. On the readings, see Chapters 1 (pp. 17–20, above) and 6 (pp. 110–20, below).

33 *Liber Famelicus*, ed. Bruce, p. 62.

34 *Middle Temple Records*, II, 629, 634, 638.

35 *Liber Famelicus*, ed. Bruce, p. 70.

36 Baker, 'Inns of Court and legal doctrine', p. 281; Prest, *The Inns of Court under Elizabeth I and the Early Stuarts, 1590–1640*, p. 120; Walter Cecil Richardson, *A History of the Inns of*

Court: With Special Reference to the Period of the Renaissance (Baton Rouge, LA: Claitor's Pubishing Division, 1973), p. 117.

37 There is no adequate study of the reading, but see my comments in *Sir James Whitelocke's Liber Famelicus*, pp. 40–9.

38 BL, Hargrave MS 91, fols 196–295^v; BL, Hargrave MS 198; BL, Hargrave MS 237, fols 5–95^v; BL, Hargrave MS 91, fols 296–319^v; CUL, MS Ll. 3. 12, fols 326–477; CUL, MS Ee. 6. 3, fols 192–225^v; Bodleian, Dep. MS d 746; Bodleian, Rawlinson MS C. 207, fols 62–96^v; Bodleian, Rawlinson MS C. 207, fols 245–70; Bodleian, Ashmole MS 1150 (1), fols 1–83; LI, Misc. MS 486 (8); LI, Law MS 14. Ii; LI, Maynard MS 79, fols 329–80; MTL, uncatalogued MS, Muniments Room; TCD, MS 853 (4); TCD, MS 733 (3); Harvard Law School, MS 1077; William Andrews Clark Memorial Library, Selden-Hale Collection MS 586.

39 Baker, 'Learning exercises', p. 22, 'Inns of Court and legal doctrine', p. 278 and *passim*.

40 *The Diary of Bulstrode Whitelocke*, ed. Spalding, p. 67.

41 Prest, *The Inns of Court under Elizabeth I and the Early Stuarts, 1590–1640*, esp. pp. 124–36, and cf. Baker, 'Inns of Court and legal doctrine', p. 281, and Thorne and Baker (eds), *Readings and Moots at the Inns of Court in the Fifteenth Century*, p. lxxi; *Pension Book of Clement's Inn*, ed. Carr, p. xxx.

42 Raffield, *Images and Cultures of Law*, p. 43.

43 *Ibid.*, p. 20.

44 *Ibid.*, p. 167.

45 *Ibid.*, p. 89.

46 *Liber Famelicus*, ed. Bruce, pp. 7–10.

47 *Ibid.*, p. 21.

48 Prest, *The Inns of Court under Elizabeth I and the Early Stuarts, 1590–1640*, p. 101.

49 *Ibid.*, pp. 105, 112–13; LI, Misc. MS 486 (8), fols 1–2.

50 Prest, *The Inns of Court under Elizabeth I and the Early Stuarts, 1590–1640*, p. 101; *Liber Famelicus*, ed. Bruce, p. 74.

51 *Middle Temple Records*, II, 629, 634, 638; BL, Additional MS 53725, fol. 110. Bruce has incorrectly identified these cupboardmen as 'Sturly' and 'Hudson' (*Liber Famelicus*, ed. Bruce, p. 74). Whitelocke may have expected some reciprocal support from Ford and Rives, whom he had earlier assisted during their own readings (*Middle Temple Records*, II, 585, 619).

52 *Middle Temple Records*, II, 646; David Lemmings, 'Ritual and the law in early modern England', in Suzanne Corcoran (ed.), *Law and History in Australia: A Collection of Papers Presented at the 1989 Law and History Conference* (Adelaide: Adelaide Law Review Association, 1991), pp. 3–19 (p. 7).

53 Prest, *The Inns of Court under Elizabeth I and the Early Stuarts, 1590–1640*, p. 226.

54 *Liber Famelicus*, ed. Bruce, p. 75.

55 LI, Misc. MS 486 (8), fol. 1.

56 *Ibid.*, fol. 1.

57 *Middle Temple Records*, II, 449.

58 Prest, *The Inns of Court under Elizabeth I and the Early Stuarts, 1590–1640*, pp. 133–4; *Middle Temple Records*, II, 640.

59 *Middle Temple Records*, II, 574–5, 643, 653–4; *The Diary of Bulstrode Whitelocke*, ed. Spalding, p. 49.

60 The quotation is the title to ch. 1 of Raffield, *Images and Cultures of Law*.

61 Bulstrode Whitelocke, *Memorials of the English affairs, or, An historical account of what passed from the beginning of the reign of King Charles the First, to King Charles the Second*, I (London: Nathaniel Ponder, 1682), 50.

62 *Table Talk of John Selden*, ed. S. W. Singer (London: John Russell Smith, 1847), p. 93.

63 *Liber Famelicus*, ed. Bruce, p. 14.

64 Christopher W. Brooks and Kevin Sharpe, 'History, English law and the Renaissance', *Past and Present*, 72 (Aug. 1976), 133–42 (137).

65 John H. Baker, 'The dark age of English legal history', in Dafydd Jenkins (ed.), *Legal History Studies: Papers Presented to the Legal History Conference, Aberystwyth, 18–21 July 1972* (Cardiff: University of Wales Press, 1975), pp. 1–27 (p. 2).

66 Whitelocke here drew his material without qualification, 'out of the observation of so grave a judge and so expert as Fortescue as in the time he lived'; see *A Collection of Curious Discourses, Written by Eminent Antiquaries upon Several Heads in our English Antiquities. Together with Mr. Thomas Hearne's Preface and Appendix to the Former Edition*, ed. Thomas Hearne, 2 vols (London: W. and J. Richardson, 1771), I, 78–81; Powell, *Sir James Whitelocke's Liber Famelicus*, pp. 62–3.

67 *The Diary of Bulstrode Whitelocke*, ed. Spalding, p. 51.

68 Raffield, *Images and Cultures of Law*, p. 85.

69 *Liber Famelicus*, ed. Bruce, p. 48.

70 John Reeve has rightly described the changes brought about by these policies as 'an uncharacteristic and in many ways an unwanted development'. 'They were', he suggests, 'the politics of a non-parliamentary England, politics which came about with the breakdown of traditional political and constitutional process' (L. J. Reeve, *Charles I and the Road to Personal Rule* (Cambridge: Cambridge University Press, 1989), p. 2).

71 Wilfrid R. Prest, 'Politics and profession in early Stuart England: the diary of Sir Richard Hutton', in *Rulers, Religion and Rhetoric in Early Modern England: A Festchrift for Geoffrey Elton from his Australasian Friends*, ed. S. M. Jack for *Parergon*, n. ser., 6 (1988), 163–77 (163).

72 See Powell, *Sir James Whitelocke's Liber Famelicus*, ch. 6, and Damian X. Powell, 'Sir James Whitelocke's advice to the Crown in 1627', *Historical Journal*, 39:3 (1996), 737–42.

73 Alan Cromartie, *Sir Matthew Hale, 1609–1676: Law, Religion and Natural Philosophy* (Cambridge: Cambridge University Press, 1995), p. 11.

74 Cromartie, 'The constitutionalist revolution', p. 118, and see his *The Constitutionalist Revolution: An Essay on the History of England, 1450–1642* (New York, NY: Cambridge University Press, 2006).

75 James Whitelocke, *A Learned and Necessary Argument to Prove that Each Subject hath a Propriety in his Goods. Shewing also the extent of the kings perogative in impositions upon the goods of merchants exported and imported out of and into this kingdome* (London: Printed for John Burroughes, 1641). Sometimes misattributed to Sir Henry Yelverton, the speech was reprinted in 1659 as *The Rights of the People Concerning Impositions, Stated in a Learned Argument: With a Remonstrance Presented to the Kings Most Excellent Majesty, by the … House of Commons … 1610 … By a Late Eminent Judge* (London: Printed for William Leak).

5

'The sinful history of mine own youth': John Donne preaches at Lincoln's Inn

Emma Rhatigan

Donne's metamorphosis from writer of witty, erotic love poetry to serious religious preacher has provoked more than one raised eyebrow. In a letter to Sir Henry Goodyer, Donne complained that Lucy Harington, Countess of Bedford, one of his earliest patrons, 'had more suspicion of my calling, a better memory of my past life, then I had thought her nobility could have admitted' and later he went so far as to coin for himself the dual identities of Jack Donne, writer of scurrilous verse, and John Donne, sober divine.[1] This strain between Jack Donne and John Donne must have been particularly apparent at Lincoln's Inn. Donne had lived and studied at Lincoln's Inn from 1592 to at least 1594, perhaps as late as 1596,[2] the period in which he wrote some of his most salacious early verse. Thus when he accepted the appointment of preacher to the Society in 1616 he was agreeing to return to the institution in which he had passed several years of his less pious youth. Indeed, in preaching to the gentlemen students of Lincoln's Inn he was effectively addressing the figures of his past self. In this chapter, I want to explore how Donne negotiated this unique preaching relationship. I will argue that Donne did not ignore or gloss over his youth, but rather deliberately used his own biography to bridge the gap between the secular and spiritual which he confronted in the Lincoln's Inn congregation.

The stereotype of the Inns of Court student was well known. A useful summary of the popular image can be found in Francis Lenton's *Characterismi* (1631). According to Lenton, an Inns of Court gentleman is 'an Infant, newly crept from the Cradle of learning … left to the view of faire vertue, and foule vice, the last of which layes siege to his tender Walls, and often makes a shrewd Battery, if not quite scales it'. His preferences are for 'Poetry instead of *Perkins*', he 'holds it a greater disgrace to be Nonsuit with a Lady, than Nonplus in the Law', and 'when he should bee mooting in the Hall, he is perhaps mounting in the Chamber'.[3] Lenton continues to explain that:

> His Recreations and loose expence of time, are his only studies (as Plaies, Dancing, Fencing, Tauerns, Tobacco,) and Dalliance (which if it be with Time, is irreuocable) and are the alluring baits of ill disposed extrauagants. He is roaring when hee should be reading, and feasting when he should be fasting.[4]

Sir John Davies, who was admitted to the Middle Temple in 1588 and called to the bar in 1595, concurs with this image in his epigram on an Inns of Court student. He writes of a student 'Leauing old Ployden, Diar, and Brooke [common law text books] alone, / To see old Harry Hunkes and Sakersone [bears]'.[5] Thomas Overbury (Middle Temple), in *His Wife* (1628), emphasises the students' concern with fashion. He claims an Inns of Court student is 'distinguished from a Scholler by a paire of silke stockings, and a Beauer Hat', 'laughes at euery man whose Band fits not well, or that hath not a faire shoo-tie', and 'is ashamed to bee seene in any mans company that weares not his clothes well'. Legal interests once again rank low in the students' priorities and Overbury explains that 'You shall neuer see him melancholly, but when hee wants a new Suite, or feares a Sergeant: At which times onely, he betakes himselfe to *Ploydon*.'[6] As Wilfrid Prest reminds us, we should be wary of taking this stereotype too far, though at the same time it was so pervasive that there probably was some degree of truth in it.[7] Certainly there is evidence that numerous Inns of Court students used their time in London to take classes in dancing, fencing, and music and were keen patrons of the theatre. In the 1650s, William Prynne recorded from personal experience, and with disapproval, the gaming and dancing that took place at Lincoln's Inn during the Christmas season and on Saturday nights with the passive approval of the benchers.[8] The Inns also functioned as important literary and cultural centres. Not only did they foster numerous poets, playwrights, and writers, such as, in addition to Donne himself, Francis Beaumont, Edmund Campion, John Davies, John Ford, Everard Guilpin, John Harrington, John Hoskins, John Marston, John Martin, Thomas Overbury, Benjamin Rudyerd and, most famously, Francis Bacon, but the circulation of manuscript miscellanies demonstrates that the Societies harboured consumers as well as the producers of literature.[9] The revels and masques held at the Societies provided perfect opportunities for the students to indulge these literary interests.[10]

It is hard to say how far Donne himself conformed to this stereotype of the dissolute student while he studied at Lincoln's Inn. It would certainly be naïve to read too much biography into the *Songs and Sonnets*, *Elegies*, and *Satires* which he wrote during the time he was living in the Inns of Court (approximately 1591–96) and the factual evidence which survives for his student days is far less sensational.[11] Richard Baker, a contemporary, remembers Donne as 'not dissolute, but very neat; a great visiter of Ladies, a great frequenter of Playes, a great writer of conceited Verses'.[12] The fact that Donne felt it necessary to construct the dual identities of Jack Donne and John Donne suggests, however, his own self-consciousness about the gap between preacher and student. The students, moreover, would undoubtedly have been sensitive to his past. In recording his notes of a sermon preached by Mr Ireland at the Temple Church, John Manningham's diary of 1602–3 specifically comments that Ireland 'about some three yeares since was a student of the Middle Temple'.[13]

Donne chooses to mediate this complicated preaching relationship not by ignoring his autobiographical connection with the student congregation, but rather by deliberately evoking it. References to his past life and, in particular, his former literary identity are a defining characteristic of the Lincoln's Inn sermons. According to Potter and Simpson this is part of a strategy of self-justification, an attempt to combat 'potential scepticism' regarding his clerical transformation. Thus when Donne ventriloquises the prophet Jeremiah in a Lincoln's Inn sermon on Psalm 38: 2 ('For thine arrowes stick fast in me, and thy hand presseth me sore') (*c*.1618), bemoaning and confessing 'the sinfull history of mine own *youth*' (II, 53), Potter and Simpson argue that he is 'imaginatively identifying himself with the prophet and justifying his own preaching against criticism, or potential criticism, that he was setting himself up as a judge over other people while a well-known sinner in his own youth'.[14]

A close examination of Donne's Lincoln's Inn sermons, however, suggests that Donne's rhetorical strategy in drawing on his biography is far more complex than Potter and Simpson make allowance for. Rather than rejecting his secular past, Donne always emphasises the manner in which the secular and the spiritual can be brought together, thus encouraging the students in the congregation to follow his own religious journey of conversion. For example, the sermon on Psalm 38: 2, which Potter and Simpson identify as a prime instance of Donne's self-justifying rhetoric, opens with a discussion of Donne's preference for the Book of Psalms and Paul's Epistles among the books of the Bible. He tells his congregation:

> I acknowledge, that my spirituall appetite carries me still, upon the *Psalms of David*, for a first course, for the Scriptures of the Old Testament, and upon the *Epistles of Saint Paul*, for a second course, for the New: and my meditations even for these *publike exercises* to Gods Church, returne oftnest to these two. For, as a hearty entertainer offers to others, the meat which he loves best himself, so doe I oftnest present to Gods people, in these Congregations, the meditations which I feed upon at home, in those two Scriptures.[15]

Donne continues by explaining that one of his reasons for this preference is 'because they are Scriptures, written in such forms, as I have been most accustomed to; St *Pauls* being Letters, and *Davids* being Poems: for, God gives us, not onely that which is meerly necessary, but that which is convenient too; He does not onely feed us, but *feed us with marrow, and with fatnesse*' (II, 49). This is an unambiguous reference to his earlier poetic career; yet Donne is not rejecting his life as a poet and a letter writer, but rather deliberately linking it to his current activity. By demonstrating that poetry and letters can be religious as well as secular, Donne breaks down the sharp divide between his current and former life. Consequently, he also breaks down the barriers between the secular world his congregation inhabits and the religious life to which he is seeking to draw it. Donne's play on the notion of 'appetite', through extended metaphors of meat and tasting, is especially ingenious. He moves from 'spirituall appetite', suggesting religious longing for God's word, to taste as in personal preference, to portraying Scripture as a form of spiritual nourishment. Moreover, in his very emphasis on his spiritual appetite, Donne also evokes the notion of sensual appetite, an idea which is reinforced by the reference to his poetry. Yet the idea of sensual appetite is suggested only through its absence, through its re-writing as spiritual appetite. In other words, Donne is using the example of his own youth in order to re-inscribe sensual appetite as spiritual appetite, to provide the secular with its more meaningful spiritual alternative.

A further example can be found in a sermon on Psalm 2: 12 ('Kisse the Son, lest he be angry') (1616–22). Donne takes the word 'kiss' and begins by expounding its negative connotations. A kiss can suggest treachery, such as the treachery of Judas, and it can also, of course, suggest licentiousness. Donne explains:

> Treachery often, but licentiousnesse more, hath depraved this seale of love; and yet … God stoops even to the words of our foule and unchaste love, that thereby he might raise us to the heavenly love of himselfe, and his Son … Take thou heed, that that ladder, or that engine which God hath given to raise thee, doe not load thee, oppresse thee, cast thee downe: Take heed lest those phrases of love and kisses which should raise thee to him, do not bury thee in the memory and contemplation of sinfull love, and of licentious kisses. (III, 318)

Licentious kissing is something with which any reader of Donne's *Songs and Sonnets* and *Elegies* is familiar. In 'Jealousie' the lovers 'kisse and play', in 'Elegie VI', the speaker talks of his mistress's 'gnawing kisses', and in 'The Comparison' Donne's portrayal of a lover's kiss as like a surgeon 'searching wounds' is compelling in its depiction of the emotional and spiritual intensity of physical intimacy.[16] The reference to 'phrases of love' specifically evokes a literary context. Donne, it appears, is not only describing first-hand kisses, but also those which can be experienced vicariously through, for example, salacious Ovidian love poetry.[17] Once again, however, Donne is not evoking the world of 'licentiousness' in order to reject it outright. Rather, he insists that secular love can be a means, like Jacob's ladder, to bridge heaven and earth. He is, moreover, not only speaking of chaste love. Even 'foule and unchaste love' can draw us to God. Donne is, of course, careful. His congregation should not become 'oppressed' with earthly love; he is not suggesting that his auditory abandon themselves to licentious behaviour. Rather, he is demonstrating how the earthly can be re-written and re-experienced as the heavenly. Thus he continues by explaining:

> There is corne under the chaffe; and though the chaffe and straw be for cattell, there is corne for men too: There is a heavenly love, under these ordinary phrases; the ordinary phrase belongs to ordinary men; the heavenly love and the spirituall kisse, to them who affect an union to God, and him whom he sent, his Son Christ Jesus. (III, 319)

Just as Christ's incarnation bridges man and God, so too can heavenly truths be found in expressions of earthly love. Contrary to appearances, the 'ordinary phrases' of Donne's youthful love poetry hold within them the 'heavenly love' and 'spirituall kisse' to which he is now dedicated to leading his congregation. Donne then makes this literary context explicit by asserting that 'S. *Paul* abhors not good and apply-able sentences, because some secular Poets had said them before' (III, 319). St Paul thus becomes the model, not only for Donne's frequent inclusion of the metaphoric world of his poetry within his sermons, but also for the bridging of secular poetry and divine preaching both within his own biography and within the Society of Lincoln's Inn.

A final example can be found in a sermon on 1 Corinthians 16: 22 ('If any man love not the Lord Iesus Christ, let him be anathema, Maranatha') (1616–22). Donne is preaching on the theme of loving Christ so far as to lay down worldly pleasures for him. The topic has obvious relevance for a congregation of Inns of Court students and Donne makes the connection explicit by taking as an example Augustine's Epistle 26 to Licentius, specifically adapting the example to fit with the congregation of students before him.[18] He tells them:

> Of the first case, of crucifying himselfe to the world, S. *Augustine* had occasion to say much to a young Gentleman, young, and noble, and rich, and (which is not, in such persons, an ordinary tentation, but where it is, it is a shrewd one) as he was young, and noble, and rich, so he was learned in other learnings, and upon that strength withdrew, and kept off from Christ … He had sent to S. *Augustine* a handsome Elegie of his making, in which *Poeme* he had said as much of the vanity and deceivableness of this world, as S. *Augustine* could have looked for, or, perchance, have said in a Homily; And he ends his Elegie thus, *Hoc opus, ut jubeas*, All this concerning this world I know already, Do you but tell me, doe you command me, what I shall doe. (III, 304)

The description of Licentius as 'young, and noble, and rich', in the context of Lincoln's Inn, works to transform him into a gentleman student of the Inns of Court. Indeed, Licentius's youthful arrogance closely recalls Overbury's description of an over-confident, fashion-conscious Inns student who 'will talke ends of *Latine* though it be false, with as great confidence, as euer *Cicero* could pronounce an Oration' and 'by that he hath read *Littleton*, he … dares compare his Law to a *Lord Chief Justices*'.[19] The careful interjection that youth, nobility, and wealth need not always be a temptation to sin, but can be a 'shrewd' one, is typical of Donne's gentle, non-confrontational tone with his congregation.

The gentleman's 'Elegie' is a wonderfully witty moment, recalling not only the manuscript and literary culture of the Inns of Court, but also Donne's own elegies written as a student. And, of course, the juxtaposition of the elegy and the homily brings to mind just the gap between student and preacher which Donne is negotiating in his sermons in the Lincoln's Inn pulpit. The idea that the 'Elegie' said 'much of the vanity and deceivableness of this world' recalls especially Donne's *Satires*. In these witty, self-conscious pieces the speaker deliberately seeks to distance himself from the corrupt world that he inhabits, presenting himself as one who can see through the social façade of the court. Intriguingly, just as in the sermon Donne claims that the 'Elegie' might well have been a sermon, so too does Donne's earlier satiric voice claim alliance with preachers:

> Preachers which are
> Seas of Wit and Arts, you can, then dare,
> Drowne the sinnes of this place, for, for mee
> Which am but a scarce brooke, it enough shall bee
> To wash the staines away;[20]

The speaker of the *Satires* is not, however, always easy to place, often seeming to be simultaneously attracted to and repulsed by vice. He 'had no suit [at court], nor new suite to shew', yet is drawn there anyway.[21] The *Satires'* condemnation of vice is far more equivocal than that provided in a sermon. Donne addresses this as he gives Augustine's response to the gentleman. Augustine, he says, replies:

> Shall I, shall *Augustine* command his fellow-servant? … Wouldst thou heare me? … Thou that art inexorable against the perswasions of thine owne soule … How well disposed a soule, how high pitched a wit is taken out of my hands, that I may not sacrifice that soule, that I may not direct that wit upon our God, because, with all these good parts, thou turnest upon the pleasures of this world? Doe not speake out of wit, nor out of a love to elegant expressions, nor doe not speake in jest of the dangerous vanities of this world; *Mentiuntur*, they are false, they performe not their promises; *Moriuntur*, they are transitory, they stay not with thee; and *In mortem trahunt*, they dye, and they dye of the infection, and they transfuse venome into thee, and thou dyest with them: … If thou foundest a chalice of gold in the earth, so good a heart as thine would say, Surely this belongs to the Church, and surely thou wouldst give it to the Church … God hath given thee a wit, an understanding, not of the gold of Ophir, but of the gold of the heavenly Jerusalem … In that chalice once consecrated to God, wilt thou drink a health to the devill, and drink a health to him in thine owne bloud, in making thy wit, thy learning, thy good parts advance his kingdome? (III, 304–5)

Donne transforms Augustine's comments on Licentius's poem into criticisms of the prevailing literary culture of the Inns. In the original, Augustine is concerned by Licentius's poem because Licentius seems to be more interested in writing about turning to Christ, than in actually relinquishing the world.[22] The poem contains words, without any intent of action. Donne uses Augustine's complaints to censure contemporary poetry which, he claims, complains about vice, but does so from an amoral perspective. He proceeds to deconstruct what could well be his own satiric persona, whose rejection of vice is never total or unequivocal. As Augustine's and Donne's voices merge, Donne condemns the prevailing literary culture of the Inns of Court with its discourse of 'wit' and 'elegant expressions'. Such earthly vanities, he insists, are false, transitory, and venomous. Donne's argument, however, is subtle. For he is not rejecting wit, the students' intellectual abilities, or learning in themselves, but rather criticising the uses to which they are put. Wit's true use is to facilitate a relationship with God and man as the chalice does in the celebration of communion. Donne thus calls on his congregation to take their wit and learning and use them to advance the Kingdom of God, rather than earthly concerns. Just as he has switched from a satirist to a preacher, so too he calls upon his congregation to re-channel their abilities into a true Christian purpose.

Arguably, Donne himself demonstrates how this should be done through the use of rhetorical ingenuity within his sermons. The same stylistic fascination with puns, verbal acrobatics, and rhetorical showmanship is as apparent in Donne's sermons as it is in his early poetry and prose. For example, throughout Donne's religious poetry he puns on 'sun' and 'son'. In 'La Corona', the poetic voice tells us to 'Joy at the uprising of this Sunne, and Sonne' ('The Ascension', line 2), while in 'Holy Sonnet II' the speaker claims 'I am thy sonne, made with thy selfe to shine' (line 4). Again, in 'Goodfriday 1613', Donne tells us that towards the East: 'There I should see a Sunne, by rising set, / And by that setting endlesse day beget' (lines 11–12). In a sermon on 1 Peter 1: 17 ('And if ye call on the Father, who without respect of persons judgeth according to every mans works, passe the time of your sojourning here in feare') (1616–22) Donne recalls – or perhaps we should say 'resurrects' – this pun which so delighted him in his verse. Having summed up all his arguments about God the Father, Donne promises his congregation 'The next day the Son will rise' (III, 291), punning on the new dawn and the next sermon in his series which will be on the second person of the Trinity, the Son. This witty, punning conclusion to the sermon would have been enhanced by the self-conscious reference to the series of sermons, reminding the congregation of their status as a community, coming together to share the sermons on a regular basis.

The wit and word play in Donne's sermons would have especially appealed to the young students at the Inns of Court. John Manningham's *Diary* (1602–3) offers us a survey of the verbal diversions of the students. His *Diary* is packed with puns, word games, linguistic puzzles, and paradoxes. He is especially keen on puns on names. In addition to the notorious pun on Donne's name, 'Dunne is Undonne', he recalls Serjeant Harris's comment when he heard that Robert Barker was called to be a serjeant that 'It is well … there should be one barker amongst soe manie byters', as well as Julius Caesar, Master of the Requests', joke to a man seeking to be heard that 'nowe thou canst be heard in noe other Court thou appealest to Cesar'.[23]

Not only would Donne's witty preaching have directly appealed to the students, but he seems in his Lincoln's Inn sermons to have deliberately foregrounded this aspect of his preaching. An important example would be his decision to preach a series of sermons on apparently conflicting biblical texts. Donne's interest in the inherent paradoxes of Christianity pervades his preaching career. Sermons such as that preached to the Lords on Easter Day 1619 on Psalm 89: 48 ('What man is he that liveth, and shall not see death?') is particularly paradoxical and riddling. Donne concludes both that all men shall die and that, through Christ, all men can live. At Lincoln's Inn, however, Donne takes his interest in the paradoxes of Christianity to a new level. He was responsible for delivering two Sunday sermons in term time, one in the morning and the other in the afternoon, and in this series he would take in his afternoon sermon a text which appeared to completely contradict that which he had taken in the morning. As he explained to his congregation: 'I think it a usefull and acceptable labour, now to employ for a time those Evening exercises to reconcile

some such places of Scripture, as may at first sight seem to differ from one another'
(II, 325). The majority of the sermons Donne preached at Lincoln's Inn form part of
a series. This was conventional preaching practice; preachers would frequently take
a unit of the Bible and develop lengthy sequences of sermons.[24] To choose to preach
a series on antithetical texts, taking as the thematic rubric not a unit of the Bible
but what was essentially a rhetorical method, would have been extremely unusual.

Only two pairs of sermons from the series survive. The first pair was preached on
30 January 1620 and deals with God's judgement, a theme particularly appropriate
for a Lincoln's Inn congregation. The first sermon is on John 5: 22 ('The Father
judgeth no man, but hath committed all judgement to the sonne') and Donne
foregrounds the apparent contradiction in the text: '*Judgement* is an unseparable
character of God the Father, being *Fons Deitatis*, the root and spring of the whole
Deity, how [then] is it said, that the Father judgeth no man?' (II, 318). Then, having
raised a seemingly irresolvable puzzle, he provides the solution, which, he explains,
lies within the Trinity: 'the Father he judges still, but he judges as God, and not as
the Father' (II, 319). Donne claims that he does not wish 'to stray into clouds, or
perplexities in this contemplation', and yet there is a degree of relish with which he
deals with the linguistic conundrums into which his explication of the Trinity has
drawn him. He tells his congregation that 'God, that is, the whole Trinity, judges
still, but so as the Sonne judgeth, the Father judgeth not, for that Judgement he
hath committed' (II, 319). His deft employment of the rhetorical figures of *conduplicatio*, in the repetition of 'judges', and *polyptoton*, in the movement from 'judges' to
'judgeth' to 'judgement', gives the argument a density and complexity reminiscent
of the prose *Paradoxes* and *Problems* (*c*.1601) or the *Songs and Sonnets* with which
Donne entertained the Inns of Court wits in his youth. Compare, for example, the
conclusion to the Paradox entitled 'That all things kill themselves', in which we are
told 'Of our Powers, remembering kills our Memory. Of affections, Lusting our
Lust. Of Vertues, giving kills Liberality'.[25] Here, as in the sermon, much of the wit
stems from the virtuosic command of rhetorical figures, in particular *parison* and
polyptoton. Donne may have refocused his abilities in the service of the Church, but
there is every indication that he still enjoyed a rhetorical challenge.

In the afternoon sermon Donne introduces his second text, John 8: 15 ('I judge
no man'), by encouraging his congregation to put the two texts into dialogue. He
tells them:

> The Rivers of Paradise did not run all one way, and yet they flow'd from one head; the
> sentences of the Scripture flow all from one head, from the Holy Ghost, and yet they
> seem to present divers senses, and to admit divers interpretations; In such an appear-
> ance doth this Text differ from that which I handled in the forenoon. (II, 325)

Once again Donne's aim here is orthodox. The senses may seem contradictory and
'divers', but in fact they all stem from the Holy Ghost and from one essential Truth.
There remains, however, a strong sense of Donne's pleasure in this diversity of sense
and interpretation and, crucially, in his own role in reconciling them. When he offers

his solution to this sermon's apparent contradiction, explaining that 'there was never any time when Christ was not Judge, but there were some manner of Judgements which Christ did never exercise, and Christ had no commission which he did not execute' (II, 326), he once again compounds figures of repetition such as *polyptoton* and *conduplicatio*. The alliteration in 'exercise' and 'execute' intensifies the sense of verbal density yet further, so Donne can emphasise the intricacy of his argument.

Again, at the end of the second sermon, his connection of the two texts seems to emphasise complexity even as he seeks to resolve it. He tells his congregation: 'Now to collect both our Exercises, and to connexe both Texts, *Christ judgeth all men* and *Christ judgeth no man*, he claimes all judgement, and he disavows all judgement, and they consist well together' (II, 333–4). Donne's conclusion is itself a contradiction. By judging at our election, justification, and final judgement, yet not involving himself in secular, unfair, or irremediable judgement, Christ both claims all judgement and rejects all judgement. And once again the very wittiness and tightness of the paradox is emphasised through Donne's virtuosic compounding of rhetorical figures of repetition. In one sentence he brings together repetition of sound in the alliteration of 'collect' and 'connexe', repetition of words in the *polyptoton* of 'judgeth' and 'judgement' and repetition of clauses in the *parison* of 'Christ judgeth all men' and 'Christ judgeth no man' and 'he claimes all judgement' and 'he disavows all judgement'. Again, the self-conscious display of wit is reminiscent of Donne's earlier Lincoln's Inn writings, especially the *Paradoxes* and *Problems*.

In the second pair of paradoxical sermons, undated but most likely preached later the same year, Donne seeks to 'reconcile' a text from Job 19: 26 ('And though, after my skin, wormes destroy this body, yet in my flesh shall I see God') and a text from 1 Corinthians 15: 50 ('Now this I say brethren, that flesh and blood cannot inherit the kingdome of God'). Once again, Donne resolves the apparent contradiction by telling his auditory that, contrary to appearances, his texts 'answer one another' (III, 133). Job and St Paul are, in fact, talking about different types of flesh. St Paul is rejecting 'sinful flesh', while Job is celebrating 'naturall flesh; that is, flesh indued with all qualities of flesh, all such qualities as imply no defect, no corruption, (for there was *flesh* before there was *sin*)' (III, 114–15). Donne's emphasis throughout is on the fact that riddles and confusion are essentially earthly in origin. Confusions are created and perpetuated by man in his frailty. He tells his congregation:

> Here, in this world, we see God *per speculum*, says the Apostle, by reflection, upon a glasse; we see a creature; and from that there arises an assurance that there is a Creator; we see him *in aenigmate*, says he; which is not ill rendred in the margin, in a *Riddle*; we see him in the Church, but men have made it a riddle, which is the Church; we see him in the Sacrament, but men have made it a riddle, by what light, and at what window: Doe I see him at the window of bread and wine; Is he in that; or doe I see him by the window of faith; and is he onely in that? still it is in a riddle. (III, 111)

Indeed, Donne is here associating riddles and confusions with unnecessary controversy and religious disputes, aligning contradictions and paradoxes with meaningless religious wrangling. In heaven, Donne explains, all such contradictions and confusions will be resolved when we see and experience the Truth. Shifting into the first person, in a powerful testimony of personal faith, Donne insists that in heaven: 'I shall see all problematicall things come to be dogmaticall, I shall see all these rocks in Divinity, come to bee smooth alleys; I shall see Prophesies untyed, Riddles dissolved, controversies reconciled; but I shall never see that, till I come to this sight … *Videbo Deum, I shall see God*' (III, 111). Riddles, paradoxes, and problems are, it seems, dismissed in favour of the absolute Truth of God. At the end of the second sermon Donne explains:

> We have done; Adde we but this, by way of recollecting this which hath been said now, upon these words, and that which hath been formerly said upon these words of *Iob*, which may seem to differ from these (*In my flesh I shall see God*) *Omne verum omni vero consentiens*, whatsoever is true in it selfe agrees with every other truth. Because that which *Iob* says, and that which *Saint Paul* says, agree with the truth, they agree with one another. (III, 132)

Truth, specifically the complete Truth of God, is set against superficial contradictions. Yet at the same time as he rejects such earthly puzzles, Donne's sermons once again reveal a preoccupation with and pleasure in such riddles, not only in the sermons' thematic structure of being dedicated to resolving paradoxical texts, but also within the prose itself. For example, Donne revels in the central Christian paradox of the resurrection that '*No man ever saw God and liv'd*; and yet, I shall not live till I see God; and when I have seen him I shall never dye' (III, 111). The figures of *plochc* (repetition of a word in an altered or more expressive sense) and *parison* deliberately draw attention to the sermon's own wit. Donne may reject theological 'riddles', but he seems to have enjoyed linguistic riddles and, by preaching a series on conflicting texts, he has given himself scope to pay especial emphasis to this aspect of his preaching style where it would have been particularly appreciated, at Lincoln's Inn.

Despite this commitment to bridging the gap between the religious world of sermons and the world of the gentleman students, however, Donne also embraces his pastoral role of leading the men towards a Christian life. Donne seems to have recognised the extent to which the Inns of Court students were especially vulnerable. Unlike the universities, the lack of a tutorial system at the Inns of Court meant students were essentially left in London with no educational or pastoral guidance.[26] Some parents made their own arrangements for their sons, but frequently this seems to have been ineffective and the students were left to find their own way. Francis Lenton draws attention to this vulnerability of the students in his *Characterismi*. His image of an Inns of Court gentleman is of 'a youth very apt to bee wrought vpon at his first entrance, and there are Fishers of purpose for such young fry'.[27]

Donne tackles these issues directly in his Lincoln's Inn sermons. In a series on Psalm 38, for example, he deals particularly with the theme of practical morality. Donne uses this psalm to explore both the temptations to which men are subjected and the crippling effects of sin. Indeed, if Potter and Simpson's dating of these sermons to summer 1618 is correct, it is tempting to suggest that Donne was referring and responding to an incident which occurred in Lincoln's Inn earlier that year. On 27 January the *Black Books*, the Society's records, note that 'The consideracion of the punishment of M[r] John Baber and M[r] John Webb for strickinge and stabbinge in the Hall, is respited.' No further details of this outbreak of violence are recorded, but it was clearly a major incident since references to it recur throughout the next five months.[28]

Despite the Inns of Court's reputation for being the breeding ground for such ill behaviour, suspensions for it seem to have been relatively rare. Certainly this was the first such incident since Donne arrived at the Society and it seems likely that it would have caused quite a stir among the community.[29] Of course it is impossible to prove a direct link between Donne's sermon series and the violence precipitated by Baber and Webb. At the same time, even if there was no connection, it is surely possible that the incident would have been evoked in his listeners' minds. The psalmist, King David, is presented by Donne as an example of a young man who has become embroiled in a sinful life of sex and violence. In the third sermon in the series, Donne introduces his text by reminding his congregation of the extent of David's depravity. He details how David seduced Bathsheba, 'that woman, who for ought appearing to the contrary, had otherwise preserved her honour, and her Conscience entire', made Uriah the instrument of his own death, 'carrying those letters, the warrants of his own execution', and exploited Joab as 'his instrument for a murder to cover an adultry' (II, 98). The world of the psalm does not seem entirely removed from that of the Inns of Court where young men resorted to 'strickinge and stabbinge'.

This pastoral commitment to rendering the experience of David relevant to his student auditory pervades the series. For example, in the first sermon in the series, Donne preaches on the second verse of the psalm ('For thine arrowes stick fast in me, and thy hand presseth me sore'). These arrows which afflict David become, in Donne's sermon, the temptations to which the young men of the Inn would be regularly exposed. Donne preaches: 'A fair day shoots arrows of *visits*, and *comedies*, and *conversation*, and so wee goe abroad: and a foul day shoots arrows of *gaming*, or *chambering*, and *wantonnesse*, and so we stay at home' (II, 62). A life of visits, comedies, conversation, gambling, and licentiousness: Donne evokes student life as it was satirised then as now. Donne's analysis of sin is, however, subtle. Thus he continues by describing how, having been shot at by the arrows of sin, we fail to withdraw the arrows properly. He argues: 'He pulls back the arrow a little way, and he sees *blood*, and he feels his *spirit* to goe out with it, and he lets it alone: He forbears his sinfull companions, a little while, and he feels a *melancholy* take hold of him, the spirit and life of his life decays, and he falls to those companions again' (II, 64). Donne's analysis of sin and temptation and of why it is that men return so easily to their sinful lives is, here, wonderfully sensitive. The tone is that of a gentle satire on the Inns of Court student who succumbs to depression on being kept away from his peers and his usual debauchery.[30] The image of the student seeking to pull the arrow out and then squeamishly abandoning the effort seems to tap into the contemporary stereotype of the Inns of Court students who, for all their bravado, were, if not exactly cowardly, certainly more talented at carrying a sword elegantly at court than using it on the battlefield. Yet while Donne is shrewd and knowing about the students' way of life in this passage, his tone is gently teasing rather than vituperative. His argument against such a life has been made more through humour than either vicious satire or condemnatory railing.

A similar example can be found in the second sermon in the series. Here Donne is preaching on the third verse of the psalm ('There is no soundnesse in my flesh, because of thine anger, neither is there any rest in my bones, because of my sinne'), a text which leads him to consider man's state of continual misery after his fall into sin. He explains:

> And by sinnes, this flesh, that is but the loame and plaster of thy Tabernacle, thy body, *that*, *all* that, *that* in the intire substance is corrupted. Those Gummes, and spices, which should embalme thy flesh, when thou art dead, are spent upon that diseased body whilest thou art alive: Thou seemest, in the eye of the world, to walk in *silks*, and thou doest but walke in *searcloth* [a waxed winding-sheet used for the dead]; Thou hast a desire to please some *eyes*, when thou hast much to do, not to displease every *Nose*; and thou wilt solicite an adulterous entrance into their beds, who, if they should but see thee goe into thine own bed, would need no other mortification, nor answer to thy solicitation. (II, 83)

Donne once again confronts directly the worldly concerns which preoccupy his student auditory. Here, however, he seeks to persuade the students to abandon their sinful and materialistic ways of life, not through gentle humour, but through the shock tactics of deconstructing the image of a young gallant before our eyes. The physical imagery of bodies, flesh, disease, noses, and eyes make this passage extremely vivid, an effect which would have been amplified in oral delivery by the direct address of 'Thou' and the repetition of 'Thou seemest', 'Thou hast', and 'thou wilt' in the *parison* of the final phrases. There is clearly a great deal of potential here for Donne to have made eye contact with specific members of his congregation. Donne thus engages directly with the world of the students, using by turn both ironical humour and denunciatory rhetoric to persuade his congregation to reform.

Donne does, however, show an awareness of the difficulties with which his congregation are faced. For example, in the third sermon on Psalm 38 Donne sensitively addresses the theme of what we would call 'peer pressure'. He tells his listeners: 'If any good purpose arise in us, we dare not pursue it, for fear of displeasing those, with whom we live, and to whom we have a relation, and a dependence upon them … We sin, and sin, and sin, lest our abstinence from sin, should work as an increpation, as a rebuke upon them that doe not sin' (II, 101). Donne demonstrates, here, a clear understanding of the psychology of his congregation and the pressure to conform which they experienced through living in a tight community such as one of the Inns of Court. The Inns' carefully cultivated sense of corporate identity found expression in a variety of practices, ranging from the benchers' insistence on attendance at chapel and the learning exercises through to participation in the revels.[31] Bulstrode Whitelocke, for example, describes being 'by the unanimous consent of the young gentlemen of the middle Temple chosen M[aste]ʳ of the Revells' and relates how 'with much importunity[,] & reluctancy for diversion from his study[,] he att length was prevayled with, to accept'.[32]

As Donne's sermon demonstrates, however, life in such a close community could also create a pressure to sin. Donne continues by invoking the voice of Augustine to emphasise how even the most holy of men are subject to such social pressures. He tells how Augustine confesses, 'I was fain to sin, lest I should lose my credit … I would bely my self, and say I had done that, which I never did, lest I should be under-valued for not having done it' (II, 107). Moreover, as Donne continues, Augustine's voice seems to merge with his own. He tells us, 'I saw it was thought wit, to make Sonnets of their own sinnes … I sinn'd, not for the pleasure I had in the sin, but for the pride that I had to write feelingly of it' (II, 107–8). Augustine's *Confessions* is a perfect model for Donne to suggest in his efforts to draw his congregation from a sinful youth to an adulthood devoted to God. While Augustine describes the social pressures drawing him towards sin, however, he makes no mention at all of writing poetry, let alone sonnets. Donne thus takes Augustine and transforms his passage into a commentary specific to the Inns of Court, vividly suggesting not only Donne's own poetry, especially his elegies with their intensely experienced sexual encounters, but also the wider manuscript culture of the Inns of Court.[33] Donne goes on to reveal his understanding of the extent to which sin is part of a gentleman's lifestyle. He admits that it is seen to be a 'sordid, a *yeomanly* thing, still to be plowing, and weeding, and worming a conscience; a mechanicall thing, still to be removing logs, or filing iron, still to be busied in removing occasions of tentation' (II, 107). The analogy of a sinful life and social pretensions must have resonated particularly strongly with the first generation of the gentry and the merchants' sons whose attendance at the Inns of Court was part of their strategy to escape their yeoman roots.[34] Yet at the same time that Donne shows he understands the pressures of the social world in which his congregation are living, he is insistent that they cannot be used as an excuse. Once again adopting the first person to show that he is speaking as much to himself as his auditory, Donne is emphatic, 'I cannot discharge my sins upon the *Times*, and upon the present ill disposition that reigns in men nowe, and doe ill, because every body else does so', warning his congregation 'if thou think it enough to say, I have but liv'd, as other men have liv'd, wantonly, thou wilt finde some examples to die by too; and die, as other old men, old in years, and old in sins, have died too, negligently, or fearfully' (II, 103–4). Donne has shown that he understands the temptations to which the young are subjected, but he remains adamant that the students must resist 'the heats, and impetuous violence of youth' (II, 104).

In the middle of *2 King Henry IV* Justice Shallow and Justice Silence take a moment to reminisce. Wistfully, Justice Shallow recalls his youthful days at the Inns of Court, reminding Silence 'I was once of Clement's Inn, where I think they will talk of mad Shallow yet' (III.ii.12–14), and evoking an unlikely image of a drinking, gambling, and licentious youth. Shallow's recollections serve as a pertinent reminder that reminiscing about the good old days of student life is never an objective process; such memories are usually bound up with a healthy dose of exaggeration and distortion and frequently re-shaped for the polemical demands of the present moment. In Donne's Lincoln's Inn sermons, I believe we see a particularly self-conscious example of this process. When he ascended the Society's pulpit, Donne harnessed his autobiography and transformed it into a complex and highly effective rhetorical strategy to bridge the gulf between the secular and the spiritual which he confronted at Lincoln's Inn. In his review of John Stubbes's biography, *John Donne: The Reformed Soul* (2006), Colin Burrows argued that 'a sense of performance, rather than of confession' runs through Donne's work.[35] This captures precisely the mode of the Lincoln's Inn sermons, where we see no denial of the apparent contradictions in his biography, nor any awkward efforts at self-justification, but rather a deliberate attempt to employ and, indeed, perform, the discontinuities of his life in order to engage the particular congregation before him.

Notes

1 John Donne, *Letters to Severall Persons of Honour*, a facsimile reproduction, introd. M. Thomas Hester (Delmar, CA: Scholars' Facsimiles and Reprints, 1977), pp. 218, 21–2. This approach was continued by Izaak Walton, who emphasises the complete break between Donne the witty poet and Donne the preacher. See Izaac Walton, *The Lives of John Donne, Sir Henry Wotton, Richard Hooker, George Herbert and Robert Sanderson*, ed. George Saintsbury (Oxford: Oxford University Press, 1927).

2 On a portrait of Donne that was 'almost certainly on display in a private chamber of a member of Lincoln's Inn', see Cooper's chapter, pp. 172–4, below, and Plate 3.

3 Lenton is most likely referring to John Perkins (d.1545?), the legal writer who, according to J. H. Baker, became a 'household name' for generations of legal students. See J. H. Baker, 'Perkins, John (d. 1545?)', *Oxford Dictionary of National Biography*, Oxford University Press, Sept. 2004; online edn, Jan. 2008 www.oxforddnb.com/view/article/21970 (accessed 24 Feb. 2009). He could, however, also be referring to William Perkins, the Cambridge Puritan.

4 F[rancis] L[enton], *Characterismi: Or Lentons Leasures* (London: I. B. for Roger Michell, 1631), sigs F4ʳ–F6ʳ. Francis Lenton was a poet who seems to have been part of the poetic coteries centred on the Inns of Court during the 1620s and 1630s. Jerome de Groot, 'Lenton, Francis (*fl.* 1629–1653)', *Oxford Dictionary of National Biography*, Oxford University Press, Sept. 2004, www.oxforddnb.com/view/article/16468 (accessed 24 Feb. 2009).

5 *Poems of Sir John Davies*, a facsimile reproduction, introd. Clare Howard (New York, NY: Columbia University Press, 1941), pp. 55–6.

6 Thomas Overbury, *His Wife. With Additions of New Characters, and Many Other Wittie Conceits Neuer Before Printed* (London: Robert Allot, 1628), sigs K4[r]–K5[r]. Donne himself contributed to Overbury's *Characters* before his ordination. See Geoffrey Keynes, *A Bibliography of Dr. John Donne*, 4th edn (Oxford: Clarendon Press, 1973), pp. 167–8.

7 Wilfrid R. Prest, *The Inns of Court under Elizabeth I and the Early Stuarts, 1590–1640* (London: Longman, 1972), pp. 137–9. On the interests of Inns of Court students in the period, see also Philip J. Finkelpearl, *John Marston of the Middle Temple: An Elizabethan Dramatist in his Social Setting* (Cambridge, MA: Harvard University Press, 1969).

8 William Prynne, *A Briefe Polemical Dissertation Concerning the True Time of the Inchoation and Determination of the Lords Day-Sabbath* (London: T. Mabb for Edward Thomas, 1655), sig. A2[r]. Prynne had been admitted to Lincoln's Inn in 1621 and called to the bar in 1628.

9 On the Inns of Court as centres of literary production, see Finkelpearl, *John Marston*, pp. 19–31, Arthur F. Marotti, *John Donne, Coterie Poet* (Madison, WI: University of Wisconsin Press, 1986), pp. 25–95, and Prest, *The Inns of Court under Elizabeth I and the Early Stuarts, 1590–1640*, pp. 153–8. On manuscript circulation in the Inns of Court, see Mary Hobbs, *Early Seventeenth-Century Verse Miscellany Manuscripts* (Aldershot: Scolar Press, 1992), esp. pp. 90–3.

10 On the revels, see Finkelpearl, *John Marston*, pp. 32–61. These 'non-legal' interests did not, of course, mean the students were not open to sermons. See, for example, John Manningham's diary which juxtaposes lewd jokes, witty poetry and prose, and tales of womanising, drinking, and gaming with extensive sermon notes. When preaching to the students, Donne's dilemma was not that of confronting a congregation that was antagonistic to sermon attendance. His challenge, rather, was to address an auditory with extremely high standards when it came to sermons and yet whose lifestyle seems not always to have been so religious. See *The Diary of John Manningham of the Middle Temple 1602–1603*, ed. Robert Parker Sorlien (Hanover, NH: The University Press of New England, 1976).

11 It is difficult to date Donne's poems, most of which were not printed until after his death. However, it is generally agreed that most of the *Elegies*, the first two *Satires*, and some of the *Songs and Sonnets* were written during this period.

12 Richard Baker, *A Chronicle of the Kings of England* (London: Printed for Daniel Frere, 1643), p. 156.

13 *Diary of John Manningham*, ed. Sorlien, p. 115.

14 *The Sermons of John Donne*, ed. George R. Potter and Evelyn M. Simpson, 10 vols (Berkeley; Los Angeles, CA: University of California Press, 1953–62), II, 8–9, 18–20. On psalm translation in the period, see Hannibal Hamlin, *Psalm Culture in Early Modern English Literature* (Cambridge: Cambridge University Press, 2004). Although no research has yet been undertaken on psalm translating taking place within the Inns of Court, it is noticeable that a number of the translators mentioned in Hamlin's study had connections with the Inns. For example, Francis Bacon (Gray's Inn), John Davies (Middle Temple), John Denham (Lincoln's Inn), George Gascoigne (Gray's Inn), Edwin Sandys (Middle Temple), George Sandys (Middle Temple), Edmund Waller (Lincoln's Inn), and George Wither (Middle Temple).

15 *The Sermons of John Donne*, ed. Potter and Simpson, II, 49. All subsequent references to Donne's sermons are to this edition.

16 *The Poems of John Donne*, ed. Herbert J. C. Grierson, 2 vols (Oxford: Oxford University

Press, 1912; repr. 1953), 'Jealousie', l. 24, 'Elegie VI', l. 27, and 'The Comparison', l. 51. Unless stated otherwise, all subsequent references to Donne's poetry are to this edition.

17 For recent work on Donne and Ovid, see, for example, M. L. Stapleton, '"Why should they not alike in all parts touch"? *Donne* and the elegiac tradition', *John Donne Journal*, 15 (1996), 1–22.

18 Donne claims his source is Letter 39, but it is, in fact, Letter 26. For a translation and commentary on this letter from Augustine to Licentius, see *The Works of Saint Augustine: Letters 1–99*, ed. John E. Rotelle, trans. Roland Teske (New York, NY: New City Press, 2001), pp. 78–84.

19 Overbury, *His Wife*, sigs K4ʳ–K5ʳ.

20 *Donne: The Satires, Epigrams and Verse Letters*, ed. W. Milgate (Oxford: Clarendon Press, 1967), 'Satire IV', ll. 237–41.

21 *Ibid.*, l. 7.

22 Augustine was probably equally disturbed by Licentius's confusion of Roman mythology and the Bible.

23 *Diary of John Manningham*, ed. Sorlien, pp. 150, 173, 186.

24 Other series Donne preached at Lincoln's Inn include one on Psalm 38, one on the persons of the Trinity, and one disputing Catholic theology.

25 *Paradoxes and Problems*, ed. Helen Peters (Oxford: Clarendon Press, 1980), pp. 1–2. It seems likely Donne wrote his *Paradoxes* while a student at the Inns of Court. Indeed, two, or possibly three, of his paradoxes are included in Manningham's *Diary*.

26 Prest, *The Inns of Court under Elizabeth I and the Early Stuarts, 1590–1640*, pp. 138–41. See also Finkelpearl, *John Marston*, pp. 12–15.

27 Lenton, *Characterismi*, sig. F5ᵛ.

28 *Black Books*, II, 119, 200, 201, 204–5.

29 The *Black Books* record no suspensions in the years 1615–17. In 1616, there were two potentially violent incidents. On 12 February, it is recorded that the principal cook abused a bencher, and on 11 June it is noted that there was disorder at the reader's table. In neither case, however, does the violence seem to have reached the levels that it did between Baber and Webb.

30 On the importance of community and the construction of social identities in the Inns of Court, see Michelle O'Callaghan, *The English Wits: Literature and Sociability in Early Modern England* (Cambridge: Cambridge University Press, 2007), pp. 10–34. On the ways in which satirists in the Inns framed themselves as both isolated and embedded within a community, see Lawrence Manley, *Literature and Culture in Early Modern London* (Cambridge: Cambridge University Press, 1995), esp. pp. 378–9.

31 See O'Callaghan, *The English Wits*, esp. pp. 10–12.

32 *The Diary of Bulstrode Whitelocke, 1605–1675*, ed. Ruth Spalding, Records of Social and Economic History, New Series XIII (Oxford: Published for the British Academy by Oxford University Press, 1990), p. 57.

33 For a translation of this passage of Augustine's *Confessions*, see *The Works of Saint Augustine: The Confessions*, ed. John E. Rotelle, trans. Maria Boulding (New York, NY: New City Press, 1997), p. 66.

34 On the gentry at the Inns of Court, see Prest, *The Inns of Court under Elizabeth I and the Early Stuarts, 1590–1640*, pp. 23–32, 40–6.
The idea of removing logs as being an especially 'sordid' and 'yeomanly' activity

strikingly recalls *The Tempest*, III.i, in which Prospero sets Ferdinand to the base labour of piling logs. Donne's own father was, of course, an ironmonger, who claimed gentle birth even as he spent his days 'filing iron'. See R. C. Bald, *John Donne: A Life* (Oxford: Clarendon Press, 1970; repr. 1986), pp. 19–22.

35 Collin Burrows, 'Recribrations', *London Review of Books*, 28:19 (5 October 2006), 3–6 (6).

6

Readers' dinners and the culture of the early modern Inns of Court

Wilfrid R. Prest

It is flattering to be invited to revisit an era – the sixteenth and seventeenth centuries – and a subject – the Inns of Court – on which I first worked many years ago. Yet nostalgic retrospection can be a risky business. A Middle Temple student remarked in February 1602 that 'Yf you put a case in the first bookes of the lawe to the auncientes, you may presume they may have forgotten it; yf in the newe bookes, you may doubt whether they have reade it.'[1] Our knowledge of the early modern Inns of Court has grown by leaps and bounds since the mid-1960s. Meanwhile, my own interests have moved forward chronologically and diversified both geographically and thematically. Hence it is only too likely that I have not read, or if read not remembered, all that is requisite for the task to which the first part of this chapter is committed, a brief overview of recent work on the early modern Inns. Nevertheless, having thus attempted to lay the groundwork, the second and more substantial part will consider what might be termed the 'alimentary hypothesis' for the collapse in the later seventeenth century of what was then a long-established system of legal education by means of aural 'learning exercises'.[2]

Recent work on the early modern Inns of Court

When Desmond Bland's *Bibliography of the Inns of Court and Chancery* appeared in 1965, historians in general (as distinct from legal historians) were beginning to show some interest in the early modern Inns of Court, especially their role in educating those who would eventually fight the English civil wars.[3] But apart from a pioneering doctoral thesis by Eric Ives on the late Yorkist and early Tudor Inns and legal profession, the best account of the sixteenth- and seventeenth-century Inns then available was still that provided by the legal historian W. S. Holdsworth in two books of his multi-volume history of English law first published in 1924.[4]

Things are very different today. We have general histories which largely cover the Tudor and Stuart centuries, despite some remaining gaps and unevennesses of treatment.[5] J. H. Baker and Chris Brooks have also cast much light on the basic organisation and structure of the upper and lower echelons of England's so-called 'third university', Serjeant's Inn and the Inns of Chancery, as well as on their members, respectively the serjeants at law and judges, and the attorneys and solicitors, the 'lower branch' of England's two-tiered legal profession.[6] Numerous articles, chapters, and monographs contribute to what is now a large body of specialised studies on such topics as the post-Reformation religious history of the Inns, the political and social networks of which they were part, and the education, both legal and non-legal, provided to their students.[7] Biographies of lawyers and other members have made further contributions.[8] Besides the unexpurgated modern edition of John Manningham's Middle Temple diary cited at the outset of this chapter, we now have Baker's comprehensive account of *Readers and Readings in the Inns of Court and Chancery*, together with some useful guides to archival material and records.[9] While it takes time for such work to show up in the general literature, the Tudor and Stuart Inns of Court now seem to enjoy a markedly more prominent place in outline surveys and syntheses than once was the case.[10]

It is fair to say that this growth over the past forty years in general and legal-historical treatment of the early modern Inns of Court remains by and large unmatched by a comparable outpouring of scholarship on their artistic, cultural, and literary roles. That judgement may possibly reflect my disciplinary blinkers and consequent ignorance of work in other fields. But literary scholars at least, much quicker off the mark in this respect than their historian colleagues, long ago recognised the salience of the Inns and their members in what can be broadly termed the Elizabethan Renaissance and its early Stuart sequel or continuation. Hence the substantial sections in Bland's 1965 *Bibliography* on 'Drama' and 'Literature', listing the work of, among others, F. S. Boas, Muriel Bradbrook, L. B. Campbell, E. K. Chambers, A. W. Green, Alfred Harbage, Lesley Hotson, E. M. W. Tillyard, Enid Welsford, and Frances Yates, not to mention G. M. Young, R. J. Schoeck, and Bland himself. Of course since 1965 there have been some important studies of individual authors, literary communities, and genres associated with the early modern Inns of Court, together with work which explores the specific contribution of an Inns of Court context to the distinctive characteristics of individual texts and other cultural artefacts.[11] But this body of writing on cultural, literary, and intellectual aspects of the early modern Inns of Court, because it built on already substantial foundations, could hardly represent such a fundamental change in knowledge and understanding as has occurred with respect to their legal, and general, or social history.

Legal, social, cultural and literary historians concerned with the early modern Inns of Court make use of each other's work in various ways, while remaining committed to distinctively different assumptions, priorities, questions, and methodologies. Legal historians have been primarily concerned with the Inns' contribution to legal doctrine and learning, to legal education, and to the legal profession. While political and social historians may share some of these interests, they tend to focus on other issues, such as the extent to which the Inns inculcated a distinctive political outlook, or functioned as channels of upward social mobility. Again, those who look at the Inns as sites of cultural and literary production usually rely on other accounts of the composition and structure of those societies, as a means to their end of better interpreting the associated texts. Such division of labour, while in some ways regrettable, may well be inevitable. The early modern Inns of Court were themselves heterogeneous, loose-knit institutions, liminal even in their topographical and social location between City, suburbs, West End, and country-side. Incorporating aspects of humanistic academy, boarding or fraternity house, casino, gentleman's club, university college, law school, professional office, theatre, and guild or trade union, they have – unsurprisingly – attracted the attention of a correspondingly diverse range of scholars.

In 1972, after expressing some disdain for the 'antiquaries and domestic chroni-clers' who then dominated the historiography of the Inns of Court, I announced my own rescue operation, which sought to relate developments within the walls of the late Tudor and early Stuart Inns to the wider world outside.[12] Yet historians of all people should know that yesterday's *nouvelle vague* is tomorrow's old hat. Within twenty years of that book's publication the legal scholar Peter Goodrich was calling for a history of the common law 'that exceeds the merely antiquarian', and 'a social history of ... England's self-appointed third university, the Inns of Court'.[13] By now the linguistic, narrative, and post-structural turns were upon us. Thus when Goodrich wrote of 'social history', he plainly envisaged something rather different from what I had attempted. So his 1991 article 'Eating law: commons, common land, common law' asserted – via a process of hermeneutic textual analysis – that it was 'through dining' that early modern Inns of Court 'students trained in the Law', and 'through feasting that each further qualification in law is ceremonially inscribed upon the body of the Law, into its physical presence and community'.[14] This somewhat startling conclusion was built upon an impressively exotic range of reference, from Dionysius and Exodus, via the Venerable Bede and an assortment of sixteenth- and seventeenth-century texts, to Freud, Merleau-Ponty, Foucault, Bataille, and Derrida, not to forget 'the eminent Russian geographer Woeikof', and Australia's own Michael Symons (disguised as one 'M. Symmons') writing in *Meanjin* on 'A Gastronomic Interpretation of Christianity'. The author's allusive prose and exclusive focus on printed sources further emphasised his distance from the conventional norms of historical scholarship. A comparable vision and method-ology inform the more recent book-length study by Paul Raffield.[15]

Exploring the cultural life of the Inns of Court in its relations to the role and image of law in early modern England is a wholly admirable objective. But shall we best pursue this desirable goal by depending upon twentieth-century theory and the interrogation of a limited range of printed materials? Exposition and selective inter-pretation supported by assertion, analogy, and the invocation of authority, rather than a survey of the widest possible range of relevant evidence, recasts history as an imaginative literary art, 'about anticipating the past rather than fondly imagining we can reconstruct it', to quote another contemporary theorist.[16] Yet most histor-ical writing in the Rankean (our normal science) tradition can reasonably aspire to add at least some increment of factual information to the common store and on-going dialogue. Whether recently fashionable alternative modes of approaching or apprehending the past are capable of this limited achievement seems to me doubtful at best.

Nevertheless, to paraphrase Hugh Trevor-Roper, in so far as it succeeds in furthering debate and enquiry, fertile error may indeed be preferable to sterile accuracy, or orthodoxy.[17] Goodrich's 1991 focus on what he then termed, following Mikkel Borch-Jacobson, 'the homosociality of eating rites at the inns of court', did highlight a lack of attention by historians to the everyday 'details of life, rites and exercises at the inns'.[18] While Goodrich's claim that a hermetic, hierarchical, and misogynistic communal-professional ethos was formed 'through and across rites of eating' seems extravagant, the consumption of food and drink at the early modern Inns of Court is surely no less worthy of examination than the construction of legal argument there. Unfortunately, the cultural and social, or 'non-metabolic aspects of food' (as distinct from its biological, economic, and material manifestations) have until recently attracted little attention from historians, as distinct from anthropologists and other social scientists, although there are now some heartening signs of more receptive academic attitudes.[19]

The alimentary hypothesis

My concern for the rest of this chapter is not, however, with the Inns' commons or everyday meals, but rather the entertainment provided at the twice-yearly 'readings' (or lectures), the most elaborate, prestigious, and prolonged form of 'learning exercise'.[20] These last developed (probably as conscious imitations of the medieval universities' declamations, disputations, and lectures) to instruct would-be pleaders at the bar in the form and content of legal argument. But during the mid to later seventeenth century, the whole complex formal structure of aural learning and teaching faltered and collapsed. Readings at the Inns of Court ceased in the late 1670s. By the early 1700s, the lesser moots and other case-argument exercises, where they were still performed, had become largely meaningless and educationally worthless rituals, revenue raisers for the Inns rather than instructional resources for their students.

Historians have naturally sought to explain the causes of this momentous development. No shortage of possibilities present themselves, from the proliferation of printed law books, compilations and treatises, through an Elizabethan-early Stuart litigation boom with its accompanying pressures on both learners and teachers, to changes in legal procedure which placed ever more emphasis on written as distinct from oral argument. But recently a consensus has emerged that the critical precipitant of the final cessation of readings at the Inns of Court was none other than a mounting burden of conspicuous gastronomic consumption. Thus, Baker writes:

The expense which led readers to curtail their performance was incurred in the increasingly elaborate provision of food and wine which the audience expected for the duration [of the reading]. It is a strange reason for the collapse of a prominent university, but the fact seems to be that the alimentary aspects of the readings came to outbalance the educational, and the former proved too costly for individuals to undertake with equanimity.[21]

In his important study of the Inns of Court and the bar during the later seventeenth and early eighteenth centuries, David Lemmings similarly proposed that 'ruinously expensive reading feasts' were a major reason why readings ended in the 1670s.[22] These views echo Holdsworth's brief account of Sir Francis North's extravagant reading at the Middle Temple in 1671, which concludes with the suggestion that the prospect of incurring 'such enormous expense would make most persons far prefer to pay a moderate fine' instead of reading.[23] Since Holdsworth wrote, legal education at the medieval and early modern Inns of Court and Chancery has been intensively studied – but not so the hospitality dispensed by readers. Eric Ives has noted that in the later fifteenth century, a 'reading was also a festive occasion, an opportunity for "wining and dining the right people" … The reader's dinner was an elaborate affair, and he often entertained outsiders as well as members and former members.'[24] But unfortunately Ives did not pursue his own suggestion that the hospitality which readers dispensed had cultural and social functions as well as financial and gastronomic significance.

Besides some possible sense that the topic was unworthy of serious attention, historians may well have been deterred by evidential complexities and difficulties. The records of the early modern Inns contain frequent references to attempts to regulate the hospitality dispensed by readers. They also regularly list the names of barristers and students appointed as stewards of the readers' dinners, suppers, and drinkings, whose role seems to have been both to organise and subsidise the entertainment provided. Surviving financial accounts also occasionally cast light on catering arrangements at readings. But the cryptic and formal nature of all these records often obscures their meaning. Other miscellaneous references are scattered through a wide variety of sources external to the Inns. Fragmentary and random in occurrence though they may be, such material can usefully supplement, indeed flesh out, the often bare, formal, and stylised entries in the records of the Inns themselves. A third class of evidence, hitherto largely unexploited, was created by or on behalf of the readers themselves. Such documents vary enormously in form and scope. But sufficient survives to permit at least a partial reconstruction for comparative purposes of the nature and costs of hospitality provided at five individual Inns of Court readings between the 1590s and the 1670s. Four of these readings were delivered at the Middle Temple, by Henry Haule in 1595, Francis Moore in 1607, James Whitelocke in 1619,[25] and Francis Bramston in 1668; the other items relate to Henry Sherfield's Lincoln's Inn reading of 1624.

While historians have emphasised the growing financial burdens borne by readers, the main common element found in all these latter sources is not an itemised expenditure account, but detailed enumerations of gifts in cash and kind made to readers to defray their costs and assist their hospitality. In other words, the readers themselves were evidently less interested in recording their financial outlays than the various kinds of tangible support provided for them on the occasion of this important professional milestone by friends, neighbours, colleagues, family and relatives, clients, and patrons. Indeed it is only the papers relating to Francis Bramston's Restoration reading, chronologically the last in our series, which provide a detailed record of an individual reader's expenses; and as we shall see, the story they tell does not altogether support the hypothesis of an intolerable and uncontrolled escalation in readers' outlays after 1660.

Readers' gifts and feasts

Let us look first at the four pre-civil war readings, when the system was still in full force. All four readers had relatively modest family backgrounds: the Haules were ancient but minor Kent gentry, Moore and Sherfield came from yeoman farmer stock, while Whitelocke's father was a London merchant whose early death had saddled his widow with responsibility for a large brood of children. On the other hand, Moore and Whitelocke went on to achieve far greater professional eminence – as, respectively, the long-term leading counsellor at the Chancery bar through much of James I's reign, and a puisne justice of the Common Pleas – than did Haule, whose highest office was as retained counsel to the town of Maidstone, or Sherfield, who despite holding the prestigious recorderships of Salisbury and Southampton, died bankrupt after his prosecution before Star Chamber in a *cause célèbre* of the early 1630s.[26]

These career differences may well be reflected in the nature of the various gifts which the different readers received.[27] Thus in 1623 Sherfield collected the smallest total amount of cash (at £33 7s. 0d. less than half what James Whitelocke had received four years before); moreover his takings came in generally smaller dribs and drabs, with nothing like the large lump sums that Whitelocke was presented with by the Bishop of Durham (£22), Merton College, Oxford (£11), and Eton College (£10). Sugar loaves feature prominently among Sherfield's receipts. Unfortunately he provided no valuations for these or any other gifts in kind which he received, but Whitelocke (who did) put a standard one-mark (13s. 4d., two-thirds of a pound) price on each of the fourteen loaves he was given. (Sugar remained a 'great rarity' in the early seventeenth century; its price does not seem to have fallen much before the 1640s.)[28] Given his office as Recorder of Southampton – a seaport with strong French and Portuguese commercial connections – Sherfield acquired less wine than we might expect, and in general appears to have accumulated a more homely and miscellaneous assortment of foodstuffs than either Moore or Whitelocke.

One striking if possibly accidental omission from both Moore's and Sherfield's lists is venison, the premier high-status feasting fare of medieval and early modern

England. While venison could be lawfully acquired only by or from someone who actually possessed a deer park or otherwise enjoying hunting privileges, a 'well-organized, although illegal market for venison and game was taking shape by about 1600'.[29] Yet most of the venison consumed during Inns of Court readings before the civil wars may well have been lawfully obtained. Readers enjoyed a cash allowance from their Inn to pay the fees, gratuities, or rewards given to the gamekeepers and other persons who brought in gifts of venison. In 1513, the rulers of the Middle Temple, concerned that readers were receiving too many bucks and overburdening the house with the resultant fees, prescribed that henceforth only twelve deer would be accepted at the charge of the house, with the cost of payments for any additional venison to be borne by the reader himself. The limit was raised to fifteen animals in 1556 and was doubled to thirty in 1570.[30] But in the mid-1590s, Haule appears to have accepted nearly sixty bucks, mostly from colleagues and country neighbours, paying the messenger or porter who brought the meat a standard fee of ten shillings in all but four cases (it is unclear how much if any of this expenditure he was able to claim back from the house).[31] A quarter-century later, the tally of eighty-three bucks sent to Whitelocke's reading suggests that he personally paid all the rewards, which totalled over £40. In 1614, the standard allowance for Gray's Inn readers seems to have been rewards for thirty bucks and two stags, together with thirty bushels of flour and no less than thirty pounds of pepper, which would doubtless have produced a large quantity of spicy venison pasties. This may however represent a scaling back of the house contribution, since in 1584 the allowance was for 'xx brace of bucks and a lease of stags'.[32]

Two other features of these gift lists deserve comment. First, the donors were a very mixed group of kinsfolk, neighbours, clients, and colleagues. Their gifts plainly functioned to cement reciprocal ties of friendship and obligation, bonds which might well extend beyond the nominal donor and recipient, as shown by an undated note from Henry Dacre to his relative Sir Nicholas Carew, of Beddington, Surrey:

> My good cosin yt falleth out thys yeare yt both ye readers of ye Temples are my countryemen & good kynd neyghbours, unto whom as ye manner ys I have promised some buckes, & yf I might be behoulding unto yow for one, yow should doe me a verye great favour, & yf yow should please at anye tyme to comand the lyke or a far greater curtesye at my handes I shall take yt for an argument of your loue towards me[33]

Second, despite the overwhelming maleness of the exchange networks to which the gift lists bear witness, women are not wholly absent from the lists of donors, except at Sherfield's reading. Thus Moore records receiving a turkey from 'Mris Grunter', and 'a fatt shepe and a fat lamb' from 'my sister Apleton', while Whitelocke had a sugar loaf from 'Mrs Jenkinson', '6 capons, 12 partriches, 12 quayles, 5 trouts' from 'the Lady More' and £5 in cash from his mother-in-law. Coupled with the wide geographical and social range of the donors, this evidence of female participation in the readers' hospitality networks suggests that the 'homosociality' of the Inns of Court was less than total.[34]

Finally, no gifts were identified by their recipient as specifically intended for his dinner, or feast, rather than as contributions to the general hospitality provided during the reading. Indeed, what the Inner Temple's rulers characterised in 1661 as 'great and excessive cost and charges in undue feasting and entertainments' seems not to have been due primarily to a spirit of competitive emulation centred around the Grand Day dinner, usually held on the last Wednesday or Thursday of the reading, when readers entertained their most aristocratic and influential guests. Robert Brerewood's manuscript account of the Middle Temple in the 1630s insists that although this event was commonly known as the reader's dinner or feast, that terminology was misleading, since the bill was not picked up by the reader, but by the four junior members appointed as stewards of the reader's dinner.[35] Moore may have been an exception; his own summary account of his reading indicates that although his four stewards 'paid £8 contribution … I performed the feast at myne owne costes'.[36] But then Moore was a very wealthy man, and his explicit mention of taking personal financial responsibility for his feast suggests that this was not yet the accepted or customary practice.

From 1660, when readings resumed following a break of nearly twenty years, readers may possibly have assumed more responsibility for the expenses of their feast, since it evidently became usual for those appointed as stewards of the reader's dinner to pay a fee to compound for the office (although the Inns possibly passed on that money to the reader). Nevertheless, it must be emphasised that the mounting costs of staging a reading were not attributable to a single event known as the 'reader's dinner' or 'feast', but rather reflected rising expectations and demands on all the reader's hospitality throughout the entire course of his reading, and sometimes preceding its formal commencement. This is clearly shown by the judges' orders of 1627, which sought to restrict to three per week the additional courses (known as 'exceedings') served at the reader's expense to the Inns' entire membership assembled in their respective halls, as also to limit the numbers of servants in attendance on readers to a maximum of ten. The same themes recur in the final set of orders agreed on by the rulers of the Inns fifty years later, in their last efforts to prevent the collapse of the readings. By now, however, claims on the reader's hospitality had become in effect boundless: hence the prohibition on providing more than two liveries for attendants, offering any entertainment or exceedings before readings began (other than biscuits and wine before church on the immediately preceding Sunday), having more than two Grand Days (or feasts) during the course of their reading (now limited to a week), serving more than two courses during those Grand Days, entertaining anyone other than members of the Inn in hall on the other three days, providing breakfasts or suppers, bringing wine in bottles into the hall, and serving wine after their own table had risen from dinner.[37]

These last-ditch regulations date from 1678, ten years after Francis Bramston's Middle Temple reading, for which a uniquely detailed set of accounts survives. Seemingly compiled by Bramston's clerk, this enumeration of expenditure and receipts includes summary statements and a few original bills for comestibles and utensils supplied by numerous tradesmen – including a grocer, butcher, cheese-monger, oilman (who dealt in olives, capers, vinegar, salt, and anchovies as well as 'best oyll'), confectioner, fishmonger, poulterer, potter (who provided pans, pitchers, and dishes, as well as pots and porringers), fruiterer, and herbwoman, together with a note of the wages paid to the cooks and their assistants who actually prepared the meals. These are in addition to 'an account of what came from your chamber', which seems to complement if unfortunately not duplicate a further list (in another hand) of the donors of gifts of food (predominantly venison) received on Bramston's behalf. There are also bills of fare for each day of the reading, running from Sunday 2 to Monday 10 August, and another list – also unique – of 'Presents sent forth'.[38]

Following an unpropitious start – he was called to the bar in June 1642, on the very eve of civil war – Francis Bramston (*bap.*1619, *d.*1683), the younger son of a chief justice of the King's Bench, had risen rapidly in his profession from 1660 onwards. His ample resources are reflected in the munificence of the daily bills of fare provided to his table throughout his reading. For the first day's dinner on Sunday 2 August, two courses were provided to three messes of diners (probably twelve persons in all, mostly members of the Inn's ruling Parliament). The first course included the following: 'A dishe of pigeons Boyld venison Grand Sallett Rost Chines of veale and mutton Bakt venison Roste Venison Battalia pye Oranges and Lemans Butterd Samon Stewed Carpes Rost Turkeys A Made dish Fresh samon quince pye Westphalia bacon Cold bakt meate Rost Capons Hansh of Veale Neates tongue & udder A custard'. The second course consisted of 'Boyld pyke Rost partridges Gellys of sortes Harterchoke pye Fryd soules Rost Chickens Orangadoe pye Dryd Tongues Sturgeon Rost pewits Tartes of Sortes Anchoveys & Botargoe Cold Neates tongue pye Fruites of sorts Marchpanes'. The gentlemen waiters who had the honourable task of serving this remarkable banquet doubt-less fully deserved their 'Boyled pidgeons Rost beefe venison pasty Fresh samon Made dish Rost Capon [and] Custard', while 'Venison pastys' and 'Rabbetts' were provided as 'Exceedings for the hall' – that is, additional courses for those not sitting at the bench table. And so it continued, with little apparent variation, for the next eight days: a menu dominated by huge quantities of largely non-butchers' meat, always including venison, together with various other kinds of game, seafood, the occasional 'made dish' or stew, meat, bird or fish pies, and a 'grand sallet'. The bill of fare for the reader's feast on Thursday 6 August is distinguished from the rest only by an additional list of dishes 'for ye Lords gentlemen' (presumably those who waited on the numerous peers who attended as Bramston's guests), and a 'Bankett' of various sweetmeats, puddings, and fruit offered as an additional course, which included 'A Rocke of Candyes', assorted 'Gellys', 'Creame Tarte Blamage Oranges & Lemans A mount of fruite Creame in Cullers A dish of fruite Fresh Cheeses & Creame A Rocke of snow sweet Baktmeate Marchpane'.

Stephen Mennell has observed that 'the sheer volume and indeed waste of food' provided at medieval feasts was 'inherent in and necessary to' their social function. In the seventeenth century, courtly banquets 'remained occasions for fairly unsophisticated quantitative display and for prodigious feats of meat-eating':

> The flocks of sheep, herds of cattle, gaggles of geese, shoals of fish and schools of porpoise mustered for the occasion bore only a remote and incidental relation to the nutritional requirements and capacities of the principal guests. Rather it was almost the other way round: the number of mouths would be in a sense determined by the quantity of food it was deemed necessary to distribute.[39]

Bramston exploited still further opportunities to demonstrate his capacity for conspicuous consumption and munificent hospitality by sending out presents of venison, in the form of sides, haunches, and pasties, both great and small, to a diverse group of recipients. Those so favoured included family members (Lady Bramston, Sir Mundiford Bramston, and a person identified only as 'Mr yor Kinsman'), great men and women (including the Countess of Nottingham and the speaker of the House of Commons), legal colleagues and neighbours (Mr Arthur Turner, Dr Ball, Master of the Temple Church, and Mr Bucke, the aptly named under-treasurer of the Middle Temple), dependants, and servants ('yeoman of the wineseller', 'Mr Pettit yor man', and 'Mary', who received respectively a side of venison, a hanch of venison, and '1 small pasty').

So Francis Bramston's 1668 reading might well seem to epitomise the almost obscenely prodigal extravagance which characterised and supposedly accelerated the last declining phase of the old aural exercise system at the Inns of Court. An entry in John Evelyn's diary for 3 August 1668 records that: 'Mr Bramstone ... now Reader at the Middle Temple invited me to his feast which was very extravagant & greate as the like had not been seene at any time: Here were the Duke of Ormonde; [Lord] Privy-seale; [Earl of] Bedford, [Lord] Belasis, [Viscount] Halifax & a world more of Earles and Lordes.' 'The expense necessary to satisfy the appetite of these grandees', comments Lemmings, 'was clearly a great burden to many of the readers.'[40]

As a long-standing member of the Middle Temple, Evelyn was possibly better placed than most to compare Bramston's hospitality with that of his predecessors. Yet Sir John was also something of a prig, whose judgement may have been warped by strong disapproval of the various forms of excess he associated with the returned Cavaliers. For the expenditure recorded in the detailed accounts of Bramston's reading appears to amount to some £332. This was unquestionably a huge sum of money, especially since it includes no allowance for wine, and given that Bramston's reading only lasted for just over a week. But when Bramston's costs in 1668 are compared with those of Whitelocke, who in 1619 read for the first two weeks in August, the difference is not so great. Whitelocke's own summary account shows that he personally laid out some £183 on 'cates' (i.e. provisions or supplies). But then he received numerous gifts, amounting by his own estimate to the sum of £130 in cash and kind. And if Whitelocke's spending on wine was any guide, Bramston's outgoings under this head would not have added very much to his final bill, since for just over £11 Whitelocke could purchase a hogshead of claret, an eighteen gallon runlet of sack, seventeen gallons of canary, and a gallon of Rhenish wine.[41]

The value of the gifts of provisions received by Bramston is difficult to calculate. However, it seems likely that he was less favoured in this respect than Whitelocke, acquiring on the most conservative reading only fifty-three bucks from thirty-eight donors, as against the eighty-three bucks, one stag, and a side of venison which Whitelocke accumulated from a total of seventy-six benefactors. In the final analysis, Whitelocke calculated his net reading expenditure (that is, after subtracting all gifts received) at just over £239. As we have already seen, the accounts submitted and paid on Bramston's behalf fifty years later totalled £332. But we do not know how far these payments were offset by gifts of cash, or indeed provisions. From the viewpoint of the house and future readers (as distinct from his own pocket), Bramston's spending had clearly exceeded the upper limit of £300 imposed by the judges in 1664,[42] but perhaps not by an insupportable or outrageous margin. And if Brerewood's testimony from the 1630s is to be trusted, that limit was unrealistically low, since he claimed then that 'some have spent above six hundred pounds in … the usual time of Reading'.[43] Of course Brerewood may have exaggerated the profligacy of his professional colleagues. Further, comparisons between outlays on hospitality in the 1630s and the 1660s can be valid only if they take account of trends both in prices and barristers' earnings. While food prices fluctuated markedly from year to year, and the inflationary pressures of the early seventeenth century had eased somewhat by the later 1660s, the fee income of successful barristers seems to have risen substantially from the 1650s onwards. Indeed, even if Bramston's net expenditure on food and drink had actually amounted to double what Whitelocke paid out – which on the evidence surveyed above seems highly unlikely – it is probable that his personal earning capacity had grown by no less a proportion.[44]

The detailed documentation of entertainment expenses at the readings of Bramston and Whitelocke is highly unusual in itself. Nor have we any way of knowing whether the cost and scale of hospitality which that evidence reveals was itself at all representative of other readings from the same period. What can be said with some confidence is that organising the provision, cooking, and service of food and drink during a reading was no small undertaking. It is not even clear how far readers could rely on their Inn and its domestic staff for basic necessities like crockery and linen: in August 1595, Henry Haule had to spend more than £16 on laundry and hiring linen and plate 'all the readinge', with another £2 to the pewterer, 'for lones and losse'.[45] But while such requirements were presumably readily available in London, securing adequate supplies of appropriate foodstuffs might be another matter. A couple of letters sent to the reader-elect Henry Sherfield at Lincoln's Inn during January 1624 by the attorney Ambrose Prewett, his nephew and general agent in Salisbury, provide a graphic glimpse of the difficulties which could arise.

Prewett began by seeking clarification of numbers and dates:

> But towchinge yor direccons for my Journey into the Isle of Wight, had I not therein
> conceyved some doubte towchinge even the mayne pointe of yor L[ette]re, I shold
> before this tyme have bine takeing my Journey thither. W[hi]ch doubt is this.
>
> After yo[u]r declaracon of the quantity of Lobsters w[hi]ch yow desire to have against
> the last daye of the Terme w[hi]ch yow mencon to be one hundred you saye
>
> And in the Reading tyme I would have 66 lobsters or 70 for wednesday dynner and
> Fryday dinner the first weeke, and the like for mondaye and wednesdaye of the second
> weeke.
>
> Now whether yor desire and meaninge is to have 66 or 70 for wednesday and soe
> many more for fridaye of the first weeke and soe for mondaye and wednesdaye of the
> second weeke, or whether to have onely 66 or 70 for twoe dynners I desire certenley
> to understand from yow.
>
> Neither doe yow mencon in yo[u]r l[ette]res nor is it knowne to me the certen daye
> when yo[u]r Readinge doth begynne[46]

No doubt Prewett's uncle was able to sort out these issues of numbers and timing,
and perhaps he was not excessively depressed by his nephew's gloomy news that
local suppliers of partridges, quails, and ducks 'cannot assure me of any at all'. In
response to Sherfield, Prewett began his second letter ten days later, on 17 January,
by explaining that he has just returned from the Isle of Wight, 'allthough I was
enformed at Southampton by the waye that noe good was to be done there at this
season'.[47] Nevertheless, being a determined person, 'for better satisfaction I repayred
my selfe to divers places in the Island', only to discover that 'theire tyme and season
for taking of Lobsters comes not in till June or afterwards ... till thend of May there
are none to be had in any of those partes upon any termes'.

Having drawn a blank with Isle of Wight lobsters, the enterprising Prewett turned
his attention to other seafood options:

> I have therefore since my Retorne from thence made further enquiry of others which
> travell for transportinge of fishe from the Isle of Purbecke and other coasts neere
> Exeter.
>
> Where as I understand If the season for greate extreme Frosts hinder not, stoare may
> be had at r[eas]onable rates. But to knowe certenley the Rates or the precise size of
> the Fishes It beinge casuall as the tymes and the manner of takeinge maye fall out Is
> that which I cannot be resolved of.

Fortunately, Ambrose did find someone who might be able to help: 'one Covert
whoe is nowe an Innkeeper at the Signe of the Lambe in Salisbury who hath himself
heretofore bine only a Driver and transporter of fishe from those westerne partes
but nowe keepeth servantes and horses for that purpose'. Mr Covert, 'understanding
the provision to be for yow', was very willing to assist 'at as lowe rates as possibly he
Canne', and indeed ready to venture to the Isle of Purbecke, having been acquainted
with the numbers of lobster, mullet, and plaice Sherfield required. This seemed
to Ambrose far better than going himself, since 'I have seene by conference with
fishermen in the Isle of Wight ... they are most uncerten in the[i]r dealinges with

those which are not familiarly acquainted with their employment'. Meanwhile he had also sent:

> A message into Gloucestershire to severne there for Salmons if any shall be seasonable besides which partes there are none to be had for this tyme that I canne by any meanes learne of.

> I have made the best enquiry and meanes I could for Partridges & Quayles but cannot be yett certen of what quantityes I shalbe provided but they are very scarce in this Country and I feare the rates wilbe very highe.

Well might his master endorse this missive: 'Noe Lobsters to be had in the Isle of Wight at this Season'.

Last course

What created a financial burden for Inns of Court readers in the sixteenth and seventeenth centuries was almost certainly not a single massive binge in the form of the reader's feast or Grand Day, but rather the costs of hospitality extended throughout the whole course of a reading, especially the provision of exceedings to supplement ordinary commons. Nor can the eventual cessation of readers' feasts and readings themselves in the later seventeenth century be regarded as the culmination of a self-destructive potlatch gift-cycle, in which the pressure of ever-rising expectations eventually persuaded potential readers to opt out of the game rather than risk financial ruin. In fact complaints about 'excessive' hospitality at readings go back to the early sixteenth century,[48] while under Elizabeth and the early Stuarts inability or unwillingness to bear the costs of reading was often cited as the reason for barristers either refusing nomination or being passed over in the choice of readers. It is hard to see why the financial pressures should suddenly have become absolutely unbearable in the 1670s, especially when Bramston's list of presents sent forth shows him employing a hitherto unrecorded and possibly novel means of extending his hospitality beyond the walls of the Middle Temple, even on the verge of the system's final collapse. Moreover, it is clear from Bramston's papers that after 1660 the logistical effort of getting in food and drink for a reading had been considerably eased by the catering services available in London from various merchants and tradesmen.

Perhaps the real problem was not so much rising costs as the decreasing benefits of reading hospitality. The care with which readers tallied up the gifts of cash, drink, and foodstuffs received from kinsfolk, fellow-practitioners, neighbours, and clients suggests that they fully recognised the reciprocal, symbolic, and more than merely market-driven character of the hospitality they provided. If the number and value of incoming gifts to readers did indeed tend to decline between the early and later seventeenth century, we may infer not only the advance and thickening of a commercial economy, but some diminution in the cultural and social value accorded to the forms of hospitality which readers had traditionally extended.[49]

Finally, the moribund state of academic learning exercises (lectures and disputations) at eighteenth-century Oxford and Cambridge argues against any implicit inference that legal education by learning exercise at the Inns of Court might have continued to 1700 and beyond if only potential readers had not been deterred by the cost and scale of the hospitality they felt obliged to provide.[50] Indeed the demise of the learning exercises is a classically over-determined event. Ever-growing accessibility and variety of printed law books, diminishing professional benefits of call to the bench (for which reading was the traditional qualification), the disruptions of the civil wars and Interregnum (meaning that few barristers had an interest in preserving a system which they had not experienced as students, while those due to read in order of seniority were much further advanced along their careers), and the ever-present temptation for the unendowed and unincorporated Inns to commute academic obligations into cash fines: given this formidable assemblage of disincentives, prospective high-cost hospitality at readings seems a relatively marginal issue, especially given the rising professional incomes of later Stuart barristers. So I am driven to conclude that the alimentary hypothesis for the collapse of the learning exercise system is little more than a red herring.

Notes

1 *The Diary of John Manningham of the Middle Temple 1602–1603*, ed. Robert Parker Sorlien (Hanover, NH: The University Press of New England, 1976), p. 194.

2 John H. Baker, *Readers and Readings in the Inns of Court and Chancery* (London: Selden Society, 2000), p. 7.

3 *A Bibliography of the Inns of Court and Chancery*, comp. Desmond S. Bland (London: Selden Society, 1965). While my criticisms (*Law Quarterly Review*, 84 (1968), 142–3) still seem largely justified, I regret the acerbity of that review.

4 Eric W. Ives, 'Some aspects of the legal profession in the late fifteenth and early sixteenth centuries' (PhD dissertation, University of London, 1955); William S. Holdsworth, *A History of English Law*, 12 vols (London, Methuen, 1903–52), IV, VI.

5 Walter Cecil Richardson, *A History of the Inns of Court: With Special Reference to the Period of the Renaissance* (Baton Rouge, LA: Claitor's Publishing Divison, 1978); Wilfrid R. Prest, *The Inns of Court under Elizabeth I and the Early Stuarts, 1590–1640* (London: Longman, 1972); Thomas W. Evans, 'Study at the Restoration Inns of Court', in Jonathan A. Bush and Alain Wijffels (eds), *Learning the Law: Teaching and Transmission of English Law, 1150–1900* (London: Hambledon Press, 1999), pp. 287–302; David Frederick Lemmings, *Gentlemen and Barristers: The Inns of Court and the English Bar 1680–1730* (Oxford: Clarendon Press, 1990). The earlier sixteenth century and the mid-seventeenth century are major remaining gaps.

6 cf. John H. Baker, *The Common Law Tradition: Lawyers, Books and the Law* (London: Hambledon Press, 2000), p. 3; John H. Baker, *The Order of Serjeants at Law: A Chronicle of Creations with Related Texts* (London: Selden Society, 1984); and Christopher W. Brooks, *Pettyfoggers and Vipers of the Commonwealth: The 'Lower Branch' of the Legal Profession in Early Modern England* (Cambridge: Cambridge University Press, 1986). See also Chapter 1, pp. 8–24, above.

7 Only a selection of such material can be cited: but see R. M. Fisher, 'The reformation of church and chapel at the Inns of Court, 1530–1580', *Guildhall Studies in London History*, 3 (1979), 223–47 (and numerous other articles by the same author, derived from his 'The Inns of Court and the Reformation' PhD dissertation, University of Cambridge, 1974); Jason T. Pacey, 'Led by the hand: manucaptors and patronage at Lincoln's Inn in the seventeenth century', *Legal History*, 18 (1997), 26–44; Louis A. Knafla, 'The law studies of an Elizabethan student', *Huntington Library Quarterly*, 32 (1969), 221–40; Louis A. Knafla, 'The matriculation revolution and education at the Inns of Court in Renaissance England', in Arthur J. Slavin (ed.), *Tudor Men and Institutions* (Baton Rouge, LA: Louisiana State University Press, 1972), pp. 232–64; Margaret McGlynn, *The Royal Prerogative and the Learning of the Inns of Court* (Cambridge: Cambridge University Press, 2003); Michael C. Mirow, 'Bastardy and the statute of wills: interpreting a sixteenth-century statute with cases and readings', *Mississippi Law Journal*, 69 (1999), 345–71; Richard J. Ross, 'The memorial culture of early modern English lawyers: memory as keyword, shelter, and identity, 1560–1640', *Yale Journal of Law and the Humanities*, 10 (1998), 229–326; Terence K. Shaller, 'English law and the Renaissance: the common law and humanism in the sixteenth century' (PhD dissertation, Harvard University, 1979).

8 Allen D. Boyer, *Sir Edward Coke and the Elizabethan Age* (Stanford, CA: University of California Press, 2003); Michael A. R. Graves, *Thomas Norton: The Parliament Man* (Oxford: Blackwell, 1994); Paul E. Kopperman, *Sir Robert Heath 1574–1649: Window on an Age* (London: Royal Historical Society, 1989); Vivienne M. Larminie, *Wealth, Kinship and Culture: The Seventeenth-Century Newdigates of Arbury and their World* (Woodbridge: Boydell Press, 1995); Hans Scott Pawlisch, *Sir John Davies and the Conquest of Ireland* (Cambridge: Cambridge University Press, 1985); Damian X. Powell, *Sir James Whitelocke's Liber Famelicus, 1570–1632: Law and Politics in Early Stuart England* (Bern; New York, NY: Peter Lang, 2000); Ruth Spalding, *The Improbable Puritan: A Life of Bulstrode Whitelocke 1605–1675* (London: Faber, 1975); *Notes of Me: The Autobiography of Roger North*, ed. Peter Millard (Toronto; London: University of Toronto Press, 2000); Baird Whitlock, *John Hoskyns Serjeant-at-Law* (Washington DC: University Presses of America, 1982).

9 Clare M. Rider, 'The Inns of Court and the Inns of Chancery and their records', *Archives*, 24 (Oct. 1999), 27–36; Guy Holborn, *Sources of Biographical Information on Past Lawyers* (Warwick: British and Irish Association of Law Librarians, 1999).

10 cf. James A. Sharpe, *Early Modern England: A Social History 1550–1760* (London: Edward Arnold, 1987); Malcolm Smuts, *Culture and Power in England 1585–1685* (Basingstoke: Macmillan, 1999); and Geoffrey Holmes, *August in England: Professions, State and Society 1680–1730* (London: Allen and Unwin, 1982).

11 For example, Marie Axton, *The Queen's Two Bodies: Drama and the Elizabethan Succession* (London: Royal Historical Society, 1977); William R. Elton, *Shakespeare's Troilus and Cressida and the Inns of Court Revels* (Aldershot: Ashgate, 1999); Philip J. Finkelpearl, *John Marston of the Middle Temple: An Elizabethan Dramatist in his Social Setting* (Cambridge, MA: Harvard University Press, 1969); Michelle O'Callaghan, 'Literary commonwealths: a 1614 print community, *The Shepheards Pipe* and *The Shepherds Hunting*', *The Seventeenth Century*, 13 (1998), 103–23; Patrizia Grimaldi Pizzorno, *The Ways of Paradox from Lando to Donne* (Florence: L. S. Olschki, 2007); Robert W. Wienpahl, *Music at the Inns of Court during the Reigns of Elizabeth, James and Charles* (Ann Arbor, MI: University Microfilms

International for the Department of Music, California State University, Northridge, 1979); Jessica Winston, 'Expanding the political nation: *Gorboduc* at the Inns of Court and succession revisited', *Early Theatre*, 8 (2005), 11–34.

12 Prest, *The Inns of Court under Elizabeth I and the Early Stuarts, 1590–1640*, p. vii.

13 Peter Goodrich, *Languages of Law: From Logics of Memory to Nomadic Masks* (London: Weidenfeld & Nicolson, 1990), p. 52, and review of Wilfrid R. Prest, *The Rise of the Barristers: A Social History of the English Bar, 1590–1640* (Oxford: Clarendon Press, 1986), in *Social and Legal Studies*, 1 (1992), 427.

14 Peter Goodrich, 'Eating law: commons, common land, common law', *Journal of Legal History*, 12 (1991), 246–67.

15 Paul Raffield, *Images and Cultures of Law in Early Modern England: Justice and Political Power, 1558–1660* (Cambridge: Cambridge University Press, 2004).

16 Alun Munslow, 'History and biography: an editorial comment', *Rethinking History*, 7:1 (2003), 1–11 (6).

17 'In humane studies there are times when a new error is more life-giving than an old truth, a fertile error than a sterile accuracy' (Hugh R. Trevor-Roper, *History: Professional and Lay* (Oxford: Clarendon Press, 1957), p. 22).

18 Goodrich, 'Eating law: commons, common land, common law', 247; 'Review', 427.

19 Peter Garnsey, *Food and Society in Classical Antiquity* (Cambridge: Cambridge University Press, 1999), p. xi; *Food, Culture and History* (1993–).

20 On the readings, see Prest, *The Inns of Court under Elizabeth I and the Early Stuarts, 1590–1640*, ch. 6, and Chapter 1, pp. 17–20, above.

21 Baker, *Readers and Readings in the Inns of Court and Chancery*, p. 7.

22 Lemmings, *Gentlemen and Barristers*, pp. 83–7.

23 Holdsworth, *History of English Law*, VI, 491–2.

24 Eric W. Ives, *The Common Lawyers of Pre-Reformation England. Thomas Kebell: A Case Study* (Cambridge: Cambridge University Press, 1983), p. 50.

25 On Whitelocke's 1619 reading, see Chapter 4, pp. 81–3, above.

26 Biographical detail from *ODNB* and *Henry Haule's Notebook, 1590–95*, ed. Felix Hull, in *Kent Records*, n. ser., 4 vols (Maidstone: Kent Archaeological Society, 1990–94), I, 1–93 (1–7).

27 As listed in Hampshire Record Office, Winchester (HRO), 44M69 L51/i 'Guiftes from Frendes at my Reading in Lent 1623' (Sherfield); BL, Additional MS 53725, printed as *Liber Famelicus of Sir James Whitelocke, a Judge of the Court of King's Bench in the Reigns of James I and Charles I*, ed. John Bruce (London: Camden Society, 1858), pp. 70–3; CUL, MS Hh.3.2, fols 2–3ᵛ (Moore), printed in Gareth H. Jones, *The History of the Law of Charity, 1532–1827* (Cambridge: Cambridge University Press, 1969), pp. 242–3; *Henry Haule's Notebook, 1590–95*, ed. Hull, pp. 18–19, 39–42.

28 Richard Pares, *Merchants and Planters* (Cambridge: Cambridge University Press, 1960), p. 40; Sidney W. Mintz, *Sweetness and Power: The Place of Sugar in Modern History* (New York, NY: Penguin Books, 1985), pp. 159–60.

29 Roger B. Manning, *Hunters and Poachers: A Social and Cultural History of Unlawful Hunting in England, 1485–1640* (Oxford: Clarendon Press, 1993), p. 11.

30 John Bruce Williamson, *The History of the Temple, London*, 2ⁿᵈ edn (London: Murray, 1925), pp. 131–2.

31 *Henry Haule's Notebook*, ed. Hull, pp. 39–42.

32 *Pension Book of Gray's Inn*, I, 64, 211 (a lease or leash = three). Haule spent £8 on 34 bushels of flour (*Henry Haule's Notebook*, ed. Hull, p. 18). While Lincoln's Inn may have followed a parallel practice, the first explicit mention of rewards occurs in 1670, when Sir John Churchill was granted 'the same allowance for venison as hath formerly been accustomed to have been allowed for other readers' (*Black Books*, III, 70).

33 Berkshire Record Office, Reading, D/ELl c1/97.

34 For evidence of a female gardener employed at Lincoln's Inn, see Chapter 9, p. 183, below.

35 *Inner Temple Records*, III, 61; MTL, Brerewood MS, fol. 21; Jones, *History of the Law of Charity*, p. 241.

36 CUL, MS Hh.3.2, printed in Jones, *History of the Law of Charity*, p. 241.

37 William Dugdale, *Origines Juridiciales or, Historical Memorials of the English Laws* (London: F. & T. Warren, 1666), p. 319; *Black Books*, III, 120.

38 Essex Record Office, Chelmsford, D/DEb 60, unfoliated; begins 'The Rt. Worshipfull Francis Bramston Esquire Reader of the Middle Temple his Accompt beginning ye 2d of August 1668'.

39 Stephen Mennell, *All Manners of Food: Eating and Taste in England and France from the Middle Ages to the Present* (Oxford: Basil Blackwell, 1985), pp. 58–9, 63.

40 Lemmings, *Gentlemen and Barristers*, p. 84, quoting *The Diary of John Evelyn*, ed. E. S. de Beer, 5 vols (Oxford: Clarendon Press, 1955), III, 512. Evelyn characterised the Middle Temple revels in January 1668 as 'an old but riotous Costome, & has relation to neither Virtue nor policy', while he found Sir Henry Peckham's reader's feast the following year 'a pompous Entertainment' (*ibid.*, III, 504, 536–7).

41 *Liber Famelicus*, ed. Bruce, p. 73.

42 *Black Books*, III, 488.

43 MTL, Brerewood MS, fol. 19.

44 On barristers' fees, see Lemmings, *Gentlemen and Barristers*, pp. 151–4.

45 *Henry Haule's Notebook*, ed. Hull, p. 18.

46 HRO, 4459/48/12, 7 Jan. 1624.

47 HRO, 44M69/48/13, 17 Jan. 1624.

48 See Williamson, *The History of the Temple, London*, pp. 131–2.

49 See Anna Bryson, *From Courtesy to Civility: Changing Codes of Conduct in Early Modern England* (Oxford: Clarendon Press, 1998); Felicity Heal, *Hospitality in Early Modern England* (Oxford: Clarendon Press, 1990).

50 See Lucy S. Sutherland, 'The curriculum', in Lucy S. Sutherland and L. G. Mitchell (eds), *The History of the University of Oxford. Vol. V: The Eighteenth Century* (Oxford: Clarendon Press, 1986), pp. 471–6, and Paul Langford, *A Polite and Commercial People: England, 1727–1783* (Oxford: Oxford University Press, 1989), pp. 79–80, 89–90.

Part II

Art, architecture, and gardens

Introduction

The art, architecture, and gardens
of the early modern Inns of Court

Elizabeth Goldring

The visual splendours of legal London and the Inns of Court were much remarked upon by visitors to early modern England. The Netherlandish painter Lucas de Heere, who lived in England in the late 1560s and early 1570s, included drawings of justices of the Queen's Bench in a notebook in which he recorded sights that struck him as both remarkable and distinctively English.[1] (See Plate 1) Thomas Platter, a Swiss medical student who travelled to England in 1599, noted the 'beautiful gardens' of the Inner and Middle Temples and 'the roof ... made of a certain excellent wood' of the hall of 'the court of justice'.[2] Justus Zinzerling, a native of Thuringia who journeyed to London in about 1610, also found the Middle and Inner Temples' 'pretty grounds by the banks of the river Thames' worthy of comment.[3] As late as 1763, the barrister and diarist James Boswell, newly arrived in London from Scotland, echoed such sentiments, praising the Temple complex as 'a pleasant academical retreat', with 'good convenient buildings' and 'handsome walks'.[4] Yet for all the interest that the early modern Inns and their inhabitants aroused in contemporary viewers, the visual culture of these institutions and their members has been largely overlooked by art historians.[5] The chapters in this section of the present volume – by Mark Girouard, Tarnya Cooper, Paula Henderson, and Geoffrey Tyack – begin to redress that balance by opening up for investigation the architecture, art, and gardens of legal London in the sixteenth, seventeenth, and early eighteenth centuries. Examining the Inns' halls in the Elizabethan and Jacobean periods, Girouard identifies many of the artificers who worked on these projects and traces lines of descent from the Inns to early seventeenth-century domestic and collegiate building works. Cooper surveys the visual culture of the Inns *circa* 1600, as well as the painted portraits that judges, barristers, and students at the Inns were beginning to commission of themselves. Henderson charts the evolution of the Inns' gardens over the course of the sixteenth, seventeenth, and early eighteenth centuries, relating developments at each of the Inns to domestic and collegiate gardens of the period, as well as to changes in the wider London landscape. Finally, Tyack explores the rebuilding of the Inns in the late seventeenth and early eighteenth centuries in response to a variety of factors, including commercial pressures and fire. This brief introduction draws out some larger themes that emerge from these chapters and concludes by suggesting ways forward for future research.

The visual aesthetic of the Inns of Court

Is it possible to define a visual aesthetic characteristic of the Inns of Court in the early modern period? Viewed as a whole, the chapters in this section suggest that, though the visual culture of the Inns was innovative in some ways – the decorative detail on the screen installed in Middle Temple Hall in the 1570s was up to the minute, while the portrait of John Donne that hung at Lincoln's Inn in the early seventeenth century was in many respects ahead of its time[6] – overall, the visual culture fostered by the Inns was, rather like the law itself, conservative. (See Plates 2 and 3) The basic layout of the Inns' halls, as Girouard notes, was 'traditional in character'.[7] So, too, as Cooper reveals, were many of the images that adorned the Inns' interiors, such as painted coats of arms and painted cloths.[8] Outside, as Henderson observes, 'sobriety' ruled, for there was less emphasis on architectural and sculptural ornament than in most contemporary gardens.[9] When, in the late seventeenth century, a succession of fires necessitated rebuilding on a large scale, the resulting façades, as Tyack argues, were characterised by 'their air of restraint'.[10]

But perhaps the best overarching description of the Inns' visual aesthetic in this period is 'bookish', for an interest in learnedness – and, perhaps more importantly, in *displaying* that learnedness – permeates numerous aspects of the Inns' (and their individual members') artistic patronage. The screen in Gray's Inn Hall, for example, seems to have drawn inspiration from illustrations in Sebastiano Serlio's *Regole generali d'architettura*, first printed in Venice in 1537; while at Middle Temple, the treatment of the Doric order on the lower storey of the hall screen is indebted to John Shute's illustration of the Roman Doric in his *First and Chief Groundes of Architecture* (London, 1563), the first vernacular treatise on any of the visual arts to have been printed in England.[11] Of course, not all viewers would have made such connections on their own. But someone like Sir Thomas Tresham, a member of the Middle Temple, presumably would have done.[12] Not only did Tresham's private library include copies of both Serlio and Shute, but he himself was a keen architect who undertook numerous building projects in his native Northamptonshire.[13]

The use of architectural pattern-books for decorative inspiration was commonplace in sixteenth-century England. Such visual quotations, as Christy Anderson has noted, served to reinforce 'the sophistication of the patron' in the eyes of viewers with personal knowledge of the source texts or access to 'a knowledgeable guide in the shape of the owner' (or, in an institutional context like the Inns, a knowledgeable dining companion in Hall).[14] Thus, the presence of allusions to Serlio and Shute is not, in and of itself, indicative that the visual culture of the Inns was more 'bookish' than that of Renaissance England as a whole. But an examination of the Inns' and their members' wider patronage of the visual arts suggests that the label is an apt one.

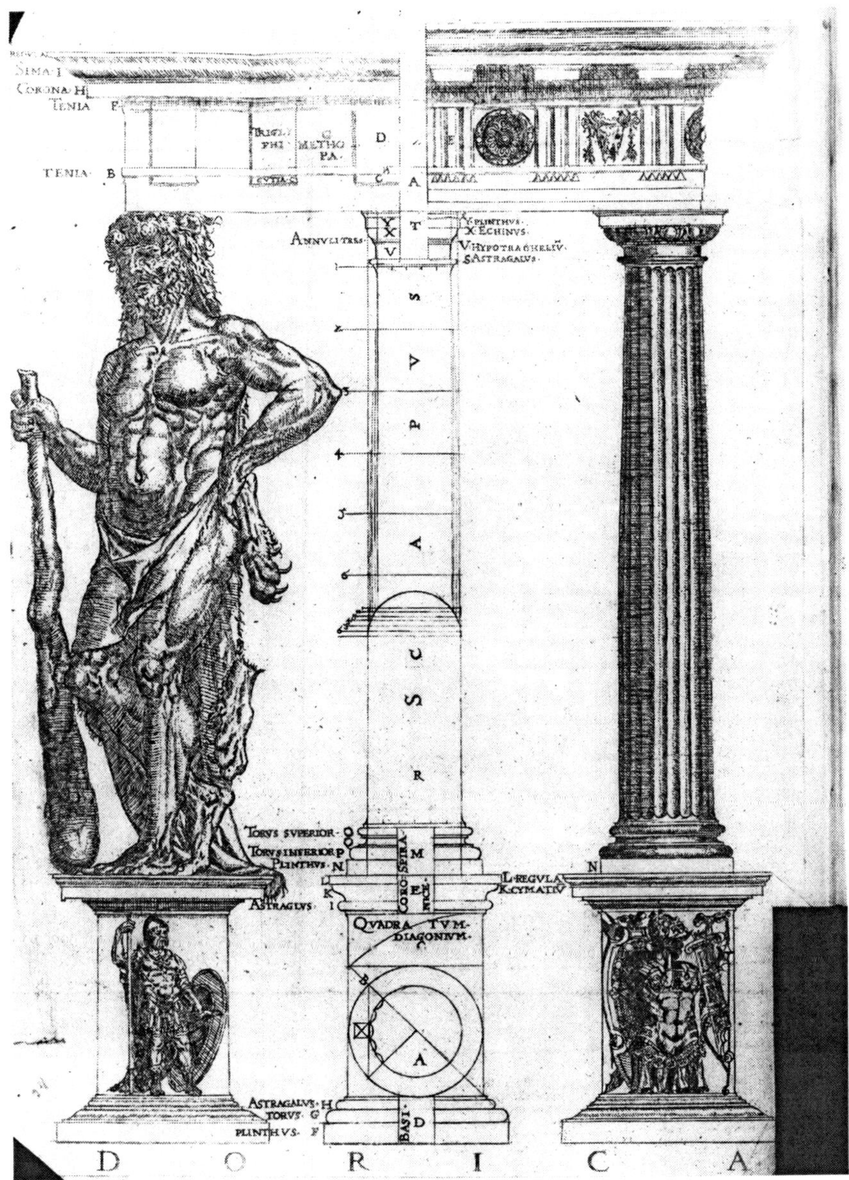

1 The Roman Doric order, as illustrated in John Shute, *The First and Chief Groundes of Architecture* (London: Thomas Marshe, 1563)

The paintings associated with this milieu, for example, tend to use Latin, as opposed to English, inscriptions. The Middle Temple's painting of the Judgement of Solomon, executed *circa* 1570–1600, features fourteen lines of Latin text explicating the biblical scene depicted and relating it to the business of the Middle Temple:

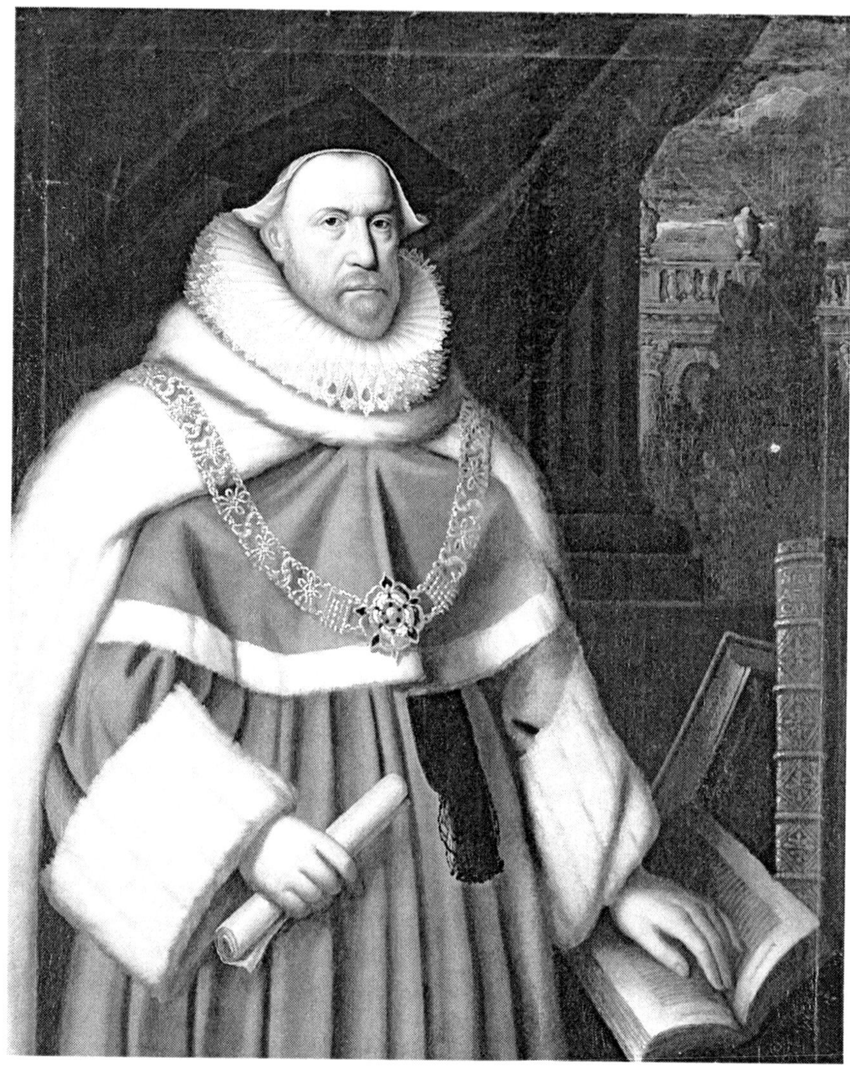

2 *A portrait of Sir John Walter*, by an unknown artist, *c.*1630, oil on canvas, 1270 × 1015 mm

the dispensation of justice.[15] (See Plate 4) By contrast, contemporary parallels such as the wall paintings depicting biblical scenes relevant to the craft of carpentry, commissioned by the Carpenters' Company in the 1560s or 1570s, feature brief inscriptions in English.[16]

This linguistic dichotomy extends to other types of painting as well. The portraits that judges in sixteenth- and early seventeenth-century England commissioned of themselves, in common with contemporary images of university and college founders, are notable for their predilection for Latin inscriptions.[17] But whereas Latin was still prevalent at Oxford and Cambridge as the institutional lingua franca in which most business and teaching were conducted, this was not the case to the same extent at the Inns in this period – a distinction which might suggest that the use of Latin inscriptions in paintings produced for the Inns and their individual members constituted a particularly concerted display of 'bookishness'.[18]

Early modern legal portraits – again in common with contemporary images of university and college founders – sometimes include additional signifiers of their sitters' learnedness in the form of scrolls or even books.[19] A portrait of the judge Sir John Walter, Chief Baron of the Exchequer (1625–30), provides a good example.[20] Executed *circa* 1630 by an unknown artist and now in the collection of the Inner Temple (to which Walter had been admitted in 1583), this painting depicts its subject in three-quarter length, wearing judicial robes. In Walter's right hand is a parchment scroll, while his left rests on an open book. Visible on the table next to him are two additional volumes, one of which may be identified from the Latin inscription on its spine ('Stat: An: Re. Car. I') as a book of statutes from the first year of Charles I's reign.[21] In contrast to images like Walter's, portraits of early modern mayors and livery company worthies are less likely to include props such as scrolls and books.[22]

The Inns of Court, as Cooper demonstrates, do not seem to have displayed portraits of judges and other leading legal figures in their halls and other public spaces in the sixteenth and early seventeenth centuries. This is in sharp contrast to what is known of institutions such as the universities and the livery companies. Several Oxbridge colleges were adorned from at least the sixteenth century onwards with portraits of their founders or benefactors, while in London, the Haberdashers' Company commissioned painted portraits of several worthies for display in its hall as early as 1598 – a practice emulated over the next few decades by numerous other livery companies.[23] But not until the second half of the seventeenth century does one start to find written evidence for the display of portraits of leading legal figures at the Inns of Court. In the early 1660s, for example, the Inner Temple seems to have acquired paintings of two recently deceased members – Edward Littleton, Chief Justice of the Common Pleas, and Sir Edward Coke, Lord Chief Justice – from Coke's daughter.[24]

Strikingly, one of the first portraits commissioned by and for an Inn was a painting not of a judge or even a bencher. Rather, its subject was a reluctant barrister: the Middle Templar Robert Ashley. Owing in part to the free time afforded by his less than thriving practice, Ashley amassed one of the largest book collections of his day. He also travelled extensively on the Continent and published translations from French, Spanish, and Italian literature. When he died in 1641, Ashley left the Middle Temple some five thousand books covering virtually every branch of learning, or, as he himself put it, 'the principall writers in their severall languages, espetially such as had opportunitie to be acquainted with the moste remote and unknowne partes'.[25] In addition, Ashley left the Inn £300 for the maintenance of his books.

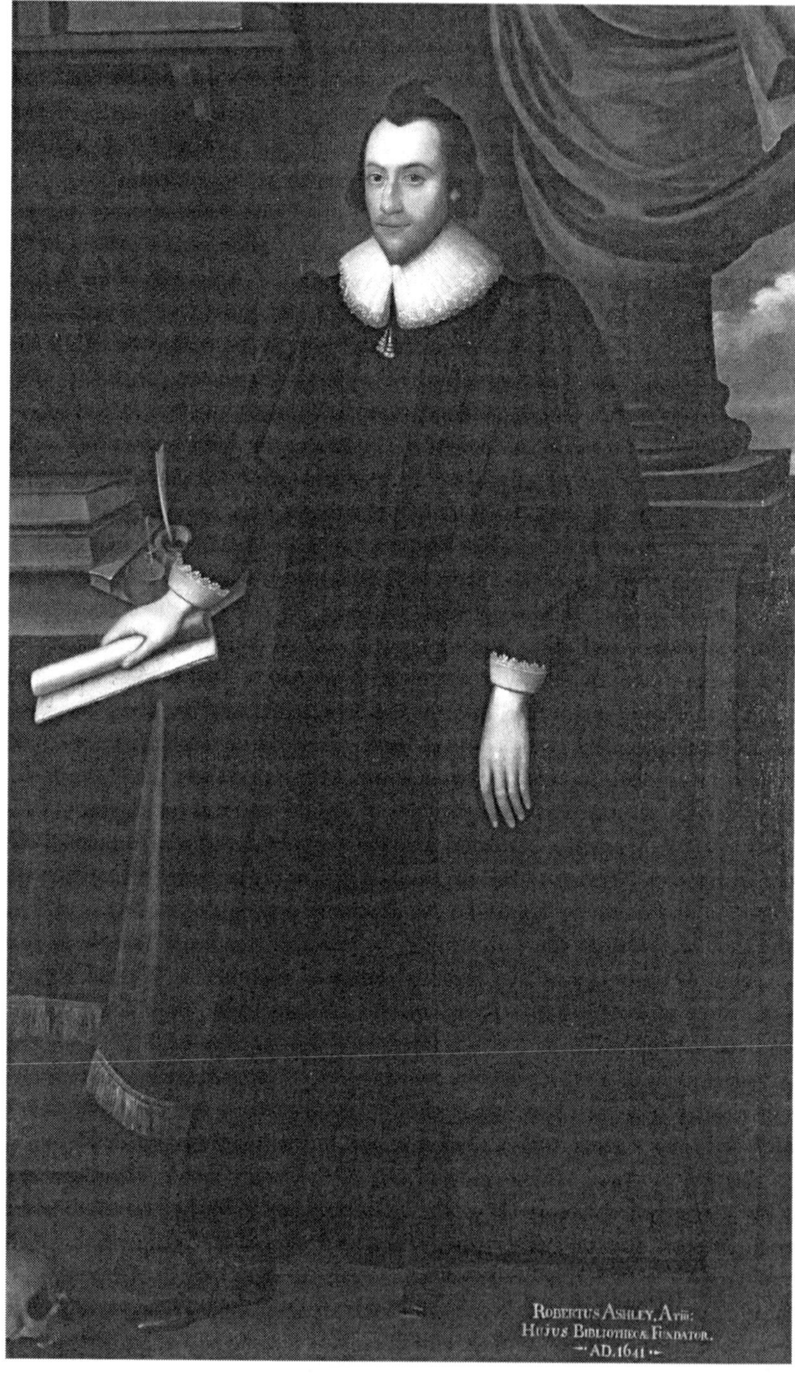

3 *A portrait of Robert Ashley,* by Thomas Leigh, 1655/56, oil on canvas, 1930 × 1205 mm

In commemoration of this bequest, the Middle Temple in 1655/56 commissioned a portrait from Thomas Leigh, who was paid £11 for painting Ashley's picture.[26] The resulting image, which remains on display in Middle Temple library, depicts Ashley life-sized and in full-length. Inscribed 'ROBERTUS ASHLEY, ARM: HUJUS BIBLIOTHECÆ FUNDATOR. A.D. 1641',[27] it shows him not as the septuagenarian he was in 1641, but rather as a young man. In his right hand he holds a parchment scroll on which words are visible, but not legible; a pen and inkwell and two books may be seen on the table next to him. Additional books are partially visible on the shelf above Ashley's head. If, as Stephen Orgel has suggested, 'the most enlightening part of any collection in the period is not what is bought but what is commissioned',[28] then this portrait celebrating a life devoted not to the law *per se*, but to scholarship, provides a window into the soul of the Inns, or at least the Middle Temple, *circa* 1655/56.

Even the gardens of the early modern Inns might be said to have displayed signs of 'bookishness'. Recreational features such as bowling alleys and tennis courts, as Henderson notes, were either late in coming to the Inns' gardens or never came at all: at Lincoln's, for example, a bowling alley was not built until some point between 1609 and 1632, while plans for a tennis court – discussed in the mid-seventeenth century – never materialised.[29] By contrast, many of the London livery companies had gardens that were well equipped from an early date with sporting facilities: the Ironmongers had a tennis court from the fifteenth century, while the Bakers, the Carpenters, and the Drapers had bowling alleys as early as the sixteenth.[30] As Henderson suggests, the emphasis on long walks and groves in the gardens of the Inns – as at the universities – seems to have been self-consciously designed, following ancient models such as the Stoics, to foster contemplation and learned, philosophical discourse.[31]

Aesthetic formation

Who helped to shape the visual aesthetics of the early modern Inns of Court? Undoubtedly, senior figures at each Inn influenced how artistic patronage was dispensed. In 1616, for example, the benchers of Lincoln's agreed that the Inn should donate £20 towards the cost of Sir Thomas Bodley's Schools Quadrangle at Oxford, perhaps the most overtly 'bookish' building project of its day.[32] This decision was reached on the basis that £20 was 'as much as the most of any other Houses in Court have donne', the benchers of the Inner Temple having donated £20 to the same undertaking a year or so earlier.[33]

More than anyone else, however, the individual treasurers of the Inns – many of whom remained in post for several years in this period – were in a position to shape artistic practices. Edmund Plowden, as Girouard demonstrates, played a pivotal role in the building and fitting out of Middle Temple Hall, both during his tenure as treasurer (1562–67) and for several years thereafter. Not only did Plowden oversee the raising of funds for this project, but he also took the lead, on at least one occasion, in the sourcing of craftsmen.[34]

In many cases it is possible to make connections between the known aesthetic interests of a given treasurer and the expenses incurred during his tenure. For example, William Rastell's 1554–55 treasurership at Lincoln's Inn included payments 'for an image of S. Richard, and for painting the images of Blessed Mary and S. Richard'.[35] Rastell was a committed Catholic who seems to have had more than a passing interest in religious art and relics.[36] A gold locket containing Sir Thomas More's portrait was one of his prized possessions, and in 1554 – recently returned to England from religious exile in Louvain – Rastell gave Lincoln's a large Deposition on panel, specifying that the painting should be hung above the altar in the Inn's chapel.[37]

Sir Francis Bacon's tenure as treasurer of Gray's Inn (1608–17) provides another example of the ways in which an Inn's visual culture – and related expenditures – reflected its treasurer's interests: in this instance, garden design, a topic Bacon later explored in 'Of Gardens', published in 1625 (alongside its companion essay, 'Of Building') as one of his *Essays or Counsels, Civill and Morall*. Bacon's period of office was marked by numerous improvements to the outdoor spaces at Gray's. Between 1608 and 1610, for example, the Inn spent more than £250 (out of a total outlay of just under £490) on the walks alone.[38] Expenditures ranged from 'settinge sicamore elme & birche trees' to creating a mount,[39] the latter of which, as Henderson suggests, may have been the model for that described in 'Of Gardens'.[40] (See Figure 21)

Roger North's treasurership at the Middle Temple (1683–84) offers yet another case in point. North was a keen reader of Vitruvius and Palladio, a collector of mathematical and scientific instruments, and the author of an essay on perspective.[41] North's year as treasurer, as Tyack discusses, was marked by the erection of a new gateway to Fleet Street that he himself had designed.[42] (See Figure 27) But North's interests extended beyond architecture to painting. A friend of Sir Peter Lely, North in 1680 served as executor of Lely's estate, in which capacity he oversaw the dispersal of the painter's own picture collection.[43] It is, thus, probably not a coincidence that North's tenure as treasurer saw the purchase by Middle Temple of new portraits of Charles I and the future James II painted in the style of Lely.[44]

Conclusions

The visual culture of the early modern Inns of Court, together with the role of the Inns as patrons of the visual arts, are rich topics which are by no means exhausted by this volume. It is hoped that this Introduction, and the chapters that follow it, will give rise to new questions and serve as a spur to further research, particularly when viewed within the wider interdisciplinary context of this volume as a whole. Future work might test out the hypothesis set forth here – that the Inns' visual aesthetic in this period was self-consciously, even performatively, 'bookish' and learned – perhaps delineating the distinctions between the individual Inns as patrons of the visual arts and drawing out, where relevant, the ways in which patronage of the visual arts provided an outlet for competition between them.

Other topics that might reward new research include the relationship between art and religion at the Inns, an extremely broad topic which encompasses subjects ranging from the art and architecture of the Inns' chapels, to tomb sculpture, to the Inns' responses (as manifested in their artistic patronage) to fluctuations in the official religion in this period. Further consideration of the links between the Inns and the College of Arms would also be welcome, for both the Inns (as institutions) and their individual members – many newly ennobled and, thus, in need of painted coats of arms – must have been among the College's best, and most regular, sources of patronage in this period. Finally, additional consideration of the artistic relationships between the early modern Inns of Court and parallel institutions such as the Inns of Chancery, the City livery companies, and the universities of Oxford and Cambridge – to say nothing of the Scottish and Continental universities – would not only provide a broader context within which to view the activities of the Inns of Court, but would also contribute to the ongoing scholarly recovery of the activities of the 'middling sort' in this period.

Notes

1 See BL, Additional MS 28330, fol. 29^r, and Chapter 8 (pp. 166–7, below).

2 *Thomas Platter's Travels in England, 1599*, ed. and trans. Clare Williams (London: Jonathan Cape, 1937), pp. 166, 178. The 'court of justice' is Westminster Hall.

3 *England as seen by Foreigners in the Days of Elizabeth and James the First*, ed. William Brenchley Rye (London: John Russell Smith, 1865), p. 133.

4 *Boswell's London Journal, 1762–1763*, ed. Frederick A. Pottle (New York: McGraw-Hill, 1950), p. 234.

5 Some consideration of the Inns' visual culture may be found in the secondary sources cited in the notes here and in the following chapters.

6 For Middle Temple Hall screen, see below and Chapter 7 (pp. 147–9, below); for Donne's portrait, see Chapter 8 (pp. 172–4, below).

7 Chapter 7 (p. 143, below).

8 Chapter 8 (pp. 158–60, below).

9 Chapter 9 (p. 192, below).

10 Chapter 10 (p. 210, below).

11 See Anthony Wells-Cole, *Art and Decoration in Elizabethan and Jacobean England: The Influence of Continental Prints, 1558–1625* (New Haven, CT; London: Yale University Press/The Paul Mellon Centre for Studies in British Art, 1997), p. 170; and Chapter 7 (p. 148, below).

12 Admitted to the Middle Temple in 1560, Tresham lived there through to 1568 (*Middle Temple Records*, I, 128, 138, 162). He was still an occasional visitor to the Temple complex in the 1590s (*Historical Manuscripts Commission Report on Manuscripts in Various Collections. Vol. III* (London: HMSO, 1904), pp. 83, 106).

13 See Lucy Gent, *Picture and Poetry, 1560–1620: Relations between Literature and the Visual

Arts in the English Renaissance (Leamington Spa: James Hall, 1981), Appendix: 'Books on art, perspective, and architecture in English Renaissance Libraries, 1580–1630', pp. 66–86 (p. 84).

14 Christy Anderson, 'Learning to Read Architecture in the English Renaissance', in Lucy Gent (ed.), *Albion's Classicism: The Visual Arts in Britain, 1550–1660* (New Haven, CT; London: Yale University Press/The Paul Mellon Centre for Studies in British Art, 1995), pp. 239–86 (p. 241).

15 See also Chapter 8, pp. 160–1, below; and John Bruce Williamson, *Catalogue of Paintings and Engravings in the Possession of the Honourable Society of the Middle Temple* (London: Middle Temple, 1931), pp. 15–16.

16 Fragments of three of the Carpenters' paintings have survived, while a fourth is known through a nineteenth-century watercolour sketch by F. W. Fairholt. See B. W. E. Alford and T. C. Barker, *A History of the Carpenters' Company* (London: George Allen and Unwin, 1968), pp. 225–8 and frontispiece, which reproduces Fairholt's watercolour. The Carpenters' paintings are also discussed in Robert Tittler, *The Face of the City: Civic Portraiture and Civic Identity in Early Modern England* (Manchester; New York, NY: Manchester University Press, 2007), p. 56; and Ian W. Archer, 'Discourses of history in Elizabethan and early Stuart London', *Huntington Library Quarterly*, 68 (2005), 205–26 (207). Another institutional parallel – perhaps indicative of a vogue, in early modern London, for the display of religious narrative pictures relevant to the craft or profession of a given institution – may be found in the Vintners' Company's commission of a painting of the marriage at Cana for display in its hall in the early 1620s. This picture is not known to be extant. See Anne Crawford, *A History of the Vintners' Company* (London: Constable, 1977), pp. 97–8; and Archer, 'Discourses of history', 207. I am grateful to Julie Tancell, Archivist of the Carpenters' Company, and Stephen Freeth, Archivist of the Vintners' Company, for assistance with my queries.

17 For the use of Latin in portraits of university and college founders, see Tittler, *Face of the City*, p. 136.

18 I owe this observation to Sarah Knight.

19 In addition to the images reproduced in this volume as Plate 1 and Figures 2, 3, 14, and 16, other early modern portraits of judges and barristers depicted with books and/or scrolls include paintings of: Richard Pate (1516–88), barrister, recorder and member of Lincoln's Inn, now in the Gloucester City Museum and at Corpus Christi College, Oxford; William Lambarde (1536–1601), barrister and member of Lincoln's Inn, now in the National Portrait Gallery and in a private collection; and Richard Brownlow (1553–1638), member of Middle Temple and Prothonotary of the Common Pleas, now at Belton House. A Continental parallel may be found in Guercino's portrait of Francesco Righetti, executed *circa* 1626–28 and now in a private collection. I would like to thank Tarnya Cooper and Robert Tittler for discussing these images with me.

20 I would like to thank Celia Pilkington, archivist of the Inner Temple, for assistance with this painting.

21 The English inscription in the lower right corner of the painting, 'Lord chief Baron Walter', appears to be a later addition.

22 See Tittler, *Face of the City*, pp. 124–7.

23 *Ibid.*, pp. 37–47, 55–6.

24 *Inner Temple Records*, III, 11, 315. See also *Catalogue of the Paintings, Engravings, Serjeants'*

Rings, Plate, Stained Glass, Sculpture, etc. belonging to the Honourable Society of the Inner Temple (London: Printed by Order of the Masters of the Bench, 1915), pp. 20–1, 55–6.

25 For Ashley's bequest, see *Calendar of the Middle Temple*, p. 72; and *Middle Temple Records*, II, 917–18. I am grateful to Lesley Whitelaw, archivist of the Middle Temple, for assistance with this painting.

26 *Calendar of the Middle Temple*, p. 165. For Leigh, see Stephanie Roberts and Robert Tittler, 'Discovering "T. Leigh": tracking the elusive portrait painter through Stuart England and Wales', forthcoming in the *British Art Journal*.

27 Translation: 'Robert Ashley, Esquire, Founder of this Library, 1641.'

28 Stephen Orgel, 'Idols of the gallery: becoming a connoisseur in Renaissance England', in Peter Erickson and Clark Hulse (eds), *Early Modern Visual Culture: Representation, Race, and Empire in Renaissance England* (Philadelphia, PA: University of Pennsylvania Press, 2000), pp. 251–83 (p. 266).

29 Chapter 9 (p. 193, below).

30 Elizabeth Glover, *A History of the Ironmongers' Company* (London: The Worshipful Company of Ironmongers, 1991), p. 13; Sylvia Thrupp, *A Short History of the Worshipful Company of Bakers of London* (Croydon: Galleon Press, 1933), p. 165; *Records of the Worshipful Company of Carpenters*, ed. Bower Marsh and John Ainsworth, 7 vols (Oxford: Oxford University Press, 1913–68), V, 27; A. H. Johnson, *The History of the Worshipful Company of Drapers of London*, 5 vols (Oxford: Clarendon Press, 1914–22), II, 224.

31 Chapter 9 (pp. 193–4, below).

32 For the Schools Quadrangle, see Geoffrey Tyack, *Oxford: An Architectural Guide* (Oxford: Oxford University Press, 1998), pp. 92–5.

33 *Black Books*, II, 182; *Inner Temple Records*, II, 93.

34 Chapter 7 (pp. 144–5, below). See also Geoffrey de Parmiter, *Edmund Plowden: An Elizabethan Recusant Lawyer* (Southampton: Catholic Record Society, 1987), pp. 61–9.

35 *Black Books*, I, 312–13.

36 First elected treasurer in 1549, Rastell shortly thereafter fled to Catholic Louvain, for which he was fined £10 for having gone 'to foreign parts without leave' (*Black Books*, I, 291, 293). After Elizabeth I's accession, Rastell again would seek religious refuge in Louvain, living there from 1563 until his death two years later.

37 The locket is listed in Rastell's will, for which, see John H. Baker's *ODNB* entry. For the 'greate image or pycture in a Table of the takyng downe of Cryste fro the Crosse', see *Black Books*, I, 308–9. A 1562 inventory of Rastell's personal effects at Serjeants' Inn suggests that his interest in the visual arts extended beyond religious art, for the walls of Rastell's chambers there were adorned with four maps, as well as numerous painted cloths. See *Law Magazine*, 31 (1844), 57–60.

38 *Pension Book of Gray's Inn*, I, 491.

39 *Ibid.*, I, 491.

40 Chapter 9 (p. 184, below).

41 See *Notes of Me: The Autobiography of Roger North*, ed. Peter Millard (Toronto; London: University of Toronto Press, 2000), pp. 129–42, 237–53.

42 Chapter 10 (pp. 206–7, below).

43 *Notes of Me*, ed. Millard, pp. 237–53.

44 *Calendar of the Middle Temple*, p. 181; and Williamson, *Catalogue of Paintings and Engravings*, pp. 16–17. These paintings remain on display in Middle Temple Hall today.

7

The halls of the Elizabethan and early Stuart Inns of Court

Mark Girouard[1]

London under Elizabeth I was a teeming, in many ways chaotic, but here and there sumptuous, city. But of the many new buildings put up during Elizabeth's reign, almost nothing is left today. The fire of 1666 blotted out a great portion, while in subsequent centuries, ever-growing prosperity – combined with the westward move of London's fashionable quarters – led to the rebuilding of surviving, mainly half-timbered, houses and to the descent of the great mansions along the Thames and elsewhere into tenements, decay, and subsequent demolition.[2] During the Second World War, German air raids destroyed much of what remained.

One small group of buildings, however, is outstanding among the few survivors: the legal halls, of Gray's Inn, the Middle Temple, and Staple Inn, together with the medieval 'Old Hall' at Lincoln's Inn, as enlarged and embellished in the Elizabethan and early Stuart decades.[3] These buildings have all been repaired and reconstructed to varying degrees over the years.[4] But they nonetheless form a rare and precious link to sixteenth- and early seventeenth-century London.[5] They also provide impressive evidence of the growing prosperity of the law as a profession and source of education in the Tudor-Stuart period. Middle Temple Hall, for example, was the biggest of all the Elizabethan great halls, rivalling in scale and richness the early Tudor halls at Christ Church, Oxford, and Hampton Court Palace. (See Plate 2)

The Inns' halls combined the traditional and the up-to-date in a way that must have seemed apposite to members of the legal profession: open timber roofs and arched or traceried (i.e. ribbed) windows in the late Gothic manner – as established in collegiate and domestic architecture of the period – combined with ebullient Mannerist or Classical screens and other embellishments, including heraldic glass, executed by the best available craftsmen. The influence of these halls on late sixteenth- and early seventeenth-century English architecture has been underestimated. But lines of descent may be traced from the Inns of Court to the domestic great halls of Elizabethan Longleat, Burghley, Wiston, and Wollaton; to the early seventeenth-century collegiate halls at Wadham College, Oxford, and Trinity College, Cambridge; and to the elaborate Jacobean hall screens at Knole, Hatfield, Audley End, and elsewhere.

The halls of the Inns of Court: an overview

At the Inns of Court, as in the colleges of Oxford and Cambridge, the great halls were used on a day-to-day basis for eating and drinking as well as, in the case of the Inns, for practical, pedagogical exercises like mooting.[6] During festive periods and on special occasions such as royal visits, the Inns' halls – like their counterparts at

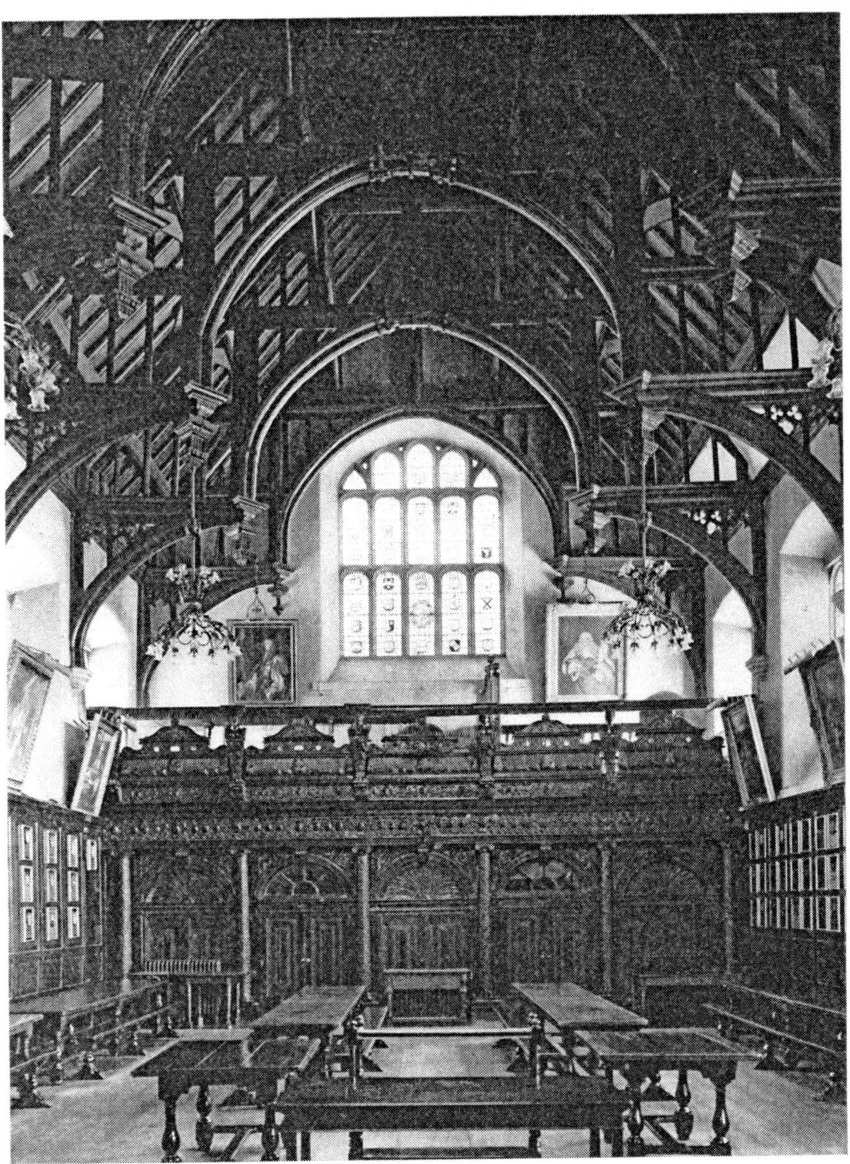

4 The interior of Gray's Inn Hall, photographed in the early twentieth century

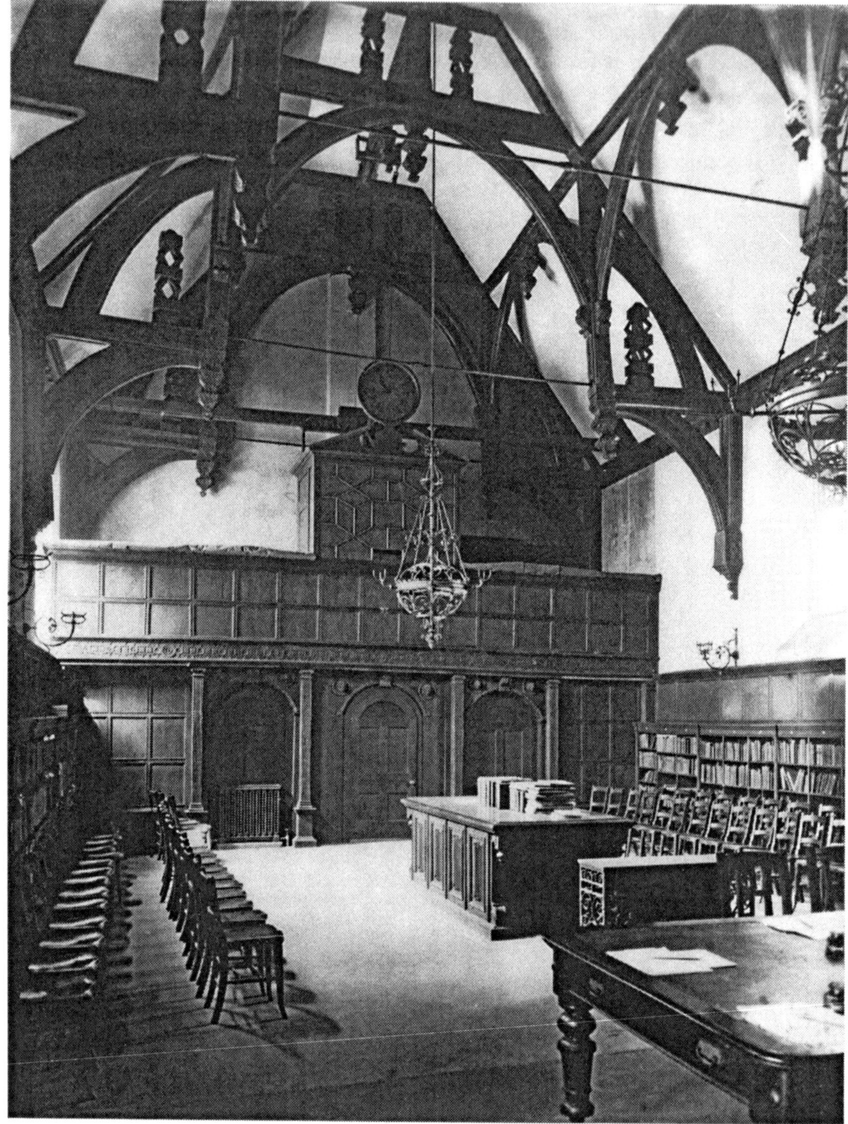

5 The earliest known photograph (*c.*1890) of the interior of Staple Inn Hall

the universities and, indeed, in the houses of the greatest nobles – also served as performance spaces in which masques and other entertainments were mounted.[7] At each Inn, as at the colleges of Oxford and Cambridge, the hall was at the heart of a complex of institutional buildings, including a chapel and lodgings, all arranged around one or more courtyards.

All of the Inns of Court initially possessed medieval halls that had been taken

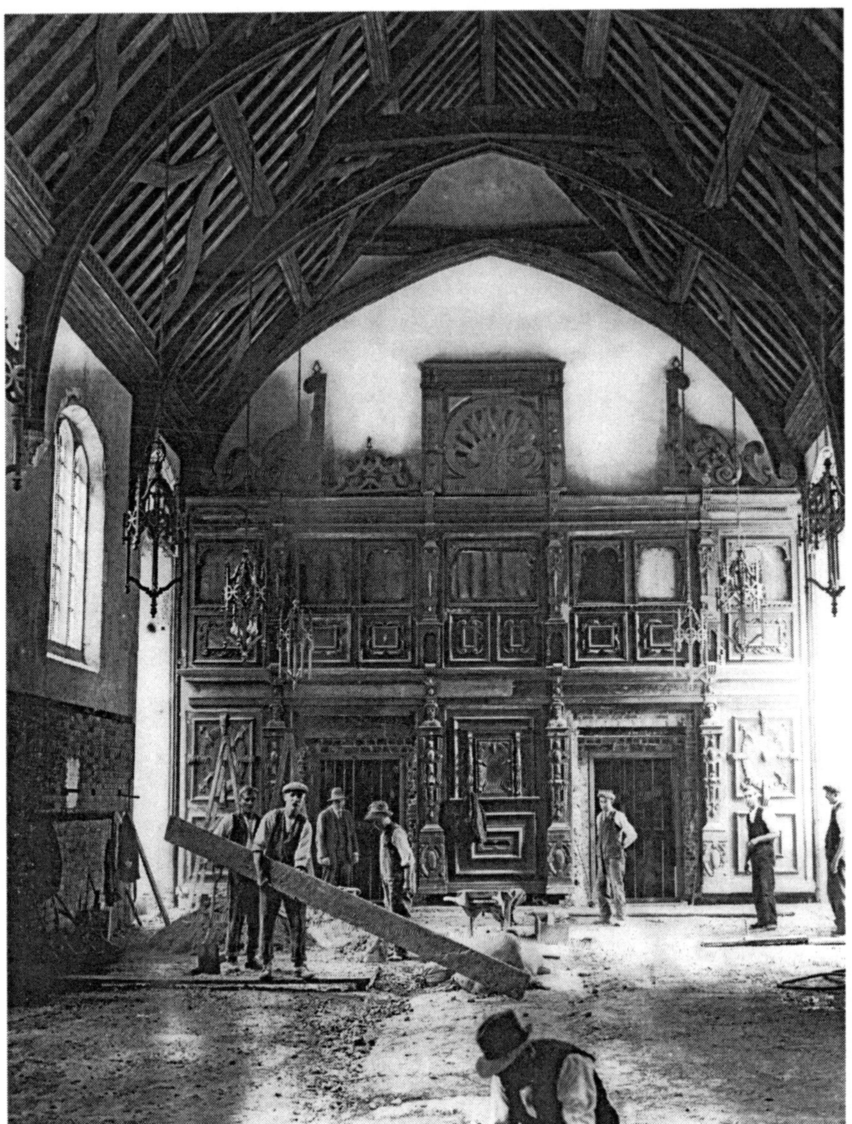

6 The interior of Lincoln's Inn 'Old Hall', showing the south bay and screen,
during reconstruction, *c.*1928

over from other bodies: the 1st Baron Grey de Wilton's Manor of Purpoole in the case of Gray's Inn; the Bishopric of Chichester in the case of Lincoln's Inn; and the Knights Templar in the case of the Middle and Inner Temples. The so-called 'Old Hall' at Lincoln's Inn, built between 1489 and 1492, is 'the earliest surviving secular building' in any of the Inns, yet was itself a replacement for an even earlier structure, the hall of the palace of the Bishop of Chichester.[8] Virtually nothing is known of the Bishop of Chichester's hall or any of the other original halls of the Inns, which were variously rebuilt, enlarged, and embellished during the second half of the sixteenth century and the early decades of the seventeenth – a period that witnessed a dramatic increase in the numbers of young men admitted to the Inns.[9]

Gray's was the first of the Inns to rebuild its hall after the Reformation. Work on this project began in 1556 and was completed four years later at a total cost of £868 10s. 8d.[10] The new hall, measuring about eighty by thirty-eight feet, was roomy enough, and certainly an enlargement of its predecessor, but it was soon outshone, perhaps deliberately, by the huge hall of the Middle Temple, measuring 101 by 41

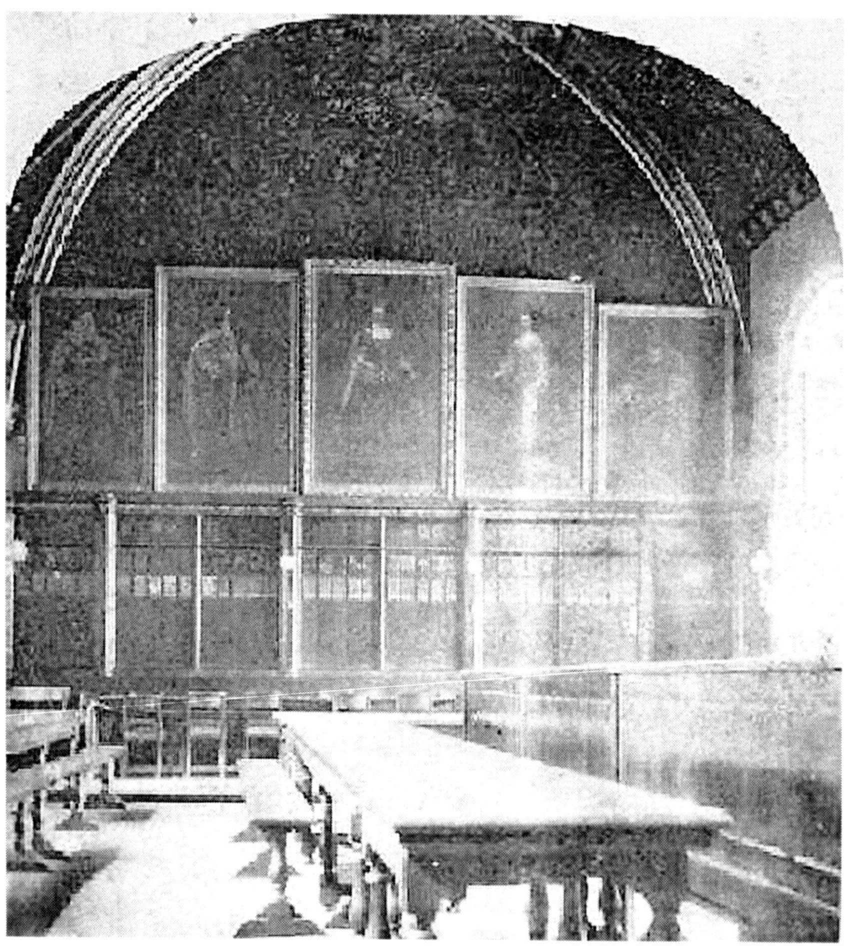

7 The interior of Inner Temple Hall as it appeared in 1867, two years before the medieval building (with early nineteenth-century embellishments) was demolished to make way for a new, Victorian one

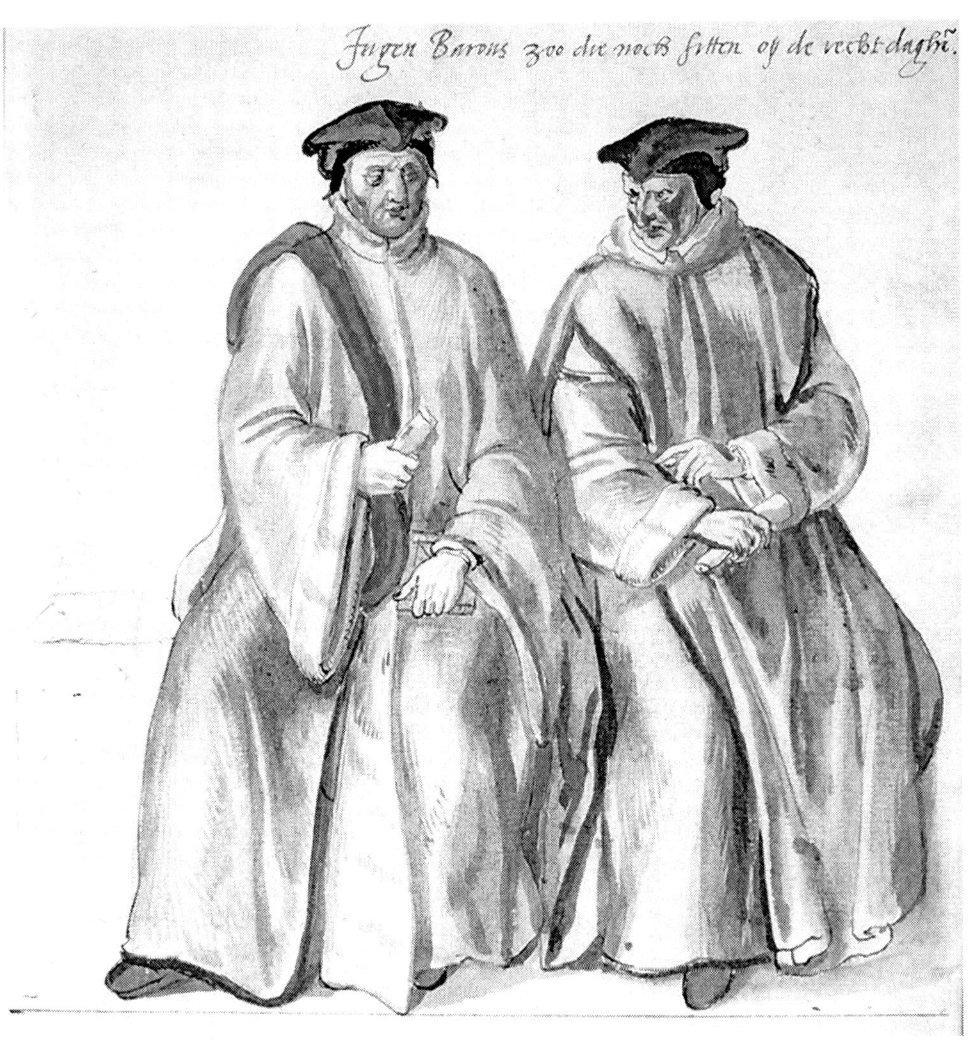

1 *Judges of the Queen's Bench*, by Lucas de Heere, *c.*1574, brush and wash on paper, 320 × 204 mm

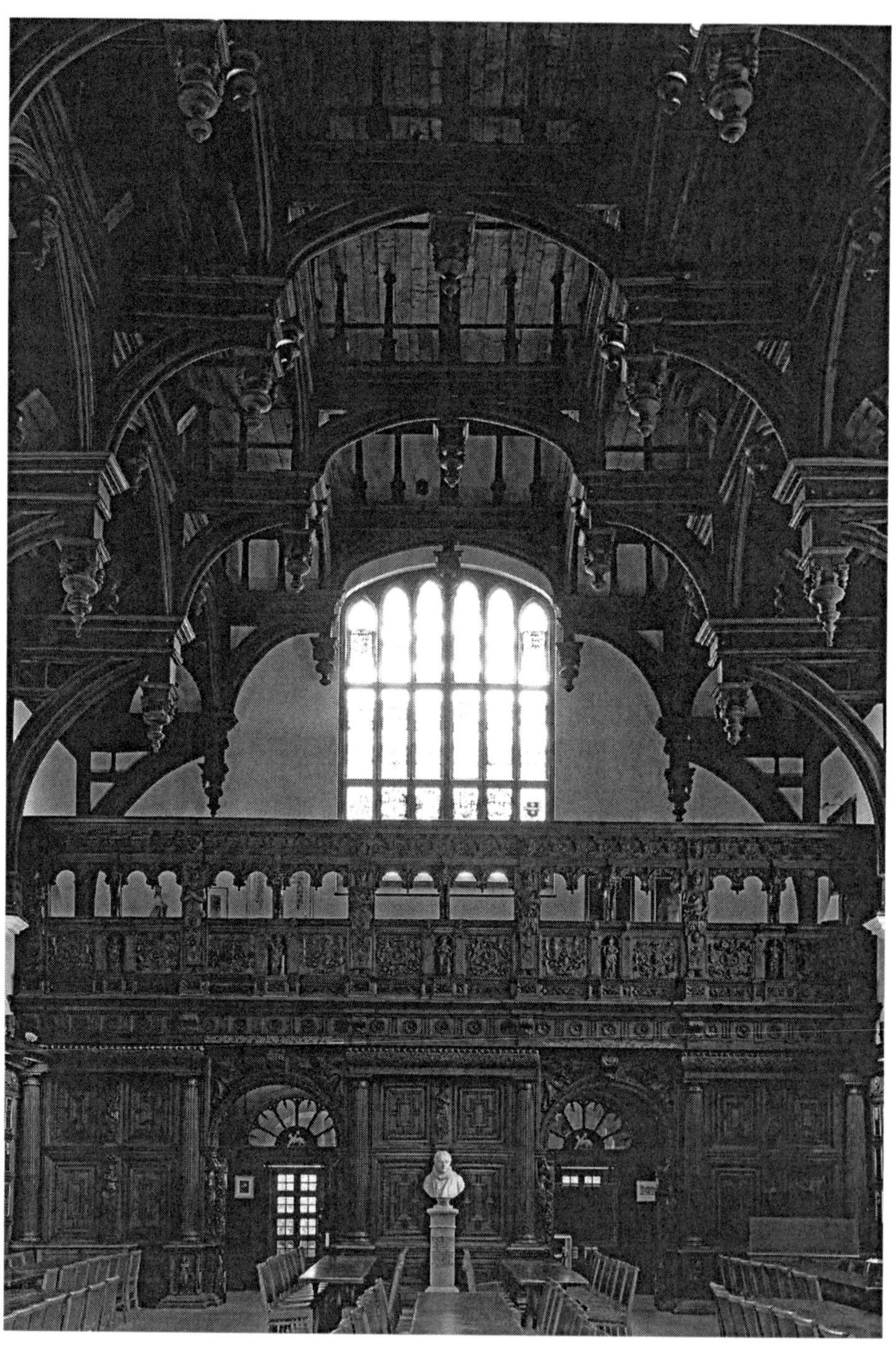

2 The interior of Middle Temple Hall, showing the screen

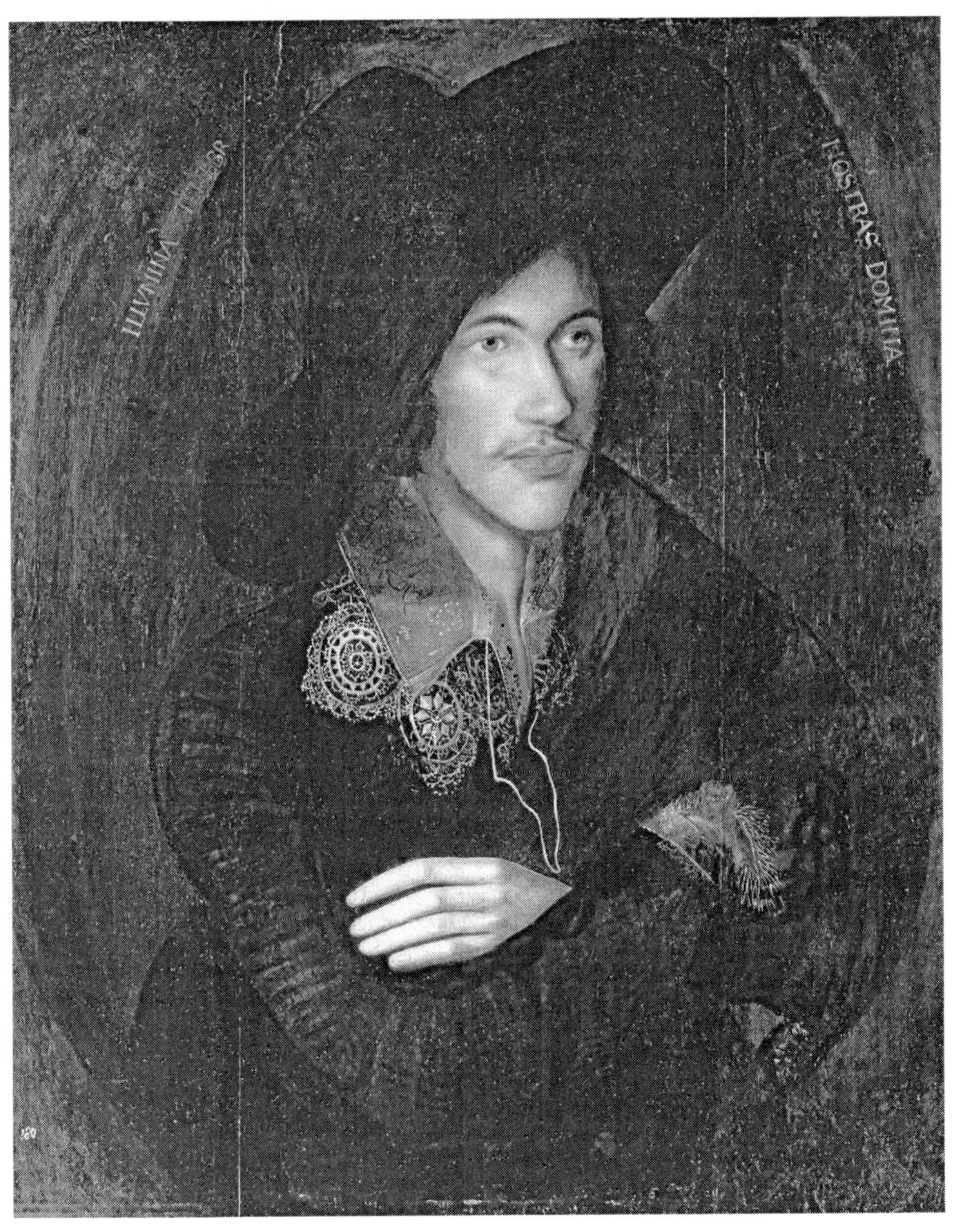

3 *A portrait of John Donne,* by an unknown English artist, *c.*1595,
oil on panel, 771 × 625 mm

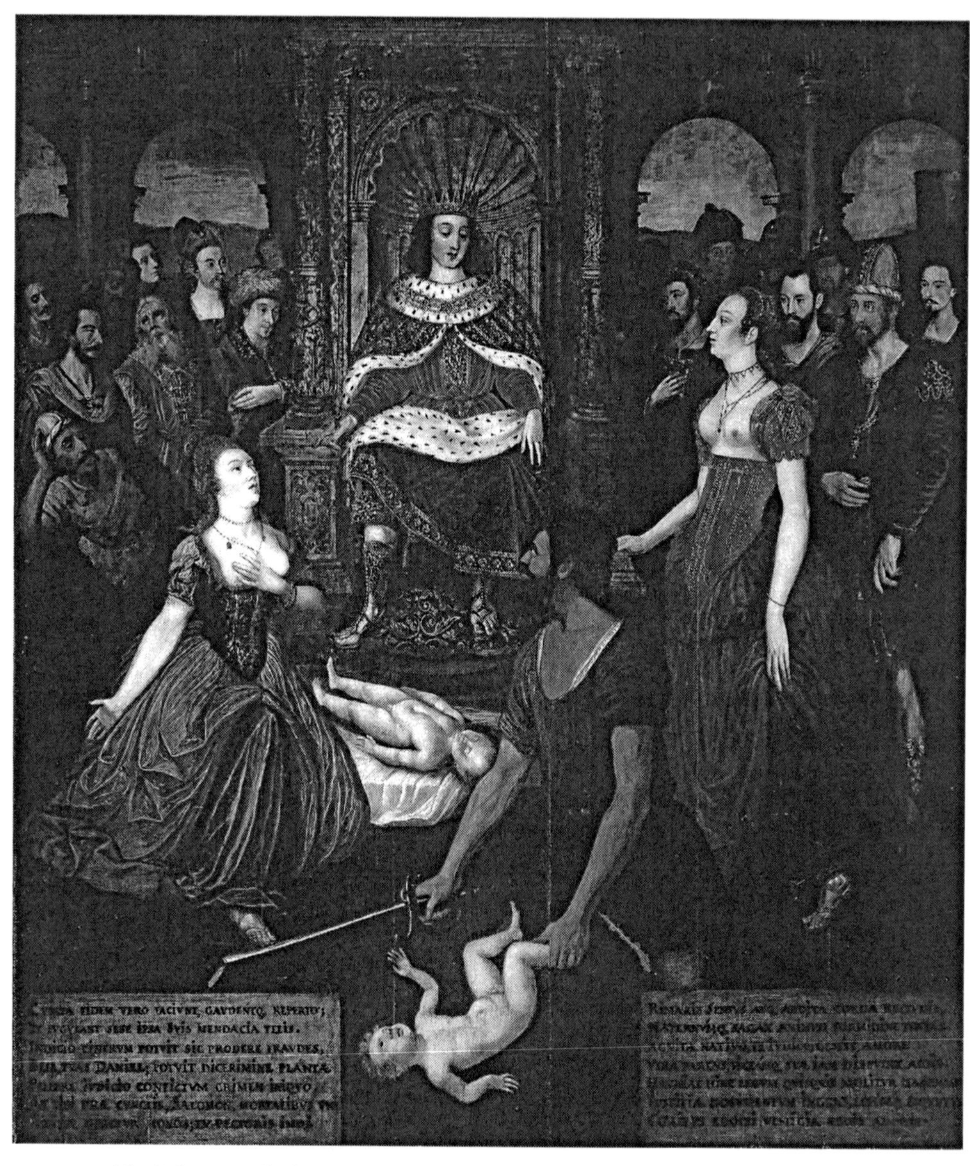

4 *The Judgement of Solomon*, by an unknown Anglo-Netherlandish artist, *c.*1570–1600, oil on panel, approximately 1270 × 1270 mm

feet. Middle Temple Hall seems to have been started in 1562 or soon after, but to have been built over a period of eight to ten years. The modest hall of Staple Inn, modest because it was not an Inn of Court, like the others, but one of the smaller Inns of Chancery, followed in or around 1581. In 1583, the late fifteenth-century 'Old Hall' of Lincoln's Inn was extended by one bay to the south. The current elaborate screen, on the south wall, was not introduced until 1624.

The Inner Temple, by contrast, remained satisfied with the fourteenth-century hall of the Knights Templar, which it had taken over as its own. But the Inner Temple did make some additions to its hall during the reign of Elizabeth. According to William Dugdale, the seventeenth-century antiquary, a 'great carved Skreen' was put up in Inner Temple Hall in 1574.[11] In the nineteenth century, the Inner Temple's medieval hall was first altered and then demolished and rebuilt; the new Victorian hall was in turn destroyed during the Second World War and then reconstructed afterwards. All that remains today of the medieval hall is the refaced buttery at the west end of the post-war hall, together with the crypt beneath it. But some sense of Inner Temple Hall's appearance in the medieval and early modern periods can be gleaned from a stereoscopic print dating from 1867.

The Inns, unlike the colleges of Oxford and Cambridge, had little or nothing in the way of endowment, and their halls necessarily were built and fitted up slowly, as money came in from their members.[12] In the case of the Middle Temple, for example, various ingenious methods were devised both to reduce the Inn's expenditures and to generate funds for the ongoing work on the new hall. In 1562, it was ordered 'that until the New Hall be completed, each member shall bear the cost of the repairs of his own chamber on pain of forfeiture'.[13] Contributions towards the building costs were also expected, and the following year, three Middle Templars lost their chambers for failing to comply.[14] In 1571, members were required to lend the Inn money on a sliding scale ranging from £3 (for benchers) to forty shillings (for utter barristers, common attorneys, and officers in the great courts) to twenty shillings (for 'others of the fellowship').[15] Also in 1571, it was ordered that pensions (i.e. taxes) would be levied for the next three years. Once again, a sliding scale was applied, in this case ranging from benchers (assessed at ten shillings per term) to those who had joined the Inn via special admissions (in which cases the treasurer was simply to 'get what he can').[16] Further subscriptions were imposed in 1574, and when, the following year, the 'debts of the Inn and the new hall' remained unmet, the subscriptions were increased.[17] (This last seems to have been intended to meet the costs associated with the hall screen.)

All of the Inns' halls in the early modern period were traditional in character and faithfully followed the general formula worked out in the fourteenth century for domestic halls, and taken over for collegiate halls at Oxford and Cambridge: an open timber roof; entry through a carved, wooden screen at one end of the hall; and the placement of a raised dais for a high table at the other end of the hall. The formula – so beautifully suggestive of an ordered, united but hierarchic society – disappeared quite early on from domestic architecture: from the late fifteenth century onwards the family increasingly abandoned the high table and ate elsewhere, and by the late seventeenth century servants had been banished to a servants' hall. But it has survived in a collegiate context, and at the Inns, down to the present day, with dons and benchers occupying the top table at each institution.

Roofs

As in the Middle Ages, the Elizabethan legal halls were originally all heated from a central brazier with smoke going out through a louver in the roof. The surviving examples of roofs are in the late Gothic tradition in much of their detail, too. They have buttresses, windows with arched lights, and roofs of hammerbeam construction, in the medieval manner. But they are also decorated with varying amounts of Classical ornament.

A mixture of this kind had already appeared in the roof of the great hall at Hampton Court Palace, built for Henry VIII in 1531–36, especially on the pendants hanging from the springing of the central arches. These are embellished with balusters and heraldry, in a pretty, Early Renaissance manner. However, the presence of Classical detail in the roofs of the Inns of Court reflects a new development: the English discovery of the five Classical orders of architecture, mainly from illustrated pattern-books such as Sebastiano Serlio's five books on architecture, printed in Venice between 1537 and 1547, and John Shute's *First and Chief Groundes of Architecture*, first printed in London in 1563 and subsequently reprinted in 1587.[18]

At Gray's Inn, the pendants in the roof of the great hall are treated like the capitals and entablature of square Doric piers. At the Middle Temple, the pendants followed a similar pattern, but were freely treated and embellished, and circular rather than square; the horizontal timbers above them are carved with a Doric frieze, and in addition, the spaces between the main timbers and the slope of the roof are filled with rows of slender Doric columns. The timbers spring from stone bracket consoles of Classical design. At Staple Inn, the timbers of the hall rise from stone consoles in the Serlian manner, derived from the Roman originals, which are repeated in wood in the roof; the pendants, however, follow a similar pattern to that seen at Gray's Inn and the Middle Temple. In the 'Old Hall' at Lincoln's Inn, the extension to the roof added on in the early 1580s has no Classical detail, because it exactly copies the fifteenth-century roof – just as the oriel windows to the east and west beneath it copy the fifteenth-century oriels at the other end of the hall.

Apart from Lincoln's Inn, all the halls suffer from the disappearance of the relevant building or other accounts, which would supply an exact chronology of projects undertaken, together with the names of the artificers employed. For Middle Temple Hall there is some indirect evidence, though, in the form of a letter dated 23 June 1562 from Edmund Plowden, who had just become treasurer of the Inn, to Sir John Thynne (1512/13–80).[19] At the time, Thynne was mired in litigation, and various members of the Middle Temple, including Plowden, were acting against him. Thynne was also in the process of building what was to become perhaps the most important and influential of the great Elizabethan prodigy houses: Longleat, in Wiltshire, a building which, with its symmetrical façade adorned with Classical pilasters, 'came as near as anything in England in the sixteenth century to a truly Renaissance house'.[20] Though geographically remote, Longleat nonetheless was 'the centre of the Elizabethan building world'.[21] Plowden's letter of June 1562 shows that Thynne's carpenter, John Lewis, who had been summoned by the Queen to employment in the Royal Works, had been diverted with her permission to work on the building of the new Middle Temple Hall. The Catholic Plowden wrote expressing his appreciation to the Protestant Thynne: 'althoghe some of the house (as I my selffe) be agenst you in some things yet hereafter this your gentlenes shall occasyon me and my felowes to give to you our fryndly furtherance in your matters hereafter to be attempted or begonne'.[22]

Lewis had come to work for Thynne in 1553. There is good reason to suppose that he had previously been employed by Thynne's old master, Edward Seymour (c.1500–52), Duke of Somerset, perhaps on roofing the hall of Syon House in Middlesex. In the course of Longleat's complex development – the building and, owing to fire, rebuilding of which stretched over a 37-year period – Lewis may have constructed no fewer than three successive hall roofs, including the roof that is there today which probably dates from the late 1570s. Apart from his London interval, Lewis appears to have remained at Longleat until he was buried in nearby Frome churchyard in 1585.

It is likely that Lewis was responsible for the basic design and initial construction of the great Middle Temple roof. But he was back at Longleat by 1565, well before work on the hall was completed. However, at least two other eminent artificers linked to Sir John Thynne – Lewis Stocket and William Spicer – may also be connected with the construction of Middle Temple Hall.

Lewis Stocket was a joiner by training, who filled the top post in the Elizabethan building world as Surveyor of the Royal Works from 1563 until his death in 1579, and was also Master of the Joiners' Company in 1571. He was clearly a competent administrator, but, as so often in the Elizabethan building world, remains a somewhat shadowy figure. He had worked for Thynne in 1559, not at Longleat but in London, when he charged nearly £21 – a sizeable sum in terms of money values of those days – for wainscoting the great chamber at Thynne's house in Cannon Row in the City of Westminster.[23] In 1564, Stocket supplied the joinery and carving for Queen Elizabeth's first coach, a fanciful piece of design which suggests that he was more than an administrator.

The evidence for Stocket's possible involvement at the Middle Temple is two-fold. First, we know that, in at least 1566 and 1567, he was not only occupying a house in Temple Lane, leading down from Fleet Street to the site of Middle Temple Hall, but renting 'a pece of grounde' adjoining it from the Middle Temple.[24] Second, in 1574/75, Stocket's son and heir, John, was admitted to the Inn 'specially'.[25] But however suggestive these fleeting references, the possibility that Stocket was employed as the surveyor of building works for Middle Temple Hall, or that he himself supplied carved work for the roof and screen, must remain surmise.

And what of William Spicer? A mason from the village of Nunney, in Wiltshire, Spicer had worked at Longleat, beginning in 1555 as a junior craftsman and rising rapidly through the ranks before falling out with Thynne and leaving Longleat in 1563. In the early 1570s, Spicer oversaw Robert Dudley, Earl of Leicester's lavish building works at Kenilworth Castle, in Warwickshire. Perhaps owing to Leicester's influence, Spicer went on to be appointed Surveyor of the Queen's Works at Berwick in 1584. Twelve years later, in 1596, he 'captured the plum of the Elizabethan building world, the Surveyorship of the Royal Works in London'.[26]

In Spicer's case, there is firm evidence that his services were requested by the Middle Temple. Writing to the Earl of Leicester from Kenilworth in June 1571, Spicer noted: 'thaye of the tempell haue wryten to me to come to them thys terme but I haue sent them worde by may man that yf they cane get leve of your lordship I will be Redy other wyse I may not'.[27] In light of the date, the project in question surely must have been the new hall. But whether Spicer accepted the Middle Temple's invitation is unknown. As is clear from the letters from Spicer to Leicester that have survived,[28] not only were the building works at Kenilworth behind schedule in the summer of 1571, but when the Middle Temple's request arrived, Spicer had only just returned to Kenilworth after having spent the previous week 'A pone my lord shandoes bylldinge' – presumably a reference to the building works of Edmund Brydges, 2nd Baron Chandos, at Sudeley Castle, in Gloucestershire.[29] Whether Spicer was able to 'get leve' of Leicester – either during the summer of 1571 or a subsequent legal term – is unknown.

Where the 'Old Hall' at Lincoln's Inn is concerned, however, one is out of the region of surmise, for relevant payments for building projects are recorded in the so-called 'Black Books' of accounts. In 1549–50, for example, 'one Parys, a joiner' was paid £4 11s. for making a screen and a 'portall' in the hall, while an unspecified painter received 8s. for painting the screen.[30] In the Inn's Minutes for 30 April 1583, it was directed that, in extending the hall, 'the plott [i.e. plan] of Symons [is] to be preserued as nere as may be, and he [is] to be used for his advise touchinge the same buildinge'.[31] In 1624, a payment of 30s. was made 'to the carpenter and joiner for removing the screen in the Hall' (i.e. that by 'Parys') and a second payment, of £40, made to 'Robert Lynton, joiner, for the new screen in the Hall'.[32] A few years later, another payment, this one for £5, was made 'for the top of the screen in the Hall'.[33]

'Parys' may be the same as (or possibly the father of) the 'Parris' who provided delicate carved work in Northamptonshire for the Middle Templar Sir Thomas Tresham in 1594–98 at the Triangular and Hawkfield Lodges at Rushton and at Lyveden New Bield.[34] He may also be the Andrew Paris, or Parris, carver, who worked on the King Edward III Great-Gates at Trinity College, Cambridge in 1600–1, and died while he was at work there.[35] 'Symons' was John Symonds, a protégé of Lewis Stocket, who first appears working under Stocket as early as 1547. He was a 'carver' who could work in stone, wood, and plaster, but he was also a designer, who could make drawings or 'plotts', as was the case at Lincoln's Inn. As Symonds was not a carpenter, however, the actual structure of the roof extension would have been made and installed by an artificer whose name is not recorded. As for Robert Lynton, he was a leading joiner of his day, warden of the London Joiners' Company in 1622, and its Master in 1627. Lynton had a history of patronage by the Inns of Court, having been employed by the Inner Temple as early as 1608 or 1609 in 'making new pews in the church, and wainscotting the treasurer's study'.[36]

Hall screens

As noted, it was traditional, from the fourteenth-century onwards, for a great hall – whether domestic or institutional – to be entered via a wooden screen positioned at one end of the rectangular hall space. Typically, the screen was an elaborately carved, two-storey structure. Sometimes, its second storey was occupied by a minstrels' gallery. If, as already suggested, the Inns' halls were entirely conventional in terms of their basic layout, their screens by contrast were in the new, Flemish manner, with no hint of traditional detail. The earliest is probably the screen at Gray's Inn, though there is no documentation. The Inner Temple screen, if Dugdale is to be relied on, dated from 1574, and was probably elaborate.[37] At the Middle Temple, as noted, money was being raised for a screen in 1575. Staple Inn seems never to have raised the money for an elaborate screen, and Lincoln's Inn, as we have seen, installed and painted a new screen in the mid sixteenth century, before installing the present screen in the 1620s.

In their detail, the Inns of Court screens are among the most efflorescent to have survived from the Elizabethan and Jacobean periods. They are joiners', not carpenters', work. Joiners, engaged in providing ornamental rather than structural woodwork, were less conservative than the carpenters, and more stylistically adventurous. Many of the joiners in sixteenth-century London were in fact foreigners, religious refugees from the Low Countries who had brought to England numerous Continental fashions, such as the vogue for decorative strapwork (i.e. the intricate depiction on wood, among other surfaces, of interlaced leather straps). These émigrés congregated especially on the South Bank in Southwark, outside the jurisdiction of the City of London and its livery companies, or guilds. Although the foreigners were much resented as interlopers, in fact English-born artificers were quick to imitate their style or to employ them in their workshops.

It is quite possible that Flemish joiners were working on the Gray's Inn and Middle Temple screens, but one cannot be certain.[38] The screens certainly show the influence of Flemish fashions and the Flemish engravings which were in circulation in England at the time to provide craftsmen with ideas and images.[39] The strapwork ornament which covers the columns and fills the friezes of the Gray's Inn screen, for example, is typical of the way in which Flemish designers and craftsmen embellished the Classical orders. The pedimented features along the top, on the other hand, have lifted elements from Serlio's designs for Doric and Composite chimneypieces.

The ebullient and indeed amazing Middle Temple screen suggests a more complicated and puzzling story: a possible two-stage development. The basic element of the lower half of the screen is formed by a row of Doric columns, with Hercules figures on the pedestals, and a Doric entablature of triglyphs and metopes – all of which are indebted to Shute's illustration of the Roman Doric order in his *First and Chief Groundes of Architecture*.[40] (See Plate 2 and Figure 1) But between the capitals of the columns and the frieze, a second quite unclassical frieze has been inserted. The upper storey is a riot of Flemish ornaments – strapwork, terms (i.e. statues

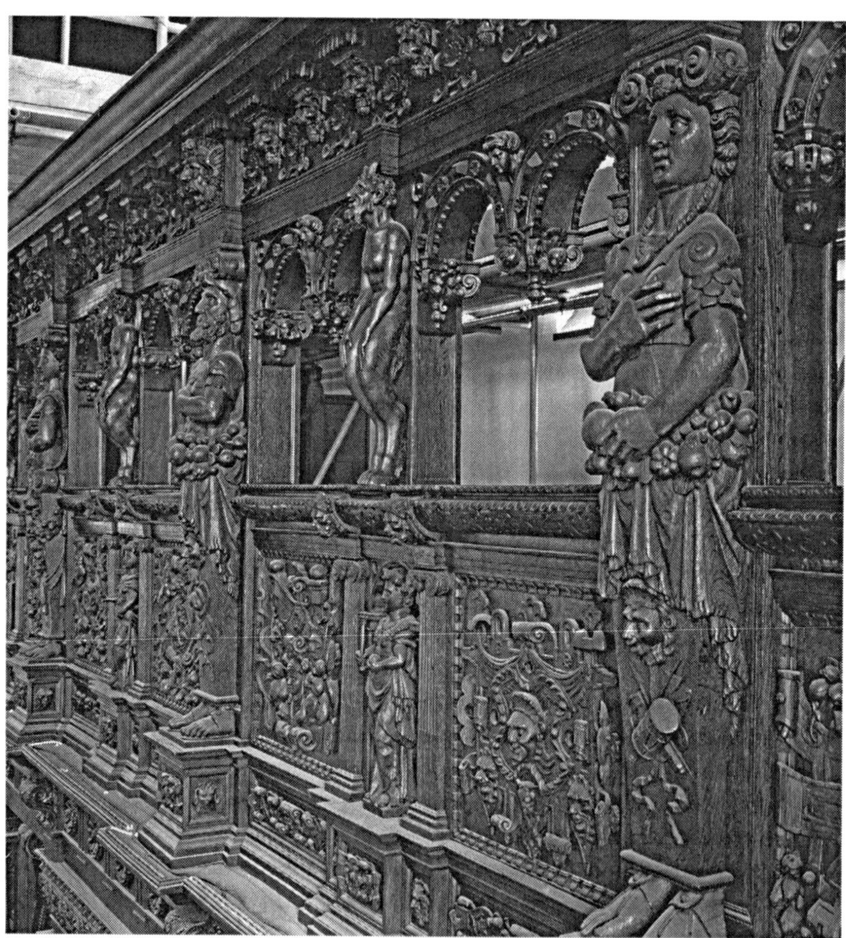

8 A detail of the upper storey of Middle Temple Hall screen

representing the upper part of the body), imps, and grotesque masks – in which smaller Ionic pilasters and capitals are submerged. Was the whole screen designed at one time? Or was the first design one for a sober Doric screen – perhaps even made and ready in the workshop – which was subsequently added to, enlarged, and embellished as tastes changed or more money came in?

The present screen in the 'Old Hall' at Lincoln's Inn reflects the changing taste of the 1620s, when strapwork was being replaced by a curious but distinctive ornamental language of *trompe-l'œil* perspective, ovals, knobs, and bosses (i.e. protrusions of stone or, in this case, wood). Though not as ebullient as the Middle Temple screen, it is an impressive object.

Heraldic glass

In addition to the roofs and the screens, a third element was added to the richness of the Inns' halls in the form of heraldic stained glass.[41] As at Oxford and Cambridge, where it was the practice throughout the sixteenth century to place the arms of college benefactors in the glass of hall windows,[42] so the Inns of Court honoured those who

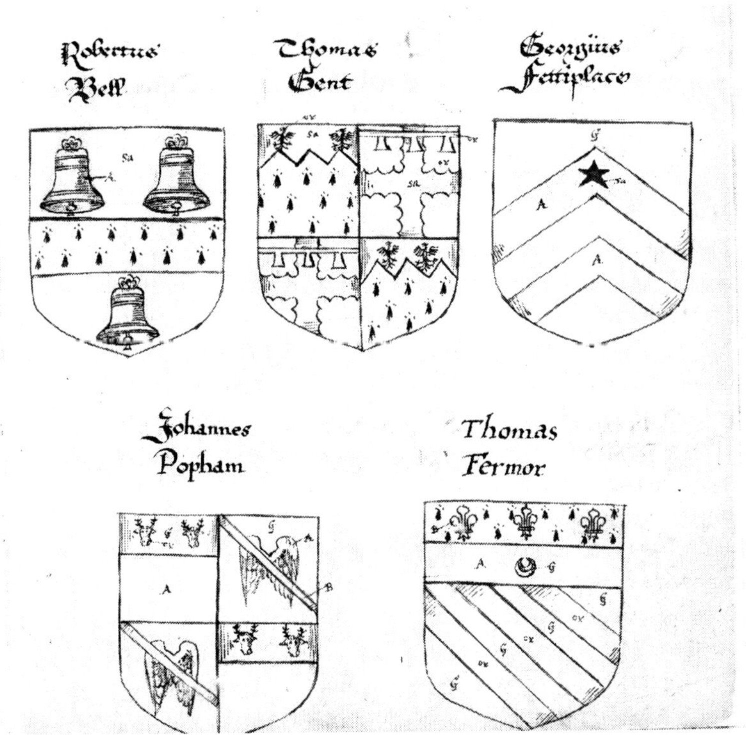

9 Detail from a heraldic manuscript of *c.*1602 recording the coats of arms in the painted glass in Middle Temple Hall

had made important contributions of one variety or another by displaying their arms in painted glass in the hall. In Middle Temple Hall, an early surviving example is a pane inscribed '1573' which features the coat of arms of Edmund Plowden, who, during his tenure as treasurer and afterwards, supervised the building of the new hall, including the raising of funds for this project.[43] Plowden's window not only contains his arms, but also has a Latin inscription noting the great care with which he brought to completion these building works. Today, the windows of the Inns' halls are filled with a splendid array of panes of heraldic glass installed over the centuries. But even by the end of Elizabeth's reign, these windows with their colourful glass must have made a handsome show.

Although heraldic glass had certainly existed before the mid-sixteenth century, the growing displays of it in the legal halls and at the universities must have encouraged similar displays in country houses, of which the windows in the great chamber at Gilling Castle in Yorkshire, a blaze of heraldic display inaugurated in 1585, are the outstanding but not the only surviving example. Two other excellent examples, both dating from the final years of the sixteenth century, may be found at Montacute House in Somerset and at Stoneleigh Abbey in Warwickshire.[44] In the case of Montacute, built to showcase the rising fortunes of the barrister (and future Speaker of the House of Commons) Sir Edward Phelips, there may be a direct debt to the Inns of Court, for Phelips was a Middle Templar who had made his money and his name practising at the chancery bar and in the court of Star Chamber.

Lines of descent

It is not just in the realm of heraldic glass that a possible line of descent can be traced from the Inns of Court to other contemporary building projects. The Inns' roofs, for example, are the first known in a sequence of country house and college roofs of similar scale and stylistic mix. Among country houses, this list includes Longleat (c.1572) in Wiltshire; Wiston (1573–75) in West Sussex; Burghley (c.1578) in Lincolnshire; and Wollaton (1580) in Nottinghamshire. Among colleges it includes Trinity College, Cambridge (1604–5) and Wadham College, Oxford (1612–13).[45]

Can any of the patrons and artificers associated with these domestic and collegiate building works be linked to the world of the Inns of Court? The roof at Wiston, built during the tenure of Sir Thomas Sherley, is an especially close copy of that of Middle Temple Hall. Although nothing is known of Sir Thomas's education, it is not inconceivable that he was a Templar, for his sons Thomas and Anthony are known to have been admitted to the Inner Temple in the early 1580s. At Burghley, William Cecil, like all the Cecil men in this period, was a member of Gray's Inn. In the case of Longleat, it is not known whether Sir John Thynne had an Inn affiliation. But the Longleat roof was the work of John Lewis, who, as noted, had been involved in the early phase of building at Middle Temple Hall. And his son, John Lewis junior, worked under another Longleat carpenter, Richard Crispin, on the roof at Wollaton, built for Sir Francis Willoughby (whose Inn affiliation, if any, is, like Thynne's, unknown).

In the case of Wadham College, Oxford, it may not be entirely irrelevant that the college's co-founders, Nicholas Wadham (1531/32–1609) and his wife Dorothy (1534/35–1618), both had ties to the world of the Inns of Court. Nicholas, though dead by the time building work on the college commenced, had been admitted to

10 A detail of the hall screen at Knole, in Kent

the Inner Temple in 1553, while Dorothy Wadham, who was closely involved in the design of the college and the selection of the craftsmen who were to build it, was the daughter of the distinguished civil and canon lawyer Sir William Petre. Whether Thomas Bolton, the artificer responsible for the college's hammerbeam roof, had ever undertaken work for any of the Inns of Court is unknown.[46]

At Trinity College, Cambridge, where the hall seems to have been envisioned from the outset as a theatre as well as a place for eating and drinking, the roof was deliberately built to identical dimensions to that at the Middle Temple.[47] This project was overseen (and probably also designed) by Ralph Symonds, a local master mason who previously had been involved in building works at Whitehall, as well as at various other Cambridge colleges, including Emmanuel, Sidney Sussex, and St John's.[48] Additional details of Ralph Symonds's biography are obscure. But the possibility that he was a kinsman of the John Symonds discussed earlier in this chapter in connection with designs for the roof extension at Lincoln's Inn 'Old Hall' in 1583 is a tantalising one. So too is the possibility that one or both men were related to the 'Ralph Symondes' listed in the *Black Books* as having been paid thirty-one shillings for repairs to the same hall in 1551–52.[49]

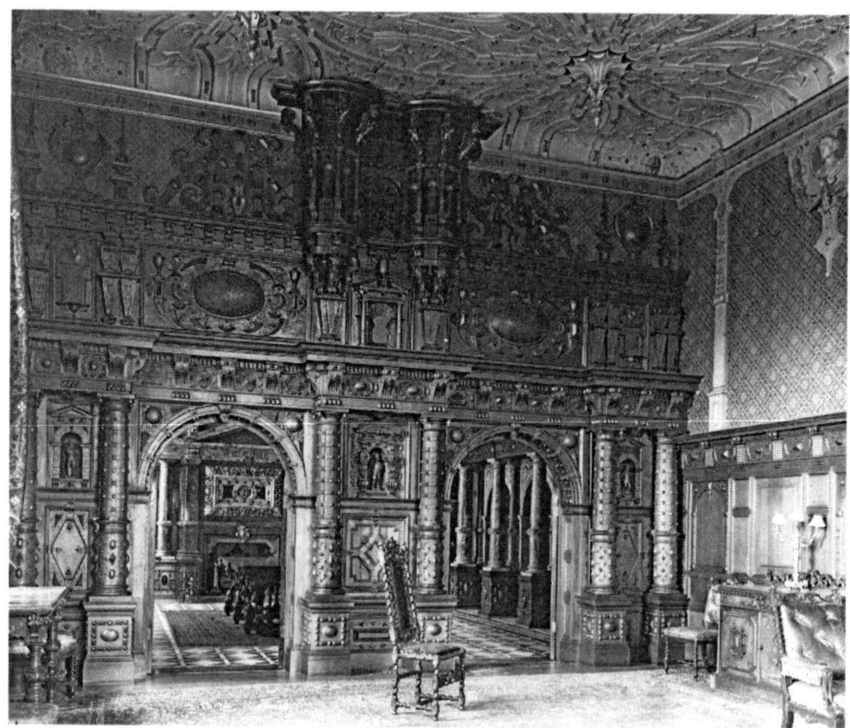

11 The hall screen at Crewe Hall, in Cheshire

Just as the roofs of the Inns' halls influenced domestic and collegiate architecture in the late Elizabethan and Jacobean periods, so the screens at Gray's Inn and especially at the Middle Temple seem to have inaugurated a series of wooden screens in country houses and colleges, mostly, though not all, of two storeys, and all richly, not to say overpoweringly, ornamented with strapwork, terms, and grotesques. This series starts with the screen at Longleat (*c.*1580), and carries on into the early seventeenth century with country house screens at Knole in Kent, Audley End in Essex, and Hatfield in Hertfordshire, as well as with collegiate screens at Trinity College, Cambridge, and Wadham College, Oxford. A little later, the screen at Crewe Hall in Cheshire, built by the judge Sir Randolph Crewe between 1615 and 1636, is close enough to that in Lincoln's Inn to suggest that it may be the work of Robert Lynton, the master joiner who, as noted, was responsible for the screen erected in the 'Old Hall' at Lincoln's in 1624.

Many of the patrons who oversaw these building works were embedded within the culture of the Inns of Court. At Knole, Thomas Sackville, 1st Earl of Dorset, had been admitted to the Inner Temple in 1554 and had co-authored *Gorbuduc*, one of the plays performed in Inner Temple Hall during the 1561–62 Christmas revels; his sons William, Robert, and Thomas were also Inner Templars.[50] At Hatfield, Robert Cecil, like his father and brothers, was a Gray's Inn man, having been admitted in 1580. At Crewe Hall, Sir Randolph Crewe had been a bencher of Lincoln's Inn since 1600. As for Sir John Thynne and Longleat, their connections to the building works at Middle Temple Hall already have been discussed.

Epilogue

Inigo Jones's Banqueting House (1619–22) in Whitehall introduced a new type of great room, grandly Classical, with a flat coffered ceiling and no Gothic elements. Halls with open timber roofs quickly went out of fashion. Perhaps the last in the sequence was the great hall (now the library) at Lambeth Palace, built *circa* 1660–63 to replace its predecessor, which had been demolished under the Commonwealth, and described by Samuel Pepys in 1665 as 'a new old-fashion Hall'.[51] But legal conservatism, combined with the high quality of the buildings, kept the halls at Gray's Inn, the Middle Temple, Lincoln's Inn, and Staple Inn intact.[52] And when, in the nineteenth century, the Gothic revival and romantic neo-feudalism brought the building of halls with open timber roofs back into fashion, it was fitting that one of the earliest examples – and the earliest in London – was the 'New Hall' at Lincoln's Inn (1843–45), a great deal bigger, though not necessarily better, than the 'Old Hall', which was piously preserved across the courtyard.

Notes

1 Citations from manuscripts at Longleat House, Wiltshire are provided by kind permission of the Marquess of Bath; I would like to thank Kate Harris, archivist at Longleat, for providing the transcriptions cited here. I am also most grateful to Elizabeth Goldring for her contributions to this essay, including extensive work on the footnotes when I was incapacitated in hospital and convalescing.

2 For a detailed discussion of these points with particular reference to the built environment of the Inns of Court, see Chapter 10 (pp. 199–213, below).

3 The medieval hall of Barnard's Inn – like Staple Inn, another of the Inns of Chancery – does not, strictly speaking, fall into this category, for, unlike the 'Old Hall' of Lincoln's Inn, it is not known to have been expanded in the early modern period. But the late fourteenth-century hall of Barnard's Inn is of note as the oldest surviving secular building in the City of London.

4 Although Gray's Inn Hall was gutted in 1941, it was reconstructed after the Second World War and its painted glass and shields, which had been removed to safety, reinstated. The interior of Middle Temple Hall, including its celebrated screen, also suffered severe damage during the Second World War – though, as at Gray's Inn, a reconstruction was undertaken after the war. Staple Inn Hall was destroyed in 1944, but later reconstructed using as many of the original parts and materials as it had been possible to salvage. Although the 'Old Hall' at Lincoln's Inn emerged from the Second World War intact, it had been taken apart and put back together, using the original materials, in the 1920s, at which point it had been in danger of collapse. During these building works, a plaster ceiling installed in the eighteenth century was removed, thereby revealing the previously hidden timbers of both the medieval roof and an Elizabethan extension to it.

5 There is, for example, no comparable body of surviving buildings for the London livery companies, as their early modern halls were decimated first by the Great Fire of 1666 and then by the Blitz (and, in many cases, by intervening fires as well).

6 For references to mooting in, for example, Lincoln's Inn 'Old Hall', see *Black Books*, I, 102, 263, 316. For the function of the halls at Oxford and Cambridge colleges in this period, see John Newman, 'The physical setting: new building and adaptation', in James McConica (ed.), *The History of the University of Oxford. Vol. 3: The Collegiate University* (Oxford: Clarendon Press, 1986), pp. 597–632 (pp. 616–18); and Christopher Brooke, 'The buildings of Cambridge', in Victor Morgan with Christopher Brooke, *A History of the University of Cambridge. Vol. 2: 1546–1750* (Cambridge: Cambridge University Press, 2004), pp. 13–62 (pp. 37–40).

7 For a discussion of some of the dramatic revels staged in the Inns' halls in the sixteenth and early seventeenth centuries, see Chapter 2, above, and Chapters 12 through 15, below.

8 Robert Fookes and Richard Wallington, 'The buildings: long history and picturesque variety', in Angela Holdsworth (ed.), *A Portrait of Lincoln's Inn* (London: The Honourable Society of Lincoln's Inn/Third Millennium Publishing, 2007), pp. 25–45 (p. 27).

9 As Wilfrid R. Prest has noted, annual admissions to the four Inns quadrupled between 1500 and 1600 (*The Inns of Court under Elizabeth I and the Early Stuarts, 1590–1640* (London: Longman, 1972), p. 7).

10 *Pension Book of Gray's Inn*, I, 497, 498.

11 William Dugdale, *Origines Juridiciales* (London: Christopher Wilkinson, Thomas Dring, and Charles Harper, 1666), p. 146.

12 For a discussion of the same issue with respect to building projects at the post-Restoration Inns, see Chapter 10 (pp. 199–213, below).

13 *Middle Temple Records*, I, 137. A similar policy had been followed at Gray's Inn when it rebuilt its hall in the 1550s. See *Pension Book of Gray's Inn*, I, 497.

14 *Middle Temple Records*, I, 140.

15 *Ibid.*, I, 176.

16 *Ibid.*, I, 176.

17 *Ibid.*, I, 197, 206.

18 See Elizabeth Goldring's Introduction, pp. 128–9, above. *The First and Chief Groundes* may also have been reprinted in 1580 and 1584. See Gerald Beasley's entry for Shute in the *ODNB*.

19 Plowden was selected as treasurer on 20 June 1562. See *Middle Temple Records*, I, 131.

20 Mark Girouard, *Robert Smythson and the Elizabethan Country House* (New Haven, CT; London: Yale University Press, 1983), p. 41.

21 *Ibid.*, p. 40.

22 Longleat, Records of Building II, fol. 100[r].

23 Longleat, Box LXXVI, Book 146, fol. 16[v].

24 *Middle Temple Records*, I, 153, 432.

25 *Ibid.*, I, 203–4.

26 Girouard, *Smythson*, pp. 44–5.

27 Longleat, Dudley Papers II, fol 321[r]. I would like to thank Elizabeth Goldring for alerting me to the contents of this letter.

28 Only two letters from Spicer to Leicester are known to have survived: the one cited in the main text above, together with another, dated 15 July 1571 at Kenilworth (Longleat, Records of Building III, fol. 161[r]).

29 Longleat, Dudley Papers II, fol. 321[r].

30 *Black Books*, I, 295.

31 *Ibid.*, I, 428.

32 *Ibid.*, II, 253. I owe this and other references to the Inns' records to Elizabeth Goldring.

33 *Ibid.*, II, 274.

34 *Historical Manuscripts Commission Report on Manuscripts in Various Collections. Vol. III* (London: HMSO, 1904), pp. xxxvi–xxxix, xli, xlvi.

35 John Willis Clark, *The Architectural History of the University of Cambridge and of the Colleges of Cambridge and Eton*, 3 vols (Cambridge: Cambridge University Press, 1988; facsimile of 1886 edition), II, 482, n. 5; 487, n. 1.

36 *Inner Temple Records*, II, 45.

37 However, a passing reference in the Inner Temple's accounts for 1619–20 suggests that, at that date at least, the screen was painted: 'To the painter, for painting the wainscot in the hall and buttery; for painting the screen' (*ibid.*, II, 121). See also the accounts for 1623–24, which record a payment of £32 10s. 'To John Feild, carpenter, and John Ramsey, the joiner, for new boarding all the hall and the passage below the screen, for boards, nails, and timber' (*ibid.*, II, 146).

38 For the activities of painters from the Low Countries at the early modern Inns of Court, see Chapter 8 (pp. 158–61, below).

39 For the dissemination of Flemish fashions via prints in England in this period, see Anthony Wells-Cole, *Art and Decoration in Elizabethan and Jacobean England: The Influence of Continental Prints, 1558–1625* (New Haven, CT; London: Yale University Press/ The Paul Mellon Centre for Studies in British Art, 1997), pp. 43–124.

40 *Ibid.*, pp. 169–70.

41 For other forms of decoration in the Inns' halls in this period – including paintings, hangings, and wooden panelling adorned with coats of arms – see Chapter 8 (pp. 158–61, below).

42 See, e.g., Newman, 'The physical setting', p. 618; and Victor Morgan, 'Cambridge and "The Country"', in Morgan and Brooke, *History of the University of Cambridge. Vol. 2*, pp. 181–240 (p. 210).

43 Although Plowden was succeeded as Treasurer in 1567, he remained 'Collector for the building of the new Hall' (*Middle Temple Records*, I, 159).

44 See Wells-Cole, *Art and Decoration*, pp. 217–18.

45 For links between the Inns' gardens and those of Trinity College, Cambridge and Wadham College, Oxford in this period, see Chapter 9 (pp. 193–4, below).

46 For Dorothy Wadham and Wadham College, see Geoffrey Tyack, *Oxford: An Architectural Guide* (Oxford: Oxford University Press, 1998), pp. 98–101. For Bolton and Wadham College, see Geoffrey Tyack, *Blue Guide: Oxford and Cambridge* (London: A & C Black/ New York, NY: W. W. Norton, 1999), p. 86.

47 See Brooke, 'The buildings of Cambridge', pp. 38–40.

48 John Summerson, *Architecture in Britain, 1530 to 1830* (New Haven, CT; London: Yale University Press, 1953; repr. 1993), pp. 161–2; Tyack, *Blue Guide: Oxford and Cambridge*, p. 192.

49 *Black Books*, I, 301–2.

50 For *Gorboduc*, see Chapter 12 (pp. 256–7, below).

51 *The Diary of Samuel Pepys*, ed. Robert Latham and William Matthews, 11 vols (London: Bell and Hyman, 1970–83), VI, 164.

52 For a discussion of legal conservatism in the building projects undertaken by the post-Restoration Inns, see Chapter 10 (pp. 199–213, below).

8

Professional pride and personal agendas: portraits of judges, lawyers, and members of the Inns of Court, 1560–1630

Tarnya Cooper[1]

During the second half of the sixteenth century, portraiture gradually became a popular genre of painting in England, not only for depicting those within aristocratic court circles, but also – and increasingly – in representing the middling sort of people and urban elites. From the 1560s onwards, numerous portraits of judges, barristers, and legal students were painted from the life, a visual display of professional pride that coincided with a dramatic increase not only in the numbers of those engaged in the legal profession, but also in the wealth and status of those who reached its upper echelons.[2] To date, such images have been little studied. One reason for this is the fact that survival rates for English paintings of this period are low, with the result that the available visual evidence remains suggestive rather than conclusive. Moreover, where sitters of the middling sort are concerned, the surviving portraits usually cannot be attributed to specific artists, with the result that such images have largely been considered to be outside the canon of British art.

Yet early modern legal portraits, as we shall see, were meaningful for the sitters and the patrons who commissioned them, as well as for their contemporary audiences. Such images can add to our understanding of the ways in which middle elites in sixteenth- and early seventeenth-century England used painted imagery to present themselves to their peers and to wider publics. They also provide a visual register for the cultural and social confidence of members of the legal profession at a time when its members were becoming the subject of increasing criticism by Puritan ministers. This chapter explores the visual culture of the early modern Inns of Court, with particular reference to the various ways that members of the legal profession and others associated with the Inns chose to be represented in painted portraits during the sixteenth and early seventeenth centuries. To that end, it begins by considering the role played by painted imagery at the Elizabethan and Jacobean Inns of Court, before turning to the wider cultural context to examine the modes of visual representation deployed by judges, barristers, and members of the Inns in this period.

Visual imagery within the Inns of Court, *circa* 1600

Determining how the interior spaces of the Inns of Court were decorated in the sixteenth and early seventeenth centuries is not straightforward, as the surviving evidence – visual as well as written – is scarce. Although painted portraits of early modern judges and other worthies hang on the walls of the Inns today, these images were acquired, with very few exceptions, from the later seventeenth century onwards, with the majority having been bequeathed to or purchased by the Inns in the nineteenth and twentieth centuries. Moreover, such portraits, as we shall see in the next section of this chapter, are likely originally to have been commissioned for display in domestic spaces and in the service of personal, rather than institutional, agendas. To the extent that accounts for the Inns have survived from the sixteenth and early seventeenth centuries, they give little indication that portraits of judges and other leading legal figures were on display. Indeed, such documents make only occasional mention of paintings of any variety – though, given that pictures were often considered relatively low-value items in this period, it may be the case that their presence was not routinely recorded.

Pictorial and documentary sources indicate that painted coats of arms were displayed within the libraries and probably within some of the main halls of the Inns in the early modern period. Some examples dating from the late sixteenth century may be seen today in Middle Temple Hall, where several centuries worth of painted coats of arms have culminated in the decoration of the entire wall space of the hall panelling. Records for Lincoln's Inn show that coats of arms were occasionally directly commissioned. In 1594–95, for example, the Inn paid ten shillings for the 'insignia', or coat of arms, of Sir John Puckering,[3] the Lord Keeper of the Great Seal and a leading figure at Lincoln's.[4] A year later, several payments for painted coats of arms of various nameless key worthies are recorded in the large payment of £3 6s. 8d. made to Joseph Elstrack, a member of a well-known family of Dutch émigré artists, for 'five coats of arms'.[5] The reasonably large price would indicate that these were probably sizeable works.

In addition, the Inns of Court displayed painted hangings, or painted cloths, a ubiquitous and relatively inexpensive form of wall decoration also common in domestic interiors in England in this period. When, for example, the buildings of Lincoln's Inn were remodelled in June 1607, the fixtures removed from the 'Shorte Gallerye' included 'shelves, tables, seates, paintinge clothes [i.e. painted cloths], and wainscott workes'.[6] The 'paintinge clothes' may have featured narrative scenes of allegorical or religious subjects or simple decorative schemes.[7] The reference to 'wainscott workes' probably describes wooden panelling painted with some type of design such as a simple *trompe l'œil* device or a feigned marble pattern.

In the case of Lincoln's Inn and Middle Temple, there is also some written evidence for the display and ownership of actual pictures – in the modern sense of paintings on panel or canvas designed to be hung on the wall – across the fifteenth and sixteenth centuries. As early as 1441, the chaplain of Lincoln's Inn delivered to the Society 6*s*. 8*d*. arising from 'the sale of divers pictures', which presumably had been hanging within the Inn's premises.[8] Just over a decade later, in 1450–51, Richard Drax, a long-standing member of Lincoln's, was specially admitted to a repast following his gift of money towards projected building works and his promise

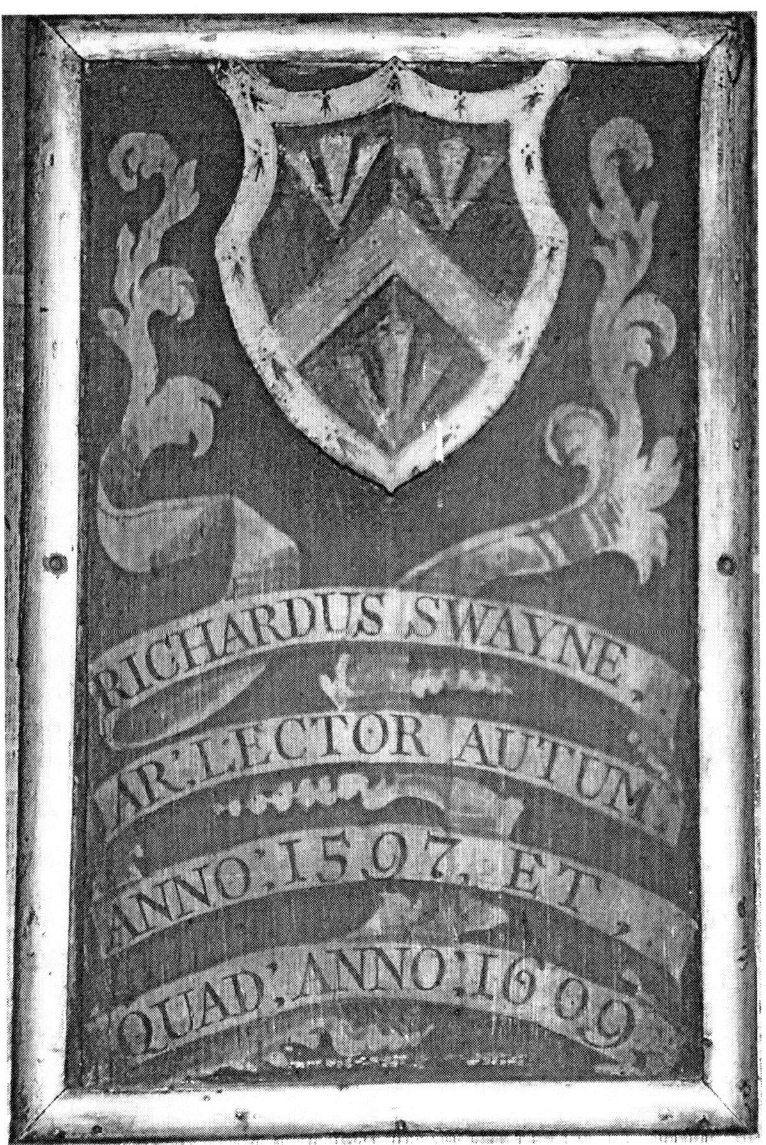

12 The painted coat of arms of Richard Swayne, a double reader at Middle Temple (1597 and 1609), is one of the oldest surviving examples of its kind. Currently in Hall, it was one of 113 panels moved there in 1697 from the then Parliament Chamber

to 'give the Society in a short time a new picture'.[9] Taken together, these brief references might indicate that, in the middle decades of the fifteenth century, the internal decorative scheme at Lincoln's was remodelled and new paintings hung in the hall or library.

Meanwhile, at Middle Temple, the authorities seem to have been collecting pictures – perhaps only on an *ad hoc* basis – at least as early as 1516. In that year, one 'Whytyng' was offered exemption from some of the charges of his membership in the Middle Temple in exchange for presenting 'one good picture well painted, to hang in the Hall'– a reference which might indicate the existence of an emerging custom of paintings being given to the Inn by its members.[10] Certainly, it is unlikely that Whytyng's picture for Middle Temple or Drax's produced decades before for Lincoln's Inn were the only painted images hanging in the Inns' halls at these dates. Yet what the subjects of the paintings were or whether they were displayed alongside other narrative, religious, or allegorical paintings is unknown. Frustratingly, the documentary references are fragmentary and at no point does a clear sense of picture holdings or a possible pattern of acquisitions emerge. It is conceivable, however, that a number of paintings were displayed at the Inns, but simply omitted from the written records: pictures at this date were of comparatively little monetary value and thus, as insubstantial gifts, they may not have been recorded. After all, there are no references to the bequest or commission of the painted cloth hangings that we know were at Lincoln's Inn in the 'Shorte Gallerye' before 1607 – which would indicate that, for Lincoln's, decorative fittings were not routinely listed in the *Black Books*.

Although the evidence for the existence of visual imagery at the early modern Inns of Court is, in the main, extremely limited, one significant exception is a late sixteenth-century narrative painting of the Judgement of Solomon. (See Plate 4) This picture is recorded as hanging in the hall at Middle Temple from the mid seventeenth century, and it remains within the Society's collection today.[11] On the grounds of style, the painting can be identified as the work of a Netherlandish mannerist artist and dated to *circa* 1570–1600,[12] a period when many artists and craftsmen from Flanders and the northern Netherlands sought refuge in England from religious persecution by the Spanish. Given that Middle Temple Hall itself was completed in the early 1570s,[13] it seems likely either that this painting was commissioned by the Middle Temple around the time the building works came to an end or that it was given to the Inn at some point during the next twenty to thirty years.[14]

The subject of this picture merits some comment, for the Judgement of Solomon was considered to be highly relevant to the legal profession. On the Continent in the late sixteenth century, it was the most frequently represented scene in the life of this Old Testament king, and the subject had come to be seen as emblematic of the idea that wise governance is the foundation for a stable state. In the case of the Middle Temple painting, there are two lengthy blocks of text which spell out the meaning of the scene in Latin. The relevance of this image to a specifically legal audience is made plain by the last few lines:

HAVRIAT HINC LEGVM QVISQVIS MOLITVR HABENAS / IVSTITIÆ DOCVMENTVM INGENS, LONGEQVE SEQVVTVS / CŒLITVS EDOCTI VESTIGIA REGIS ADORET.

(And now whoever holds the reins of justice let him learn this mighty lesson of just decision, and at a distance let him adore the footsteps of the King fully taught of God.)[15]

Thus, the painting and its inscription appear to have been intended to encourage and instruct Middle Templars to 'learn this mighty lesson of just decision' – presumably the importance of eliciting truthful information – while dining in their new hall.

Portraits of judges

Paintings of men in official robes and gowns became a standard, formulaic portrait 'type' in late sixteenth-century England, not only for judges, but also for the officers of livery companies and for men of civic office, such as aldermen and mayors.[16] Two portraits now in the National Portrait Gallery may be used to illustrate and explicate some of the key features typically encountered in portraits of judges in this period. One of these depicts Sir James Dyer (1510–82), a member of the Middle Temple who was appointed Judge of the Common Pleas in 1557 and Chief Justice of the Common Pleas in 1559.[17] The other depicts Sir William Daniel (d.1610), a member of Gray's Inn and a judge of the Common Pleas.[18] Although Daniel's image appears to date from soon after he became a judge in 1604, many other surviving examples of the genre show that – while portraits of members of the judiciary were usually painted at some point during the height of their sitters' careers[19] – this was not necessarily done on their initial appointment to the bench. Some extant portraits of judges are later copies of now-lost originals, indicating a demand for the replication of these images over a reasonably long period (sometimes extending well beyond a given sitter's death). Dyer's portrait, for example, is probably a late sixteenth-century copy of an earlier picture.[20]

Many early modern judicial portraits follow a relatively formulaic pattern and show the sitters in the red robes of office against a plain, dark background. Often, as in the Daniel and Dyer portraits, coats of arms are painted in one of the upper corners. As with many types of portraiture at this date, contemporary inscriptions are frequently employed, sometimes to record a date or a family motto. In Daniel's portrait, for example, the words 'Nec spe: nec metu' ('Neither with hope, nor with fear') appear at the top right. It is notable that the basic size and format – head and shoulders in the case of Dyer, three-quarter length in the case of Daniel – do not in any way correlate to judicial rank.[21] Rather, this choice would have been determined by the cost painters charged for portraits of varying size, and possibly also by the intended space for which the painting was commissioned.

Judicial dress appears to have become formalised in the fifteenth century, when scarlet robes displaced green for full-dress occasions. These robes were edged – and

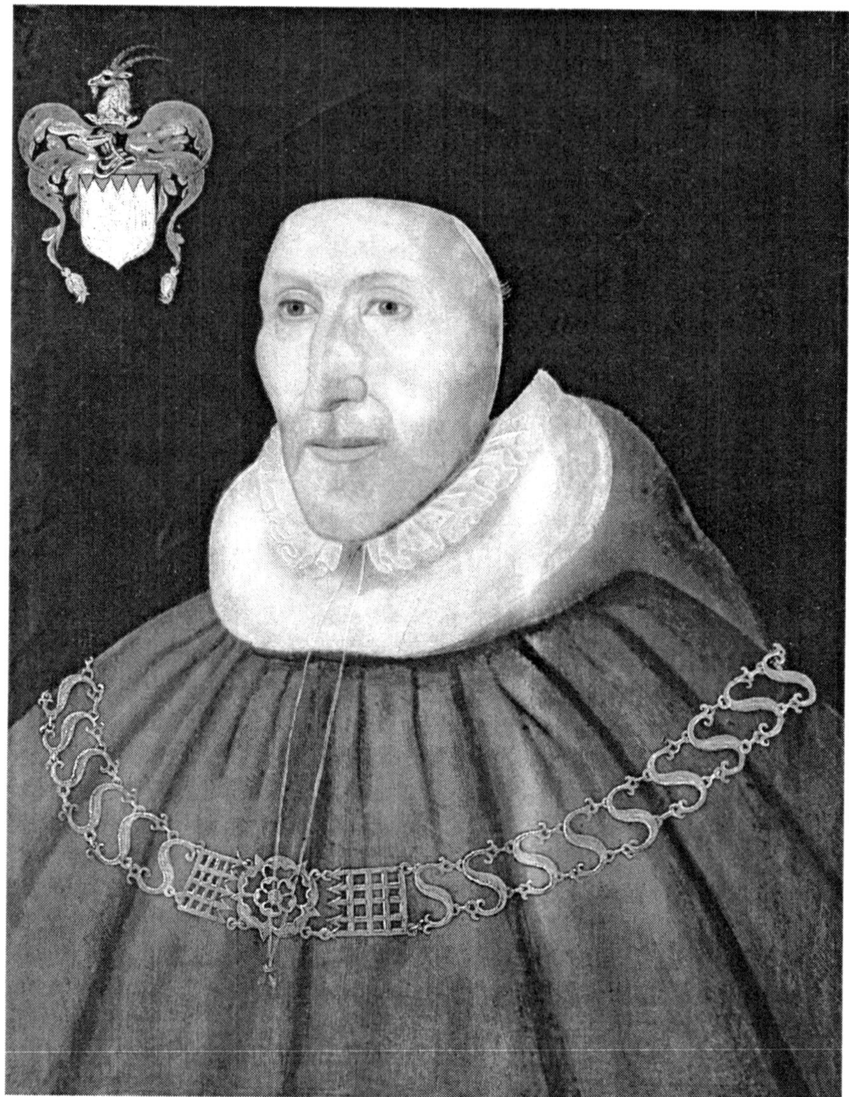

13 *A portrait of Sir James Dyer*, by an unknown English artist, after 1575,
oil on panel, 533 × 422 mm

may even have been lined – with white miniver fur, which can often been seen at
the edges and cuffs in surviving portraits. The full dress of judges must have been
extremely cumbersome and hot and would perhaps have been worn in its entirety
only on official occasions. It included a collobium or long tunic tied at the waist
with a silk sash; a short shoulder piece or hood finishing at the chest (the key part
of the costume seen in the Dyer portrait); and an 'armelausa', or long mantel, which

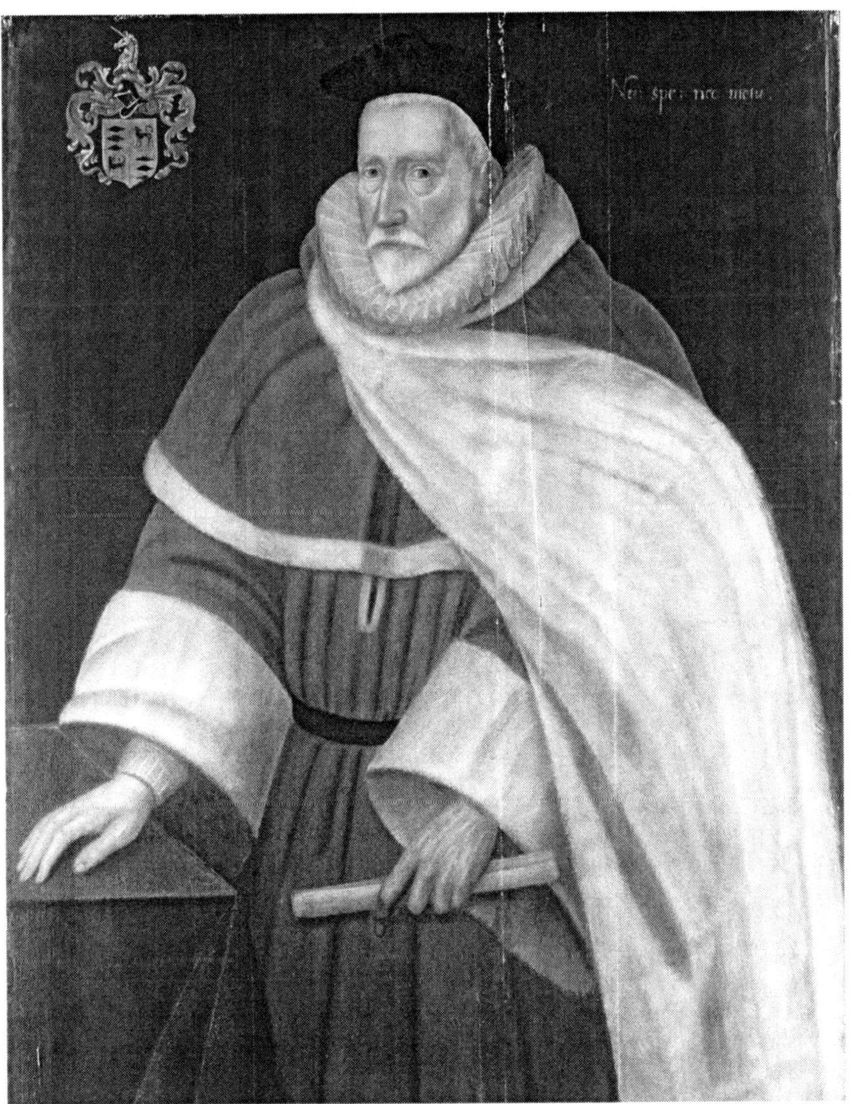

14 *A portrait of Sir William Daniel,* by an unknown English artist, 1604,
oil on panel, 1143 × 832 mm

opened down one side to reveal the white fur lining, as shown to full effect in the
portrait of Daniel. Ruffs of the size and fashion of the day can be also seen in most
judicial portraits. A fur-lined hood often is seen hanging down the back, like a 'great
bag of miniver'; one of these can just be glimpsed over the shoulder of Dyer.[22] A
square black four-cornered cap worn over a white coif and a skull cap completed
this impressive display of legal authority. Sometimes, as with Dyer, chief justices

are shown wearing a chain of office made of 'S's with a portcullis either side of a central rose. These chains were worn by the most senior judges on formal occasions, as well as by several other official servants of the Crown.[23] Other common attributes of early modern judicial portraits include the depiction of the sitter holding gloves or parchment rolls. Occasionally, the hands are shown placed upon books of legal texts. Features and poses such as these would have been decided upon in

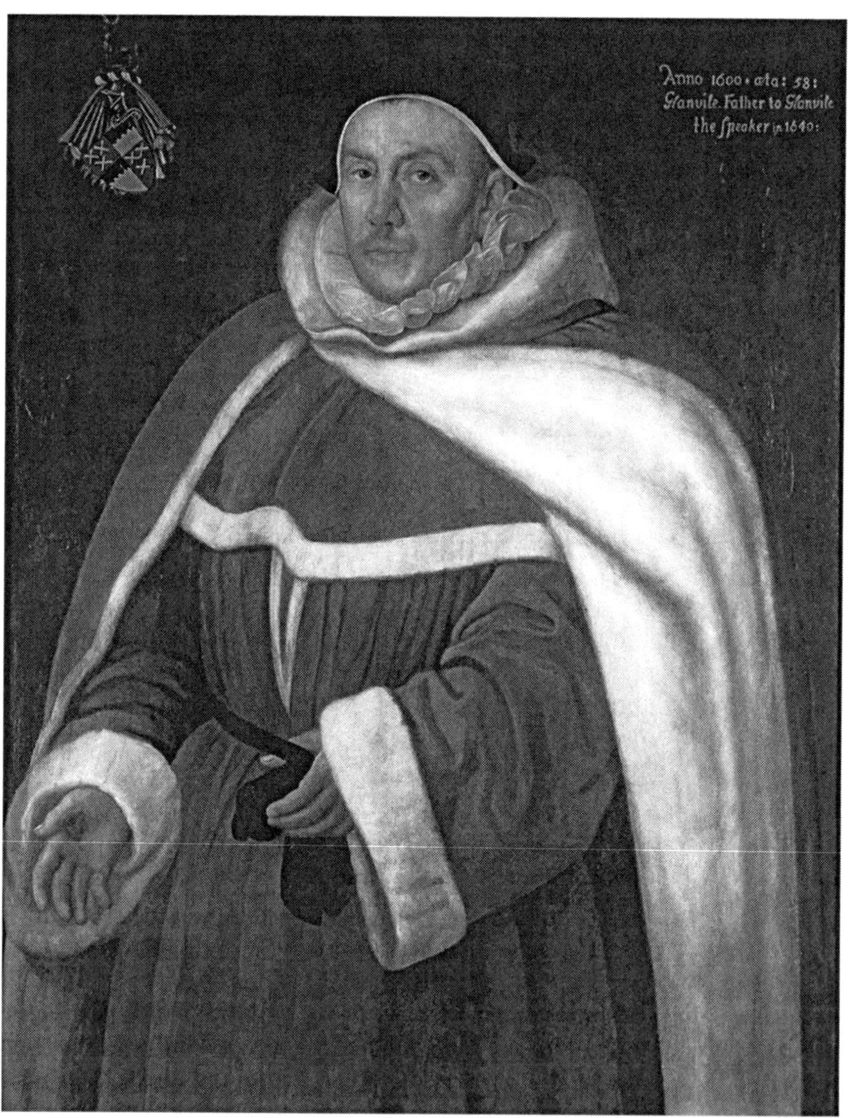

15 *A portrait of John Glanville the Elder*, by an unknown English artist, *c.*1590s, oil on panel, 1118 × 813 mm

consultation between the sitter and the artist, perhaps relying upon templates of previous judicial portraits seen in an artist's studio or in a model book.

In spite of the fact that numerous judicial portraits are extant today, there is, as noted, no documentary evidence that portraits of judges hung at the Inns of Court in the Tudor or Jacobean periods. So, how and where were they displayed? While portraits of robed judges look remarkably similar to modern eyes, particularly when seen hanging together in the Inns today, they were almost certainly not originally designed to be displayed collectively in institutional spaces. In the case of several surviving portraits, the combined evidence of provenance and later family inscriptions indicates that the majority of these images were displayed in the personal estates of the sitters shortly after their completion. A painting of John Glanville (1542–1600), a member of Lincoln's Inn and a judge of the Common Pleas, provides a good case in point. Now in Lincoln's Inn, this painting bears a later inscription at the top right: 'Anno 1600, æta: 58: Glanvile. Father to Glanvile the Speaker in 1640'. The reference to the sitter's son – Sir John Glanville the Younger (1585/86–1661) – suggests that, within decades after it was first painted, the portrait was displayed in a domestic context, alongside other dynastic, family portraits.[24]

However, there is some evidence to suggest that judges on occasion may have displayed visual images, including portraits, in their chambers. The commonplace book of John Manningham (c.1575–1622), compiled in 1602 and 1603 while Manningham was a third-year student at Middle Temple, includes a passing reference to a portrait that had once been on display in the study of the judge William Fleetwood (c.1525–94). Fleetwood, who was a member of Middle Temple and (from 1571) Recorder of London, had antiquarian interests, and the portrait in question depicted the historian and antiquary John Stowe (1524/25–1605). The reference in Manningham's diary reads as follows:

> I was with Stowe the Antiquary. He told me that a modell of his picture was found
> in the Recorder Fleetwoods study, with this inscription or circumscription: *Johannes
> Stowe, Antiquarius Angliae*, which nowe is cutt in brasse and prefixed in print to his
> Survey of London.[25]

The version of Stow's portrait in Fleetwood's chambers was apparently a drawn study for the engraving that accompanied the 1603 edition of Stow's *Survay of London*, perhaps even the original design for the printed image.[26] Although this commentary is simply a slight anecdotal reference, it is possible that Fleetwood's portrait of Stow appeared alongside other personal effects and visual memorabilia in his study. And, while we do not know how typical Fleetwood was in having displayed portraiture of one variety or another in his chambers, it may be that painted portraits occasionally hung – if only for short periods after their completion by a London painter – in a judge's London chambers.

Yet, as noted, it is likely that most Tudor and Jacobean judicial portraits were intended for display on the walls of the newly built country houses of this increasingly enriched class of men. In the context of a country house setting, it is tempting to see the display of portraiture as a direct emulation of the nobility. However, judges in this period chose to be depicted in ways that made their elite professional status unmistakable. A portrait of a judge distinctively clothed in an expensive red robe trimmed with fur represented a remarkable individual: the all-powerful bodily representative of temporal authority, unquestionably worthy of respect due to his learning and righteousness, rather than to inherited titles or blood ties. Such portraits do not attempt to assimilate their sitters into the conventions of display common to the nobility or gentry, in which the subject often is depicted in an elaborate, richly furnished interior space, occasionally, for example, with Classical pillars, embroidered curtains or pillows, items of armour, or accompanying dogs. Rather, Tudor and Jacobean judicial portraits, with their sober, unadorned backgrounds, use costume and the occasional inscription to insist upon their sitters' distinctive status as members of an elite and learned order of men.[27] For example, the original frame for Sir James Dyer's portrait bears a lengthy Latin inscription which reads in part:[28]

> Iudicis effigiem iusti, vultusque verendi / Conspice, qui legis, luxque decusque fuit. / Quem diues loculis, lachrimis quem pauper doctis / Iusticeæ a norma flectere non potuit.
> (Look upon the portrait of an upright judge, who was both the light and the ornament of the Law: whom neither the rich man with his wealth, nor the poor man with his flowing tears, could turn aside from the strict line of justice.)[29]

This text is being used to express Dyer's personal standing as a man of absolute integrity, whose principal concern, outside all considerations of rank or privilege, was with the letter of the law. This portrait is extremely rare in retaining its original sixteenth-century frame, a space where additional inscribed text sometimes was placed. It is likely that many other sixteenth-century portrait frames would have included celebratory text of this type. Indeed, professional men and all middle elites without hereditary coats of arms may have been more inclined to make use of picture frames to champion their exemplary characters and thereby to justify their right to present their likenesses in portraiture.

Even in the urban context, judges and their dress must have presented a highly distinctive visual spectacle. The Netherlandish artist Lucas de Heere (1534–84), who lived in England in the late 1560s and early 1570s, undertook numerous pen and ink drawings of notable features of the British Isles, including types of citizens, such as aldermen. A page from de Heere's sketchbook of around 1574, now in the British Library, depicts what are described as two judges of the Queen's Bench.[30] (See Plate 1) This drawing and the numerous others in the volume – which include images of nobles and a mayor, as well as of the wives of both nobles and citizens of the middling sort – have the appearance of studies from the life.[31] De Heere's judges are shown seated, as if in conversation, and holding papers and a book. No clues are provided as to their location. The judges are dressed in slightly different robes: the figure on the right wears a full mantle with the opening to the side, while the one on the left has a simpler tunic, sash, and wider sleeves. The significance of this difference in costume is not clear, but it might indicate either that the judge without a mantle was newly appointed or that de Heere's inscription is not quite accurate. As this drawing was undertaken as part of an artist's working sketchbook, it probably would have been seen only by those with whom de Heere chose to share his work. But it constitutes interesting informal evidence about the visual depiction of judges in early modern England.

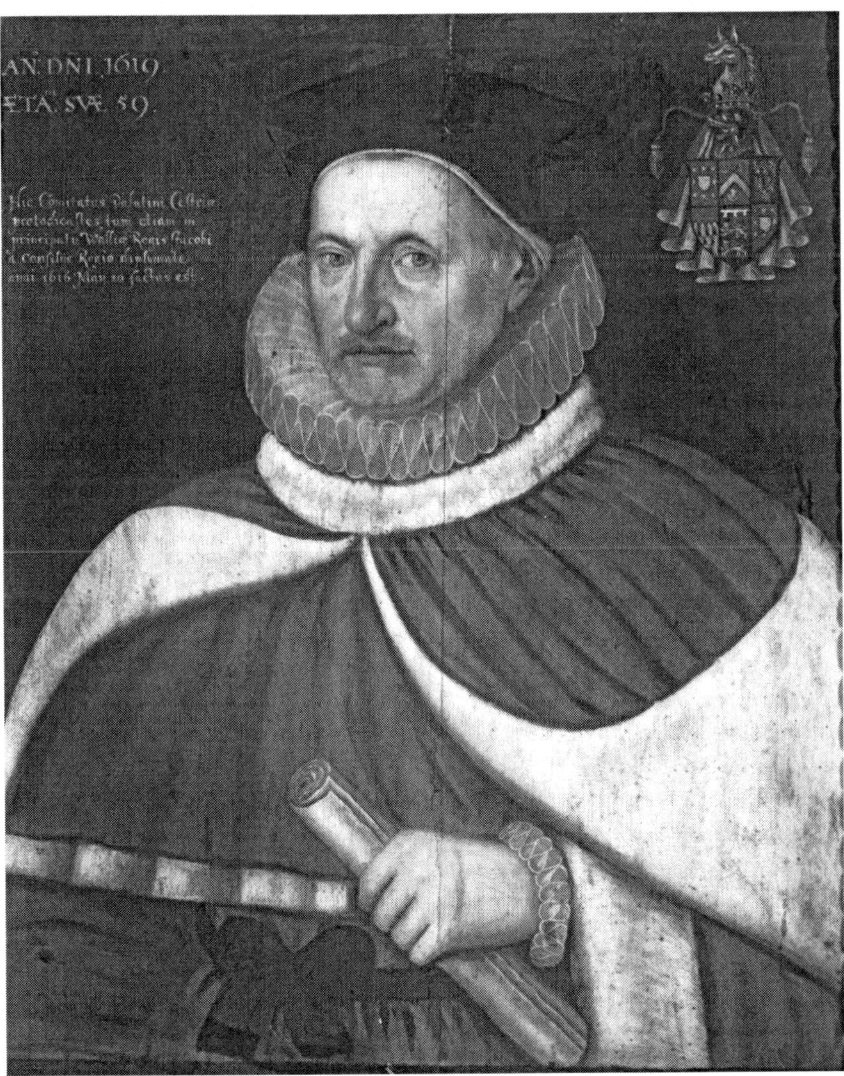

16 *A portrait of Sir Thomas Chamberlain,* by an unknown English artist, 1619, oil on panel, 700 × 570 mm

Occasionally, portraits of members of the legal profession were painted to hang collectively as part of a specific decorative scheme. An existing group of at least ten portraits of judges was almost certainly commissioned *circa* 1619 by Sir Thomas Chamberlain (d.1625), a member of Gray's Inn appointed Recorder of Banbury (1608), Chief Justice of Chester (1616), and a judge of the King's Bench (1620). The surviving portraits in this set include two now at Lincoln's Inn, which depict former members of Lincoln's: Sir Peter Warburton (*c.*1540–1621), who was confirmed as a judge shortly after James I's accession in 1603, and Thomas Egerton (1540–1617), Lord Ellesmere, who was appointed Lord Chancellor at about the same time. At least eight other portraits from this series remain in private hands. Their subjects are: Sir Christopher Wray (*c.*1522–92), a member of Lincoln's, who was appointed Chief Justice of the Queen's Bench in 1574; Sir David Williams (1550–1613), a member of the Middle Temple who was appointed a justice of the King's Bench in 1604 and whose image is encased in a double frame with that of Wray; Sir John Denham (1559–1639), a member of Lincoln's who was appointed Chief Justice of Ireland in 1612; a judge described as 'Lee', perhaps Sir James Ley (1550–1629), later 1st Earl of Marlborough, a member of Lincoln's who was named Lord Chief Justice of the King's Bench (1622–24) not long after this portrait was painted;[32] Sir Henry Hobart (*c.*1554–1625), a member of Lincoln's who had been appointed Attorney-General in 1606 and Chief Justice of the Common Pleas in 1613; Sir Thomas Foster (1548–1612), a member of Inner Temple and (from 1607) puisne justice of the Common Pleas; Sir Thomas Walmsley (1537–1612), a member of Lincoln's and, from 1589 until his death, a judge of the Common Pleas, whose image shares a double frame with that of Foster; and Thomas Chamberlain himself, whose portrait bears a Latin inscription and the date 1619.

Each portrait in the group was executed in approximately the same half-length, life-sized format on wooden panel. Each has an original arched top (now adapted into a standard rectangular space), with a simple one-word inscription bearing the sitter's surname in pale lettering: for example, 'Wray', 'Denham', 'Foster', etc. The consistent format and comparable painting style indicate that the images were devised as a group for a single decorative scheme, perhaps to be seen at a distance. Although Chamberlain's estate at Northbrook House near Kirtlington, Oxford-shire was demolished *circa* 1742 to make way for a new house, this series of judicial portraits, probably originally designed to hang within niches in the upper recesses of the main hall at Northbrook, survived.[33] It is not clear why the group was commis-sioned; however, it is possible that Chamberlain, at the height of his legal career, sought to commemorate his position among the elite of his profession by presenting judges in a collective format similar to the groups of portraits of Classical muses, philosophers, or monarchs known to have adorned the walls of some aristocratic Elizabethan and Jacobean houses. As lord of the manor, Chamberlain held his first court here in 1625, perhaps even in the hall where the portraits were displayed.

Personal portraits of lawyers and legal students

It was not, however, simply judges who were commissioning portraits of themselves in this period. Practising barristers and even some legal students are known to have done so. Such activities may be seen within an emerging pattern of increased access, among urban elites, to modes of visual portrayal. By the 1560s and 1570s, gentlemen were beginning to commission portraits of themselves for display in their own homes, often to record a particular moment in time.

Surviving inventories of the personal possessions of Tudor and Jacobean men of the legal profession are exceptionally rare.[34] But a post-mortem inventory of the household effects of the serjeant at law William Lovelace (*c.*1525/30–76) is suggestive. This document reveals that Lovelace's own portrait hung in his bedroom in his large and well-furnished house in Canterbury, while his study in London contained a desk covered with green fabric, a standing desk, law books, and painted hangings (but no pictures) upon the walls.[35] This example reflects what is known about other portraits of the middling sort and it is highly likely that portraits of barristers, like those of judges, were mainly commissioned for display in domestic rather than institutional settings in this period.

In contrast to portraits of judges, which were reasonably formulaic in the sixteenth and early seventeenth centuries, portraits of practising lawyers cannot be considered to conform to a fixed 'type'. Nor can portraits of students at the Inns. Instead, the format, pose, and dress of each sitter were shaped primarily by the individual and his particular interests and personal concerns, as well as by the depth of his pockets. But it is possible to make some generalised observations. Many extant portraits of lawyers and legal students, for example, are notable for their use of witty epigrams or well thought-out and curious iconographic devices. Dress also merits comment here. Those who had been called to the bar wore no official costume at this date, but simply adopted the black gowns of lay fashion.[36] Not surprisingly then, the clothes seen in extant portraits of barristers are not necessarily immediately distinctive as vocational dress, but rather identify the sitters simply as wealthy professional men.

It is also the case that several surviving portraits of barristers and legal students – in common with images of other urban elites outside the nobility in this period – show an interest in the careful presentation of Christian credentials and the search for Christian salvation. In this context it is also worth noting that lawyers, together with merchants, attracted the censure of Puritan preachers. Criticism of members of the legal profession can be found in sermons and treatises of this period, as well as in satirical plays.[37] Barristers were attacked for their greed and their pride, which was seen as out of proportion with their social status. In 1550, for example, the Puritan Robert Crowley noted the capacity of barristers to prolong cases to their benefit, having become 'so passing gredy, That Gods feare is out of thy syght'.[38]

One example of a barrister-to-be visibly demonstrating his Christian concern for salvation is the portrait of William Naylor, dated 1562, the current location of which is unknown.[39] Naylor was admitted to Lincoln's Inn in 1556 and was, at the

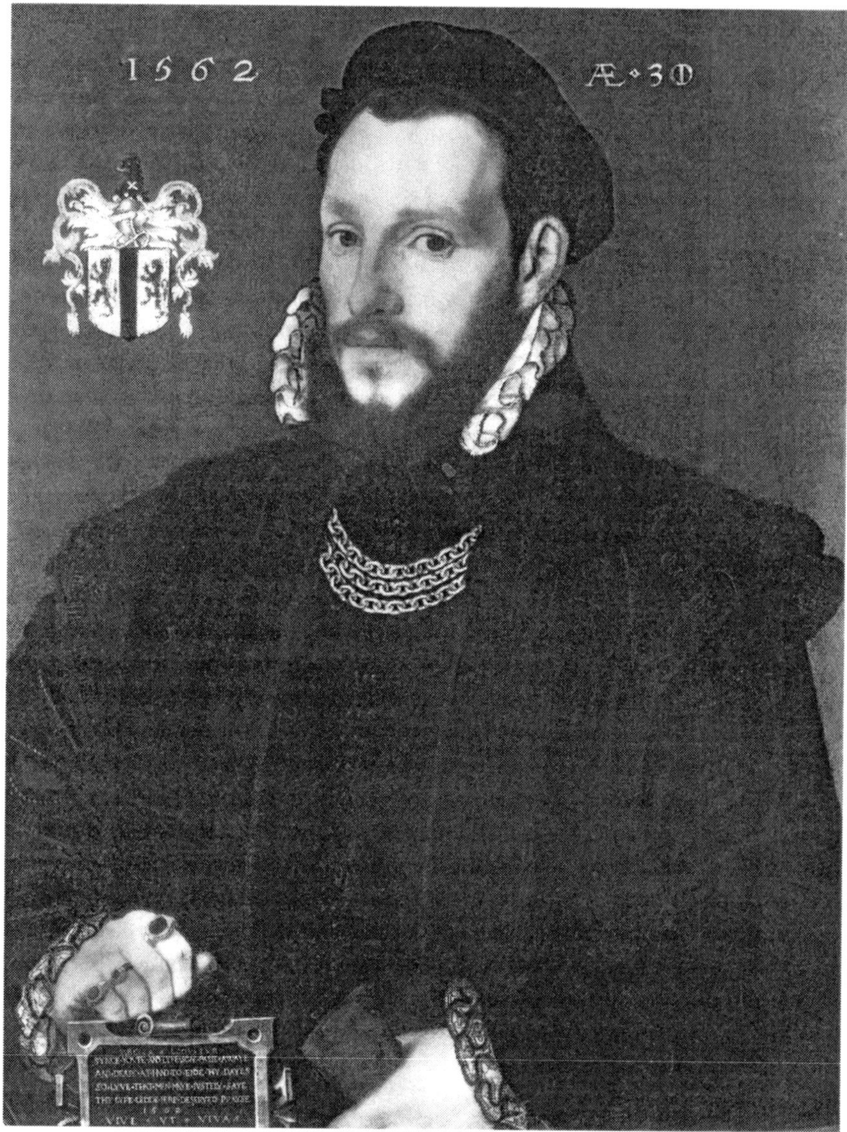

17 *A portrait of William Naylor*, by an unknown Anglo-Netherlandish artist, dated 1562,
oil on panel, dimensions unknown

time this painting was executed, an inner barrister (i.e. student), the most junior
rank of membership in the Inn. (In 1565, he would be called to the bar as an utter
barrister.)[40] Naylor is shown elaborately attired in the manner of a gentleman of
some means. He wears a black gown either trimmed or lined with fur, three bands
of gold chain, three gold rings, and a fashionable white ruff embroidered and edged

with a delicate blackwork design. The portrait is by a talented, but unknown, Anglo-Netherlandish artist and shows Naylor holding a plaque inscribed with text – an unusual device in English portraits of this date, but one occasionally seen in Netherlandish art. The words, which might be understood as if spoken aloud by Naylor himself, read as follows:

> SYNCE . YOU . … AND . LYFE. SORE PASSE . AWAYE / AND . DEAT[H] . AT . HAND . TO . END. THY DAYES. / SO LYVE THAT . MEN . MAYE . IVSTELY . SAYE. / THY LYFE . LEDDE . HERE . DESERVED . PRAYSE. / 1562 / VIVE . VT VIVA.[41]

These sentiments not only express Naylor's desire to be recognised as an exemplary Christian, but also highlight the important role, in Protestant theology, of stable and virtuous conduct to the attainment of salvation through predestination. Such conduct did not earn salvation for the sitter as in a Roman Catholic context, but the clear evidence of virtue proved the sitter's suitability (or predestined status) for election to salvation.[42]

Another, more complex, variation on this theme is a portrait of William Burton (1575–1645), the elder brother of Robert, the author of *The Anatomy of Melancholy*. Dated 1604, this painting, which shows Burton wearing a black gown, may have been intended to commemorate its subject's short-lived legal career. Burton was admitted to the Inner Temple in 1593 and called to the bar in 1603. However, owing to ill health, he retired to his estates in the country the following year. Perhaps in reflection of Burton's precarious health at the time that this portrait was executed, it features an unusually large number of allusions to death. In the painting's upper right corner, for example, is an oval cartouche encasing a skeleton, together with a Latin inscription:

> Willmus Burton filius natu maximus Radulfi Burton de Lindley com: Leic: Armig: socius Interioris Templi et Apprenticius legum Angliæ . 25 . Aug: 1604 . An: Æt. 29. (William Burton first-born son of Ralph Burton of Lindley, Esquire, of the county of Leicestershire, member of the Inner Temple and apprentice of the laws of England 25 August 1604 aged 29.)

Under Burton's coat of arms is another Latin inscription, this one reading 'LVX, VITA:' ('Light, Life'). Elsewhere, a banner within an oval pendant hanging from a ribbon reads, in Spanish, 'Mira lo galardon' ('I see the reward'), while inscribed upon the coffin slab is yet another Latin inscription: 'Hic terminus ad Quem' ('This is the end of it'). It is likely that Burton not only instructed the artist about the picture's overall iconography, but also composed the epigrams himself. Therefore, the resulting portrait might be seen not only as a vivid demonstration of Burton's desire for salvation, but also as a means of constructing an identity for himself as a man of classical education and erudition with a cosmopolitan talent for European languages – just the sort of qualities one associates with the intellectual milieu of the Inns of Court in this period.

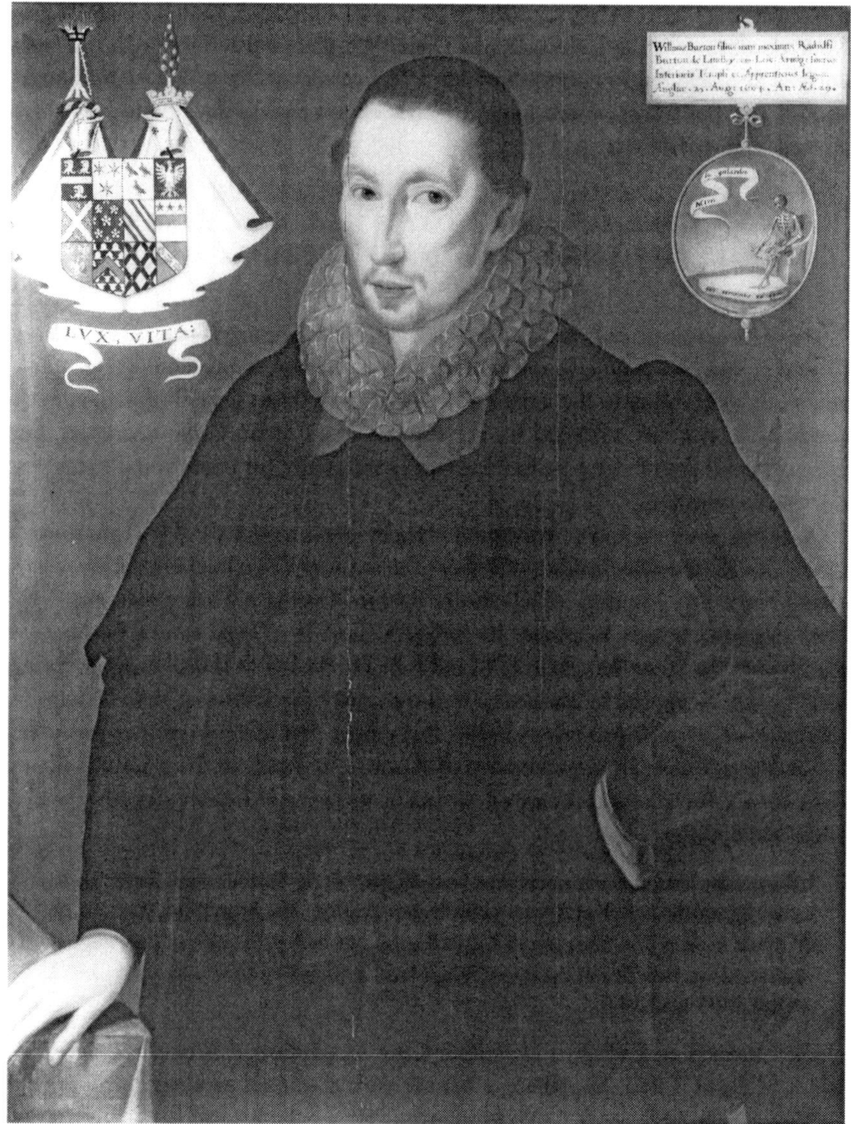

18 *A portrait of William Burton*, ascribed to William Segar, 1604, oil on panel,
902 × 724 mm

Exploring the wider context of portraiture in and around the early modern Inns
also allows us to consider a remarkable portrait of the poet John Donne, who, having
been admitted to Lincoln's Inn in 1592, left at some point between late 1594 and
early 1596, only to return as Reader in Divinity from 1616 to 1622.[43] (See Plate 3)
Painted by an unknown artist around 1595 and now in the National Portrait Gallery,

this picture thus depicts Donne as a young legal student, probably around the time he was writing the early *Elegies*.[44] As Donne must have been closely involved in determining the composition and format of the picture, it should be regarded as, at least in part, his own product. Some time between 1595 and Donne's death in 1631, this portrait was almost certainly on display in a private chamber of a member of Lincoln's Inn. The picture appears to have been seen by Thomas Morton, Bishop of Durham in the chamber of one of Donne's friends at the Inn. Morton describes it as a portrait of Donne 'all envelloped with a darkish shadow, his face and feature hardly discernable, with this ejaculation and wish written thereon: *Domine illumine tenebras meas* [Lord, light my darkness]'.[45] The inscription is slightly different from that found on the portrait today, but it is probable that it was misremembered by Morton.[46] One possible theory is that the portrait, when Morton saw it, was in the possession of Christopher Brooke (*c.*1570–1628), who, having entered Lincoln's Inn in 1587, forged a lifelong friendship with Donne, with whom he shared chambers at the Inn in the 1590s. Although Donne may well have left the Inn by the time Morton visited, it is not inconceivable that Donne had left his portrait behind with Brooke, perhaps for safe-keeping when he sailed to Cadiz in 1596 as part of the English expedition against the Spanish. Whatever the case, the picture was back in Donne's possession at his death in 1631, for it is listed in his will as 'that Picture of myne wch is taken in Shaddowes and was made very many yeares before I was of this profession [i.e. a minister]'.[47]

As a portrait, Donne's painted likeness does something quite original which anticipates portraiture of a later date. He appears in a feigned oval – one of the earliest uses of this format recorded – which provides the illusion of a darkened oval window. We see him in a highly self-conscious pose playing an obviously adopted role rather than presenting a carefully observed outward conventional likeness, as we saw for example in the portrait of Naylor. To a degree, all sitters in portraits play self-conscious roles, but Donne places himself in a position where he cannot be clearly observed, and the resulting dramatic effect has more in common with stagecraft than with conventional portraiture at this date. The young poet plays his part as a man of literary promise by positioning himself retiring in shadows, with his arms crossed and his shirt undone as if in a private candlelit dressing chamber, sulkily recalling thoughts to mind like a melancholic lover.[48] Rather than playing at presenting himself in his outward 'public' state, Donne engages in another layer of pretence, allowing the viewer a tantalizing glimpse of his inner state of mind. It is possible that the portrait had some private purpose and that it was originally painted for a lover or close friend, as the inscription, itself a reworking of a psalm ('O Lady lighten our darkness'), might suggest.

Epilogue

Whatever the Donne painting's original purpose, it is striking that the early flowering of a new type of portrait that engages in role play, in introspective analysis of personal identity, and in the presentation of a subjective self should have emerged in the environment of the Inns of Court, where a rich literary and dramatic culture fostered new ideas about self-presentation.[49] Into the 1620s and well beyond, the concept of role play in portraiture was to become increasingly fashionable. Stuart courtiers delighted in presenting themselves in paint in various dramatic guises. Lord George Stuart, for example, was painted by Anthony Van Dyck as a shepherd *circa* 1638, while Barbara Villiers and her son posed for Peter Lely as a Madonna and child in 1664.[50] At this later date, role play in portraiture was an amusing way for courtiers to style their *personae*, licensed by a droll sense of etiquette sponsored by Stuart court culture. Although many aspects of the visual culture produced by and for the early modern Inns of Court and their members were, as we have seen, traditional, even conservative, Donne's portrait was in its own time innovative and rather radical, making a witty and playful use of religious texts and employing illusionistic devices for private, dramatic ends.

Notes

1 I am particularly grateful to the archive and library staff at the Inns of Court – specifically Lesley Whitelaw (Middle Temple), Guy Holborn (Lincoln's Inn), Clare Rider (Inner Temple), and Theresa Thom (Gray's Inn) – for their help with the research for this chapter. I would also like to thank the editors of this volume for their helpful suggestions and Jane Cunningham of the Courtauld Picture Survey for her assistance in locating paintings in private collections. In addition, I am grateful to my former curatorial intern, Margaret Zoller, for her help compiling a survey of portraits of lawyers held in the archive of the National Portrait Gallery (hereafter 'NPG').

2 Christopher Brooks notes a 'ten-fold increase between 1485 and 1640 in the number of men qualified to practice as attorneys or barristers' in England ('Professions, ideology and the middling sort in the late sixteenth and early seventeenth centuries', in Jonathan Barry and Christopher Brooks (eds), *The Middling Sort of People: Culture, Society and Politics in England, 1550–1800* (London: Macmillan, 1994), pp. 113–40 (p. 113)).

3 *Black Books*, II, 43.

4 Puckering had been admitted to Lincoln's Inn in 1559, appointed under-treasurer in 1569, and made a governor at some point prior to 1575.

5 *Black Books*, II, 49. This record of institutional patronage on the part of Lincoln's Inn provides evidence not only about the visual culture of the early modern Inns of Court, but also about the range of different types of production undertaken by artists in this period. The Elstrack family were originally glaziers who had come to England in 1552 from Liège in the southern Netherlands, and one of the native-born sons, Renold, became an established engraver in London during the period 1570–1630. Although heraldic painting was officially the domain of the College of Arms, it is probable that all types of painters regularly undertook this task, either on contract from painter heralds or,

more likely, by simply copying existing coats of arms from copybooks. Although it is not entirely surprising that the Elstracks were also turning their hands to this type of work, it is rare to find documentary evidence of this type in which mention is made of the patron, artist, price, and type of painting. (I am grateful to Robert Yorke, archivist at the College of Arms, for his advice on the issue of the heralds' jurisdiction and their involvement with painters who independently painted coats of arms.)

6 *Black Books*, II, 107.

7 For painted cloths in early modern England, see Tessa Watt, *Cheap Print and Popular Piety, 1550–1640* (Cambridge: Cambridge University Press, 1991; repr. 1996), pp. 197, 200, 211–12, 219–20; and Anthony Wells-Cole, *Art and Decoration in Elizabethan and Jacobean England: The Influence of Continental Prints, 1558–1625* (New Haven, CT; London: Yale University Press/The Paul Mellon Centre for Studies in British Art, 1997), pp. 275–6.

8 *Black Books*, I, 10.

9 *Ibid.*, I, 20.

10 *Minutes of the Middle Temple*, I, 49.

11 The picture may have been hanging in the hall from the late sixteenth century, when it was painted; however, no early inventories survive. In 1658–59, the Society paid £7 for 'beautifying and repayring the picture of Solomons Judgement in the Middle Temple Hall'. A further sum was paid in 1698–99 for cleaning and repairing the picture, which was still hanging at 'the upper end of the hall'. For these extracts from the 'Treasurers' Receipt Books', 1658–59 (Bill 156) and 1698–99 (Bill 77), see John Bruce Williamson, *Catalogue of Paintings and Engravings in the Possession of the Honourable Society of the Middle Temple* (London: Middle Temple, 1931), pp. 15–16.

12 An important and unusual narrative picture for an English context, this painting is one of a type that was almost certainly once more common than the few surviving religious narrative examples indicate. Narrative imagery was sometimes the subject of tapestries and wall painting, but very few examples of independent pictures painted on panel or canvas for a sixteenth-century British setting have survived.

13 For the building of Middle Temple Hall, see Chapter 7 (pp. 142–3, above).

14 Previous historians have assumed that the picture was commissioned specifically for Middle Temple Hall, and, while there is nothing to contradict this view, equally there is no firm evidence to support it.

15 The English translation is taken from Williamson, *Catalogue of Paintings and Engravings*, pp. 15–16.

16 See Robert Tittler, *The Face of the City: Civic Portraiture and Civic Identity in Early Modern England* (Manchester; New York, NY: Manchester University Press, 2007). Tittler's chapter on 'Audience and display' (pp. 148–65) considers the possible locations for the display of institutional portraiture within the context of civic and charitable institutions. He also briefly considers some portraits of lawyers and judges, pp. 126–7.

17 The portrait of Dyer is partly damaged and abraded in the face, as the sitter once wore a beard and moustache, remnants of which are still evident. Another version of Dyer's likeness may be found on his tomb in St Andrew's Church, Great Staughton, Huntingdon. See Roy Strong, *Tudor and Jacobean Portraits*, 2 vols (London: HMSO, 1969), I, 79–80.

18 The portrait of Daniel was presented to the NPG from Barnard's Inn when it was dissolved

in 1884. It is the only known sixteenth-century portrait of Daniel. See Strong, *Tudor and Jacobean Portraits*, I, 59–60.

19 For the commemorative aspects of portraiture in this period, see, for example, Lorne Campbell, 'The Functions and Uses of Portraits', in *Renaissance Portraits: European Portrait-Painting in the 14th, 15th and 16th Centuries* (New Haven, CT; London: Yale University Press, 1990), pp. 193–225; and Jennifer Fletcher, 'The Renaissance portrait: functions, uses and display', in Lorne Campbell, Miguel Falomir, Jennifer Fletcher, and Luke Syson (eds), *Renaissance Faces: Van Eyck to Titian* (London: Yale University Press for the National Gallery, 2008), pp. 46–63.

20 See Strong, *Tudor and Jacobean Portraits*, I, 80.

21 There are also extant examples of early modern judges painted in half length. See, for example, the portraits of Sir John Popham (?1531–1607), Chief Justice of the King's Bench, now in the NPG and reproduced in David Saywell and Jacob Simon (eds), *Complete Illustrated Catalogue National Portrait Gallery* (London: Unicorn Press/NPG, 2004), pp. 501, 690.

22 W. N. Hargreaves-Mawdsley, *A History of Legal Dress in Europe until the End of the Eighteenth Century* (Oxford: Clarendon Press, 1963), pp. 46–60 (54–5).

23 The chain was a device of the house of Lancaster and originally indicated service in the royal household. It also appears in the following legal portraits: NPG 468 (Sir Henry Hobart, Bt, c.1545–1625, Chief Justice of the Common Pleas, oil on canvas, after an unknown artist); NPG 475 (Sir Roger Manwood, 1524/25–92, judge and Lord Chief Baron of the Exchequer, early nineteenth-century watercolour copy by George Perfect Harding after an unknown artist); NPG 461 (Unknown Man, formerly known as Sir Nicholas Hyde, c.1572–1631, Chief Justice of the King's Bench, oil on canvas by an unknown artist). For reproductions of these images, see Saywell and Simon (eds), *Complete Illustrated Catalogue*, pp. 305, 409, 690. A more elaborate example, albeit from the early sixteenth century, may be found in the portrait of Sir Thomas More, by Hans Holbein the Younger, dated 1527, in the Frick Collection, New York. For an illustration of this painting, which shows More in courtly dress, see Susan Foister, *Holbein and England* (New Haven, CT; London: Yale University Press/The Paul Mellon Centre for Studies in British Art, 2004), p. 77. The portrait was executed two years before More, a Lincoln's Inn man, was appointed Lord Chancellor.

24 The fact that the painting was only acquired by Lincoln's Inn in the early nineteenth century also argues for its having been originally intended for display in a domestic rather than an institutional setting. (I am grateful to Guy Holborn, Librarian of Lincoln's Inn, for sharing details of the painting's provenance.)

25 *The Diary of John Manningham of the Middle Temple 1602–1603*, ed. Robert Parker Sorlien (Hanover, NH: The University Press of New England, 1976), p. 154.

26 Although most surviving copies of the 1603 edition lack Stow's portrait, the image was reproduced in the *Gentleman's Magazine* (1 (1837), 48).

27 An exception is judges who were raised to the peerage, particularly in the second and third decades of the seventeenth century, who are occasionally painted in a more courtier-like manner of portraiture. See, for example, Daniel Mytens's full-length portrait of the judge James Ley, 1st Earl of Marlborough, which was executed in 1627, the year after Ley was raised to the peerage. For an illustration of this painting, now at Harvard University Law School, see Wilfrid Prest's entry on Ley in the *ODNB*.

28 Following uncertainties about the date of this frame, it has recently been re-examined and the current evidence indicates that the frame is original to the portrait. The inscription has been re-painted and would appear to conform to an identical or very similar earlier inscription beneath.

29 This transcription and translation are taken from Strong, *Tudor and Jacobean Portraits*, I, 80.

30 BL, Add MS 28330 ('Corte Beschryvinge van England, Scotland, ende Irland'), fol. 29[r].

31 See *ibid.*, fols 28[r]–34[r] for de Heere's depiction of assorted English men and women.

32 I am grateful to Elizabeth Goldring for her suggestion that this portrait might represent Sir James Ley.

33 Northbrook Manor House, thought to have been built after 1579, was purchased by Thomas Chamberlain in 1610 for £3,000 (*The Victoria History of the County of Oxford (Vol. VI Ploughley Hundred)*), ed. Mary D. Lobel (London: Oxford University Press for the University of London/Institute for Historical Research, 1959), p. 220). I am also grateful to unpublished correspondence supplied by the current owner of the paintings.

34 For discussion of another example, however, see Elizabeth Goldring's Introduction, p. 13[?], n.3[?], above.

35 'The chamber where Mr. Serjante laye ... the pyture of hym self' (NA, Prob 2, fol. 404[v]). In this period, the position of serjeant at law was the last stage in a barrister's career before appointment as a judge.

36 Barristers adopted ordinary black Tudor gowns, usually without sleeves (Hargreaves-Mawdsley, *A History of Legal Dress*, pp. 87–8). See also Wilfrid R. Prest, *The Inns of Court under Elizabeth I and the Early Stuarts, 1590–1640* (London: Longman, 1972), pp. 50–1.

37 See, for example, E. F. J. Tucker, *Intruder into Eden: Representations of the Common Lawyer in English Literature, 1350–1750* (Columbia, SC: Camden House, 1984).

38 Robert Crowley, *Epigrams, A.D. 1550; Voyce of the Last Trumpet, A.D .1550; Pleasure and Payne, A.D.1551; Way to Wealth, A.D. 1550; An Informacion and Peticion*, ed. J. M. Cowper (London: Early English Text Society, 1905) (first published 1872), p. 82. Other more general commentaries on conduct for young city gentlemen include: Thomas Lupset, *An Exhortation to Yonge men perswadyng them to walke in the pathe way that leadeth to honestie and godnes ...* (London: Thomas Bertheleti, 1544); Thomas Lupton, *All For Money, A moral and pitieful comedie, plainly representing the manners of men and the fashion of the worlde nowdayes* (London: Roger Warde & Richard Mundee, 1578); Stephen Bateman, *A christal glasse of christian reformation wherein the godly may beholde the coloured abuses vsed in this our present tyme collected by S. Bateman* (London: John Day, 1569); and Barnaby Rich, *Favltes, Favlts and nothing else but Favltes* (London: Jeffrey Chorleton, 1606).

39 I have also discussed this painting in 'Predestined lives? Portraiture and religious belief in England and Wales, 1560–1620', in Tara Hamling and Richard L. Williams (eds), *Art Re-formed: Re-assessing the Impact of the Reformation on the Visual Arts* (Newcastle: Cambridge Scholars' Publishing, 2007), pp. 49–64 (p. 54).

40 *Records of Lincoln's Inn*, I, 62; *Black Books*, I, 346.

41 Translation: 'Live that you may live.'

42 Numerous theological texts considered this question, one of the most influential being Théodore de Bèze's 'An Excellent Treatise Comforting Such as Troubled by Predestination', in William Perkins, *The Golden Chaine ...* (London: E. Alde for E. White, 1591). For a modern commentary, see D. Dewey Wallace Jr., *Puritans and Predestination Grace*

in the English Protestant Theology 1525–1695 (Chapel Hill, NC: The University of North Carolina Press, 1982).

43 For Donne at Lincoln's Inn, see David Colclough's entry in the *ODNB*, as well as Chapters 3 and 5 (pp. 51–74 and 90–106, above) and Sarah Knight's Introduction to Part III, pp. 217–22, below.

44 See Tarnya Cooper (ed.), *Searching for Shakespeare*, exhibition catalogue (London: NPG, 2006), pp. 175–6.

45 Geoffrey Keynes, *A Bibliography of Dr John Donne Dean of St. Paul's* (Oxford: Clarendon Press, 1973), p. 373. See also Richard Baddeley, *The Life of Dr. Thomas Morton* (York: Stephen Bulckley, 1666), pp. 101–2. The picture is also mentioned by William Drummond. See Maureen Sabine, 'Illumina Tenebras Nostras Domina – Donne at Evensong', *John Donne Journal*, 19 (2000), 19–40 (21).

46 The current inscription reads: 'ILLVMINA TENEBR[AS] NOSTRAS DOMINA'.

47 For a transcript of Donne's will, see R. C. Bald, *John Donne: A Life* (Oxford: Clarendon Press, 1970; repr. 1986), pp. 563–7 (here at p. 567). Tantalisingly, Brooke, at his death in 1628 bequeathed a number of paintings to 'my deere and ancient freind D[o]c[t]or Dunn the Deane Pawles', for which, see Michelle O'Callaghan's entry on Brooke in the *ODNB*. I am grateful to Elizabeth Goldring for this observation.

48 For a reading of this image within the wider context of the late sixteenth- and early seventeenth-century vogue for melancholic poses, see Roy Strong, 'The Elizabethan malady: melancholy in Elizabethan and Jacobean portraiture', *Apollo*, 79 (1964), 264–9; reprinted in Roy Strong, *The Tudor and Stuart Monarchy: Pageantry, Painting, and Iconography*, 3 vols (Woodbridge: Boydell, 1995), II, 295–302.

49 For the literary and dramatic culture of the Inns in this period, see Chapter 2 (pp. 32–50, above), as well as the chapters in Part III.

50 For reproductions of these images, both now in the NPG, see Saywell and Simon (eds), *Complete Illustrated Catalogue*, pp. 129, 596.

9

The evolution of the early gardens
of the Inns of Court

Paula Henderson

The gardens of the four Inns of Court are a remarkable survival of open land in London. The history of the development of these gardens from the medieval period to the early eighteenth century – as documented in the Inns' records and visualised in the earliest maps of London – reveals much about life in the Inns on various social levels. For the garden historian, a study of the Inns' gardens provides an opportunity to consider how contemporary garden design was adapted for the use of an elite professional society in an increasingly confined urban environment.

The Inns of Court and the early landscape of London: the visual evidence

The evolution of the gardens of the Inns of Court in the early modern period parallels the dramatic changes that occurred in the greater landscape of London itself. These changes – and schematic illustrations of the Inns' gardens – are seen in the early maps of the City, of Westminster, and of the suburban areas outside the City walls.[1] The Braun and Hogenberg map of 1572, for example, shows the compact, walled City, with further building spreading out in ribbons along the main access roads to the north and west and the remarkably rural character of much of the rest of London. Open fields surround the City to the north, east, and west, while large gardens and parks occupy the southern banks of the Thames.

It is this open, rural aspect of greater London that was to change so radically over the course of the sixteenth century. In one of the three surviving sections of the Copperplate map of *circa* 1553–59, on which other early maps (including the Braun and Hogenberg) were based, the importance of this open land is evident with common people enjoying leisure activities (walking, practising archery and musketry), as well as carrying out mundane domestic chores, such as drying laundry, driving pigs to market, and caring for the livestock that grazes in the open fields.[2] In a period in which few English artists were attempting to depict the life of ordinary people, this is a unique and invaluable evocation of life outside the cramped Tudor city. The effect on life in London was marked by John Stow, who wrote at the end of the sixteenth century that 'pleasant fields, very commodious for Citizens therein to walke, shoote, and otherwise to recreate and refresh their dulled spirites in the

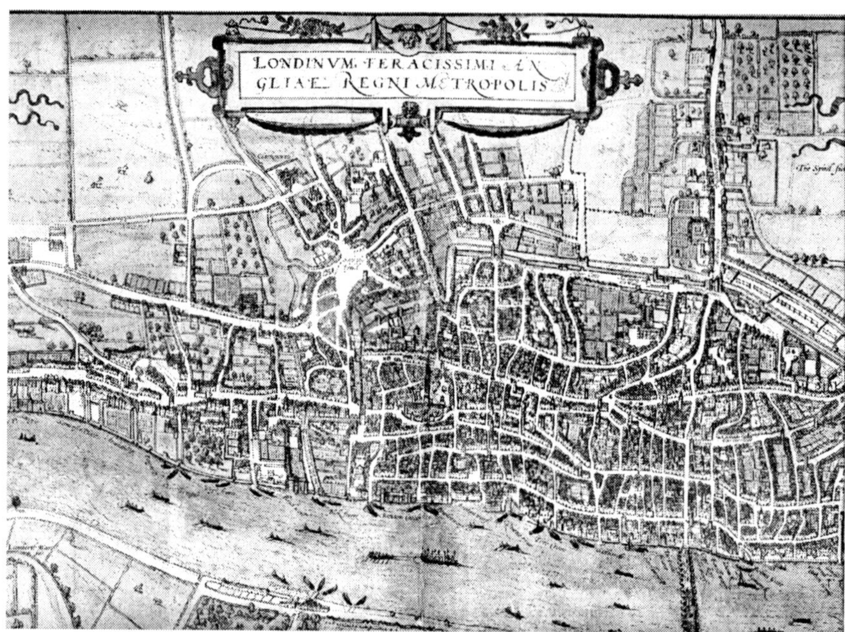

19 Detail of Braun and Hogenberg's map of London from *Civitates Orbis Terrarum*, 1572, showing the rural nature of sixteenth-century London. The Inns' gardens are visible, particularly the dense plantation of trees in the Temple garden (in the lower left on the north side of the Thames).

sweete and wholesome ayre ... [are] nowe within few yeares made a continuall building throughout'.[3]

Later maps – particularly John Norden's map of Westminster of 1593 and Wenceslaus Hollar's bird's-eye view of Covent Garden of *circa* 1658 – show how rapidly this part of London changed, the result of large-scale development in the early seventeenth century.[4] In Norden's view, one can still see animals grazing in fields to the north of the Strand and to the west of the Inns. The Temple is just visible in the lower right hand corner, adjacent to the easternmost of the great Strand palaces that were once the inns (or London mansions) of medieval bishops, but had been, since the Reformation, owned either by the Crown or by great Tudor courtiers. All of these mansions had fine gardens, particularly those on the south side of the Strand, where the land sloped down to the banks of the Thames.

By the mid-seventeenth century, much of the land northward had been developed and the open lands and gardens shrunk drastically: Covent Garden (originally the garden of the convent of Westminster) was now reduced to an enclosed square or piazza (just above the Earl of Bedford's private garden). Except for Moorfields, St Giles, and Lincoln's Inn, the open fields had largely been built on. The events and conditions that led to the loss of open lands – particularly the rapidly growing

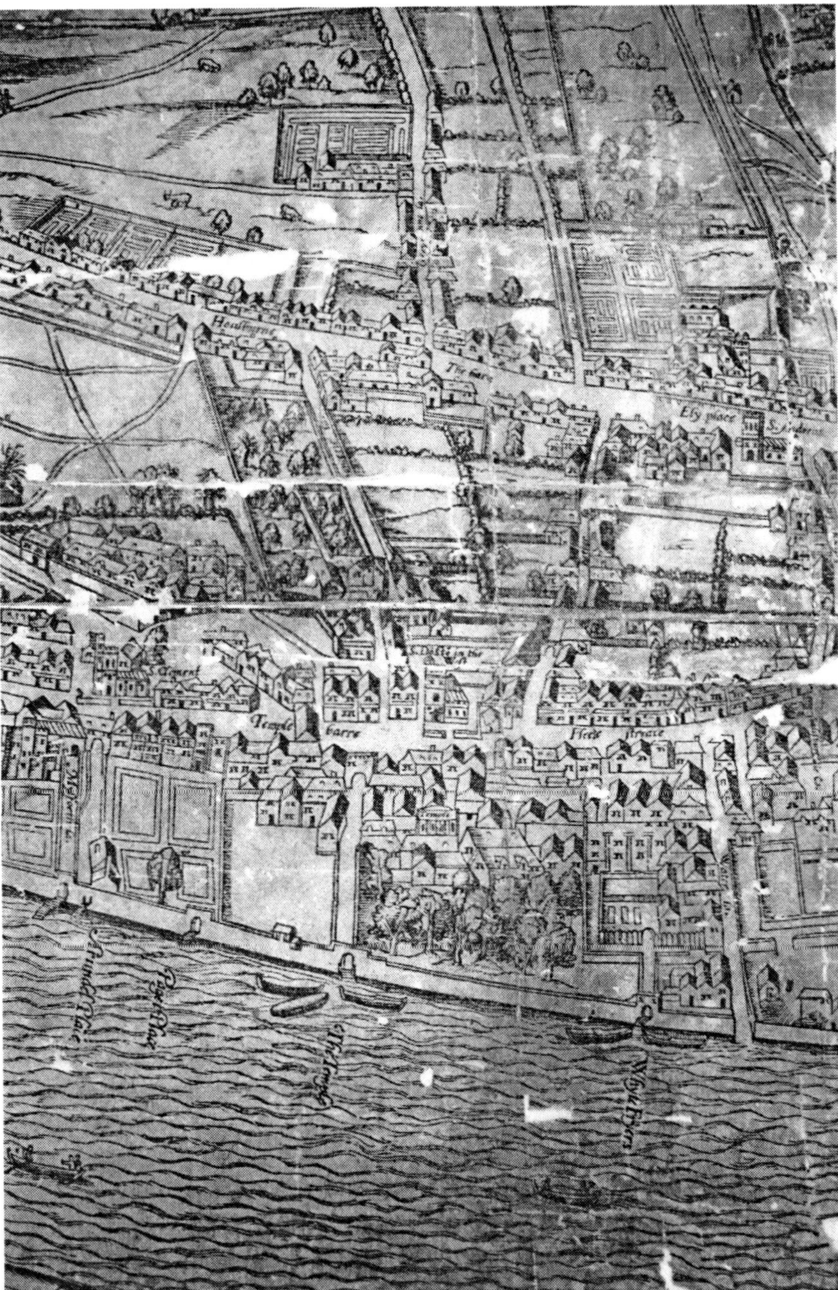

20 Early seventeenth-century copy of the so-called 'Agas' map (*c*.1562), showing the Inns of Court: Inner and Middle Temple in the lower right; the walled gardens and cross walks of Lincoln's Inn at centre left; and the walled garden of Gray's Inn at the top.

population and the need for more housing – were analogous to the increased number of students that were taken into the Inns and the necessity for more buildings and chambers. The gardens and fields around the Inns would also be affected.

Just as early maps show clearly how the metropolis evolved in the sixteenth and seventeenth centuries, they also show in varying degrees of detail how the Inns' gardens developed. While the three remaining sheets of the Copperplate map do not depict any of the Inns, the two most important maps derived from it – the so-called 'Agas' map of *circa* 1562 and the Braun and Hogenberg map of 1572 – show them all.[5] Norden's map of Westminster stops just west of the Temple gardens. In the seventeenth century, Faithorne and Newcourt's map of 1658 shows Gray's and Lincoln's Inns, but not the Temple. Hollar's map of *circa* 1658 records Lincoln's Inn in remarkable detail, just as Leake's survey of the post-fire City of 1667 records the Temple. John Ogilby and William Morgan's map of 1676 reveals much about all of the Inns' gardens, as well as the changes in other open areas, particularly Moorfields. As we shall see, these maps provide very important visual information, not just about the evolution of the Inns' gardens, but also about how they relate to other London gardens in the period.

Written accounts and records of the Inns' gardens

The other major sources of information are the Inns' records and accounts, though, as other contributors to this volume have noted, they are neither complete nor continual. In the accounts, references to gardeners – their wages, duties, punishments, and sometimes rewards – far outnumber references to any other aspect of the Inns' gardens. Gardeners were paid for planting, weeding, building hedges, making gravel paths, building sheds, and for purchasing plants and equipment. They were sacked for a variety of reasons. In 1545, a contemporary record informs us, the gardener at Inner Temple 'shall no longer occupy the garden because he often has sickness and the plague in his house, keeps ill rule, and cuts down trees'.[6] In 1616, John Mortimer (also gardener at Inner Temple) was fired for unspecified 'lewd behaviour'.[7] Initially, the Inns rented out the land to be gardened. In 1445, Lincoln's Inn leased its 'long garden' to Richard Benet, Cook of the Inn, for ten years; he paid 13*s*. 4*d*. twice yearly (at Easter and Michaelmas).[8] The Society retained all profits from herbs, fruits, and nuts. In 1556, John Rede, the gardener at Middle Temple, leased the garden for a term of thirty years for 20*s*. per annum.[9] Later accounts suggest that some gardeners continued to pay for the land they worked, but more often they were waged and provided with a shed or small house in the garden. In 1594, the gardener at Middle Temple was to be paid £6 13*s*. 4*d*. yearly and to be provided with lodging.[10] At Inner Temple, John Mortimer was given the reversion of the dwelling house of Mrs Mason with the 'garden plot thereto belonging' in 1595.[11]

Reflecting the growing rate of crime in London – itself a reflection of the rapidly expanding population of the metropolis – gardeners at the Inns were eventually given other responsibilities, particularly for security. In 1580, the following charge was made to the gardener of Inner Temple:

> Where it is affirmed that heretofore the ancient rent of the garden was 4*li* and in respect that the gardener should keep the House from rogues and beggars which he found very dangerous both in respect of health as for robbing of chambers, it is ordered that either the said rent of 4*li* shall yearly be paid as it was wont to be, or otherwise the gardener shall keep the House as free from such dangers as much as in him lieth.[12]

During Christmas celebrations in 1581–82, the gardener's men and the under-cooks made 'privy searches' within the precincts for 'rogues, and help to carry them to Bridewell or to some other place of punishement'.[13] Ten years later, the gardener, John Russell, asked for more money to pay for an extra man to protect the gate; he was given an augmentation of £5.[14] At Gray's Inn, one of the gardener's duties was to make sure that 'not boyes gerles rude or beggarly people to pester the walkes nor laundresses nor others to dry clothes on the boulinge Greene or rayles and hedges thereof'.[15] Laundresses posed a problem to all the Inns, as they constantly needed land on which to dry the laundry and the gardens were ideal. In 1613, the porter at Lincoln's Inn was charged with 'lookinge to such nusances as shall happen in the House by the sluttishness of laundresses and others' and 'in case hee finde any such nusance in the Garden or Backside, to admonishe the Panierman and Gardiner respectivelie thereof'.[16]

One series of accounts relates to the gardener at Lincoln's Inn, Robert Cooke, who in 1623 was paid £20 per annum (without any allowance for bread or beer).[17] The next year, it was reported that there were six applicants for the 'late gardener's place', but that 'no stranger shall have the place, but one of this Howse'.[18] That turned out to be Robert Cooke's widow, who in 1625 was awarded 'the gardener's place at the pleasure of the Bench'. If she proved an 'efficient substitute', she would be paid £16 a year (£4 less than her husband).[19] This is, as far as I know, a unique example of a woman being named gardener of any important house or institution in the Tudor or early Stuart periods. The story does not have a happy ending, though, as by 1628/29, John Rye was appointed gardener if he proved fit and if 'the garden be better kept than it hath lately been since Cooke, his master's, decease'.[20] In any case, Rye clearly did his job well, for twenty-seven years later, in 1655, he was described as 'an ancient servant to this Society' and was awarded 20*s.* in charity and 5*s.* a week, as he was 'disabled to worke by reason a dead palsey hath taken him in his lymbs'.[21] It is in accounts such as these that we get a glimpse of the workforce of the Inns and of the occasional compassion for old retainers.

As for the form of the early gardens, references to various fields and yards suggest that some were named according to what was being grown there – Inner Temple's 'Le nutgardeyne' and 'Fig Tree Court' – or by their function – the 'pannierman's yard', the 'woodyard', or the 'coneygarth', the latter suggesting that at least in the earliest period, benchers raised rabbits for food and fur. Larger fields and yards that may have been used initially to raise produce for the table disappeared, perhaps because it became easier to obtain supplies from local market gardens but also because the land was needed for other purposes. Although there are records of purchases of seeds and herbs for kitchen gardens by both cooks and gardeners, the emphasis was increasingly on ornamental plants, hedging materials and, especially, trees, a subject to which I shall return.

The first references to hard-landscaping or architectural features in gardens were to walls, the earliest of mud but later of brick. Gates were also built (at Lincoln's Inn in 1562) and fitted with keys.[22] The enclosure of the gardens and the guarding of the entrance by the erection of a gate demonstrate that, although gardens were to be places of recreation and pleasure, this was increasingly available to only a select few.

The gardens of the individual Inns of Court

Gray's Inn

The earliest view of the gardens at Gray's Inn appears in the 'Agas' map, which shows a rectangular enclosure to the north of the Inn with rows of narrow beds, all adjacent to open fields. In the 1570s, a railed 'walk' was built from an opening in 'Chapel Court' into the fields.[23] In the 1580s and 1590s, the 'walks' were regularised and enclosed. The future Lord Chancellor, Francis Bacon, who had been admitted to Gray's Inn in 1576, became one of the surveyors of the ground in 1591, when a wall was built to enclose 'our back field'.[24] In 1597 and the next few years, payments were made for 'levelling the walks' (in what would become the 'lower walks'), for planting trees (132 in 1598 and 58 more in 1601), and for adding stairs (presumably leading to the 'upper walks'), rails, and seats.[25] Plants listed in the accounts included trees (elm, birch, and cherry); 'quicke setts' for hedges; and ornamental plants (eglantine, standard roses, and 'violetts & primroses').[26] There was a principal gardener (either John Mortimer or Richard Brooks) and 'other gardeners' and 'labourers', all paid by the day.[27] In 1608, Bacon paid Brooks £2 to make a mount, a feature found in many Tudor gardens from Henry VIII's Hampton Court to the pairs of mounts that still survive at Sir Thomas Tresham's Lyveden New Bield, in Northamptonshire.[28] In the 1560s, William Cecil, the future Lord Burghley (who, like Bacon, was a member of Gray's Inn), had erected a high, snail mount in the corner of the garden of Cecil House in the Strand.[29] A mount 'thirty foot high … [with] some fine banqueting-house' would be the centrepiece of the 'Princely Garden' Bacon described in his famous essay, 'Of Gardens', published in 1625.[30] Bacon's model may have been the mount at Gray's Inn, on which he had a banqueting house built, capped with a griffin – the emblem of Gray's – and dedicated to his friend Jeremy Bettenham, who had been treasurer of the Inn in 1595.[31] The mount and banqueting house are shown in several of the early maps, including the Faithorne and Newcourt map of 1658, which shows knots or labyrinths on either side of the mount, which would have been best viewed, of course, from that elevated position.

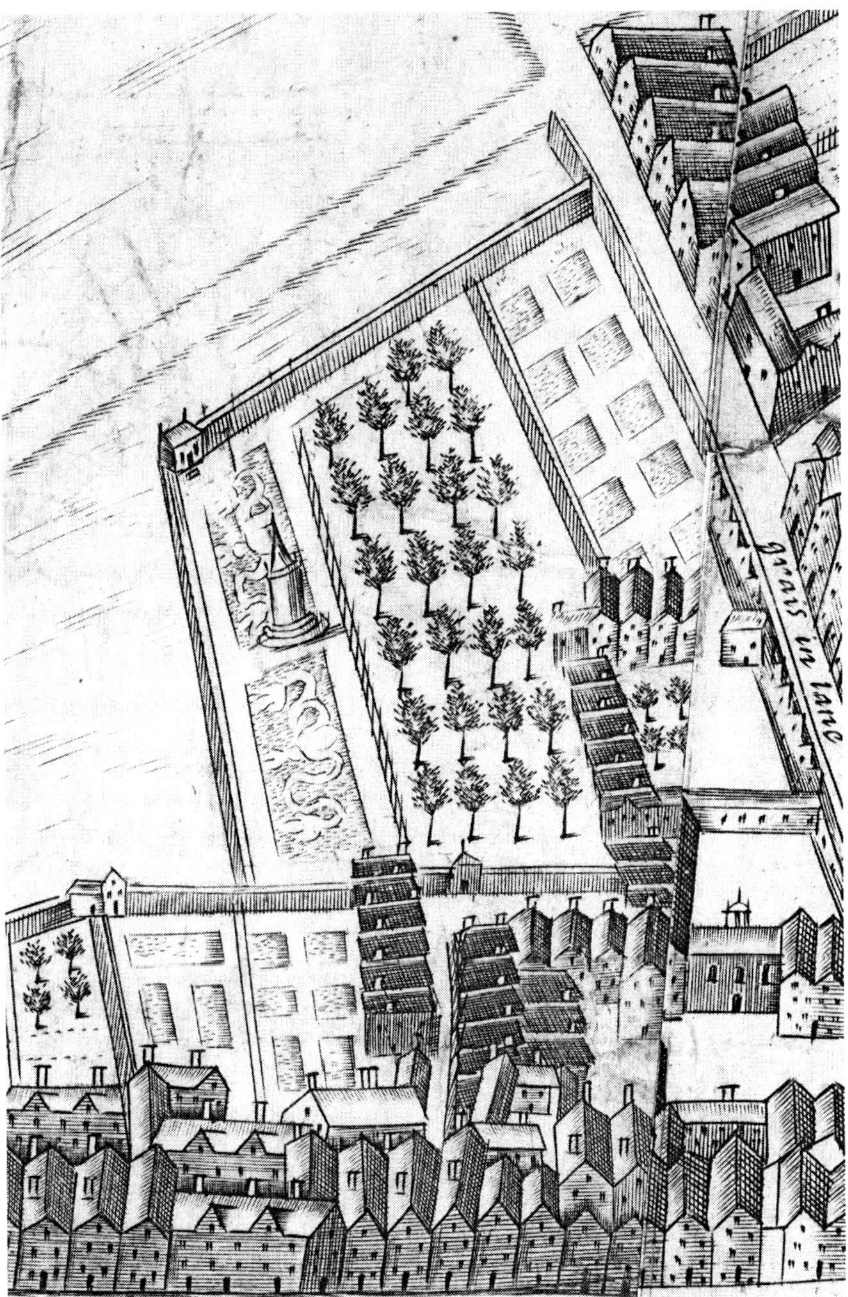

21 Detail of the map of London by Richard Newcourt, engraved by William Faithorne, 1658, showing Gray's Inn, including the banqueting house on the mount built by Sir Francis Bacon.

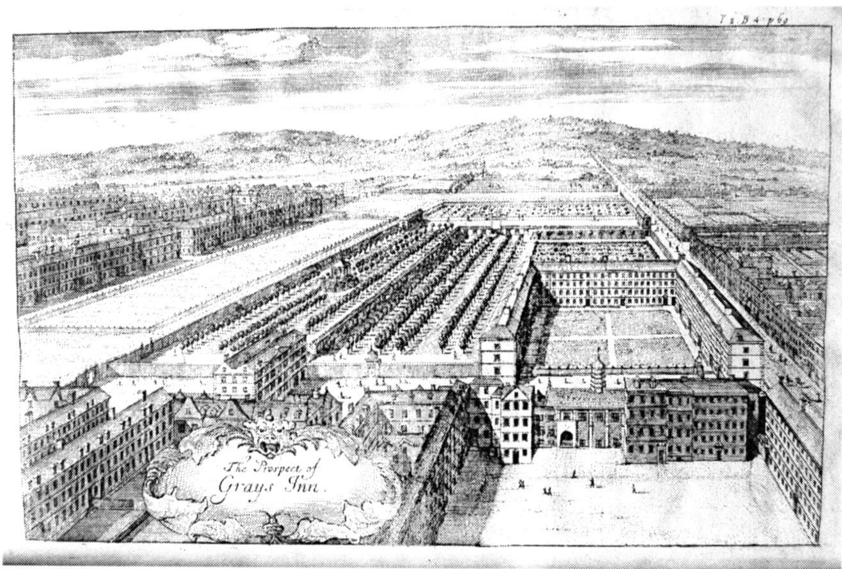

22 'The Prospect of Gray's Inn', from John Stow's *Survey of the Cities of London and Westminster*, reprinted and enlarged by John Strype, 1720.

More improvements followed. In 1610, Brooks was paid to make a bowling alley north of the terrace walk and, later, a small summer house was built in the north-west corner of the garden.[32] This and another, matching banqueting house are shown in the Ogilby and Morgan map of 1676, as are the walks and the kitchen gardens to the north (shown as quartered with each compartment planted in a 'Union Jack' design). Much of this survived well into the eighteenth century and a fine illustration appeared in John Strype's 1720 edition of Stow. Strype wrote:

> The chief ornament belonging to this Inn, is its spacious Garden, with curious Walks, as well those that are shady by the lofty Trees, as those that are raised higher, and lie open to the Air, and the enjoyment of a delightful prospect of the Fields. And this Garden hath been, for many years, much resorted unto, by the Gentry of both Sexes.[33]

The magnificent views of the Highgate Hills shown in the view would be jealously guarded and early attempts to develop the land between them and the Inn were originally thwarted. The gardens themselves, however, would soon be radically changed, as so many were in the mid-eighteenth century by landscape 'improvers'. Between 1755 and 1770, the terraces and mount were levelled, the banqueting house demolished, and the planting 'simplified' by a 'Mr. Brown', identified by David Jacques as the famous 'Capability' Brown.[34]

Inner Temple

The earliest references to the Temple gardens date to the early sixteenth century. In the 1530s, a wall was built between the Thames and the garden (visible in the 'Agas' and Braun and Hogenberg maps, which also show the gardens planted densely with trees).[35] In the 1540s, to avoid the 'displeasure, annoyance and disturbance of the gentlemen of the House' from the 'common recourse of all sorts of people into the House and garden by a door through the yard', further walls were erected around the garden.[36] In 1576, Robert Dudley, Earl of Leicester – who had been admitted to the Inner Temple in 1561 and maintained a close connection to it[37] – was granted rooms for the 'Alienations Office' (he was head of the Office of Compositions for Alienations). Behind these he created a small, enclosed garden, known for the next 350 years as the Alienation Office Garden. Leicester was granted permission by the Inner Temple

> to enclose and convert into a garden plot, all that plot or parcel of vacant ground environed with buildings, lately made in the time of the said Mr. Fuller … on the west side, the brick wall of Serjeant's Inn on the north side, the White Friars on the east side and [on the south side] the said new erected buildings … and that the said earl and such other as he, his heirs, or executors shall so admit, as aforesaid, by his or their denomination, as aforesaid, shall have and enjoy the same in severalty during the time there shall be admittances of the said buildings, without disturbance, interruption, or impediment of any person or persons, etc.[38]

In 1585, an order was made that all doors leading into 'the Earl of Leicester's garden near his office in the Temple … be walled up … by the owners of the chambers … and from henceforth there shall be no doors … out of the said chambers into the said garden'.[39] The owners of the chambers, however, were permitted 'to make windows into the said garden' and also make 'any jettied study', as long as it projected from an upper storey. It seems that Leicester – even though his own house, Leicester House in the Strand, and garden were a short walk away – had a firm hold on the pleasures of his private garden in the Inn.

In 1592, the annual allowance for the upkeep of the gardens at Inner Temple was increased from £10 to £15, reflecting work being carried out on the 'new faire garden plot'.[40] The garden was to be enclosed by 'a stronge brick wall' and have 'large and lovely walks … to be [ornamented] with beautiful banks, curious knots and beds of fragrant flowers, and sweet herbs of sundry sents and sorts'.[41] There would be 'strong and stately rails of timber carved work upon twelve of these rails was artificially wrought and placed, the figures of the 12 celestiall signs, very lively and artificially cutt'.[42]

In 1610, the riverside gardens were divided by buildings (the Heyward's Buildings, now Paper Buildings): in 1611–12, the east side was planted with trees (now King's Bench Walk).[43] In 1619, a 'pound' (presumably a pond) was created and a sundial added.[44] In the 1620s, seats were built around trees and a summer house was erected in 1630.[45] Some of these features appear in the Ogilby and Morgan map,

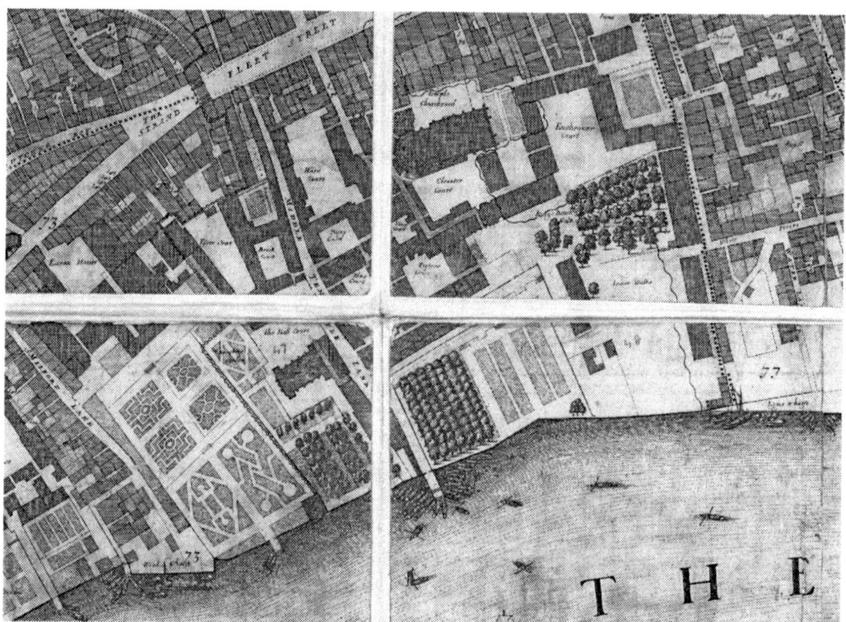

23 Detail of the map of London by John Ogilby and William Morgan of 1676, showing the Temple gardens and walks in the centre and the elaborate design of the gardens of Essex House to the left.

which shows two large areas planted with trees ('King's Bench Walk' and the garden adjacent to the river at Middle Temple Lane) and a terrace to the north of the lower gardens with stairs down to two parallel pairs of garden beds. The simplicity of these gardens contrasts dramatically with the highly stylised, intricate walks and patterns of the fashionable gardens at nearby Essex House, formerly Leicester House.[46]

Middle Temple

Again, the earliest view is the 'Agas' map, but the enclosed garden is shown empty, unlike the neighbouring garden at Inner Temple. Records begin in the mid-sixteenth century with the lease of the gardens to John Rede for a term of thirty years (20s. yearly).[47] Little of interest is recorded again until 1611, when a mason, William Wilson, was paid for purbeck stone for the walk, new doorway, and steps for the garden.[48] A new brick wall was built in 1614, and in 1615 more stone was laid in 'the new Temple private garden.'[49] In 1615, the gardener was paid for 'the new knott' and germander; pinks and unspecified 'seeds' were also purchased.[50] Payments were made for 'the new making of the garden in the Benchers' walk' (£11 11s. 3d.) and for earth 'to raise the level of the ground'.[51] The large amount of £36 23s. 10d. was paid out on the garden *circa* 1617, including 'digging, trenching and levelinge' the new garden; purchasing seeds (for the kitchen garden), as well as flowers, pinks, 3,000 whitethorns, 1,000 sweet briar, and ivy; and wire 'to bind the hedge'.[52] Eight vines and 'four double honeysuckle' were purchased, along with wire, nails, and twigs to bind them to the wall.[53] This was clearly a major renovation of the garden. Finishing touches to a pair of banqueting houses included painting and gilding the wild man 'which standeth upon on [i.e. one] of the banqueting houses in the garden' and the 'great liones standing upon the other banqueting house'.[54] Like lions, wild men were often used to support shields and coats of arms; they became increasingly popular as garden ornament in the Tudor period.[55] In 1683, a building was being erected on the north-east side of 'the Fountain … where an old Banquetting House stood lately', suggesting that the pair survived almost to the end of the century.[56] In any case, neither they nor the fountain appear on the Ogilby and Morgan map, the best visual record of the Temple gardens. The gardens of both Inner and Middle Temples must have been affected by the tides of the Thames in the early modern period, though this would end with the building of the Embankment in the nineteenth century, something that would also terminate the intimate relationship between the gardens and the river.

Lincoln's Inn

Records for Lincoln's Inn survive from the Middle Ages with accounts for leasing the gardens, as already noted above.[57] The visual records for Lincoln's Inn are the

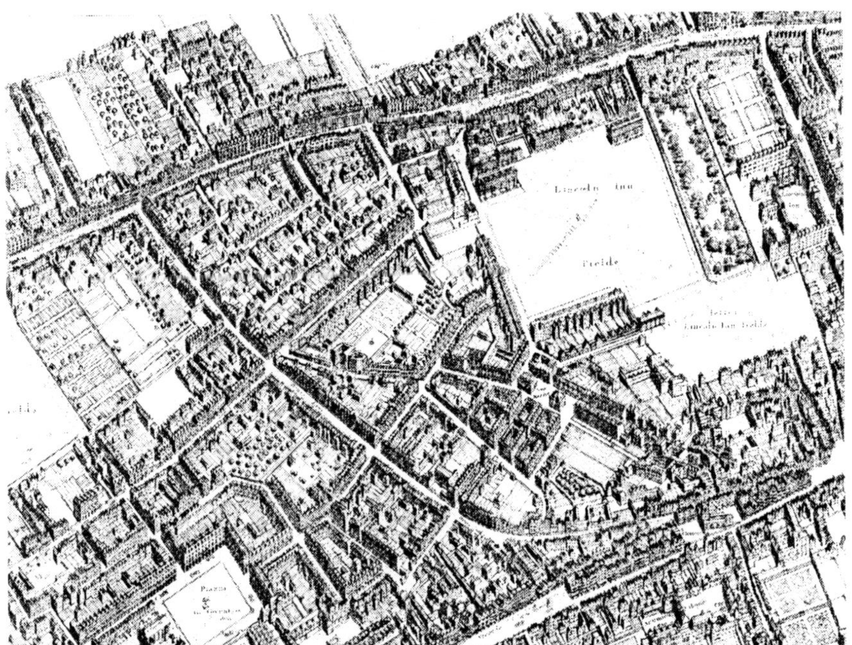

24 Detail of Wenceslaus Hollar's view of Westminster in *circa* 1658, showing the gardens and fields of Lincoln's Inn.

most detailed of all, again with the 'Agas' and Braun and Hogenberg maps clearly showing enclosed gardens near the Inn and the vast 'fields' with their numerous paths to the west. Hollar's plan of Covent Garden of *circa* 1658 provides the most detailed view of the fields and gardens with the later seventeenth-century maps showing subsequent changes.

The first accounts from the sixteenth century are for locks and keys for the garden gate in 1562.[58] A shed (or 'gardener's house') was built in 1571, perhaps in preparation for a major planting campaign in 1572, when a ditch was dug, thousands of quickset ordered, and 3,000 unidentified plants ('at iiis and iiij*d* the thousand') were brought in.[59] A hedge was planted around the 'Conyngrye' (rabbit warren) and trees removed from it. In 1580, seats were built in various gardens (one identified as the *hortus* and the other as *gardinum*).[60]

In 1608–9, Richard Wheler, Esq., was paid £74 6*s.* 5*d.* 'for making the new garden and walks' at Lincoln's Inn.[61] The gardener's wages were £4. Payments to Wheler continued at least until 1611. Hollar's slightly later engraving includes people walking through the Fields and around the garden, as well as young women laying out and drying laundry, very much like the Copperplate map of one hundred years earlier. Obviously, the orders to keep laundresses away from the Inns' gardens were not all that effective.

Most prominent at Lincoln's Inn were 'the fields', originally made up of several open fields: Cup Field, Fickett's Field to the south (sometimes called 'Lesser Lincoln's Inn Fields'); and Purse Field to the west.[62] In the Middle Ages, the fields were well-known places for exercise, including jousting. Cup and Purse fields became crown property in 1537 and executions were carried out on the site until the end of the seventeenth century. In 1617, a petition was made to King James that Lincoln's Inn Fields might be converted into walks in the manner of Moorfields, 'to the pleasure and benefit of the City', and a commission was appointed to ensure that '[the] small remainder of Ayre in those partes' would remain undeveloped.[63] One of the commissioners was Inigo Jones and, although nothing really came of it, Jones has often been credited with laying out the walks through the Fields. Houses were eventually built around the Fields (their number increasing with each later map), but even so, the Fields were considered 'ill kept and unsafe'.[64] Things only improved slightly in the mid-eighteenth century, when the Fields were enclosed by iron railings.[65]

The Inns and contemporary garden design

Although the images and documents we have considered are helpful, there are certain aspects of the Inns' gardens in the early modern period that remain elusive. The early maps show rather plain, squared compartments in most gardens, some of them probably planted with grass ('grass plots', as they were commonly called), an easy and evergreen solution to garden design. In a number of the Inns' accounts, 'rollers' were purchased, presumably for the grass plots.[66] Although we know that 'knots' were planted at both Inner and Middle Temples, we have no images of them. Knots are shown in the Faithorne and Newcourt view of Gray's Inn, illustrated above. Otherwise, apart from what might be described as a 'Union Jack' design in the kitchen gardens at Gray's Inn, other indications of planting are cursory. In contrast, nearby private gardens – such as those shown in such detail on both the Hollar and the Ogilby and Morgan maps – demonstrate all the variety and intricacies of seventeenth-century garden design. This is true not only for the houses of wealthy Londoners, but also for the livery companies, whose gardens show up quite clearly in some early maps.[67]

Similarly, there is not the great emphasis at the Inns of Court on the types of architectural ornament that were so ubiquitous in private gardens in this period. Walls and gates are prominent on the maps and views of the Inns, but they were built by necessity. Garden buildings or 'banqueting houses' are recorded for most of the Inns: one on the mount at Gray's Inn; the pair of banqueting houses at Middle Temple and a later 'summer house' at Inner Temple, the latter with wainscoting and seats.[68] Small buildings – such as the 'convenient howse, or shed' built for the gardener at Lincoln's Inn in 1571 at the upper end of the garden 'near the buttes ... for the better kepinge of the garden' – were also quite common.[69] Still, apart from the views of the banqueting house and mount at Gray's Inn, these garden buildings are not given the emphasis that they are in views of private gardens, where architectural ornament (banqueting houses, elevated viewing platforms, and even grottoes) provided dramatic punctuation and emphasis to garden design.[70]

The same is true of sculptural ornament. Apart from the figures of 'the twelve celestial signs' and the sundial itemised in the accounts at Inner Temple, there is little evidence of sculpture. Yet dials were the most common method of timekeeping in the period and one would have expected references to others. Also at Inner Temple, a carver was paid in 1618 for two pairs of figures, each with a Pegasus (the emblem of Inner Temple) and a Griffin (the emblem of Gray's Inn) to celebrate the special alliance of the two Inns in the period. The figures were painted and gilded, along with the posts and rails around the gates, upon which the figures were placed.[71] Again, this type of heraldic ornament was ubiquitous in contemporary gardens and there must have been other examples. Almost all early gardens had a fountain or conduit of some sort, yet none is mentioned in accounts of Gray's Inn or Inner Temple. The fountain referred to in the accounts of Middle Temple was not built until the early 1680s.[72] Similarly, at Lincoln's Inn it was not until 1682 that there was a discussion 'concerneing the bringing in the New River water into the Garden of this Society, and erecting a fountaine there'.[73] Yet the next extant reference to a fountain isn't until 1706, when the treasurer of Lincoln's announced that the cost of a fountain in the great garden would be £95 and 'a subscription list' to pay for it was opened.[74] In Tudor and early Stuart gardens, one would have expected to find something similar to the early seventeenth-century fountain at Trinity College,

Cambridge, which was not only an emphatic architectural ornament to the grand courtyard but, through taps at the side of the octagonal basin, a source of water for the collegiate community.[75] According to the records of the Inner Temple, water from the river was used for basic purposes, while water for drinking and cooking was initially obtained from the conduit in Fleet Street.[76] In 1594, an arrangement was made with a Mr Bulmer for a pipe to provide water to the Inn at a rent of 40*s.* per annum.[77] Perhaps the difficulties of obtaining water precluded the building of fountains until the late seventeenth century, when presumably the supplies were more accessible.

As for the planting of the gardens, accounts refer to items for kitchen gardens, as well as to those for pleasure gardens. In February 1621/22, the gardener of Gray's Inn was 'to furnishe the house with all manor of herbs roots and sallets upon Grand Dayes, Reading Weekes, and all other tymes in the yeare as need shall require to furnishe the kitchene'.[78] The ornamental plants purchased for these gardens were – where specified –mostly indigenous and common: roses (eglantine), pinks, violets, primroses, germander, and double honeysuckle, for example.[79] Given the proximity of the Inns to the gardens and nurseries of the great plantsmen of the day – John Gerard (who was raising 'all manner of strange trees, herbes, rootes, plants, flowers, and other such rare things') in Holborn, the Tradescants at Lambeth, and John Parkinson at Long Acre, just to name a few – it is odd that there is no reference in any of the accounts to exotic plants or bulbs like those being purchased for other great gardens of the period.[80] Perhaps it had something to do with the atypical role of the Inns' gardeners, who sometimes rented the land they worked and apparently owned the plants they introduced. In 1639, the gardener at Gray's Inn was dismissed and ordered to 'remove his plants and setts by the sixt of November next'.[81] He did not do so, and on 20 November 1639, it was ordered that:

> The Queenes gardiner of Somerset House is to view the gardiners plants and the vallue of them, and the successor gardiner is to give accordeing to that rate and the steward and butler to put the new gardiner in possession.[82]

The largest numbers of plants purchased were for hedging materials – privet, whitethorn, and quickset (3,000 whitethorns were ordered for Middle Temple in 1618). Hedges were used to border and divide gardens and also for mazes and labyrinths. The most costly plants purchased were the trees. Trees were purchased for orchards (apples and pears were common) but the most magnificent were the trees 'of great stature, and well grown, such as were lately in the *Groves* in the several Inns of Court', as the diarist John Evelyn, a member of Middle Temple, described them.[83] These were perhaps the definitive characteristic of the Inns' gardens, eclipsing ephemeral planting schemes, elegant pleasure buildings, and witty sculptural ornament. It is this sobriety that seems to distinguish the gardens of the early modern Inns of Court from contemporary gardens, a fact which may also help us understand exactly how the gardens were used and perhaps what they represented.

The gardens and life at the Inns

Walking remained one of the most convenient forms of exercise for city dwellers. Great open spaces, like those visible in the Copperplate map of greater London, dwindled rapidly in the Elizabethan and early Stuart periods. One only need trace the fate of Moorfields, so open and full of life in the mid-sixteenth century and so shrunk and rigid a hundred years later. It should not be surprising, then, that the Inns' gardens became popular for social promenades, mentioned in contemporary diaries and accounts. John Evelyn's praise for the walks has been mentioned above. Evelyn's contemporary and fellow diarist Samuel Pepys frequently referred to the walks, particularly at Gray's Inn. Typical is his entry for 27 June 1661:

> Hence I to Graye's Inn Walk all alone, and with great pleasure, seeing the fine ladies walk there. My self humming to myself (which now-a-days is my constant practice since I begun to learn to sing) the trillo, and found by use that it do come upon me.[84]

Keeping the students at the Inns physically active was important. In 1552–53, three men were fined 12*d.* each for 'playing ball in the Hall and breaking some glass windows' at Lincoln's Inn.[85] Archery butts were easily erected in open fields and accounts show that they were added to the bowling alley at Gray's Inn in 1632.[86] In 1609, 'some consideration shall be had of a bowling place for the young gentlemen' at Lincoln's Inn, which was clearly created at some point, for in 1632 payments were made for posts and a seat at 'the bowling green'.[87] There was some discussion, too, of a tennis court in the Fields at Lincoln's Inn in the 1650s, but apparently that was never built.[88] One wonders if students at the Inns, particularly at Inner and Middle Temples, might have used the sporting complex associated with nearby Cecil House in the Strand which featured a large, enclosed tennis court and bowling alley.[89] William Cecil may have had this in mind when he had a separate entrance to these facilities created conveniently on the Strand.

But providing a place to exercise – be it walking or engaging in sports – was only one of the purposes of the gardens. The long walks and groves must also have been linked with 'learned discourse', inspired by the antique tradition of philosophical arguments and discussions in covered walks (the ancient Athenian Stoics, for example, whose name came from the colonnaded *stoa* under which they walked and conversed). In *Silva*, John Evelyn devoted several chapters to groves and their historical significance: to poets ('the Delight the Poets took in Groves') and to philosophers ('An Historical Account of the Sacredness and Use of Standing Groves, Etc.').[90] Certainly, walks and groves were integral to the gardens and parks of the 'first two' universities, Oxford and Cambridge (the Inns have been called 'the third'). Loggan's prospects, plans, and views show a number of colleges with long, tree-lined walks and groves.[91] In his 1688 plan of Cambridge, there are many long walks shown, particularly at the colleges with gardens along the banks of the Cam (Queens', King's, Clare and Trinity).[92] Loggan's copy of a plan of Cambridge by John Hammond, dated 1592, suggests that these walks were introduced well before the end of the sixteenth century, possibly providing inspiration a couple of decades later for Francis Bacon, who had studied at Trinity College, Cambridge, in the 1570s.[93] Other colleges had densely planted groves, like those shown in views of the Temple: Trinity, St John's, and Wadham, all at Oxford, are good examples.[94]

Members of the Inns were meant to behave properly in the garden, although the rules for the garden were sometimes more lax than those for the buildings. At Lincoln's Inn in 1489, the following order was made by the governors of the Inn:

> that if any one now or in future … shall henceforth commit fornication with any woman [in his chamber] or shall carnally know her, he shall pay a fine of 100s to the Society as often as he shall be so found … And if he shall have her or enjoy her in such a way in the garden, the Coneygarth or in the lane near the Inn … he shall pay a fine of 20s.[95]

In later years, what one wore in the garden was important. The following rule was laid down at Inner Temple in 1594:

> And it is also enacted that if any fellow of this House, being in commons or lying in the House, shall wear either hat or cloak in the Temple Church, Hall, Buttery, or at the Buttery bar, or at the dresser, or in the Garden, he shall forfeit for every time that he shall so offend 6s 8d.[96]

Typically, gardens provided privacy. In *1 Henry VI* (*circa* 1590), Shakespeare famously set the scene of the protagonists of the War of the Roses – who found the Temple's hall 'too loud' – in the 'more convenient' garden, where each plucked a rose, red or white, to establish his loyalties (II.iv).[97] Perhaps for the same reason, 'finding the hall too loud', benchers of Inner Temple are recorded as having met 'in the garden' to consider 'minor matters' in 1641.[98] Clearly, the gardens offered a discrete and relatively quiet place for conversations of personal or professional matters.

Conclusions

In the end, what is most remarkable about the gardens of the Inns of Court is that they have survived into the twenty-first century. The same is not true of the magnificent private mansions and gardens that originally bordered on the Inns: they have all – without exception – disappeared because their owners succumbed to the pressure and financial rewards of land developers. The fact that the Inns have retained their gardens is another compelling, if subtle, reminder of their enduring power, determination, and wealth. As a result, the gardens of the Inns of Court continue to provide open space in an overcrowded city for the pleasures of their members and the public alike.

Notes

1 This essay is concerned with the gardens of the four Inns of Court up to *circa* 1700. Evidence of gardens at the early Inns of Chancery – such as Furnival's Inn, Staple Inn, and Barnard's Inn – is also found in the early maps and deserves further consideration. Such material, however, is beyond the scope of the present study.

2 See Ann Saunders and John Schofield (eds), *Tudor London: A Map and a View* (London: London Topographical Society Publication 59, 2001), esp. plate 1.

3 John Stow, *A Survey of London* (1598, rev. 1603), introd. and notes C. L. Kingsford, 2 vols (Oxford: Clarendon Press, 1908), I, 127.

4 The maps are illustrated in Jill Husselby and Paula Henderson, 'Location, location, location!: William Cecil's House in the Strand', *Architectural History*, 45 (2002), 159–93 (see fig. 2 for Norden's full map and fig. 3 for a detail of Hollar).

5 Although it is now known that Ralph Agas did not execute the 'Agas' map, it is still known by his name. For a full view and excellent details, see http://mapoflondon.uvic.ca/map. php, sections B3 and C3 of which show the Inns of Court.

6 *Inner Temple Records*, I, 40. The treasurer was then charged to let the garden to someone else.

7 *Ibid.*, II, 90. He was given a chance to defend himself, but apparently to no avail.

8 *Black Books*, I, 16.

9 *Calendar of the Middle Temple*, p. 13.

10 *Ibid.*, p. 27.

11 *Inner Temple Records*, I, 405.

12 *Ibid.*, I, 303.

13 *Ibid.*, I, 317.

14 *Ibid.*, I, 382.

15 *Pension Book of Gray's Inn*, I, 306 (for June 1631).

16 *Black Books*, II, 161.

17 *Ibid.*, II, 241. In 1616, his wages had been set at £25 per annum 'so that he make no more demands for increase' (*ibid.*, II, 180).

18 *Ibid.*, II, 252.

19 *Ibid.*, II, 258.

20 *Ibid.*, II, 280.

21 *Ibid.*, II, 406.

22 *Ibid.*, I, 338. There was a gate in the garden wall that was repaired in 1527, but there is no evidence that it was locked (*ibid.*, I, 218).

23 Repairs were made in July 1579. *Pension Book of Gray's Inn*, I, 39.

24 *Ibid.*, I, 90.

25 *Ibid.*, I, xxxviii, 138, 145–6, 148 and Appendix I (the Accounts), 490–1.

26 *Ibid.*, I, Appendix I.

27 *Ibid.*, I, Appendix I, 490.

28 *Ibid.*, I, Appendix I, 490. On mounts and earthworks, see Paula Henderson, *The Tudor House and Garden: Architecture and Landscape in the Sixteenth and Early Seventeenth Centuries* (New Haven, CT; London: Yale University Press, 2005), pp. 124–8.

29 See Husselby and Henderson, 'Location, location, location!', fig. 4.

30 On the relationship between Bacon's essay and his gardens, see Paula Henderson, 'Sir

Francis Bacon's essay, "Of Gardens", in context', *Garden History*, 36:1 (Spring 2008), 59–84.

31 John Aubrey transcribed the Latin inscription and date (1609) that were on the frieze of the banqueting house (Bodleian, Aubrey MS 6, fol. 67). Bentenman or Bettenham was far older than Bacon and may have been his mentor in his early years at the Inn. See Francis Cowper, *A Prospect of Gray's Inn*, 2nd rev. edn (London: Published by Graya on behalf of Gray's Inn, 1985), p. 12; and *Pension Book of Gray's Inn*, I, Appendix III.

32 On the bowling alley, see *Pension Book of Gray's Inn*, I, 492. Payment was made to Richard Snetham for the banqueting house, for which, see *ibid.*, I, 492.

33 John Stow, *A Survey of the Cities of London and Westminster*, ed. John Strype, 2 vols (London: Printed for A. Churchill, J. Knapton, R. Knaplock, J. Walthoe, E. Horne, [and 5 others in London], 1720), I, 253 (i.e. I, bk 3, 253); quoted in David Jacques, '"The Chief Ornament" of Gray's Inn: the walks from Bacon to Brown', *Garden History*, 17:1 (Spring 1989), 41–67 (52). Jacques's article has very useful reconstruction plans for the gardens: see his figs 2, 3, and 8.

34 Jacques, '"The Chief Ornament"', 57–61.

35 In addition to *Inner Temple Records*, see Conway Davies (ed.), *Collection of Manuscripts in the Library of the Honourable Society of the Inner Temple* (London: Oxford University Press for the Masters of the Bench of the Inner Temple, 1972). See also Tia Sedley, 'Inner Temple garden: "A New Faire Garden, Environed *with* Stronge Brick Walls"', *The London Gardener or The Gardener's Intelligencer*, 7 (2001–2), 46–51. A drawing of the Temple dated 1563, mentioned in the introduction to *Inner Temple Records* (I, 106) has since been lost (communication from Dr Clare Rider, Archivist to the Honourable Society of the Inner Temple).

36 *Inner Temple Records*, I, 151.

37 For Leicester's special relationship with the Inner Temple, see Marie Axton, 'Robert Dudley and the Inner Temple revels', *Historical Journal*, 13:3 (1970), 365–78 (365); as well as Chapter 2 (pp. 34–42, above).

38 *Inner Temple Records*, I, 286–7.

39 *Ibid.*, I, 335–6.

40 See Sedley, 'Inner Temple garden', 46–50 (49), citing ITL, *Miscellaneous Manuscripts*, 32f 12v.

41 *Ibid.*, 49, citing ITL, *Miscellaneous Manuscripts*, 32f 12v.

42 *Ibid.*, 49, citing ITL, *Miscellaneous Manuscripts*, 32f 12v.

43 *Inner Temple Records*, II, 161–2.

44 *Ibid.*, II, 116. The dial cost 15*s.* and the carpenter, John Feilde, was paid £19 for 'the pound'.

45 *Ibid.*, II, xxxvi.

46 The squiggly paths through the dense plantings near the river are typical of *bosquets* or wildernesses in the period, influenced by Versailles and found in most private gardens.

47 *Calendar of the Middle Temple*, p. 13.

48 MTL, MT.2/TUT/3, Bills, *c.*1611–*c.*1619, 1 (bill dated 29 September 1611). This coincided with the acquisition of stone for new building works, as well. I am grateful to the Archivist at Middle Temple, Lesley Whitelaw, for generously providing me with unpublished accounts, bills and financial papers relating to the gardens.

49 MTL, MT.2/TUT/3, Bills, *c.*1611–*c.*1619, 2 (bill dated 13–26 August 1614).

50 MTL, MT.2/TUT/3, Bills, *c.*1611–*c.*1619, 9 (bill dated 1615).

51 MTL, MT.2/TUT/3, Bills, *c*.1611–*c*.1619, 9 (bill dated 1615).

52 MTL, MT.2/TUT/3, Bills, *c*.1611–*c*.1619, 12 (bill datable to the treasurership of Laurence Hyde, which ran from 22 November 1616 to 21 November 1617).

53 MTL, MT.2/TUT/3, Bills, *c*.1611–*c*.1619, 21–22 (bill not dated).

54 MT.2/TUT/9, Bills, *c*.1611–*c*.1619, 9 (1617).

55 For a full account of the significance of wild men, see Henderson, *Tudor House and Garden*, pp. 193–5 and 203–6.

56 *Calendar of the Middle Temple*, p. 130.

57 *Black Books*, I, 16.

58 *Ibid.*, I, 338.

59 *Ibid.*, I, 378 and Appendix, 450.

60 *Ibid.*, I, 417 and n. The *hortus* was also called 'the Backsyde' (previously 'Coney garth') and the editor of the *Black Books* has speculated that the *gardinum* was identical with 'Cotterel's Garden'.

61 *Ibid.*, II, 143.

62 On the later history of Lincoln's Inn Fields, see Susan Palmer, 'From fields to gardens: the management of Lincoln's Inn Fields in the eighteenth and nineteenth centuries', *The London Gardener or The Gardener's Intelligencer*, 10 (2004–5), 11–27. Today, Lincoln's Inn Fields is the largest garden square in London (7.25 acres).

63 *Ibid.*, 11.

64 *Ibid.*, 12.

65 *Ibid.*, 14–16.

66 For example, in 1621 a new stone roller in an iron frame was purchased for the Inner Temple, *Inner Temple Records*, II, xxxvi, 134. The stone roller cost 15*s*. 6*d*. The iron frame 'weighing 53 lb' cost 4*d*. per pound, or 17*s*. in total.

67 See, for example, the gardens of the Drapers' Company and the Clothworkers' Hall in John Schofield, 'City of London gardens, 1500–c. 1620', *Garden History*, 27:1 (Summer 1999), 73–88, figs 4 and 5.

68 In *Inner Temple Records*, II, 192 (1630–31, payment to William Newman, plasterer, for 'work done about the summer house in the garden, 10*s*' and to John Ramsey, joiner, 'for wainscot and seats'.)

69 *Black Books*, I, 378. In 1655, another gardener's house was built 'in the farthest corner of the Walkes next to the garden on the outside' (*ibid.*, II, 409).

70 See, for example, Henderson, *Tudor House and Garden*, pp. 143–77.

71 *Inner Temple Records*, II, xxxvi and 110. The carver was paid £4; Bowen, the painter, was paid £20 for the painting and gilding. These two badges still appear on the respective garden gates of the Inner Temple and Gray's Inn.

72 The fountain is visible in the illustration of the Temple in the 1720 edition of Stow, *Survey of the Cities of London and Westminster*, I, bk. 3, page opposite 271.

73 *Black Books*, III, 136.

74 *Ibid.*, III, 225.

75 On the Trinity College fountain, see Henderson, *Tudor House and Garden*, pp. 186–8, fig. 214.

76 Inner Temple Records, II, xxxvi.

77 For subsequent sources of water, see *ibid.*, II, xxxvii–xxxviii.

78 See *Pension Book of Gray's Inn*, I, 245 (11 February 1621/22).

79 *Ibid.*, I, Appendix I, 490.

80 John Gerard's list of the plants that he grew in his Holborn garden was printed in 1596. See *A catalogue of plants cultivated in the garden of John Gerard in the years 1596–1599*, edited with notes, references to Gerard's *Herball*, the addition of modern names and a life of the author by Benjamin Daydon Jackson (London: Privately printed, 1876). On the plants that John Tradescant the Elder purchased for Robert Cecil at Hatfield, see, for example, Prudence Leith-Ross, *The John Tradescants: Gardeners to the Rose and Lily Queen*, rev. edn (London: Peter Owen, 1998), pp. 33–8.

81 *Pension Book of Gray's Inn*, I, 334.

82 *Ibid.*, I, 337.

83 John Evelyn, Silva, or a Discourse of Forest-Trees, and the Propagation of Timber, 2 vols (London: Robert Scott, 1706), I, 245.

84 Samuel Pepys, *Diary and Correspondence*, ed. Richard Lord Braybrooke, 4 vols (London; New York, NY: George Bell & Sons, 1894), I, 197–8.

85 *Black Books*, I, 304.

86 *Pension Book of Gray's Inn*, I, 309.

87 *Black Books*, II, 121, 305.

88 *Ibid.*, II, 414–17, 421. Apparently, buildings were put up on the land intended for the court.

89 See Husselby and Henderson, 'Location, location, location!', pp. 179–81.

90 John Evelyn, *Silva*, I, 324–55.

91 David Loggan, *Oxonia illustrata* (Oxford: Theatro Sheldoniano, 1675), pl. 17 (Oriel) and 29 (Magdalen). David Loggan, *Cantabrigia illustrata* (Cambridge: n. pub., *c.*1690), pl. 25 (Christ's College) and 19 (Gonville and Caius).

92 Loggan, *Cantabrigia illustrata*, pl. 6.

93 *Ibid.*, pl. 28[A].

94 Loggan, *Oxonia illustrata*, pl. 28, 29, 32.

95 *Black Books*, I, 89–90.

96 *Inner Temple Records*, I, 396.

97 William Shakespeare, *1 Henry VI*, in *The Oxford Shakespeare: The Complete Works*, ed. John Jowett, William Montgomery, Gary Taylor, and Stanley Wells, 2nd edn (Oxford: Oxford University Press, 2005).

98 *Inner Temple Records*, I, 396. Similarly, the benchers met 'in the garden' at Middle Temple on 20 May 1641 (*Calendar of the Middle Temple*, p. 71).

10

The rebuilding of the Inns of Court, 1660–1700

Geoffrey Tyack

Walking through the Inns of Court today, it soon becomes obvious that physical evidence of their appearance in the sixteenth and the first half of the seventeenth centuries is quite sparse: the Temple Church, Middle Temple Hall, and the old quadrangle and chapel at Lincoln's Inn are the only major buildings that survive reasonably intact from this period. The relative dearth of early buildings can largely be explained by later rebuildings, most recently after the Second World War, when the Inns – especially the Inner Temple and Gray's Inn – suffered grievously. The most important of these rebuildings, however, took place in the thirty years after the Restoration of 1660, and it established the visual character that the Inns still, in large part, retain.

One reason for the rebuilding is obvious: fire, not only the Great Fire of 1666, which affected only one of the Inns (the Inner Temple), but also a series of later fires which devastated two of the others (the Middle Temple and Gray's Inn), destroying most of their timber-framed buildings and sparing only the halls and chapels. But this was not the whole story. New buildings also went up because they were profitable, and because they satisfied a demand. To understand why, we need to establish what the Inns were, and what they were in the process of becoming.

For anyone used to Oxford and Cambridge, the most tempting analogy is with the universities and their colleges which, with their halls, chapels, and quadrangles, in many respects resemble the Inns. William Noy, the Attorney-General, remarked in 1632, for which year he served as treasurer of Lincoln's Inn, that 'every inn of the court was an university of itself':[1] a place of legal learning, focusing (unlike Oxford and Cambridge) on common law, and providing a practical training for barristers as well as an agreeable place in which the aristocratic *jeunesse dorée* could prolong their adolescence. One might therefore expect a large-scale rebuilding programme to be related in some way to an expansion of legal education. Yet, just as the number of students in Oxbridge declined in the late seventeenth century, the number of law students at the Inns went down too, and even more dramatically.[2] The lawyers, as the legal historian John H. Baker has observed elsewhere in this collection, 'left in droves' during the civil wars.[3] Lectures or 'readings' were reinstated in the 1650s, but they ended in the 1670s, along with the 'moots' or discussions which now became, in Baker's words, 'little more than a formalised ritual'.[4] Writing in the early eighteenth century, Roger North, a former treasurer of the Middle Temple, observed that the Inns retained 'the outward show or pretence of collegiate institutions, yet in reality, nothing of that sort is to be found in them'.[5] By the middle of the eighteenth century, the great lawyer Sir William Blackstone (1723–80), a member of the Middle Temple, could write that 'all sorts of regimen and academical superintendance ... are found impracticable and [are] therefore entirely neglected'.[6] Instead, aspiring barristers had to rely on informal instruction from older lawyers, supplemented by individual study.[7]

The post-Restoration Inns

If formal legal education was declining in the post-Restoration period, the number of professional lawyers and would-be lawyers was not. For all their academic lassitude, the Inns retained one vital prerogative: the control of admissions to the bar. They were at the centre of legal London, and there was still a demand for chambers – flats rather than student lodgings – for trainee and practising barristers, for judges and, increasingly in the eighteenth century, for private individuals with no particular connection to the law. Chambers did not belong to an Inn as a corporate entity – the Inns were never technically incorporated – but to individual benchers, who could rebuild and sub-let them.[8] In this sense the Inns, as organisations, were somewhat like the aristocratic landlords of the rapidly expanding western suburbs of London or the City livery companies (or guilds) who owned land in London; they wanted to profit from their land, but with minimal financial outlay. They did not have large landed endowments like the Oxford or Cambridge colleges, depending instead on rents and fees. And they could not rebuild without the consent of all of the benchers. All this implied an architecture in which the principles of commodity and firmness prevailed over that of delight.

New residential building in post-Restoration London inevitably meant Classical elevations – however loosely interpreted – and the use of brick rather than timber. The first known brick building in the Inns was the Old Hall of Lincoln's Inn (1489–92),[9] but most of the residential construction undertaken in the sixteenth and early seventeenth centuries seems to have been of timber. Then, in 1629–30, a new brick block went up in Crown Office Row, part of the Inner Temple, looking south over the garden and the River Thames. Unusually in the light of earlier developments, this was conceived not by individuals but by the Inn as a whole and was financed 'with the treasure of the house', which recouped part of the cost of £2,682 19*s*. 9*d*. by letting the chambers, the rest coming from a tax on members.[10] Rebuilt in the eighteenth century, and destroyed in the Second World War, it was one of the largest building projects of its time in London, five storeys high and no fewer than twenty-three bays wide, with a roofline enlivened by pedimented gables, then at the height of architectural fashion.[11] Similar buildings went up in the Middle Temple to the north. One of them, of 1637–40, was praised for its 'graceful situation, convenience and uniformity',[12] qualities which were to characterise many of the new buildings of the post-Restoration period.

The Inner and Middle Temples and the fires of 1666 and 1677

Next came the Great Fire, which spread from the crowded slums of White-friars to the Inner Temple and the Master's House next to the Temple Church. The Master's House was rebuilt in 1667 as a neat brick Classically proportioned box of the comfortable, instantly recognisable type that was to proliferate throughout England in succeeding decades. It was followed almost immediately by the Lamb Building, a severely plain four-storeyed block of chambers put up by the Middle Temple on a site between the church and Inner Temple Hall.[13] Soon afterwards the fire-damaged buildings of the Inner Temple were rebuilt in a similar style, their frontages looking out on to the open spaces of Exchequer Court and King's Bench Walk, newly laid out with formal walks and avenues of Franco-Dutch inspiration, as shown in a birds-eye view of 1671.[14] Of these buildings, the only survivor is Nos. 1–2 King's Bench Walk, possibly the block of chambers promoted in 1670 by Francis Phelips, a bencher, and built by Edward Tasker, 'a skilful surveyor and contriver of buildings'.[15] But no sooner were they completed than another fire of 1677 made

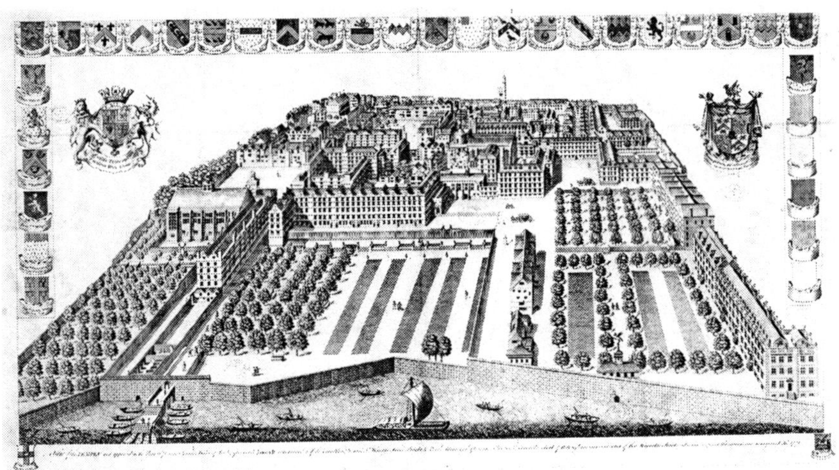

25 A bird's-eye view of the Inner Temple and Middle Temple in 1671, re-engraved in 1770. This shows the two Inns after the Great Fire of London, but before the two more localised fires of 1677 and 1679. King's Bench Walk (Inner Temple) is on the right, Middle Temple Hall on the left, and to the right of it, Crown Office Row (Inner Temple). Inner Temple Hall is in the middle of the picture and, behind it, hemmed in by other buildings, the Temple Church.

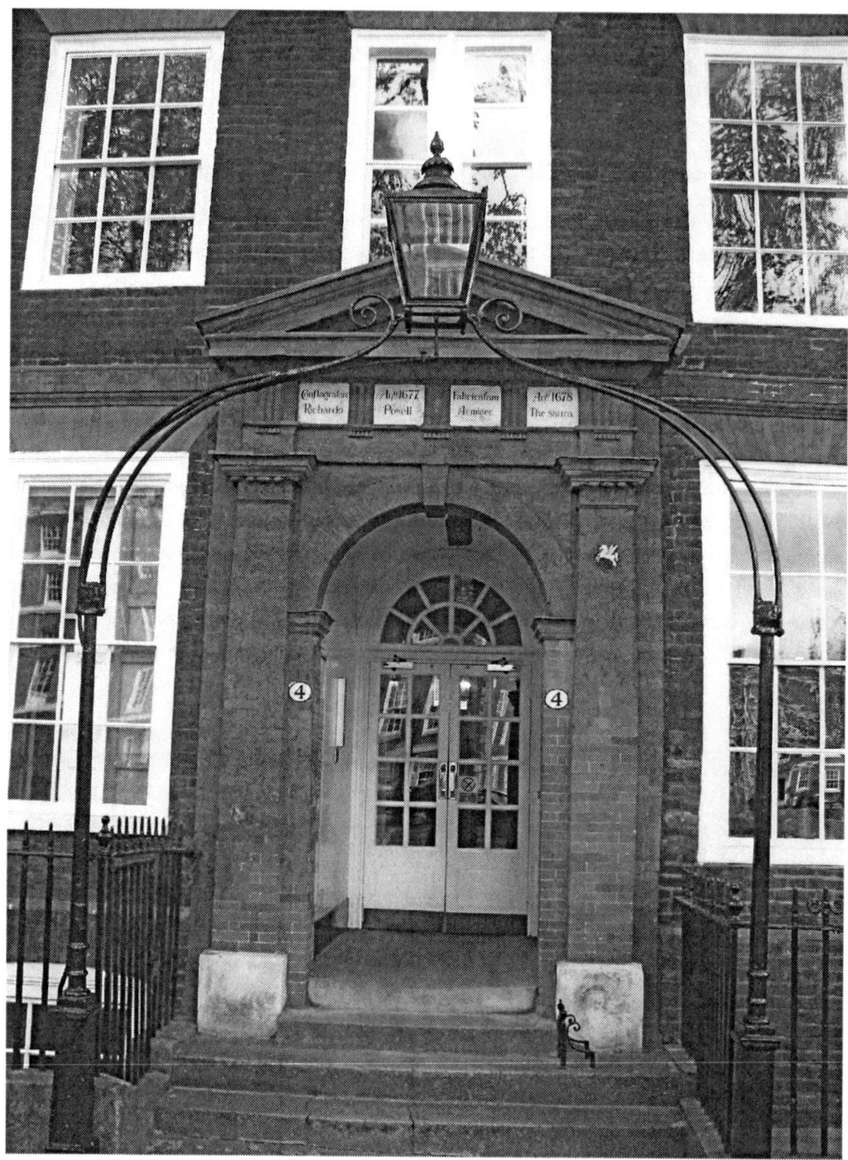

26 The doorway of No. 4 King's Bench Walk (Inner Temple). It carries the date 1678,
following the rebuilding of the chambers after a fire. The range is built of brick, and
the doorcase in gauged red brick exemplifies the spread of classical architectural ideas
following the London Rebuilding Act of 1667.

it necessary to rebuild Nos. 3–6 King's Bench Walk again. The new buildings here were four rather than three storeys high, and their brickwork is of especially high quality, above all in the splendid Classical doorcases (i.e. frames) of specially cut gauged and rubbed red brick; they presumably reflect the tastes of the individual benchers who promoted the buildings, one of whom (at No. 4) arranged to have the date, 1678, and the name of the Treasurer, Richard Powell, recorded over the doorway. The doorways lead to staircases which give access to the sets of chambers, the largest of which were made up of sets of four rooms – one for the clerk, an office/study, a sitting room, and a bedroom – panelled in wood, and with a heavy outer door for privacy.

The new buildings in the Temple established a new paradigm for architecture in the Inns of Court and Chancery, which remained unchallenged until the nineteenth century.[16] Sober and undemonstrative, they showed the influence of the 1667 Rebuilding Act for the City of London, which stipulated the standardisation of façades and the external use of brick instead of timber to minimise fire risk.[17] King's Bench Walk is the best example of post-Fire domestic architecture left in the City, its elevations anticipating later speculative developments such as Bedford Row on the fringe of Gray's Inn, begun *circa* 1690, and Queen Anne's Gate, Westminster (*c*.1704). The staircase layout of the new buildings here and elsewhere in the Temple recalls the blocks for gentleman commoners that recently had been put up in Oxford and Cambridge colleges, such as the Fellows' Building at Christ's College, Cambridge (1640–43) and Sir Christopher Wren's new building at Trinity College, Oxford, of 1665–68. But the overall effect is generally more austere, and one early nineteenth-century writer on the buildings of the Inns was reminded not so much of the English universities as of the apartment buildings of Paris and Edinburgh.[18]

We do not know who built most of the post-Restoration buildings in the Inner Temple, but we do know who was responsible for the exactly contemporary expansion of the Middle Temple. He was the most famous, or notorious, of all post-Restoration London builders: Nicholas Barbon.[19] Born in about 1640, the son of the Puritan zealot Praise-God Barebones, who gave his name to one of Cromwell's short-lived parliaments, Barbon studied medicine at the University of Leiden before applying his talents to the development of fire insurance and, in the 1670s, to property development, especially around the fringes of the City. He lived in Crown Court, off Fleet Street, and in 1674 he began to plan the development of Essex Street on the site of Essex House and its garden, south of the Strand and immediately west of the Middle Temple. This led to an outcry from the benchers who feared the loss of amenity and 'the decay, if not the ruin, of the Society'.[20] But Barbon was a persuasive and ruthless man – described by Roger North, one of the benchers of the Middle Temple, as 'full of law'[21] – and the benchers clearly decided that if they could not beat him, they would do well to join him. So in 1676 Barbon was employed to build New Court, a detached four-storeyed block like the earlier Lamb Building, on part of Essex House garden, and this was followed in 1677 by Essex Court. Both have plainer elevations than King's Bench Walk, though the external severity was belied by the elaborate decoration of some of the rooms.[22]

The fire of 1679 and the rebuilding of the Middle Temple

In 1679 came yet another fire which devastated much of the Middle Temple's older buildings, in Brick Court, Elm Court, and Pump Court, next to the Inner Temple.[23] North tells us that the benchers' first response was to prepare a plan for a complete rebuilding along more rational, Classical lines. But, like the merchants confronted by Wren's plan for the rebuilding of the City after the Great Fire of 1666, the owners of the chambers failed to agree on compensation for their old premises, and nothing came of the project. So the opportunity to completely re-plan a set of haphazard medieval and post-medieval buildings, as happened at Queen's College, Oxford, in the early eighteenth century, was lost. Barbon now, in North's words:

> proposed that a new model should be made of the whole Temple, making the best of the ground, but preserving the courts and gardens ... That every one should have a chamber in the new building, in the same height as the old was, and as neer the scituation, as could be. And that if any had more demension then before, he should pay, if less receiv a certein rate ... That there should be 4 floors in the building, all 10 foot high except the upper which should be 9 and every chamber have a cellar ... Here was a seeming equality, to answer all pretenders; if another has more he pays, if less, he is payd for it, if high the charg is less then lower; who can assign a juster rate? ... In short wee agreed, I [North] made the articles, had them ingrost [engrossed], allowed by the bench, and the model annext, and wee being setled in the modell, went to work briskly.[24]

The brick buildings, like those of New Court and Essex Court, followed the stipulations of the London Rebuilding Act of 1667 for what was described in a court case as 'houses of the third or best rate of houses fronting principal streets'.[25] Barbon's builders must have worked to pre-arranged elevations, though in the absence of drawings or accounts it is impossible to say who prepared them. They ensured a high degree of visual uniformity, but the old, complex, intricate plan of the Inn was preserved, and it is this that has delighted lovers of the picturesque down to the present day.

Barbon did more than anyone else to shape the architectural character of the Inns. In some ways he was the forerunner of such luminaries of the building profession as Thomas Cubitt, one of the most prolific property developers in nineteenth-century London. Barbon was a quintessentially modern figure, accumulating land, borrowing money on a large scale – he was an early exponent of deficit financing – and employing large numbers of labourers as well as master craftsmen like John Fitch (1679) and the carpenter John Foltrop (1681).[26] Barbon had a talent for manipulating his clients, though arguably, as at the Middle Temple, to their mutual advantage; Roger North called him 'an exquisite mob-master'.[27]

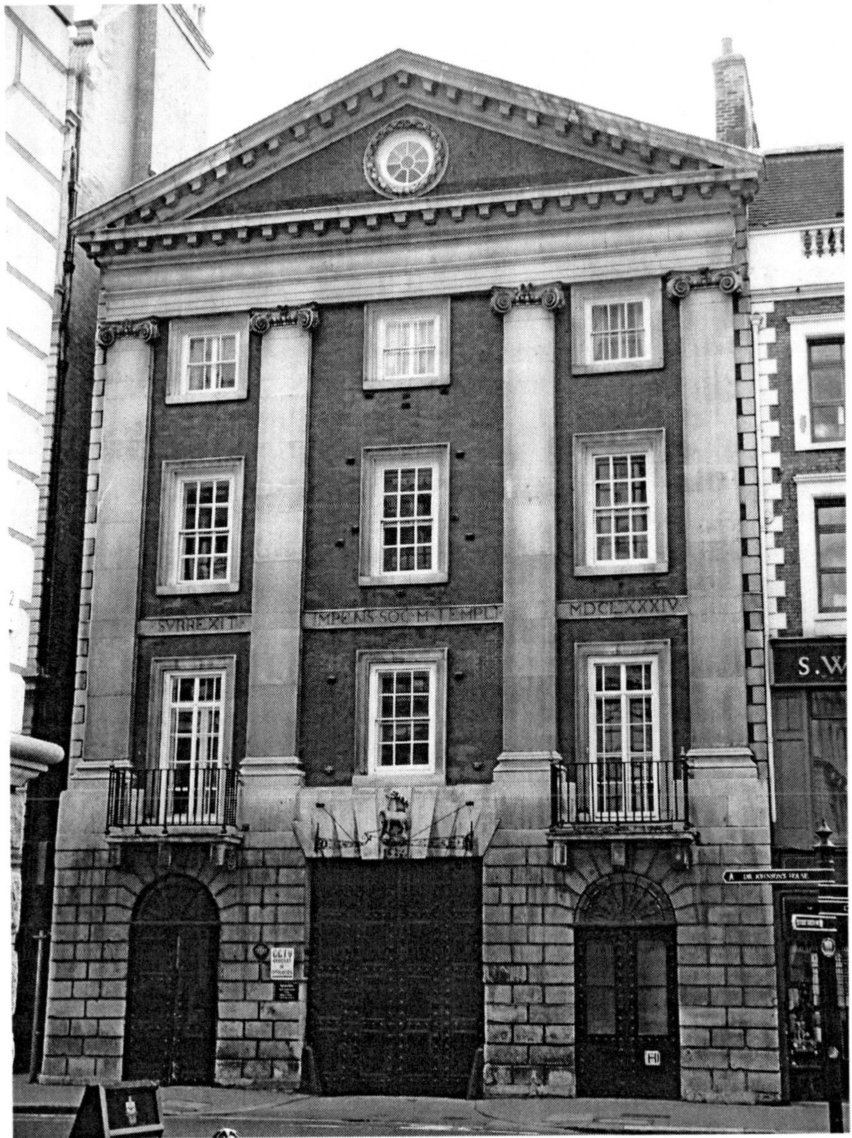

27 Middle Temple Gateway. This exercise in pure Classicism (1683–84) was designed by
the Treasurer, Roger North, who had previously negotiated on behalf of the Inn
with Nicholas Barbon, builder of New Court, Pump Court, etc. The dominating feature
is the pediment, carried on Ionic pilasters which stand on a rusticated base.

But Barbon did not always get his own way. After the 1679 fire, he proposed building another block of chambers on the site of the 'cloister' at the east end of Pump Court, where in the past students had walked in the evenings and 'put cases'.[28] This outraged the benchers of the Inner Temple, whose property lay immediately to the east, and, following an appeal to Heneage Finch, the Lord Chancellor – who was one of their number – a Classicised 'cloister' was retained, with round arcades and a row of Doric columns inside supporting the three-storeyed block of chambers above. The new design was provided by no less an architect than Sir Christopher Wren, who had already done surveying work for the Inner Temple in King's Bench Walk, and had recently designed a similar 'cloister' under the new library at Trinity College, Cambridge; the Middle Temple block went up in 1680–81.[29]

In 1683–84, when Roger North became treasurer (i.e. head of the Society, usually for a one-year term) and decided that the Inn needed a new public face in the form of a gateway to Fleet Street, he chose not to go to Barbon, or even to Wren, but to design it himself. North had already taught himself the rudiments of architecture by reading Vitruvius, Palladio, and other approved authorities, and he discovered

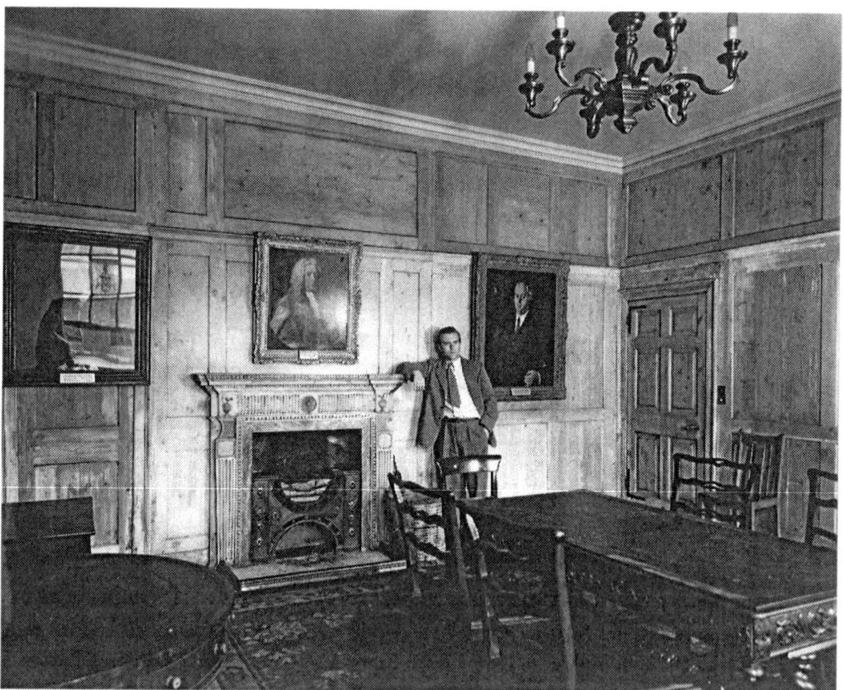

28 The interior of a chamber in the Inner Temple, showing plain late seventeenth-
or eighteenth-century wood panelling and a chimneypiece of *c.*1760–1800.
The room is typical of chambers in all the Inns after their rebuilding in the second
half of the seventeenth century.

'the joys of designing and executing' by 'drawing the model of my litle chamber, and making patterns for the wainscote'.[30] We do not know what his chamber looked like, but the new gateway was an exercise in pure Classicism, purged of the Mannerist embellishments found in some of the City's post-Restoration public buildings, such as the then-adjacent Temple Bar (1670–72), and with none of the Baroque bravura of Wren's later architecture. North's own account of the gateway suggests that he would have liked to treat it as a Classical portico, like the one which Nicholas Hawksmoor was to build in front of the Clarendon Building in Oxford in 1712–13. But funds did not permit the use of free-standing columns, which would in any case have blocked the narrow street.[31] And in order to give the building the requisite dignity, North was 'forc't to raise it very high, the houses being so on each side'.[32] This meant that he had to substitute pilasters for columns and to stand the 'temple-front' on a rusticated plinth with an opening into Middle Temple Lane in the centre and shops on either side: an expedient similar to that which Wren later found himself having to employ on the new east front of Hampton Court in order to allow a passage between Fountain Court and the garden. But despite these offences against the strictest 'Vitruvian' standards, North's gateway is, from an architectural point of view, the most ambitious and impressive of all the post-Restoration buildings at the Inns.

Gray's Inn and Lincoln's Inn

The Middle Temple Gateway is the only piece of 'public' architecture put up by the post-Restoration Inns. Elsewhere pragmatism ruled. Gray's Inn was rebuilt piece-meal in the style pioneered by Barbon, starting in 1676 and continuing after fires in 1680, 1684, and 1687; the work seems to have been finished by 1693.[33] Gray's lay on the edge of Barbon country, and in June 1684 some two hundred of Barbon's employees, 'shouting and ahallowing … and raising their hats', fought a pitched battle on the site of Red Lion Square – one of his largest speculations – with the members of the Inn, accompanied by between fifty and sixty 'gentlemen in gowns' who feared the loss of the open space where they had been accustomed to walk since time immemorial.[34] Here ancient precedent triumphed over modern commerce, and the square was left open. The Inn's own new buildings, which may or may not have been put up by Barbon himself, were as sober as those at the Middle Temple, with immensely long, unadorned frontages to the gardens. In contrast to the conge-ries of small courtyards at the Middle and Inner Temples, there were two main courtyards, separated by the hall and chapel: South Square and Gray's Inn Square, the latter created from two smaller courtyards (Coney Court and Chapel Court) after the demolition in 1685 of a range that had separated them. In both court-yards the plainness of the brick walling was relieved by stone doorcases with broken segmental pediments enclosing little stone balls on plinths originally displaying the numbers of the staircases: a motif also found in New Square at Lincoln's Inn. Both courts have an inward-looking, collegiate character, though for John Strype, writing in 1720, '[Grays Inn] Court, being the best situate, as to an open Air, especially the West and North sides, which look into the Garden and adjacent Fields, is of most esteem, and hath the best Buildings':[35] a judgement that can be echoed today, despite extensive war damage and later rebuilding.

Lincoln's Inn was the only Inn not to suffer from disastrous fires in the late seventeenth century, doubtless because its older buildings were of brick and not timber. But, as at the other Inns, there was a demand for more chambers, and this was met *circa* 1685–93 by the building of a new and spacious open-ended courtyard (New Square) on the site of an open space called Ficketts Field or Little Lincoln's Inn Fields, south-west of the Inn and looking north on to its garden. Beyond was Lincoln's Inn Fields, a fashionable residential area whose open character had been successfully preserved from intensive housing development by the lobbying of earlier generations of benchers.[36] The promoter of New Square was Henry Serle, a barrister but not a bencher of Lincoln's Inn, and his original idea, first mooted in 1680, was for a private development.[37] But, like the members of the Middle Temple

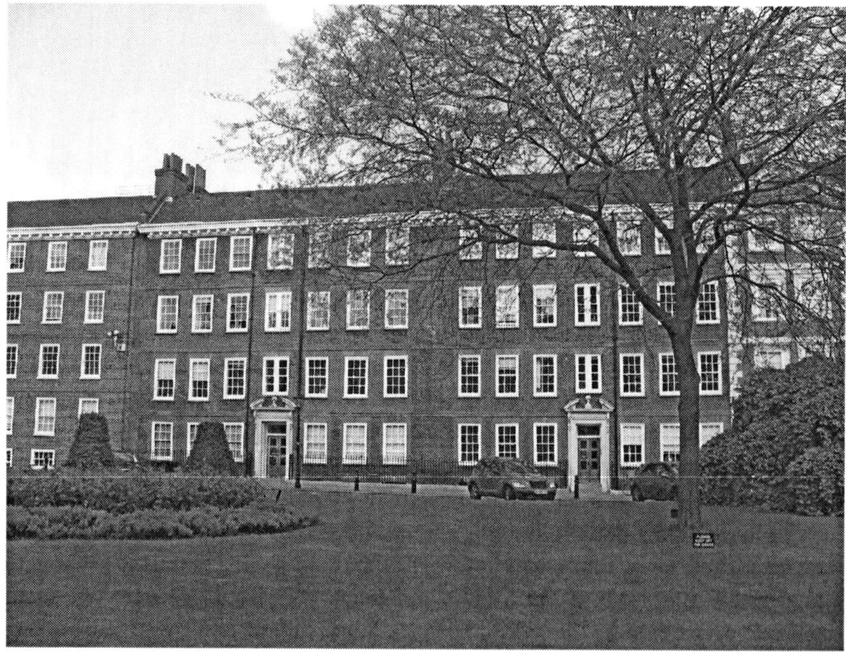

29 Gray's Inn Square, the east range. The buildings, in the austere manner of Nicholas Barbon – if not by Barbon himself – went up over a period of ten years, starting in 1679, on the site of two older courtyards. Embellishment is confined to the stone doorcases and the wooden cornice. The open space in the foreground was created after the demolition of the range separating the older courtyards in 1685.

and Gray's Inn when first confronted by Barbon's activities, the benchers objected because of the possible loss of their rights of way, and an agreement was made in 1682 that the area would be developed as eleven blocks of chambers or 'lodgings for the use of the Society' around 'three parts of a square'; the square itself was to be kept open 'for the prospect and recreation of the said Society and members thereof'.[38] The buildings are as plain as those of Gray's Inn, save for the inner face of the gateway to Carey Street, embellished like Temple Bar with a curved (segmental) pediment and scroll-like volutes: a far cry from the sober Classicism of the Middle Temple Gateway. The project was finished off by Barbon – yet again – after Serle's death in 1690, and the first chambers were occupied in 1692, but Barbon did not succeed in persuading the lawyers to let him build an office for the Six Clerks of the Court of Chancery in the middle of the square, and the integrity of the open space has been maintained ever since.[39]

In some respects, Lincoln's New Square echoes the aristocratic squares of the burgeoning western and north-western parts of London, such as St James's Square and – closer at hand – Bloomsbury Square, both begun in the 1660s, though New Square is architecturally more uniform than they originally were. But a closer analogy is with the Garden Quadrangles at New College (1682–1707) and Trinity College (1668), Oxford, in both of which the buildings form three sides of a square. This was

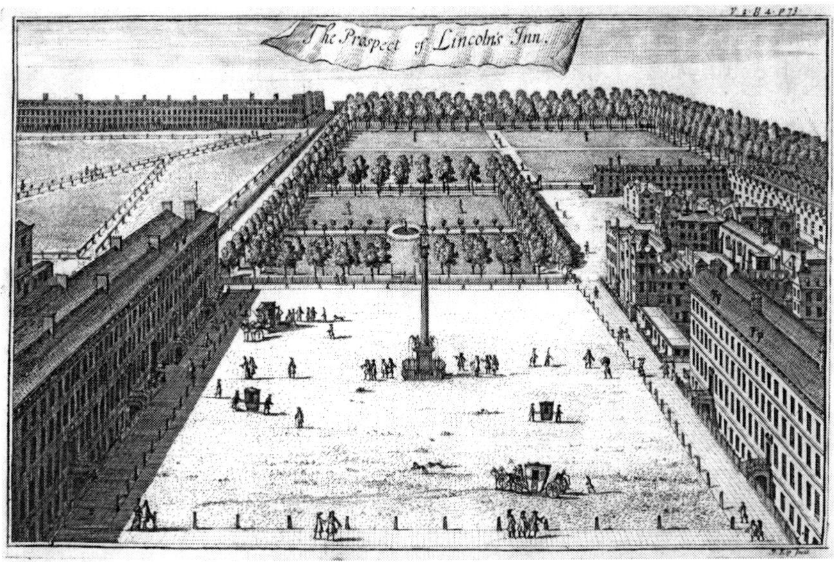

30 New Square, Lincoln's Inn in 1720, from Strype's edition of Stow's survey of London. The 'square' – in fact, an open-ended courtyard – was begun in 1682 and finished, by Nicholas Barbon, in the 1690s. It looks north on to a formal garden created in the 1660s, with Lincoln's Inn Fields to the left. The older buildings of the Inn are on the right of the picture.

a different kind of urbanism to that espoused by Gray's Inn: less cellular and introverted, more attuned to the notion of an open, airy public space first formulated in the Renaissance. This effect is captured in the illustration in Strype's 1720 edition of John Stow's *A Survey of the Cities of London and Westminster*, showing a Corinthian column and sundial in the middle of the open space, with the Inn's formal garden to the north and the houses on the north side of Lincoln's Inn Fields in the distance.[40] After this there was relatively little new building at any of the Inns until 1774–80, when Sir Robert Taylor put up the two handsome Classical blocks known as Stone Buildings to the north of the old core of Lincoln's Inn, the fruits of an architectural competition held three years earlier.[41]

Conclusions

The late seventeenth-century rebuilding of the Inns of Court is revealing not only for what it tells us about the Inns as institutions but also for the light it throws on post-Restoration London, and England. London was a city in which commerce flourished as part of a dynamic, globalising economy. Old institutions such as the Inns of Court had to adapt to a new economic and cultural climate in order to survive. The livery companies became in essence charitable institutions, and as such they continue to flourish. The universities of Oxford and Cambridge increasingly took on the character of finishing schools for the aristocracy, assuming some of the functions that had been performed by the Inns in their sixteenth- and early seventeenth-century heyday. The post-Restoration Inns became residential compounds for lawyers, and their changing functions and aspirations are echoed and displayed in their architecture. Avoiding grandiose Baroque planning gestures, they opted to rebuild on their old sites, retaining their existing halls and chapels and, as we have seen, their existing haphazard plans and their jealously preserved garden settings. Their new residential buildings did not follow the fashions of the court, the Church, or the aristocracy. They were plainer and more utilitarian in appearance than most contemporary buildings in the universities,[42] and less exuberantly decorated than the public buildings of the City, such as Temple Bar or the post-fire Royal Exchange. With their air of restraint and their sober, almost minimalist Classicism, the post-Restoration buildings of the Inns of Court spoke the language of sober calculation that made London one of the fastest-expanding cities of its time. In that sense the law – that most pragmatic of professions – found in the buildings of Barbon and his contemporaries its ideal architectural embodiment.

Notes

1 BL, MS Harley 980, fol. 153, quoted in John H. Baker, *The Third University of England: The Inns of Court and the Common-Law Tradition* (London: Selden Society, 1990), p. 4; reprinted in Baker, *The Common Law Tradition: Lawyers, Books, and the Law* (London: Hambledon Press, 2000), pp. 3–28; and in *The Selden Society Lectures 1952–2001* (Buffalo, NY: W. S. Hein, 2003), pp. 565–614.

2 Lawrence Stone, *The University in Society*, 2 vols (Princeton, NJ: Princeton University Press, 1974), I, 37; David Lemmings, *Gentlemen and Barristers: The Inns of Court and The English Bar 1680–1730* (Oxford: Clarendon Press, 1990), pp. 9–11. The decrease in the number of students was most marked at Gray's Inn.

3 Baker, *The Third University of England*, p. 4. See also Chapter 1 (pp. 8–26, above).

4 Baker, *The Third University of England*, p. 21.

5 Roger North, *A Discourse on the Study of the Laws* (London: Baldwyn, 1824), p. 1; quoted by Thomas W. Evans, 'Study at the Restoration Inns of Court', in Jonathan A. Bush and Alain Wijffels (eds), *Learning the Law: Teaching and the Transmission of Law in England, 1150–1900* (London: Hambledon Press, 1999), pp. 287–302 (p. 287).

6 Quoted in Baker, *The Third University of England*, p. 22. See also Francis Cowper, *A Prospect of Gray's Inn*, 2nd rev. edn (London: Published by Graya on behalf of Gray's Inn, 1985), pp. 73–4.

7 Lemmings, *Gentlemen and Barristers*, pp. 78–92.

8 The system is explained in *Notes of Me: The Autobiography of Roger North*, ed. Peter Millard (Toronto; London: University of Toronto Press, 2000), pp. 116–17. See also Clare M. Rider, 'The Inns of Court and Inns of Chancery and their records,' *Archives*, 24 (Oct. 1999), 27–36; and Lemmings, *Gentlemen and Barristers*, pp. 31–42, 50–1.

9 For the Old Hall at Lincoln's Inn, see Chapter 7 (pp. 138–56, above).

10 Geoffrey Tyack, 'The buildings of the Inner Temple', in Clare Rider and Val Horsler (eds), *The Inner Temple: A Community of Communities* (London: Third Millennium Publishing, 2007), pp. 60–77 (p. 64).

11 As for instance in the Dutch House in Kew Gardens (Kew Palace), of 1631: for an illustration, see Nicholas Cooper, *Houses of the Gentry* (New Haven, CT; London: Yale University Press, 1999), p. 176.

12 Quoted in Wilfrid Prest, *The Inns of Court Under Elizabeth I and the Early Stuarts 1590–1640* (London: Longman, 1972), p. 19.

13 It was destroyed in the Second World War and not rebuilt. See *An Inventory of the Historical Monuments in London*, ed. Royal Commission on Historical Monuments (England), 5 vols (London: HMSO, 1924–30), IV, pl. 190.

14 It is only known in a re-engraved version of 1770, when it was described as a 'View of the Temple as it appeared in the Year 1671'. See Figure 25.

15 Howard M. Colvin, *A Biographical Dictionary of British Architects 1600–1840*, 4th edn (New Haven, CT; London: Yale University Press, 2008), p. 1014; *Inner Temple Records*, II, 64, 72.

16 For example, Clifford's Inn, north of Fleet Street, demolished in 1891 and now only known from photographs. See Hermione Hobhouse, *Lost London* (London: Macmillan, 1971), p. 120.

17 John Summerson, *Georgian London*, rev. and ed. Howard Colvin (New Haven, CT;

London: Yale University Press, 2003), pp. 37–8. See also T. F. Reddaway, *The Rebuilding of London after the Great Fire* (London: Cape, 1940).

18 William Herbert, *Antiquities of the Inns of Court and Chancery* (London: Vernor and Hood, 1804), p. 193. An early Edinburgh example is Milne's Court in the Lawnmarket, by Robert Mylne (1690).

19 For Barbon, see N. G. Brett-James, 'A speculative London builder of the seventeenth century', *Transactions of the London and Middlesex Archaeological Society*, new series 6 (1933), pp. 110–45; Summerson, *Georgian London*, pp. 29–35; Elizabeth McKellar, *The Birth of Modern London: The Development and Design of the City, 1660–1720* (Manchester: Manchester University Press, 1999), pp. 42–6.

20 *Fourth Report of the Royal Commission on Historical Manuscripts* (London: Eyre and Spottiswoode for HMSO, 1874): petition from the Middle Temple to the King, 24 February 1674.

21 *Notes of Me*, ed. Millard, p. 126.

22 *Calendar of the Middle Temple*, pp. 121–5; John Bruce Williamson, *The History of the Temple, London* (London: John Murray, 1924), p. 519. One of the rooms is illustrated in *An Inventory of the Historical Monuments in London*, ed. Royal Commission on Historical Monuments (England), IV, pl. 200.

23 The fire also destroyed the adjacent Hare and Fig Tree Courts, both of which were rebuilt by the Inner Temple.

24 *Notes of Me*, ed. Millard, pp. 127–8.

25 NA, C8/230/72: complaint of John Thacham, gent., 3 May 1680. I owe this reference to Frank Kelsall.

26 For Fitch, see Colvin, *A Biographical Dictionary of British Architects 1600–1840*, pp. 377–8. For Foltrop, see McKellar, *The Birth of Modern London*, pp. 101–3.

27 *Notes of Me*, ed. Millard, p. 123.

28 *Lives of the Norths*, quoted in Walter George Thornbury, *Old and New London*, 6 vols (London: n. pub., 1879–85), I, 162. Roger North's *Lives of the Norths*, written in manuscript in the early eighteenth century, contains biographies of Francis (Lord Guildford, Keeper of the Great Seal), Dudley, and the Rev. John North. After Roger North's death, the work was edited for publication by his son, Montagu.

29 *Calendar of the Middle Temple*, pp. 128–9; *Country Life*, 103 (28 May 1948), pp. 1,072–3. It was destroyed in the Second World War but reconstructed afterwards.

30 *Notes of Me*, ed. Millard, p. 129. North left a detailed manuscript account of the gateway project (BL, Additional MS 32540, fol. 37ᵛ), reprinted in *Of Building: Roger North's Writings on Architecture*, ed. Howard M. Colvin and John Newman (Oxford: Oxford University Press, 1981), pp. 51–2. See also Howard M. Colvin, 'Roger North and Sir Christopher Wren', *Architectural Review*, 110 (Oct. 1951), 257–60 (258–9).

31 'I acknowledge also that pilastering is a defect. Nothing comes up to the grandure of a massy collume. The purse I managed would not reach it. And the publick would not permitt such an incroachmentt on the street' (North, *Of Building*, ed. Colvin and Newman, p. 52).

32 *Ibid.*, p. 52.

33 William Douthwaite, *Gray's Inn: Its History and Associations* (London: Reeves and Turner, 1886), pp. 101–2; 'Gray's Inn – II', *Country Life*, 82 (13 Nov. 1937), 492–8; Cowper, *Prospect of Gray's Inn*, pp. 75–6; Bridget Cherry and Nikolaus Pevsner, *The Buildings of*

England. London 4: North (London: Penguin Books, 1998), p. 283.

34 *Seventh Report of the Royal Commission on Historical Manuscripts* (London: HMSO, 1879), p. 481: John Verney to Sir Richard Verney, 16 June 1684. See also McKellar, *The Birth of Modern London*, pp. 28–9, 198. For the importance of the Inns' gardens as spaces for contemplation, see Chapter 9 (pp. 193–4, above).

35 John Stow, *A Survey of the Cities of London and Westminster*, ed. John Strype, 2 vols (London: Printed for A. Churchill, J. Knapton, R. Knaplock, J. Walthoe, E. Horne, [and 5 others in London], 1720), I, 253.

36 McKellar, *The Birth of Modern London*, pp. 195–7.

37 William H. Spilsbury, *Lincoln's Inn: Its Ancient and Modern Buildings*, 2nd edn (London: Reeves and Turner, 1873), p. 91; Robert Fookes and Richard Wallington, 'The buildings: long history and picturesque variety', in Angela Holdsworth (ed.), *A Portrait of Lincoln's Inn* (London: The Honourable Society of Lincoln's Inn/Third Millennium Publishing, 2007), pp. 25–45 (p. 28).

38 NA, C10/214/19, C8/379/4; I am grateful to Frank Kelsall for supplying me with transcripts of this and other relevant documents. Work had begun by 1685.

39 Fookes and Wallington, 'The buildings', p. 30; 'The Quincentenary of Lincoln's Inn', *Country Life*, 52 (23 Dec. 1922), 851.

40 The column, which no longer exists, went up in 1696. See *Country Life*, 52 (23 Dec. 1922), 851.

41 Robert Hradsky, 'The 1771 competition for rebuilding Lincoln's Inn', *Georgian Group Journal*, 17 (May 2009), 95–106.

42 Compare, for instance, the north range of Gray's Inn with the pilastered west range of Clare College, Cambridge (begun 1669), both overlooking gardens.

Part III

Literature and drama

Literature and drama at the early modern Inns of Court

Sarah Knight

> Away thou fondling motley humourist
> Leave me, and in this standing wooden chest,
> Consorted with these few books, let me lie
> In prison, and here be coffined, when I die.[1]

John Donne wrote his first 'Satire' as a student at Lincoln's Inn during the early 1590s, and carefully locates his poem within his institutional context, representing the Inns – as did many of his contemporaries – both as privileged institutions associated with the venerable laws by which civic order is maintained, and as a convenient *pied-à-terre* for hedonistic spirits eager to indulge in the social excess available to them in London. 'Consorted with these few books' (3), Donne's speaker initially aligns himself with the academic life of the Inns, often described as 'the third university',[2] but his subsequent actions jettison him from study into a contrasting milieu of misrule. The poem illuminates the overlapping worlds inhabited by residents at the Inns, who were ensconced within these institutions of learning but also situated within the city, subject to its cultural influence and social distractions. 'Satire 1' brilliantly epitomises the kind of satire then fashionable at the Inns, but satire was just one form in which writers and dramatists there experimented. This introduction briefly traces a few of those trends, to identify what was innovative about literary and dramatic work at the Inns during this period, treating Donne's poem as a revealing window on to the distinctive world of the early modern Inns, and considering how the essays in this section will contribute to our awareness of Inns cultural life.

During this period, the Inns were a unique formative context for the composition of works authored by men both living within their walls and writing from outside for an Inns audience. The essays in this section examine such works in all their diversity, from the start of Elizabeth's reign until the closing of the theatres in 1642. Jessica Winston looks at the early Elizabethan Inns both as professional community and as epicentre of literary networks, considering how the poems written there 'helped [Inns writers] to establish and reinforce their sense of themselves as members of a homogeneous and like-minded group'.[3] Lorna Hutson considers how concepts of law and forms of legal discourse, such as 'evidence' and 'proof', shaped plays with an 'evidential plot' written for the Inns by authors such as Gascoigne and Shakespeare.[4] Bradin Cormack and Richard McCoy explore (as does Hutson) one of the most celebrated of Inns plays, *The Comedy of Errors*. Cormack examines how the culture of 'legal revelling' at the Inns helped to shape distinct representations of authority in the plays performed there,[5] while McCoy discusses how plays written for the Inns often came to stage a 'mediation of the conflicts dividing the Elizabethan ruling class'.[6] Alan Nelson's new archival research for the forthcoming Records of Early English Drama *Inns of Court* volumes shows how misrule at the Inns' dramatic performances caused collision with local authorities, and suggests how innovative Inns theatre could be.[7] These essays illuminate the richness of writing and performance at the early modern Inns, highlighting the new literary forms and trends that helped to make the cultural life of the Inns so idiosyncratic.

The contemporary cityscape, particularly the areas nearest to the Inns, looms over many of these texts. Donne's 'Satire 1' is a striking example of such graphic evocation – through the law student's eyes – of urban locations and the characters which people them; the poem demonstrates a keen attention to the human variety of late Elizabethan London, which Mary Bly has called the 'social architecture' of the city, that we often encounter in Inns writing.[8] In Donne's poem, the speaker becomes a kind of reluctant tour guide to the various contexts inhabited by young men at the Inns, from the 'wooden chest' (2) of the study, to the 'street' (67) where his companion 'creeps to the wall' (68), keeping out of the way of grubby splashes from the road, to the rowdy gathering where his friend 'quarrelled, fought, bled' (110), to the Inn once more, to which they limp back sore and hung-over. Donne's speaker's curiosity in 'Satire 1' about the world outside Lincoln's walls, and, particularly, less salubrious locations nearby, was shared by other fictionalised law students: in his *Micro-cosmographie* (1628), a book of 'Characters', John Earle expands the world of the Inns to include the tavern, described as 'the Innes a Court mans entertainment' (sig. C6ᵛ).[9] In this collection, this inter-permeability of Inns and surrounding city is explored: Cormack's reading of Shakespeare's *Comedy of Errors* and the *Gesta Grayorum*, for instance, shows us how important the physical setting of the Inns in Elizabethan London was for understanding the particular idiom of their dramatic texts.[10] Nelson provides a later example of dramatic cross-pollination with other city institutions besides the tavern: James Shirley's masque *The Triumph of Peace* was first performed on 3 February 1634 at Whitehall by members of the Inns, then repeated only ten days later at the Merchant Taylors' Hall, a few miles to the east.[11]

Inns students were frequently associated with play-going, both because they were known for regular attendance at the public playhouses, and because the Inns constituted one of the main centres of private theatrical performance in early modern London. Even more than at the contemporary universities, a two-way traffic of authorship and influence ran between the Inns and the public theatres, which proved pivotal in shaping Inns drama. Receptive to trends on commercial stages, while also offering authors the opportunity to demonstrate their educational credentials, the Inns witnessed many different kinds of dramatic entertainment during this period, ranging from neoclassical works of *imitatio* like Gascoigne and Kinwelmersh's *Jocasta* (Gray's Inn, 1566), a version of Euripides' *Phoenissae* by way of Ludovico Dolce's *Giocasta* (1549), to romantic comedies like *The Comedy of Errors* and *Twelfth Night*, to politicised Senecan tragedy such as Thomas Sackville and Thomas Norton's *Gorboduc* (Inner Temple, 1561–62), to lavish and frequently licentious in-house revels, characterised by what Richard McCoy calls an 'odd blend of unruly energies and sumptuous ceremonial'.[12] The 1616 book *Sir Thomas Ouerburie his wife*, a selection of 'Characters' begun by Overbury and augmented by John Davies, hints that familiarity with the theatre distanced the 'Innes of Court man' from the university student just as much as his new legal training did: 'By that he hath heard one mooting, and seen two plaies, he thinkes as basely of the *Vniuersity*, as a young *Sophister* doth of the *Grammer-schoole*' (sigs H1^v–H2^r). Whether these 'plaies' were performed within Inns halls or on public stages, satirical fiction illuminates contemporary reputation: the claim that the Inns man has seen more plays than he has attended legal exercises rests on this reputation for taking a lively interest in the contemporary theatre.

While Donne's poem looks outward from Lincoln's Inn to the 'middle street' (15) beyond the Inn's walls, it also remains conscious of its institutional origin: the 'velvet Justice with a long / Great train of blue coats' (21–2), a judge surrounded by liveried servants, is one of the first characters for whom the speaker imagines his friend abandoning him, which suggests an alertness to power hierarchies and patronage networks in play within the legal system. Sharing a tendency of his Inns contemporaries towards institutional self-referentiality, Donne scatters legal terms throughout his poem which would resonate with his Lincoln's readers – 'jointures' (36), 'pardoned' (65), 'judge' (97), 'liberty' (70) – and such subtle play with legal discourse is a consistent feature of literature and drama produced at the Inns. Cormack and McCoy both examine the nuances of the term 'liberty' in Inns drama,[13] and Hutson considers how comic plays of the same period engage with the terms and concept of legal proof.[14] This sensitivity in such plays to legal discourse, which one imagines would be warmly received by an Inns audience or readership, is striking, as is the sophistication with which writers like Donne, Gascoigne, and Shakespeare, as well as 'in-house' authors of the revels, use legal terminology not just as a succession of in-jokes, but also as a medium for advancing complex ideas about law, language, and ethical responsibility.

Widespread, too, is a form of literary engagement common during the Renaissance, the *imitatio* of classical models, cleverly adapted in this case to the specific context of the Inns, as discussed here by Winston and Hutson. Winston examines how familiarity with classical lyric and pastoral models was central to the poetic training Inns writers received: she notes how Barnabe Googe, for instance, subverts the pastoral form to include other elements, such as ghostly Senecan visitors, and she emphasises the influence of neo-Latin writers such as Mantuan as inter-mediary between Virgil and Googe.[15] Hutson's essay also considers how dramatists at the Inns engaged with classical models, in their case Plautine comedy as filtered through the Ariostan *commedia erudita*, to produce a new kind of English comedy that turned Roman and Italian legal situations into plays concertedly adapted to the institutions of English law.[16] Later Inns satire also rests on institutionally specific *imitatio*: Donne's 'Satire 1' is based on Horace's *Satire* I.9, in which a bothersome acquaintance ambushes Horace's speaker and leaves him alone only when he is obliged to attend a legal case,[17] but Donne's adaptation of his Latin model places his poem within the Inns. Although legal matters intrude into Horace's poem's climax, Donne's representations of legal discourse and institutions are clearly contem-porary rather than retrospective. By transposing the speaker, friend, and context from Augustan Rome to late Elizabethan England, Donne reinvents a well-known classical model as something topical and new, in a flourish typical of Inns *imitatio*.

The combination of an interest in the demotic 'social architecture' of early modern London and such concerted displays of erudition suggests that the Inns were both literally and culturally poised between the city just outside their walls and the universities which many Inns residents had only recently left.[18] To this dichotomy we can add the royal court: geographically, the Inns were relatively near to the royal court (when the monarch was in London), and, like the universities, benefited from their affiliations with court dignitaries. In Overbury's *Characters* the 'Innes of Court man' is described 'as farre behinde a *Courtier* in his fashion, as a scholler is behinde him' (sig. H2ʳ),[19] implying that the Inns are more worldly than the universities, yet not as sophisticated as the court. Yet the worlds of Inns and royal court *did* overlap, as we see in McCoy's essay, which focuses on the courtly and political overtones of revels at the Inns, the negotiation with concepts of power and government in drama like *The Comedy of Errors* and the *Gesta Grayorum*, and the participation of leading courtiers in Inns dramatic culture.[20] Time spent at the Inns could be seen as transitional between these worlds, as the young men moved away from the more sequestered world of the universities which many of them had attended beforehand, and looked towards their adult careers, whether in the spheres of law, politics, or church.

The Inns provided a suitable transitional space for many students to exercise their creativity, whether as poets, dramatists, or actors. For some who exercised their creativity in this way, a literary career that began at the Inns was not merely transi-tional: Francis Beaumont (Inner Temple, 1600), for instance, was the son of a judge but made his living as a playwright.[21] For others, relationships formed at the Inns were later parlayed into careers and patronage. Touching on questions of friend-ship and sociability, Winston discusses the formative and often beneficial impact of institutional networks on literary production at the Inns earlier in the sixteenth century, looking at writers such as George Gascoigne and Barnabe Googe.[22] We might compare this tendency with the representation of Inns sociability in 'Satire

1', where Donne's speaker moves within a network of friends – however 'headlong, wild uncertain' (12) these may be – and his first priority is to get his friend to 'swear by thy best love in earnest ... / Thou wilt not leave me' (13–15). This speaker's ardour for his friend is a particularly heightened example of how friendships can function in an exclusive institutional microcosm, where coteries and networks are paramount, and play a significant part in shaping cultural as well as social life there.

That studies of literature and drama at the Inns have gathered momentum over the last few years suggests that this is a burgeoning area of critical enquiry. Recent publications by Cormack, Hutson, Mukherji, and Winston, in particular, have enhanced our understanding of how the Inns helped to shape early modern literary and dramatic culture, and have initiated a critical conversation with which other scholars can fruitfully engage.[23] Yet more work remains to be done. The publication of the *Inns of Court* volumes in the Records of Early English Drama series will no doubt prompt closer investigations of the staging practices and dramaturgy at the early modern Inns, while the accounts of Inns events in the new critical edition of John Nichols's *Progresses and Public Processions of Queen Elizabeth I* will prompt fresh research into the associations between Inns and royal court, and between Inns revels and other forms of Tudor and Stuart ceremonial. More detailed investigations of the Inns' literary and dramatic relations with other city institutions, such as the livery companies and the guilds, have long been due, and fuller explorations of the continuities and divergences between education at the Inns and the university training which often preceded this would also be welcome. The essays in this section individually address the varied nature of literary and dramatic production at the Inns, insisting on the Inns' particularity as a creative microcosm, uniquely shaped by their situation in the heart of the early modern city, and as institutions formed by their dynamic inter-relations with academic, courtly, and plebeian life: hopefully, these essays will stimulate further questions and investigations into the rich and unique cultural context of the early modern Inns.

Notes

1 John Donne, 'Satire 1', in *Selected Poetry*, ed. John Carey (Oxford: Oxford University Press, 1996), 1–4. All line references are to this edition.

2 See Chapter 1, pp. 8–24.

3 See Chapter 11, pp. 223–44 (p. 224).

4 See Chapter 12, pp. 245–63.

5 See Chapter 13, pp. 264–85.

6 See Chapter 14, pp. 286–301 (p. 297).

7 See Chapter 15, pp. 302–14.

8 Mary Bly, 'Playing the tourist in early modern London: selling the liberties onstage', *PMLA*, 122:1 (2007), 61–71 (61).

9 John Earle, *Micro-cosmographie, or, A peece of the world discovered in essayes and characters* (London: William Stansby for Edward Blount, 1628).

10 See Chapter 13, pp. 268–72.
11 See Chapter 15, pp. 303–4.
12 See Chapter 14, p. 286.
13 See Chapters 13, pp. 267–81, and 14, pp. 289–96.
14 See Chapter 12, pp. 249–56.
15 See Chapter 11, pp. 228–9.
16 See Chapter 12, pp. 246–50.
17 Horace, *Satires, Epistles and Ars Poetica*, ed. H. R. Fairclough (Cambridge, MA; London: Harvard University Press/William Heinemann, 1926, repr. 1978), pp. 103–11.
18 Stephen Porter, 'University and society', in Nicholas Tyacke (ed.), *The History of the University of Oxford*, 8 vols (Oxford: Clarendon Press, 1984–2000), IV, pp. 25–104: Porter argues that the Inns functioned 'both as an alternative to the universities and as a supplement to them' (p. 26).
19 *Sir Thomas Ouerburie his wife with new elegies vpon his (now knowne) vntimely death: whereunto are annexed, new newes and characters / written by himselfe and other learned gentlemen* (London: Edward Griffin for Laurence L'isle, 1616). Begun by Thomas Overbury, the 'Characters' were augmented by John Davies.
20 See Chapter 14, pp. 290–6.
21 For a fuller discussion of Beaumont at the Inns, see Subha Mukherji, *Law and Representation in Early Modern Drama* (Cambridge: Cambridge University Press, 2006), pp. 2–3.
22 See Chapter 11, pp. 224–39.
23 Bradin Cormack, *A Power to Do Justice: Jurisdiction, English Literature, and the Rise of Common Law, 1509–1625* (Chicago, IL: University of Chicago Press, 2008); Lorna Hutson, *The Invention of Suspicion: Law and Mimesis in Shakespeare and English Renaissance Drama* (Oxford: Oxford University Press, 2007); Mukherji, *Law and Representation*; Jessica Winston, 'Seneca in early Elizabethan England', *Renaissance Quarterly*, 59:1 (2006), 29–58; Jessica Winston, 'Expanding the political nation: *Gorboduc* at the Inns of Court and succession revisited', *Early Theatre*, 8:1 (2005), 11–34.

11

Lyric poetry at the early Elizabethan Inns of Court: forming a professional community

Jessica Winston

Between 1560 and 1660, the Inns of Court were one of the most vibrant literary communities in England. They were associated with writers such as Thomas Sackville and Thomas Norton, John Donne, John Marston, Ben Jonson, and Francis Bacon, as well as with the production of drama, ranging from one of the earliest English tragedies, *Gorboduc* (1562) to Shakespeare's *Comedy of Errors* (1594) and *Twelfth Night* (1602) to the most expensive masque ever performed in Caroline England, James Shirley's *The Triumph of Peace* (1634).[1] While the Inns of Court were rich social, legal, and literary communities over the entire period, they were hardly static or homogeneous over time. Wilfrid Prest has shown that the cultural status of the Inns changed through the early modern period, turning from 'small, inward looking professional fraternities' into 'large, complex, quasi-public institutions'.[2] The literature of this community changed too, shifting according to academic, courtly, and popular taste. While didactic poetry, translation, and tragedy were popular in the 1560s and 1570s, Ovidian-style erotic poetry and satire were in the 1590s, masques and pastoral in the 1610s, and masques and closet drama in the 1630s and 1640s.[3] This chapter looks at the poetry written at the Inns in the decade when a circle of writers first formed at the law schools, the 1560s. The writing and sharing of poetry among men at the Inns in this decade was a complex social practice, one that helped to create and solidify a professional community at the schools.

Over the early modern period, the Inns of Court were an increasingly careerist milieu, attended by young, ambitious men from the aristocracy and gentry who wished to pursue law and, often more urgently, to make contact with the social world of early modern London and patrons at court. As Prest explains, the Inns'

> geographical location made them ideally suited to introduce young men to the exciting world of London, already the mecca of ambition and talent, the kingdom's administrative, commercial and political hub. The inns provided convenient communal accommodation midway between City and Court. For most young gentlemen who wished to spend some time in London, an inn of court was the logical place to stay.[4]

This community of self-consciously ambitious men began to form at the law schools in the 1560s, and the composition and circulation of poetry helped the members to take their first steps along a professional path, allowing them to enter into and move within the social world of the Inns of Court themselves. Poetic composition allowed Inns of Court men to create and affirm social connections with each other and to shape the attitudes and values of the community that would, in turn, partly define who they were to others.

This chapter explores the poetry of three main writers at the Inns in the 1560s: Barnabe Googe (1540–94), George Turberville (1543–97?), and George Gascoigne (1534?–77), while drawing on the writings of Hugh Plat (1552–1608), Timothy Kendall (*fl.*1572–77), and John Grange (*b.*1556/57, *fl.*1577).[5] Such authors wrote poetry that was similar to the sorts of verse they were required to write in school days on set themes that affirmed the importance of work, friendship, duty, humility, and the like. As we shall see, such poetry confirmed the writers' shared social and professional aspirations and helped to establish and reinforce their sense of themselves as members of a homogeneous and like-minded group, a collection of dutiful, responsible, serious, moral, religious, and civically minded men, who were ready to take on important careers.

Two kinds of poetry

The communal significance of Inns of Court poetry comes into focus if we understand the values associated with such writing. Men at the Inns wrote various kinds of poetry, including eclogue, epitaph, epigram, dream vision, song, and sonnet. Some such as Gascoigne and Grange also wrote prose narratives that were peppered with innovative and traditional verse forms. Most of these genres appeared commonly in schoolroom exercises: poetic composition and adaptation was part of the grammar school and university curriculum and central to education in the arts of rhetoric. In grammar schools and the first years of the university, students often worked with short poetic forms (e.g. epigraphs, sonnets, epigrams) and longer verse assignments often accompanied exercises in prose.[6] For instance, at the Durham School, one ordinance required that the schoolmaster read 'versifying rules' aloud and that 'every second day' students 'make certain verses upon certain argument[s] which shall be given them'.[7] Such an assignment appears in George Gascoigne's play *The glasse of governement* (written c.1565) in which the schoolmaster, Gnomaticus, asks his university-bound students to versify a list of precepts on duty to their king, country, and parents, since 'Artes *Poetrie* giveth greatest assistaunce unto memorie'.[8] One student creates a set of verse precepts, 'adding neither dilations, allegories, nor examples', while another 'dilate[s] and enlarge[s] everie point' (55–6). Gnomaticus is pleased with both, praising each for having 'so well accomplished [his] dueties' (58). Later, the two go off to the university and then on to productive and respectable careers in the Church and university.

The episode conveys one purpose for poetry. For the reading and writing of poetry was part of a larger curriculum which helped to prepare one for a life of service to the state, the principal goal of a humanist education.[9] Thus in his *Boke named the governour* (1531), Thomas Elyot describes the education of those who are 'to haue authoritie in a publike weale', arguing for the importance of poetry in a reading programme involving the works of Ovid, Martial, and Homer, which provide 'incomparable wisedoms and instructions for politike gouernaunce of people'.[10] Likewise, in his *Scholemaster* (1570), Roger Ascham presents a programme to prepare youth to 'serve God and country by virtue and wisdom', extending Elyot's views on reading classical poetry to the importance of translating, paraphrasing, and writing it (along with prose).[11] Thus poetry was identified with a broader civically orientated educational project. As Richard Helgerson observes: 'Classroom verse-making aimed at furthering eloquence and strengthening morals, not at producing poets.'[12] Such activities helped to develop in students 'the qualities of temperament and training necessary to magistrates and gentlemen, the "governors" of the realm'.[13] At grammar schools and universities, poetry helped to prepare one for the duty of a life in civil affairs.

Yet lyric poetry was not linked solely with morality, duty, 'God and country', but with activities and values that were culturally the opposite of these things, with lechery, idleness, and delinquency. The *Glasse of governement* demonstrates these other associations as well, in the characters of two other students (elder brothers to the first set) who write poetry too. Unlike the younger men, these two ignore the schoolmaster's assignment and create love poetry and epic verses, writing 'loving sonnets' and 'verses in praise of Marshiall feates and pollycies' (60). Such activities are the first of many that lead the two to a life of crime. In *The glasse of governement*, poetry is associated with both duty and delinquency. Each kind of writing – we might call it 'humanist' or 'romance' poetry – augers the students' futures, marking them out as men of respectable or prodigal affairs. As Richard Helgerson argues, the two terms existed in a 'dialectic of opposites', with humanism 'represent[ing] paternal expectation, and romance, rebellious desire'.[14] Thus Christopher Gaggero observes that Gascoigne shows: 'If young men are to learn their duty, it seems they must renounce the pleasures of poetry, if not – and this is an important distinction – poetry itself'.[15]

While they did not renounce poetry altogether, students at the Inns renounced some of its 'pleasures' (those amorous and heroic topics), using their poetry instead to place themselves on the path of service to God and country. Mid-Tudor Inns of Court poetry has some characteristics that follow from its association with humanist educational practices: a certain impersonal tone and ponderous moralising, as well as an extensive development of aphorisms and didactic commonplaces, heavy metre, and an advisory tone. In addition, the metre and diction of the poems, as G. K. Hunter puts it, has a moral as well as aesthetic quality, creating an effect of 'weight and solidity' as well as 'plainness'.[16] Hence, in the words of Panofsky: 'The distinctive voice of the early Elizabethan poet is that of the schoolmaster exhorting or reminding possibly wayward youths'.[17]

Why did members of the Inns continue to write such poetry once they left the grammar schools and universities? They could have stopped or imitated other models, ranging from the generically multifarious poetry of Chaucer, to the Latinate and popular works of Skelton, to the satires and sonnets of Thomas Wyatt and Henry Howard, Earl of Surrey. Why would they continue essentially schoolroom exercises as part of their extracurricular activities? One might think that Inns of Court authors continued because they remained in an educational environment, but poetry was not a part of the training offered at the Inns.[18] Another possibility is that they composed verse to be closer to the world of the court, to imitate and become a part of the social life of this other milieu.[19] Yet the poetry at court in the period was primarily written in Latin.[20] If students at the Inns had wanted to imitate life at court, they would have (as they could have) written in Latin as well.

A more likely possibility lies in the opposing social meanings of lyric poetry, those linked with the divergent values of 'humanism' and 'romance'. As men such as Googe, Turberville, and Gascoigne moved into and within the social world of the Inns of Court, the writing of poetry allowed them to associate themselves with 'humanism', with those ideals supposedly instilled by their parents or in their schooling – duty, responsibility, public mindedness, and the like – and to distance themselves from 'romance', those values linked with love poetry and even epic: the rebellious rejection of duty, the prioritisation of the beloved over scholarly and professional responsibilities, and dramatic assertions of individual importance.[21] Through their verse, mid-Tudor poets at the Inns constructed themselves both with and against the social meanings of the form in which they wrote. Like the good students in Gascoigne's *Glasse*, they marked themselves out – as individuals and as a community – as dutiful rather than profligate men.

Barnabe Googe's *Eglogs* and the negation of the erotic

Barnabe Googe's *Eglogs* illustrate how one Inns of Court man defines himself both with and against the social meanings of the form in which he wrote. In these, Googe writes about love, but also against it, using pastoral poetry to warn readers of the dangers of erotic entanglements. Throughout the *Eglogs*, the author announces his connection with the values of his humanist education, and he does so through a negation of romantic attraction. Born in 1540, Googe was the son of Robert Googe, a landowner in Kent. Like many members of the gentry of his generation, Googe probably received a grammar school education. We know that he attended Christ's College, Cambridge as a pensioner between 1555 and 1559. By 1559, he had entered Staple Inn, one of the Inns of Chancery affiliated with Gray's Inn, where he became 'a full participant in the burgeoning cultural life of that community'.[22] Googe was recognised in his own day as a translator, but he also published a miscellany, the *Eglogs epytaphes, and sonettes* (1563).[23]

This collection contains eight eclogues in imitation of Virgil and Mantuan; four epitaphs, including one on the death of the translator of Virgil, Thomas Phaer, and one on the poet Nicholas Grimald; a series of shorter poems (his 'sonettes'); and a dream vision titled 'Cupido Conquered'. Googe's poetry has been recognised primarily for its role in literary history.[24] As the first eclogues in English and the first collection of poetry published by a living English author, the volume had some influence on Spenser's *Shepheardes Calender* (1579), yet it is also important to consider this collection as Inns of Court poetry. To be sure, not all of the poems were written at the Inns. At least two, 'Going Towards Spain' (43) and 'Coming Homeward out of Spain' (45) were written during an embassy to that country in 1561, but the collection contains a number of verses written to and by members at the Inns, and Googe himself associated the whole work with this milieu, dedicating it to William Lovelace, a reader at Gray's Inn.

The *Eglogs* show how Googe used poetry to define himself as a dutiful and serious man. The eclogue is a pastoral genre, built on the premise of a distinct contrast between rustic and urban life, often expressing nostalgia for the simplicity of rural life in an ideal natural setting and containing celebrations of virtuous country over decadent city living. The theme may have had some personal significance for Googe, who (although writing in an urban institution) may have seen the pastoral world as an idealised retreat from the vices of the urban environment. Also importantly, pastoral poetry often takes up the subject of love, featuring shepherds who idly pass their time discussing the triumphs and pains of romance.[25] In his *Eglogs*, Googe conforms to these conventions and defies them, altering the bucolic genre into severely moralising, admonitory, and didactic poetry.

The alteration is evident in 'Egloga Prima'. A young shepherd, Daphnes, asks an older one, Amintas, to tell him a tale to pass the time. Amintas agrees, offering a story about love. But the tale is not a happy, or even melancholy, musing about love. Instead, it is a lengthy lecture on the debilitating physical and psychological effects of erotic desire, followed by a sermon on the necessity of avoiding love altogether. After introducing his subject, 'the cause of lovers' pain' (5.60), Amintas describes the effects of love. The lover falls into a 'fervent humour', suffering from a 'frenzy' while 'poison' 'infects the blood about and boils in every part'. Ultimately, the lover falls into 'bondage', captured by affection in a 'slavish, servile yoke' (5.65–94). The description repeats Petrarchan conventions, in which lovers describe themselves as slaves to the tyrant love. But while the Petrarchan lover is often a masochist who enjoys such enslavement, Amintas is horrified by it, using his tale about love as a warning. The lecture is the sort that Daphnes wants. When Amintas is done, the younger shepherd thanks him, handing Amintas a whistle that once belonged to his father. With this gesture, Daphnes makes Amintas into something of a father figure and signals the way that Googe has turned the eclogue into a didactic type of parental admonition to the young shepherd.

A similar alteration takes place in the fourth eclogue, which develops the story of Dametas, who, in an earlier sequence, kills himself for love, and now appears as a ghostly fury, clothed in black, before the shepherd Melibeus to warn him:

> O Melibei, take heed of love
> > of me example take,
> That slew myself, and live in hell,
> > for Deiopeia's sake.
> I thought that death should me release
> > from pains and doleful woe,
> But now, alas, the troth is tried
> > I find it nothing so,
> For look what pain and grief I felt
> > when I lived here afore,
> With those I now tormented am,
> > and with ten thousand more.
>
> > > > (8.53–64)

Ghostly visitors appear in other pastoral works, for instance in Boccaccio and Mantuan, but Googe alters the genre, introducing a 'tormented' ghost more akin to those in Seneca's tragedies (which were translated by men affiliated with the Inns) or the *Myrrour for magistrates* (1559), which circulated there.[26] In the *Myrrour*, the ghosts of former English rulers warn kings and magistrates about appropriate behaviour. Like them, Dametas admonishes Melibeus to avoid romantic love. Googe brings tragedy to the pastoral, pressing the genre into Senecan form and incorporating a tirade on the dangers of erotic attraction.

Other *Eglogs* likewise warn against romance. The fifth describes the shepherdess, Claudia, who like Dametas kills herself in a fit of passion. The sixth presents the shepherd Felix who counsels his companion Faustus to let reason rule him in matters of love. The seventh contains yet another tale of unrequited love, and the eighth and final eclogue warns lovers to avoid Cupid ('Cupido's camp' (12.4)) and to focus on God. The eclogues end with the shepherd Cornix, who turns away from the subject of love altogether and speaks in language approaching that of devotional prayer, concluding that one should 'love and fear the mighty God that rules and reigns on high' (12.239–40). In this final turn, Cornix (and by extension Googe) seems to suggest that religious piety is important for pastoral tranquility.[27]

Critics concur that Googe altered the pastoral. Paul Parnell says that Googe 'wrote the *Eglogs* as a sort of refutation of the pastoral tradition'; William Sheidley similarly argues that Googe put 'the pastoral to work to solve the problem of literary love'; and Simon McKeown observes that Googe 'harnessed the eclogue for his own didactic agenda, using the form to expound moral, political, religious, and sexual dogma.'[28] Yet Googe's treatment of pastoral is not unique. The mode was used for social, political, and religious commentary, and Googe's work in particular adapts that of the Italian writer Mantuan (Baptista Spagnolo Mantuanus, 1448–1516), whose ten neo-Latin eclogues were a common text in European schools in the sixteenth and seventeenth centuries, and translated by Googe's friend and fellow Inns of Court man George Turberville in 1567.[29] Moreover, Mantuan's 'moralistic tone' influences Googe's.[30]

Even with the precedent of Mantuan, one wonders why Googe chose to write eclogues, removing any pleasure from the pastoral world and creating stern and moralistic scenes. One suggestion is that Googe was a poet and that eclogues, the genre of Virgil's earliest literary endeavours, represented an appropriate way to begin a poetic career.[31] But Googe did not have ambitions to be a national poet (as Virgil did). Instead, from the Inns, he went on to earn regular employment at court, to hold a seat in parliament (1571), and to serve two stints as a civil servant in Ireland (1582–83 and 1584–85). Moreover, in his literary endeavours, he did not follow Virgil's example and move to epic. Instead he wrote only occasional poetry, his dream vision ('Cupido Conquered'), and a Christian allegorical poem, *The shippe of safegard* (1569), as well as translations of several moral and religious works. A more probable response is that Googe wrote pastoral poetry because it was associated with romance and idleness. By turning the genre to moral, didactic ends, Googe defined himself as a man who was *not* a lover or even a poet, but rather one interested in duty, responsibility, morality, and religion. In his revision of the pastoral, Googe portrays himself as a man concerned with religious and moral reform, not as a man of amours. At the same time, it is possible that Googe wrote the *Eglogs* because he could make it fulfil the admonitory role that the literature of his schooling performed: the improvement of youth and the creation of better servants of the state. In the *Eglogs*, Googe takes a community of shepherds and turns them into severe, moralising men. As we shall see, by circulating such works among his colleagues at the Inns, he aimed to shape the values of the community there as well.

Creating community in Googe's answer poetry

Googe's *Eglogs* show how one Inns of Court man defined himself with and against the meanings of the form in which he wrote. Yet Googe and other poets at the Inns also shared their verses with each other in order to display their ideas and values and to shape those of their fellow students. As in Googe's pastoral poetry, where a community of shepherds communicates its ideas through poetry, poetic composition at the law schools was a kind of conversation, one in which Inns of Court men shared their attitudes about romance, duty, discipline, friendship, fidelity, pride, and the like in order to mould the values of the community as a whole.

Such poetry originally circulated in manuscript, none of which exists today, so it is necessary to reconstruct such circulation from printed sources. This is not difficult, since the collections of Googe and other Inns of Court writers, such as Turberville, Gascoigne, Kendall, and Grange, call attention to their origins in manuscript, and there are close affinities between manuscript poetry and printed miscellanies. As Mary Hobbs observes: 'the first printed [i.e. early Elizabethan] anthologies evidently derive from manuscript anthologies.'[32] For example, George Gascoigne's *Hundreth sundrie flowres* (1573) contains a series of poems, written at the request of members of Gray's Inn in the early to mid-1560s. Since the poems were written

ten years before the volume appeared in print, it is likely that they were circulated in manuscript. In addition, in the preface to Barnabe Googe's *Eglogs epytaphes, and sonettes*, Laurence Blundeston explains that he published Googe's 'paper bunch' (4.41), when the poet was out of town. This word choice indicates that the poems were initially in manuscript compilation. It is difficult to tell whether the story is true. However, in a discussion of a similar preface in Gascoigne's *The adventures of master F.J.* (1573), Arthur Marotti observes that such prefaces often replicate 'the circumstances of the production, transmission, and preservation or collection of social verse, calling attention to the social and biographical circumstances in which lyrics were typically written'.[33]

One popular genre at the schools, the answer poem, which circulated in manuscript, shows how such poetry helped to define the community at the Inns. Answer poetry is verse that explicitly responds to a poem written by someone else usually well known to the author. E. F. Hart observes that this kind of poetry generally falls into four separate categories: 'The answer proper, in which the theme or arguments of a poem are criticized as a whole, or (more usually) refuted one by one', 'imitations', 'extension poems [that] develop or amplify some idea, image, or characteristic rhythm or style of the original poems', and 'mock-songs'.[34] Describing the social function of this kind of poetry, Marotti contends that such verse highlights the occasional origins of sixteenth- and seventeenth-century verse. Answer poetry 'foregrounds the social ... character of poetic composition, marking poetic discourse ... as continuous with other forms of communication'.[35]

Examples of answer poetry and related genres, such as verse epistles, appear in several poetry collections from the period. Googe's collection, which he calls in his dedication 'the numbered heaps of sundry friendships' (2.35–6), contains verse written to and received from friends Alexander Neville and Laurence Blundeston, as well as a number of verse epistles, such as 'To George Holmedon of a Running Head' (29).[36] George Turberville's *Epitaphes, epigrams, songs and sonets* (London: Henry Denham, 1567) contains poems addressed to Barnabe Googe, such as 'Maister Googe his Sonet on the paines of Love' and 'Turberuiles aunswere and distick to the same' (sig. B7ᵛ), and 'Mayster Googe his Sonet' ('Accuse not Gode if fansie fonde') and 'Turberuiles aunswere' (sig. C2ʳ). And Timothy Kendall's *Trifles*, printed at the end of his *Flowers of epigrammes* (1577) has many poems addressed to men at universities and the Inns of Court, such as 'A Letter Written to T.W. Gent, when he was a Scholler in Oxford' (sig. P4ᵛ), 'Preceptes Written to his frend Richard Woodwards Praierbooke, Sometime his Companion in Oxford' (sig. D6ʳ) and 'To his dere brother Iohn Sheppard Gent. of Grayes Inne' (sig. S4ᵛ). As these titles suggest, Inns men wrote answer poetry to a range of people, including their peers at the Inns of Court and universities. All such poetry helped to create and continue connections between the poets and others, but a significant number of the poems helped students at the Inns to connect and negotiate their relationships with members of the law schools.

The importance of such poetry is evident if we look at some of the sonnets (the shorter poems) in Googe's *Eglogs epytaphes, and sonettes,* considering how he uses the answer poem to converse with other members of the Inns about their attitudes and ideas. Take, for instance, an exchange between Googe and Alexander Neville, his cousin and fellow member of the Inns.[37] In 'To Alexander Neville', Googe advises his relative to avoid idleness:

> If thou canst banish idleness, Cupido's bow is broke,
> And well thou mayest despise his brands clean void of flame and smoke.
> What moved the king Aegisthus once to love with vile excess?
> The cause at hand doth straight appear: he lived in idleness.
>
> (Poem 29)

Googe repeats the move in the *Eglogs*, writing about love in order to warn against it, counselling Neville to 'banish idleness', since doing so will help him to avoid romantic entanglements. He illustrates his point using an extreme example of love-in-idleness: King Aegisthus who, left in charge of Argos when Agamemnon went to the Trojan war, fell in love with Clytemnestra, Agamemnon's wife, and with her murdered her husband upon his return from war. The poem is short, but conveys Googe's own ideas, while attempting to shape those of Neville through admonitory advice.

Neville replies to Googe in 'The Answer of A. Neville to the Same', also published in the *Eglogs epytaphes, and sonettes*:

> The lack of labour maims the mind,
> And wit and reason quite exiles,
> And reason fled, flames fancy blind,
> And fancy she forthwith beguiles
> The senseless wight, that swiftly sails
> Through deepest floods of vile excess.
> Thus vice abounds, thus virtue quails,
> By means of drowsy idleness.
>
> (Poem 29a)

Neville observes the dangers of idleness, describing the way that 'lack of labour' makes one into a 'senseless wight'. He departs from the form of Googe's verse, responding to the fourteeners with tetrameter and in a rhyme scheme that also differs from the original. Also departing from Googe's end-stopped lines, Neville uses enjambment in lines four through six to emphasise the unstoppable effects of fancy. Yet even with such changes, Neville's reply is in accord with Googe. Using an equally elevated diction, Neville agrees that idleness should be avoided, writing a physiological and psychological explanation of Aegisthus' actions, showing that 'lack of labour' leads to the vicious acts that Aegisthus committed. In the end, Neville agrees with Googe's sentiment: 'vice abounds' and 'virtue quails' because of 'drowsy idleness'.

Another example of the use of poetry to confirm social values appears in an exchange between Googe and Laurence Blundeston, a member of Gray's Inn.[38] Googe's collection contains a prefatory poem by Blundeston, as well as two sets of verse to and from him. In one, Googe praises his friend for his ability to 'rule affections right' and Blundeston replies in kind. Googe writes:

> Some men be counted wise that well can talk,
> And some because they can each man beguile,
> Some for because they know well cheese from chalk,
> And can be sure, weep whoso list, to smile.
> But Blund'ston, him I call the wisest wight,
> Whom God gives grace to rule affections right.[39]

(Poem 21)

Blundeston replies:

> Affections seeks high honour's frail estate,
> Affections doth the golden mean reprove,
> Affections turns the friendly heart to hate,
> Affections breed without discretion love;
> Both wise and happy he, Googe, he may be hight,
> Whom God gives grace to rule affections right.

(Poem 21a)

Like the previous exchange, this one is a form of social converse and confirmation. Blundeston repeats the form, moral content, and tone of Googe. Both poems are written in iambic pentameter and contain four general statements followed by two lines of praise. Both have the same rhyme scheme (ab ab cc). Moreover, Blundeston repeats the rhyme at the end of the verse, using 'hight' to respond to 'wight' and reiterates Googe's praise, likewise congratulating his friend for his ability to 'rule affections right'. Overall, the exchange is a playful and genial confirmation of their mutual esteem and comparable values.

In Googe, community is created through the explicit confirmation of likeness. In this way, his answer poetry differs in tone from the poems in this genre described by E. F. Hart and Arthur Marotti. Hart writes that answer poems have much in common with 'forms of parody' and that the genre was popular with the 'gentlemanly amateur in an age when lyric and song were fashionable'. Moreover, he emphasises that the most common kinds of answer poems are 'critical' of the recipient, and while most of these verses never go beyond 'friendly chaff' some 'amount to gentle satire'.[40] Marotti, describing the spirit of 'competitive versifying' that characterises answer poetry, suggests that some poems went much further. In particular, the poetry of the Sidney circle probably originated as a 'coterie game' and poetic exchanges among the members of this group were often 'quite hostile'.[41]

Both critics suggest that satire, hostility, and competition between men is the norm in the answer poetry circulated in male literary communities, and such an assessment makes sense, given the way that competition of various sorts (particularly over women) is often central to communities of men, helping to create and sustain, while also threatening, homosocial bonds.[42] Thus Wendy Wall finds that Renaissance sonnets – typically written to women, but exchanged among men – represent poetic exchange as a form of courtship, and more precisely show an understanding of poetic composition as a competition among men, played out in the field of verse writing for women.[43] But it is noticeable in this regard that Googe's answer poetry (and most of his other writing) is not competitive or erotic, but appears instead as a form of genial, if morally stringent, conversation. Googe and his friends do not cement a literary community through the medium of love poetry. They negate the presence of women and avoid competition. Cathy Shrank observes of Googe's collection that 'woman' is 'decentered' further than we might expect from reading Wall: 'The poems either avoid the subject of love entirely or counsel against it, celebrating instead the rational life of studiousness and male fellowship.'[44] Googe's poetry suggests that he primarily wants to establish his similarities with his fellow authors, to affirm his like-minded attitudes and ideas, and more broadly to attempt to bring about the homogeneity of the community as a whole.

Indeed, instead of competitive, Googe's poems are subtly coercive: the implied expectation that his interlocutor respond in kind cuts off the possibility of genuine dialogue. In her analysis of Googe's *Eglogs*, Jennifer Richards shows that the conversations between shepherds leave little room for disagreement or dissent. In most, an older man advises his younger companion to control his desires. In so doing, they present 'a cycle of exchange – represented by the "thanks" owed to a senior shepherd by a junior for advice given – which entails an expression of satisfaction with the status quo'. There is no expectation that the junior shepherd will disagree, and there is, therefore, no chance for free-flowing ideas in critical conversation.[45] Like the *Eglogs*, Googe's answer poetry neither invites nor represents dissent. Googe and his respondents insist on their similarity in a way that closes off difference, affirming likeness and, by extension, promoting the homogeneity of their community.[46]

The answer poetry of Turberville and Gascoigne: negotiating friendships

While never hostile, critical, or competitive, the answer poetry by members of the early Elizabethan Inns does not always achieve such easy (even if required) conviviality, as we can see in an exchange between Googe and his fellow poet and Inns of Court man, George Turberville, who like Googe published a collection of poetry, the *Epitaphes, epigrams, songs and sonets*. Like Googe's *Eglogs*, Turberville's poems are, as Panofsky observes, 'frankly occasional and social': 'Here are found poems addressed to friends or "answers" to the poems by friends, epitaphs, epigrams, and in the amatory poems are recorded – though artificially – the daily emergencies in a lover's life.'[47] Several of the poems are exchanges between Turberville and Googe, or responses by Turberville to verses only printed in Googe's collection, such as 'Out of Sight Out of Mind' and 'Of Money' (35, 42). Turberville's answer to 'Of

Money' shows two Inns of Court men speaking about another value, friendship, and creating and confirming their own friendship through this process. Yet the reply registers some of Turberville's anxiety. In 'Of Money', Google writes:

> Give money me, take friendship whoso list,
> For friends are gone come once adversity,
> When money yet remaineth safe in chest,
> That quickly can thee bring from misery,
> For face shows friends, when riches do abound,
> Come time of proof, farewell, they must away;
> Believe me well, they are not to be found,
> If God but send thee once a louring day.
> Gold never starts aside, but in distress
> Finds ways enough to ease thine heaviness.

William Sheidley remarks that much of Google's wit comes from his creative combination of two commonplaces: the first that friendship is worth more than money and the second that false friends are unfaithful in times of need.[48] Google brings the logic of the two together, concluding that money is worth more than friendship, since it never 'starts aside' in distress and 'finds ways enough to ease thine heaviness'. Critics have seen 'Of Money' as an expression of personal sentiment. Donald L. Peterson praises the 'personal conviction that comes through in its unrelieved severity of statement'. Sheidley writes, 'the poet seems to have come from a friend who has just let him down'. And one contemporary poet repeats this collapse of poet and fictional persona in his distich, 'Google / Is Scrooge'.[49]

It is more helpful to see the poem as an extension of the educational exercise of *refutatio*, writing against a claim or *thesis*, an activity defined by Panofsky as 'the writing on a general issue either favoring or denying a given position'.[50] For Google seems less to offer a personal opinion than a presentation of his rhetorical and intellectual abilities in *refutatio*. He piles up a series of statements that as a result of the numerous end-stopped lines reads like a collection of definitive moral truisms. Nevertheless, together they refute the two commonplaces about friendship and money and add up to a proof of the unexpected thesis that money is worth more than friendship.

Google's poem is a skilfully told joke. Yet it is difficult to tell whether Turberville replied because he got the joke or missed it. In his response, he follows Google's lead: treating the first poem as the *thesis* and refuting 'Of Money's' position by showing that accusations of faithlessness are more fittingly applied to money:

> Friend Googe, giue me the faithful friend to trust,
> And take the fickle Coine for moe that lust.
> For friends in time of trouble and distresse
> With help and sound aduise will soone redresse
> Eche growing griefe that gripse the pensiue brest,
> When Moneie lies lockt vp in couert Chest.

> Thy Coine will cause a thousand cares to grow,
> Which if thou hadst no Coine thou couldst not know.
> Thy Friend no care but comfort will procure,
> Of him thou mayst at neede thyselfe assure.
> Thy Monie makes the Theefe in waite to lie,
> Whose fraude thy Friende & falsehood will descrie.
> Thou canst not keepe vnlockt thy carefull Coine,
> But some from thee thy Monie will purloine:
> Thy faithfull Friend will neuer start aside,
> But take his share of al that shall betide.
> When thou art dead thy Monie is bereft
> But after life thy trustie Friend is left:
> Thy Monie serues another Maister than,
> Thy faythful Friend lincks with no other man.
> So that (Friend Googe) I deeme it better I,
> To choose the Friend and let the Monie lie.

(sigs. Q2–Q2^v)

Turberville echoes Googe in both his form and diction, writing in a series of end-stopped aphorisms and incorporating phrases from Googe's poem, such as 'lockt vp in couert Chest' and 'start aside'. But he departs in tone, writing something more serious than 'Of Money'. The couplets in combination with the end-stopped lines make the statements about friendship and money seem even more absolute than those of the first poem. In addition, while the apostrophe to 'Friend Googe' addresses the Scrooge-like Googe ironically and humorously with the name of 'friend', the twice repeated phrase feels insistent as well, as much an assertion that Googe is a friend as a recognition of him as such. Indeed, the length of Turberville's reply (it is more than twice as long as the original) suggests something of his seriousness, making it seem as though he could not stop writing without first making sure that he had made his point. In the end, Turberville comes across as anxious about friendship, writing in order to connect with 'Friend Googe' and to ensure that they value friendship in the same way. The poem corrects Googe and attempts to assert a connection with him.

Turberville's response reflects an anxiety about male friendship, which appears throughout his poetry in his ambiguous use of the word 'friend'. Take the instance of the poem 'To his Friend Ryding to Londonward' (sigs K6–K6^v). The title makes one think that the poem concerns the departure of a male friend. The verse itself, however, compares the friend's departure toward London to Cressida's departure from Troy, which suggests that it is, instead, about the departure of a female friend, but we cannot be sure. What initially seems to be a poem about the loss of male friendship quickly becomes a verse on the loss of romance, or one that codes a discussion of friendship in romantic language.

The ambiguous presentation of friendship and romance underscores the aspect of mid-Tudor Inns of Court poetry that we saw in Googe, the extent to which friendship and romance are mutually dependent, but opposing, terms. Men at the Inns reinforced their sense of communal identity and belonging in sometimes romantic terms, at the same time warning against women and, more specifically, the threat that women might distract from friendship and even a public career. As Shrank writes: 'In the case of Googe's and Turberville's sonnets, that is, amorous experience is analysed in order to learn a lesson which is then passed on to other men. It is consequently the absence or rejection, rather than the presence, of the woman that forms the trope by which male sociability is consolidated.'[51] Thus women are often the focus of anxiety and harsh judgements. In one poem, Googe calls a 'Mistress A.' a Gorgon, accusing her of having been raised by wolves and possessing a tiger's heart (25.11–25). To be sure, given the proximity of the Inns to brothels, and the social reality of liaisons between Inns of Court men and local women, we can assume that some of the men were involved with women, and such involvement is partly what Googe aimed to prevent. Yet despite such derisive words, it is important to recognise that women *per se* were not the problem. Rather, in the poetry, a cluster of terms and topics – woman, love, romance, desire, lust – represent individual experiences or feelings that distract from participation in the community. As Richards writes of Googe's *Eglogs*, the shepherds criticise love, since 'sexual desire, heterosexual and homosexual, is equated equally in the *Eglogs* with other types of desire (including social aspiration and the lust for power), all of which entail an assertion of will that is dangerous to the commonwealth'.[52] Like the shepherds, Googe and Turberville express anxiety about romantic relationships with women, cautioning their friends to avoid personal distractions and admonishing them to focus on the end goal, public duty and service to the commonwealth (as opposed to individual gain and private joys). Of course, that such warnings occur frequently suggests the difficulty of preventing those kinds of desires and ambitions that threatened the coherence of the group. Thus, in his poetry, Turberville links anxiety about friendship with romantic troubles. In so doing, he conveys a level of anxiety about the fragility of his connections with other men. Poetry is a way to make and continue friendships, while expressing concern about sustaining such bonds.

Whatever ideas answer poetry helped to circulate, or anxieties it helped to negotiate, members of the Inns were self-consciously aware that their writing helped to establish social connections, something that is evident in the poetry of George Gascoigne. Gascoigne was born *c.*1534 and was, like Googe and Turberville, a member of the gentry. He attended Cambridge (which college is unknown), was admitted to Gray's Inn in 1555, and returned to the schools sometime in the early to mid-1560s. Gascoigne's professional life was not the success that he might have wanted. As Gascoigne himself points out in his poem 'Gascoigne's Woodmanship', he shot 'ofte awrie' at everything, for instance squandering his fortune, involving himself in many lawsuits, and failing to obtain royal patronage.[53]

Gascoigne wrote in a broad range of literary forms, including translations, estates satire, epigram, epitaph, sonnet, and prose narrative, and much of his work was published in the miscellany *A hundreth sundrie flowres* (1573), and later reprinted in *The posies* (1575). Describing the work performed by all of Gascoigne's poetry, Pigman has observed that 'Gascoigne published his writings primarily as a means of seeking preferment', and the Inns of Court answer poems in *A hundreth sundrie flowres* were part of this larger goal.[54] These are five 'sundry theames', which Gascoigne composed for members of Gray's Inn in the mid-1560s, when (after an unsuccessful attempt at farming), he returned to the schools to pursue a career in law.[55]

G. T., the presumably fictional editor and compiler of the *Hundreth sundrie flowres*, introduces the 'sundry theames' (as he does all of the poems in the volume), describing the occasion for their composition:[56]

> I have herde master Gascoignes memorie commended by these verses following, the which were written upon this occasion. He had (in the middest of his youth) determined to abandone all vaine delights and to retourne unto Greyes Inne, there to undertake againe the study of the common lawes. And being required by five sundrie gentlemen to wrighte in verse somewhat worthy to be remembered, before he entred into their fellowship, he compiled these five sundry sortes of metre upon five sundry theames which they delivered unto him. (58.0.01–0.11)

G. T. states that Gascoigne was 'required' by 'sundrie gentlemen' at Gray's Inn to write poems on set themes in order to return there. Critics have questioned the truth of G. T.'s statements throughout *Flowres* and the G. T. material is usually described as a fictional frame, which sets Gascoigne's poetry within occasional contexts that may or may not have existed. The frame may be fictional, but G. T.'s comments have some relationship to real situations, since – as we have already seen – members of the Inns wrote poems to each other on themes related to personal behaviour and comportment (such as Googe's poems to Neville and Blundeston on idleness and lust). Moreover, it is likely that the events G. T. describes really occurred, since this is one of the few points in the *Hundreth sundrie flowres* when he uses the names of real men: the themes are assigned by and written to Francis Kinwelmersh, Anthony Kinwelmersh, John Vaughn, Alexander Neville, and Richard Courtop.[57] The request to write on set themes 'somewhat worthy to be remembered' recalls the assignment that the schoolmaster Gnomaticus gave to his students in the *Glasse of governement*, asking them to write verses on various precepts or themes, since 'Artes *Poetrie* giveth greatest assistaunce unto memorie', and underscores that poetry at the Inns in the 1560s was an extension of the sorts of versification assignments given to students in grammar schools.[58] At the same time, G. T.'s statement that Gascoigne was 'required by five sundrie gentlemen to wrighte in verse … before he entred into their fellowship' reinforces the idea that this sort of composition was a common practice at the Inns and a way of establishing (or in this case reconfirming) social connections.

Initially, the 'sundry theames' reveal more about Gascoigne's reluctance to rejoin this community than his desire to connect himself to it. Gascoigne's poetry, in the words of Fred Inglis, is marked by his characteristic 'scornful, truculent resignation'.[59] Such scorn and truculence come across strongly, since the content and tone of the 'sundry theames' create the sense that Gascoigne is resistant to the demands of the assignments given to him. The first of them, a sonnet on the theme 'audaces fortuna iuvat' ('fortune helps the brave'), a theme that, according to G. T., Francis Kinwelmersh, a member of Gray's Inn, 'delivered' to Gascoigne, provides one example of this 'truculent resignation'.

> If yelding feare, or cancred villanie,
> In Caesars haughtie heart had tane the charge,
> The walles of Rome had not bene reared so hye,
> Nor yet the mightie empire lefte so large.
> If Menelaus could have ruled his will
> With fowle reproch to loose his faire delight,
> Then had the stately towers of Troy stood still,
> And Greekes with grudge had dronke their own despight.
> If dread of drenching waves or feare of fire,
> Had stayed the wandring Prince amidde his race,
> Ascanius then, the frute of his desire
> In Lavine lande had not possessed his place,
> But true it is, where lottes doe light by chaunce,
> There Fortune helpes the boldest to advaunce.
>
> (58.1–14)

Gascoigne describes the fates of Caesar, Menelaus, and Aeneas. Yet it is curious that the theme, 'fortune helps the brave', applies to only one of his examples. Caesar's might results from his ability to control his 'haughtie heart'. Menelaus brings down Troy because he is unable to 'rule his will'. Only Aeneas, as a figure who overcomes 'dread' and 'feare' to conquer Rome ('Lavine lande'), stands as an example of bravery. Yet the phrase 'But true it is, where lottes doe light by chaunce' in the second-to-last line calls attention to the fact that none of Gascoigne's examples prove the theme well, since in each case it is resolution (or the lack therof) that affects the outcome (637). Gascoigne writes on the maxim given to him, but in a way that seems to challenge, rather than address, the assignment.

Gascoigne's resistance is evident as well in his fourth theme on the topic 'no haste but good', which (again according to G. T.) was 'delivered' to him by Alexander Neville (whom we saw exchanging poetry with Barnabe Googe). In response to the maxim, which he interprets to mean 'haste makes waste', Gascoigne writes seven sonnets concerning Gascoigne's/the narrator's rise and fall from favour at court. G. T.'s introduction to the poem notes that all of the sonnets themselves were written very, very quickly:

> Alexander Nevile delivered him this theame, *Sat cito, si sat bene*, whereupon he [Gascoigne] compiled these seven Sonets in sequence, therin bewraying his owne *Nimis cito*: and therewith his *Vix bene*. (61)

G. T. tells us that Gascoigne wrote '*Nimis Cito*', 'too fast', and therefore '*Vix bene*', 'hardly well' (640). Of course, the quality of the sonnets is open to the reader's judgement, and we do not know how quickly Gascoigne wrote, but G. T.'s comment implies that Gascoigne's composition proves the theme on which he writes, showing that haste, 'too fast', indeed makes waste, 'hardly well'. At the same time, G. T. suggests Gascoigne's refusal to live by the precepts that he has been assigned to versify, pointing to his calculated unwillingness to act in accordance with the very lesson he has been asked to explain.

Looked at in another way, Gascoigne's disregard is less a sign of his indifference and unwillingness to connect than an indication of the similarity of his personality and attitudes to those for whom he writes. The 'sundry theames', as I suggested above, has the feel of a grammar school academic assignment, such as the requirement from the Durham School that students 'make certain verses upon certain argument which shall be given them'. In response, Gascoigne shows his understanding of the task 'delivered' to him, dutifully completing 'themes' while affecting the 'truculent resignation' of a schoolboy. Together, the men at the Inns and Gascoigne seem to engage in a knowing imitation and mild parody of such academic assignments. Gascoigne's affected disregard indicates that he understands their request, and displays his shared understanding of the form being mocked. Gascoigne connects to the members of the Inns by demonstrating his willingness to complete the task, while expressing his sense of humour.

Communal poetry

Gascoigne's 'sundry theames' returns us to the question of why the men at the Inns continued the poetic practices of the grammar school and university. Writing poetry and attending the Inns played an analogous role in the lives of the men themselves. In the grammar schools, poetic composition was supposed to help one to acquire the skills and attitudes that would allow one to become an active participant in public life. At the same time, men came to the Inns in order to effect this transition, to become officers, secretaries, parliamentarians, and ambassadors in service to the state. Both activities were central to the creation of oneself as an active member of the realm. By continuing to write on set themes and commonplaces at the Inns, the men there continued to practise and memorise the ideas and attitudes they associated with professional responsibility. At the same time, by doing such work on their own, they self-consciously and knowingly took on the qualities of men who considered questions about duty, service, appropriate public behaviour, and the like. Thus, as we have seen in the poems discussed in this chapter, they wrote about 'idleness', 'lust', 'friendship', and 'courage', as well as 'hasty' work. If versification helped to turn precepts into memory, then the continuation of this activity helped to turn memory into personality. Writing poetry allowed the authors to take on the personas of dutiful servants to the state that they learned and wrote about in their schooling.

Yet it was not enough for members of the Inns to write verses on duty, responsibility, thriftiness, and the like, and, therefore, to put themselves on the path to respectable careers. They also had to write amorous poetry and turn the amorous path into the dutiful one as well. Indeed, they displayed both their poetic abilities and moral steadfastness by writing both kinds of verse, and turning both to the same end. More important, members of the Inns were not writing for themselves, but also for their peers, in an effort to shape a homogeneous community of like-minded men. For them, the way to do this was to counsel each other about appropriate behaviour by both describing and affirming the values that they wanted to uphold, and by illustrating the dangers of other ways of being. By writing and circulating lyric poetry, they defined themselves as individuals and as a community. Hence, lyric poetry at the Inns served a social as well as psychological function, allowing men to enter into, connect with, and shape the social world of the Inns of Court. And once they were established at the Inns, the community then furnished them with the incentive, authorisation, and credentials to begin to make contacts in the professional and political world of the Elizabethan government, and it fostered the production of other forms of writing that they could use to make these contacts.

Notes

1 On the literary connections of the Inns, see A. Wigfall Green, *The Inns of Court and Early English Drama* (1931; repr. New York, NY: Benjamin Blom, 1965); Philip Finkelpearl, *John Marston of the Middle Temple: An Elizabethan Dramatist in his Social Setting* (Cambridge, MA: Harvard University Press, 1969); Christopher Paul Baker, 'Ben Jonson and the Inns of Court: the literary milieu of *Every Man Out of His Humor*' (PhD dissertation, University of North Carolina, 1974); Arthur F. Marotti, *John Donne: Coterie Poet* (Madison, WI: University of Wisconsin Press, 1986), esp. pp. 25–95; Brent Whitted, 'Legal play: the literary culture of the Inns of Court, 1572–1634' (PhD dissertation, University of British Columbia, 2000); W. R. Elton, *Shakespeare's Troilus and Cressida and the Inns of Court Revels* (Aldershot: Ashgate, 2000); Anthony Arlidge, *Shakespeare and the Prince of Love: The Feast of Misrule in the Middle Temple* (London: Giles de la Mare, 2000); Michelle O'Callaghan, *The 'Shepheardes Nation': Jacobean Spenserians and Early Stuart Political Culture, 1612–1625* (Oxford: Oxford University Press, 2000); and Stella P. Revard, 'Thomas Stanley and "A Register of Friends"', in Claude J. Summers and Ted-Larry Pebworth (eds), *Literary Circles and Cultural Communities in Renaissance England* (Columbia, MO: University of Missouri Press, 2000), pp. 148–72.
2 Wilfrid Prest, *The Inns of Court under Elizabeth I and the Early Stuarts, 1590–1640* (London: Longman; Totowa, NJ: Rowman and Littlefield, 1972), p. 4.
3 On the shifting literary tastes of members, see Prest, *The Inns of Court under Elizabeth I and the Early Stuarts, 1590–1640*, pp. 153–73.
4 *Ibid.*, p. 21.
5 The collections by Googe, Turberville, and Gascoigne will be discussed later in the essay. Hugh Plat's collection is *Flouers of Philosophie* (London: H. Bynneman and F. Coldocke, 1572), Timothy Kendall's is *Flowers of epigrammes* (London: J. Shepperd, 1577), and John Grange's is *The golden Aphroditis* (London: H. Bynneman, 1577).
6 Richard Panofsky, 'A descriptive study of mid-Tudor short poetry, 1557–1579' (PhD

dissertation, University of California, Santa Barbara, 1975), p. 5: referred to hereafter as 'Mid-Tudor short poetry'.

7 Quoted in Richard Foster Watson, who cites numerous grammar school statutes on verse-making in the curriculum, *The English Grammar Schools to 1660: Their Curriculum and Practice* (Cambridge: Cambridge University Press, 1908), pp. 473–4. For further discussion of literary composition and grammar school curricula, see also Peter Mack, 'Rhetoric in the grammar school', in *Elizabethan Rhetoric: Theory and Practice* (Cambridge: Cambridge University Press, 2002), pp. 11–47; Lynn Enterline, 'Rhetoric, discipline, and the theatricality of everyday life in Elizabethan grammar schools', in Peter Holland and Stephen Orgel (eds), *From Performance to Print in Shakespeare's England* (Basingstoke: Palgrave Macmillan, 2006), pp. 173–90.

8 *The Glasse of Governement* in *The Complete Works of George Gascoigne*, ed. John W. Cunliffe, 2 vols (Cambridge: Cambridge University Press, 1910), II, 1–90 (47). Further references to the *Glasse* will be to page numbers in this edition.

9 Kenneth Charlton discusses the emphasis on civic duty and service to the state in Renaissance educational theory in *Education in Renaissance England* (London: Routledge and Kegan Paul, 1965), esp. pp. 41–85. Anthony Grafton and Lisa Jardine show that there was a disconnect between theory and practice, the idea that 'successful drilling in *copia* and *methodus* will guarantee a classroom product of moral uprightness and good characters': see *From Humanism to the Humanities: Education and Liberal Arts in Fifteenth- and Sixteenth-Century Europe* (Cambridge, MA: Harvard University Press, 1986), p. 149.

10 Thomas Elyot, *Boke named the governour*, ed. Henry H. S. Croft, 2 vols (New York, NY: Burt Franklin, 1967), I, 28 and 58.

11 Roger Ascham, *The Schoolmaster*, ed. Lawrence V. Ryan (Charlottesville, VA: University Press of Virginia, 1967), p. 35.

12 Richard Helgerson, *Elizabethan Prodigals* (Berkeley, CA: University of California Press, 1976), p. 32.

13 Panofsky, 'Mid-Tudor short poetry', p. 5.

14 Helgerson, *Elizabethan Prodigals*, p. 41.

15 Christopher Gaggero, 'Pleasure unreconciled to virtue: George Gascoigne and didactic drama', in Lloyd Edward Kermode, Jason Scott-Warren, and Martine van Elk (eds), *Tudor Drama Before Shakespeare, 1485–1590: New Directions for Research, Criticism, and Pedagogy* (Houndsmills: Palgrave, 2004), pp. 167–94 (p. 170).

16 G. K. Hunter, 'Drab and golden lyrics of the Renaissance', in Reuben A. Brower (ed.), *Forms of Lyric: Selected Papers from the English Institute* (New York, NY: Columbia University Press, 1970), pp. 1–18 (pp. 10–11).

17 Panofsky, 'Mid-Tudor short poetry', p. 7.

18 Kenneth Charlton surveys this training in 'Education and the Inns of Court in the sixteenth century', *British Journal of Educational Studies*, 9 (1960), 25–38.

19 J. W. Saunders asserts that 'professional poets' (he implies, those not associated with court) in the sixteenth century tried 'as best they could to imitate the Courtier's habits' in 'From manuscript to print: a note on the circulation of poetic MSS in the sixteenth century', *Proceedings of the Leeds Philosophical Society*, 6 (1951), 507–28 (509) and 'The stigma of print: a note on the social bases of Tudor poetry', *Essays in Criticism*, 1 (1951), 139–64. In the 1590s, Inns of Court men did imitate poetic forms popular at court (see Marotti, *John Donne*, pp. 25–95).

20 Stephen May, *Elizabethan Courtier Poets* (Columbia, MO: University of Missouri Press, 1991), pp. 43–5.

21 That duty, responsibility, care for the state, the active life, etc. were indeed educational values is evident in many Renaissance educational and political treatises. J. H. Hexter shows that 'questions of responsibility' are of the utmost importance to such treatises, which describe the 'responsibility through education' for young men, particularly aristocrats, to prepare themselves for office, and emphasise, 'their responsibility to turn the education they get to the service of the public weal' in *Reappraisals in History* (Evanston, IL: Northwestern University Press, 1961), p. 67. Referring specifically to Elyot's *Boke named the governour*, Charlton points out that 'duty, responsibility, obligation' are the 'key concepts' (*Education in Renaissance England*, p. 83). More specifically, through the speaker Lupset, Thomas Starkey suggests that educated men must use their learning in service to the state, or they 'regardeth not [their] office and duty': see *A Dialogue Between Pole and Lupset*, ed. T. F. Mayer (London: Royal Historical Society, 1989), p. 2.

22 *The Shippe of Safegarde (1569) by Barnabe Googe*, ed. Simon McKeown and William E. Sheidley (Tempe, AZ: Arizona Center for Medieval and Renaissance Studies, 2001), p. xviii.

23 Biographical information taken from Mark Eccles, 'Barnabe Googe in England, Spain, and Ireland', *English Literary Renaissance*, 15:3 (1985), 353–70; Judith M. Kennedy's introduction to Barnabe Googe, *Eclogues, Epitaphs, and Sonnets*, ed. Judith M. Kennedy (Toronto: University of Toronto Press, 1989), pp. 1–31. All references to Googe's poetry collection will be to numbered entries in this volume.

24 Simon McKeown is an exception to this trend, discussing how Barnabe Googe reworks and reflects his own and contemporary religious and political beliefs: 'Barnabe Googe: poetry and society in the 1560s' (PhD dissertation, Queen's University, Belfast, 1993).

25 On the characteristics of pastoral, see Frank Kermode, *English Pastoral Poetry: From the Beginnings to Marvell* (London: George G. Harrap, 1952), pp. 11–44.

26 On the *Myrrour* at the Inns of Court, see Jessica Winston, '*A Mirror for Magistrates* and public political discourse in Elizabethan England', *Studies in Philology*, 101 (2004), 381–400.

27 J. D. Alsop suggests that for Googe 'quiet country refuge' is necessary 'until God restore[s] the true order': 'The sixth eclogue of Baptista Mantuan and the Elizabethan poet Barnabe Googe', *Cahiers Élisabéthains*, 25 (1984), 1–8 (1).

28 Paul Parnell, 'Barnabe Googe: a Puritan in Arcadia', *Journal of English and Germanic Philology*, 60:2 (1961), 273–81 (281); William Sheidley, *Barnabe Googe* (Boston, MA: Twayne, 1981), p. 74; McKeown, 'Barnabe Googe', p. 96.

29 Helen Cooper, 'Mantuan', *The Spenser Encyclopedia*, ed. A. C. Hamilton (Toronto: University of Toronto Press, 1990), pp. 452–3 (p. 452).

30 Kennedy, introduction to Googe, *Eclogues, Epitaphs, and Sonnets*, ed. Kennedy, p. 21.

31 Virgil began his career with his pastoral *Eclogues*, moved on to the *Georgics*, and then wrote the epic *Aeneid*. His movement, from pastoral to epic, became in the words of Lawrence Lipking, the 'pattern of a career to so many later poets', the so-called *rota Virgilii* or *cursus Virgilii*. See Lipking, *Life of the Poet: Beginning and Ending Poetic Careers* (Chicago, IL: University of Chicago Press, 1981), p. xi, and Edward Kennedy, 'Virgil', *The Spenser Encyclopedia*, ed. Hamilton, pp. 717–19 (p. 717).

32 Mary Hobbs, *Early Seventeenth-Century Verse Miscellany Manuscripts* (Aldershot: Scolar

Press, 1992), p. 21.

33 Arthur F. Marotti, *Manuscript, Print, and the English Renaissance Lyric* (Ithaca, NY: Cornell University Press, 1995), p. 222.

34 E. F. Hart, 'The answer-poem in the early seventeenth century', *Review of English Studies* n.ser. 7 (1956), 19–29 (22; 24–25).

35 Marotti, *Manuscript*, pp. 159–60.

36 'Running' means 'flighty' or 'giddy' (see Googe, *Eclogues, Epitaphs, and Sonnets*, ed. Kennedy, p. 171). Holmedon appears to be a fellow student and friend of Googe's, since he is addressed as 'my Holmedon' (26.8) and told that a 'running head' is 'the vilest plague that students can sustain' (26.6).

37 Born in 1544, Neville matriculated at St John's College, Cambridge in 1559. His name does not appear on the roles at the Inns, but it is assumed that he attended because, as we shall see further below, he is one of the five men for whom Gascoigne had to write 'sundry themes' on his return to Gray's Inn in the early to mid-1560s.

38 Franklin B. Williams, *Index of Dedications and Commendatory Verses in English Before 1641* (London: Bibliographical Society, 1962), p. 19. It is possible that Blundeston was a fellow student with Googe at Christ's College, Cambridge. See Kennedy's note to 'L. Blundeston to the Reader' in her edition of Googe, *Eclogues, Epitaphs, and Sonnets*, p. 139.

39 The phrase 'cheese from chalk' describes things that are dissimilar, as in the expression, 'No more alike than cheese and chalk'. Frank Percy Wilson, *Oxford Dictionary of English Proverbs*, 3rd edn (Oxford: Clarendon Press, 1970), p. 113.

40 Hart, 'Answer-poem in the early seventeenth century', 19.

41 Marotti, *Manuscript*, p. 162.

42 See, for instance, Eve Kosofsky Sedgwick, *Between Men: English Literature and Male Homosocial Desire* (New York, NY: Columbia, 1985), pp. 1–27.

43 Wendy Wall, *The Imprint of Gender: Authorship and Publication in the English Renaissance* (Ithaca, NY: Cornell University Press, 1993), esp. pp. 38–50.

44 Cathy Shrank, '"Matters of love as of discourse": the English sonnet, 1560–1580', *Studies in Philology*, 105 (2008), 30–49 (36).

45 Jennifer Richards, *Rhetoric and Courtliness in Early Modern Literature* (Cambridge: Cambridge University Press, 2003), pp. 154–5.

46 Laurie Shannon argues that the literary community at the Inns in the 1560s also fosters the formation of an egalitarian political community, one modelled on male friendship relations. Yet it is worth recognising that, if this is the case, the community does not welcome critical deliberation or disagreement. See 'Minerva's men: horizontal nationhood and the literary production of Googe, Turberville, and Gascoigne', in *Oxford Handbook of Tudor Literature, 1485–1603*, ed. Mike Pincombe and Cathy Shrank (Oxford: Oxford University Press, 2009), pp. 437–54. Moreover, such insistence on homogeneity underscores a difference between the poetry at Inns in the 1560s and in the 1590s, when much of the poetry, usually satirical, expressed hostility toward other Inns of Court men and other authors and often, in Lawrence Manley's view, conveyed the poet's isolation from others. See Manley, chapter 7 'Essential difference: the projects of satire', in *Literature and Culture in Early Modern London* (Cambridge: Cambridge University Press, 1995), pp. 372–430. Such differences in the tone of 1560s and 1590s poetry reinforce the need to examine different periods of literary production at the Inns in their immediate institutional and communal contexts.

47 Richard Panofsky, 'Introduction', George Turberville, *Epitaphes, Epigrams, Songs and Sonets (1567) and Epitaphes and Sonnettes (1576)* (Delmar, NY: Scholars' Facsimiles and Reprints, 1977), pp. v–xv (p. vi).

48 Sheidley, *Barnabe Googe*, p. 53.

49 Donald L. Peterson, *The English Lyric from Wyatt to Donne: A History of Plain and Eloquent Styles* (Princeton, NJ: Princeton University Press, 1967), p. 137; Sheidley, *Barnabe Googe*, p. 53; and John Peck, quoted in Sheidley, *Barnabe Googe*, p. 53.

50 Panofsky, 'Mid-Tudor short poetry', p. 127.

51 Shrank, '"Matters of love as of discourse"', 37.

52 Richards, *Rhetoric and Courtliness*, p. 155.

53 George Gascoigne, *A Hundreth Sundrie Flowres*, ed. G. W. Pigman III (Oxford: Clarendon Press, 2000), 72.2 and p. xxiv. References to the text of the *Hundreth Sundrie Flowres* refer to numbered entries in this edition, to Roman numeral pages in Pigman's 'Biographical introduction', or to Arabic numeral pages in the notes.

54 Pigman, 'Biographical introduction', Gascoigne, *Hundreth Sundrie Flowres*, ed. Pigman, p. xxiii.

55 For more on these poems and their role as 'an initiation into a literary clique' see Gillian Austen, '*Gascoigne's Memories* (1565)', in *George Gascoigne* (Cambridge: D.S. Brewer, 2008), pp. 36–48.

56 Most commentators, including most recently Austen, *George Gascoigne* (p. 36), assume that G.T. is fictional, but there is a possibility that the initials stand for George Turberville.

57 Not much is known about these men: Francis Kinwelmersh (1538–1600) was admitted to Gray's Inn in 1557. He collaborated with Gascoigne on *Jocasta* (1566) and may also have been the brother of Anthony Kinwelmersh, who was admitted to Gray's Inn in 1561. John Vaughn was admitted to Gray's Inn in 1562/63. No record of Alexander Neville's (1544–1614) admission to the Inns exists. He translated Seneca's *Oedipus* (1563) and, as we have seen, wrote some of the poetry published in Googe's *Eglogs epytaphes, and sonettes* (1563). Richard Courtop was admitted to Gray's Inn in 1559. For biographical information, see Gascoigne, *Hundreth Sundrie Flowres*, ed. Pigman, pp. 636–41.

58 For more on poetic assignments in the schools, see Watson, *English Grammar Schools*, esp. ch. 29 ('Verse-making with a note on the Flores Poetarum'), pp. 468–82.

59 Fred Inglis, *The Elizabethan Poets: The Making of English Poetry from Wyatt to Ben Jonson* (London: Evans Brothers, 1969), p. 159.

12

The evidential plot:
Shakespeare and Gascoigne at Gray's Inn

Lorna Hutson

The Inns of Court in the sixteenth century were, among other things, centres of experiment in the composition and performance of new kinds of vernacular drama influenced by classical models. The significance literary critics accord to this fact has largely depended on their sense of the importance of academic or neoclassical drama for the development of Shakespeare's art. In this chapter, I will focus on the relationship between one neoclassical comedy, composed and performed at Gray's Inn in 1566 – George Gascoigne's *Supposes* – and another, Shakespeare's *Comedy of Errors*, performed in the same place nearly three decades later, in 1594. As I will show, a relative lack of literary critical interest in any dialogue between these two Inns of Court plays stems from a more general tendency to underplay or even deny altogether the importance of neoclassical dramaturgy to the development of the Shakespearean stage at the end of the century. Yet, as I hope to demonstrate, treating the legal setting of the plays seriously helps us assume a less dismissive attitude towards the 'rules' of neoclassical drama, enabling us to understand another aspect of its theatrical dynamism. For both classical and neoclassical comedy depend for their sophisticated effects of realism on a rhetoric of probable conjecture, or evidence evaluation, which has very direct links not only with the daily work of lawyers at the Inns of Court, but, via England's participatory justice system, with reforms in popular legal culture in England more generally.[1]

Gascoigne, Shakespeare, and neoclassical comedy

George Gascoigne's *Supposes* falls squarely into the definition of that kind of academic or neoclassical comedy that Shakespeare is said, on the whole, to have rejected for a more fluid and imaginative 'native' tradition. For *Supposes* is a humanistic translation of Ludovico Ariosto's *I Suppositi*, which was composed and performed in Ferrara in 1509.[2] Ariosto's earliest dramatic works, *La Cassaria* (1508) and *I Suppositi* (1509), are generally accorded the status of the first real 'modern' comedies in Italian – the first, that is, to fashion the models of coherent dramatic intrigue offered in the recently rediscovered corpus of Plautine and Terentian comedy into original, attention-compelling and realistic plays.[3] Although Ariosto's achievement antedated the development of Italian neoclassical theory on the importance of the dramatic unities – unity of time, place, and action – it anticipated such theory in practice. As well as unified dramatic action, these plays' staging (for which Ariosto was responsible) called, like earlier Ferrarese performances of Plautus and Terence, for a unified theatrical space. In addition to perspective backdrops painted by Pellegrino da Udine and later by Raphael, Ariosto made use of a modified version of the traditional set described by Elena Povoledo as the '*città ferrarese*', which involved a shallow proscenium stage on which juxtaposed houses, with functional doors, provided the illusion of a street in the city.[4] This kind of 'fixed-locale staging', as Alan Nelson has shown, became (without painted backdrops) the norm in sixteenth-century English academic drama at Oxford, Cambridge, and the Inns of Court. Indeed, Nelson cites the performance of Gascoigne's *Supposes* in the hall of Gray's Inn as 'a perfect example of academic staging'.[5] In academic staging, as opposed to on the Elizabethan popular stage, the dramatic space cannot be imaginatively transformed from indoors to outdoors, from one part of the city or forest to another. 'The stage platform', as Nelson writes, 'is always and only the main street of a named city or town, for example, Florence or Bordeaux. A house once assigned to a given mater- or pater-familias retains its identity unchanged to the end of the play. A particular exit is understood as leading to a particular forum or port, and nowhere else.'[6] And the object of this staging convention, as with the compositional dramatic unities of time, space, and action, was the maximisation of verisimilitude.[7]

For anglophone critics, educated in the Shakespearean tradition, it has been easy to overlook what the generically, temporally, and scenically permissive theatre of Shakespeare and his successors owes to these strict conventions. The Shakespearean 'Muse of fire', audaciously ready to bring 'the vasty fields of France' on to the stage by way of the audience's imagination seems to transcend the clumsy straining after verisimilitude that motivated the earlier neoclassicists at the universities and the Inns, as if all Shakespeare had to do was to look back to a native, English tradition to find all the dramaturgical techniques he needed.[8] Indeed, the extent to which most critics emphasise Shakespeare's rejection of classical dramaturgy makes it hard to appreciate why he engaged with it at all. Thus, for example, Anne Barton introduces *Comedy of Errors* in the influential *Riverside Shakespeare* by writing, 'Shakespeare may well have felt … that it would be a useful discipline to submit himself to the three unities even … if he saw no subsequent need to employ them'. Likewise, Helen Cooper states, 'Shakespeare opened his career with evident humanist ambitions. *The Comedy of Errors* is more classical than anything Ben Jonson ever produced', but this, she continues, 'show[s] how Shakespeare found classical dramatic and dramaturgical models inadequate to generate the kind of theatre he wanted to produce'.[9]

While both these critics are correct in observing that Shakespeare did not consider himself bound by neo-Aristotelian dramatic unities, this does not mean that he rejected other aspects – particularly rhetorical aspects – of neoclassical dramaturgy. Indeed it is, as I will show, more persuasive to put Cooper's argument the other way around, to propose that while Shakespeare was drawn to the scope and intensity that he found in Corpus Christi cycles, he knew that to translate such cosmic drama into causally complex narratives of specific individuals, he would need to draw on the forensic rhetoric – the rhetoric of proof, probability, conjecture, and circumstance – that asks audiences to infer or imagine what cannot be staged. In the tradition of erudite comedy, such inferences and conjectures are generated by very strict limitations on what can be staged, as well as by the plots of intrigue. Shakespeare, however, saw that inference and conjecture were more than compensations for the limitations of the unitary stage, and that, dissociated from intrigue, they could become the resources of a credible inwardness (what we call 'psychology') in dramatic characters.

Erudite comedy, with its conventions of fixed-locale staging and of unified, continuous time, is much more than a sterile set of rules. The apparent limitations of the neoclassical stage were also generators of conjecture, stirring up the audience to *imagine* (sometimes salaciously) what was going on behind those doors leading always to the same houses of procurers, brothels, and bourgeois fathers with nubile daughters. We need to recover the combination of knowingness and novelty and the sense of fun that must have greeted Gascoigne's play when it was first performed to an audience as well-versed in Latin comedy as the lawyers of the Inns. Laughter would almost certainly have greeted the metatheatrical joke of the opening speech of *Supposes*, which plays with the fact that, in the fixed-locale staging of academic drama, all conversations have to take place outdoors. Thus, with ludicrous impropriety, the nursemaid, Balia, initiates the action of Ariosto's and Gascoigne's comedy by beckoning the (apparently) maidenly Polynesta out of the house to talk, on the pretext that the walls have ears:

> Here is no body, come foorth, *Polynesta*, let us looke about to be sure least any man heare our talke: for I thinke within the house the tables, the plankes, the beds, the portals, yea and the cupboards them selves have eares.[10]

'Least any man heare our talke' … ! The audience would enjoy the sense of the conversation's being both risqué (the nurse and Polynesta are about to discuss the latter's secret affair) and theatrically *avant-garde*: for the first time, the audience of an English comedy was being told by the *dramatis personae* that it would henceforth, in imitation of Latin comedy, be completely ignored. And a further new dramatic effect is hinted at in Balia's opening words: in this kind of drama the audience can know the interiors of houses, and the intriguing activities that go on in them, only by *conjecture*, and by the scenes evoked in characters' descriptions of an imagined interior. This encourages an imaginative resourcefulness – a reliance on the conjectural scene-painting and describing of unstaged locations and events – that will, in fact, become a crucial component even in the more permissive theatrical space of the popular theatre. And it also encourages an awareness of the importance of false conjecture (people being mistaken in their beliefs in the circumstances that lead to a particular person or thing being in a particular location) as a resource in the dramatic portrayal of emotion and character. What characters themselves are persuaded to believe about unstaged events can engage the audience in imagining the psychology of the character in question.

The received critical wisdom on Shakespeare's *Comedy of Errors* is, as we have seen, that it represents a kind of apprentice-work, an early exercise in mastering the discipline of Roman comic form. It is frequently noted, for example, that *The Comedy of Errors* expertly fuses the plots of two distinct comedies by Plautus – *Amphytrion* and *Menaechmi* – just as Ariosto's *I Suppositi* blends the plots of Plautus' *Captivi* and Terence's *Eunuchus*.[11] What has been less often noticed, however, is the extreme way in which the play's opening signals its distance from the *mood* of the licentious, amorous plots of Roman New Comedy. Onstage in Gray's Inn in 1594 appear not a lovesick adolescent and his slave, nor a nurse and her amorous charge, but a Duke, a prisoner, and a jailer.[12] The Duke speaks first, enjoining the prisoner – a merchant – to accept his fate at the hands of the law:

> Merchant of Syracusa, plead no more.
> I am not partial to infringe our laws.[13]

He explains that atrocities committed by Syracusans against Ephesians have caused the latter to inflict a penalty of death on any Syracusan who ventures into Ephesus, unless a thousand marks can be found to ransom him. It appears that Egeon has no means of coming by the ransom. 'Therefore', concludes the Duke, 'by law thou art condemned to die' (1.1.25).

Shakespeare's ostentatious departure from the usual amorous opening seems to signal a polemical engagement with the tradition, especially within this legal context. Why a scene of judgment at all? And why, in particular, does this opening insist, contrary to the very *raison d'être* of forensic rhetoric, that the pleading of particular circumstances will have no effect on the judge's sentence? While at Gray's Inn, Gascoigne wrote a poem in which he addressed Death as his judge, and asked him to judge his 'cause'. Here, the poem anticipates (playfully, of course) a 'gentle' or more equitable sentence as a result of considering the circumstances:

> Be judge then gentle death, and take my cause in hand
> Consider every circumstance, marke howe the case doth stande.[14]

When Shakespeare's Duke invites Egeon to 'say in brief the cause' (1.1.29) of his being in Ephesus, however, it has already been decided against him. The affecting circumstances do no more than persuade the Duke to 'limit' (1.1.151) the merchant the space of a day to raise a thousand marks for his ransom. The inception of the play's action thus weirdly proposes equivalence between the neoclassical 'day' – the day that limits the scope of dramatic action – and the day as the possibility of reprieve from *death*. It's hard not to see this as another metatheatrical joke, as if the trial is, in fact, of the neoclassical comic day – or, indeed, of the possibility of comedy like Gascoigne's. Shakespeare seems to be putting neoclassical intrigue comedy – comedy like *Supposes* – on trial.

In fact, the affinity Shakespeare here foregrounds – likening the judicial examination of a 'cause' to the action of a Roman comedy – was not as bizarre as the grim extremity of his version makes it seem. *The Comedy of Errors* seems to be engaging, in a generically self-conscious way, with the ambivalence of previous English dramatists', including Gascoigne's, response to what Adele Scafuro has called the 'forensic disposition' manifest in the characters and situations and plots that formed the staple features of Roman New Comedy and its Italian imitations.[15] We must briefly turn to the forensic rhetoric of Roman comedies and of Ariosto's *La Cassaria* and *I Suppositi*, so as to be able to consider first, how this rhetoric might contribute to the drama's probability and second, how Inns of Court men might have had an especial interest in this kind of rhetorical probability.

Forensic rhetoric in classical and neoclassical comedy

Gascoigne's and Shakespeare's audiences at the Inns were men who were all taught Latin at school through the reading of what is called 'Roman New Comedy', a corpus of six plays by Terence and twenty by Plautus, deriving from Greek models which, as Adele Scafuro has written, dramatised 'the litigious activity of fourth-century Athenians, known to us through the speeches of the fourth-century orators and codified for us in such works as the *Rhetorike pros Alexandron* and Aristotle's *Rhetorike*'.[16] It is hard to exaggerate the prominence of legal scenarios and references to litigation and forms of proof in Roman New Comedy; indeed, historians of Roman law draw heavily on Plautus and Terence for evidence of legal practice in the mid-Republican period.[17] In Plautus and Terence, characters *use* the law, or use the threat of legal action, as a means to achieve their desires. This accounts, as Scafuro argues, for the theatricality, the role-play, of much of the communication between characters. Characters develop 'forensic strategies' in their interactions with one another, calling witnesses to ensure the legal force of their actions, acting as arbitrators, and offering slaves for examination under torture, as legally admissible evidence to prove their confidence in their own case.

Typically, in the plays of Plautus and Terence, young men and wily slaves strategically engage legal procedure, or the threat of it, as part of a plot to extract a beautiful young woman from the clutches of a pimp, or slave-dealer, and/or to ward off the consequences of paternal displeasure with the amorous affair. In addition, however, the resolution of the plot usually involves a mimetic sleight-of-hand by which the dramatist reveals that the lovers may marry after all, that their affair is not illicit, by introducing what would now be called a 'back-story', that is, a narrative of kinship *proving* that their wedding is legally and morally acceptable. In effect, what this means is that, in these plays, the morally suspect use of legally probable arguments by cunning slaves and by lovesick young men to deceive procurers or kinsfolk is *no different in kind* from the dramatically probable narrative of kinship employed by the dramatist to resolve the legal dilemma of the plot. Moreover, sixteenth-century dramatists, many of whom had legal training, realised and emphasised the analogy between the dramatist's 'probable' resolution of the plot through circumstantial narrative, and the young lovers' deceptions, which were facilitated by equally probable, but false, circumstantial narratives.

Thus, for example, Ariosto's first play, *La Cassaria* (1508) bases its plot on a legal scam featured in Plautus' *Poenulus* ('The Little Carthaginian'). In Plautus' play, Agorastocles is in love with a courtesan being kept in the house of his next-door neighbour, a pimp. His slave suggests that they entrap the pimp by sending one of Agorastocles' other slaves to him, dressed up as a Carthaginian soldier in search of a good time. When the slave hands over Agorastocles' money to the pimp for a girl, hired witnesses will be able to prove to the praetor, or judge, that the pimp, according to the Roman law of *furtum manifestum*, or manifest theft, is guilty of taking Agorastocles' property.[18]

Ariosto's modification of this plot of entrapment uses conjectural rhetoric to emphasise its analogy with the *trompe l'œil* of neoclassical theatre. In his play, the young lover likewise lives next door to a pimp and loves a courtesan in that house. To gain this courtesan, his servant plans to leave a valuable trunk (*cassaria*) in the pimp's house on the pretext of its being security for a girl, and then, having arranged for the police to break in and find the stolen trunk, he anticipates that the judge will be more ready to believe a narrative of the trunk's theft than the unlikely story of such a wealthy prize being left as a paltry down payment. Thus, excising the hired witnesses who in Plautus testify to the theft, Ariosto makes the success of the entrapment turn on what legal rhetoricians called 'artificial proof' – the use of arguments from the circumstantial topics of time, place, motive, opportunity, and character – to make people believe a narrative account of what no one could have seen, *because it is a lie*.[19] But the success of the entrapment (and it does succeed, after a fashion) is equivalent to the success of the dramaturgical illusion, the neoclassical verisimilitude. Just as the audience can never see beyond the door of the pimp's house, but will imagine the 'interior' where the coffer (with its equally evocative and illusory interior) snugly nestles, so the judge, lacking witnesses to give an account of how the coffer came to be there, will believe what the generative rhetorical topics of artificial proof lead him to think most probable.

Ariosto, who had studied civil law (as well having practical experience in performing in Roman comedies) clearly relished the power of what Italian legal treatises on proof referred to as *indicia* – the signs drawn from topics of circumstance that might be adduced when a 'full proof' (confession or two unimpeachable witnesses) was lacking.[20] When the servant's clever plan goes horribly wrong in *La Cassaria*, for example, and the young man's father finds his trunk missing, the servant tries to persuade him to go to the governor and complain that it's been stolen by the pimp. 'What evidence, what proof [che indizio, che prova] can I give him to convince him that this is so?', says the father, quite reasonably (since there is none). But the servant, desperately confident, says that if they just go to the governor's house, he will present 'tali indizii e conietture e prove, che non potrà, se ben volesse, negare di crederti' (so many indications and conjectures and proofs that even if he didn't want to he couldn't help but believe you).[21]

'What nedeth me more evident tokens?': the subversion of proof in *Supposes*

When George Gascoigne, studying English common law at Gray's Inn, decided to produce a version of Ariosto's *I Suppositi* for the Candlemas Revels in 1566, he was responding to a poet who, as a reluctant law student himself, had seen and exploited the dramaturgical possibilities of the legal rhetoric of proof and probability. But the play of Gascoigne's choice, *I Suppositi*, is a more mischievous and unsettling exposure of the moral scandal of this evidential plot than is Ariosto's earlier play, *La Cassaria*. Moreover, Gascoigne's translation of Ariosto's play into an English common-law context gave it a different kind of resonance as a cultural event. England had a participatory system of criminal law that relied for its administration on voluntary, untrained officers and on the evidence evaluation of unlearned juries. In England, *indicia* were, as Sir Thomas Smith wrote in the 1560s, 'what we call in our language evidence against the malefactor', to be evaluated by the jury.[22] So in England, unlike in Italy, France, or Germany, *indicia* were not part of a complexly codified tariff of proof to be deployed by learned professional judges, but were probabilities to be decided by unlearned laymen. A new vernacular literature which would help with the evaluation of such probabilities would be written – one example is Richard Bernard's *Guide to Grand Jurymen* of 1627 – but this literature lay in the future, and would itself be informed by a familiarity with classical and neoclassical comedy (Bernard translated the plays of Terence).[23] At the point at which Gascoigne was turning Ariosto's scandalous play of adulterous sex and multiple thefts of identity into English, however, other members of the Inns were wrestling with the problems of administering justice effectively by means of the existing participatory system. In 1562, for example, Sir Nicholas Bacon (who had entered Gray's Inn by 1532) devoted most of his opening speech to parliament as Lord Keeper to the want of discipline and good local governance arising from twin problems of an unlearned clergy and corruption among Justices of Peace. To remedy the want of justice in the localities, he suggested a royal commission to 'examine by all meanes and wayes the offences of such as have not seen to the due execucion of lawes accordeing to the offices and chardges committed to them by the prince'.[24]

Ariosto's second play could be seen as touching on these very concerns about the due execution of laws, since it was set, not in some vague and fictitious city, but in the Ferrara in which his first audience lived, and it involved a foreigner's difficulty in legally proving his case. The very setting of the play in a simulacrum of the audience's own city, and the transformation of the 'returning father' motif of Roman New Comedy into the arrival of a disoriented foreigner unfamiliar with the city's judicial institutions are elements which work to disturb the Roman comic tradition and to skew *I Suppositi*'s putative function as an idealising celebration of the *città ideale*. In other words, the play Gascoigne chose mischievously *emphasises* the disturbance to good civic governance potentially posed by the amorous plot of New Comedy.

Erostrato, a Sicilian studying in Ferrara, has changed identities with his servant, Dulippo, in order to infiltrate a bourgeois Ferrarese household and deflower the daughter of the house; between them, master and servant plot to counter the dowry negotiations of the daughter's other lover, the lawyer, Cleander, by persuading a visiting Sienese merchant to pose as the false Erostrato's father and sign a false bond. The arrival of Erostrato's real father from Sicily is then met with disbelief by the Ferrarese citizens, who refute his claims with those of the fakes (Dulippo and the Sienese merchant) while Ferrara's magistrates and laws prove incapable of helping him prove his identity or find the son whom he begins to think must have been murdered by Dulippo.

Richard Andrews, commenting on Ariosto's plays as achievements in the Italian vernacular, reminds us what a new experience it would have been for an audience to try to follow 'a brand-new intrigue of this sort in performance conditions'.[25] The same point needs to be made about the vernacular form of Gascoigne's *Supposes*: while some of Gascoigne's audience would have read Ariosto, his plays were not, like Terence and Plautus, school texts, and very few plays written in the English language had, by 1566, required their audiences to follow a complicated plot for the first time in performance.[26] So, in Act 2, scene 1 Dulippo – dressed as Erostrato, and living as a wealthy foreign law student in Ferrara – offers an elaborate narration to the real Erostrato (dressed as Dulippo, and serving in a Ferrarese household) detailing the outrageous yet plausible lies by which he has just convinced a Sienese merchant to pose as Philogano, Erostrato's father.[27] He told the Sienese that Este hostility to people of his city was so great that if he wanted to stay in Ferrara he'd better pose as a Sicilian, and that the identity of Philogano, rich father to a student in Ferrara, would do admirably. In Act 2, scene 2 the Sienese merchant, posing as Philogano, enters the door of the false Erostrato's house, and the audience awaits further developments. In Act 4 – the usual act in which such a crisis occurs – the real Erostrato's real father, Philogano and his servant Litio (Gascoigne's alteration of Ariosto's 'Lico' may involve a pun on the Latin *lis, litis*, or 'lawsuit'), wearied by their long journey from Sicily, arrive at this very door. Their knocking, however, arouses the hostile response of the false Erostrato's cook, Dalio, who claims that the lodgings are full, indeed that Philogano himself is already *inside*. Then the Sienese imposter issues forth and rehearses, as his own life story, the circumstances leading up to Philogano's arrival in Ferrara. The real Philogano splutters in disbelief as Dalio shuts the door in his face.

At this moment, when Philogano, instead of meeting his longed-for son, finds himself shut out of his son's house, the object of Dalio's obscenities, the effect is more disturbing than anything comparable in Roman comedy. And the peculiar nature of the disturbance derives from the relationship between the increasingly demented, disorienting evidential contradictions, and the invocation of a Ferrara as a civic ideal. For it is also at this point, having witnessed Philogano's experience as a stranger – bullied, abused, and told infuriating lies by a man occupying his accommodation and claiming to be him – that the audience first meets the citizen, the 'Ferrarese' of the cast list, who speaks patriotically for the city's good government, and especially for its judicial system. After a dig at the proverbial falsehood of the Ferrarese, Litio accuses the bystanding Ferrarese citizen of belonging to a city without due respect for law, where officers allow such cheating to go on. 'What know the officers of this?', asks the Ferrarese, 'thinke you they knowe of every fault?' 'Nay', replies Litio, 'I think they will knowe as little as may be, specially when they have no gaines by it, but they ought to have their eares open to heare of such offences' (4.4.10–14). Litio's words echo the concerns of Sir Nicholas Bacon and those of other Inns of Court authors – for example, William Fleetwood (Middle Temple, 1547) and Thomas Norton (Inner Temple, 1555) – on the subject of corrupt local officers, promoters, and informers.[28]

It is, however, when the Ferrarese citizen attempts to vindicate the honesty of his city by reuniting the Sicilian foreigner with his son Erostrato that the most marked – if still darkly comic – departure from the Roman tradition takes place. In this moment we experience not only an unsettling subversion of the play's discourse of civic idealism, but, in our sympathy with Philogano, a brush with the everyday possibility of tragedy. The well-meaning Ferrarese introduces the *fraud*, the disguised Dulippo, to Philogano, telling him that this is his son. Philogano thus suddenly realises that the man whom all Ferrara takes to be his son is the servant in whose company Erostrato left Sicily. With dawning horror, he conjectures the scenario most likely to explain such a bizarre situation:

> Out and alas, he whom I sent hither with my sonne to be his servaunt, and to give attendance on him, hath eyther cut his throate, or by some evill meanes made him away, and hath not only taken his garments, his bookes, his money and that which he broughte out of *Sicilia* with him, but usurpeth his name also, and turneth to his owne commoditie the bills of exchaunge that I have alwayes allowed for my sonnes expenses. Oh miserable *Philogano*, oh unhappie olde man: oh eternall god, is there no judge? no officer? no higher powers whom I maye complaine unto for redresse of these wrongs?
>
> (4.8.25–34)

No *senex* figure of Roman comedy sounds quite so distraught on discovering how he's been made a dupe in his absence. The difference from Roman comedy lies in Ariosto's brilliant exploitation of the horror of surmise: Philogano's imagined scenario of his son's murder is indeed more likely than the play's 'real' explanation, and its pathos plumbs unexpected emotional depths in the comic convention of paralogism, or mistaken conjecture.

Another shadowy element of disturbance to the comedy, however, lies in what

Philogano's plight exposes about the limitations of human proof, the possibility of fundamental error that haunts all questions of identity, legitimacy, and paternity once they become questions.[29] Though the Ferrarese gamely insists on the infallibility of Ferrara's legal system – 'Yes, sir, we have potestates, we have Judges, and above all, we have a most juste prince, doubt you not, but you shall have justice, *if your cause be just* [my emphasis]' (4.8.35–7) – Litio has already pointed out the technical problem with such idealism: 'If there be many such witnesses in this country, men may go about to prove what they will in controversies here' (4.8.14–15). When, in Ariosto's play, Filogono (Philogano) cried out for a '*podestà*', Ariosto, too, was acknowledging the problem Litio perceived – the *podestà*, or senior judge, was, in most northern Italian cities, a non-native appointment, who was explicitly forbidden to enter into kinship relations with local inhabitants.[30] In both Ariosto's and Gascoigne's versions, however, the father's prospects only look bleaker when he finds his case being handled by a lawyer who is none other than Cleander, rival suitor to the man claiming to be his son. Cleander, far from expressing confidence in his client's case, declares that it will be almost impossible to prove:

> Yea, but how will you prove that he is not *Erostrato*, having suche presumptions to the contrarie? or how will it be thought that you are *Philogano*, when an other taketh upon him the same name, and for proofe bringeth in him for a witnesse, which hath bene ever reputed here for *Erostrato*?

> (5.5.1–5)

Gascoigne here follows Ariosto's use of '*presunzione*' or presumption, a Roman and Italian civil law term for the judge's ability to assume the truth of a certain matter for the purposes of inquiry.[31] The fact that Gascoigne chooses to use this term speaks of his alertness to the technical legal vocabulary favoured by Ariosto (Ariosto's modern translators simply render '*la publica presunzione*' as 'everybody knows') but it is also a telling indicator of the process, documented by historians like Barbara Shapiro and Michael McNair, by which English common law was responding to the need to refine the evidentiary concepts and gradations of proof used by justices and juries in a participatory system, by assimilating the evidentiary vocabulary used by professional judges in Romano-canon tradition.[32]

What happens, of course (the real Erostrato, meanwhile, lying imprisoned in Polynesta's father's house), is that Cleander's anticipation of the problematic, expensive, and ultimately ineffective nature of the mode of proof Philogano proposes becomes redundant as the conjectural work of the denouement's 'recognition' takes over: Cleander begins to piece together clues and fragments of proof which suggest that Dulippo is, in fact, the son he lost long ago at the battle of Otranto. The predictable romance denouement obviates the need for dwelling further on the legal impasse momentarily glimpsed in the discussion of how inadequate Philogano's testimony and proofs would be, but it no less clearly raises further questions of likelihood and probability. As Cleander finds out from Philogano that Dulippo's former name, as a foundling, was 'Carino', he immediately claims that 'Carino' was the name of his own son, whom he lost at Otranto. From the perspective of the strangers to Ferrara, however, this simply looks like another trick, another set of circumstantial lies, like those produced by the law student Erostrato, to prove a false identity and kinship. As soon as Cleander asks Philogano for details of Dulippo's origins, Litio is on guard, 'Sir, have I not told you enough of the falsehood of *Ferrara*? this gentleman will not only picke your purse, but beguile you of your servaunt also, and make you beleve he is his sonne' (5.5.99–101). When Cleander comes to his 'recognition' finale, Gascoigne's Litio voices an obscene response (unspoken in Ariosto) to the lawyer's request to see the birthmark that would clinch the story that Dulippo and Carino are one and the same person. 'What nedeth me more evident tokens?' exclaims Cleander, 'this is my sonne out of doubt whom I lost eighteen years since, and a thousand, thousand times have I lamented for him: he should have a mould on his left shoulder' (5.5.127–31). Litio replies acidly, displacing the audience's urge to laugh at the pat rehearsal of these proofs: 'He hath a moulde there in deede: and an hole in an other place, too. I woulde your nose were in it' (5.5.132–3).

'For lacke of proofe I am able to go no furder':[33]
Gascoigne's *Glasse of governement*

Ariosto's comedy playfully foregrounds the unlikelihood of the proofs by which its ending contrives to avert the scandals of Polynesta's affair and Dulippo's crimes. The play's ingenuity made it a favourite for translators in France, where it was turned into French by three separate authors.[34] In England, however, Gascoigne's was the only – rather belated – translation, and it was followed, in Gascoigne's own oeuvre, by a play which used the same neoclassical rhetoric of conjecture to very different moral and political ends – *The glasse of governement* (pub. 1575). This play was dedicated to Gascoigne's kinsman at Gray's Inn, Sir Owen Hopton (Gray's Inn, 1580) who was also a veteran of Guildhall sessions of *oyer and terminer* (commissions to hear and determine specific offences) and 'privy searches' or secret investigations made at Burghley's command to keep law and order in London.[35] In the play dedicated to Hopton, Gascoigne shows his skill in using characters' conjectures and inferences to manipulate emotion, instilling anxiety and eliciting pathos, but he avoids having characters use conjectural arguments to deceive and go unpunished, as Erostrato and Dulippo do. All deliberately deceptive 'supposes' become clues in a plot of magisterial detection, and are punished by law. The action is set in Antwerp, and involves the machinations of a prostitute to ensnare a studious young burgher's son by pretending to engage him in a legitimate amorous courtship. A key figure in the denouement is the representative of civic justice whose absence from *Supposes* is so keenly noted in Philogano's lament. This figure, the Markgrave, having arrested the prostitute's pimp on suspicion, is not initially able to sentence him because, as one critic notes, 'he makes a great point of *finding direct evidence*, not executing summary punishment [my emphasis]'.[36] The play, in fact, thus adapts the forensic structure of intrigue comedy, transforming the wily slave's heroic improvisation of lies into the heroic magistrate-detective's capacity to gather and evaluate the evidence on which to condemn those lies. Dramaturgically, intrigue becomes the material on which the retrospective work of detection thrives. Politically and morally, however, the dramaturgy of intrigue and conjecture (or 'supposing') is in fact *condemned to death*, along with the hapless youths who found themselves seduced by the pimps and prostitutes of Antwerp. For whereas Gascoigne's earlier play celebrated the ambivalence of merely probable judgments – the fact that the 'evident tokens' which seem to prove that Dulippo is Cleander's son were no more irrefutable, as proof, than the public presumption on which all Ferrara mistook Dulippo for Erostrato – his later play insists that proof be conclusive. In the second last scene of the play, the virtuous magistrate complains that, to rid the town of the pimp and his prostitute, 'I have done my best … to apprehend them, and I have examined them also, but truly I can not finde hitherto any proof against them, whereby they ought to be punished'. Providentially, in the ensuing dialogue, legally sufficient proof emerges, and the magistrate rejoices, 'by this means I have good cause to punish them'.[37]

'This sympathized one day's error':[38] *The Comedy of Errors*

Gascoigne's second play seems never to have been performed. Nevertheless, it is an original product of his pen and one that clearly strives to adapt the forensic rhetoric of neoclassical comedy to the legal-political concerns expressed by men of the Inns of Court in the 1560s and 1570s. Before concluding this chapter with some thoughts on its implications for reading Shakespeare's *Comedy of Errors*, then, it is worth turning to these legal-political concerns and their relationship to dramatic writing in the period.

Recent work by Jessica Winston on translations of Seneca in the 1560s and 1570s at the Inns of Court has broadened and complicated our understanding of these writings as political interventions. Winston convincingly demonstrates that the deliberative rhetoric of Thomas Sackville and Thomas Norton's *Gorboduc* (Inner Temple, 1561) offers 'an altered understanding of the sorts of people and institutions that could legitimately contribute to conversations about the governance of the realm'.[39] The question of 'governance', however – a term defined by Steve Hindle as referring to a specific 'conflation of judicial and administrative functions within early modern government' – was not limited to that of the Elizabethan succession.[40] It involved, particularly in the first troubled decade after the reign of Mary Tudor, urgent debates on local judicial administration, and the roles of voluntary local officers (Justices of Peace, constables) and traditional parish authorities (ecclesiastical courts, ministers, and churchwardens) in maintaining justice and order in the localities. For men with governmental responsibilities, questions focused on the issue of who could best evaluate evidence in different circumstances: when administering penal statutes, when allocating responsibility for bastards, etc. Many of the men who debated these questions were, oddly enough, all connected, one way and another, with the writing of neoclassical – or rhetorically probable – plays.

Thus, for example, in a debate in 1571 on a bill to penalise non-attendance at divine service once a quarter, those who spoke at length on the question of who should administer it (whether promoters, Justices of Peace, churchwardens or other officers) included William Fleetwood of the Middle Temple, and Sir Owen Hopton of Gray's Inn, while Thomas Norton of the Inner Temple and Christopher Yelverton of Gray's Inn were vocal on the same day on a bill concerning the prosecution of slander against the Queen.[41] Christopher Yelverton wrote the epilogue to Gascoigne and Kinwelmersh's *Jocasta*, also performed in 1566 at Gray's Inn. Thomas Norton was the author of *Gorboduc*. Sir Owen Hopton, as we have seen, received the dedication of Gascoigne's reformed neoclassical comedy, and his friend, William Fleetwood of the Middle Temple, was to receive the dedication of another reformed neoclassical comedy on the subject of magistrates and judicial administration in 1578. This was George Whetstone's *Promos and Cassandra* (on which Shakespeare's *Measure for Measure* (1604) was based): a play that, like Gascoigne's *Glasse of Governement*, self-consciously linked the idea of the forensic rhetoric of neoclassical comedy with the reforming magistrate's equitable consideration of circumstances in applying the law.

Interestingly enough, Whetstone's preface to Fleetwood engaged in a kind of critical manifesto for English academic theatre. On the one hand, Whetstone criticised Italian intrigue comedies for being 'lascivious' in condoning adultery; on the other, he lambasted the native English morality play, with its devils and angels, for lacking the rhetorical probability of Italian intrigue comedy. 'The *Englishman*', he wrote, 'groundes his work on impossibilities: ... he ... bringeth Gods from Heaven, and fetcheth Deuils from Hel'.[42] His own play's action, though not tied to unity of place, aimed at circumstantial probability, just as it was thematically concerned with the upright magistrate who administered justice by evaluating circumstances. In Act 3, scene 3 of the second part of the play, the King of Hungary asks his chief justice whether provision has been made for Justices of Peace 'to heare and determine' suits between a corrupt magistrate and a 'poore man' who has been abused by him.[43] Another author who was probably at the performance of Gascoigne's *Supposes* in 1566 was Philip Sidney (Gray's Inn, 1567). His *Old Arcadia* (*c*. 1579) would, like Gascoigne and Whetstone, adapt the forensic structure of Terentian comedy to a trial conducted by an equitable magistrate, and would include topical criticism of negligent 'shepherds', or Justices of Peace.[44]

Just as the rhetoric of evidence, probability, and equity dominated Inns of Court fiction and drama of the 1570s, so it did in the legal literature of the Inns. The trial scenes of the *Old Arcadia* and of *Promos and Cassandra* are marked by the same interest in equitable interpretation and evidence evaluation that is such a prominent feature of the *Commentaries or Reports* published in 1571 by Fleetwood's friend and colleague in the Middle Temple, the great lawyer, Edmund Plowden. Indeed, in

1578, the year of Whetstone's play, Plowden's *Reports* were reprinted with a 'table of notable contents' composed by Fleetwood. In 1577 Fleetwood had composed the first of a new genre in local judicial administration – the handbooks for the Justices of Peace – in which he included material on the equitable interpretation of penal statutes.[45] In Plowden's work, too, a new interest in the evaluation of evidence according to probabilities emerges. A jury, he wrote, 'may find their Verdict upon that which appears most probable, and by the same Reason, that which is most probable shall be good Evidence'.[46] And it appears that as part of the building of Middle Temple Hall, carried out under Plowden's treasurership in the 1560s, a painting of the Judgement of Solomon was commissioned which made the difficulties and responsibilities of evaluating evidence into its particular theme.[47]

If we come back, at this point, to the opening of Shakespeare's *Comedy of Errors* in Gray's Inn, 1594, it begins to seem a little less egregious, and a little more like a comment on developments in the adaptation of neoclassical comedy to the reformed evidential plot of the 1570s. Only, what happens in *The Comedy of Errors*, of course, is that the magistrate is called upon to investigate a series of allegations of fraud, adultery, false-witness, theft, and violence in which no one turns out to be actually guilty.

After the confusions of Acts 2 and 3, which feature a suspected adultery where none took place and an arrest for debt where the defendant owed nothing, the whole of Acts 4 and 5 are given over to vociferous, impassioned conflict of testimony as to what exactly has just taken place. The language in these two acts is filled with oaths and accusations of forswearing: 'God doth know' (4.4.66), 'sooth to say' (4.4.70), 'Pardie'(4.4.72), 'Sans fable'(4.4.74), 'So befall my soul / As this is false' (5.1.208–9) 'Ne'er may I look on day nor sleep on night' (5.1.210), 'I never saw the chain, so help me heaven' (5.1.268). Phrases insisting on first hand, ear- and eye-witnessing are no less frequent: 'These ears of mine … did hear thee' (5.1.26), 'I will be sworn these ears of mine / Heard you confess' (5.1.260–1). The word 'perjured' occurs twice, 'witness' occurs four times, versions of 'swear' and 'forswear' appear seven times.

What is it, after all, that placates the law, and lifts the sentence of death against Shakespeare's Egeon? One could say it was the romance of recognition – the fact that Egeon is reunited with his wife and sons, and that the brothers Antipholi and Dromio embrace one another. But that romantic reunion would itself appear wholly improbable and unengaging, were it not for the passionate crescendo of accusations of false witnessing, adulteries, thefts, and assaults that comes, eventually, to the ears of the Duke as he makes the apparently inexorable journey towards the place where Egeon is to die. For the Duke consents to hear and 'determine' Adriana's cause first, before seeing to the execution of Egeon according to the Ephesian law which he announced, at the play's opening, that he could not infringe out of partiality (5.1.167). And in the course of determining the cause between husband and wife, Antipholus and Adriana, we, as audience, begin to infer more inward, and psychological causes for their readiness to believe the worst of one another, thus making us believe in them as characters and engaging us, emotionally, in desire for reconciliation expressed so powerfully in the play's ending.

When, in Act 5, the Duke enters with Egeon of Syracuse, ominously '*bare-headed, with the* Headsman and other Officers', he is interrupted by two long narrations, one spoken by Adriana, impeaching her husband, and one by Antipholus of Ephesus, accusing her. Each of these narratives, though perfectly reasonable as an account of the day's crazy events, acquires its plausible coherence from the mutual suspicion that we infer from the couple's interpretation of the day's mystifying contradictions, supplemented by the glimpse we have had of the tensions of their domestic life. In this way, then, Shakespeare's play both conforms to the model of the reformed neoclassical plot of the 1570s, where the magistrate hears and evaluates evidence, and transforms it into the resource of an entirely new kind of psychological drama, in which what really matters is not a display of justice being done, but an engagement of the audience in inferences about the histories and motives of the characters.

The *Comedy of Errors* was the first English neoclassical comedy to be played at Gray's Inn after George Gascoigne's *Supposes* was performed there in 1566. It reveals the influence of 1570s literature, with its emphasis on equitable magistrates and evidence evaluation, but it also heralds a new age of freedom in the uses of 'supposes' – false or mistaken conjectures – in what we might call the English 'theatre of the psyche'.

Notes

I would like to thank the editors, Jayne Archer, Elizabeth Goldring, and Sarah Knight for their meticulous attention to earlier versions of this paper, and for permitting me to rewrite it after the original argument (presented at their excellent conference in 2006) had been generally incorporated into my book, *The Invention of Suspicion: Law and Mimesis in Shakespeare and English Renaissance Drama* (Oxford: Oxford University Press, 2007). What follows here draws somewhat on that argument, but with new material and a new emphasis.

1 The importance of the legal setting of *The Comedy of Errors* is not only discernible in the play's rhetoric of probable conjecture. In this volume (pp. 264–85), Bradin Cormack brilliantly demonstrates how the play's apparently universal concerns of familial relation and individual identity thematised in the romance of reunited twins and reconciled spouses may be read as emerging from the preoccupations of the Inns of Court revels with the jurisdictional constitution of person, office, and authority. Also in this volume (pp. 286–301), Richard McCoy's fine analysis of the political rather than jurisdictional resonances of 'liberty' in *The Comedy of Errors* reveals the importance of attending to the play's legal location and occasion.

2 For the manner of Gascoigne's translation, and his use of both prose and verse versions of Ariosto's play, see George Gascoigne, *A Hundreth Sundrie Flowres*, ed. G. W. Pigman III (Oxford: Clarendon Press, 2000), pp. 471–2. At the conference on 'The Intellectual and Cultural World of the Inns of Court' (London, 14–16 September 2006), at which a version of this argument was delivered, Professor Alan Nelson objected to subjecting

Gascoigne's play to critical analysis as it was 'merely' a translation of Ariosto. I am a great admirer of Professor Nelson's work, but his objection seems extreme in its historical positivism, and I hope this essay will persuade him of the worth of exploring the translation of Ariosto's comedy, with its legal concerns, into an English Inns of Court context.

3 See Douglas Radcliffe-Umstead, *The Birth of Comedy in Renaissance Italy* (Chicago: University of Chicago Press, 1969), p. 64; Richard Andrews, *Scripts and Scenarios: The Performance of Comedy in Renaissance Italy* (Cambridge: Cambridge University Press, 1993), pp. 31–47.

4 Nino Pirrotta and Elena Povoledo, *Music and Theatre from Poliziano to Monteverdi*, trans. Karen Eales (Cambridge: Cambridge University Press, 1982) pp. 299–334, esp. pp. 316–20; see also Sergio Costola, 'Ludovico Ariosto's theatrical machine: tactics of subversion in the 1509 performance of *I Suppositi*' (PhD dissertation, University of Los Angeles, 2002), pp. 79–88.

5 Alan H. Nelson, 'The universities: early staging in Cambridge', in John D. Cox and David Scott Kastan (eds), *A New History of English Drama* (New York, NY: Columbia University Press, 1997), pp. 59–67 (p. 65). For detailed speculation on the position of the stage in Gray's Inn Hall in 1594, see Margaret Knapp and Michal Kobialka, 'Shakespeare and the Prince of Purpoole: the 1594 production of *The Comedy of Errors* at Gray's Inn Hall', in Robert S. Miola (ed.), *The Comedy of Errors: Critical Essays* (New York, NY: Garland; Routledge, 1997), pp. 431–45.

6 Nelson, 'The universities: early staging in Cambridge', p. 64.

7 Peter Womack, 'The comical scene: perspective and civility on the Renaissance stage', *Representations*, 101 (Winter, 2008), 32–56 (36–7).

8 *Henry V*, Prologue, lines 1–12, in *The Riverside Shakespeare*, ed. G. Blakemore Evans, J. J. M. Tobin *et al.*, 2nd edn (New York, NY: Houghton Mifflin, 1997), p. 979.

9 Anne Barton, Introduction, *The Comedy of Errors*, in *The Riverside Shakespeare*, ed. Blakemore *et al.*, p. 111; Helen Cooper, 'Shakespeare and the Mystery Plays', in Stuart Gillespie and Neil Rhodes (eds), *Shakespeare and Elizabethan Popular Culture* (London: Arden, 2006), pp. 18–41 (p. 34).

10 George Gascoigne, *Supposes, Hundreth Sundrie Flowres*, ed. Pigman, Act 1, scene 1, lines 1–4, pp. 471–2. Further references to act, scene and line in this edition will be given in the text.

11 See, for example, Robert S. Miola's excellent *Shakespeare and Classical Comedy: The Influence of Plautus and Terence* (Oxford: Clarendon Press, 1994), pp. 19–38; on Ariosto's blending of *Eunuchus* and *Captivi*, see Pigman in Gascoigne, *Hundreth Sundrie Flowres*, ed. Pigman, p. 471.

12 The first text we have of *The Comedy of Errors* is that of the First Folio, where the Stage Direction appears, '*Enter the Duke of Ephesus, with the Merchant of Syracuse, Iaylor, and other Attendants*' (see *Mr William Shakespeares Comedies, Histories and Tragedies* (London: Isaac Jaggard and Edward Blount, 1623), p. 85. We cannot, of course, be sure that what appears in the Folio text records the play as performed on 28 December 1594. For the circumstances of the first performance as recorded in the *Gesta Grayorum*, see 'The *Gesta Grayorum* Account [at Gray's Inn, 1594]', in Miola (ed.), *Comedy of Errors: Critical Essays*, pp. 425–9. See also Cormack's and McCoy's extensive discussions of the revels in this volume (see n.1).

13 Shakespeare, *The Comedy of Errors*, ed. Charles Whitworth (Oxford: Oxford University

Press, 2002), 1.1.3–4. Further references to act, scene, and line in this edition will appear in the text.

14 Gascoigne, *Hundreth Sundrie Flowres*, ed. Pigman, p. 270.

15 Adele C. Scafuro, *The Forensic Stage: Settling Disputes in Graeco-Roman Comedy* (Cambridge: Cambridge University Press, 1997).

16 Scafuro, *Forensic Stage*, p. 10.

17 For example, J. M. Kelly, *Roman Litigation* (Oxford: Clarendon Press, 1966), pp. 62–4; other examples are given in Scafuro, *Forensic Stage*, p. 6.

18 Plautus, *Poenulus* ('The Little Carthaginian'), lines 185–6, in *Plautus*, trans. Paul Nixon, 5 vols (Cambridge, MA: Harvard University Press, 1932), IV, 18–19. On *furtum manifestum*, see Alan Watson, *The Law of Obligations in the Later Roman Republic* (Oxford: Clarendon Press, 1965), pp. 230–2; Scafuro, *Forensic Stage*, pp. 458–60.

19 On 'artificial proof' in legal rhetoric, see Barbara J. Shapiro, 'Classical rhetoric and the English law of evidence', in Victoria Kahn and Lorna Hutson (eds), *Rhetoric and Law in Early Modern Europe* (New Haven, CT: Yale University Press, 2001), pp. 54–72.

20 On *indicia*, see Barbara J. Shapiro, *'Beyond Reasonable Doubt' and 'Probable Cause': Historical Perspectives on the Anglo-American Law of Evidence* (Berkeley, CA: University of California Press, 1991), pp. 120–1; John Gilissen, 'La Preuve en Europe (XVIe–XIXe S.)', in *Recueils De La Société Jean Bodin Pour L'Histoire Comparative Des Institutions*, vol. 17, *La Preuve: Moyen Age et Temps Modernes* (Brussels: Librairie Encyclopédique, 1965), pp. 755–833, esp. pp. 759–69; John F. Langbein, *Prosecuting Crime in the Renaissance: England, Germany, France* (Cambridge, MA: Harvard University Press, 1974), pp. 272–9.

21 Ludovico Ariosto, *La Cassaria*, 4.2.148–9; 4.2.159–61, in *Tutte Le Opere di Ludovico Ariosto*, ed. Cesare Segre, 5 vols (Milan: Mondatori, 1974), V, 38.

22 Sir Thomas Smith, *De Republica Anglorum* (written 1562–65), ed. Mary Dewar (Cambridge: Cambridge University Press, 1982), p. 114.

23 Richard Bernard, *A Guide to Grand Jurymen* (London: Felix Kingston for Edward Blackmore, 1627); Bernard, *Terence in English: Fabulae Comici Facetissimi* (Cambridge: John Legate, 1598). For a more detailed treatment of this literature and its relation to drama, see Hutson, *The Invention of Suspicion*.

24 *Proceedings in the Parliaments of Elizabeth I*, vol. 1, *1558–1581*, ed. T. E. Hartley (Leicester: Leicester University Press, 1981), p. 82.

25 Andrews, *Scripts and Scenarios*, p. 43.

26 An exception might be *Gammer Gurton's Needle*, possibly performed in Christ's College, Cambridge in 1550–51, 1553–54 and 1559–60. See Alan H. Nelson, *Records of Early English Drama: Cambridge*, 2 vols (Toronto: University of Toronto Press, 1989), II, 897. This play interestingly transforms the amorous intrigue of Roman New Comedy into concerns with jurisdiction and evidence evaluation in the post-Reformation parish.

27 As Charles Ross points out, Ariosto added the detail of Erostrato's being a law student when he rewrote *I Suppositi* in verse. See Charles Ross, 'Ariosto in prose: nuancing Shakespeare's *Taming of the Shrew*', *Prose Studies*, 29:3 (2007), 336–46.

28 See, for example, Thomas Norton's advice written in 1577 to Walsingham on executing the laws not by informers, but by 'men of best credit and note of uprightnes' who can 'examine the qualitie of every such offence, with all the circumstances bothe of the facte and of the state, and manner of the offender', in *Illustrations of Old English Literature*, ed. J. Payne Collier, 3 vols (London: privately printed, 1866), III, 20–1. See also Fleetwood's

advice to parliament in 1571 on a bill mandating attendance at divine service once a quarter, 'that the penallty of the statute should not goe to promoters' (*Proceedings*, ed. Hartley, p. 200).

29 See Terence Cave, *Recognitions: A Study in Poetics* (Oxford: Clarendon Press, 1988), p. 252.

30 See David S. Chambers and Trevor Dean, *Clean Hands and Rough Justice: An Investigating Magistrate in Renaissance Italy* (Ann Arbor, MI: University of Michigan Press, 1997), pp. 49–50.

31 See James Bradley Thayer, *A Preliminary Treatise on Evidence at the Common Law* (Boston, MA: Little, Brown, 1898), pp. 314–15, discussing Andrea Alciati's definition.

32 Shapiro, *'Beyond Reasonable Doubt'*, 120–56; Michael R. T. McNair, *The Law of Proof in Early Modern Equity* (Berlin: Duncker and Humblot, 1999), p. 263.

33 *The Complete Works of George Gascoigne*, ed. John W. Cunliffe, 2 vols (Cambridge: Cambridge University Press, 1910), II, 82.

34 Jacques Bourgeois (1545), Jean-Pierre de Mesmes (1552), and Jean Godard (1594). See Brian Jeffrey, *French Renaissance Comedy 1552–1630* (Oxford: Clarendon Press, 1969), pp. 21, 38 and 46.

35 For Hopton's judicial work, see *Queen Elizabeth and her Times, A Series of Original Letters Selected from the Inedited Private Correspondence of the Lord Treasurer Burghley, the Earl of Leicester, the Secretaries Walsingham and Smith, Sir Christopher Hatton*, ed. Thomas Wright, 2 vols (London: Henry Colburn, 1838), II, 17, 63, 68, 187; for the dedication, see *The Complete Works of George Gascoigne*, ed. Cunliffe, II, 3.

36 Linda Bradley Salamon, 'A face in *The Glasse*: Gascoigne's *Glasse of Government* re-examined', *Studies in Philology*, 71 (1974), 47–71 (68).

37 *The Complete Works of George Gascoigne*, ed. Cunliffe, II, 82–3.

38 Shakespeare, *Comedy of Errors*, 5.1.398 (Abbess).

39 Jessica Winston, 'Expanding the political nation: *Gorboduc* at the Inns of Court and succession revisited', *Early Theatre* 8:1 (2005), 11–34 (17, 27). See also Jessica Winston, 'Seneca in early Elizabethan England', *Renaissance Quarterly*, 59:1 (Spring, 2006), 29–58.

40 Steve Hindle, *The State and Social Change in Early Modern England, c. 1550–1640* (London; New York, NY: Macmillan Press, 2000), p. 3.

41 *Proceedings*, ed. Hartley, pp. 201–2, 203–4, 205–6.

42 George Whetstone, 'To his worshippfull friende, and Kinseman, William Fleetwood Esquier, Recorder of London', *The Right Excellent and famous Historye of Promos and Cassandra* (London: John Charlewood for Richard Jones, 1578), sig. Aii^v.

43 *Ibid.*, sig. K3^r.

44 See Katherine Duncan-Jones, *Sir Philip Sidney: Courtier Poet* (London: Hamish Hamilton, 1991), p. 48; Blair Worden, *The Sound of Virtue: Philip Sidney's* Arcadia *and Elizabethan Politics* (New Haven, CT: Yale University Press, 1996), pp. 71, 200, 204. See also Robert W. Parker, 'Terentian structure in Sidney's original *Arcadia*', in Arthur F. Kinney (ed.), *Sidney in Retrospect* (Amherst, MA: University of Massachusetts Press, 1988), pp. 151–8.

45 William Fleetwood, *The Office of a Justice of Peace* (London: W. Lee, D. Pakeman, and G. Bedell, 1655). For the date of composition, see *Queen Elizabeth and her Times*, ed. Wright, II, 64: 'Peradventure your Lordship would knowe how myself is occupied. I am in very deed, my Lord, at presente, at the request of dyvers of my frends, setting down an order

how justices of peace shall use themselves in theire offices … At Bacon Howse, in Foster-Lane in London this 30 July, 1577'.

46 *The Commentaries or Reports of Edmund Plowden of the Middle Temple, esq.* (London: Edward Brooke, 1779), p. 412.

47 The painting is reproduced in Hutson, *Invention of Suspicion*, p. 197. On the rebuilding of Middle Temple Hall, see Mark Girouard's chapter in this volume (pp. 144–6), and on the painting, see Tarnya Cooper's chapter (pp. 160–1) and Plate 4.

13

Locating *The Comedy of Errors*: revels jurisdiction at the Inns of Court

Bradin Cormack

The first recorded performance of Shakespeare's *The Comedy of Errors* dates to 28 December 1594, during the Christmas revels at Gray's Inn, an extended fictional event performed by the students in honour of their lord of misrule, the Prince of Purpoole.[1] As represented in the *Gesta Grayorum* (1688), the production was something of a substitute for the serious or 'good Inventions' that the students had planned in honour of a visit paid their court by student representatives from the Inner Temple. Things, however, got out of hand when rowdy visitors to the festivities mobbed the hall's performance space: 'there arose such a disordered Tumult and Crowd upon the Stage, that there was no Opportunity to effect that which was intended'. The Templarians left in disgust, and the students improvised:

> In regard whereof, as also for that the Sports intended were especially for the gracing of the Templarians, it was thought good not to offer any thing of Account, saving Dancing and Revelling with Gentlewomen; and after such Sports, a Comedy of Errors (like to *Plautus* his *Menaechmus*) was played by the Players. So that Night was begun, and continued to the end, in nothing but Confusion and Errors; whereupon, it was ever afterwards called, *The Night of Errors*.[2]

So the story goes. But the fit between crisis and solution is so good as strongly to suggest a staged event. In that case the question arises of the play text's relation to this particular performance context. Links between *The Comedy of Errors* and the content of the students' revels – both, for example, are deeply interested in sorcery as a causal explanation for their staged 'errors' – have led many scholars to argue that at a minimum the students devised part of their festivities in response to the commissioned play.[3] It is also possible that our text of *The Comedy of Errors* represents, in turn, Shakespeare's revision in response to a commission from Gray's Inn. My essay contributes to that second hypothesis by disclosing a dimension of the play and of the culture of legal revelling that might be said to dramatise the formation and transformation of authority.

Certainly, the revels context is suggestive for some of the changes that Shakespeare made to his primary source in Plautus. Most famously, of course, *The Comedy of Errors* extends the comedy of bringing on to stage a pair of long-separated twins who share the same name, Menaechmus in Plautus and Antipholus in Shakespeare, by adding, as servants to the protagonists, a second pair of twins, two Dromios, whose presence alongside their masters marks Shakespeare's vernacular stagecraft as a small overpowering of the classical past.[4] The changes I want to highlight, however, concern what might be thought of as the narrative frames Shakespeare imagines for his action. In each case what turns out to be at issue is *jurisdiction*, the legal administrative principle or practice that defines the scope of a particular judicial power over a given matter or territory: having jurisdiction means having authority, less as a given, however, than as the effect of administrative delimitation itself.[5] Shakespeare's framing moves are interesting, first, because jurisdiction is itself conceivable as a frame, an order that subtends the very possibility of legal authority and judgment. The concept of jurisdiction broadens the significance of the Gray's Inn performance, not just because jurisdiction is a technical matter of interest to lawyers, but also because the student revels are themselves imaginable, I think, as a jurisdictional exercise, a cultural practice for articulating the nature of the Inns' authority as self-regulating professional associations. In this context, jurisdiction helps us appreciate how an event like the student revels or the production of *The Comedy of Errors* could operate culturally as a meditation on the distribution of authority, including the extended authority of the stage or of fiction.

My essay falls into four parts. After sketching in the jurisdictional dimension of *The Comedy of Errors* and, in the second section, the Inns' legal and professional status within London, I describe the institutional character of the revels generally, with attention to each of the three lavish or 'grand' Christmases in the Elizabethan period for which extensive documentary evidence survives: those at the Inner Temple in 1561–62, at Gray's Inn in 1594–95, and at the Middle Temple in 1597–98. In a final section, I return to *The Comedy of Errors* and the jurisdictional cast of its account of relation. Throughout, I will be tracking the work fictions do within a complex of multiple jurisdictions. In so locating these texts, I identify literary representation with the analytical amplification of authority's internal dynamics, this at a moment in which the *differentiated* character of authority was manifest as authority's very ground.[6] So, whereas René Girard, for one, has meditated at great length on the problem provoked by twins as a symbol of non-differentiation and the potential therein for social violence, I mean to draw attention to the implications of what might be called twinned or twin systems, regimes of authority that are at once different and same.[7] In that kind of system, social stabilisation happens not through the sacrifice of the mimetic double that threatens the differentiated order, but rather in the ongoing acknowledgement of the doubling of identity into relation (a process for which the twin is also symbol), and of the social potential inherent in that distributive function.

Twins, places: jurisdiction in *The Comedy of Errors*

Among all the other doubles in *The Comedy of Errors*, the law, too, is a twin.[8] At the play's opening and conclusion and in related scenes in Acts 2 and 3, Shakespeare indexes the doubling of legal norms by exploiting space to index the importance of jurisdictional heterogeneity for the conception and operation of law. In place of Plautus' prologue, which explains the narrative background to the confusions about to unfold, Shakespeare's play opens at a liminal moment in a legal case, as argument is giving way ('Merchant of Syracusa, plead no more' (1.1.3)) to the judgment that condemns Egeon to death, first for having entered Ephesus and then for lacking the money required to ransom his now forfeited life. As the Duke explains, Ephesus has made a law to exclude all merchants of Syracuse just to the extent that merchants of Ephesus, according to an ongoing conflict, are on punishment of death excluded by 'rigorous statutes' from Syracuse (1.1.9). A striking element in the legal catastrophe the Duke relates is that the cities' enactments are at once insistently discrete and insistently mirrors of one another. In effect, the conflict has issued in a parody of natural and international law, in which shared legal norms, deriving not from nature but from positive law, work not to regulate exchange, but to exclude it:

> It hath in solemn synods been decreed
> Both by the Syracusians and ourselves
> To admit no traffic to our adverse towns.
> Nay, more: if any born at Ephesus
> Be seen at Syracusian marts and fairs;
> Again, if any Syracusian born
> Come to the bay of Ephesus, he dies,
> His goods confiscate to the Duke's dispose,
> Unless a thousand marks be levièd
> To quit the penalty and to ransom him.
>
> (1.1.13–22)

Inside the passage's repetitions and recursions, content and form are in scrupulous tension. On the one hand, as a correlative to the absence of commercial traffic, there is no legal traffic between the laws – each operates in its own formal sphere, as the expression of its city's peculiar jurisdiction. On the other, there is only traffic between the two laws, insofar as their contents simply repeat one another. How does it matter, the play opens by asking, that jurisdiction twins the law?

Mirroring this jurisdictional opening, the play concludes with a scene played out in front of a priory overseen by the Abbess who will turn out to be Egeon's wife and mother to the Antipholi. After Antipholus and Dromio of Syracuse (S) flee into the priory to escape the legal mess and violence that, unwittingly, they have helped cause, the Abbess insists on the inviolability of sanctuary, refusing either to surrender Antipholus S or to admit Adriana, the wife of Antipholus of Ephesus (E), within her walls. Her language makes the priory a place of ecclesiastical privilege, a 'peculiar' or 'private' law (Latin *privus + lex*) cognate with the Duke's authority: 'He took this place for sanctuary, / And it shall privilege him from your hands / Till I have brought him to his wits again, / Or lose my labour in assaying it' (5.1.94–7). Against the Abbess's claim here that her jurisdiction operates for the cure of souls, Adriana's sister Luciana urges Adriana to 'Complain unto the Duke of this indignity' (5.1.113), a generic sentiment that parses out also as a quasi-technical claim, insofar as 'dignity' (Latin *dignitas*) is a term for the honour of a held office or privilege.[9] The Abbess has committed an *in*dignity by claiming the dignity of this jurisdiction over Antipholus and within her house. In this sense, Luciana's quibble corresponds to the particular terms of Adriana's appeal to the Duke, as to a regulatory power, for 'justice … against the Abbess' (5.1.134), a statement implying that, by dealing in *in*justice, the Abbess's jurisdiction (which in theory is *for* justice) violates the Duke's superior jurisdiction. Against *The Comedy of Errors'* opening figuration of law as it relates to distinct sovereign entities, the play's final scene represents the city's internal order in terms of the historical tension between the temporal and spiritual jurisdictions over the subject.

In the middle of the play, finally, Shakespeare uses the division of stage space to frame a third crisis, this one jurisdictional in an extended rather than strictly legal sense. When Adriana wonders why her husband has not returned home for supper, her sister Luciana remarks that a wife's role is not so to question her husband, but rather to recognise that, as 'master of his liberty' (2.1.7), a man cannot belong to the domestic sphere in the same way as a woman does. 'Why should their liberty than ours be more', Adriana asks, to which Luciana replies, 'Because their business still lies out o'door', a rhyme that isolates as the play's principal topology the division of world (and stage space) into inside and outside (2.1.10–11). Luciana avers, moreover, that for women a 'headstrong liberty is lashed with woe', insofar as 'There's nothing situate under heaven's eye / But hath his bound in earth, in sea, in sky' (2.1.15–17). As a term for freedom generally and, more technically, for a privilege granted by the sovereign to a person or corporate body, the repeated keyword 'liberty' nicely captures the passage's jurisdictional undertow.[10] The world, in Luciana's telling, is made up of bounded institutional realities nested inside the bounded realities pertaining to nature. In the following act, this tension between bounded and unfettered liberties gives Shakespeare one of the play's most successful scenes, in which Antipholus S gets his twin's supper and Antipholus and Dromio E return home, hungry, only to find the door to their house locked against them and a second Dromio guarding the door, having usurped his twin's place as porter. When Dromio S, inside, defiantly identifies himself to the would-be intruders as 'The porter for this time, sir, and my name is Dromio', Dromio E ignores the qualification by which his twin claims only a temporary role, and replies, 'O, villain, thou hast stolen both mine office and my name' (3.1.43–4).

In two ways, then, and along gender lines, the play's division of domestic and public space helps describe jurisdiction's differently inflected consequences for identity. As Adriana complains, female freedom is compromised insofar as a purely domestic authority is inefficacious when, outside its walls, it enters the place of broader public exchange. As Dromio expresses it, male freedom is differently vulnerable: to the extent that it operates, as it were, between portals, it opens one to the possibility of finding oneself outside the orders that bestow office and name. The city and house are the source of the liberties that constitute freedom, and to be shut out of their economies is to be in a space where anything might happen. As a stranger, Egeon is outside Ephesian liberties. Even more darkly, the communal decision in Act 4 to hand over Antipholus and Dromio E to the rigorous exorcist/mountebank Dr Pinch makes madness and its social consequences into an emblem for the terror of this loosening of jurisdictional identity. The 'dark and dankish vault' where Antipholus and Dromio are imprisoned is at once the underside of 'home' and a frighteningly anti-jurisdictional space (5.1.248).[11]

Twinhood in *The Comedy of Errors* cuts obliquely across these jurisdictional boundaries, mixing and confusing the orders of governance and identity that, Duke-like, the characters unwittingly struggle to keep apart. Only in Act 5 when they come to see the interpenetration of apparently stable and discrete spheres does the action of the play become legible to them. In sum, Shakespeare defines the play's action, its 'errors', and the resolution to those errors, as the effect of the interaction among jurisdictionally distinct spheres of activity and judgment. What can we make of this? As is well known, English law in the Tudor period was less a homogeneous whole than still a system of multiple and interconnected jurisdictions, both in relation to the hierarchical distribution of authority from the central down to the local common-law courts, and with respect to the different non-common law tribunals that operated alongside the common-law forums.[12] Jurisdiction in and around the city of London was especially complex, and we can best illuminate the jurisdictional turn in Shakespeare's dramatic thinking, as well as the significance of the 1594 performance, by noting the ways in which liberty and jurisdictional privilege were live institutional questions for Londoners generally and, within a professional context, specifically so for the lawyers and students at the Inns. I turn now to this context.

Placing the Inns

The four Inns of Court, as well as the subordinate Inns of Chancery, lay outside the medieval city's western walls, in an area that early on was informally known as *Ultra Fletam*, since it lay 'beyond the Fleet River', which emptied into the Thames at the wall.[13] Parts of this area came to be included within the administrative boundaries of London proper early in the thirteenth century, when the city successfully extended its jurisdiction as far west as Temple Bar. The Temple, along with the two Inns therein (Inner Temple and Middle Temple), was found here, and by the Tudor period was counted as being within the London ward of Farringdon Without, a precinct bounded to the west by Temple Bar and divided by the city wall from

Farringdon Within to the east. Slightly further north, Lincoln's Inn (in Chancery Lane) and Gray's Inn ('situate within the mannor of Pirpoole [Purpoole, Portpoole] in Holborn'[14]) were both accounted part of the county of Middlesex, falling as they did just outside the municipal and 'county of city' boundaries that differentiated London both from the suburbs and from the county within which the city was geographically (although not juridically) situated.

Jurisdiction in this area, and especially in Farringdon Without, is best thought of as a palimpsest of alternative liberties. Of prime importance were the fiercely defended 'ancient liberties' of London itself, including its jurisdiction and various legal privileges against county and national authority.[15] Inside the London boundaries that exempted London from other jurisdictions, however, there were in turn various liberties vis-à-vis the city – privileged areas, mostly ecclesiastical in origin, whose inhabitants (as was the case for all liberties in and around the city) remained 'in important respects exempt from the jurisdiction of the Lord Mayor and from the legislation of Common Council [the legislative court at Guildhall]'.[16] The Temple (and its two Inns) was counted among these exempt areas, as was the liberty of Whitefriars, a precinct on the site of a former Carmelite foundation lying immediately to the east of the Temple and linked to it through the Temple's eastern gate. In the Elizabethan period, Whitefriars retained the privileges that until the dissolution had exempted the ecclesiastical foundation from temporal and spiritual jurisdiction. The common lawyers made their home, then, in a space of competing liberties. Crossing a street or passing through a gate might bring a law student from under county-of-city jurisdiction into Middlesex jurisdiction; or into a space such as Whitefriars that, according to a commission report of 1597, seemed to operate 'without any certaine and knowen officer' at all;[17] or into an Inn (as both school and home) whose academic and professional status privileged it in ways similar to London's private jurisdictions more generally.

We can distinguish three effects of this complex play of jurisdiction on the legal culture of the Inns. A first point is simply that the intersection of county, municipal, and private jurisdictions made the experience of legal rule in London uneven. In an illuminating article on the Whitefriars as a disreputable place exploited on the London stage in order to attract audiences to the liberty and its theatre, Mary Bly has emphasised that, far from being legal accidents, the liberties within London 'were specific legal entities, free from the Lord Mayor's jurisdiction and – crucially – self-governed'.[18] Even after a charter in 1608 placed by name a number of these exempt places squarely under the Lord Mayor's jurisdiction, certain of these precincts (including Whitefriars and, within the medieval walls, Blackfriars) retained a great deal of *de facto* autonomy, in addition to certain recognised powers of self-governance, as for the 'keeping and cleaning the public ways in their areas'.[19] The most important privilege pertaining to Tudor Whitefriars was that of sanctuary, an exemption that made visible a historical-temporal unevenness in the city's relation to its pre-Reformation past. As Bly notes, Londoners would have carried with them, as part of local knowledge, the historical fact that when Henry VIII dissolved the Carmelite order in 1538, he 'allowed the area to keep the privilege of sanctuary', a right that 'by 1600 … had evolved into immunity for debtors, escaped felons, illegal foreigners, and sex workers'.[20] This means that in late Tudor London, sanctuary was as likely to be a secular phenomenon indexing the city's layered ecclesiastical history as it was to be an immediately ecclesiastical one. In this context, it is easy to imagine, for example, that the early audience of *The Comedy of Errors* would have felt invited by the play's jurisdictional frames to relate the Abbess's Ephesian priory not just, as Laurie Maguire argues, to the temple of Diana at Ephesus,[21] but also, in a submerged bawdy register, to a liberty such as Whitefriars or Clerkenwell, a former priory lying east of Gray's Inn and just outside London's administrative boundaries: places where, beyond London jurisdiction, prostitutes lived and *laboured*, albeit differently from the Abbess (cf. *Errors*, 5.1.97), on behalf of men. Thus Bly notes that 'Nun in White Fryers' had some currency on stage as a term for Whitefriars prostitutes;[22] and, closer to Shakespeare's play, D. S. Bland notes among the Prince of Purpoole's subjects in the Gray's Inn revels one '*Lucy Negro*, Abbess *de Clerkenwell*', a topical allusion to a brothel keeper there, Lucy Morgan (*Gesta*, pp. 17; 94–5).[23]

A second point is that, within the complex of London jurisdictions, the legal status of the Inns themselves emerged as an identifiable issue. Important here is the fact, as J. H. Baker has laid out, that the lawyers promoted their interests within the London community by structuring their communities as self-regulating, voluntary, but *unincorporated* associations.[24] The strikingly informal arrangement allowed the lawyers to avoid the potentially disadvantageous legal consequences falling on corporations, and to benefit especially from a greater administrative flexibility than would have been possible with a binding charter. When, for example, the lawyers insisted, in the face of an imposed tax, that they were 'to be assessed as separate bodies so that they could apportion the total sum themselves' (both within each Inn and among the four Inns), they gave as their reason 'that wee are noe corporation'.[25] The greater autonomy adhering to the associations as essentially personal rather than artificial bodies meant, however, that the protection of their privilege was less predictable than it would otherwise have been, working chiefly, in Baker's formulation, through 'a combination of trust, agency, contract and custom, and also – perhaps most important – by endeavouring to prevent awkward questions from coming to the fore'.[26]

The relation of the Inns to their environs was one such awkward question. This was especially the case for the Temple, which, as a place of ecclesiastical origin, claimed jurisdictional exemption through a strikingly similar history to that of Whitefriars. The Temple had originally belonged to the Knights Templar, and by papal bull was exempted from temporal or spiritual jurisdiction, standing instead as a 'papal peculiar' immediately under the Roman see. Following the abolition of the order in 1308, the Temple was granted in 1324 to the order of the Hospitallers, from whom the common lawyers leased the site for their institutional use. When

Henry VIII dissolved the Hospitallers in 1540, and thereby brought possession of the Temple into his own hands, he resisted the City of London's attempt to absorb the Temple's privilege into its jurisdiction, and instead allowed the Temple to retain its special status, as now a 'royal' peculiar and as such a place exempted from all jurisdictions subordinate to the Crown's.[27] As a royal peculiar, the Inner Temple and Middle Temple could claim, first, to be extra-parochial, a status that the lawyers took seriously in part because it allowed them to avoid the burden of tithes. One memorable sign of the lawyers' thinking in this regard is that, from some point soon after the passage of the 1601 poor laws (which required parishes to provide for children abandoned within their limits), the Temple lawyers collectively undertook to support infants left at Temple gate, paying for their upbringing and, from a little later in the seventeenth century, according them the surname of Temple. This was an act of charity, but also the lawyers' way of asserting that no parish was jurisdictionally in a position to do the job.[28] With respect to Gray's Inn and Lincoln's Inn, Baker has found evidence in later periods that both associations similarly claimed extra-parochial status, although this was certainly on shakier grounds than for the Temple, given that these associations had no 'peculiar' ecclesiastical history in respect of their territories.[29]

The Temple's relation to temporal jurisdiction was especially vexed, and Baker notes that the lawyers' argument that the Temple fell outside 'the authority and jurisdiction of the city of London', was 'frequently contested by the lord mayors of the city'.[30] (Gray's Inn and Lincoln's Inn, local to Middlesex, were not so situated as to have to answer London jurisdiction in the same way.) Two cases Baker cites are of particular interest. Taken from 1556 and 1669, these involve the attempts of junior members to protect the legal status of the Temple against the Lord Mayor's entering the precinct attended by a sword-bearer 'carrying the sword erect'. As Baker explains, 'the sword was carried in this way, point upwards, within the bounds of the city only, and therefore the lord mayor's coming in this manner was taken as formally asserting a claim to jurisdiction'.[31] On both occasions, and in a particularly impressive skirmish in 1669, students met the affront by pulling the sword down and thereby asserting the Inns' jurisdictional privilege. In 1556, the enthusiastic student seems to have been expelled. In the 1669 case, on the other hand, far from violating Inn norms, the rowdiness seems to have given voice to a position dear to the entire association, and Baker wryly notes that the benchers or senior members arranged for 'dinner at Inn expense for the ringleaders'.[32]

The third and most important point about the Inns' status in London is that, within London's complex jurisdictional scene, the system of professional governance *internal* to an Inn could itself be seen to constitute a jurisdiction, even if the governing members' authority had no formal sanction beyond the voluntary agreement of the members themselves. The laws regulating the lawyers' communities inevitably intersected with those organising the broader polity. As was the case for the livery companies, whose administrative jurisdictions the central common law recognised and allowed as an efficient means to regulate commercial life, the central government had a declared interest in promoting the regulation of the Inns; and W. R. Prest interestingly describes during the Tudor period a process of centralisation in the Inns' internal governance that helped sustain governmental centralisation generally, since it put in place a useable 'command chain' for the implementation of policy.[33] In this sense, the internally constituted authority of the Inns' governing members produced a visible jurisdiction. Moreover, the lawyers' professional sense of themselves was intimately linked to their capacity for self-governance. This point is given powerful expression, for example, in a 1585 legal action brought in Common Pleas by the treasurers of Gray's Inn against a non-paying member, Cotton Gargrave (*d*.1588). The plaintiffs' action has a double orientation to the question of jurisdiction. Emphasising the 'immemorial' customs that allowed the Inn's governors to 'constitute decrees, laws and ordinances for the good rule and governance' of the members and, when those laws were breached, to 'impose pecuniary penalties … according to their wholesome discretions', the plaintiffs' language establishes as a matter of professional pride that the Inn has regular jurisdiction over its members, even as it demonstrates that, for lack of enforceability, the Inn's authority proved in this case simply ineffective (hence the move to common law).[34]

In sum, jurisdiction at the Tudor Inns involved the operation of association norms in their encounter with the other systems of authority that, taken together, rather messily constituted legal rule in London. Internal governance at the Inns produced an image and order of power that perceptibly twinned the orders of governance outside.

Revels jurisdiction

The jurisdictional status of the Inns in London is suggestive for legal revelling and its relation to political life. First, there is a continuity between the implicit licence (as traced by Baker) granted the students bent on protecting Temple jurisdiction and the explicit licence granted the students at all the Inns during their Christmas celebrations. To a modern eye, the extent of the latter liberty seems astonishing. D. S. Bland, in his edition of the *Gesta Grayorum*, reprints from the official Admission Register of Gray's Inn an entry from 6 January 1595 that admits John Spencer, Mayor of the City of London, into 'the society of this inn (*in societatem huius hospitii*)', and which is signed, in an enormous hand, by 'Henrie Helmes Pr[ince of] Purpoole'.[35] The concept of jurisdiction helps make sense of the exemplary tension here between very playful and very serious institutional forms. The point is less that the governors may 'really' have ceded their authority to the student prince during the Christmas period than that the prince's sovereign 'rule' amplifies the jurisdictional cast of authority as a lateral encounter between internally regulated systems, each sovereign in its sphere. Even as they seem to subvert the good order of the school, the revels are legible as a jurisdictional performance on behalf of that order. Viewing the revels in this way extends their politics to include not just the topical content of the plays or masques coordinated by the students, but also the revels' overall theatricalisation of professional privilege as one sign of the active dispersion or distribution of political authority.[36] I would argue, then, that within a specific institutional context the revels functioned much like the commercial drama that self-consciously represented London on the stage and thereby, in Jean Howard's formulation, helped to '*construct* the city and make it intelligible for those *un*familiar with its places or the uses to which they can be put'.[37] Analogously, the revels worked as institutional activations of the physical and conceptual space in which the junior members of an Inn now found themselves. The students' fictive reconfiguration of their professional milieu *represents* a political content, but also *enacts* the jurisdictional scene in which delimited action or practice issues in authority.[38]

As mentioned earlier, there are three Elizabethan 'grand' Christmases for which we have extensive documentary evidence: the 1561–62 revels at the Inner Temple come down as a prose summary reported in the final section of Gerard Legh's *Accedens of Armory*, a popular manual of heraldry first published in 1562; the revels at Gray's Inn in 1594–95 survived in an unusually complete manuscript that was printed in 1688 as the *Gesta Grayorum*; and the Middle Temple revels of 1597–98 come down in a printed version from 1660 based on a surviving manuscript written by Benjamin Rudyerd while he was a student at the Middle Temple and in all probability a participant in the festivities. In each of these, the jurisdictional character of the revels is exemplified through the double representation of office and of territory. In relation to the first, indeed, the most characteristic element in the students' revels was the appointment of a group of fictive officers – the 'revels' Lord Chancellor, Lord Treasurer, Lord Admiral, and so on – to assist the Christmas prince in his festive reign. A first political function of this fictive assumption of office is clarified in a 1540 royal report on the Inns written by Sir Nicholas Bacon, who at thirty was already an 'ancient' or senior member at Gray's Inn. That text concludes (in tacit defence of the frivolities) that the students take up offices mimicking real ones 'onely to the intent, that they should in time to come know how to use themselves'.[39] The judgement implies that the revel fictions were a form of educational practice, with the assumption of authority by the revels council operating as a rehearsal for more serious scenes.[40] Alongside this pedagogical rehearsal of power, however, was the *institutional performance* as such, since between the fictive sovereignty of the student prince and the sovereignty of the monarch and her court there fell the regular order of the Inn. And in relation to that governance, the students' performance staged the normative status of the Inn's self-governance.

The revel prince's authority was refracted not only in his officer-delegates, but also in alternative sovereign figures whose authority mirrored his own. This explicitly jurisdictional dynamic issues in an intensified apprehension of the Inn as a place whose authority is territorially delimited. To take the latest of the three Christmases first, the 1597–98 Middle Temple revels, overseen by the Prince d'Amour, revolved around the defence of the prince's title as sovereign of love, a thematic that responded to the fact that revelling at the Inn (and thus the validity of the prince's title) had been suspended for a number of years. Predictably, the students first measure the prince's authority against the senior members of the Inn, such that it can be said of his revels subjects that 'if any man do maintain … the Authority of the Benchers or utter Barristers within his Excellencies Dominons, this is high treason'.[41] In the elaborate proclamation of the prince's title that opens the revels, the jurisdictional scope of the prince's authority is twice foregrounded in relation to local and national authority. The orator begins with recent history: 'It is not unknown how for these eight years past, the youthful, couragious, and victorious state of the Knights Templars hath been ruined … For who of late hath taken the honorable course of Love, or so much as set foot in the pathway of Chivalry?' The knight who 'relieth more on his Manly courage, than on witty evasions to shift off a quarrel' (a reference, surely, to the forensic arts) 'is now esteemed unexpert and Fool-hardy'. As a consequence of this decline, the orator concludes, 'the merciless troops of Catchpoles dare now make Inrodes to the very Gates of our Cities, where the *Aqueduct in Platea fletensi* had wont to be the uttermost border of their approach' (pp. 129–30). The local reference here is to the Temple's gates, especially the eastern one that gave on to Whitefriars, and to the Fleet River at medieval London's western walls. Catchpoles are sheriff's officers whose role was to track down debtors. So the lament is that a neighbouring authority, taking advantage of the prince's absence, has attempted to erode the prince's territorial jurisdiction. In this playful history, the students mirror back to the Inn the image generally of the Temple's liberties with respect to the city and its officers.

The jurisdictional tenor of this opening unfolds in a different direction when a 'strange Knight' challenges the prince's title by insisting that the 'Regal Title of Prince *d'Amours* [*sic*]' belongs of right, not to the prince, but, predictably enough for a 1590s production, to 'my dread Soveraign', the 'Lady of that fortunate Island', whose 'Kingdom seated in the midst of the Waters, gives the Winds free liberty to spread her glorious fame every where' (pp. 130–1). Faced with this challenge to his authority, the prince decides not 'to expose the tryal of his Title to the hazard of a single combat', and instead turns to the elaboration of those political offices relevant to his own authority: 'the tryal by Combat being upon this occasion put off, the Prince began to settle his Estate in a peaceable form of Government, and to that end caused all his Officers to assemble themselves together, and caused to be read unto each of them … his several charge and duty' (pp. 134–6). A potential jurisdictional crisis between 'sovereigns' issues in the regularisation of governance within the prince's realm. This is a telling result; no clearer emblem could be found for the jurisdictional proposition that authority stages itself not just in the hierarchical division of a *given* sovereign power, but also, bottom up, through the regular practice of power within delimited spheres.

Three years earlier, in the Gray's Inn revels that included the production of *The Comedy of Errors*, territory and office were even more clearly on display. The Prince of Purpoole (a name referencing the ancient manor of Portpoole on which Gray's Inn was sited) reigned for a full six weeks, served by some forty officers and dozens more followers. In this time, the prince made a royal progress through the city; issued formal pardons for licentious behaviour within his realm; received official letters from subordinate rulers (representing the Inns of Chancery associated with Gray's Inn) detailing possible insurrections among the prince's subjects; and entertained embassies both from other kingdoms (Inns) and, in the most elaborate fiction of the whole programme, from Russia, to which the prince, in addition, was supposed to travel on a military mission against the Tartars between 7 January and 3 February. These revels were so grand that they threatened to tumble into the regular school year: 'it was intended that the Prince's "return" from Russia should be celebrated by two further nights of revelling [on 4 February]', Bland writes, even though in the event the senior members of the Inn dismantled 'the stage and spectators' scaffolds. The most he was able to do was to ride in triumph through the City where he was entertained with a Latin oration by a scholar of St. Paul's school.'[42] This curtailing of the programme did not prevent the Queen from wittily acknowledging her revels-cousin upon his return from 'Russia' and, as late as Shrovetide, receiving the prince at court for the performance of *The Masque of Proteus*.

As suggested in this brief summary, the Gray's Inn revels consistently identify the prince's authority as a relation between his kingdom and other territories. At one point, for example, in a playful reference to the virtues of credit as a kind of inter-national glue, his knights are instructed to 'be much in the Books of the worshipful Citizens of the principal City, next adjoining to the Territories of Purpoole' (*Gesta*, p. 41). The revels also included a list of 'tributaries', subjects holding 'Signories, Lordships, Lands, Privileges, or Liberties under his Honour', among whom, for example, we find (in possible tension, as already suggested, with Shakespeare's Abbess) '*Lucy Negro*, Abbess *de Clerkenwell*', who holds the 'Nunnery of Clerken-well, with the Lands and Privileges thereunto belonging, of the Prince of *Purpoole* by Night-service in *Cauda*' (p. 17). The joke pivots on the two puns on 'knight service' and the 'tail' that translates the Latin *cauda*. For the present argument, the most interesting aspect of the joke is that it effectively repeats the Inn's professional privileges, but now in reverse, with the Inn taking the place of the sovereign on whom the Inn's actual liberties depended. The prince's progress through the city similarly indexes the association's status by mimicking the territorial performance of power in the progresses made through London by the Lord Mayor and, of course, the Queen.[43] Territoriality, finally, is the frame in which I would also understand the students' interest in Russia as an alternatively sovereign space and as a military destination for their prince. The text identifies the expedition against the Tartars as being religiously inspired (p. 62), but, as Bland notes, Russia's commercial impor-tance to England is certainly also significant (p. 102). At once religious, diplomatic, and commercial, the prince's journey against the Tartars evokes not only Protestant militarism and English diplomatic journeys undertaken on behalf of the Queen, but also the efforts of the recently incorporated Muscovy company, which, as one alternative to the lawyers' own (unincorporated) association, supported a mercantilist, rather than legal, performance of the nation's territorial identity.[44]

The most complex interplay between office and the territorialisation of privilege occurs in the 1561–62 Inner Temple revels, an event whose textual record constitutes a meditation on the very idea of privilege as delimited private law. These impressive revels were explicitly political in motivation, since the Templars in that year honoured Lord Robert Dudley, in gratitude for his help in resolving an internal jurisdictional dispute with one of the other Inns, by granting him special admission to the Society and electing him Marshall and Constable of the Inn and Christmas Prince. Interceding directly with Elizabeth against two of her judges, Dudley had prevented the Middle Temple from usurping control over Lyon's Inn, one of the three Inns of Chancery traditionally under Inner Temple control. As Prince Pallaphilos, Dudley was assisted by a council of around twenty, including, unusually for festivities generally in the hands of the students, several senior members of the Inn.[45]

As already noted, Gerard Legh's allegorical prose account of the Inner Temple revels appears at the end of his heraldic handbook. My point now in turning at somewhat greater length to Legh (and especially to a curious doubling of names whose significance for the text has been overlooked) is that the textual environment in which these revels are contained clarifies a logic of office and delegation according to which the revels fiction might work seriously to reflect back to the Inn its status as a professional jurisdiction. Legh casts the Christmas celebrations as a dialogue between two characters, both apparently named for himself, whose conversation structures the handbook generally. 'G' (for Gerard) points his interlocutor, 'L' (for Legh), to 'a famous escutcheon of renown' that 'beareth azure, a Pegasus argent'. Recurring to the myths around Pegasus, Gerard explains that the muses associated with Pallas Athena are now to be found in London's 'old forworn Temples', a place where a famous soldier presides: 'Pallaphilos, the High Constable of the Goddess herself, Marshall of the Inner Temple', who sits there with his 'magnificent court'.[46] Legh asks for an account of this wonderful being, and Gerard reports on his visit to the prince's palace, this being the hall where the festivities honouring Prince Pallaphilos – that is, Robert Dudley – took place.

Gerard relates how, upon returning to London from his travels in eastern parts, he was alarmed to hear cannon fire. An 'honest citizen' informs him, however, that this is but a 'warning shot to the officers of the Constable Marshall of the Inner Temple, to prepare to dinner'. The important word here is 'officers', since what follows is a meditation on the Marshall's own office: '"Why", said I, "what is he of that estate, that seeketh not other means to warn his officers, than with such terrible shot in so peaceable a country?"' In response, the citizen says that 'he uttereth himself the better to be that officer, whose name he beareth' (p. 27). The exchange interrogates what it means for the Constable and Marshall of an Inn to be a constable and marshall at all, or a revels Prince a prince. The citizen is pointing out that Gerard has misunderstood the logical relationship between status and action, in supposing that the Constable's action in firing the cannon is explicable through reference to his given 'estate', when in fact his estate is itself made full only through practice: 'he uttereth himself the better to be that officer, whose name he beareth'. The order of the Inns, in other words, is an order of names that do not belong naturally to those who carry them, but which become theirs through the practice of delegation. Gerard's reaction to this account of office is to ask after its particular scope: 'I then demanded what province did he govern that needed such an officer. He answered me the province was not great in quantity, but ancient in true nobility: "A place", said he, "privileged by the most excellent princes[s], the high governor of the whole land"' (p. 27). In response to Gerard's enquiry, the citizen defines the privilege of the Inn as a distributive hierarchical relationship among higher and lower governors.

The following day, Gerard returns to the Temple, where, as he stands marvelling at the arms on display in the Temple Church, he encounters the figure who will guide him further into the law's mysteries: 'There came unto me a herald, by name Pallaphilos, a King of Arms, who courteously saluted me saying, for that I was a stranger and seeming by my demeanour a lover of honour, I was his guest of right' (p. 28). This is an unsettling passage. For, as Legh narrates it, the herald carries the same name as the prince he serves, a curiosity whose force is emphasised by the herald's identification as 'a *King* of Arms', that is, a chief herald, a rank inside the real College of Arms, which, as a royal corporation founded in 1483, had jurisdiction over all matters armorial. Complicating the already complex performance of office, Legh's figure thus merges the two functions of heralds, the messenger of state and the guardian of the aristocratic hierarchy.

What are we to make of the textual play that has a Pallaphilos serve Pallaphilos, and a king the prince? Rather than a confusion, I take this ripple in Legh's text to be a primary guide to the cultural work undertaken by the revellers in their fiction-making. The text ably keeps the two names apart, as though withholding a joke whose shape the reader has begun to see, until the moment when, with Gerard looking in on the feast from a side gallery, the herald formally announces Dudley's presence to the assembled revellers: 'But to proceed. This herald Pallaphilos, even before the second course came in standing at the high table, said in this maner: "The mighty Pallaphilos, Prince of Sophie, High Constable-Marshall of the Knights Templers, Patron of the honourable order of Pegasus"' (p. 33). The herald's attribution of his own name to the prince brings together the two orders for which the name stands, thereby differentiating and coordinating the worlds in which Pallaphilos and Pallaphilos diversely govern. As such, the name at the centre of Legh's text of the revels helps measure the meaning of offices whose efficacy resides exactly in not collapsing into one another. This picture of authority's production inside coordinated spheres of practice makes particularly good sense of the revel fiction that Legh's text records. As a function undertaken within bounds, office yokes together the students' jurisdiction and the political world their jurisdiction playfully reconfigured. First and foremost, the students' fictive assumption of authority operates within *its* bounds. As a fiction about sovereignty, moreover, it also amplifies, more generally, the concept of jurisdictional differentiation through which a prince's authority is cognate with a herald's authority, and both of these with, say, the lawyer's authority as that emerges through his professional practice. Authority, Legh's system of names insists, is everywhere an experiment in jurisdiction.

Notably, Legh subjects his intersecting hierarchies of office to an extreme spatial zoning. Upon first encountering Gerard in the Temple Church, the herald Pallaphilos invites him, as stranger and guest, for a drink and 'such cheer as the time and country will yield us' (p. 28). The herald's rooms are so ordered as to signify degrees of professional authority through degrees of privacy. Each of these is marked by the prestige of the material book proper to the place: 'comely couched books of ancient gests' in an outer office; and 'further within', in a 'private study, wherein sat his Herald Marshall, . . . four ledgers of huge volume, all of single coats [of arms]' (p. 28). In the herald's office, the herald is king; and if the revels prince is Marshall of the Inn, the herald, here, has his own marshall, as a refraction of his authority. Herald Pallaphilos is to these rooms as Prince Pallaphilos is to the palace or Temple Hall, a point Legh now makes explicit when Pallaphilos is said to lead Gerard from the professional 'order of his study' towards the sovereign order of another room, 'the palace of his Prince' (p. 29).

The juridical-administrative process of delegation that coordinates the hierarchies of study, Inn, and state is emblematised, finally, in the very name the herald shares with his prince, a name that in fact allegorises (as an erotic bond) the administrative relationship between *Pallas*'s authority and the delegated authority her authority makes possible in a loving servant (*Pallas-philos*). At the end of the dinner, (Prince) Pallaphilos asks (Herald) Pallaphilos to present him with twenty-four worthy knights of the new order of Pallaphilos. What unfolds between the two protagonists is a dizzying exchange of status and favour between the two officer-delegates. Calling the herald forward to 'understand his pleasure', the prince instantly places that pleasure within a broader hierarchy of pleasure, noting in his own regard that 'it hath *pleased* the high Pallas to think me to demerit the office of this place' (pp. 33–4, emphasis added). Pleasure is an administrative signifier, placing the men in the political-erotic relation to Pallas's anterior authority that their name, too, hints at. The name of Pallaphilos, then, is the name of an office or, better, of office itself – understood both as a hierarchical distribution of authority from the sovereign and as a lateral distribution of authority within a broad jurisdictional field. In that double structure, political action emerges as an always local tension – Prince Pallaphilos says he holds the 'office of *this* place'– between the command that one 'do his office' and the free or loving doing of it (p. 34). In sum, as refracted in Legh's textual meditation on office, and in his conflation of legal authority, the authority of heraldry as an office about office, and the fictive authority of the revels court, professional privilege at the Inn emerges as one constituted jurisdiction among a plurality of jurisdictions; and also as the movement *within* jurisdiction between the freedom to exercise power and the binding command that makes that freedom articulate.

Twins, again: relation in *The Comedy of Errors*

We are now in a stronger position to see *The Comedy of Errors* as a play whose narrative exploitation of jurisdiction is deeply in conversation with a culture that defined authority according to the twinned and delimited spheres in which authority takes shape. In its 1594 Gray's Inn performance, the play's virtuoso doubling of names and of office would have resonated with the complex doublings whereby the revel prince and his court amplified the professional authority of the Inn relative to its governmental others outside the lawyers' walls. Jurisdiction, in other words, is the twin that makes possible the play twins' unsettling disruption and, then, consolidation of status, office, and authority. That dynamic penetrates the play's conception of dramatic action. Specifically, I want to suggest that jurisdiction, as expressed both in the Inns' relation to the London polity and in the students' delimited sovereignty at their festivities, gave Shakespeare a language for representing identity as a relational dynamic between freedom and boundedness.

In a ground-breaking study of how Elizabethan dramatists exploited the forensic, circumstantial narrative of classical Roman comedy at a historical moment when evidentiary norms were undergoing rapid change in the common law, Lorna Hutson has argued that Shakespearean character emerges as one effect of an audience's being asked, in the manner of a jury, to sort through the narrative 'evidence' presented on stage.[47] In her reading of *The Comedy of Errors*, the improbabilities specifically of its romance plot intensify the stakes and formal effect of the characters' forensic activity: 'The play's forensic or legal inquiry into the purely *imaginary* villanies, lewdnesses, and betrayals with which characters are charged' encourages the audience 'to infer more inward and psychological causes for the nature of those imaginings, which, in turn, precludes our sceptical dismissal of the romance denouement, grounding it firmly in our sense of what is emotionally credible'. According to Hutson, then, the *reality effect* that goes under the name of character is the back formation of a mimetic process of inductive reasoning in which the audience is asked to discover, according to probability, hidden causes adequate to the outrageous errors they witness, errors 'so clearly shaped by the creative powers of intense emotional vulnerability'.[48] This is a brilliantly convincing argument about the play and, more generally, the invention of psychological depth on the early modern stage. But if *The Comedy of Errors*, in Hutson's reading, effects a mimesis of characterological depth through the practice of legal *adjudication*, it is also a play whose engagement with legal *jurisdiction* generates a cognate horizontal complexity, instantiated in the character's relation to its others. I conclude by briefly considering this question in relation to the play's treatment of marriage.

Each of the play's two troubled marriages stages the relation between identity and freedom as a jurisdictional question. Adriana's lament is that her husband has become alienated or 'exempt' from her – a word that means both outside her control and, in the context I have been adducing, beyond her jurisdiction, this in the same way that Whitefriars or the Temple were *exempt* from the Lord Mayor's authority. Curiously enough, freedom, here, constitutes an injury, as Adriana makes clear in urging Antipholus S, the twin she thinks her husband, not to add legal wrong to the wrong already done within their marriage:

> Be it my wrong, you are from me exempt;
> But wrong not that wrong with a more contempt.
> Come, I will fasten on this sleeve of thine.
> Thou art an elm, my husband, I a vine,
> Whose weakness, married to thy stronger state,
> Makes me with thy strength to communicate.
>
> (2.2.162–7)

The wife's dependence upon the husband is a cultural convention and, under coverture, a legal reality. But in her opening concession, Adriana argues that it is the husband who has been wronged by being exempted from his jurisdictional dependence upon her. The implication is that his self-identity depends on a correlative self, hers, whose identity is similarly relational. If we take Adriana's 'exemption' seriously as jurisdictional privilege, legal identity is most fully expressed, not as autonomy, but as relational boundedness. To be exempt, here, is to be something other than a self, a point Adriana makes also by drawing on the language of legal incorporation, which allows her to say that Antipholus, in being apart from her, has become 'estrangèd from thyself':

> Thyself I call it, being strange to me
> That undividable, incorporate,
> Am better than thy dear self's better part.
>
> (2.2.111–14)

The model of marriage Adriana articulates is one in which selfhood is premised not on sovereign autonomy, but on a play of jurisdictional relation among parts.

In the case of the play's second marriage, the Abbess/Emilia makes a similar argument about the nature of freedom, but in the opposite direction. Confronted in the public space before her priory with the image of Egeon as a subject literally bound by the Duke's temporal authority, she declares, as Egeon's long-lost wife, that Egeon can be made her husband only by regaining his 'liberty', that is, his autonomy from a superior jurisdiction:

> DROMIO S. O, my old master! Who hath bound him here?
> ABBESS   Whoever bound him, I will loose his bonds,
>   And gain a husband by his liberty.
>
> (5.1.339–40)

According to the Abbess's formula, however, Egeon's liberty from one jurisdiction frees him to be possessed in another. If Adriana articulates freedom as a tension among jurisdictions rather than an exemption from them, the Abbess also makes jurisdictional boundedness a precondition of the sovereign legal identity that, in another of its aspects, is an *unbinding*. Jurisdictional differentiation gives legal expression to the notion that identity is a twinned play in the subject between command and freedom.

In my reading of the legal revels at the Inns of Court, I have argued that the students' fictions are less a direct rehearsal of the political authority a young lawyer might aspire to than an oblique performance of the twinned and twinning jurisdictional order subtending legal authority generally. In *The Comedy of Errors'* dark exploration of the slipperiness of identity within a suspended space of unacknowledged relations, Shakespeare's hidden protagonist may similarly be, not just those characters whose confusions, longings, and injuries call up the bounds that make for their discrete identities, but, as a legal expression of relation's priority, the jurisdictional frame and form that both tragically shapes those bounded identities and comically loosens them.

Notes

Thanks to Jayne Archer, Elizabeth Goldring, and Sarah Knight for their suggestions and for organising the 2006 conference at which I first presented the argument. I am also grateful to J. H. Baker for his kindness with some questions arising for me from his written work on the Inns, and to Bill Brown and Stephen Orgel. For their comments and their invitations to share my work, I thank Janet Halley, Jeannie Suk, and the Law and Humanities Colloquium at Harvard Law School; and Bernadette Meyler and the Law and Humanities Colloquium at Cornell Law School.

1 William Shakespeare, *The Comedy of Errors*, ed. T. S. Dorsch, rev. and introd. Ros King (Cambridge: Cambridge University Press, 2004). All citations are from this edition. On the staging of *The Comedy of Errors* at Gray's Inn, see Margaret Knapp and Michal Kobialka, 'Shakespeare and the Prince of Purpoole: the 1594 production of *The Comedy of Errors* at Gray's Inn Hall', in Robert S. Miola (ed.), *The Comedy of Errors: Critical Essays* (New York, NY: Garland; Routledge, 1997), pp. 431–45.

2 *Gesta Grayorum* (London: W. Canning, 1688). Cited from the modernised text in *Gesta Grayorum or the History of the High and Mighty Prince Henry Prince of Purpoole, Anno Domini 1594*, ed. Desmond Bland (Liverpool: Liverpool University Press, 1968), pp. 31–2. All further references to the *Gesta* are to this edition. On dramatic confusion of the kind recorded in the *Gesta Grayorum*, see William N. West, '"But this will be a mere confusion": real and represented confusions on the Elizabethan stage', *Theatre Journal*, 60 (2008), 217–33.

3 The best account of *The Comedy of Errors* as an Inns of Court drama is Lorna Hutson, *The Invention of Suspicion: Law and Mimesis in Shakespeare and English Renaissance Drama* (Oxford: Oxford University Press, 2007), ch. 4, esp. pp. 147–57. For an extension of the argument in relation to neoclassical drama at the Inns, see also Hutson's essay in

this collection, pp. 245–63. In light of Hutson's work on *supposition* or 'merely probable inferences' in relation to George Gascoigne and Inns comedy generally (*The Invention of Suspicion*, pp. 185–202 (p. 192)), it seems likely that the staging of sorcery at the Inn, whether in the revels or *The Comedy of Errors*, had a legal epistemological, rather than only thematic, dimension. Magical thinking about cause operates, namely, both as an antitype to the law's rational account of causation and, curiously, as a dark analogue to the law's inevitably probabilistic 'conjuring' of cause through the retrospective adjudication of evidentiary signs. For sorcery in the play and the revels, see Richard C. McCoy's essay in this collection, pp. 286–301 (296–7). On the connections between *The Comedy of Errors* and the Gray's Inn revels as evidence of an orchestrated revels event, see also Douglas Lanier, '"Stigmatical in Making": the material character of *The Comedy of Errors*', in Miola (ed.), *Comedy of Errors: Critical Essays*, pp. 299–334; Ros King, 'Introduction', in Miola (ed.), *Comedy of Errors: Critical Essays*, pp. 32–3; and Elizabeth Rivlin, 'Theatrical literacy in *The Comedy of Errors* and the *Gesta Grayorum*', *Critical Survey*, 14:1 (2002), 64–78. On the possible topicality of *The Comedy of Errors* in its Gray's Inn performance, see Maureen Godman, '"Plucking a Crow" in *The Comedy of Errors*', *Early Theatre*, 8:1 (2005), 53–68.

4 On the late Elizabethan stage in relation to classical comedy and specifically the classical forensic plot, as writers exploited it in light of changes within English law in the adjudication of circumstantial evidence, see Hutson, *The Invention of Suspicion*; on vernacular poetry of the 1590s in relation to the classical past, see Sean Keilen, *Vulgar Eloquence: On the Renaissance Invention of English Literature* (New Haven, CT: Yale University Press, 2006).

5 On jurisdiction as a practice, see Richard T. Ford, 'Law's territory (A history of jurisdiction)', *Michigan Law Review*, 97 (1999), 843–930.

6 On the Tudor and Jacobean literary response to jurisdictional multiplicity as an indicator of law's unevenness and of the instability of sovereignty, see Bradin Cormack, *A Power to Do Justice: Jurisdiction, English Literature, and the Rise of Common Law, 1509–1625* (Chicago, IL: University of Chicago Press, 2008).

7 René Girard, *Violence and the Sacred*, trans. Patrick Gregory (Baltimore, MD: Johns Hopkins University Press, 1977). See also Girard, *A Theater of Envy: William Shakespeare* (South Bend, IN: St. Augustine's Press, 2004).

8 On doubling in relation to the unity of Christian marriage and the duplicity of Ephesian magic, see Laurie Maguire, 'The girls from Ephesus', in Miola (ed.), *Comedy of Errors: Critical Essays*, pp. 355–91. On twinning and the doubleness of the image subtending memory and mercantilism, see Shankar Raman, 'Marking time: memory and market in *The Comedy of Errors*', *Shakespeare Quarterly*, 56:2 (2005), 176–205.

9 See, for example, John Cowell's definition of jurisdiction itself: 'Jurisdiction is a dignity which a man hath by a power to doe Justice in causes of complaint made before him.' Cowell, *The Interpreter* (Cambridge: John Legate, 1607), sig. Oo4ᵛ.

10 See, for example, Cowell's definition of *quo warranto* as 'a writ that lyeth against him, which usurpeth any *Frawnchis* or libertie against the king … without good title'. Cowell, *The Interpreter*, sig. Hhh2ʳ.

11 For a study of early modern subjectivity in relation to territorial, social, and economic displacement, see Patricia Fumerton, *Unsettled: The Culture of Mobility and the Working Poor in Early Modern England* (Chicago, IL: University of Chicago Press, 2006). The

classic account of the relation of liberty to juridical identity and citizenship is Hannah Arendt, *The Origins of Totalitarianism* (New York, NY: Harcourt Brace, 1951).

12 On jurisdiction at the national and central level, and in relation especially to the writ through which the common-law courts controlled other jurisdictions, see Charles M. Gray, *The Writ of Prohibition: Jurisdiction in Early Modern English Law*, 2 vols (New York, NY: Oceana Publications, 1994). For a description of the jurisdictional complexity of English law during the Tudor period, presented as an extended description of the various courts and their jurisdictions, see Sir John Baker, *The Oxford History of the Laws of England*, vol. 6 (1483–1558) (Oxford: Oxford University Press, 2003), pp. 117–319.

13 On the *Ultra Fletam*, see Lord Silsoe, *The Peculiarities of the Temple* (London: Estates Gazette, 1972), pp. 3–6.

14 George Buc, *The Third Universitie of England* (London, 1615), appended to John Stow and Edmund Howes, *The Annales or a Generall Chronicle of England* (London: Thomas Dawson for Thomas Adams, 1615), p. 974.

15 On the city's jurisdiction as an expression of its own liberties and as limited by other liberties, see Penny Tucker, *Law Courts and Lawyers in the City of London, 1300–1550* (Cambridge: Cambridge University Press, 2007), pp. 27–46.

16 Valerie Pearl, *London and the Outbreak of the Puritan Revolution: City Government and National Politics, 1625–43* (Oxford: Oxford University Press, 1961), pp. 23–37 (p. 24).

17 Cited in Virginia Gildersleeve, *Government Regulation of the Elizabethan Drama* (New York, NY: Columbia University Press, 1908), p. 145.

18 Mary Bly, 'Playing the tourist in early modern London: selling the liberties onstage', *PMLA*, 122:1 (2007), 61–71 (62). On the liberties outside London's administrative borders, see Steven Mullaney, *The Place of the Stage: License, Play, and Power in Renaissance England* (Chicago, IL: University of Chicago Press, 1988). A particularly fine account of London theatre in relation to the city's historical jurisdictions (including Whitefriars and Blackfriars) is Janette Dillon, *Theatre, Court and City, 1595–1610: Drama and Social Space in London* (Cambridge: Cambridge University Press, 2000), esp. ch. 4 and 5.

19 Pearl, *London and the Outbreak of the Puritan Revolution*, p. 32. For the gap between *de jure* and *de facto* autonomy in the Whitefriars, see Gildersleeve, *Government Regulation of the Elizabethan Drama*, pp. 146–8. The continuously odd status of such privileged places within London is nicely expressed in the fact that Whitefriars in the late seventeenth century came to be known as Alsatia, this in reference to the disputed territory of the Alsace-Lorraine on the border between France and Germany. On Alsatia, see Gildersleeve, *Government Regulation of the Elizabethan Drama*, p. 147; George Drake, 'Tom Jones and *Alsatia*', *Notes and Queries*, 44:2 (1997), 200–1; Clare M. Rider, 'Alsatia: the Inner Temple's lawless neighbour', *Inner Temple Yearbook*, 2004–5 (London: Inner Temple, 2005), pp. 6–9. I am grateful to Dr Rider for alerting me to this highly suggestive name for the later Whitefriars.

20 Bly, 'Playing the tourist', 63. Gildersleeve, *Government Regulation of the Elizabethan Drama*, pp. 147–8, notes that the Whitefriars pretended to rights of sanctuary even after sanctuary was abolished nationally in 1623–24.

21 Maguire, 'The girls from Ephesus', pp. 364–6.

22 On the Whitefriars nun, see Bly, 'Playing the tourist', 63–5.

23 See Richard C. McCoy's essay in this collection, p. 287.

24 John H. Baker, 'The Inns of Court and Chancery as voluntary associations', in Baker,

The Legal Profession and the Common Law: Historical Essays (London: Hambledon Press, 1986), pp. 45–74.

25 *Ibid.*, p. 62.

26 *Ibid.*, p. 74.

27 Silsoe, *The Peculiarities of the Temple*, pp. 7–20.

28 On the Temple's support of abandoned children, datable to as early as 1617, see Frank Douglas MacKinnon, 'The Temple Family', in *Inner Temple Papers* (London: Stevens and Sons, 1948), pp. 24–9; also Silsoe, *The Peculiarities of the Temple*, pp. 82–3.

29 Baker, 'The Inns of Court and Chancery as voluntary associations', p. 61.

30 John H. Baker, 'The Inn and the City of London', in Baker, *An Inner Temple Miscellany: Papers Reprinted from the Inner Temple Yearbook* (London: The Honourable Society of the Inner Temple, 2004), pp. 122–7 (p. 122).

31 *Ibid.*, p. 123.

32 *Ibid.*, p. 124.

33 W. R. Prest, *The Inns of Court under Elizabeth I and the Early Stuarts, 1590–1640* (London: Longman; Totowa, NJ: Rowman and Littlefield, 1972), p. 74.

34 *Treasurers of Gray's Inn* v. *Gargrave* (Common Pleas, 1585). The translated text is given in J. H. Baker, 'The Old Constitution of Gray's Inn', in Baker, *The Legal Profession and the Common Law*, pp. 39–43 (p. 42).

35 *Gesta Grayorum*, ed. Bland, p. x. I am grateful to Alan Nelson, who at the conference on which this volume is based emphasised the visual impact of this and similar entries in the Admission Register.

36 On the theoretical importance of jurisdiction's distributive function, see Peter Goodrich, *Law in the Courts of Love: Literature and Other Minor Jurisprudences* (London: Routledge, 1996); Cormack, *A Power to Do Justice*, esp. pp. 1–10.

37 Jean Howard, *Theater of a City: The Places of London Comedy, 1598–1642* (Philadelphia, PA: University of Pennsylvania Press, 2007), p. 23. Howard's superb study of London localities describes the theatre's exploitation of an uneven distribution of urban experience similar to the unevenness I am identifying with jurisdictional heterogeneity.

38 On the ways in which Inns drama tracked basic constitutional questions in order to promote the place of the common lawyers therein, see, for example, Jessica Winston, 'Expanding the political nation: *Gorboduc* at the Inns of Court and succession revisited', *Early Theatre*, 8:1 (2005), 11–34; Paul Raffield, *Images and Cultures of Law in early Modern England: Justice and Political Power, 1558–1660* (Cambridge: Cambridge University Press, 2004). Whatever the topical force of a play like *Gorboduc* (Inner Temple, 1561–62) or *The Misfortunes of Arthur* (Gray's Inn, 1588–89), I would also argue that its ideological work is best understood as taking place in a field whose primary political force is the jurisdictional frame itself.

39 Edward Waterhouse, *Fortescutus Illustratus* (London: Thomas Roycroft for Thomas Dicas, 1663), p. 546. Cited in Marie Axton, *The Queen's Two Bodies: Drama and the Elizabethan Succession* (London: Royal Historical Society, 1977), p. 6.

40 See Richard C. McCoy's essay in this collection, pp. 286–301 (290–1).

41 Benjamin Rudyerd, *Le Prince d'Amour* (London: William Leake, 1660). Cited from the modernised text provided in Anthony Arlidge, *Shakespeare and the Prince of Love: The Feast of Misrule in the Middle Temple* (London: Giles de la Mare, 2000), Appendix II, pp. 126–64 (pp. 152–3). All further references to the MT revels are to this edition.

42 *Gesta Grayorum*, ed. Bland, p. xv.

43 On political progresses in London, see, for example, William Leahy, *Elizabethan Triumphal Processions* (Aldershot: Ashgate, 2005); Hester Lees-Jeffries, 'Location as metaphor in Queen Elizabeth's coronation entry (1559): *Veritas Temporis Filia*', in Jayne Elisabeth Archer, Elizabeth Goldring, and Sarah Knight (eds), *The Progresses, Pageants and Entertainments of Queen Elizabeth* (Oxford: Oxford University Press, 2007), pp. 65–85. It seems likely that the law students' revel procession also invoked, now within a narrower institutional context, the rituals associated with the annual induction of senior lawyers to the order of serjeant. Like the revels, this ceremony involved obligatory feasting, highly ritualised clothing, and an impressive procession in which the gathered legal community led the new serjeants to Westminster Hall for their admission to the order. See John H. Baker, *The Order of Serjeants at Law: A Chronicle of Creations with Related Texts* (London: Selden Society, 1984), pp. 84–107, esp. pp. 88–92.

44 On Russia and the Muscovy Company in relation to early modern drama, see Daryl W. Palmer, *Writing Russia in the Age of Shakespeare* (Aldershot: Ashgate, 2004); Felicia Londré, 'Elizabethan views of the "Other": French, Spanish, and Russians in *Love's Labour's Lost*', in Felicia Hardison Londré (ed.), *Love's Labour's Lost: Critical Essays* (New York, NY: Garland, 1997), pp. 325–44.

45 On the background and organisation of the revels, see Marie Axton, 'Robert Dudley and the Inner Temple revels', *Historical Journal*, 13:3 (1970), 365–78; also D. S. Bland (ed.), *Three Revels from the Inns of Court* (Trowbridge: Avebury, 1984), pp. 12–17; Olga Horner, 'Christmas at the Inns of Court', in Meg Twycross (ed.), *Festive Drama* (Cambridge: D. S. Brewer, 1996), pp. 41–53.

46 Gerard Legh, *The Accedens of Armory* (London: Richard Tottil, 1562). Cited from the modernised text in Bland (ed.), *Three Revels from the Inns of Court*, pp. 9–46 (pp. 35–6). All further references to the IT revels are to this edition. On Legh's record of the revels, see Paul Raffield's essay in this collection, pp. 32–50.

47 Hutson, *The Invention of Suspicion*, p. 155.

48 *Ibid.*, pp. 155–6; 154.

14

Law sports and the night of errors: Shakespeare at the Inns of Court

Richard C. McCoy

The revels at Gray's Inn in the winter of 1594–95 were a very grand affair, lasting from 20 December to Shrovetide, 3 March, 'So that our *Christmas* would not leave us, till such time as *Lent* was ready to entertain us'.[1] They attracted England's greatest and brightest, from Queen Elizabeth and the Earl of Essex to William Shakespeare and Francis Bacon. Throughout its various 'grand nights', these stars of the Elizabethan world picture were ready for their close-ups, and their alignment was unusually harmonious. Within a few years, that harmony would be shattered as Essex and his followers drifted towards open rebellion, but, for this occasion, everyone was on their best behaviour. Still, the word 'revel' is rooted in rebellion, and, in their odd blend of unruly energies and sumptuous ceremonial, the revels at Gray's Inn help highlight tensions pervading the Elizabethan world picture. Indeed, they provide us with striking snapshots, some formal and carefully posed and others rambunctious and confusing, of that world's major players and their conflicting agendas.

The anonymous record of these festivities, entitled the *Gesta Grayorum, or the History of the High and Mighty Prince Henry Prince of Purpoole*, was not printed until 1688, but the publisher is certain that the 'ingenious Gentlemen' who staged them intended 'to leave to succeeding Times the Memory of those Actions'.[2] The title alone suggests the ironic pomposity typical of these extravagant feasts of misrule, but members of the Inns of Court took their revels seriously, and their grandiloquence was not always ironic. As Philip Finkelpearl says, 'We will probably come close to the true tone of the revels if we see them as a mixture of disorderly conduct, mock solemnity, and a serious miming of dignified roles.'[3] He adds that the 'atmosphere in these revels is a mixture, not a compound, of youthful idealism and cynical sophistication, and the two attitudes seem to coexist comfortably.'[4] The *Gesta Grayorum* readily combines grave solemnity and rude misrule, but the mixture can still be confusing most notably on the night of the performance of Shakespeare's play which was described as a night of 'nothing but Confusion and Errors' (p. 32).

The account begins with the election of Henry Helmes, 'a very proper Man of Personage, and very active in Dancing and Revelling' (p. 6), as Prince of Purpoole, and the festivities start on 20 December with his 'glorious Inthronization' (p. 16).

The list of more than seventy 'Officers and Attendants' (pp. 10–13) in his entourage conveys the splendour of the event, as does the entry of 'the Prince's Champion all in compleat Armour, on Horse-back' into the great hall (p. 14). But ribaldry dominates the descriptions of 'Homagers and Tributaries', including Lucy Negro, Abbess of the 'Nunnery of Clerkenwell' and her 'Choir of Nuns … to chaunt *Placebo* to the Gentlemen of the Prince's Privy Chamber' (p. 17). 'Nunnery' was slang for a brothel, and young blades at the Inns of Court prided themselves on their prowess with prostitutes. Fondly recalling his own time at the Inns, Justice Shallow boasts in *2 King Henry IV* that 'we knew where the bona-robas were, and had the best of them all at commandment' (3.2.20–1).[5] For the coronation of the Prince of Purpoole, another tributary is ordered to present him with 'Cunny-Furr … to line his night-Cap, and face a pair of Mittins' (*Gesta*, p. 18). By contrast, the revels conclude on 3 March, Shrovetide, with 'a very stately Mask' (p. 86) in honour of Elizabeth, 'the greatest Queene / That hath or shall a Regall scepter sway' (p. 85). Raunchy accounts of sea battles against Amazons in their ship, 'the *Rowse-flower*; wherein the Merchant came up with her in such close manner, that he brake his Boltsprite in her hinder Quarter' (p. 66), are followed by Petrarchan professions of love for the 'Excellent Queene, trew adamant of Hartes' (p. 83). Laws are laid down and abruptly abrogated, pardons are issued and voided by multiple exceptions, and pageants are disrupted by rowdy disorders, most dramatically on the night when the *Comedy of Errors* was performed in the great hall of Gray's Inn.

This 'next grand Night was intended to be upon *Innocents-Day*' (p. 29), 28 December, and the splendour of the coronation the week before stirred such excitement that a 'great Presence of Lords, Ladies, and worshipful Personages, that did expect some notable Performance at that time' (p. 29) filled the great hall to capacity. Unfortunately, according to the *Gesta Grayorum*, 'there was no convenient room for those that were Actors' (p. 29), and 'there arose such a disordered Tumult and Crowd upon the Stage, that there was no Opportunity to effect that which was intended' (p. 31). Apparently put out by the crowds, the 'Lord Ambassador' from the Inner Temple and his entourage concluded 'that they were not so kindly entertained, as was before expected', and they departed in a huff, 'discontented and displeased' (p. 31). This segment concludes by recording that it was

> thought good not to offer any thing of Account, save Dancing and Revelling with Gentlewomen; and after such Sports, a Comedy of Errors (like to *Plautus* his *Menaechmus*) was played by the Players. So that Night was begun, and continued to the end, in nothing but Confusion and Errors; whereupon, it was ever afterwards called, *The Night of Errors*. (pp. 31–2)

This is, rather shockingly, our first recorded review of a Shakespeare play, described here as a feeble substitute for some truly 'notable Performance' by the members of Gray's Inn; the members are presumably the 'Actors' for whom 'there was no convenient room', and they are not to be confused with the Lord Chamberlain's 'Players'.

The contempt for these players gets even harsher in the mock-trial of those deemed responsible for this 'mischanceful Accident' (p. 32) launched the next night. Because it was seen as 'a great Discouragement and Disparagement to our whole State', an official inquiry by 'a Commission of *Oyer* and *Terminer*' (p. 32) arraigns the 'Sorcerer or Conjurer' (p. 32) supposedly responsible for the 'Throngs and Tumults, Crowds and Outrages' (pp. 32–3).[6] He is also charged with foisting upon the assembly 'a Company of base and common Fellows, to make up our Disorders with a Play of Errors and Confusions' (p. 33). The description of Shakespeare and his company as 'base and common Fellows' recalls Robert Greene's notorious jibe at Shakespeare as an 'upstart Crow' made just two years earlier.[7] Greene was featured prominently in *The Phoenix Nest*, an Inns of Court anthology published the year before, where he was described as a 'worthy Gentleman, *a braue Scholler, and M. of Artes in both Vniuersities*'.[8] Behind such insults is the university wits' snobbish disdain for actors and others deemed their social and intellectual inferiors.

Scholars continue to argue about whether the 'Errors and Confusions' of the 'grand Night' of 28 December were staged or genuine. Leslie Hotson believes that the disorders were deliberately arranged as a 'necessary prologue' to an inevitable restoration of harmony, and Helen Ostovich also sees such disruptions as part of the pattern of misrule.[9] On the other hand, D. S. Bland, the most recent editor of the *Gesta Grayorum*, is certain that the 'record leaves no doubt that the disorders were quite unexpected', and Douglas Lanier argues that, for Gray's Inn, 'the damage to honor and reputation … was quite real'.[10] Overcrowding and struggles among a 'host of different artistic decision makers' could cause real problems, as Graham Parry and Barbara Ravelhofer point out, and masques were usually performed in fairly chaotic circumstances.[11] Moreover, the confusion surrounding this performance of *The Comedy of Errors* makes it hard to understand its actual reception. Scorn for the play and the 'base and common Fellows' who staged it may be jocular but insult humour still stings. Shakespeare may have returned the insult in his next play. Many discern links between the *Gesta Grayorum*'s 'Ambassador from the mighty Emperor of *Russia* and *Moscovy*' (p. 59) and the masque of Muscovites in *Love's Labour's Lost* (5.2.122).[12] Lynne Magnusson sees that play's mockery of the masquers' mockery as payback for lordly derision, especially in the ladies' determination 'To dash it like a Christmas comedy' (5.2.462).[13] Yet contempt for plays and players was unlikely at the Inns of Court where many members were, like John Donne, great frequenters of plays.[14] Moreover, insults to Shakespeare had already backfired badly, as Henry Chettle recognised in his apology for Greene's slur: not only was Shakespeare an accomplished writer, but he also had the support of 'diuers of worship'.[15]

By 1594, 'diuers of worship' were providing Shakespeare with even more support, and, by late December, his career had taken off. He had recently secured the patronage of one of Gray's Inn's most glittering and exalted members, Henry Wriothesley, the Earl of Southampton (Gray's Inn, 1589), and backing from the Earl probably helped secure his play a prominent place in the festivities and could not be easily discounted. Shakespeare's dedication of *Venus and Adonis* and *The Rape of Lucrece* the year before had been well received, and both poems served up the posh, sexy, and learnedly classical fare savoured at the Inns of Court. *The Comedy of Errors* has a comparably illustrious pedigree, drawing on Plautus, one of the most respected authors of ancient Rome.[16] Even more important was the patronage of Henry Carey, Baron Hunsdon, Elizabeth's Lord Chamberlain, the official responsible for providing the Queen's Christmas entertainment. Carey had just reconstituted his own theatrical company by drawing the best actors from rival companies sidelined for years by the plague, and he and the Lord Admiral now had control over every show in town.[17] In the spring of 1594, Shakespeare became the resident playwright and shareholder in the Lord Chamberlain's Men. With the abatement of the plague, they could finally play at court for the first time in years, and, as the editor of the Oxford *Comedy of Errors*, Charles Whitworth, explains, a performance at Gray's Inn 'must have seemed to them almost as prestigious as a Court appearance, in view of the number of high-ranking dignitaries and noblemen in attendance.'[18] Gray's Inn was especially eager to put on a spectacular show because 'such Pass-times had been intermitted by the space of three or four Years, by reason of Sickness and Discontinuances' (p. 5). It was a grand venue and an auspicious moment for a spectacular debut.

Shakespeare made the most of this extraordinary opportunity. *The Comedy of Errors* fits its context perfectly and it addresses and resolves audience concerns brilliantly. Charles Whitworth sees this 'short, boisterous comedy with a joyously festive ending' as the perfect nightcap for 'an evening of carnivalesque gaiety'. For this reason, he thinks it impossible that it could have been an improvised substitution or dismal flop, adding that:

> It is very unlikely that an outside professional company could have been summoned at the last minute to replace another aborted performance in the evening's programme, as the *Gesta Grayorum* account may lead us to imagine. The 'trial' of the 'sorcerer or conjuror,' who was presumably the member of the Inn responsible for organizing the evening's entertainment ... was only a game and it was only pretended that he had 'foisted' a company of professional players upon the assembly without their prior knowledge or approval.[19]

The trial echoes many of the themes of the play and concludes with the familiar reversals of feasts of misrule. The 'Prisoner was freed and pardoned' and the prosecutors sent to the stocks, 'And this was the End of our Law-sports, concerning the Night of Errors' (p. 34). The horror and shame supposedly caused by an affront to the dignity of Gray's Inn is dissipated by 'mocking thus at our own follies' (p. 34).

Far from being a 'mischanceful Accident', Shakespeare's play illuminates its context by dramatising some of the *Gesta Grayorum*'s major themes. Noting this correspondence, Ros King contends that 'the play was chosen, and the words of the *Gesta* devised, to complement each other.'[20] 'A man is master of his liberty' (2.1.7) in *The Comedy of Errors* – 'liberty' is a term repeatedly invoked in the play – and, for the Inns of Court, liberty is an essential value.[21] Ben Jonson dedicates *Every Man Out of His Humour* 'To the Noblest Nurseries of Humanity and Liberty in the Kingdom: The Inns of Court', and says it flourishes during their law sports, 'when the gown and cap is off and the Lord of Liberty reigns'.[22] Liberties taken during the revels can be merely libertine, and *The Comedy of Errors* easily captures the *Gesta Grayorum*'s atmosphere of free-wheeling sexual licence: the description of Luce's vast, spherical proportions, encompassing entire countries, including, of course, the Netherlands (3.2.143–4), anticipates subsequent dirty jokes about the enemies of Gray's Inn from 'Gelderland', 'Netherland', 'Cleive', and the 'Low-Countries' (p. 66).[23] Shakespeare knew his audience well and could cater to their more sophomoric and bawdy tastes.

At the same time, liberty acquires a graver political significance in both the revels and Shakespeare's play. 'Revel', as noted earlier, is etymologically rooted in rebellion, and Wilfrid Prest has shown how 'outbreaks of student rebellion' at the Inns of Court were sometimes prompted by serious grievances and desires for reform.[24] At the same time, the Christmas 'parliaments' that organised the revels and elected their leaders saw the Inns' system of governance and recreation as an attractive alternative to conflict and revolt. They proudly regarded the Inns as an exemplary 'balanced polity, each part of which had a limited share in the power of government', and their customs and practices contributed to emergent ideas of rule by consent.[25] Friendship is seen as the foundation of good government, and the friendship between Gray's Inn and the Inner Temple is the virtue celebrated in the *Gesta Grayorum*'s *Masque of Amity*. In earlier court revels, such as Richard Edwards's *Damon and Pythias* (1564), it serves an explicitly political function; the friendship of the titular heroes inspires the otherwise cruel Dionysius to renounce tyranny and the 'flatt'ring sycophants' who encourage it, and the play ends with a hymn asking that God grant Queen Elizabeth, 'True friendship and true friends full fraught with constant faith' near the beginning of her reign.[26] In *The Misfortunes of Arthur*, performed at Gray's Inn in 1588, Mordred ignores this lesson at his peril. Though warned by a wise counsellor that loyalty cannot be forced and can come only from the heart, he still seeks to impose 'whatsoeuer the Soueraigne wills, or nilles' while forcing subjects to submit 'against their wills'.[27] Mordred meets the tyrant's end and dies in battle. Marie Axton has noted the doggedly admonitory function of these performances, in which flattery and advice, political speculation, and careful protest are combined.[28] More recently, Jessica Winston has described Inns of Court dramas such as *Gorboduc* as a medium for 'public discourse about governance in Elizabethan England'.[29] All the privileged participants in these law sports saw themselves as 'Lords of Liberty', using these occasions to assert their honour and autonomy and to rehearse the roles they hoped to assume in society.[30] The Inns of Court were regarded as 'a kind of aristocratic University', and their members saw themselves as the 'creame o'th kingdome'.[31] Therefore revellers at the Inns were expected to conduct themselves, in the words of an early Tudor commission, as they would 'in the King's highness house and other noble men, and this is done onely to the intent that they should in time come to know how to use themselves.'[32] As Elizabeth's reign entered its last decade, the revellers in the *Gesta Grayorum* still shared these aspirations. They too considered themselves the 'creame o'th kingdome' and hoped for an appropriately prominent role in government. The members of Gray's Inn began with festivities befitting a royal court and concluded with a visit to the Queen's actual palace at Whitehall. Undoubtedly, a good time was had by all, but some who aspired to a more permanent place at court also hoped that these extravagant celebrations would subsequently help them 'know how to use themselves'. As we shall see, such a quest was never straightforward even during the revels. The *Gesta Grayorum* concludes with the revellers yielding some of their liberty and surrendering to their sovereign. The protagonists of *The Comedy of Errors* must first lose themselves before they can learn 'to use themselves'.

In *The Comedy of Errors*, the protagonists are supposed to be 'lords of liberty', but liberty, for them, proves paradoxical and problematic. In one of the play's most declamatory passages, Luciana insists that 'A man is master of his liberty', and follows through with a cosmic defence of male supremacy:

> There's nothing situate under heaven's eye
> But hath his bound, in earth, in sea, in sky.
> The beasts, the fishes, and the wingèd fowls
> Are their males' subjects and at their controls.
> Man, more divine, the master of all these,
> Lord of the wide world and wild wat'ry seas,
> Indued with intellectual sense and souls,
> Of more preeminence than fish and fowls,
> Are masters to their females, and their lords:
> Then let your will attend on their accords.

(2.1.16–25)

As Eamon Grennan notes, Luciana's 'eloquent secular sermon on degree' offers yet another version of Tillyard's Elizabethan world picture, and patriarchal ascendancy is strenuously asserted.[33] Yet here as elsewhere and everywhere, that picture is fraught with problems, starting with assertions of man's mastery in a play where men are clueless, helpless, and continually threatened with bondage.

Bondage is both political and sexual, and the heroes' attitudes towards bondage are profoundly inconsistent, rendering their conception of liberty comparably blurred. Antipholus of Ephesus impotently rages against those who seek to bind him, but Antipholus of Syracuse is ambivalent and oddly passive. The latter may recoil in horror at the prospect of incorporation of his 'dear self's better part' (2.2.123) by the overbearing Adriana, much as his servant runs from engulfment by Luce, but he yearns for domination by Luciana: 'Teach me, dear creature, how to think and speak' (3.2.33). Simultaneously unnerved and allured, he still seems ready to surrender despite intense misgivings:

> Against my soul's pure truth why labour you
> To make it wander in an unknown field?
> Are you a god? Would you create me new?
> Transform me, then, and to your power I'll yield.
>
> (3.2.37–40)

Calling her a siren and a mermaid, he is even ready to drown himself and die: 'And in that glorious supposition think / He gains by death that hath such means to die' (3.2.50–1). His 'glorious supposition' recalls George Gascoigne's *Supposes*, an earlier comedy of errors presented at Gray's Inn, where supposes and suppositions are defined as 'nothing else but a mistaking, or imagination of one thing for an other'.[34] Such mistaken suppositions afflict almost everyone in Shakespeare's play. Antipholus's abrupt infatuation with Luciana may be just one more error among many, and, as soon as she leaves, he rapidly recoils. When he first arrived in Ephesus, he was reluctant to immerse, much less drown, himself: 'I to the world am like a drop of water / That in the ocean seeks another drop, / … So I, to find a mother and a brother, / In quest of them unhappy, lose myself' (1.2.35–40). As soon as Luciana leaves, his resistance increases because he fears that her 'gentle sovereign grace, / Of such enchanting presence and discourse, / Hath almost made me traitor to myself' (3.2.159–61). He worries that he is literally enchanted and, fearing that 'There's none but witches do inhabit here' (3.2.155), he resolves to escape Ephesus. Increasingly convinced that 'here we wander in illusions', he can only pray that 'Some blessed power deliver us from hence!' (4.3.41–2).

As the play nears its end, the errors only multiply, their liberties grow more imperilled, and the heroes' adversaries grow more sinister, seeking only to bind them tighter. The Syracusan Dromio tells his master that the arresting officer 'came behind you, sir, like an evil angel, and bid you forsake your liberty' (4.3.19–20), and they both see the courtesan as 'the devil' frightening them with 'her chain' (4.3.73–4). The worst is Doctor Pinch, a preposterous 'conjurer' called in to exorcise Antipholus of Ephesus – 'I charge thee, Satan, hous'd within this man / To yield possession to my holy prayers, / And to thy state of darkness hie thee straight' (4.4.52–4) – but he can only impose further bondage: 'Mistress, both man and master is possessed, / … They must be bound and laid in some dark room' (4.4.90–2). Adriana embraces this solution with a vengeance, and she is determined to 'bind him fast / And bear him home for his recovery' (5.1.40–1). In the midst of all this increasingly Manichaean and oppressive religious hysteria, their long-lost mother materialises to rectify all errors and 'make full satisfaction' (5.1.399). The matriarch turns out to be the only one who can make a man 'master of his liberty' and free him from bondage and confusion.

Emilia is a benign but ambiguous character. She is, on the one hand, a religious figure, garbed in the habit of a nun and an abbess and revered by the Duke as 'a virtuous and reverend lady' (5.1.134). The protection she offers is also derived from an older ecclesiastical order, now imperilled by the Reformation but not wholly suppressed.[35] Defending her son from his pursuers, she says 'He took this place for sanctuary, / And it shall privilege him from your hands' (5.1.94–5). Her ministrations are medical and spiritual, consisting of 'wholesome syrups, drugs and holy prayers', and they are deemed a 'charitable duty of my order' (5.1.104 and 107). Moreover, she takes on the role of a *dea ex machina*, imparting a sense of what Kent Cartwright calls 'immanent Providential design rather beyond the chance and fortune that typically govern comedy and farce'.[36] At the same time, the cures she prescribes are less spiritual than practical and down to earth. Unlike Doctor Pinch, she claims no supernatural powers to cast out devils or to 'conjure ... by all the saints in heaven' (4.4.55), and she binds no one.[37] Rebuking Adriana's possessive jealousy, she opposes threats of bondage with the festive liberty exalted by law sports that provide the play's occasion:

> Thou sayest his sports were hinder'd by thy brawls;
> Sweet recreation barr'd, what doth ensue
> But moody and dull melancholy ...
> In food, in sport and life-preserving rest
> To be disturb'd, would mad or man or beast.
>
> (5.1.77–84)

When reunited with her own long-lost husband, Emilia practises what she preaches, saying 'whoever bound him, I will loose his bonds / And gain a husband by his liberty' (5.1.340–1). Finally, she saves her sons and restores their identity, inviting all to a baptismal or 'gossips' feast' (5.1.405) that allows, as Reg Foakes explains, 'each of the main characters ... to be, as it were named, to discover, or rediscover, his or her real identity'.[38] This happy reunion represents a rebirth, and its emphasis on 'nativity' (5.1.404) not only is seasonally apt but it also counters her son's morbid if 'glorious supposition' that love 'gains by death that hath such means to die' (3.2.51). Despite its religious aura, the play's emphasis on 'sweet recreation' is consistent with the secular and festive energies of the *Gesta Grayorum*'s law sports. Emilia restores her husband and her sons as 'lords of liberty'.

In the end, Shakespeare's Antipholus of Syracuse learns not to relinquish his liberty too easily. When he first fell in love with Luciana, he rashly promised 'Thee will I love, and with thee lead my life' (3.2.67). By the play's end, he is more cautious, assuring her only that 'What I told you then, / I hope I shall have leisure to make good, / If this be not a dream I see and hear' (5.1.374–6). In their first encounter, Shakespeare prefaces his hero's romantic grovelling with a courtly compliment to Queen Elizabeth. Antipholus begins praising his new mistress by comparing her knowledge and grace to 'our earth's wonder, more than earth divine' (3.2.32), which can be taken as a reference to the Queen, and, if the play were performed at court, his compliment could easily have been taken accordingly.[39] Such a compliment is typical of the cult of Elizabeth, and it is echoed and amplified by the conclusion of the *Gesta Grayorum* which seems to culminate in a comparable atmosphere of romantic abjection and self-immolation. Yet the fears of a 'gentle sovereign grace

[that] … almost made me traitor to myself' (3.2.159–61) also beset many of the restless, privileged, and ambitious young men in Shakespeare's original audience. And they too ultimately resisted a complete surrender of their liberty as their revels ended.

The grand finale of the revels at Gray's Inn was the *Masque of Proteus*, a command performance at Whitehall before the Queen at Shrovetide, 2 March 1595, and it seeks to manage courtly tensions through courtly compliment. The masque's author was Francis Davison, admitted to Gray's Inn in 1593, and the son of William Davison, Francis Walsingham's principal secretary. In 1587, Davison's father had delivered the warrant for the execution of Mary, Queen of Scots, and was made the scapegoat for Elizabeth's regret, deprived of office, and sent to the Tower for more than a year. However, the older Davison's support for Walsingham's hard line caught the attention of the Earl of Essex, and, following Walsingham's death in 1590, Essex campaigned to get Davison appointed Secretary of State. Both were intent on a more hawkish foreign policy and eager for a war on Spain. The other candidate was Robert Cecil, son of Lord Burghley, and Essex's principal rival for control of the Privy Council. Elizabeth finally gave the post to Cecil in 1596, characteristically leaving it vacant for more than five years, but in 1595, the appointment was still pending.

Francis Davison wrote *The Masque of Proteus* at a point when both his father's career and his own hung in the balance, and, in a familiar pattern, it promotes their ambitions as a form of service to the Queen. That spring, he would begin working as an intelligence agent for the Earl of Essex on the Continent. He and many other young men at the Inns of Court shared his patron's enthusiasm for war and adventure, although some, like John Donne, would discover the close link between 'Honour and misery' after joining the Earl's Cadiz expedition.[40] Earlier in the *Gesta Grayorum*, the Prince of Purpoole had been exhorted to press on against the Spaniard 'in the alliance of a new war' (p. 75) and assured that victory would be easy.[41] Davison's *Masque* describes a struggle between Proteus and the Prince of Purpoole for control 'of *Neptunes* Empery' (p. 77); like the men described by Luciana in *The Comedy of Errors*, the prince and his knights also want to be 'Lord[s] of the wide world and wild wat'ry seas' (2.1.21). The prince's squire tells how the Prince of Purpoole caught Proteus asleep and held him prisoner despite this demigod's 'familiar artes and turning tricks' (p. 80). To regain his freedom, Proteus has offered his captor 'The Adamantine rock, The seas true star', assuring him that it would secure 'the wide Empire of the Ocean' (p. 82), a goal promoted by Essex and his followers. However, complete possession would come only if 'the Prince should bring him to a power / Which in attractive virtue should surpass / The wondrous force of his Ir'ne drawing rock' (p. 82). The Prince of Purpoole readily agrees, and he and seven of his knights 'enter Hostages in to his rock / When't should bee brought to the appointed place' (p. 82), namely the court of Elizabeth where reigns that 'Excellent Queene, trew adamant of Hartes'. In a predictably flattering conclusion, the Queen's attractive power trumps all, for, as the squire says to Proteus:

> What can your Iron doo without Armes of men,
> And armes of men from hartes of men doo move,
> The hartes of men, that's it thence motion springs
> Lo Proteus then Th'attractive Rock of hartes,
> Hartes which once truly touched with her beames
> Inspiring purest zeale and reverence
> As well unto the person as the Power.
>
> (p. 84)

Suitably impressed, Proteus surrenders to this higher power, yielding 'thanckes of guift, & Libertie of due' (p. 85), and he strikes the rock with his trident to release the hostages who come dancing out 'in a very stately Mask'. A second hymn is sung 'at the Departure of the Maskers into the rock' at the masque's conclusion:

> Shadowes before the shining sunne do vanish ...
> Pure holiness doth all enchantment banish
> And cullors of false Principallity
> Do fade in presence of true majesty.
>
> (p. 86)

The masque apparently ends as all masques do, according to Stephen Orgel, by moving beyond its own illusions to the triumph 'of true majesty'; in Orgel's view, 'the prince always wins'.[42] The Queen's ascendancy certainly seems absolute. When the Prince of Purpoole demands that Proteus 'Yelde victory, and liberty and thanckes' (p. 85), Proteus duly yields. And so does the Prince of Purpoole, for as the *Gesta Grayorum* tells us, 'on *Shrove-Tuesday*, at the Court, were our Sports and Revels ended', and, with the onset of Lent and repentance, his 'Principality is determined; which, although it shined very bright in ours, and other Darkness; yet, at the Royal Presence of Her Majesty, it appeared as an obscured Shadow' (pp. 88–9). The *Gesta's* last sentence assures us that the members of Gray's Inn finally and happily surrender to the Queen's higher authority much as 'the great Rivers ... [do] that triumph in the Multitude of their Waters, until they come unto the Sea. *Sic vinci, sic mori pulchrum* [thus to be conquered, thus to die is beautiful]' (p. 89). Antipholus of Syracuse embraces the same 'glorious supposition', proclaiming 'He gains by death that hath such means to die' (3.2.51).[43]

Yet the law sports at Gray's Inn do not actually end with the *Masque of Proteus* and its note of self-immolating abjection. Instead, the final scene is one of self-aggrandising aggression, for on that

> same night there was fighting at Barriers; the Earl of *Essex* and other Challengers, and the Earl of *Cumberland* and his Company Defendants: Into which number, our Prince was taken, and behaved himself so valiantly and skilfully therein, that he had the prize adjudged due unto him, which it pleased Her Majesty to deliver him with her own hands. (p. 88)

The *Gesta Grayorum* thus concludes with a grand chivalric contest, featuring the two biggest stars of the tilt-yard, the Earls of Essex and Cumberland, in their customary roles of challenger for and defender of the Queen's favour. Essex and his faction used these events to advance their own agendas while professing devotion to the Queen. The 'rites of knighthood' thus permitted a kind of 'chivalric compromise' between submission to sovereignty and aristocratic ambition.[44] The *Gesta Grayorum* seeks a similar balance between devotion and liberty. Even the most enraptured tributes to Elizabeth in the *Masque of Proteus* remind her that 'armes of men from hartes of men doo move'. Elizabeth takes this admonition to heart and responds magnanimously to the climactic show of 'Armes of men'. She awards the prize to the Prince of Purpoole 'with her own hands; telling him, that it was not her Gift; for if it had, it should have been better' and promising 'a better Reward from her self' (p. 88). Like Emilia, the Queen is a good virgin mother who encourages her dependents' autonomy.

For the men of Gray's Inn, their revels' end was almost too good to be true, their own 'Lord of Liberty' declared the victor and the Queen herself awarding the prize. Was the revels prince actually the best swordsman at the barriers? Perhaps, but in my view the revels' happy ending has the same air of contrivance and artifice as the resolution of *The Comedy of Errors*.[45] The Duke may profess astonishment that 'the parents to these children / ... accidentally are met together' (5.1.350–1), but the cause of their reunion is clearly neither accidental nor supernatural, but manifestly theatrical. That either outcome would have been a surprise seems no more likely to me than that 'The Night of Errors' was actually a 'mischanceful Accident' (pp. 31–2). Equally improbable are the accusations of 'Sorceries and Enchantments, and namely, of a great Witchcraft' made the next night (p. 32).[46] The same hysterical fears, of course, pervade *The Comedy of Errors*, and they prove equally baseless; the play's errors seem uncanny but are really perfectly ordinary. At the trial at Gray's Inn, the 'Sorcerer or Conjurer' responsible for the 'Play of Errors and Confusions' escapes punishment and turns the tables on his accusers, charging them with bringing 'all this Law-stuff on purpose to blind the Eyes of His Excellency' (p. 33). He also refutes their claim 'that those things which they all saw and perceived sensibly to be in very deed done and actually performed, were nothing else but vain Illusions, Fancies, Dreams and Enchantments, and to be wrought and compassed by the Means of a poor harmless Wretch that never had heard of such great Matters in all his Life' (pp. 33–4). In contrast to Doctor Pinch, this conjurer lays claim to no supernatural powers or anything else beyond his humble means. He thus adopts the same defence used by some of Shakespeare's theatrical conjurers like Rosalind and Prospero whose epilogues disclose that their charms are wholly theatrical. Similarly, as Jonathan Crewe suggests, although the characters in *The Comedy of Errors* believe that the forces besetting them are either supernatural or arbitrary, the audience can see 'the benign and healing theatricality that is shaping their ends'.[47] This theatricality is affirmed as a positive and efficacious force by the conjurer who insists that what his accusers call 'vain Representations and Shews' (p. 32) were 'in very deed done and actually performed'.

From one perspective, all the performances of the *Gesta Grayorum* were 'vain Representations and Shows'. The pageants and progresses of the Prince of Purpoole were splendid and many who thronged the streets to see him 'thought there had been some great Prince, in very deed, passing through the city' (p. 57), but of course he too was a mere play-actor in a longer-running play. Yet not only was such play 'in very deed done and actually performed' but it also served serious and significant purposes, primarily the mediation of the conflicts dividing the Elizabethan ruling class. Some undoubtedly saw these lengthy law sports as mere vanities, but as Luciana tells Antipholus of Syracuse, ''Tis holy sport to be a little vain / When the sweet breath of flattery conquers strife' (3.2.27–8). Many critics see her advice as a hypocritical lapse from the lofty sanctimony of her earlier praise of marriage, but I find her stance consistent with that complex mixture of what Philip Finkelpearl calls 'youthful idealism and cynical sophistication' that defines the tone of revels at the Inns of Court.[48] A similar mixture prevailed in the cult of Elizabeth in its prime. Essex and his followers, including Francis Davison, were willing to flatter the Queen as long as they retained hopes of obtaining their objectives. Once Elizabeth rejected the Earl's candidates for high office, including William Davison and Francis Bacon, their quarrels grew more heated. Factional strife intensified and flattery eventually failed despite the pretensions of the cult of Elizabeth. As Essex grew more recalcitrant and frustrated, the 'chivalric compromise' became more precarious, collapsing altogether when he revolted in 1601. The next year, in the wake of the Essex revolt and the Earl's execution, Davison put together an anthology called *The Poetical Rhapsody*, one of the most influential and valuable Elizabethan miscellanies and the last of its kind. Poems by Campion, Ralegh, Spenser, and Davies among others offer tribute to the dead heroes, Sir Philip Sidney and the Earl of Essex, and Davison's own verses bitterly castigate the Queen's mistreatment of his father under thinly veiled references to Astraea and Eubulus, the generic name for a good councillor.[49] But in 1594–95, as the *Gesta Grayorum* shows, revels at the Inns of Court could still contain rebellion while 'the sweet breath of flattery conquers strife'.

Notes

I am very grateful to Jayne Archer, Elizabeth Goldring, and Sarah Knight for inviting me to participate in the stimulating and enjoyable 2006 conference on the Inns of Court, for their hard work and editorial skill in preparing this volume for publication, and for encouraging and enabling contributors to share and compare their work.

1 *Gesta Grayorum or the History of the High and Mighty Prince Henry Prince of Purpoole, Anno Domini 1594*, ed. Desmond Bland (Liverpool: Liverpool University Press, 1968), p. 88; hereafter cited in the text. Bland calls the revels 'unreasonably protracted' in *Three Revels from the Inns of Court* (Trowbridge: Avebury, 1984). p. 24, n. 26.

2 W[illiam] C[anning], 'The Epistle Dedicatory', *Gesta Grayorum*, ed. Bland, p. 2.

3 Philip J. Finkelpearl, *John Marston of the Middle Temple: An Elizabethan Dramatist in his Social Setting* (Cambridge, MA: Harvard University Press, 1969), p. 38. See also C. L. Barber's discussion of lords of misrule in *Shakespeare's Festive Comedy: A Study of Dramatic Form and its Relation to Social Custom* (Princeton, NJ: Princeton University Press, 1959; repr. 1972): 'The man who acts as a mock lord enjoys building up his dignity, and also exploding it by exaggeration, while his followers both relish his bombast as a fleer at proper authority and also enjoy turning on him and insulting his majesty' (p. 37).

4 Finkelpearl, *John Marston*, p. 44.

5 Thomas Nashe describes the predilections of Inns of Court members for 'gameing, following of harlots, drinking, or seeing a Playe', contending that the last is the most innocuous in *Pierce Penilesse His Svpplication to the Divell* in *The Works of Thomas Nashe*, ed. Ronald B. McKerrow, 5 vols (Oxford: Basil Blackwell, repr. 1958; first pub. 1904), I, 212. Karen Newman includes 'Inns of Court men' among the clients of London's brothels in her discussion of 'Sex in the City' in *Cultural Capitals: Early Modern London and Paris* (Princeton, NJ: Princeton University Press, 2007), p. 136. References to Shakespeare's plays are to *The Norton Shakespeare*, ed. Stephen Greenblatt, Walter Cohen, Jean E. Howard, and Katharine Eisaman Maus (New York, NY; London: W.W. Norton, 1997), unless otherwise indicated.

6 A 'Commission of *Oyer* and *Terminer*' is a court charged 'to hear and determine' matters of treason, felonies, and misdemeanours.

7 Robert Greene, *Greens groats-worth of witte* (London: [J. Wolfe and J. Danter] for William Wright, 1592), sig. F1^v.

8 *The Phoenix Nest* (1593), ed. Hyder Rollins (Cambridge, MA: Harvard University Press, 1931), p. 31 and p. xx.

9 Leslie Hotson, *Mr. W. H.* (New York, NY: Knopf, 1964), pp. 50–1, and Helen Ostovitch, 'Introduction', Ben Jonson, *Every Man Out of His Humour*, ed. Helen Ostovich (Manchester: Manchester University Press, 2001), p. 32. Similarly, Bradin Cormack concludes in his contribution to this volume that 'the fit between crisis and solution is so good as strongly to suggest a staged event' (p. 264).

10 Desmond Bland, 'Introduction', *Gesta Grayorum*, ed. Bland, p. xiii and Douglas Lanier, '"Stigmatical in Making": the material character of *The Comedy of Errors*', in Robert S. Miola (ed.), *The Comedy of Errors: Critical Essays* (New York, NY: Garland; Routledge, 1997), pp. 299–334 (p. 322).

11 Graham Parry, 'The politics of the Jacobean masque', in J. R. Mulryne and Margaret Shewring (eds), *Theatre and Government under the Early Stuarts* (Cambridge: Cambridge University Press, 1993), pp. 87–117 (p. 113); Barbara Ravelhofer, *The Early Stuart Masque: Dance, Costume, and Music* (Oxford: Oxford University Press, 2006), p. 17.

12 See G. R. Hibbard, 'Introduction', *Love's Labour's Lost* (Oxford: Clarendon Press, 1990), pp. 46–7.

13 Lynne Magnusson, 'Scoff power in *Love's Labour's Lost* and the Inns of Court: language in context', *Shakespeare Survey*, 57 (2004), 196–208 (202).

14 John Marston's father bequeathed his law books and furniture from his chambers at the Middle Temple but lamented his son's 'delight in plays and vain studies in fooleries' in 1599; cited by Michael Neill, 'Introduction', *The Selected Plays of John Marston* (Cambridge: Cambridge University Press, 1986), p. x. The enthusiasm for plays at the Inns of Court persisted as William Prynne's complaint in his anti-theatrical tract, *Histrio-*

mastix (London: E[dward] A[llde, Augustine Mathewes, Thomas Cotes] and W[illiam] I[ones] for Michael Sparke, 1633) indicates: 'That Innes of Court men were undone but for Players; that they are their chiefest guests and imployment, & the sole busines that makes them afternoons men: that this is one of the first things they learne as soone as they are admitted, to see Stage-plays' (sig. **3ᵛ). (Prynne was admitted as a student to Lincoln's Inn in 1621). See also Francis Lenton's description of the habits of the Inns of Court Men in *The Young Gallants Whirligigg* (London: M[iles] F[lesher] for Robert Bostocke, 1629): 'Your Theaters hee daily doth frequent' (p. 7).
15 Henry Chettle, *Kind-harts Dreame* (London: [J. Wolfe and J. Danter] for William Wright, [1593?]), sig. A4ʳ.
16 Charles Whitworth, 'Introduction', *The Comedy of Errors* (Oxford: Oxford University Press, 2002), pp. 6 and 17; all references to the play are from this edition. For a discussion of *The Comedy of Errors*' classical sources, see Wolfgang Riehle, *Shakespeare, Plautus and the Humanist Tradition* (Cambridge: D. S. Brewer, 1990) and Robert S. Miola's 'Introduction' in Miola (ed.), *The Comedy of Errors: Critical Essays*. See also Lorna Hutson's essay in this collection, pp. 245–63.
17 Andrew Gurr, *The Shakespearean Playing Companies* (Oxford: Oxford University Press, 1996), pp. 65–77.
18 Whitworth, 'Introduction', p. 2.
19 *Ibid.*, p. 4: Whitworth argues convincingly that *The Comedy of Errors* 'was composed expressly' for performance at the Gray's Inn revels (pp. 2–5) as does Sidney Thomas, 'The date of *The Comedy of Errors*', *Shakespeare Quarterly*, 7:4 (1956), 377–84.
20 Ros King, 'Introduction', *The Comedy of Errors*, ed. T. S. Dorsch (Cambridge: Cambridge University Press, rev. 2004; first pub. 1988), p. 33.
21 'Liberty' and its variants occur seven times in the play (1.1.102; 2.1.7, 10, 15; 4.3.18; 5.1.53, 342).
22 Ben Jonson, *Every Man Out of His Humour*, ed. Ostovich, pp. 383–4.
23 Compare accounts of the 'Seige of *Sluce*, the Battery of Brest, or sacking of Maidenhead' in Benjamin Rudyerd's *Le Prince d'Amour* (London: William Leake, 1660), p. 23.
24 Wilfrid R. Prest, *The Inns of Court under Elizabeth I and the Early Stuarts, 1590–1640* (London: Longman, 1972), pp. 101–2.
25 Prest, *The Inns of Court under Elizabeth I and the Early Stuarts, 1590–1640*, pp. 110–11. Prest cautions that 'student militancy' was a complex phenomenon and rejects any effort 'to portray the inns of court revolts as so many dress rehearsals for the Great Rebellion. On the other hand, it does not seem entirely fanciful to class them among both the causes and effects of that "de-legitimation" of established authority which helped make revolution possible' (p. 114); see also his final chapter on 'The Inns of Court and the English Revolution' (pp. 220–36). For discussion of the Inns as a polity, see also Paul Raffield's essay in this collection, pp. 32–50.
26 Richard Edwards, *Damon and Pythias*, in Ros King (ed.), *The Works of Richard Edwards: Politics, Poetry and Performance in Sixteenth-Century England* (Manchester: Manchester University Press, 2001), pp. 183–4. Eubulus (Good Counsel) rebuked the flatterer who sustains 'Tyranny' in the play's final speech (p. 183).
27 Thomas Hughs *et al.*, *Misfortunes of Arthur* (2.2.78–80) in *Early English Classical Tragedies*, ed. John W. Cunliffe (Oxford: Oxford University Press, 1912), pp. 245–6.
28 Marie Axton, *The Queen's Two Bodies: Drama and the Elizabethan Succession* (London:

Royal Historical Society, 1977), pp. ix–x, p. 2, and *passim*, and 'Robert Dudley and the Inner Temple revels', *Historical Journal*, 13:3 (1970), 365–78 (374–5).

29 Jessica Winston, 'A *Mirror for Magistrates* and public political discourse in Elizabethan England', *Studies in Philology*, 101 (2004), 381–400 (382).

30 Richard C. McCoy, 'Lords of Liberty: Francis Davison and the cult of Elizabeth', in John Guy (ed.), *The Reign of Elizabeth I: Court and Culture in the Last Decade* (Cambridge: Cambridge University Press, 1995), pp. 212–28 (p. 220). See also Finkelpearl's discussion of the shifting connotations of the term 'liberty' including 'revelry, rebellion, uninhibited satire, relaxed playfulness, libertine wantonness, licensed fooling, and political freedom', in *John Marston*, p. 80. In his subtle analysis in this volume, Bradin Cormack argues for more muted and oblique aspirations since he sees the revels as exercises in managing competing jurisdictional allegiances. In both *The Comedy of Errors* and the Gray's Inn revels, 'legal identity is most fully expressed, not as autonomy, but as relational bounded-ness' (p. 280). Though I see the revellers' aspirations as more assertive, I also see liberty as a problematic legal and political aspiration since the revellers must also embrace submission and bondage.

31 Cecil Headlam, *The Inns of Court* (London: Adam and Charles Black, 1909), p. 17, and Francis Lenton, *Innes of Court Anagrammatist* (London: [T. Harper] for William Lashe, 1634), sig. A2^r, cited in Finkelpearl, *John Marston*, p. 11. See also Prest, *The Inns of Court under Elizabeth I and the Early Stuarts, 1590–1640*, regarding the 'aristocratic image and reputation' of Gray's Inn (p. 11).

32 Prest, *The Inns of Court under Elizabeth I and the Early Stuarts, 1590–1640*, p. 105.

33 Eamon Grennan, 'Arm and sleeve: nature and custom in *The Comedy of Errors*', *Philological Quarterly*, 59 (1980), 150–64 (151). For A. C. Hamilton, this mastery of every beast has an idealised prelapsarian quality; the passage provides a brief glimpse of a paradise lost when the heroes lose their connections to home and identity but then regained through the happy ending's reunion; see Hamilton, *The Early Shakespeare* (San Marino, CA: Huntington Library, 1967), pp. 107–8.

34 George Gascoigne, *Supposes* (1566) in *A Hundreth Sundrie Flowres*, ed. G. W. Pigman III (Oxford, Clarendon Press, 2000), p. 7. See Lorna Hutson's essay in this collection for an illuminating discussion of the influence of Gascoigne's *Supposes* and that play's 'false or mistaken conjectures' on *The Comedy of Errors* (p. 259).

35 John L. McMullan, 'Criminal organization in sixteenth and seventeenth century London', *Social Problems*, 29 (1982), 311–23 (313–14). For sanctuary's surprising durability in the face of efforts to suppress it, see Isobel D. Thornley in 'The destruction of sanctuary', in Robert William Seton Watson (ed.), *Tudor Studies Presented to Albert Frederick Pollard* (Freeport, NY: Books for Libraries, 1969; first pub. 1924), pp. 182–207.

36 Kent Cartwright, 'Surprising the audience in *The Comedy of Errors*', in Evelyn Gajowski (ed.), *Re-Visions of Shakespeare: Essays in Honor of Robert Ornstein* (Newark, DE: University of Delaware Press, 2004), pp. 215–30 (p. 216). See Alexander Leggatt's discussion of the play's replacement of practical deception and bewilderment with fantasy and mystery in *Shakespeare's Comedy of Love* (London: Methuen, 1974), pp. 2–3.

37 See Stephen Greenblatt who notes that the 'comedy's decorum rests upon the strict absence of supernatural agency' in 'Shakespeare bewitched', in Tetsuo Kishi, Roger Pringle, and Stanley Wells (eds), *Shakespeare and Cultural Traditions* (Newark, DE: University of Delaware Press, 1994), pp. 17–42 (p. 29).

38 *The Comedy of Errors*, ed. R. A. Foakes (London: Arden, 1962), p. 106.

39 Francis Douce was the first to suggest an implicit compliment to the Queen; cited in *Comedy of Errors*, ed. Foakes, p. 51. Foakes points out that the 'play may have been performed before her', though the records are confusing.

40 John Donne, 'The Storme: To Mr. Christopher Brooke', in *Complete Poetry and Selected Prose of John Donne*, ed. Charles M. Coffin (New York, NY: The Modern Library, 2001), l. 12 (p. 132).

41 This exhortation concludes the Latin oration by one of the scholars of St Paul's; the translation is from Basil Brown, *Law Sports at Gray's Inn* (New York, NY: privately printed, 1921), p. xxix.

42 Stephen Orgel, *The Jonsonian Masque* (Cambridge, MA: Harvard University Press, 1967), p. 19.

43 Samuel Daniel uses the same trope to describe what he calls 'th'Ocean of all-drowning Sov'raintie' in *The Civil Wars*, ed. Laurence Michel (New Haven, CT: Yale University Press, 1958), p. 240. See my discussion of this trope in 'Lords of Liberty' (219–20) and *The Rites of Knighthood: The Literature and Politics of Elizabethan Chivalry* (Berkeley, CA: University of California Press, 1989), pp. 117–18.

44 McCoy, *Rites of Knighthood*, pp. 14–19.

45 Desmond Bland notes the 'essential formality of combat at barriers' making it easier to manage than the tilt in *Three Revels from the Inns of Court*, in *Gesta Grayorum*, ed. Bland, p. 52.

46 Because Sandra Billington sees the 'Night of Errors' as a genuine embarrassment, she treats the trial as a 'semi-serious debate' aimed at establishing 'who was responsible for the unruly crowd; whether a magician had caused an illusion or whether trouble had resulted from the perennial problem of the king's officers mismanaging the commonwealth' in *Mock Kings in Medieval Society and Renaissance Drama* (Oxford: Clarendon Press, 1991), p. 51. I cannot see how any of the participants could even be 'semi-serious' in their suspicions of a 'magician'.

47 Jonathan Crewe, 'God or the good physician: the rational playwright in *The Comedy of Errors*', *Genre*, 15 (1982), 203–23 (208, 214).

48 See n. 4.

49 See my discussion of this collection in 'Lords of Liberty', pp. 223–7.

15

New light on drama, music, and dancing at the Inns of Court to 1642

Alan H. Nelson

As co-editor of the Inns of Court collection for Records of Early English Drama (REED), my job over the last several years has been to identify, transcribe, and assist in putting into print all known archival, manuscript, and printed evidence for drama, quasi-drama (including masques), dance, and secular music associated with the Inns of Court from as far back as it is possible to reach (1407) to 1642, the year of the closing of the theatres in London. This is a collection I inherited from my good friend and colleague Professor John R. Elliott, Jr, of Syracuse University, who suffered an incapacitating stroke in 2002, which led to his death some two years later. The extensive material Elliott transcribed in the late 1980s remained as yet unprocessed when I came on board in 2004.[1] In this chapter I will outline the existing state of scholarship on Inns of Court performances, and will discuss some of the new discoveries made during our research for the Records of Early English Drama *Inns of Court* volumes.

An overview of recent scholarship on Inns drama

An early base-line for determining what is 'new' in Inns of Court drama scholarship is A. Wigfall Green, *The Inns of Court and Early English Drama* (1931), the first and still the only comprehensive survey of its subject. Of intermediate date are Philip J. Finkelpearl, *John Marston of the Middle Temple* (1969), and Wilfrid R. Prest, *The Inns of Court under Elizabeth I and the Early Stuarts, 1590–1640* (1972).[2] Of recent date are Anthony Arlidge, *Shakespeare and the Prince of Love: The Feast of Misrule in the Middle Temple* (2000), and John H. Baker, 'Christmas in the Inns of Court and Chancery' (2004).[3] All contain material which was distinctly new at the time of publication. Some topics which I present here as 'new' are touched on by these or other scholars, but have not yet been incorporated into more comprehensive studies of dramatic performance at the Inns.

In addition to these historical studies, significant recent archival research into the political and performance contexts of Inns of Court drama has also been conducted; a most important discovery, published independently by two sets of scholars in 1995 and 1996, is a contemporary description (in British Library MS 48023, fol.

369ᵛ) of the performance of Thomas Norton and Thomas Sackville's *Gorboduc* or *Ferrex and Porrex* by the Inner Temple in 1561–62.[4] The unidentified writer claims that *Gorboduc*, or at least one of its dumb-shows, carried the message 'that yt was better for the Quene to marye with the Lord Robert knowen then with the king of Sweden'. Whether this blatant endorsement of Robert Dudley, future Earl of Leicester, as a potential husband for Queen Elizabeth was in fact understood or approved by the original audience of the play, which included Elizabeth herself, must remain open to question. The document has been further analysed by Jessica Winston in a paper published in 2005: Winston argues for a reading of *Gorboduc* as a specific political response to the 1561–62 Inner Temple revels.[5] Another newly discovered document is a set of notes bound in at the end of a legal manuscript now preserved as Cambridge University Library MS Ll.1.11. These notes, which include contemporary dance notation and lyrics as well as literal notes of music, were first reported in J. H. Baker and Jane Ringrose, *A Catalogue of English Legal Manuscripts in Cambridge University Library* (1996),[6] and are referenced by Barbara Ravelhofer in *The Early Stuart Masque: Dance, Costume, and Music* (2006), who discusses the Lincoln's Inn affiliation of the manuscript and the choreographical instructions it contains.[7]

New manuscript sources

The research we have conducted for the *REED: Inns of Court* volumes has led to other archival discoveries: among 'new' records identified by REED research is a letter from William Gawdy to his father dated 19 February 1634 (British Library MS Add. 36989, fol. 72), touching on James Shirley's *Triumph of Peace*, first performed on 3 February at Whitehall by members of the Inns, probably the best-documented English theatrical event prior to the Restoration. Gawdy's letter does not so much reveal something new, as consolidate and re-emphasise important facts already known:

> Sir you injoyned mee to send you a briefe relation howe I got into the masque and howe I was placed: Sir Edmund Varney by the mediation of my cosen Charles got mee a ticket and placed mee very well in the midle gallery. The scene did farre exceed ours, I think Inigo Iones did strive in this to bury the mention of the former whiche hee made for us. as for the masque it selfe the booke (whiche you shall receive withe this letter) will informe you.

Gawdy's reference to tickets as a method of controlling admission to a theatrical event antedates the earliest *Oxford English Dictionary* citation (1673) by almost forty years.[8] Probably the tickets of 1634 were not offered for sale but carefully distributed by Inns of Court authorities. A contemporary letter reveals that admission was further controlled by a 'turning chair', probably a kind of turnstile.[9] The 'middle gallery' in which Gawdy took his seat was evidently part of a three-storey scaffold erected against the side walls of Merchant Taylors' Hall, where on 13 February the masque received its second performance. The 'former' masque which Inigo Jones 'made for us' was George Chapman's *The Memorable Maske of the Two Honorable Houses or Innes of Court; the Middle Temple, and Lyncolns Inne* (1613), written to commemorate the wedding of Princess Elizabeth to the Elector Palatine. Rather than describe the 1634 masque in detail Gawdy defers to 'the booke (whiche you shall receive with his letter)', doubtless Shirley's *Triumph of Peace*, entered into the Stationers' Register on 24 January and already in print at the time of performance.

Elliott found important new information concerning professional performances in the treasurers' Account Books of the Inner Temple, dating from 1605 onwards, and in miscellaneous loose receipts of the Middle Temple. An abstract of known performances is given at the end of this chapter in the form of an appendix. Here we may examine four documents or excerpts, two from the Inner and two from the Middle Temple. The first excerpt is taken from the Inner Temple treasurer's Account Book for 1612–13, where 'the same day' in lines 1 and 2 refers to All Hallows Day, 1 November 1612:

> Item payd to Musitians for theyr ffee the same day   xxs
> Item payd for a playe the same day   v li
> …
> Item payd to the Musitions for their ffee the vth of November   xiijs iiijd
> Item payd for a play on Candlemas day   vjli xiijs iiijd
> Item payd to another company of players which were appointed to play heere the same day   xxxs
> Item paid for 2 staffe torches the same day   ijs

Only with the mention of 'another company of players' in the penultimate entry does it become absolutely clear that the players on Candlemas were not Inner Temple gentlemen but professional actors; and we may infer the same for the earlier play on All Hallows Day. The Inner Temple treasurer's Account Book for 1614–15 is even more explicit:

> Item paid to the Kinges maiesties servantes for a play vpon allsaintes day 1614   vj li
> …
> Item paid for 2 staffe torches the same daye   ijs
> Item paid to Iohn Hopper for the Musitions fee the same day   xxs
> …
> Item paid to his maiesties servantes for a play vpon Candlemas daye last past   vjli xiijs iiijd
> Item paid for 2 staffe torches the same day   ijs
> Item paid for ye musitions fee ye same day   xxs

So the 'players' who performed on both 1 November 1614 and 2 February 1615 were the King's Men, who were probably also the 'company of players' from 1612–13.

Over at the Middle Temple, the earliest miscellaneous receipt of exceptional interest is written entirely in the hand of Edward Juby (*d.* 1618),[10] a well-known professional actor who had performed at the Rose and Fortune theatres from the mid-1590s onwards:

> Receved of Mr Baldwin, for a play parformd by the Palgraves Players, on Candelmas day last 1615 the Sume of twelue poundes
> (signed) By me Edward Iuby

The receipt is endorsed (in another hand): 'The players Bill for a play on Candelmas Day 1615.'[11] A similar detailed receipt survives from eighteen years later, dated 3 November 1632:

> Received of the Society of the Middle Temple London for a Playe called Hyde Parke, acted there on the feast of all Saintes last past the summe of Ten pounds I saye received as aforesaid   10 li
> (signed) By me Anthony Turner

Like Edward Juby, Anthony Turner was a well-known professional actor. As for the play, *Hyde Park* is a comedy by James Shirley, licensed 20 April 1632, printed 1637.

From these four records, and from similar records abstracted in the Appendix, we may conclude that professional performances were virtually *de rigueur* at the Inner Temple and Middle Temple, from the second decade of the seventeenth century to the closing of the theatres in 1642. Green demonstrates that professional performances resumed at the Restoration and lasted until 1687.[12] In addition to *Hyde Park*, whose text survives, three plays survive in title only: *The Oxford Tragedy*, *The Bridegroom and the Madman*, and *The City Shuffler*, performed respectively in 1608, 1619, and 1633. Companies performing at various Inns over the years include the King's Men *alias* the Blackfriars Players; the Palgrave's Men; Prince Charles's Men; the Queen's Men; and Beeston's Boys.

Shakespeare at the Inns

Two professional performances at two different Inns of Court have long been known: *The Comedy of Errors* was performed at Gray's Inn on 28 December (Innocents' Day) 1594, while *Twelfth Night* was performed at the Middle Temple on 2 February (Candlemas Day) 1602. The first of these performances is documented in *Gesta Grayorum*, not published until 1688; the second is briefly (and uniquely) documented in the contemporary diary of John Manningham, who details 'a play called "Twelue night, or What you Will", much like the Commedy of Errores, or Menechmi in Plautus, but more like and neere to that in Italian called *Inganni*.'[13] Among many issues raised by these documents, I wish to address two here. Were these one-off performances, perhaps indeed plays specially commissioned for the event? Or were they plays already in the repertory of the Lord Chamberlain's Men? Of the two plays, *Twelfth Night* more exactly fits the pattern, fully established in subsequent years, of a play performed at an Inn of Court by a professional company at Candlemas. The precise venue is slightly puzzling, as Shakespeare's company, by then the King's Men, is otherwise associated with the Inner rather than the Middle Temple. The performance of *Comedy of Errors* at Gray's Inn in 1594 on Innocents' Day is slightly more anomalous.[14]

Anthony Arlidge argues that *Twelfth Night* was 'commissioned for performance' at the Middle Temple, written, or at least adapted, for the Inn.[15] An apparent precedent lies in activities at the Inner Temple in 1561–62, when Arthur Brooke (or Broke) (*d.* 1563) was not only hired to compose a play and a masque, but rewarded for his efforts with an honorary admission to the Society. Brooke had been the first to publish a version of the Romeo and Juliet story in English, and was admitted to the Inner Temple on the recommendation of Thomas Sackville and Thomas Norton, authors of *Gorboduc*; he may have been the author of the masque *Beauty and Desire*, played alongside *Gorboduc*.[16] Inns of Court masques, moreover, were certainly commissioned from professional playwrights, including Francis Beaumont, George Chapman, Thomas Middleton, James Shirley, and William Davenant. But Inns of Court masques were by definition one-off events, typically performed first at home, then at court, and then no more. Masque texts were also short; and while they brought acclaim and financial benefit to a playwright, they brought little or none to his professional company.

The Comedy of Errors is listed among Shakespeare's plays by Francis Meres in *Palladis Tamia* (1598),[17] and was performed at court on Innocents' Day 1604,[18] while *Twelfth Night* is known to have guaranteed the financial success of the King's Men, which it could only have done as part of the company's standing repertory.[19] While I agree with Arlidge that a connection to the Middle Temple might be detected in minor textual details, including the names Curio and Fabian, I am not persuaded that *Twelfth Night* was in any exclusive sense an Inns of Court play. Its very title conflicts with its Middle Temple performance at Candlemas.

While the strong claim that *Twelfth Night* was a Middle Temple play in some foundational or original sense cannot (I think) be sustained, some evidence can be marshalled in support of Arlidge's more limited claim that Inns of Court gentlemen might have cooperated in the play's performance, for some Inns of Court entertainments were performed by a mix of amateurs and professionals. At the 'Barriers' for the Inauguration of the Prince of Wales on 4 November 1616, for example, gentlemen of the Inns were certainly involved, as revealed in a contemporary manuscript:

> Brave Mars and mighty Pallas
> Come help me to remember
> The noble acts, and worthy facts
> Performed in November.
> By Barriars stoute and sturdie
> Young Gentlemen for propper
> Whoe had their Hose, as men suppose
> bedawbed with lace of Copper.

The same poem concludes:

> But happie was this Proiect
> thrice happie was this Monday
> To Tenninges owld, and Burbige bould
> Natt Feild, and Harry Cundy.[20]

Reading 'Tenninges' as an error for 'Heminges', the happy participants were John Hemmings, Richard Burbage, Nathan Field, and Henry Condell, all members of the King's Men. Similarly, roles in Thomas Middleton's *The Inner Temple Masque: or Masque of Heroes* (1619) were played by members of Prince Charles's Company:[21]

The Parts	*The Speakers*
D Almanacke	Joseph Taylor
Plumporridge	William Rowley
A Fasting-day	John Newton
New-yeere	Henry Atwell
Time	William Carpenter
Harmonie	A Boy

Apparently the 'masque' was performed by Inns of Court gentlemen, the antimasque by professional players.

The second issue provoked by the documents now before us concerns the standing commitments of professional companies to perform plays in particular Inns of Court on particular dates each year. Taking the King's Men as the most consistently documented example, that company effectively committed itself to being resident in London, and not on the road, on 1 November and 2 February each and every year. Theatre historians must now add these dates to the itineraries of the professional companies, and explain – or explain away – any ensuing conflicts.

Misbehaviour at the Inns

My final topic concerns misbehaviour in the Inns of Court in incidents which I will call 'Chambers in the Night' and 'The Heavy Hitter'. The 'Chambers in the Night' episode is described by John Chamberlain in a letter to Sir Dudley Carleton, dated 25 January 1623. Chamberlain ascribes the activities to Lincoln's Inn:

> Sheriffe Hanford hath ben very magnificall, and one night feasted all the kings servants, and within two dayes after all the gentlemen of Lincolns ynne, who at the breaking up of theyre revells, made such a peale of ordinance or chambers at midnight, as gave a great alarme at court, and put them in feare as yf there had ben some uprore in the citie.[22]

Joseph Mede (1586–1638), a biblical scholar at Cambridge, ascribes the episode rather to Gray's Inn:

> The gentlemen of Grayes Inne to make an end of Christmas on Twelfe night, in the dead time of the night shott of[f] all the chambers they had borrowed from the Tower, being as many as filled 4 carts.
>
> The King awakened with this noise, start out of his bed, & cryed Treason Treason, &c[;] & that the Cittie was in an vprore; in such sort (as it is told) that the whole court was raised, & almost in armes; The Earle of Arundell running to the Bedchamber with his sword drawne as to rescue the Kings person. &c These are such things as I heard from Londoners. & so I leaue them[23]

One wonders why James was all that surprised, as Inns of Court gunnery can be traced back to the Inner Temple revels of 1561–62.[24]

The 'Heavy Hitter' incident of Christmas 1627–28 is elucidated by the Middle Temple Parliament Books of 1590–91, where young gentlemen of that society were accused of 'Breakinge open forciblie of divers chambers in the night season And in levyinge and takinge injuriouslie certaine sommes of monie of divers gentlemen of this house in nam[e] of the lord of mysrule his rent (as the[y] tearmed it)' (fol. 215). Again in 1612–13, Middle Temple gentlemen 'contemptuously upon the vij[th] daye of this instant moneth of Ianuary sett upp … mr Watson for their Lord of Misrule, broke open Chamber doores as well within the howse as owt of the howse, made owtcrise in the night with striking upp of drumes and blowing of hornes aswell within the howse as in the streetes and comytted other disorders'.

At the Inner Temple during the Christmas season of 1627–28 a son of the politician Sir Guy Palmes (1580–1653) (Inner Temple, 1597) was appointed Lieutenant to the Lord of Christmas.[25] This was either Stafford Palmes, admitted 2 January 1620, or – perhaps more likely – his younger brother Francis, admitted 8 February 1625. According to Joseph Mede's initial letter of 12 January 1628,[26] the Lieutenant attempted to collect 'taxes' from properties ranging along Fleet Street as far west as Temple Bar, and along Ram Alley (now Hare Court). These properties lay in what was customarily known as 'Alsatia', part of which was recognised as a liberty, technically beyond the reach of London authorities (Ram Alley was notorious for taverns and brothels).[27] Mr Palmes, according to Mede, set his tax rate at ten shillings for each property. Along with his accomplices, Palmes 'brake open late in the night all the dores … namely of such as would not open to him; and from those that would not pay, he took a distresse'. A 'distresse' was a moveable property of value which would be redeemed upon payment of a required sum. Complaints being directed to City of London authorities, the Lord Mayor with a guard of halberdiers found 'my Lord of Christmas in a Taverne' about eleven o'clock in the night. Though Palmes 'made brave resistance', he was finally knocked to the ground and taken away to one of the two London prisons known as 'counters': one was situated on Wood Street near the Guildhall, the other in the Poultry. Eventually, explained Mede, the King's Attorney fetched the malefactors from prison and brought them in his own coach to court: there the young gentlemen and the Lord Mayor were reconciled by the King himself by a 'joyning of hands'.

A second letter dated 19 January is replete with modifications and corrections.[28] Mede explains that Palmes was not himself the Lord of Christmas, but rather the 'Lord of misrules Lieutenant'. On 5 January, the eve of Twelfth Night, Palmes had attempted to gather rents 'limited' at five (not ten) shillings a house, in Ram Alley and Fleet Street. At each door the revellers 'winded the Temple horne', an instrument mentioned frequently in the Inn's financial records. If the house door was not opened at the second 'blast or summons', the Lieutenant called upon his 'Gunner', in fact 'a robust blacksmith, whose 'gun or petard' was 'an huge overgrowne smithes hammer'. At the Lieutenant's cry 'Give fire Gunner!' the blacksmith applied his hammer with such force that many a door would require subsequent repair. From inside the residence the blow must have sounded like an explosion.

The denouement is vividly described by Mede, who tells of the reactions and involvement of the Mayor, Recorder and Attorney-General. It may be helpful to know that the Lord Mayor for 1627–28 was Sir Hugh Hammersley, while the Recorder of London was Sir Heneage Finch (1580–1631), and the Attorney-General was the Inner Templar Sir Robert Heath (1575–1649):

> My Lord Mayor being complained to on Sunday morning sayd he would be with them about 11 of the clock the same night, willing that all that ward should attend him with their halberds and that himselfe, besides those that came out of his house, would bring the watches along with him. In fine his Lordship being thus attended and advanced as high as Ram-alley, forth came with their swords, and in their hose and dublets out of the Temple gate Mr Lieutenant Palmes and some other gentlemen. One bad him come to my Lord Mayor; he answered, my Lord Mayor might come to him; but in fine they agreed to meet halfe way. And as the enterview of Princes is never without danger of some ill accident, so it hapned in this: for first Mr Palmes being quarreled with by some of the Halbardiers for not putting off his hatt to my Lord Mayor, and giving crosse answeres, the halbards began to fly about his eares, and he and his company to brandish their swordes. At last being beaten to the ground, and Mr Palmes sore wounded, they were faine to yeeld to the longer and more numerous weapon. My Lord Mayor takeing Mr Palmes by the shoulder led him to the Counter and thrust him in at the prison gate with a kind of indignation etc, and so notwithstanding his hurts he was forced to lye among the Common prisoners for 2 nights. On Tuesday the Kings Atturney became a sutor to my Lord Mayor for their liberty, which his Lordship granted upon condition Mr Atturney would undertake, they should the day following submitt themselues to his Lordship. On Wednesday after dinner Mr Palmes etc came to my Lord Mayors house and there in the presence of Mr Atturney, Mr Recorder and 6 Aldermen acknowledged his fault to his Lordship and craved pardon, and besides promised to repay the money he had gathered and to do reparations upon broken dores. Thus the game ended.

Repercussions from the Palmes incident appear in the Inner Temple Acts of Parliament for 10 February 1628 (fol. 178): 'At this parliament it is specially given in charge that order be given at Alhallontide next touching Christmas.' Accordingly, under 23 November 1628 occurs an elaborate set of 'Orders concerning Christmas' restricting celebrations to a maximum of three weeks, limiting alcohol to mealtimes, and banning the sale or issue of tobacco. A final order forbids any repetition of the high-jinx of the previous year:

> That there shall not bee anie goeing abroade out of the Circuit of this howse or without any of the Gates by any Lorde or other Gentleman to breake open any howse or chamber or to take any thinge in the name of Rent or a distresse.

The 1627–28 Christmas disorders were recollected by William Dugdale:

> That, for preventing of Quarrells within the House, and that general scandal and obloquie which the House hath heretofore incurred in time of Christmas, there shall no Gentleman of this House, side with any person whatsoever, that shall offer to disturb the peace and quiet of the House, but shall indeavour to punish them, according to the old Custome of the House and that no Strangers be suffred to come within the Hall, but such as shall appear and seem to be in good sort and fashion.[29]

Palmes's conduct of his office in January 1628 was clearly the exception rather than the rule. Nevertheless, the lord of misrule tradition observed at the Inner Temple and the other three Inns did sometimes get out of hand. Only occasionally – and in this case thanks to the curiosity of Joseph Mede – do details of the misrule survive in something like their original full sweep and colour. Like most collections published by our ongoing project, *REED: Inns of Court* for the most part gathers into one place documents which have been known to scholars for decades if not centuries. With luck, however, having a fresh look at familiar documents as well as searching for 'new' documents may yield new information and new connections. In our case we believe we have discovered significant new connections to the world outside the Inns of Court, in particular, to the world of professional theatre, and to the lives of neighbours who may – or may not – have been amused by the antics of the Inns of Court.

Appendix. Chronological list of Inns of Court performances to 1642 by professional companies

This list is adapted from Alan H. Nelson and John R. Elliott, Jr. (eds), *Inns of Court*, 3 vols, Records of Early English Drama (Boydell and Brewer, 2011), appendix 8. The abbreviations GI, IT, LI, and MT refer respectively to Gray's Inn, Inner Temple, Lincoln's Inn, and Middle Temple.

1594–95	28 Dec.	GI	comedy	Shakespeare, *Comedy of Errors*
1601–2	2 Feb.	MT	comedy	Shakespeare, *Twelfth Night*
1605–6	1 Nov.	IT	play	visiting players
1605–6	2 Feb.	IT	play	visiting players
1606–7	2 Feb.	IT	play	visiting players
1607–8	2 Feb.	IT	tragedy	*Oxford Tragedy*, visiting players
1608–9	1 Nov.	IT	play	visiting players
1608–9	2 Feb.	IT	play	visiting players
1609–10	1 Nov.	IT	play	visiting players
1609–10	2 Feb.	IT	play	visiting players
1610–11	1 Nov.	IT	play	visiting players
1610–11	2 Feb.	IT	play	visiting players
1611–12	1 Nov.	IT	antics/ puppets	visiting entertainers
1611–12	2 Feb.	IT	play	visiting players
1612–13	1 Nov.	IT	play	visiting players
1612–13	2 Feb.	IT	play	visiting players
1613–14	1 Nov.	IT	play	visiting players
1613–14	2 Feb.	IT	play	visiting players
1614–15	1 Nov.	IT	play	King's Men
1614–15	2 Feb.	IT	play	King's Men
1615–16	1 Nov.	IT	play	King's Men
1615–16	2 Feb.	IT	play	visiting players
1615–16	2 Feb.	MT	play	Palsgrave's Men
1616–17	1 Nov.	IT	play	King's Men
1616–17	4 Nov.	4 Inns	barriers	Prince Charles's Creation as Prince of Wales
1616–17	Christmas	MT	play	visiting players (?)
1617–18	1 Nov.	IT	play	visiting players
1617–18	2 Feb.	IT	play	visiting players
1618–19	2 Feb.	MT	play	*Bridegroom and the Madman*, Prince's Men
1619–20	1 Nov.	IT	play	players unknown
1619–20	2 Feb.	IT	play	players unknown
1620–21	1 Nov.	IT	play	visiting players

1620–21	2 Feb.	IT	play	visiting players
1621–22	1 Nov.	IT	play	King's Men
1621–22	2 Feb.	IT	play	King's Men
1622–23	1 Nov.	IT	play	visiting players
1623–24	1 Nov.	IT	play	visiting players
1623–24	2 Feb.	IT	play	visiting players
1624–25	2 Feb.	IT	play	players unknown
1626–27	1 Nov.	IT	play	King's Men
1626–27	2 Feb.	IT	play	King's Men
1627–28	1 Nov.	IT	play	King's Men
1627–28	5 Nov.	IT	play	visiting players
1627–28	2 Feb.	IT	play	Queen's Men
1628–29	1 Nov.	IT	play	King's Men
1628–29	2 Feb.	IT	play	visiting players
1629–30	2 Feb.	IT	play	King's Men
1631–32	1 Nov.	IT	play	King's Men
1631–32	2 Feb.	IT	play	King's Men
1632–33	1 Nov.	IT	play	King's Men
1632–33	1 Nov.	MT	play	*Hyde Park*, Queen's Men
1632–33	2 Feb.	IT	play	King's Men
1632–33	2 Feb.	MT	play	Prince's Men, 'put off'
1633–34	1 Nov.	IT	play	King's Men
1633–34	1 Nov.	MT	play	*The City Shuffler*, visiting players
1634–35	1 Nov.	IT	play	King's Men
1634–35	2 Feb.	IT	play	King's Men
1635–36	2 Feb.	IT	play	King's Men
1637–38	1 Nov.	IT	play	King's Men
1637–38	4 Nov.	MT	play	Queen's Men
1637–38	2 Feb.	IT	play	King's Men
1637–38	2 Feb.	MT	play	Queen's Men
1638–39	1 Nov.	IT	play	King's Men
1638–39	1 or 2 Nov.	MT	play	Queen's Men
1638–39	2 Feb.	IT	play	King's Men
1638–39	2 Feb.	MT	play	visiting players
1639–40	1 Nov.	IT	play	King's Men
1639–40	2 Nov.	MT	play	Beeston's Boys
1640–41	2 Feb.	IT	play	King's Men
1640–41	2 Feb	MT	play	Beeston's Boys

Notes

1 For details not fully referenced in my text or footnotes, see Alan H. Nelson and John R. Elliott, Jr (eds), *Inns of Court*, 3 vols, Records of Early English Drama (Boydell and Brewer, 2011).

2 Full bibliographical details are: A. Wigfall Green, *The Inns of Court and Early English Drama* (New Haven, CT: Yale University Press, 1931; repr. New York, 1965); Philip J. Finkelpearl, *John Marston of the Middle Temple: An Elizabethan Dramatist in his Social Setting* (Cambridge, MA: Harvard University Press, 1969); Wilfrid R. Prest, *The Inns of Court under Elizabeth I and the Early Stuarts, 1590–1640* (London: Longman, 1972).

3 Anthony Arlidge, *Shakespeare and the Prince of Love: The Feast of Misrule in the Middle Temple* (London: Giles de la Mare, 2000); John H. Baker, 'Christmas in the Inns of Court and Chancery', in *An Inner Temple Miscellany: Papers Reprinted from the Inner Temple Yearbook* (London: The Honourable Society of the Inner Temple, 2004), pp. 41–7.

4 Henry James and Greg Walker, 'The politics of *Gorboduc*', *English Historical Review*, 110 (1995), 109–21; and Norman Jones and Paul Whitfield White, '*Gorboduc* and royal marriage politics: an Elizabethan playgoer's report of the premiere performance', *English Literary Renaissance*, 26 (1996), 3–16; see also Rivkah Zim, 'A poet in politics: Thomas Sackville, Lord Buckhurst and first earl of Dorset (1536–1608)', *Historical Research*, 79 (2004), 199–223.

5 Jessica Winston, 'Expanding the political nation: *Gorboduc* at the Inns of Court and succession revisited', *Early Theatre*, 8:1 (2005), 11–34.

6 John H. Baker and Jane Ringrose, *A Catalogue of English Legal Manuscripts in Cambridge University Library* (Woodbridge: Boydell Press, 1996), pp. 430–1.

7 Barbara Ravelhofer, *The Early Stuart Masque: Dance, Costume, and Music* (Oxford: Oxford University Press, 2006), pp. 37–8.

8 See 'ticket' (*n.*), 5.a. 'A slip, usually of paper or cardboard, bearing the evidence of the holder's title to some service or privilege, to which it admits him': the earliest use given in the *OED* is in the Galston Session Records of 1673, cited by Andrew Edgar, *Old Church Life in Scotland: Lectures on Kirk-Session and Presbytery Records* (Paisley and London: Alexander Gardner, 1885): 'Several hunders of tickets ar distribute' (p. 173, note). See 'ticket, *n.*', in *The Oxford English Dictionary* (Oxford: Oxford University Press), 2nd edn 1989; OED Online, http://dictionary.oed.com/cgi/entry/50252446 (accessed 3 July 2009).

9 George Garrard to Thomas Wentworth, Earl of Strafford, Sheffield Archives, MS WWM/Str P/13/207 (27 February 1633/34).

10 For a discussion of Juby's career and that of his wife Frances, see S. P. Cerasano and Marion Wynne-Davies, *Readings in Renaissance Women's Drama: Criticism, History, and Performance, 1594–1598* (London: Routledge, 1998), pp. 89–90; see also Andrew Gurr, *The Shakespearean Playing Companies* (Oxford: Oxford University Press, 1996), p. 237.

11 This receipt was noticed in 1971 by Tucker Orbison, 'Traces of two Jacobean dramatic performances at the Middle Temple', *Yearbook of English Studies*, 1 (1971), 55–62, and thus is not quite a 'new' discovery.

12 Green, *The Inns of Court and Early English Drama*, pp. 153–6 (p. 153).

13 *The Diary of John Manningham of the Middle Temple 1602–1603*, ed. Robert Parker Sorlien (Hanover, NH: The University Press of New England, 1976), p. 48.

14 See also Chapters 12 (pp. 245–63), 13 (pp. 264–85), and 14 (pp. 286–301), above.

15 Arlidge, *Shakespeare and the Prince of Love*, p. 3.

16 See Desmond S. Bland, 'Arthur Broke's *Masque of Beauty and Desire*: a reconstruction', *Research Opportunities in Renaissance Drama*, 19 (1976), 49–55.

17 See Francis Meres, *Palladis Tamia Wits treasury being the second part of Wits common wealth* (London: P. Short for Cuthbert Burbie, 1598), sig. 282[r]: 'As *Plautus* and *Seneca* are accounted the best for Comedy and Tragedy among the Latines: so *Shakespeare* among y[e] English is the most excellent in both kinds for the stage: for Comedy, witnes his *Gentlemen of Verona*, his *Errors*.'

18 Revels Office Books for 1604–5, published photographically in A. E. Stamp, *The Disputed Revels Accounts* (Oxford, 1930). These documents are no longer 'disputed' as possible forgeries.

19 Prefatory poem by Leonard Digges in *Poems: By Wm: Shakespeare* (1640), referencing 'Malvoglio that crosse garter'd gull.'

20 Oxford, Bodleian Library, MS Eng. poet. c. 11, fol. 72.

21 Thomas Middleton, *The Inner Temple Masque: or Masque of Heroes* (London: [William Stansby] for John Browne, 1619), sig. A2[v].

22 NA, SP14/137/27.

23 BL, MS Harley 389, fol. 274.

24 See Gerard Legh, *The Accedens of Armory* (London: Richard Tottill, 1562), e.g. sigs 219[v]–27[r]: for further discussions of Legh, see Chapters 2 and 13 (pp. 32–50 and 264–85), above.

25 This story is told with more exacting detail and more complete references in Alan H. Nelson, '"Give fire, Gunner!": Inner Temple high-jinx, Christmas 1627–8', *The Inner Temple Yearbook*, 2007–8 (London: Inner Temple, 2007), pp. 46–8.

26 BL, MS Harley 390, fos 339–40.

27 Clare Rider, 'Alsatia: the Inner Temple's lawless neighbour', *The Inner Temple Yearbook*, 2004–5 (London: Inner Temple, 2005), pp. 56–9.

28 BL, MS Harley 390, fos 343–4.

29 William Dugdale, *Origines Juridiciales* (London: F. and T. Warren for the author, 1666), pp. 149–50.

Select bibliography

Arlidge, Anthony, *Shakespeare and the Prince of Love: The Feast of Misrule in the Middle Temple* (London: Giles de la Mare, 2000)

Axton, Marie, *The Queen's Two Bodies: Drama and the Elizabethan Succession* (London: Royal Historical Society, 1977)

——, 'Robert Dudley and the Inner Temple revels', *Historical Journal*, 13:3 (1970), 365–78

Baker, Christopher Paul, 'Ben Jonson and the Inns of Court: the literary milieu of *Every Man out of his Humor*' (PhD dissertation, University of North Carolina, 1974)

Baker, John H., *The Common Law Tradition: Lawyers, Books, and the Law* (London: Hambledon Press, 2000)

——, 'The dark age of English legal history', in Dafydd Jenkins (ed.), *Legal History Studies: Papers Presented to the Legal History Conference, Aberystwyth, 18–21 July 1972* (Cardiff: University of Wales Press, 1975), pp. 1–27

——, 'The Inns of Court and Chancery as voluntary associations', *Quaderni Fiorentini per la storia del pensiero Giuridico Moderno*, 11/12 (Milan: Giuffrè, 1982–83), pp. 9–38

——, *An Inner Temple Miscellany: Papers Reprinted from the Inner Temple Yearbook* (London: The Honourable Society of the Inner Temple, 2004)

——, *An Introduction to Legal History*, 4th edn (London: Butterworths, 2002)

——, *The Law's Two Bodies: Some Evidential Problems in English Legal History* (Oxford; New York, NY: Oxford University Press, 2001)

——, *Learning in the Early Inns of Chancery* (London: Selden Society, 1990)

——, *The Legal Profession and the Common Law: Historical Essays* (London: Hambledon Press, 1986)

——, *Manual of Law French* (Amersham: Avebury, 1979)

——, *The Order of Serjeants at Law: A Chronicle of Creations with Related Texts* (London: Selden Society, 1984)

——, *Readers and Readings in the Inns of Court and Chancery* (London: Selden Society, 2000)

——, *The Third University of England: The Inns of Court and the Common-Law Tradition* (London: Selden Society, 1990)

——, 'The three languages of the common law', *McGill Law Journal*, 43 (1998), 5–24

——, 'Why the history of English law has not been finished', *Cambridge Law Journal*, 59 (2000), 2–84

Baker, John H. (ed.), *The Oxford History of the Laws of England*, 6 vols (Oxford: Oxford University Press, 2003)

Baker, John H., and Jane Ringrose, *A Catalogue of English Legal Manuscripts in Cambridge University Library* (Woodbridge: Boydell Press, 1996)

Bald, R. C., *John Donne: A Life* (Oxford: Clarendon Press, 1970; repr. 1986)

Barnes, Thomas G., 'Star Chamber litigants and their counsel, 1596–1641', in John H. Baker (ed.), *Legal Records and the Historian: Papers Presented to the Cambridge Legal History Conference, 7–10 July 1975, and in Lincoln's Inn Old Hall on 3 July 1974* (London: Royal Historical Society, 1978), pp. 7–28

Barton, John, 'The Faculty of Law', in McConica (ed.), *The History of the University of Oxford. Vol. 3: The Collegiate University*, pp. 257–83

Bland, Desmond S., 'Arthur Broke's *Masque of Beauty and Desire*: a reconstruction', *Research Opportunities in Renaissance Drama*, 19 (1976), 49–55

——, 'Rhetoric and the law student in sixteenth-century England', *Studies in Philology*, 54 (1957), 498–508

Bland, Desmond S. (comp.), *A Bibliography of the Inns of Court and Chancery* (London: Selden Society, 1965)

Boyer, Allen D., *Sir Edward Coke and the Elizabethan Age* (Stanford, CA: University of California Press, 2003)

Brand, Paul, *The Origins of the English Legal Profession* (Oxford: Blackwell, 1992)

Brooks, Christopher W., *Law, Politics and Society in Early Modern England* (Cambridge: Cambridge University Press, 2008)

——, *Lawyers, Litigation and English Society since 1450* (London: Hambledon Press, 1998)

——, *Pettyfoggers and Vipers of the Commonwealth: The 'Lower Branch' of the Legal Profession in Early Modern England* (Cambridge: Cambridge University Press, 1986)

——, 'Professions, ideology and the middling sort in the late sixteenth and early seventeenth centuries', in Jonathan Barry and Christopher Brooks (eds), *The Middling Sort of People: Culture, Society and Politics in England, 1550–1800* (London: Macmillan, 1994), pp. 113–40

Brooks, Christopher W., and Kevin Sharpe, 'History, English law and the Renaissance', *Past and Present*, 72 (Aug. 1976), 133–42

Brown, Basil, *Law Sports at Gray's Inn* (New York, NY: Private Print, 1921)

Chambers, David S., and Trevor Dean, *Clean Hands and Rough Justice: An Investigating Magistrate in Renaissance Italy* (Ann Arbor, MI: University of Michigan Press, 1997)

Charlton, Kenneth, 'Education and the Inns of Court in the sixteenth century', *British Journal of Educational Studies*, 9 (1960), 25–38

——, *Education in Renaissance England* (London: Routledge and Kegan Paul, 1965)

Collinson, Patrick, 'Hooker and the Elizabethan Establishment', in McGrade (ed.), *Richard Hooker and the Construction of Christian Community*, pp. 141–81

Colvin, Howard M., 'Roger North and Sir Christopher Wren', *Architectural Review*, 110 (Oct. 1951), 257–60

Cormack, Bradin, *A Power to Do Justice: Jurisdiction, English Literature, and the Rise of Common Law, 1509–1625* (Chicago, IL: University of Chicago Press, 2008)

Costola, Sergio, 'Ludovico Ariosto's theatrical machine: tactics of subversion in the 1509 performance of *I Suppositi*' (PhD dissertation, University of Los Angeles, 2002)

Cowper, Francis, *A Prospect of Gray's Inn*, 2nd rev. edn (London: Published by Graya on behalf of Gray's Inn, 1985)

Cromartie, Alan, *Sir Matthew Hale, 1609–1676: Law, Religion and Natural Philosophy* (Cambridge: Cambridge University Press, 1995)

Dever, Mark E., *Richard Sibbes: Puritanism and Calvinism in Late Elizabethan and Early Stuart England* (Macon, GA: Mercer University Press, 2000)

Dillon, Janette, *Theatre, Court and City, 1595–1610: Drama and Social Space in London* (Cambridge: Cambridge University Press, 2000)

Douthwaite, William, *Gray's Inn: Its History and Associations* (London: Reeves and Turner, 1886)

Dunseath, T. K., *Spenser's Allegory of Justice in Book V of* The Faerie Queene (Princeton, NJ: Princeton University Press, 1968)

Elton, William R., *Shakespeare's Troilus and Cressida and the Inns of Court Revels* (Aldershot: Ashgate, 2000)

Ettenhuber, Katrin, '"Take heed what you hear": re-reading Donne's Lincoln's Inn sermons', *John Donne Journal*, 26 (2007), 127–57

Evans, Thomas W., 'Study at the Restoration Inns of Court', in Jonathan A. Bush and Alain Wijffels (eds), *Learning the Law: Teaching and Transmission of English Law, 1150–1900* (London: Hambledon Press, 1999), pp. 287–302

Finkelpearl, Philip J., *John Marston of the Middle Temple: An Elizabethan Dramatist in his Social Setting* (Cambridge, MA: Harvard University Press, 1969)

Fisher, R. M., 'The Inns of Court and the Reformation' (PhD dissertation, University of Cambridge, 1974)

——, 'The origins of Divinity Lectureships at the Inns of Court, 1569–1585', *Journal of Ecclesiastical History*, 29 (1978), 145–62

——, 'Privy Council coercion and religious conformity at the Inns of Court, 1569–1584', *Recusant History*, 15 (1981), 305–24

——, 'The reformation of church and chapel at the Inns of Court, 1530–1580', *Guildhall Studies in London History*, 3 (1979), 223–47

——, 'The reformation of the clergy at the Inns of Court, 1530–1580', *Sixteenth Century Journal*, 12:1 (1981), 69–91

Ford, Richard T., 'Law's territory (A history of jurisdiction)', *Michigan Law Review*, 97 (1999), 843–930

Gaggero, Christopher, 'Pleasure unreconciled to virtue: George Gascoigne and didactic drama', in Lloyd Edward Kermode, Jason Scott-Warren, and Martine van Elk (eds), *Tudor Drama before Shakespeare, 1485–1590: New Directions for Research, Criticism, and Pedagogy* (Houndsmills: Palgrave, 2004), pp. 167–94

Girouard, Mark, *Elizabethan Architecture: Its Rise and Fall, 1540–1640* (New Haven, CT; London: Yale University Press/The Paul Mellon Centre for Studies in British Art, 2009)

Goodrich, Peter, 'Eating law: commons, common land, common law', *Journal of Legal History*, 12 (1991), 246–67

——, *Languages of Law: From Logics of Memory to Nomadic Masks* (London: Weidenfeld & Nicolson, 1990)

——, *Law in the Courts of Love: Literature and Other Minor Jurisprudences* (London: Routledge, 1996)

——, 'Laws of friendship', *Law and Literature*, 15:1 (2003), 23–52

——, *Legal Discourse: Studies in Linguistics, Rhetoric and Legal Analysis* (Basingstoke: Macmillan, 1987)

—— 'Signs taken for wonders: community, identity, and *A History of Sumptuary Law*', *Law and Social Inquiry*, 23 (1998), 707–28

Grafton, Anthony, and Lisa Jardine, *From Humanism to the Humanities: Education and Liberal Arts in Fifteenth- and Sixteenth-Century Europe* (Cambridge, MA: Harvard University Press, 1986)

Graves, Michael A. R., *Thomas Norton: The Parliament Man* (Oxford: Blackwell, 1994)

Gray, Charles M., *The Writ of Prohibition: Jurisdiction in Early Modern English Law*, 2 vols (New York, NY: Oceana Publications, 1994)

'Gray's Inn – II', *Country Life*, 82 (13 Nov. 1937), 492–8

Guy, John, *Christopher St. German on Chancery and Statute* (London: Selden Society, 1985)

——, 'Thomas More and Christopher St German: the battle of the books', in Alistair Fox and John Guy (eds), *Reassessing the Henrician Age: Humanism, Politics and Reform, 1500–1550* (Oxford: Blackwell, 1986), pp. 95–120

Hargreaves-Mawdsley, W. N., *A History of Legal Dress in Europe until the End of the Eighteenth Century* (Oxford: Clarendon Press, 1963)

Hart, James S., *The Rule of Law, 1603–1660: Crowns, Courts and Judges* (Harlow: Pearson Longman, 2003)

Headlam, Cecil, *The Inns of Court* (London: Adam and Charles Black, 1909)

Henderson, Paula, 'Sir Francis Bacon's essay, "Of Gardens", in context', *Garden History*, 36:1 (Spring 2008), 59–84

——, *The Tudor House and Garden: Architecture and Landscape in the Sixteenth and Early Seventeenth Centuries* (New Haven, CT; London: Yale University Press, 2005)

Herbert, William, *Antiquities of the Inns of Court and Chancery* (London: Vernor and Hood, 1804)

Hindle, Steve, *The State and Social Change in Early Modern England, c. 1550–1640* (London: Macmillan Press, 2000)

Holborn, Guy, *Sources of Biographical Information on Past Lawyers* (Warwick: British and Irish Association of Law Librarians, 1999)

Holdsworth, Angela (ed.), *A Portrait of Lincoln's Inn* (London: The Honourable Society of Lincoln's Inn/Third Millennium Publishing, 2007)

Holdsworth, William S., *A History of English Law*, 12 vols (London: Methuen, 1903–52)

Horner, Olga, 'Christmas at the Inns of Court', in Meg Twycross (ed.), *Festive Drama* (Cambridge: D. S. Brewer, 1996), pp. 41–53

Hradsky, Robert, 'The 1771 competition for rebuilding Lincoln's Inn', *Georgian Group Journal*, 17 (May 2009), 95–106

Hutson, Lorna, *The Invention of Suspicion: Law and Mimesis in Shakespeare and English Renaissance Drama* (Oxford: Oxford University Press, 2007)

Ives, Eric W., *The Common Lawyers of Pre-Reformation England. Thomas Kebell: A Case Study* (Cambridge: Cambridge University Press, 1983)

——, 'Some aspects of the legal profession in the late fifteenth and early sixteenth centuries' (PhD dissertation, University of London, 1955)

Jacob, E. F., *Sir John Fortescue and the Law of Nature* (Manchester: Manchester University Press, 1934)

Jacques, David, '"The chief ornament" of Gray's Inn: the walks from Bacon to Brown', *Garden History*, 17:1 (Spring 1989), 41–67

James, Henry, and Greg Walker, 'The politics of *Gorboduc*', *English Historical Review*, 110 (1995), 109–21

Johnson, Jeffrey, 'Consecrating Lincoln's Inn Chapel', *John Donne Journal*, 23 (2004), 139–60

Jones, Gareth H., *The History of the Law of Charity, 1532–1827* (Cambridge: Cambridge University Press, 1969)

Jones, Norman, and Paul Whitfield White, '*Gorboduc* and royal marriage politics: an Elizabethan playgoer's report of the premiere performance', *English Literary Renaissance*, 26 (1996), 3–16

Jordan, Constance, and Karen Cunningham (eds), *The Law in Shakespeare* (Basingstoke: Palgrave Macmillan, 2007)

Kahn, Victoria, and Lorna Hutson (eds), *Rhetoric and Law in Early Modern Europe* (New Haven, CT: Yale University Press, 2001)

Kelly, J. M., *Roman Litigation* (Oxford: Clarendon Press, 1966)

Kezar, Dennis D. (ed.), *Solon and Thepsis: Law and Theater in the English Renaissance* (Notre Dame, IN: University of Notre Dame Press, 2007)

Knafla, Louis A., 'The law studies of an Elizabethan student', *Huntington Library Quarterly*, 32 (1969), 221–40

——, 'The matriculation revolution and education at the Inns of Court in Renaissance England', in Arthur J. Slavin (ed.), *Tudor Men and Institutions* (Baton Rouge, LA: Louisiana State University Press, 1972), pp. 232–64

Langbein, John F., *Prosecuting Crime in the Renaissance: England, Germany, France* (Cambridge, MA: Harvard University Press, 1974)

Legendre, Pierre, *Law and the Unconscious: A Legendre Reader*, ed. Peter Goodrich, trans. Alain Pottage and Anton Schütz (Basingstoke: Macmillan, 1997)

Lemmings, David Frederick, *Gentlemen and Barristers: The Inns of Court and the English Bar 1680–1730* (Oxford: Clarendon Press, 1990)

——, 'Ritual and the law in early modern England', in Suzanne Corcoran (ed.), *Law and History in Australia: A Collection of Papers Presented at the 1989 Law and History Conference* (Adelaide: Adelaide Law Review Association, 1991), pp. 3–19

McConica, James (ed.), *The History of the University of Oxford. Vol. 3: The Collegiate University* (Oxford: Clarendon Press, 1986)

McCoy, Richard C., 'Lords of Liberty: Francis Davison and the cult of Elizabeth', in John Guy (ed.), *The Reign of Elizabeth I: Court and Culture in the Last Decade* (Cambridge: Cambridge University Press, 1995), pp. 212–28

McGlynn, Margaret, *The Royal Prerogative and the Learning of the Inns of Court* (Cambridge: Cambridge University Press, 2003)

McGrade, Arthur S. (ed.), *Richard Hooker and the Construction of Christian Community* (Binghamton, NY: Medieval and Renaissance Texts and Studies, 1997)

MacKinnon, Frank Douglas, 'The Temple Family', in *Inner Temple Papers* (London: Stevens and Sons, 1948)

Macnair, Michael R. T., *The Law of Proof in Early Modern Equity* (Berlin: Duncker and Humblot, 1999)

Magnusson, Lynne, 'Scoff power in *Love's Labour's Lost* and the Inns of Court: language in context', *Shakespeare Survey*, 57 (2004), 196–208

Maitland, Frederick W., *English Law and the Renaissance* (Cambridge: Cambridge University Press, 1901)

Manley, Lawrence, *Literature and Culture in Early Modern London* (Cambridge: Cambridge University Press, 1995)

Marotti, Arthur F., *John Donne, Coterie Poet* (Madison, WI: University of Wisconsin Press, 1986)

——, *Manuscript, Print, and the English Renaissance Lyric* (Ithaca, NY: Cornell University Press, 1995)

Miola, Robert S., *Shakespeare and Classical Comedy: The Influence of Plautus and Terence* (Oxford: Clarendon Press, 1994)

Miola, Robert S. (ed.), *The Comedy of Errors: Critical Essays* (New York, NY: Garland; Routledge, 1997)

Mirow, Michael C., 'Bastardy and the statute of wills: interpreting a sixteenth-century statute with cases and readings', *Mississippi Law Journal*, 69 (1999), 345–71

Morgan, Victor, with Christopher Brooke, *A History of the University of Cambridge. Vol. 2: 1546–1750* (Cambridge: Cambridge University Press, 2004)

Morrissey, Mary, 'Scripture, style and persuasion in seventeenth-century English theories of preaching', *Journal of Ecclesiastical History*, 53 (2002), 686–706

Mueller, Janel M., *The Native Tongue and the Word: Developments in English Prose Style 1380–1580* (Chicago, IL; London: University of Chicago Press, 1984)

Mukherji, Subha, *Law and Representation in Early Modern Drama* (Cambridge: Cambridge University Press, 2006)

——, '"Understood relations": law and literature in early modern studies', *Literature Compass*, 6:3 (2009), 706–25

Nelson, Alan H., '"Give fire, Gunner!": Inner Temple high-jinx, Christmas 1627–8', *The Inner Temple Yearbook*, 2007–8 (London: Inner Temple, 2007), pp. 46–8

O'Callaghan, Michelle, *The English Wits: Literature and Sociability in Early Modern England* (Cambridge: Cambridge University Press, 2007)

Orbison, Tucker, 'Traces of two Jacobean dramatic performances at the Middle Temple', *Yearbook of English Studies*, 1 (1971), 55–62

Pacey, Jason T., 'Led by the hand: manucaptors and patronage at Lincoln's Inn in the seventeenth century', *Legal History*, 18 (1997), 26–44

Palmer, Susan, 'From fields to gardens: the management of Lincoln's Inn Fields in the eighteenth and nineteenth centuries', *The London Gardener or The Gardener's Intelligencer*, 10 (2004–5), 11–27

Parmiter, Geoffrey de, *Edmund Plowden: An Elizabethan Recusant Lawyer* (Southampton: Catholic Record Society, 1987)

Pearce, Robert A., *A Guide to the Inns of Court and Chancery* (London: Butterworths, 1855)

Pocock, John G. A., *The Ancient Constitution and the Feudal Law: A Study of English Historical Thought in the Seventeenth Century* (London: Cambridge University Press, 1957)

——, *The Ancient Constitution and the Feudal Law: A Study of English Historical Thought in the Seventeenth Century – A Reissue with a Retrospect* (Cambridge: Cambridge University Press, 1987)

Powell, Damian X., *Sir James Whitelocke's Liber Famelicus, 1570–1632: Law and Politics in Early Stuart England* (Bern; New York, NY: Peter Lang, 2000)

——, 'Sir James Whitelocke's advice to the Crown in 1627', *Historical Journal*, 39:3 (1996), 737–42

Prest, Wilfrid R., *The Inns of Court under Elizabeth I and the Early Stuarts, 1590–1640* (London: Longman, 1972)

——, 'The learning exercises at the Inns of Court', *Journal of the Society of Public Teachers of Law*, n. ser., 9 (June 1967), 301–13

——, 'Politics and profession in early Stuart England: the diary of Sir Richard Hutton', in *Rulers, Religion and Rhetoric in Early Modern England: A Festchrift for Geoffrey Elton from his Australasian Friends*, ed. S. M. Jack for *Parergon*, n. ser., 6 (1988), 163–77

——, *The Rise of the Barristers: A Social History of the English Bar, 1590–1640* (Oxford: Clarendon Press, 1986)

Raffield, Paul, 'Bodies of law: the divine architect, common law and the ancient constitution', *International Journal for the Semiotics of Law*, 13 (2000), 333–56

——, *Images and Cultures of Law in Early Modern England: Justice and Political Power, 1558–1660* (Cambridge: Cambridge University Press, 2004)

Raffield, Paul, and Gary Watt (eds), *Shakespeare and the Law* (Oxford: Hart Publishing, 2008)

Ravelhofer, Barbara, *The Early Stuart Masque: Dance, Costume, and Music* (Oxford: Oxford University Press, 2006)

Reddaway, T. F., *The Rebuilding of London after the Great Fire* (London: Cape, 1940)

Rhatigan, Emma, 'Knees and elephants: John Donne preaches on ceremonial conformity at Lincoln's Inn', *John Donne Journal*, 23 (2004), 185–213

Rhodes, Neil (ed.), *English Renaissance Prose: History, Language, and Politics* (Tempe, AZ: Medieval and Renaissance Texts and Studies, 1997)

Richardson, Walter Cecil, *A History of the Inns of Court: With Special Reference to the Period of the Renaissance* (Baton Rouge, LA: Claitor's Publishing Division, 1973; 1978)

Rider, Clare M., 'Alsatia: the Inner Temple's lawless neighbour', *The Inner Temple Yearbook*, 2004–5 (London: Inner Temple, 2005), pp. 56–9

——, 'The Inns of Court and the Inns of Chancery and their records', *Archives*, 24 (Oct. 1999), 27–36

Rider, Clare, and Val Horsler (eds), *The Inner Temple: A Community of Communities* (London: Third Millennium Publishing, 2007)

Rivlin, Elizabeth, 'Theatrical literacy in *The Comedy of Errors* and the *Gesta Grayorum*', *Critical Survey*, 14:1 (2002), 64–78

Ross, Richard J., 'The memorial culture of early modern English lawyers: memory as keyword, shelter, and identity, 1560–1640', *Yale Journal of Law and the Humanities*, 10 (1998), 229–326

Scafuro, Adele C., *The Forensic Stage: Settling Disputes in Graeco-Roman Comedy* (Cambridge: Cambridge University Press, 1997)

Schoeck, R. J., 'From Erasmus to Hooker: an overview', in McGrade (ed.), *Richard Hooker and the Construction of Christian Community*, pp. 59–73

Sedley, Tia, 'Inner Temple Garden: "A new faire garden, environed *with* strong brick walls"', *The London Gardener or The Gardener's Intelligencer*, 7 (2001–2), 46–51

The Selden Society Lectures 1952–2001 (Buffalo, NY: W. S. Hein, 2003)

Shaller, Terence K., 'English law and the Renaissance: the common law and humanism in the sixteenth century' (PhD dissertation, Harvard University, 1979)

Shapiro, Barbara J., *'Beyond Reasonable Doubt' and 'Probable Cause': Historical Perspectives on the Anglo-American Law of Evidence* (Berkeley, CA: University of California Press, 1991)

——, *Rhetoric and Law in Early Modern Europe* (New Haven, CT: Yale University Press, 2001)

Shawcross, John T., *The Development of Milton's Thought: Law, Government, and Religion* (Pittsburgh, PA: Duquesne University Press, 2008)

Sheen, Erica, and Lorna Hutson (eds), *Literature, Politics and Law in Renaissance England* (Basingstoke: Palgrave Macmillan, 2005)

Lord Silsoe, *The Peculiarities of the Temple* (London: Estates Gazette, 1972)

Smuts, Malcolm, *Culture and Power in England 1585–1685* (Basingstoke: Macmillan, 1999)

Sommerville, J. P., *Politics and Ideology in England, 1603–1640* (London: Longman, 1986)

Spalding, Ruth, *The Improbable Puritan: A Life of Bulstrode Whitelocke 1605–1675* (London: Faber, 1975)

Spilsbury, William H., *Lincoln's Inn: Its Ancient and Modern Buildings*, 2nd edn (London: Reeves and Turner, 1873)

Strong, Roy, *Tudor and Jacobean Portraits*, 2 vols (London: HMSO, 1969)

Summerson, John, *Architecture in Britain, 1530 to 1830* (New Haven, CT; London: Yale University Press, 1993 repr.)

Sutherland, Lucy S., 'The curriculum', in Lucy S. Sutherland and L. G. Mitchell (eds), *The History of the University of Oxford. Vol. V: The Eighteenth Century* (Oxford: Clarendon Press, 1986), pp. 471–6

Thayer, James Bradley, *A Preliminary Treatise on Evidence at the Common Law* (Boston, MA: Little, Brown, 1898)

Thorne, Samuel E., 'Early history of the Inns of Court', *Graya*, 50 (1959), 79–96

——, *Essays in English Legal History* (London: Hambledon Press, 1985)

Thorne, Samuel E., and John H. Baker (eds), *Readings and Moots at the Inns of Court in the Fifteenth Century. Vol. 2: Moots and Readers' Cases* (London: Selden Society, 1990)

Tittler, Robert, *The Face of the City: Civic Portraiture and Civic Identity in Early Modern England* (Manchester; New York, NY: Manchester University Press, 2007)

Tucker, E. F. J., *Intruder into Eden: Representations of the Common Lawyer in English Literature, 1350–1750* (Columbia, SC: Camden House, 1984)

Tucker, Penny, *Law Courts and Lawyers in the City of London, 1300–1550* (Cambridge: Cambridge University Press, 2007)

Tyack, Geoffrey, 'The buildings of the Inner Temple', in Rider and Horsler (eds), *The Inner Temple: A Community of Communities*, pp. 60–77

Walters, Mark D., 'St German on reason and parliamentary sovereignty', *Cambridge Law Journal*, 62 (2003), 335–70

Watson, Alan, *The Law of Obligations in the Later Roman Republic* (Oxford: Clarendon Press, 1965)

Wells-Cole, Anthony, *Art and Decoration in Elizabethan and Jacobean England: The Influence of Continental Prints, 1558–1625* (New Haven, CT; London: Yale University Press/The Paul Mellon Centre for Studies in British Art, 1997)

Whitlock, Baird, *John Hoskyns Serjeant-at-Law* (Washington, DC: University Presses of America, 1982)

Whitted, Brent, 'Legal play: the literary culture of the Inns of Court, 1572–1634' (PhD dissertation, University of British Columbia, 2000)

Wienpahl, Robert W., *Music at the Inns of Court during the Reigns of Elizabeth, James and Charles* (Ann Arbor, MI: University Microfilms International for the Department of Music, California State University, Northridge, 1979)

Wigfall Green, A., *The Inns of Court and Early English Drama* (1931; repr.: New York, NY: Benjamin Blom, 1965)

Williamson, John Bruce, *Catalogue of Paintings and Engravings in the Possession of the Honourable Society of the Middle Temple* (London: Middle Temple, 1931)

——, *The History of the Temple, London* (London: John Murray, 1924)

——, *The History of the Temple, London*, 2nd edn (London: Murray, 1925)

Wilson, Luke, *Theaters of Intention: Drama and the Law in Early Modern England* (Stanford, CA: Stanford University Press, 2000)

Winston, Jessica, 'Expanding the political nation: *Gorboduc* at the Inns of Court and succession revisited', *Early Theatre*, 8:1 (2005), 11–34

Wright, Nancy E., Margaret W. Ferguson, and A. R. Buck (eds), *Women, Property and the Letters of the Law in Early Modern England* (Toronto; London: University of Toronto Press, 2004)

Index

CPSIA information can be obtained at www.ICGtesting.com
Printed in the USA
LVOW070309220513

334891LV00005B/75/P